# Educational Recommender Systems and Technologies:

## Practices and Challenges

Olga C. Santos
*aDeNu Research Group, UNED, Spain*

Jesus G. Boticario
*aDeNu Research Group, UNED, Spain*

Information Science
REFERENCE

| | |
|---|---|
| Managing Director: | Lindsay Johnston |
| Senior Editorial Director: | Heather Probst |
| Book Production Manager: | Sean Woznicki |
| Development Manager: | Joel Gamon |
| Development Editor: | Myla Harty |
| Acquisitions Editor: | Erika Gallagher |
| Typesetters: | Mackenzie Snader |
| Print Coordinator: | Jamie Snavely |
| Cover Design: | Nick Newcomer |

Published in the United States of America by
Information Science Reference (an imprint of IGI Global)
701 E. Chocolate Avenue
Hershey PA 17033
Tel: 717-533-8845
Fax: 717-533-8661
E-mail: cust@igi-global.com
Web site: http://www.igi-global.com



Library of Congress Cataloging-in-Publication Data

Educational recommender systems and technologies : practices and challenges / Olga C. Santos and Jesus G. Boticario, editors.
p. cm.
Includes bibliographical references and index.
Summary: "This book aims to provide a comprehensive review of state-of-the-art practices for educational recommender systems, as well as the challenges to achieve their actual deployment"--Provided by publisher.
ISBN 978-1-61350-489-5 (hardcover) -- ISBN 978-1-61350-490-1 (ebook) -- ISBN 978-1-61350-491-8 (print & perpetual access) 1. Educational technology. 2. Recommender systems (Information filtering) I. Santos, Olga C., 1978- II. Gonzalez Boticario, Jeszs.
LB1028.3.E3327 2012
371.33

2011038335

British Cataloguing in Publication Data
A Cataloguing in Publication record for this book is available from the British Library.

## Editorial Advisory Board



## Program Committee

# List of Reviewers

Cristina Bender, *Universidad Nacional de Rosario, Argentina*
Constanta Bodea, *Academy of Economic Studies, Romania*
Daniel Burgos, *International University of La Rioja, Spain*
Sergey Butakov, *Solbridge International School of Business, Korea*
John Champaign, *University of Waterloo, Canada*
Weiqin Chen, *University of Bergen, Norway*
Nidhi Chopra, *Indira Gandhi National Open University, India*
Claudia Deco, *Universidad Nacional de Rosario, Argentina*
Alicia Diaz, *Universidad Nacional de La Plata, Argentina*
Lucas Rêgo Drumond, *University of Hildesheim, Germany*
Thieme Hennis, *Delft University of Technology, the Netherlands*
Juha Leino, *University of Tampere, Finland*
Keith Maull, *University of Colorado at Boulder, USA*
Christos Mettouris, *University of Cyprus, Cyprus*
Regina Motz, *Universidad de la República, Uruguay*
Thai-Nghe Nguyen, *University of Hildesheim, Germany*
Ifeyinwa Okoye, *University of Colorado, USA*
Abelardo Pardo, *University Carlos III of Madrid, Spain*
Chhavi Rana, *UIET, MDU, Rohtak, Haryana, India*
Vicente A. Romero, *Atos Origin SAE, Spain*
Daniel J. Salas, *Universidad de Córdoba, Colombia*
Surendra Sarnikar, *Dakota State University, USA*
George Sielis, *University of Cyprus, Cyprus*
Jody Underwood, *Intelligent Automation, Inc., USA*

# Table of Contents

**Section 2**
**Techniques, Algorithms and Architectures to Support the Recommendation Process**

# Foreword

I am very pleased to write a few words for this timely, important, and thought provoking collection focusing on various dimensions related to educational recommender systems and technologies. The research on recommender systems in general has now spanned more than a decade, for example, early articles on recommender systems can be found in DBLP from late nineties. However, recommender systems in education lend themselves to some unique requirements that set them apart from any other domains. As identified by the editors of this volume, educational criteria are very significant factors that require serious consideration when looking at the use of recommender systems elsewhere where user preferences dominate the scene.

The research and use of recommender systems in education benefit from a number of intertwined areas that have been focus of research in recent years, both from pedagogy and technical perspectives. On one hand, the emergence of constructivist paradigm has brought the needs and preferences of individual learner at the center of the educational process, and on the other, recent advancements in Internet, mobile, and location-aware technologies have made it possible to relate learning not only to the learners' personal characteristics but also to the changes in their real-time contexts. Educational recommender systems therefore have to consider not just the technical aspects but also the actual implementation and management issues for successful and meaningful deployment of such systems to benefit individual learners.

It is pleasing to see this edited collection coming at the right time, with the right focus on both research and use of recommender systems in education. The four sections build on one another, starting from modeling of knowledge, to the actual development techniques, algorithms, and architectures, leading to the deployment in real world scenarios, and finally, looking at various challenges such systems face as research progresses further.

It is particularly noteworthy that the challenges address cognitive aspects and the emerging mobile learning, areas where our understanding is still evolving along with the advances in educational recommender system research. This makes it even more important to see the crossroads of the research in these areas and use that understanding in other evolving areas such as emotional intelligence, ubiquitous learning and 3-D environments. This collection nicely provides that opportunity.

The book contains the right balance between the research innovations and their practical use, and should serve as a solid stepping stone for both further technological developments and for reflection on the experiences that are obtained during actual deployment, particularly as the advances in technology make it further possible to integrate more and more contextual aspects in the design of such systems. The first step in this feedback loop is to look at the experiences of early adopters and identify best practice examples. This collection is a valuable step in that direction.

I have had pleasure of knowing the editors of this collection, Olga and Jesus, for some time, and I am particularly impressed with their personal innovative research. Their experiences reflect in the selection of chapters and their placement in the book, to cover a wide range of issues within the four sections. This wide range makes the book not only valuable to both researchers and practitioners, but also provides a snapshot in time which future researchers can refer to gauge the progress in this area and to identify future directions.

While writing this short piece of my thoughts, I am privy to Olga and Jesus' preface that precedes the chapters in this book. I wholeheartedly agree with them that while the chapters in this book individually provide their own viewpoint and unique wisdom, the book captures a holistic perspective that will be a significant contribution to the field of recommender systems in education.

*Kinshuk*
*Athabasca University, Canada*

**Kinshuk** *is Associate Dean of Faculty of Science and Technology and Professor of Computing and Information Systems at Athabasca University, Canada. He also holds NSERC/iCORE/Xerox/Markin Industrial Research Chair in Adaptivity and Personalization in Informatics. Before moving to Canada in August 2006, Kinshuk worked at German National Research Centre for Information Technology as Postdoctoral Fellow, and at Massey University, New Zealand as Associate Professor of Information Systems and Director of Advanced Learning Technology Research Centre. He has been involved in large-scale research projects for adaptive and mobile learning systems and by early 2011, he has published over 300 research papers in international refereed journals, conferences, and book chapters. He is the Founding Chair of IEEE Technical Committee on Learning Technology and Co-Editor-in-Chief of the SSCI indexed Journal of Educational Technology & Society (ISSN 1436-4522).*

# Preface

Recommender systems have shown to be successful in many domains where information overload exists. This success has motivated research on how to deploy recommender systems in educational scenarios to facilitate access to the wide spectrum of information. Tackling open issues in their deployment is gaining importance as lifelong learning becomes a necessity of the current knowledge-based society. Although *Educational Recommender Systems* (ERS) share the same key objectives as recommenders for e-commerce applications (i.e. helping users to select the most appropriate item from a large information pool), there are some particularities that should be considered before directly applying existing solutions from those applications. For instance, recommendations in the educational domain should not be guided only by the learners' preferences but also by educational criteria. However, most ERS approaches have focused on applying traditional recommendation algorithms in order to find relevant resources for learners in learning scenarios. While this approach is pointing at interesting open issues, there are complementary views in this field to address the current challenges, which may clarify grounds to successfully deploy ERS.

The handbook aims to provide a comprehensive review of state-of-the-art practices for ERS as well as the challenges to achieve their actual deployment. Some topics discussed in the handbook are the following: 1) State of the art of ERS, 2) Modeling issues in developing ERS, 3) Techniques and algorithms to produce recommendations in e-learning settings, 4) Methodologies to develop ERS, 5) Architectures to support the recommendation process, 6) Management of educational issues when providing recommendations to learners, 4) Evaluation methods to measure the recommendations' impact on users, 5) Challenges for providing suitable recommendations in the educational domain, 6) Application of ERS in real world scenarios, and 7) New educational related areas where ERS fit purpose.

The target audience of this handbook covers researchers interested in recommendation strategies for educational scenarios and in evaluating the impact of recommendations in learning, as well as academics and practitioners in the area of technology enhanced learning interested in supporting learners and educators in their learning and teaching tasks though personalized intelligent learning environments. Furthermore, the handbook is also targeted at teachers who are interested in using learning technologies and/or in the potential of adaptive and intelligent learning technologies.

We received 31 chapter proposals, which ended in 13 accepted chapters (42% acceptance rate) written by a total of 44 researchers working in institutions worldwide. In particular, there are papers from 3 continents and 13 countries, as follows: Netherlands, Germany, Cyprus, Romania, Spain, Norway, and Finland in Europe, Uruguay, USA, Argentina, and Brazil in the Americas, and Singapore and China in Asia. Moreover, 53 researchers have been involved in the reviewing process from diverse institutions in Europe, America, and Asia (see reviewers' list for details).

The reviewing process consisted of several phases. First, the chapter proposals were reviewed by the editors who provided feedback to the authors aimed to better fit the objectives of the handbook. The full chapters were reviewed by 4 reviewers, consisting of 1 from the Editorial Advisory Board (EAB), 2 from the Program Committee (PC), and 1 from the List of Reviewers. Editors also reviewed the chapters, made additional comments, highlighted critical issues, and asked authors of initially accepted papers to consider all comments in their revised version. The authors of papers who were considered valuable for the handbook had to submit their revised version and explain in detail how they addressed the reviewers' comments. Afterwards, reviewers and editors read through the revised version and authors' explanations. For some submissions, a second round of revision was needed. Final decisions of acceptance were taken based on the last received reviews. Additional final comments were given to authors for preparing the final version. The aim of this reviewing process was to obtain high quality chapters that properly cover relevant field issues.

With regards to the contents of the Handbook on Educational Recommender Systems and Technologies: Practices and Challenges, ERS are currently undergoing a rapid evolving process as reflected by the ongoing developments in the field. We have identified several practices taking place in two different directions. First, those focused on *design time issues*, which involve knowledge modeling to feed the recommendation process. This issue is of relevance as educational aspects are to be taken into account when developing recommender systems for educational scenarios. Second, the *runtime issues*, which deal with techniques, algorithms, and architectures that differ from those used in other domains to support the delivery of recommendations. The submissions received show that very often, design and runtime practices are still in the research arena and range from conceptual descriptions to the implementation and testing of prototypes, although gradually, recommender systems are being used in real world e-learning scenarios. Supporting this progress entails facing challenges both on addressing educational issues, and on taking advantage of increasing opportunities coming from the learner's context, such as those from mobile devices.

The contributions of this handbook are grouped into the following four sections:

- **Section 1:** Knowledge modeling for the recommendation process
- **Section 2:** Techniques, algorithms and architectures to support the recommendation process
- **Section 3:** Experiences in real world e-learning scenarios
- **Section 4:** Challenges for ERS

**Section 1** focuses on knowledge modeling for the recommendation process and presents different approaches aimed to model at design time the recommendation needs required in ERS. This modeling can be done following ad-hoc approaches, using existing modeling structures such as content or topic maps, or through ontologies. This section compiles the first four chapters of the handbook.

In **Chapter 1**, *Okoye et al.* outline a science ERS for high school students that can support student learning of science content by providing just-in-time personalized information retrieval of vetted science content to intentional learners in an informal setting. Intentional learners are learners that are intrinsically motivated to learn and seek out resources by themselves. The authors discuss a prototype system, the Customized Learning Service for Concept Knowledge (CLICK), which is an application designed to provide recommendations on digital library resources based on user's concept knowledge derived from automated evaluation and approximation of their knowledge state from essay writing. CLICK employs recommendation techniques to suggest resources to learners aiming at addressing the misconceptions and incorrect knowledge that are found by comparing automatically generated domain and learner models. Three core components to personalization in the context of intentional learning were established: first, a learner model that accounts for the learner state over time; second, a designed approach built upon a foundation of strong resources that are expert-approved and vetted; third, a recommender technology approach that supports traditional recommender techniques as well as social-based techniques. By exploring this system, the authors aim to contribute to better understand the knowledge modeling requirements to make comprehensive recommendations that account for the learner's knowledge state.

In **Chapter 2**, *Underwood* describes a recommender system that is intended to guide students to activities for which they are ready by using a framework for structuring digital learning activities in terms of knowledge, skills, and abilities. It uses a structured map of mathematics concepts and processes to power a recommender system called Metis. The Metis approach to recommender systems uses the content map to determine the knowledge of the learner and to select a set of activities the learner is ready for. Its reliability draws on a content map structured by prerequisite relations between knowledge, skills, and abilities. The approach is built on cognitively guided instruction, which has not been implemented in an automated system to date. In contrast to most tutoring systems, which take a procedural approach, Metis tries to find a good place to start rather than try to make corrections along the way. It is designed to assess in real-time how students are performing and to use this information, along with a content map, as a basis for recommending a set of activities that the learner is ready for. Metis is focused on pooling together all the digital learning content that is available on the web in order to help finding quality educational activities. This approach is intended to make activities more engaging, and thus encouraging learners' interest in the content area.

In **Chapter 3**, *Sielis et al.* describe a method to support the creativity process through context-aware recommendations. The method uses ontologies for representing the context knowledge and the topic maps technology for storing, managing, and delivering content used as recommendations. The context in which ideas are developed and the context around the user task are considered to enhance creativity. Such context can be exploited in offering context-aware recommendations to the users on relevant resources, people, ideas, projects, et cetera. These recommendations are provided to users during the creativity process and the learning involved. These authors also present the software system that has been developed to support this method. The goal of their system is to recommend suitable patterns for the current problem and its context. The recommended pattern is ontology independent and is based on problem's parameters the user is trying to solve (e.g. type of the problem, problem definition, problem complexity, if the problem is divisible, objectives, if expert knowledge is required, etc.). The evaluation carried out shows positive results.

In **Chapter 4**, *Diaz et al.* introduce an educational resource recommender that uses an ontology network to assist the modeling and execution of a system based on quality features for a given user and context. Authors show how different ontologies can be modeled as an ontology network in order to explicitly specify the relevant features for the domains identified. Such features are i) specific educational domain, ii) quality assurance domain, iii) user context domain, and iv) recommendation criteria domain. The ontology network can be tailored to specific domains and user profiles. The design aims to obtain a flexible model that is not dependent on any particular mechanism of content evaluation, such as a specific quality metric or educational domain. Whenever it is required to assess a different quality dimension or to consider another educational domain, new extensions of learning object metadata, educational resources quality and recommendation criteria ontologies might be added, keeping up the core model intact. This work shows how the ontology-based reasoning mechanism can be used to validate the recommendation criteria, thus looking for flexibility in tailoring the educational resource adequacy features called educational resource quality.

Once recommendations have been modeled for the educational domain, appropriate techniques, algorithms, and architectures have to be designed and implemented in order to provide the recommendations support in the educational system. Thus, **Section 2** covers these issues. Firstly, there are techniques to deal with the reputation of the learners or predicting the student performance. Secondly, meta-search engines supported by ontology-based clustering algorithm or multi-agent architectures can be applied to provide flexible content-based retrieval that facilitates finding educational resources. Thirdly, meta-rules are used to define set of educationally oriented rules. Finally, architecture-centric approaches support designing ERS. Six chapters have been included in this section that deal with these issues.

In **Chapter 5**, *Hennis et al.* propose a reputation model intended to support knowledge sharing and management, quality assurance, and user engagement in peer-based online learning communities. Online communities have the potential to support learning as a creative process, and reputation systems can support the process in different ways, as for motivation and quality concerns. Recommender technologies have been proposed to automatically produce recommendations based on interest and interactions in online learning environments, which use either collaborative filtering techniques or content filtering techniques. Both techniques can be combined with reputation management to improve the recommendation process. Reputation derives from learners' past, which relates to the sum of their interactions, actions, and contributions in that environment. Thus, the reputation information can be a useful input for ERS. The authors discuss that reputation management systems can be used: i) to make a contextualized picture of the individuals' interests and capability to solve problems, and ii) to motivate individuals to share knowledge in online communities, to recognize learning activities carried out in peer-to-peer communities as a complement to formal certificates.

In **Chapter 6**, *Thai-Nghe et al.* focus on the problem of predicting student performance in the context of ERS by applying state-of-the-art factorization techniques to generate the most accurate rating (or performance prediction). Moreover, as a natural fact, the knowledge of learners improves over time, so factorization methods should and can take the temporal effect into account. Experimental results show that the proposed temporal extension, i.e. tensor factorization, can improve the prediction results. Student performance data from two real data sets from the KDD Challenge 2010 were used and compared with some other baselines. In this way, authors discuss how they can deliver recommendations for many problems, such as to recommend to the students some similar exercises with the appropriate difficulty level (i.e. not too hard nor too easy for them) in order to help them improve their knowledge by learning/doing similar tasks, or to recommend similar grammar structures, vocabularies, or a similar problem/section when the student is learning or doing exercises in an English course, et cetera. The proposed method opens an approach to tackle the need of considering recommendations features different from the preferred learning activities as they might not be the pedagogically the most adequate. This is entitled to facilitate recommendation of tasks based on students' performance but not on their preferences.

In **Chapter 7**, *Bodea et al.* present a meta-search approach, meant to deliver bibliography from the Internet according to trainees' results obtained from an e-assessment task. It uses an ontology-based clustering algorithm for results' presentation that produces recommendations for the students who want to use the e-assessment tool in project management. The meta-search engine is part of an ERS, attached to an e-assessment application for project management knowledge. The procedure is included in a recommender engine, which fires recommendations each time an e-assessment application is used. Meta-search means that, for a specific query (or mistake made by the trainee), several search mechanisms for suitable bibliography (further reading) could be applied. The lists of results delivered by the standard search mechanisms are used to build thematically homogenous groups using an ontology-based clustering algorithm. Exploiting the clustering technologies improves the performance issues of the ERS attached to the e-assessment application, which is intended to gain a formative value and become a learning tool. Authors present experimentation results and discuss the efficiency of the proposed solution in the context of similar applications.

In **Chapter 8**, *Casali et al.* describe an ERS that is intended to help learners to find educational resources that are appropriate to their needs and preferences. The search is performed in different repositories of learning objects, where each object has descriptive metadata. A multi-agent architecture that includes several types of agents with different functionalities is used to support content-based retrieval, which provides an ordered list of the resources according to the user profile data. The framework is meant to be scalable and able to work with heterogeneous and distributed information from different learning object repositories, thus showing that the system architecture is feasible and can help people to find suitable objects. Authors present the design of the personalized search agent that takes a hybrid approach using content- and knowledge-based techniques. This agent is in charge of showing the retrieved items in the correct order. To evaluate the proximity between the recommended ranking and the user's own ranking, authors carried out two experimentations with resources from the Ariadne repository. Six users evaluated whether the retrieved objects were interesting for them and if the recommended order was correct, according to his/her opinion, after browsing the retrieved resources.

In **Chapter 9**, *Romero et al.* present a solution to the problem of generating recommendations for educational applications where required amount of data are not available for the algorithms. To this, they introduce a new abstraction level, meta-rules. Rules can offer specific recommendations even with no usage information. However, large rule-sets are hard to maintain, reengineer, and adapt to user preferences. Meta-rules are used as rules that generate rules, and generalize a rule-set providing bases for adaptation, reengineering, and on-the-fly generation. Authors show the process of creating a recommender for a real situation. The process is described in detail from the data collection stage to the recommender definition.

In **Chapter 10**, *Brito et al.* present an architecture-centric approach for designing ERS where quality attributes are considered in a systematic manner. The underpinning of their approach is a simple process that touches two levels of software design: i) architectural design, which deals with quality attributes in a high-level way; and ii) detailed design, which deals with lower level modeling strategies for realizing the software architecture at the source code. Authors provide a case study that shows, in a step-by-step fashion, how the software architecture can be designed and gradually refined. The proposed approach relies on architectural styles and good practices for the structural definition of the system, and design patterns for the implementation of quality attributes related to ERS (e.g., adaptability, performance and reliability) by using object-oriented programming languages.

**Section 3** reflects the current situation in the field of ERS. The inclusion of this section is expected to motivate researchers to produce more user studies, as more real-world experiences are needed to understand how users perceive recommendation-based support in e-learning. One chapter was selected to illustrate this section.

In **Chapter 11**, *Leino* presents a real-life application and discusses how recommenders can also be gamed in the context of e-learning. The author discusses his experiences of adding recommender features to additional reading materials listing page in an undergraduate-level course. The results reported show that students perceived the system as useful and did not resent compulsoriness, and that the perceived social presence promoted social behavior in many students. However, some misbehavior was also detected, as many students rated materials without viewing them, which points to the need for ERS to be robust against some students trying to get points without earning them. The lessons learned from this chapter may be applied in various e-learning settings. Moreover, this case study is a step in the direction of gathering and analyzing actual experiences of using recommender systems in e-learning to better augment the e-learning process on the learners' terms and to create an engaging e-learning experience.

Finally, **Section 4** includes a couple of papers that compile some of the existing challenges in the field, which cover two significant issues: 1) considering meta-cognitive functions in the recommendations process, and 2) taking advantage of the opportunities derived when the mobile is used for the learning process (i.e. in m-learning contexts).

In **Chapter 12**, *Zhou and Xu* analyze the challenges regarding the use of ERS to enhance meta-cognitive functioning in online learners. Meta-cognition plays a crucial role in the promotion of effective school learning, but in most of the e-learning environment designs, meta-cognitive strategies have generally been neglected. If the learning system were able to guide the student and intelligently recommend learning activities or strategies to facilitate monitoring and control of their own learning, it would favor and improve the learning process and performance. These authors identify the following five challenges: i) consider both learner attributes and the learning sequences during recommendations, ii) detect the learners' motivation and social-emotion and their changes as the task unfolds and to inform what learning strategies to recommend, iii) detect meaningful learning actions and translate them into a strategy in order to evaluate the current learning strategy and subsequently formulate recommendations, iv) identify learning activities or strategies that are more complex with multiple features instead of recommending static learning resources and v) retrieve ratings or preferences to learning strategies/activities in advance by the system by considering learner profiles, learning goals, tasks, and contexts and adapt them according to the learner's progress and performance at different learning stages. The authors propose to adopt data mining algorithms (i.e., content-based and sequence-based recommendation techniques) to meet the identified issues.

In **Chapter 13**, *Liu and Divitini* analyze the opportunities and challenges from context to provide suitable recommendation for mobile learning. Context, which can be used to characterize the situations of a learner in mobile learning environment, presents an opportunity to improve the learning efficiency of mobile learning. Recommendation approaches can provide appropriate recommendation by understanding the actual demands of learners with the help of context, which are 1) supporting new pedagogical theories, 2) satisfying changing requirements of learners, 3) tackling information overload, and 4) overcoming the shortcomings due to poor input and output capacity of current mobile devices. Context also features a challenge to recommendation approaches on input data, context modeling, algorithms, and evaluation such as 1) creating accurate learning context, 2) designing effective recommendation algorithms, 3) properly presenting recommendation results, and 4) including the context of a learner in the scope of evaluation methods. Based on this analysis from context, possible research directions and questions are identified. The application of context-based recommendation may facilitate the further development of mobile learning.

The above chapters compile practices and challenges in ERS. They intend to provide a valuable window from where to analyze the current status of the field. This handbook aims to contribute to advance the research and motivate further analysis and developments, which includes the execution of real world experiences with recommender systems in e-learning scenarios. Overall, the handbook attempts to provide alternative views on related subjects and to bring educators closer to using recommender systems to support the learning process and computer scientists developing algorithms to provide appropriate recommendation strategies.

Last but not least, we would like to deeply thank the more than 50 people that have been involved in the ERSAT project, as Editorial Advisory Board members, Program Committee members, or Additional Reviewers. They all have contributed their expertise to select the relevant contents for this handbook and have provided very valuable comments to improve the quality of the submissions received. Thanks to all of you!

*Olga C. Santos and Jesus G. Boticario*
*aDeNu Research Group, UNED, Spain*

# Section 1
# Knowledge Modeling for the Recommendation Process

# Chapter 1
# Educational Recommendation in an Informal Intentional Learning System

**Ifeyinwa Okoye**
*University of Colorado at Boulder, USA*

**Keith Maull**
*University of Colorado at Boulder, USA*

**James Foster**
*University of Colorado at Boulder, USA*

**Tamara Sumner**
*University of Colorado at Boulder, USA*

## ABSTRACT

*Recommender systems have become part of the standard toolkit of web personalization. These same tools and techniques are now making their way into educational and adaptive e-learning systems. In this chapter, we will discuss aspects of a prototype system, the Customized Learning Service for Concept Knowledge (CLICK), an application designed to provide digital library resources recommendations based on user's concept knowledge demonstrated through automated evaluation and approximation of their knowledge state from essay writing. We present the underlying concepts behind recommender systems, review learner models as they are designed within the CLICK environment, and review the lessons learned. We will discuss aspects of how CLICK supports intentional learning as well as extensions to the existing technology to improve such support. Future challenges and directions for CLICK and related technologies are also discussed.*

DOI: 10.4018/978-1-61350-489-5.ch001

## INTRODUCTION

Intentional learners are learners that are intrinsically motivated to learn and seek out resources by themselves. The information seeking behaviors of today's young learners (and arguably *all learners*) are predominantly focused online – whether through search engine queries, learning portals that provide highly structured educational materials backed by sound learning concepts or through informal learning tools. Furthermore, their behaviors suggest that they are performing their information seeking tasks in increasingly independent ways. Educational tools and resources will need to adapt appropriately to address not only the *content* requirements of today's learners and learning environments, but also the *learner's needs* – that is not only address the way they learn, but also *effective* ways to optimize their learning. To support learner needs completely, personalized models of learner states are required, including both the current state of the learner's knowledge as well as the transitions the learner makes through various knowledge states. Such a personalized model must address the behavior of the individual learner over time.

Recommender systems have become vitally important tools for addressing web personalization. They have enjoyed varying degrees of success in e-commerce contexts, such as product recommendations and movie recommendations. These systems are largely designed around recommendation filtering concepts that rely either on the ratings a user has supplied about items they have purchased or consumed, or on the content of the item itself. Recommender systems within educational contexts are now becoming more widespread, as educational materials, particularly those found online, become the principal mode of learning. Personalization of these materials will be an imperative that cannot be overlooked or under-estimated and indeed will become central to the success of these systems as they continue to gain popularity and widespread use. Social recommendation is also becoming an important feature of educational personalization. For example, the CourseRank (Bercovitz, et. al, 2009) system provides undergraduate course planning assistance to students based on both the course ratings of other students as well as on courses that have already been taken towards the student's intended major course of study. There is no doubt; tools like these will become part of the standard toolkit of future learners.

The objective of this chapter is to outline a science educational recommender system for high school students that can support robust student learning of science content by providing just-in-time personalized information retrieval of vetted science content to intentional learners in an informal setting. Supporting intentional learning has become high priority in many educational contexts, both public and private. Evidence of this can be found, particularly in the United States, where public school districts around the country are mounting concentrated efforts to reform traditional instruction, one part of which is to provide more robust curricular support for intentional learning. The need for supporting intentional learning is perhaps amplified by yet another concern, also especially relevant in the United States. Demographic trends across the country underscore the critical need to broaden access to personalized learning, highlighted by reports that suggest the next decade as the era of "extreme diversity" in K-12 classrooms, most notably in large urban school districts (KnowledgeWorks, 2006). This increasingly diverse student body possesses a wide range of background knowledge and life experiences, and an increased expectation that technology play a significant role in their learning (Hanson & Carlson, 2005). In recognition of the significance of this intellectual challenge and societal need, the National Academy of Engineering recently named personalized learning as one of 14 Grand Challenges for the 21st century, alongside providing energy from fusion and developing carbon sequestration methods (NAE,

2008). Transformational advances are needed to provide effective and affordable approaches to personalizing learning that can be flexibly applied to a wide variety of science topics, age-ranges, and instructional settings.

Aside from the many challenges that all recommender systems have, educational recommendation systems have new challenges to face. This is especially true of informal and intentional learning systems which are required to utilize prior knowledge of the learner, determine the learning goals of the learner and recommend different media formats as well as embed recommendations within a user-interface that is both intuitive and supports the learning process. In this chapter we will examine a prototype system that has been developed – the Customized Learning Service for Concept Knowledge (CLICK). By exploring this system, we hope to more fully understand the knowledge modeling requirements to make comprehensive recommendations that account for the learner's knowledge state. We will examine the details of the CLICK system and explore how it supports intentional learning. Finally, we will offer suggestions about the key components of educational recommender systems that take advantage of both high quality digital learning resources *and* the learner's knowledge state – which, we argue, must be part of any system that is to be placed in an intentional learning context.

## BACKGROUND

Traditional recommendation systems are designed to guide users to discover and make choices that are consistent with their wants and needs around products, services and activities of interest. Recommendation systems have experienced rapid growth as the Internet has expanded beyond mere static, information-only web site to dynamic, interactive and personalized content-drive sites. Commercial systems such as Amazon.com now commonly recommend products to users for purchase, while Netflix.com has built an impressive movie recommendation platform that provides its users rental recommendations that fit their prior viewing habits as well as the habits of others with similar tastes and interests.

Recommendation systems are customarily designed around three key recommendation concepts: (a) *collaborative filtering*: recommending items that match items a user has rated before, (b) *content-based filtering*: recommending items based on the kinds of items a user has purchased or viewed before, and (c) *knowledge-based filtering*: recommending items that are based on a user model or profile of interests that may have been captured as a result of explicit feedback or built from behavioral or interaction data. Systems built by combining these techniques have enjoyed interest early in the development of recommendation technologies (Burke, 2000). They continue to grow in popularity as more profile information is extracted from user behavior the longer they interact and consume items from the same systems. A fourth recommendation concept that is gaining recent success, *social filtering*, must also be mentioned. Social filtering might indeed be considered a variant of collaborative filtering, except that social filtering relies on the details of the social cohort a user belongs to and the role they (and others) may play in shaping the interests of that social grouping. Social networks are now becoming an ubiquitous technology through the rapid adoption of social networking sites such as Facebook, Orkut, MySpace, and LinkedIn. Thus, the activities and interests of the social groups represent huge opportunities to develop and extend recommendation techniques.

While recommendation systems have enjoyed a great deal of success in e-commerce systems as well as peer-to-peer social networks, their benefits are being proven in other areas. Recommendation systems are being developed and deployed in a number of diverse areas – personalized learning and education being one such area. Personalized learning has been recognized as an important advancement for learning and in the digital era, it follows that educational recommender systems form the backbone of any true personalized learning engine, particularly those that are built on top of the web. These web-based learning engines can provide free, ubiquitous, instant and continuous access to online learning opportunities that are adapted and customized to each learner's individual needs.

Educational recommender systems may differ based on the formal or informal learning goals of the system, the type of learners it expects (latent or intentional), the topics and domains it's designed to cover, and the expected age and technological proficiency of its users, among other features. Two scenarios below outline the type of recommendation system we will be discussing in the rest of the chapter.

## Scenario A: Formal Learning

*Thirteen year old Jonathan is taking an earth systems class this semester. As part of the class, Jonathan is given a website where he has to read and complete the test questions for the module that was taught in class the week before. The teacher reminds the students at the end of each week about which module they should work on. On Saturdays, Jonathan logs into the system online using his school given username and password. He navigates to the module for the week, goes through the material, takes the quiz and prints out his score report to hand in to his teacher on Monday.*

We consider this a formal learning context, where the goal of the system is to ensure each student completes a specified curriculum. The materials which might make up the "recommended resources" are usually organized in modules which reflect a curriculum sequence and may be pre-determined and prescribed to every student without personalization. Assessments, usually in multiple choice formats, are provided at the end of each module and a user is required to get some percentage of the questions correct. At which point, the user can move on to the next module. Since the assessments are normally in multiple choice formats, the feedback to the user is "correct" or "incorrect". The learning that goes on in this context can be said to be latent or unintentional since the user's goal is to complete the assessment and print the report for the teacher.

The Educational Recommender system that we're proposing in this chapter is very different from the above system and is illustrated by the following scenario.

## Scenario B: Informal Learning

*Fourteen year old Molly recently moved to Johnstown with her parents who are visiting scholars at Highskill University. Molly has been watching the national news coverage of the recent earthquakes in California. The news reports keep showing video footage of the destruction caused by the earthquake, a number associated with the severity of the earthquake and some information about where the earthquake was felt. Molly wants to know a little more: What caused this to happen? Can it happen in Boulder where we live? Is there some way to stop it from happening again? And what does the number indicating severity mean? What is the difference between a 7.5 or 5.7 earthquake? Who decides what number it is? She starts asking questions and her busy scholar parents write down "http://www.dlese.org" on a piece of paper and tell her this website will have useful and accurate information about earthquakes.*

*She goes to the website, types in "earthquakes" and 1000 hits come back. Which link should she go to? Which one will tell her what she wants to know in the vocabulary she understands as an 8th grader?*

In the above scenario, what is needed is a system to better assist intentional learning. Specifically, a system designed to help the user understand concepts within a domain by recommending useful resources that might help her achieve her learning goals. The materials and resources in this system should be loosely coupled, redundant, unstructured, and have a wide spectrum of users and learning styles they can cater to. Assessment might be open-ended because there isn't a particular module's content that is being assessed.

The rudiments of such a system can be found in CLICK, the goal of which is to help intentional learners better understand concepts in a specific domain (Ahmad et al, 2007). CLICK works by providing students the opportunity to write essays about Earth systems topics. It assesses the learner's essay and deduces the misconceptions and knowledge gaps of the learner relative to a domain model for the topic. The knowledge gaps are then presented to the user along with digital library resources that may be valuable in understanding those misconceptions. Users are encouraged to visit those resources and upon sufficient review, revise and re-write their essays for re-evaluation. Since there is no lesson plan, the feedback to the user provides a personalized structured-learning path through which the learner can make more sense of the domain content. This type of system promotes a cognitive perspective around how people learn, taking into account that different users may have different content knowledge. By acknowledging that everyone is not on the same learning path, the system allows each learner to navigate through the recommended resources they find most interesting and/or useful until they adequately demonstrate deeper understanding.

We have now outlined the different ways formal latent educational recommender systems are different from the CLICK informal intentional learning educational recommender system. The rest of the chapter will explore the finer details of the system and extensions to it as an educational recommender system.

## CLICK

The Customized Learning Service for Concept Knowledge (CLICK) was designed to be a scalable online service that recommends resources to student users based on the user's conceptual understanding (Ahmad et al, 2007). CLICK uses the Digital Library for Earth Systems Education (DLESE) to support learners' understanding of earth science content. CLICK first extracts a list of concepts that a learner should know about Earthquake and Plate Tectonics from a collection of documents that are grade level appropriate. Next, CLICK diagnoses the learner's incorrect, incomplete and fragmented conceptual knowledge. Finally, CLICK recommends digital library resources that might help the learner remedy the diagnosed deficiencies. The biggest difference between CLICK and other Educational recommender systems such as those proposed by Karampiperis & Sampson (2005) and Shen & Shen, (2004) is that all the work in CLICK is supposed to be done algorithmically. In other systems, the construction of the domain ontology and the domain concept map is done manually and requires tremendous resources in terms of expertise, time and money. Thus, such systems are difficult to replicate for other domains and hence the benefits of the system are not easily transferred – that is the system only works within the domain for which it was developed. CLICK is designed to overcome domain dependence by providing an architecture that can be applied and extended to a number of domains. The four main components of the CLICK system are the *domain concept map generator module*, the *student concept map generator module*, the *misconception identification module* and the *instructional plan generation module*. In this section, we will address each of these components and the details of their operation within the CLICK architecture (Figure 1).

*Figure 1. The CLICK architecture*

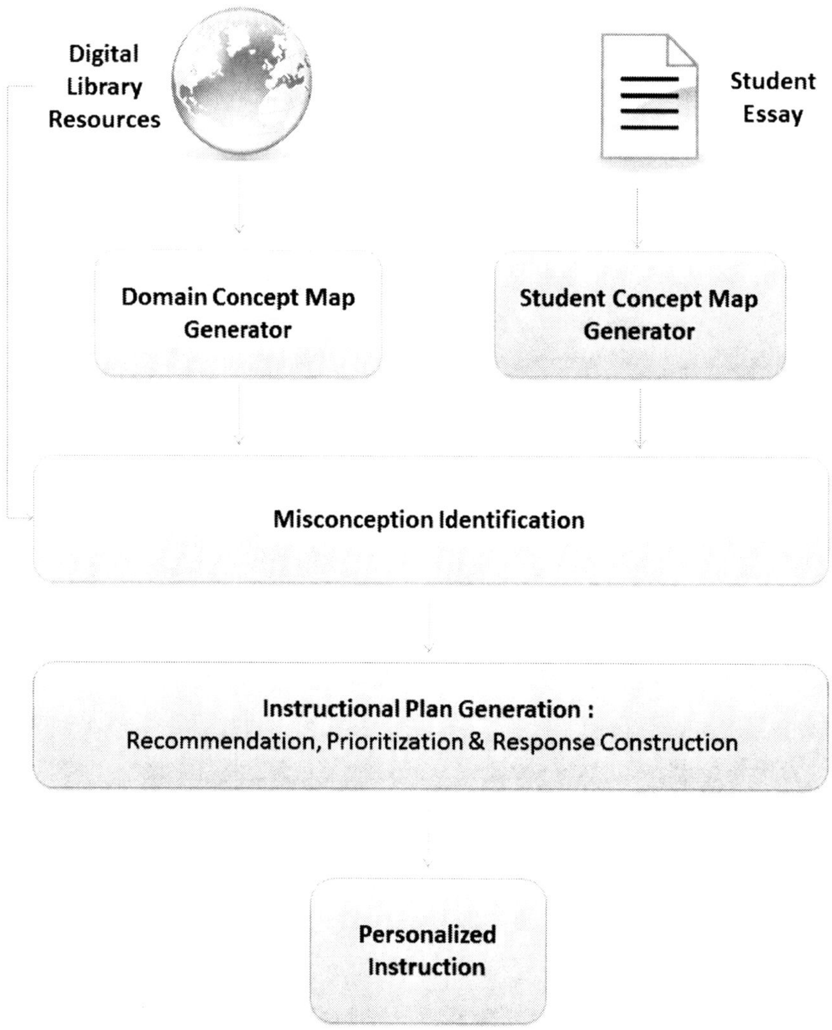


## DOMAIN CONCEPT MAP GENERATION

The domain concept generation process is captured in an architectural module called COGENT, explained in full detail elsewhere (de la Chica, 2009). In this section we will provide a summary of the key features of COGENT and how they relate to the CLICK architecture and process flow. The creation of the domain concept map is divided into two processes – *sentence extraction* or deciding which sentences to include from the digital resources and *sentence linking* or deciding which extracted sentences to link together.

*Figure 2. Sentence selection overview*

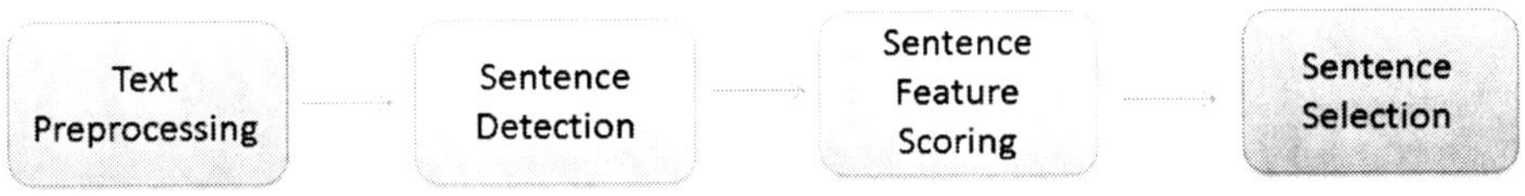


## Sentence Extraction

The sentence extraction is performed using multi-document summarization techniques based on MEAD (Radev et al., 2004). Custom features have been added based on domain content, document structure, and sentence length (de la Chica, 2009). These custom features were developed to reproduce the process of human expert annotators in choosing which sentences to include in a concept map. The selection process involves four primary steps: (1) HTML document resources are first converted to plain text, (2) sentence boundaries with the document are identified, (3) sentences are assigned scores based on features, resulting in a single score and ranking for each sentence, and (4) redundant sentences are eliminated and the resulting ranked sentences are outputted. Figure 2 shows the overview of the selection process.

Since sentence extraction is a crucial component of the CLICK process flow, we will review the three feature partitions of sentence selection based on domain content features, document structure features and sentence-level features.

Domain content features expose the essential features of the domain and are divided into three essential sentence features. First, the default MEAD *centroid* feature is used which assigns scores to sentences that contain words that are statistically significant to the group of documents being summarized. This provides an initial baseline of sentences to be selected, but does not provide enough contextualized detail to capture more subtle features of the documents being analyzed. Thus, the *educational standards* feature is developed to compare each sentence to the learning goals and educational standards as described by the relevant AAAS (American Association for the Advancement of Science) Benchmarks and National Science Education Standards for the domain. A score is assigned based on term frequency-inverse document frequency (Salton & Buckley, 1988), which boosts sentences that are related to the learning goals and educational standards of the domain and penalizes those that are not. Finally, the *gazetteer* feature compares named entities in each sentence to a list of pre-populated locations. The intuition of this feature is simple: named-entities are often crucial to detailed scientific explanations and examples. Thus capturing these would likely improve the accuracy of sentence selection. *Gazetteer* scores are assigned based on the uniqueness of a location, where locations listed infrequently receive higher scores.

Document structure features aim at exploiting the features of HTML documents to score sentences. For example, the default MEAD *position* feature assigns a higher score to sentences that appear earlier within a document. Similarly, the *hypertext* feature leverages the hierarchical structure of HTML tags by assigning a higher score to sentences that occur earlier in a paragraph, paragraphs that occur earlier within a document, and sentences with higher level HTML headings. Finally, sentence-level features are examined to score sentences based on lexical features. The default MEAD *length* feature eliminates sentences that have less than a certain cut-off number of words. The *content word density* feature classifies each word in a sentence as either a semantically important content word, or a syntactic function word that contributes little semantic information. Only sentences that have a ratio of content words to function words of at least 50% are considered for inclusion in the concept map.

As mentioned previously, the output of the sentence extraction process is a ranking of sentences largely based on the domain content, document structure and sentence-level features already discussed. Sentences are assigned a cumulative score based on all of the features and ranked, with redundant sentences eliminated using the MEAD cosine re-ranker and a cutoff similarity value of 0.7. Finally, the top ranked sentences are extracted until the cumulative word count is 5% of the total word count in the group of original documents. These extracted sentences are passed on to the Concept Linking Classifier (de la Chica, 2009) to be linked into the concept map structure.

## Evaluation

To evaluate the quality of COGENT's sentence extraction module, its performance is compared to two baselines. The random baseline simply selects a random set of sentences from the digital resources. The default baseline is the default configuration of MEAD which uses only the centroid, position, and length features. The COGENT configuration uses all of the default and custom features described above. The random, default, and COGENT configurations all use the same word compression factor of 5% to create summaries of comparable length.

The ROGUE package (Lin & Hovy, 2003) is used to assess the quality of the three configurations. ROGUE is based on common *n*-gram counts and the longest common subsequence. ROGUE-1 (unigrams), ROGUE-2 (bigrams), ROGUE-W-1.2 (weighted LCS), and ROGUE-S*(skip bigrams) are reported. The results are shown in Table 1.

## Sentence Linking

Once a subset of sentences has been extracted from the digital library resources, they must be linked together to form the concept map structure. Sentence linking is implemented by the Concept Linking Classifier, which uses a supervised machine learning technique, support vector machines (SVM), to decide if two sentences should be linked. The classifier takes as input labeled training data produced by human annotators and learns weights for features extracted from the sentences. These weights are then applied to features extracted from new, unlabeled pairs of sentences to determine if they should be linked. The following is a description of the features developed to represent the relevant characteristics of sentence pairs. They include lexical, syntactic, semantic, and document structure features.

Lexical features examine word overlap, word relations and *n*-gram features. The *word overlap*

*Table 1. COGENT evaluation showing ROGUE-1 (R-1), ROUGE-2 (R-2), ROGUE-W-1.2 (R-W-1.2) and ROUGE-S* (R-S*). F=F-measure, R=Recall and P=Precision. (de la Chica, 2009).*

| | RANDOM | | | DEFAULT | | | COGENT | | |
|---|---|---|---|---|---|---|---|---|---|
| | *F* | *R* | *P* | *F* | *R* | *P* | *F* | *R* | *P* |
| **R-1** | 0.4939 | 0.4855 | 0.5026 | 0.5308 | 0.4976 | 0.5688 | 0.6054 | 0.6073 | 0.6034 |
| **R-2** | 0.0988 | 0.0972 | 0.1006 | 0.1409 | 0.1321 | 0.1510 | 0.1901 | 0.1907 | 0.1895 |
| **R-W-1.2** | 0.1157 | 0.0929 | 0.1533 | 0.1228 | 0.0951 | 0.1733 | 0.1453 | 0.1185 | 0.1877 |
| **R-S*** | 0.2566 | 0.2481 | 0.2657 | 0.2969 | 0.2620 | 0.3424 | 0.3796 | 0.3820 | 0.3772 |

feature computes the number of word token overlaps between two sentences and normalizes the score based on sentence length. The *lexical chain* feature compares words between two sentences connected by the thesaurus relations repetition, synonymy, hypernymy, and hyponymy. The *n-gram* features compute the unique unigrams and bigrams that appear in the pair of sentences being considered. Syntactic features used by the linker are based on part of speech tags, parse trees, head noun phrase pairs, head verb phrase pairs, and their combinations. These features require each sentence to be part of speech tagged and parsed. Semantic features for sentence linking are built on top of MEAD's default cosine similarity that is used to score semantic distance between sentences. Finally, to extract document structure features, the *sentence distance* feature is used to calculate the distance between a pair of sentences based on their locations in the original digital library resources. Sentences from different resources are assigned a binary value for this feature – 1 if they are found within the same resource, otherwise 0. For sentences within the same resource, the *paragraph* feature is used to assign binary values to sentences that are found within the same paragraph.

## Evaluation

In a comparison of the link classifier to human expert created links from single digital resources, the most promising features for each feature group were identified as: common token count (lexical), common part of speech token count (syntactic), cosine (semantic), and sentence distance (document structure). These features were used to evaluate the performance of the link classifier on multi-document sentence linking. Table 2 describes the performance of the multi-document link classifier trained on these features compared to a majority-rules (all disconnected) baseline. Because the vast majority of sentence pairs were not linked by the experts, as expected the majority-rules baseline (all disconnected) performs very well. In its current implementation, the link classifier is more aggressive than necessary when linking, as evidenced by a nearly four-fold increase in the number of generated links under experimental tests. This weakness is part of future work to improve the linking algorithm.

# STUDENT CONCEPT MAP GENERATION

In CLICK, the learner's knowledge is represented by a concept map that is compared to a reference domain concept map. To construct the learner concept map, the learner's essay is first segmented into sentences. Each sentence in the learner's essay is treated as a concept node. Then a linking algorithm based on lexical chains (Morris & Hirst, 1991) is used to connect concept nodes into a graph structure. Nouns identified by a syntactical parser are used as candidate words for forming chains. The linking algorithm connects sentences

*Table 2. Link classifier evaluation results (de la Chica, 2009)*

| Feature | Accuracy | F-Measure | Recall | Precision |
|---|---|---|---|---|
| majority-rules (all disconnected) baseline | 0.9956 | N/A | N/A | N/A |
| sentence distance | 0.9651 | 0.0626 | 0.2623 | 0.0355 |
| common token count | 0.9375 | 0.0284 | 0.2061 | 0.0153 |
| cosine | 0.6234 | 0.0125 | 0.5386 | 0.0063 |
| Common POS token count | 0.0216 | 0.0083 | 0.9204 | 0.0042 |

that share these stemmed nouns, or that share synonyms, hypernyms, or hyponyms of these nouns using WordNet (Miller et al, 1990). Nouns from the previous four sentences are considered in creating these lexical chains. If a sentence cannot be linked using the lexical chain technique, it is attached to the preceding or following sentence.

### Evaluation

The learner knowledge map construction process is evaluated against maps created by human experts. The two measures of comparison are sentence selection (which learner sentences to include in the concept map) and sentence connectivity for 12 learner essays. For sentence selection, experts had an average recall, precision, and f-score of .92 when compared against each other. Since the automated algorithm includes all student sentences, it has a recall of 1.00, a precision of .87, and an F-measure of .93. For sentence connectivity, the experts had a recall of .66, precision of .67, and F-measure of .66 when compared to each other. The algorithm had a recall of .52, precision of .39, and F-measure of .44. These evaluation results indicate the algorithm has room for improvement when compared to the expert judgments.

## MISCONCEPTION IDENTIFICATION

The misconception identification module which is built on shallow (statistical) NLP techniques generates part of the user model. In CLICK, aside from pre-established information about the user such as age and grade, the user's conceptual knowledge is the most important element in the user model that guides resource recommendation. There are three types of misconceptions identified in CLICK – incorrect statements, incomplete understandings and fragmented knowledge. Below we briefly summarize how each of these misconceptions is identified, but the complete discussion on misconception identification in CLICK, including system design, algorithms, implementation specifics, and evaluation is fully documented in (Ahmad, 2008).

The core operation for the misconception identification module in CLICK is an alignment of the student concept map to the domain concept map. Each concept in the student concept map is aligned to concepts in the domain concept map using key terms and context. The alignment is done using Lucene's implementation of a vector space model. For each concept in the domain concept map, all neighboring concepts that are 1 distance from it are included as part of the concept. Synonyms and hypernyms for the head verb and head noun for the main domain concept text are also included if their number of senses are below a certain threshold. All of these features together form one document in the Lucene index. Queries to the index are generated from the student concept map and include the head word and named entities within a student concept, vocabulary terms determined from a domain glossary, and synonyms and hypernyms for the head noun and head verb. Executing all the generated queries against the Lucene index results in an alignment of the student concept map to the domain concept map, and the top fifteen results are retrieved.

Incorrect statements are identified by being in direct conflict with an aligned domain concept or having a wrong definition. To find concepts that are in direct conflict, the head nouns and head verbs of a concept in a student concept map are matched against head nouns and head verbs in its aligned domain concept counterparts. If the modifier of either the head noun or the head verb is found to be opposite to the one in the domain concept as determined from WordNet (Miller et al, 1990), the student concept is said to be incorrect. Hand-crafted rules for identifying definition swaps were developed and checked for fidelity against definitions in the student concepts to the definitions in the domain concept map. All student concepts that are not identified as being incorrect are passed on to the incomplete understanding and fragmented knowledge identification modules.

To identify students' incomplete understanding, important concepts are identified in the domain concept map using social networking and text analysis techniques. The resulting important concepts are composed from an intersection of the concepts identified via page rank and the HITS algorithm, concepts with an in/out degree higher than 6 and concepts with term-density higher than 0.5. All important concepts that were not aligned to any of a student's concepts (from the alignment stage) are marked as missing knowledge for the student. For the important concepts that were aligned, if there is less than a 50% overlap with the student concept, the student concept is labeled as having insufficient details. The missing knowledge and insufficient details constitute the student's incomplete understanding.

We classify two concepts in the student's essay as being fragmented if they should be connected based on their aligned counterparts in the domain concept map but are not connected in the student concept map. Two concepts in the student concept map are also considered to be fragmented if their shortest path distance is greater than 3 while their aligned counterparts in the domain concept map have a path distance of less than or equal to 3.

## Evaluation

Each misconception identification sub-module was evaluated separately but they all began with the data from the same study that is described next. Twelve students were asked to write an essay on earthquakes and plate tectonics with a word count of between 250 and 300 words. The essays were turned into concept maps using the student concept map generation module. Then four high school earth science teachers who were considered experts in the domain of earth science were recruited to assess the resulting student concept maps with reference to the domain concept map. Each student's concept map was assessed by two experts.

For all three sub-modules, the gold standard was taken to be the union of the two experts' assessment. The inter-expert agreement was calculated by assuming each expert's assessment was the gold standard and measuring the other expert's assessment against that and then averaging over all students work and experts. The baseline for the incorrect statement module was that all the student's concepts were incorrect. For the incomplete understanding module, the baseline was that every student concept constituted an incomplete understanding and for the fragmented knowledge module, the baseline was established by labeling all unconnected student concepts as fragmented. The results are shown in Table 3 with F standing for F-measure, R for recall and P for precision. The results show that the algorithm does reasonably well in detecting misconceptions.

## INSTRUCTIONAL PLAN GENERATION

The instructional plan generation module comprises prioritizing the misconception remediation,

*Table 3. Misconception identification evaluation F=F-measure, R=recall and P=precision. (Ahmad, 2008).*

| | EXPERT | | | ALGORITHM | | | BASELINE | | |
|---|---|---|---|---|---|---|---|---|---|
| | *F* | *R* | *P* | *F* | *R* | *P* | *F* | *R* | *P* |
| **Incorrect statement** | 0.69 | 0.69 | 0.69 | 0.69 | 0.87 | 0.57 | 0.48 | 1.0 | 0.31 |
| **Incomplete understanding** | 0.61 | 0.60 | 0.61 | 0.55 | 0.52 | 0.58 | - | 1.0 | 0.46 |
| **Fragmented knowledge** | 0.58 | 0.58 | 0.58 | 0.63 | 0.76 | 0.54 | - | 1.0 | 0.01 |

identifying resources that have the potential to help learners remedy their knowledge gap, and presenting the results of these analyses back to the learner in a pedagogically appropriate manner. To date, only the recommendation sub-module has been implemented in CLICK. Both the misconception prioritization and the presentation format are currently hard coded. Below, we summarize how the recommendation module works and discuss its evaluation.

There are four inputs to the recommendation module; a list of the student's misconceptions, the portion of the student's concept map where the misconceptions occurred, the portions of the domain concept map which were used to detect the student's misconceptions, and the digital library resources. The domain and student knowledge map representations are each converted into concept matrices that show how close a pair of key terms are in their respective maps. A concept graph of the student's understanding is then generated where nodes represent key terms and vertices representing the user's competence in understanding the key terms. A concept graph for each of the resources is also generated. Then using the maximum sub-graph as the similarity measure, the three resource graphs most similar to the student concept graph are selected for recommendation as the top-level URL. Resource graphs for each of the pages within each of the three resources are also generated and compared to the student's concept graph., which generates the "specific web page" in the recommendation. For a full discussion of the recommendation module, refer to Gu (2009). Currently, the only features of the learner profile that are used to make the recommendations are grade level and prior knowledge. Furthermore, the features of the resource that are used are its description and intended grade level.

## Evaluation

To evaluate the recommendation, first experts manually select the three most important misconceptions each of the 12 students had, thereby manually doing the misconception sequencing. Then, for each of the misconception each student had, the system recommended three online resources from DLESE whose content could help the student remedy the misconception. The system recommended the main URL for the resource – termed "online resource" and the exact URL within the online resource termed "specific web page" which contained the information the student needed. Then, an Earth science education expert was asked to rate the recommended resources as "highly relevant", "somewhat relevant" or "not relevant". During analysis, "highly" and "somewhat relevant" resources were merged into a single category "relevant". Based on analyzing the results from this evaluation, we were able to improve the recommendation algorithm and do another round of evaluations of new recommendations. The graph below (Figure 3) shows that our algorithm made an improvement of about 20% in terms of recommending resources that would be considered highly or somewhat relevant to the misconception.

## ASSESSING THE IMPACT OF CLICK PERSONALIZATION ON LEARNING

The working theory behind educational recommendation is that personalizing the recommendation will improve learning for the users in some way, be it by reducing the time it takes the users to find the resource, by helping the users determine what content they still need to learn and helping them learn it or perhaps by making their learning more robust by being able to transfer knowledge. Based on this observation, we carried out a study to determine if this theory that personalization helps learning held true for the users of our system. The study is fully documented in Butcher & Sumner (2010). The subject pool of 12 freshmen students were divided into control and experiment. Both groups were asked to write an essay and then were

*Figure 3. Comparison of two iterations of recommendations (Gu, 2009)*

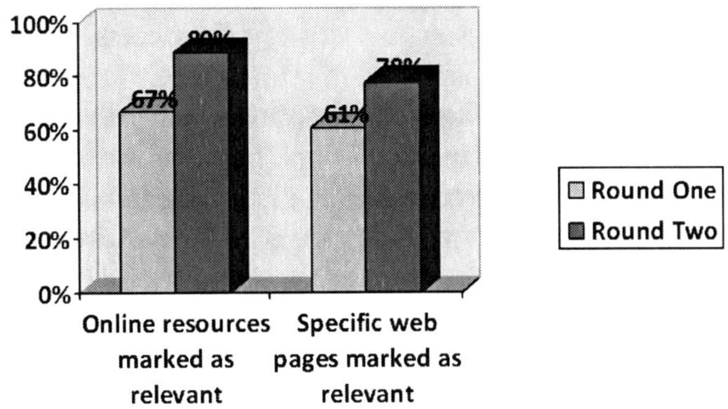


asked to make changes to their essay based on the feedback they were given. The control group had access to their top 3 identified misconceptions and a search interface into DLESE. While the experimental group had access to their top 3 identified misconceptions and recommended resources that were aligned to specific problematic sentences in their essay. Results showed that the students in the experimental group explored the resources more, performed deeper content revision of their essays and were more likely to recognize that they needed new knowledge. The students in the experimental condition liked the system and asked if they could use it for their other classes. From this we can deduce that learning actually occurred in the experimental condition and thus that personalization, even when done by a computer, can help students' learning.

## ADDRESSING THE CHALLENGES FOR EDUCATIONAL RECOMMENDER SYSTEMS FOR INTENTIONAL LEARNING

As mentioned earlier, educational recommender systems for intentional learning have to deal with determining prior knowledge, determining the learning goals, recommending different media formats, and ensuring the user interface is very usable. Each of these will be addressed separately in the context of CLICK described so far.

### Prior Knowledge

It is difficult to model a learner's prior knowledge because assessments in any format can only approximate a learner's knowledge. The formats currently being used in online settings are: multiple choice and short constructed responses and essays. Which format will give us the best information needed to make a recommendation? What is needed is information on what concepts a student understands well, the concepts the student doesn't understand and the knowledge gaps the student has. Almost any assessment format can give us this information if we structure it correctly.

To elicit learner prior knowledge in CLICK the essay format is used. Each user is asked to write a 250- 300 word essay on plate tectonics and earthquakes. Next, CLICK uses the algorithms described earlier in the chapter to convert the essay into a concept map representation and then detect the student's misconceptions. Instead of generating a definite representation of what the student knows, a representation of what the student *does not know*, based on the learning goals is generated.

We do acknowledge that the task used to elicit the user's prior knowledge was not well designed. We asked users to write everything they knew about Earth systems. Then, to find the problematic sentences in the students' work, their work was compared to a domain concept map consisting of everything students should know about earth science. The fact that the expected work output from the students was well below the amount of content they were assessed on virtually guaranteed that knowledge gaps, if not misconceptions would be found in the students' work. Since the primary interest is in improving student understanding of science concepts, it seemed appropriate to ask students to construct concept maps of their understanding as a more effective way to elicit what students know. This way, their command of a specific language does not significantly affect their expression of their prior knowledge. But creating concept maps is not a task that students are accustomed to so they might find it difficult to express themselves using this medium. A constructed response seems like the most viable method. It targets specific knowledge areas so we can compare students' work with just the part of the domain knowledge map that is targeted by one constructed response task. It is also less involved than writing an essay so perhaps students who are not native English speakers would be better served by this assessment format. The tradeoff of using a constructed response is that questions must be created that target specific topics and learning goals.

## Learning Goals

People have different goals when they come to an informal intentional learning system. Some might come to simply learn about a phenomenon for example "what causes tsunamis" or "why does California have lots of earthquakes and Connecticut hardly any"? Others might come because they have an upcoming exam in school and they want to learn more about something they don't fully understand and on which they will be tested. Others yet might have ended up in the system from browsing the web. In all of these cases, the recommender system is recommending resources based on some identified learning intention and criteria for success.

In CLICK, we assume that the users of our recommender system are high school students and their goal is to meet the standard of competence in Earth systems as defined by the American Association for the Advancement of Science (AAAS) standards. We use the AAAS standards because it is not tied to a particular school district or curriculum. Different school districts have different curricula which are designed to be taught in a school year. So it makes sense to use an idealized curriculum that is not constrained to what can be taught in a school year and that is not influenced by what region of the world a person resides. AAAS is a respected "international non-profit organization that is dedicated to advancing science around the world. AAAS has many publications and programs that raise the bar of understanding for science worldwide" (Science, 1993).

It is conceivable that at the beginning of each session with users are asked for their learning goal. They could, for example, select between "school-related" and "personal". For the school-related goals, the AAAS standards might be used as the model learning goals, and for the personal goals, it might be less important to determine the student's prior knowledge or learning goals and instead concentrate on recommending resources that match their expressed content need.

## Media Formats

Content-based recommendation requires a model of resources, which might be based on the words used in the resource, as in traditional word-document matrix information retrieval (Manning et al, 2008). However, word-based approaches cannot be applied to non-verbal resources such as images, animations, and simulations. Yet, as the semantic web becomes a new source of rich data, systems are being developed (Zhuhadar & Nasraoui, 2008) to manipulate these new resource descriptions. However, the current state of the art still relies on detailed metadata descriptions to help characterize these document-based and digital non-verbal resources. For resources with video, animations, and simulations, CLICK relies on analyzable word-based content within the resource, along with its metadata, to construct domain representations and recommend resources.

We can divide metadata characterizations into two categories: descriptive and evaluative (Vuorikari et al, 2006). Descriptive characteristics include objective information like the author, publication year, language, and type of resource (whether text, image, animation, etc). Evaluative characteristics include more subjective information such as quality rating, pedagogical utility, and ease of use. Metadata can further be classified as authoritative or non-authoritative (Recker & Wiley, 2001). Authoritative metadata is usually contributed by the creators or authors of a resource, and typically includes descriptive information about the resource such as author, content, technical requirements, and rights management. Non-authoritative metadata is usually contributed by users, and includes evaluative information such as rating, as well as crowd-sourced information such as usage metrics. Non-authoritative metadata allows users to add value to the resource with evaluative annotations such as how the resource was used, its usefulness in particular instructional contexts, how it relates to other resources, and perhaps an average rating of quality.

These quality evaluations can come from subject experts, educational professionals or end users (Vuorikari et al, 2006). Alternatively, quality indicators can be assessed automatically. One such method uses natural language processing and machine learning techniques to assess resource quality on the dimensions of: has prestigious sponsor, content is appropriate for age, has sponsor, identified learning goals, has instructions, identifies age range, and organized for learning goals (Wetzler et al 2009). Within CLICK, resource quality has been controlled by the source of the resources: NSDL, where particularly within the library collections in use within CLICK, the resources are vetted by domain experts.

## User Interface

The user interface is an important component of an educational recommender system because if the system cannot easily be used, then it may undermine the necessary support for learners. There are many heuristics for designing good user interfaces such as: emphasize recognition over recall; the system's status should always be visible and have a minimalist design; and be consistent in the use of symbols, among many others (Nielsen, 1994).

During the design of CLICK, emphasized participatory design was emphasized by engaging with our projected users. The interface design was iterated several times before settling on the current design.

Figure 4 shows the current CLICK user interface running within a web browser. A student writes in the left pane which has basic word processing capabilities. When the student clicks on *Find problems and Recommendations*, the problems and recommendations are displayed in the top right panel. In addition to all the heuristics outlined in Nielsen (1994), two design issues came to the forefront when trying to ensure the system was usable. The first was that the information about misconceptions and the recommendations should be conveyed simply and quickly. The second was that it was necessary to support the way participants worked when writing an essay on a scientific topic. Below, we outline how the CLICK system deals with these issues.

## Conveying Information Simply and Quickly

The *problem* buttons (*problem 1* and *problem 2* in the figure above) let users know immediately how many learning problems were detected in

*Figure 4. The CLICK user interface*

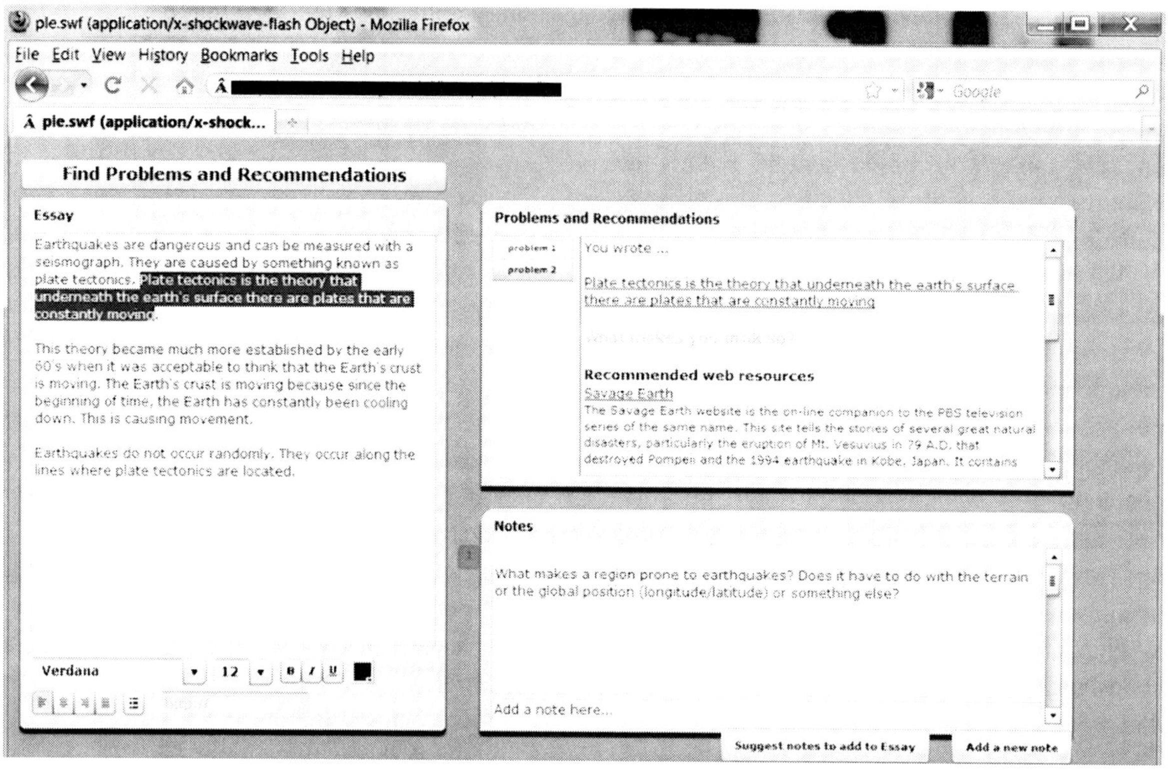


their work. When the user clicks on a numbered problem button – for example, *problem 1* – the pane to the right of the problems pane displays the problematic sentence, a prompt to help the user revise the sentence, and three recommended resources that can help users remedy their problems. Clicking on the problematic sentence in the "problems and recommendations" pane highlights the sentence within the student's essay. All these convey information quickly and simply to the user.

## Support the Learners' Work Process

During the user interface design, students were observed working with resources when writing an essay. It was found that student took notes from various resources and pasted them at the bottom of their essay. At some point during the writing phase, they worked the note into their essay. The notes panel is our solution to supporting this process. It gives students a place to take notes from a resource. It was also discovered that some students forgot to cite the source when the note is already within their essay. A pink button associated with a note can be dragged into the essay. Double-clicking on it opens a pop-up window that contains the text of the note. This helps students to remember to cite their sources since the text and font is different from that of the essay. Though the "Suggest notes to add to Essay" button functionality has not been implemented, when it is implemented it will suggest other notes that students have previously written that should be added to their essay to make it better. This will help students know when they have all the content they need within their work space.

The current user interface results from the initial decisions made on how to detect misconceptions. Since students were required to write an essay, a writing pane was provided to have a cohesive system. Depending on what sort of learning goals that will be supported in the future, it might be valuable to include search engine features when the learning goal is "personal" as opposed to "school centered". In any case, a number of improvements to the user interface are planned to address the issues identified here and elsewhere.

## NEXT STEPS FOR CLICK

There are three main areas of current work underway on CLICK: 1) the generalization of the algorithms to other domains, 2) identifying core concepts in the domain concept map, and 3) prioritizing the misconceptions.

### Generalization

One major goal for the next iteration of CLICK is to generalize the algorithms to work with new domains. Ideally, the automated approach to domain representation given a set of high-quality digital resources could be ported to many subject areas with minimal manual intervention. Rather than hand-crafting domain ontologies, we want to focus on domain-independent approaches to support a wide variety of STEM topics and age ranges. Our current expansion has been to two domains: weather and climate (near domain) and biological evolution (far domain). Our algorithms show promising results so far, but are hampered by some domain-specific implementation aspects such as the gazetteer feature in concept extraction stage. Generalizing our approach will enable rapid, inexpensive, high-quality domain representations that can be flexibly embedded in a range of learning applications.

### Core Concept Identification

Another major goal for CLICK is to identify core concepts in the domain. These are the "big ideas" that are vital to support deep science learning and transfer. AAAS learning goals will be used to inform the design and evaluation of our algorithms. We are conducting an expert annotation study to label core concepts in the digital resources, which will help us develop automatic methods for core concept identification. These core concepts will be represented as highly interconnected nodes in the concept maps with labels that are pedagogically useful to model deep understanding. They will be used to prioritize instructional interventions and provide feedback to enable robust learning.

### Prioritization

Prioritization of the misconceptions is important because all learning needs are not equally important. Students should see marked improvements in their work early on as this can motivate them to learn more. Good teachers know and already prioritize the misconceptions they report back to students on their work. So it is essential that we prioritize the misconceptions so that users can tackle the big problems first. For example, it is more important that a student understands how and why earthquakes are formed than knowing that earthquakes occur frequently in Indonesia.

Because of the way CLICK is structured, at the far end of the system, CLICK generates a list of student misconceptions and recommended resources that can remedy the student's problems. At the time of this writing, CLICK does not address the notion of the importance of each of the learner's problems. In the evaluation of the recommendation, we had experts manually select the top-3 misconceptions that each student should work on. So to CLICK, not understanding how Earthquakes are formed has the same importance as not knowing that earthquakes occur in Indonesia. By prioritizing the misconceptions, we are trying to model effective formative feedback. To do so, it is essential to give students an idea of where and how their effort should be concentrated in order to see an increase in learning.

With CLICK prioritization is done bottom-up. In the expert study, experts were provided with students' problematic sentences and asked in what order the students should go about remedying the problems. The inter-rater reliability, which was chosen as the upper bound for any algorithmic implementation of the expert process, was very low. The reason for this low reliability was primarily a function of the small number of students in the study. Another solution that has been tried was to identify up to 13 misconception categories (Ahmad, 2008). If the misconception types can be sequenced, then doing the prioritization would be reduced to a classification task. However, there is not yet enough data to train and test such a misconception classifier. When we do obtain more data, this direction will be explored more thoroughly. A more viable option, however, might be to do top-down prioritization by prioritizing the concepts to be learned. Following this line of thinking requires constructing a more hierarchical domain knowledge map, which is currently underway.

Learning science has highlighted the important role of "critical knowledge components" in supporting robust learning (VanLehn et al, 2006). Focusing on "big ideas" or "linchpin ideas" is an important strategy for developing enduring understanding that transfers to new domains (Wiggins and McTighe, 2005). Building on these ideas, the domain knowledge map can be prioritized by identifying and representing "core concepts," that is, the critical ideas necessary to support deep science learning and transfer. These core concepts can then be used to prioritize instructional interventions and provide pedagogical feedback to enable robust student learning. The order presented in sources such as textbooks, syllabus from various school districts and vetted online resources can also be used to figure out what these core concepts should be and in what order a user should learn them. A combination of the information from these sources will provide an ideal path which can be further tailored to each student.

## SUMMARY OF NEXT STEPS

In addition to the three main next steps of generalization, core conception detection and misconception prioritization, we also hope to improve the extraction, misconception detection and the recommendation during the next iteration of the project. For all the above, during this next phase of the project, we will use better software pieces such as summarizers, chunkers, named-entity recognizers, parsers and semantic role labelers that are tuned for our data. In addition, for the extraction, we are exploring ways to increase the confidence of the extractions, reduce extraneous/non-important concepts and reduce the total number of concepts extracted while increasing the ability of the domain concept map to help in misconception diagnosis by being able to resolve all references to people, events and phenomena.

For the misconception detection, our error analysis (which is not reported in this chapter) showed that alignment of student concepts to domain concepts was the biggest problem facing the misconception detection module. Hence we are working on improving the alignment of student concepts to domain concepts. We are also exploring other ways we can determine the truth value of a student's concept. For the recommendation, we are considering other ways in which we can recommend resources. For example, we are exploring the notion of analogies to help in making recommendations. So if a user understands an analogy that simplifies a hard-to-grasp concept, we can recommend that simplified analogy as a building block for the student before they are recommended the difficult piece.

## FUTURE RESEARCH DIRECTIONS

Architectures to support learner models and knowledge have appeared in adaptive e-learning systems (Brusilovsky et al, 2005; Brusilovsky, 2004). The variation presented in our work with

CLICK is to expand support for intentional modes of learning. As students spend more and more time on the internet, it would be useful to integrate informal, intentional learning into the rest of their online experience. Emerging technologies such as OpenID (Recordon & Reed, 2006) could facilitate the integration of educational recommender systems with social networks such as Facebook. Furthermore, Attention Profile Markup Language (APML) might be used to develop student interest profiles that could be used by the learner model, and potentially shared across learning applications. Collecting information from a student's participation in other online activities such as social networking and web-based research would inform the learner model and could enable better, more targeted educational resource recommendations (Vuorikari et al, 2010). Social recommendation is an area that CLICK could benefit from greatly, for example, in understanding the relationship between resources that are commonly used among users with similar profiles would provide a powerful new way to learn about resources that affect learners in similar ways. Finally, since CLICK does not currently process non-text media formats, for example, video or audio resources, these formats should become part of the larger set of resources available for recommendation. For example, exploiting metadata formats that include video, audio or other non-textual material so that these types of resources could become part of the resource recommendation would broaden the appeal and effectiveness of recommendations to various learners and learning styles.

As the web quickly transitions from Web 2.0 to Web 3.0, where personalization becomes even more important and "me-onomies" develop that target the preferences, interests and behaviors of individual users, further research in CLICK should take advantage of personalized learning opportunities that will be essential to the future of learning. To facilitate lifelong learning, informal intentional educational recommender systems such as CLICK should not only gather information from learners' online activities, but also embed such information into their web experience. The web could be augmented by embedding videos, engaging simulations, and links to educational resources that relate the content on the webpage to the personalized learner model of the end-user. Students may then be more motivated to deeply explore topics they encounter throughout their everyday web experience when customized learning resources are unobtrusively embedded within that web experience.

## CONCLUSION

In this chapter we have presented the CLICK system and some of its inner workings. CLICK provides *automatic* generation of personalized resources that are designed to address a user's specific needs in an intentional learning setting. CLICK employs recommendation techniques to suggest resources to learners that address the misconceptions and incorrect knowledge that are found by comparing automatically generated domain and learner models. Three core components to personalization in the context of intentional learning have thus been established. First, any system that is designed to support intentional learning needs to have a flexible learner model that accounts for the learner state over time. This model also needs to account for user behavior within the system and how that behavior supports knowledge gains. Second, the system designed for intentional learning needs to be built upon a foundation of strong resources that are expert-approved and vetted. Within the CLICK system, a well-maintained digital library based on high metadata standards provides such resource support and demonstrates the value of such vetting in educational contexts where it is crucial. Finally, the system needs to be designed around sound recommender technology that supports traditional recommender techniques as well as social-based techniques. Learners today are engaged socially with one another and support for the interaction of online social communication, collaborative learning, and sharing are paramount.

E-learning environments have come a long way in supporting learners in formal settings. As the Internet continues to transform the lives of learners engaged in formal learning activities and opportunities, so too will it transform informal learning. Systems like CLICK must be developed and expanded that support the information seeking behaviors of learners who are motivated, but must rely on overwhelming amounts of digital materials available to them. Tomorrow's educational tools and techniques must be able to meet the challenges of a new generation of learners in a new era of mobile intelligent technology, ubiquitous social connectivity, and persistent information access.

## REFERENCES

Ahmad, F. (2008). *Generating conceptually personalized interactions for educational digital libraries using concept maps*. PhD Dissertation, Department of Computer Science, University of Colorado at Boulder.

Ahmad, F., de la Chica, S., Butcher, K., Sumner, T., & Martin, J. H. (2007). Towards automatic conceptual personalization tools. In *Proceedings of the 7th ACM/IEEE-CS Joint Conference on Digital Libraries* (pp. 452–461).

American Association for the Advancement of Science. (1993). *Benchmarks for science literacy*.

Bercovitz, B., Kaliszan, F., Koutrika, G., Liou, H., Mohammadi Zadeh, Z., & Garcia-Molina, H. (2009). CourseRank: A social system for course planning. In *Proceedings of the 35th SIGMOD International Conference on Management of Data* (pp. 1107–1110).

Brusilovsky, P. (2004). KnowledgeTree: A distributed architecture for adaptive e-learning. In *Proceedings of the 13th International World Wide Web Conference, Alternate Track Papers & Posters* (pp. 104–113).

Brusilovsky, P., Sosnovsky, S., & Shcherbinina, O. (2005). User modeling in a distributed e-learning architecture. *User Modeling, 12*, 387–391. doi:10.1007/11527886_50

Burke, R. (2000). Knowledge-based recommender systems. *Encyclopedia of Library and Information Systems, 69*(Supplement 32), 175–186.

Butcher, K. R., & Sumner, T. (2010). Self-directed learning and the sensemaking paradox. *Human-Computer Interaction*, 26.

Collins, M. (1999). *Head-driven statistical models for natural language parsing*. Ph.D. dissertation, Department of Computer Science, University of Pennsylvania.

de la Chica, S. (2009). *Generating conceptual knowledge representations to support students writing scientific explanations*. PhD Dissertation, Department of Computer Science, University of Colorado at Boulder.

Gu, Q. (2009). *Personalized information seeking to support intentional learning*. PhD Dissertation, Department of Computer Science, University of Colorado at Boulder.

Hanson, K., & Carlson, B. (n.d.). *Effective access: Teachers' use of digital resources in STEM teaching*. Gender, Diversities, and Technology Institute, Education Development Center, Inc. Retrieved from http://www2.edc.org/gdi/publications_SR/EffectiveAccessReport.pdf

Karampiperis, P., & Sampson, D. (2005). Adaptive learning resources sequencing in educational hypermedia systems. *Journal of Educational Technology & Society, 8*(4), 128–147.

KnowledgeWorks. (2006). *2006-2016: Map of future forces affecting education* (p. 8). Institute for the Future and KnowledgeWorks Foundation.

Lin, C. Y., & Hovy, E. (2003). Automatic evaluation of summaries using n-gram co-occurrence statistics. In *Proceedings of the 2003 Conference of the North American Chapter of the Association for Computational Linguistics on Human Language Technology,* vol. 1 (pp. 71–78).

Manning, C. D., Prabhakar, R., & Hinrich, S. (2008). *Introduction to information retrieval*. Cambridge University Press. Retrieved from http://www.amazon.ca/exec/obidos/redirect?tag=citeulike09-20&path=ASIN/0521865719

Miller, G. A., Beckwith, R., Fellbaum, C., Gross, D., & Miller, K. J. (1990). Introduction to WordNet: An on-line lexical database. *International Journal of Lexicography*, *3*(4), 235. doi:10.1093/ijl/3.4.235

Morris, J., & Hirst, G. (1991). Lexical cohesion computed by thesaural relations as an indicator of the structure of text. *Computational Linguistics*, *17*(1), 21–48.

NAE. (2008). *Grand challenges fir engineering*. National Academy of Engineering. Retrieved April 2008, from http://www.engineeringchallenges.org/

Nielsen, J. (1994). Usability inspection methods. In *Conference Companion on Human Factors in Computing Systems* (pp. 413–414).

Radev, D., Allison, T., Blair-Goldensohn, S., Blitzer, J., Celebi, A., Dimitrov, S., et al. (2004). MEAD-A platform for multidocument multilingual text summarization. In *Proceedings of LREC* (Vol. 2004).

Recker, M. M., & Wiley, D. A. (2001). A non-authoritative educational metadata ontology for filtering and recommending learning objects. *Interactive Learning Environments*, *9*(3), 255–271. doi:10.1076/ilee.9.3.255.3568

Recordon, D., & Reed, D. (2006). OpenID 2.0: A platform for user-centric identity management. In *Proceedings of the Second ACM Workshop on Digital Identity Management* (pp. 11–16).

Salton, G., & Buckley, C. (1988). Term-weighting approaches in automatic text retrieval. *Information Processing & Management*, *24*(5), 513–523. doi:10.1016/0306-4573(88)90021-0

Shen, L., & Shen, R. (2004). Learning content recommendation service based-on simple sequencing specification. *Advances in Web-Based Learning–ICWL*, *2004*, 293–323.

Stein, N. L., & Levine, L. J. (1990). *Making sense out of emotion: The representation and use of goal-structured knowledge. Psychological and biological approaches to emotion*, (pp. 45–73).

Vanlehn, K., et al. (2006). The PSLC theoretical framework.

Vuorikari, R., Manouselis, N., & Duval, E. (2006). Using metadata for storing, sharing and reusing evaluations for social recommendations: The case of learning resources . In Goh, D., & Foo, S. (Eds.), *Social information retrieval systems: Emerging technologies and applications for searching the Web effectively*. Hershey, PA: Idea Group Publishing.

Vuorikari, R., Poldoja, H., & Koper, R. (2010). Comparison of educational tagging systems–Any chances of interplay. *International Journal of Technology Enhanced Learning, 2*.

Wetzler, P. G., Bethard, S., Butcher, K., Martin, J. H., & Sumner, T. (2009). Automatically assessing resource quality for educational digital libraries. In *Proceedings of the 3rd Workshop on Information Credibility on the Web - WICOW '09* (p. 3). Presented at the 3rd workshop, Madrid, Spain.

Wiggins, G. P., & McTighe, J. (2005). *Understanding by design*. Association for Supervision & Curriculum Development.

Zhuhadar, L., & Nasraoui, O. (2008). Semantic information retrieval for personalized e-learning. In *2008 20th IEEE International Conference on Tools with Artificial Intelligence* (pp. 364–368).

## ADDITIONAL READING

Adomavicius, G., & Tuzhilin, A. (2005). Toward the next generation of recommender systems: A survey of the state-of-the-art and possible extensions. *IEEE Transactions on Knowledge and Data Engineering*, 734–749. doi:10.1109/TKDE.2005.99

Ahmad, F., de la Chica, S., Butcher, K., Sumner, T., & Martin, J. H. (2007). Towards automatic conceptual personalization tools. In Proceedings of the 7th ACM/IEEE-CS joint conference on Digital libraries (pp. 452–461).

Aleven, V. A., & Koedinger, K. R. (2002). An effective metacognitive strategy: Learning by doing and explaining with a computer-based Cognitive Tutor. *Cognitive Science*, *26*(2), 147–179. doi:10.1207/s15516709cog2602_1

Basu, C., Hirsh, H., & Cohen, W. (1998). Recommendation as classification: Using social and content-based information in recommendation. In Proceedings of the National Conference on Artificial Intelligence (pp. 714–720).

Boyd, D. M., & Ellison, N. B. (2008). Social network sites: Definition, history, and scholarship. *Journal of Computer-Mediated Communication*, *13*(1), 210–230. doi:10.1111/j.1083-6101.2007.00393.x

Brusilovsky, P., Kobsa, A., & Nejdl, W. (2007). *The adaptive web: methods and strategies of web personalization*. Springer-Verlag New York Inc.

Chi, M., Feltovich, P., & Glaser, R. (1981). Categorization and representation of physics problems by experts and novices. *Cognitive Science*, *5*, 121–152. doi:10.1207/s15516709cog0502_2

Csikszentmihalyi, M., & Csikzentmihaly, M. (1991). *Flow: The psychology of optimal experience*. HarperPerennial New York.

Haghighi, A., & Vanderwende, L. (2009). Exploring content models for multi-document summarization. In *Proceedings of Human Language Technologies: The 2009 Annual Conference of the North American Chapter of the Association for Computational Linguistics* (pp. 362–370).

Jurafsky, D., & Martin, J. (2008). *Speech and Language Processing: An Introduction to Natural Language Processing, Computational Linguistics and Speech Recognition*. Prentice-Hall.

Laudauer, T., Foltz, P., & Laham, D. (1998). An introduction to latent semantic analysis. *Discourse Processes*, *25*, 259–284. doi:10.1080/01638539809545028

Mestre, J. (2002). Probing adults' conceptual understanding and transfer of learning via problem posing. *Journal of Applied Developmental Psychology*, *23*(1), 9–50. doi:10.1016/S0193-3973(01)00101-0

Nenkova, A., & Adviser-Mckeown, K. (2006). *Understanding the process of multi-document summarization: content selection, rewriting and evaluation*. Columbia University.

NRC. (2000). *How People Learn: Brain, Mind, Experience, and School: Expanded Edition*. Washington, DC: National Research Council: Commission on Behavioral and Social Sciences and Education, National Academy Press. 374 pp.

O'Donnell, A., Dansereau, D., & Hall, R. (2002). Knowledge Maps as Scaffolds for Cognitive Processing. *Educational Psychology Review*, *14*(1), 71–86. doi:10.1023/A:1013132527007

Razzaq, L., & Heffernan, N. (2010). Is it Better to Give or Wait to be Asked? In *Intelligent Tutoring Systems* (pp. 349–358). Hints. doi:10.1007/978-3-642-13388-6_39

Sarrafzadeh, A., Alexander, S., Dadgostar, F., Fan, C., & Bigdeli, A. (2008). "How do you know that I don't understand?" A look at the future of intelligent tutoring systems. *Computers in Human Behavior*, *24*(4), 1342–1363. doi:10.1016/j.chb.2007.07.008

Schenker, A. (2005). *Graph-theoretic techniques for web content mining*. World Scientific Pub Co Inc.

Shardanand, U., & Maes, P. (1995). Social information filtering: algorithms for automating "word of mouth". In Proceedings of the SIGCHI conference on Human factors in computing systems (pp. 210–217).

VanLehn, K. (1996). Cognitive skill acquisition. *Annual Review of Psychology*, 47.

Vekiri, I. (2002). What Is the Value of Graphical Displays in Learning? *Educational Psychology Review*, *14*, 261–312. doi:10.1023/A:1016064429161

Wade-Stein, D., & Kintsch, E. (2004). Summary Street: Interactive computer support for writing. *Cognition and Instruction*, *22*(3), 333–362. doi:10.1207/s1532690xci2203_3

Wang, D., Li, T., Zhu, S., & Ding, C. (2008). Multi-document summarization via sentence-level semantic analysis and symmetric matrix factorization. In *Proceedings of the 31st annual international ACM SIGIR conference on Research and development in information retrieval* (pp. 307–314).

Wertheimer, R. (1990). The geometry proof tutor: An "intelligent" computer-based tutor in the classroom. *Mathematics Teacher*, *83*, 308–317.

## KEY TERMS AND DEFINITIONS

**CLICK:** Conceptual Learning Service for Concept Learning. A prototype automatic personalized learning system that analyses student-written essays and suggests useful digital resources. CLICK functions as an informal, intentional recommender system.

**COGENT:** Concept Model Generation Engine. A module of CLICK that extracts key concepts from a set of digital resources and links them together to automatically create a knowledge map of the learning domain.

**Concept:** For the purposes of CLICK, each sentence is treated as a concept.

**Core Concept:** A linchpin idea which is central to understanding a set of other concepts. In the domain map, they are represented as strongly interconnected clusters of nodes where the relations between nodes are typed in pedagogically useful ways. A cluster corresponds to a critical knowledge component, identifying highly related ideas and important relationships between them.

**DLESE:** Digital Library for Earth Science Education. A curated repository of high-quality digital resources covering the earth science domain for use by students and teachers. Resources include text as well as multimedia information such as animations and interactive simulations.

**Intentional Learning:** A situation where learners are intrinsically motivated to learn. This encompasses learning situations where the learner wants to understand a concept for the sake of knowing or while getting ready for a test. The key aspect of this is that the learners seek out the resources on their own. Aka self-directed learning.

**Knowledge Map:** A variation of concept maps that consist of a network of nodes and links where the nodes contain clauses or sentences and the links contain a limited set of relationship types between the nodes.

**MEAD:** Multi-document summarization tool that has been extended with customized features for CLICK.

**Metadata:** Information about a resource such as its author, subject, and copyright.

**Misconception:** This refers to incorrect statement, fragmented knowledge and incomplete understanding (knowledge gaps).

# Chapter 2
# Metis:
# A Content Map-Based Recommender System for Digital Learning Activities

**Jody S. Underwood**
*Intelligent Automation, Inc., USA*

## ABSTRACT

*Recommender systems in e-learning contexts typically try to "intelligently" recommend actions to a learner based on the actions of previous learners. One of the limitations of such systems is that a lot of data is needed in order to recommend meaningful activities. This chapter describes one approach for addressing this limitation in a framework that uses a structured map of mathematics concepts and processes to power a recommender system that will recommend to students digital learning activities for which they are ready. This recommender system is called Metis, for the Greek goddess of good advice, and is currently in the design phase. Metis takes seriously the idea that to build on the knowledge, skills, and abilities (KSAs) that a student has, it is essential to identify those KSAs. Trying to build on KSAs that a student does not have is misguided. Metis recommends activities linked to KSAs that students are ready to learn, and more standard recommender algorithms further refine the list of recommended activities. Taking this approach has the potential to make activities more engaging, which can lead learners to greater interest in the content area.*

## INTRODUCTION

*"We are leaving the information age and entering the recommendation age."--Chris Anderson, author of The Long Tail (p. 107)*

DOI: 10.4018/978-1-61350-489-5.ch002

Imagine a classroom where all students are at the same level, where they all pick up whatever topic the teacher is teaching. Students would all be engaged and interested, there would be less clowning around, and the teacher's job would be to teach content and not have to do behavior management. In this chapter, we present a framework to help achieve this goal.

As Mark Twain said about the weather, "Everybody talks about it but nobody does anything about it," it is widely understood that people can most easily learn something that they almost know. But "doing something about it" requires finding out what each individual student is ready to learn and tailoring lessons appropriately. Only with great difficulty, and perhaps only in theory, can a teacher conduct this kind of assessment and instruction for 30 students simultaneously. Human tutors can help individual students learn, with varying approaches and levels of success, but they are expensive. Some intelligent tutoring systems have displayed impressive results in laboratory studies (Shute & Psotka, 1996), but their approach is to create a single software application as a solution to help all students learn. We posit that no single activity can be a solution for everyone since students have different background knowledge and take different approaches to learning. Some researchers are developing educational games (e.g., Plass, et al., 2010), and some practitioners have developed videos (e.g., http://khanacademy.org) that focus on singular concepts perhaps for the same reason. Multiple activities that take different approaches to learning single concepts and processes, structured in easily accessible ways, would help individuals learn in their own ways. Our approach will focus on singular concepts, which is the basis for allowing us to determine what people know and provide them with material they are ready for.

Some mathematics educational content portals (e.g., onlinemathlearning.com, exploremath.com, some textbook publishers) have activities that focus on individual content areas. A learner can browse the activities according to content area and sometimes genre (e.g., games, worksheets), but the activities are not structured to help students and teachers locate activities that are geared to their existing knowledge and learning preferences. Moreover, each content area typically has a single activity, that is, takes a single approach to learning; there are not multiple activities, where each would take a different approach to help students learn the material, in tune with different learning preferences. In addition, these sites do not provide descriptions for required prior knowledge for an activity, which would help guide learners to activities they are ready for.

This chapter describes a recommender system that will guide students to activities for which they are ready by using a framework for structuring digital learning activities in terms of knowledge, skills, and abilities (KSAs). This recommender system is called Metis, for the Greek goddess of good advice. The Metis approach provides a unique environment for underperforming learners in which their learning paths are individualized. Our explanation for underperforming students is that they are not given enough time to master material before they move on to more complex material. Metis will suggest to these students only activities they are ready for. For example, in mathematics, if a learner is having a lot of difficulty with an activity that uses ratios for comparison, Metis will recommend activities that focus on comparing and ordering numbers or understanding the concept of ratios and proportions, both of which are prerequisites for using ratios for comparison. If they are having some difficulty with this activity, they will be directed to an activity of a different genre that teaches the same KSA. Similarly, if the learner finds a 'using ratios for comparison' activity easy, suggestions will be made for activities that build on that concept. Such a prerequisite content map-based recommender system, where achievement is individually defined and measured, has the potential to strengthen overall attitudes toward and self-efficacy in math-related tasks (Schoenfeld, 2002), which in turn can bolster achievement.

After presenting reviews of research in support of the underlying cognitive pedagogical approach of Metis, we describe the modules of the recommender system and then expound on it via an example.

## BACKGROUND

Recommender systems use ratings or popularity as a guide, but these approaches need a large amount of data before they can be useful (Burke, 2000). Many efforts in educational recommender systems similarly use usage data and ratings to create recommendations for learners (e.g., Geyer-Schulz, Hahsler, & Jahn, 2001; Recker, Walker, & Lawless, 2003). Some of the identified shortcomings of such systems are biased recommendations, "free riding" (where students just consume recommendations and do not contribute), and positive/ negative feedback effects (where a few early positive or negative recommendations may affect the life of a learner's experience). One of the problems with these educational recommender systems is that they focus only on surface features and not on understanding the content for which learners are ready, a goal for educational recommender systems noted by Drachsler, Hummel, and Koper (2008). Supplying a content-based framework for a recommender system may alleviate the impact of these problems, even if they do not remove them entirely. One thing that can be assured is that mapping relationships between math concepts, while assessing what students know while they interact with digital content, can provide the basis to guide students to activities appropriate to their level.

To support our approach to a content map-based recommender system, we review the literature on cognition and learning (specifically on mastery learning and cognitive load), assessing learner knowledge, and the structure of knowledge for the purpose of individualizing learning.

### Cognition and Learning

Researchers have attempted to individualize learning in academic subjects with a good deal of success. Bloom (1983), for one, explored mastery learning in his educational research. Mastery learning refers to the notion that, given clear instructional objectives, periodic diagnostic assessments, and sufficient time, any learner can acquire the knowledge and skills being taught (Shute, Lajoie, & Gluck, 2000). Bloom found that if students in a class show up with the same level of prerequisite knowledge, they will end up with the same level of achievement, and if they show up with different levels of prerequisite knowledge they will more likely end up with different levels of achievement. The ERIC database lists nearly 2,000 articles on mastery learning, and five of the six major research syntheses substantiate the method's positive effect on student achievement (referenced in Martinez & Martinez, 1999). In another line of research, prior knowledge has been found to be a very reliable predictor of depth, breadth, and efficiency of training (Tobias, 1989; 1994). Those who already have a declarative and procedural foundation for a topic are likely to learn it faster, remember it longer, and transfer what they have learned to new situations (Chi, Glaser, & Rees, 1982; Shute, 1994; White & Frederiksen, 1986). Metis's approach to linking activities to a prerequisite content map will help individual students gain the foundational prerequisite knowledge they need to learn the material currently being taught in class.

Research on cognitive load suggests that learning happens best under conditions that are aligned with general theories of human cognition. We define a "simple" explanation as one that: (1) is expressed in terms of things the student already knows (i.e., the student's existing schemas; Sweller, 1988), and (2) is small enough to fit into short-term memory (Miller, 1956). Complex explanations, in contrast, are those that string together many steps, including some concepts that students may not have yet mastered. Some homework help systems use this complex explanation approach (e.g., webmath.com). Research has shown that students learn best when the explanations presented to them are simple ones (Kluger & DeNisi, 1996; Bangert-Drowns, Kulik, & Morgan, 1991). Metis prefers activities that provide simple explanations by focusing on single topics so they can be recommended in response to evidence of a student having the prior knowledge necessary to understand them.

## Assessing Learner Knowledge

For the user to be engaged, recommended activities must be neither too easy (promoting boredom) nor too hard (discouraging continued play). Learning is optimized when the difficulty of the task lies in the user's zone of proximal development (Vygotsky, 1978) and the flow of the activity is undisturbed (Csikszentmihalyi, 1990). To achieve this optimization, assessment of what the student knows needs to occur during an activity without affecting the flow, and recommendations made that are at the right level of difficulty for the learner.

As a matter of pedagogy, it is important to find out *what* students know, as opposed to (1) how much they know, which reflects a more traditional, summative approach to assessment; or (2) what they "know" that happens to be wrong, which typically reflects assessments that focus on identifying common errors and providing feedback based on those determinations. We take seriously the idea that to build on the knowledge, skills, and abilities (KSAs) possessed by a student, it is essential to first find out what KSAs a learner has. Trying to build on KSAs that a student does not have is misguided.

Since video games designed for entertainment actually provide an environment in which players learn (Gee, 2003), the educational research community has been experimenting with the use of educational games as a way to teach curricular material (e.g., Barab, Arici, & Jackson, 2005). Designing assessments into games and other digital learning environments is one of the critical gateways to creating learning paths that are individualized and therefore maximally engaging for the learner, using sound pedagogical methodology as a foundation. Efforts have begun to assess what students are actually learning in these game environments (e.g., Hickey, 2009). Both the Digital Media Collaboratory (out of U. Texas at Austin) and the EduMetrics Institute advocate addressing assessment issues as an initial part of serious game design (Chen & Michael, 2005). Shute et al. (2008) propose an approach for embedding assessments into games to reveal what is being learned during the gaming experience, where the focus is not only on content knowledge, but also higher-order skills. Some efforts are interested in analyzing a sequence of events to infer abilities such as problem-solving strategies (e.g., Ketelhut, Nelson, & Schifter, 2009). Others have begun to implement embedded assessments to gauge content learning (e.g., Zapata-Rivera, 2009). PIXELearning creates sophisticated training simulations that give the player appropriate feedback so players come to understand the connection between their within-activity actions and the outcomes (Chen & Michael, 2005). While Metis does not solely contain games, we view games as having the potential to engage learners. They are also good environments to assess how learners perform while they are learning. With all these sophisticated approaches to embedded assessment in nascent states, activities in Metis, which include games, simulations, videos, and text, will use simple embedded assessments to gauge performance by associating score, time on task, and other relevant characteristics for each activity to determine what a student's KSAs are.

## Embedded Assessment

Embedded assessment is the process of measuring knowledge and ability as *part* of a learning activity rather than after the fact, when it is only an approximation of learner behavior. Student actions can be evaluated within context while carrying out tasks, or otherwise interacting in a digital environment. These actions can be collected, viewed, and analyzed immediately. Embedded assessments can focus on such things as content knowledge, process and procedures, and higher-order 21st century skills such as collaboration and strategic thinking (Underwood, Kruse, & Jakl, 2010). Stakeholders may obtain reports detailing student proficiencies and challenges – who needs help in teamwork, who is accelerating in particular math skills, and how well individuals compare with the larger population taking a course. Parents, teachers, administrators and others may gain valuable information that can be elusive during the course of traditional instruction.

Interactive digital learning activities lend themselves easily to end state-activity assessment, which can be used to give information to a recommender system. For non-interactive activities, like video or texts, data can be collected about events such as time on task, the educational goal of the activity (though, without really knowing if it was achieved), and the genre. The educational goal of the activity for Metis will be directly linked to KSAs in the content map. Genre can be used to determine whether a particular activity is better suited to a learner than another, and therefore more highly recommended.

For interactive activities, such as games or simulations, the final state of the activity should be collected in addition to the types of data collected for non-interactive activities. The activity should be designed so that a final score will communicate, as much as possible, the level of student achievement of the educational goals. For example, scores should meaningfully reflect achievement levels, which could be numeric or some other designation (e.g., "super-awesome"), for performance on each KSA to communicate this information both to the learner and to the learner profile.

If the goal of the activity is to teach problem-solving (e.g., in a game or simulation), then the final state may not give enough information about the types of difficulties or progress a learner is experiencing. In this case, within-activity assessment can be performed. Similarly, for activities that focus on more than one concept or are complex in other ways, more detailed and specific information can be collected via assessments embedded in the activity. It is more difficult to design such environments – for example, some efforts that focus on immersive, complex environments have decided to include pop-up quizzes that have little to do with the in-game problems being solved, apparently not been able to truly embed assessment in the fabric of the game (e.g., DimensionM, http://www.dimensionu.com/math/). There are other efforts that successfully collect data about specific moments and events to enable reasoning about a learner's performance (e.g., Underwood, Kruse, & Jakl, 2010). With in-game embedded assessment, as soon as a determination is made that a student is having difficulty or is bored, recommendations can be made to direct learners to more appropriate material, even before the activity is completed. This level of embedded assessment is beyond the scope of this version of Metis; it is included for completeness on the types of embedded assessment that can be done.

## Automated Diagnosis and Tutoring

The past several decades have seen numerous approaches toward automated diagnosis and tutoring of students engaged in mathematics problem solving. These approaches, which represent the state of the art in instructional systems, typically involve detailed analyses of potential solution paths for problems, formal representations of correct and incorrect answers, error analysis to identify common misconceptions and misunderstandings, and support in the form of focused feedback or detailed explanations to students during the process of solving a problem. While many of the systems have displayed impressive results in laboratory studies (Shute & Psotka, 1996), the analyses necessary to develop these approaches are expensive to produce (Anderson, Corbett, Koedinger, & Pelletier, 1995) and are therefore not easily scalable (Underwood, 2007). In addition, focusing on misunderstandings and misconceptions may not be the best approach to helping students learn. Cognitively Guided Instruction (CGI; Carpenter, Fennema, & Franke,

*Table 1. Automated tutoring systems reviewed for knowledge structure and recommendations*

| System | Reference | Content area |
|---|---|---|
| Adaptive Content for Evidence-based Diagnosis (ACED) | Shute, Hansen, & Almond, 2007 | Algebra (sequences as patterns) |
| Assessment and Learning in Knowledge Spaces (ALEKS) | Falmagne, Cosyn, Doignon, & Thiery, 2004 | Algebra, arithmetic |
| Assistments | Razzaq, Feng, Nuzzo-Jones, Heffernan, Koedinger, Junker, et al., 2005 | Algebra |
| Cognitive tutors | Anderson, Corbett, Koedinger, & Pelletier, 1995 | Algebra, geometry, LISP programming, other areas |

1996) is a teacher professional development effort that builds on what students are able to do. It does this by working back from errors to find out what valid conceptions students do have so that the instruction can help students build on their existing knowledge.

Metis will follow the CGI approach, which up until now has only been used with (human) teachers and not yet automated. It will use embedded assessment of student KSAs to recommend activities of different genres that would be appropriate to help a particular student learn. This approach has the potential to be less expensive to automate than the previously-mentioned existing automated tutoring efforts, and ultimately scalable.

## The Structure of Knowledge

The structure of the content map is central to creating an effective recommender system. To determine how best to do so, we will now review the research literature for knowledge structures used by automated tutoring systems. Diagnosis of knowledge is performed for different purposes in the reviewed systems, including determining overall KSA proficiency, identifying errors that are commonly made, and selecting the next task. We briefly review some representative systems here, describe their knowledge structure and the use of it to select activities for learners, and show that having a prerequisite structure would be better suited to the goals of each of these systems, and in particular, for recommending appropriate activities for a learner.

The systems we are reviewing are ACED, ALEKS, Assistments, and Cognitive Tutors. See Table 1 for full names, references, and content area that each tutor covers.

ACED has a proficiency model that structures KSAs in terms of general-to-specific relations. For example, 'understands sequences as patterns' is the most general KSA that ACED has in its proficiency model and 'can extend a geometric sequence' is at the most specific level. The general-to-specific relation is defined by part-of links—for example, 'can extend a geometric sequence' is part of its parent KSA, 'solves problems using geometric sequences'. This structure allows the system to make inferences about student knowledge of more general KSAs based on performance on tasks for more specific KSAs. That is, if a student can extend a number of geometric sequences, the system can say with some confidence that this student knows something about sequences as patterns in general. ACED uses a Bayesian inference network to compute probabilistic estimates of a student's proficiency in all the KSAs based on his performance on each task. At any point, the system has a snapshot of the student's estimated proficiency for all KSAs. ACED uses a weight of evidence algorithm to select an activity that will provide the most new information about a student. Results of student learning showed no difference in learning between adaptive and linear sequencing of tasks (Shute, Hansen, & Almond, 2007). This result likely occurred because the algorithm used in ACED focused on maximizing the *precision* of proficiency estimates and not the educational value of selecting the "next task." With the powerful analysis mechanisms ACED uses, it would be worth investigating whether the knowledge structure is where the weakness lies. If they had used a prerequisite structure, the selected activities could have been more in tune with what a student is ready for.

ALEKS uses a precedence network to structure its KSAs. To create the precedence model, experts were asked to determine the answers to the following two questions. A precedence structure is created based on the answers.

Q1. Suppose that a student is not capable of solving problem *p*. Could this student nevertheless solve problem *p'*?
Q2. Suppose that a student has not mastered problems *p1*, *p2*,. . ., *pn*. Could this student nevertheless solve problem *p'*?

Falmagne et al. (2004) showed an example from the resulting precedence network where 'word problems on proportions' precedes 'multiplication of monomials,' which in turn precedes 'graphing a line through a given point with a given slope.' While the two questions imply a direct prerequisite relation from one item type to another, the resulting precedence model seems to be more general than a prerequisite relation, in that, as Falmagne et al. pointed out, some concepts are taught in a particular order even though there may be no logical or pedagogical reason to do so (p. 4). That is, ALEKS bases its KSA relations on the order they are generally taught (i.e., based on scope and sequence, or curriculum).

ALEKS starts a session with a student by administering an adaptive assessment. This initial assessment is adaptive in that the choice of each new question is based on an aggregate of responses to all previous questions. Using its knowledge structure and the initial assessment, ALEKS probabilistically determines the KSAs the student has mastered and a set of problem types he is ready to learn. It maintains a persistent student model that keeps track of performance on KSAs through all sessions with a student. If a student is unable to solve a problem, ALEKS can switch to a related but easier problem, where *easier* is defined in terms of precedence. If both problems require a KSA that the student does not have, ALEKS has no way of identifying it. Again, having a true prerequisite structure would address these issues.

Assistments have links from tasks to KSAs, defined by experts, but no connections between any of the KSAs. The amount and nature of the assistance that students receive while solving a problem is used to approximate student KSA strengths and weaknesses with the goal of providing increasingly accurate predictions of how students will perform on a particular standardized mathematics test. While one can imagine this system making recommendations to students for courses of action based on predictive achievement, they do not do that nor use it to select or recommend tasks for students. That is, Assistments have a predetermined order in which to present tasks to students.

The Cognitive Tutors use production systems to model knowledge. Each rule in the production system represents a KSA that can be used to solve a problem or make progress in solving a problem. Each problem has links to the KSAs necessary to solve that problem, but there are no links between the KSAs themselves. The Cognitive Tutors estimate students' mastery of the mathematics skills in its rule base by using a Bayesian procedure that computes the probability the student has learned each of the KSAs. They accordingly assign students new problems that target deficient skills.

While each of these systems tutors students in math, none of them has a strict model of how KSAs relate to each other. Some take a statistical approach to approximating knowledge, and at least one of those systems did not show a benefit in learning (Shute, Hansen, & Almond, 2007). We argue that the use of prerequisite content maps would be beneficial in designing any system that is intended to individualize learning. Building on this idea, and after a short aside describing what this chapter does not address, we will describe the underlying technology and then the design of Metis.

## What this Chapter Does Not Address

Metis is currently in its design phase. This chapter is meant to describe the aspects of the content map and the associated approach to assessment that complements a traditional recommender system. As such, it does not address the specific recommender algorithms used to incorporate ratings of activities into Metis or how learner profiles are captured (other than keeping track of the KSAs in which the learner shows proficiency or has weakness), but assumes that an appropriate algorithm will be used. Similarly, it does not address the validity of ratings. Since the content map is being designed by math educators using math topics useful to student learning that can be found in math textbooks, no specific links to curriculum are being made. When deployment begins, these issues may need to be addressed more fully. Finally, this chapter is not about games for learning, though a brief review of research in this area is included, particularly as they relate to embedded assessment.

## Underlying Metis Technology

To date, most educational researchers interested in within-activity performance collect log data and then go through a tedious process of tagging and evaluating the logs by hand. This is a place where computers can do better than humans. Pragmatic Solutions has developed software that allows a developer to collect within-activity data, automatically tag it, reason about it during the data collection process, and deliver individual recommendations to the learner, all in near real-time. This section describes the technological capabilities of Leverage in support of the Metis recommender system.

Leverage™ is an SDK, originally created by Pragmatic for game developers to collect end-state activity data, analyze it in real-time through a rule-based system, mine the data for behaviors, and adapt the games to individual preferences and behaviors (Underwood, Kruse, & Jakl, 2010). Done in real-time, in-game data is collected to update learner profiles without impeding the flow of the environment (Csikszentmihalyi, 1990), a requirement that is critical to fostering both engagement and the potential for learning (Shute, et al., 2008). Leverage supports the dynamic delivery and modification of any and all elements in a game (for example, recommendations in the form of within-activity feedback), with the capability of providing individualized content to a large user base in near real-time. Leverage will capture performance data from the Metis activities, including such data as math goals and associated final scores, number correct/incorrect, and time to solve problems.

MygameIQ™ (http://mygameiq.com), also developed by Pragmatic, is a content delivery system with a collection of educational and other serious games. This site can serve as a repository for games and activities that do not otherwise have public homes, like those developed as part of research projects or individuals wanting to contribute educational games for public use. In MygameIQ, users can rate activities based on how well they like them. The existing game set, which continues to grow, comes from Dole, Starlight Foundation, GlobalKids, and Math Snacks (http://mathsnacks.com; Chamberlin, 2003), and users can select games based on genre or popularity. The Metis recommender system will be built on top of MygameIQ, recommending games and other activities learners are ready for, using the prerequisite content-map and the learner profile.

## METIS: CROSS-ACTIVITY RECOMMENDATIONS

In this section, we describe the Metis recommender system (see Figure 1), which includes the following components: a prerequisite-based content map, learning activities linked to content map KSAs via metatags, embedded performance assessments related to how students perform on activities as they relate to KSAs, a learner profile that keeps track of the performance assessment results as well as demographics and other learning preferences, and the recommender that uses the content map and learner profile for recommending appropriate activities. We will describe main components of Metis and then paint a scenario of how it will work.

### Content Map

As we indicated, our explanation for students not interested in mathematics is that they were moved ahead faster than they should have been in terms of not having mastered the material; in other words, they are lacking the prerequisite skills needed to progress. To address this, we propose a map of mathematics that supports accepted mathematics knowledge, skills, and abilities (KSAs). This map defines a "neticulum" (Underwood, 2005), where a learning path is individualized to every person, the KSAs of which are all part of any math curriculum. Mapping the prerequisite relationships between math concepts, while assessing what students know while they interact with digital content, can provide the basis to guide students to activities appropriate to their knowledge. It is also possible for a teacher to initialize the process by indicating which KSAs seem problematic for a learner.

The Metis content map uses prerequisite links between relevant KSAs (see Figure 2). The portion of the map shown in the figure includes processes related to ratios, proportions, and their prerequisite KSAs including equivalent fractions, factors, and number order.

For example, in order to *use ratios for comparison*, one needs to know how to *compare and order numbers* as well as *understand the concept of ratios and proportions*, the two prerequisites shown in the map. We have included in this abbreviated map KSAs that cover the set of learning activities we will use in our example below. All the additional KSAs in the map are there to show connections and extensions in different directions, and in no way imply completeness. The "clouds" signify sets of as yet undefined KSAs. This math content map will continue to get filled out as more learning activities are included.

Each KSA is listed in the form of a mathematical process, for example, *use ratios for comparison*. We have found that putting knowledge concepts in this grammatical form (e.g., using a verb to specify how the KSA will be achieved) simplifies the process of identifying prerequisites and of mapping activities to them. Having KSAs that are more general – for example, *ratios* – makes it difficult to identify all the respective prerequisite KSAs, so we posed the question of what a KSA needs to look like in order to solve this prerequisite identification problem. The map will get large, but Metis should be easy to work with as long as the KSAs are represented well, there is a good interface, and it has rich search capabilities.

### Learning Activities

Digital learning activities include such genres as text, videos, animations, games (which themselves have many genres), worksheets, and simulations. To make the most of a content map-based recommender system, an activity should focus on a single concept, which also allows the designer of activities to assume mastery of its prerequisites. That is, if a learner does not perform well in an activity, the designer does not have to create ways for the learner to focus on them within the activity; the

*Figure 1. Metis recommender system design*

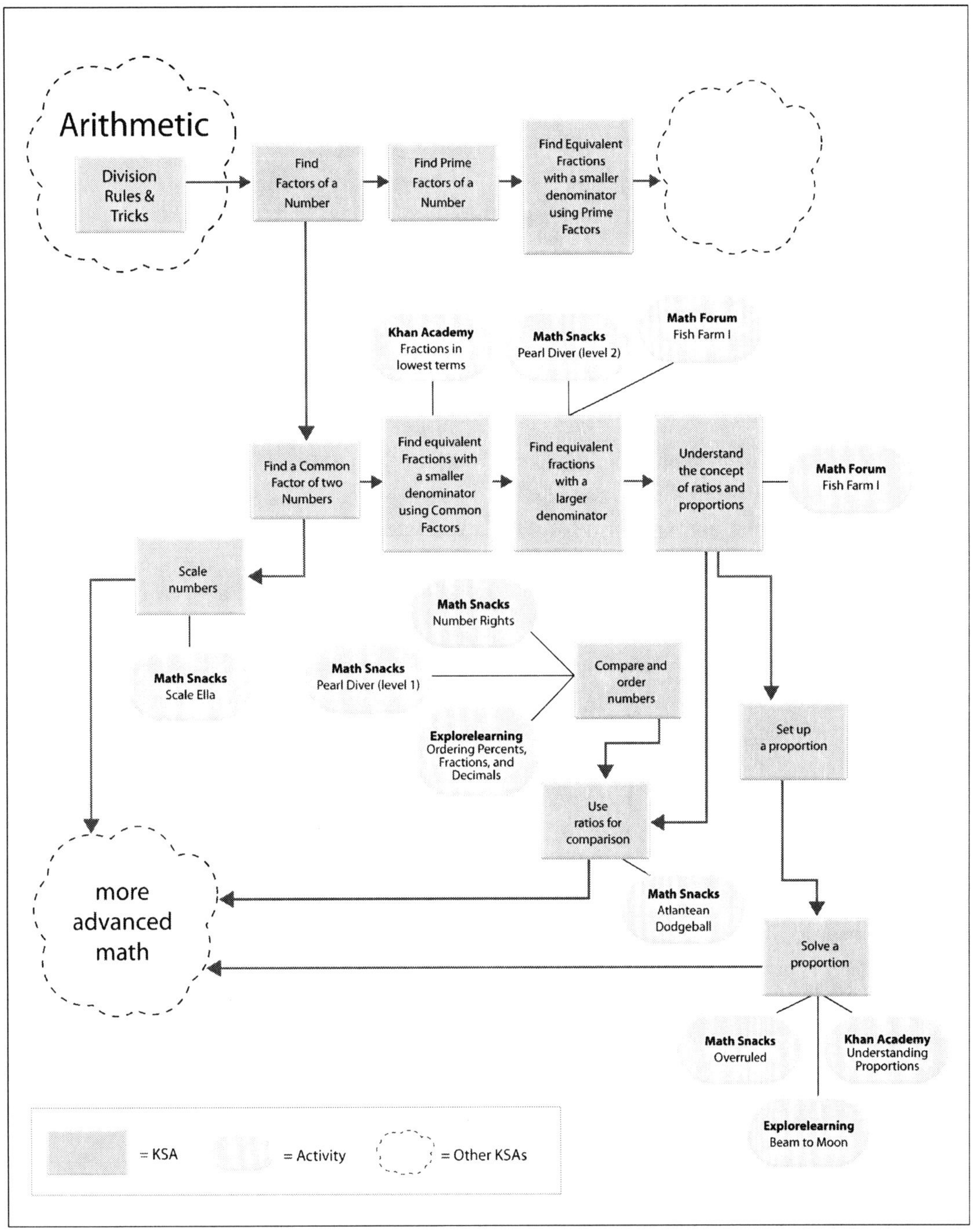


recommender system will make recommendations based on the prerequisites of that activity.

Each learning activity used in Metis focuses on a single KSA and is connected to the content map via the KSA (see Figure 2). Activities with multiple levels may focus on more than one KSA, though each level typically focuses on an individual KSA.

*Figure 2. Portion of a Metis content map for mathematics*

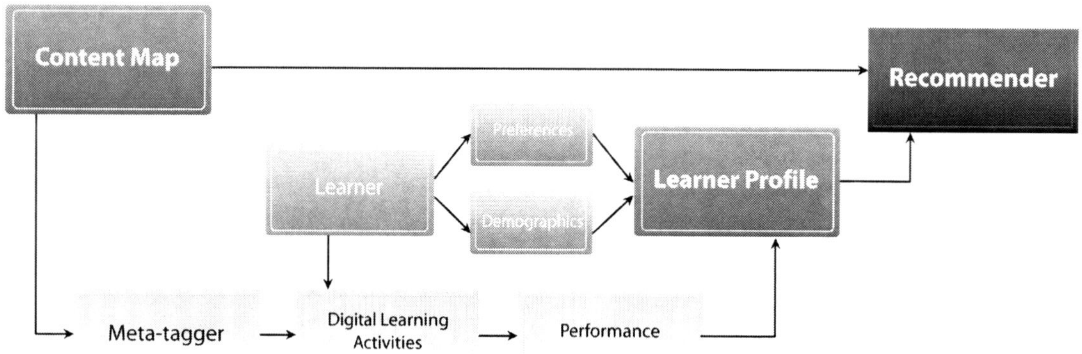


In our experience, though there may be exceptions, texts and videos teach KSAs (i.e., concepts and processes), while animations, games, worksheets, and simulations give students ways to practice those KSAs. Similarly, different students have preferences in the way they learn best. Therefore, it is important to have multiple activities linked to each KSA, each taking a different approach to learning in those content areas. The activities should also be structured in easily accessible ways in addition to just by content area, for example, by genre or by designer. After use, learners will be asked to rate the activity for enjoyableness and relevance.

Metis's approach of linking activities to a prerequisite content map provides the foundation for recommending activities to help individual students gain the foundational prerequisite knowledge they need to learn the material currently being taught in class. The other important piece is the learner profile, which keeps track of learner preferences and activity performance.

## Learner Profile

The learner profile collects learner performance data for each of the activities and associates it with the KSAs in the content map. It also keeps track of learner demographics and preferences, which include things mined from actual performance (e.g., what genres this person spends the most time on or performs best on) as well as preferences selected directly by the learner. Demographics can be used to mine performance data to learn about trends in learners interacting with the digital activities, for example, age, gender, whether they like math, whether they are good at math, and computer and game use (see Appendix A for a demographic survey we have used with some of our games, which learners can fill out upon using Metis). At the end of any activity, the learner profile is updated to note the level of mastery achieved in the current KSA.

Digital learning activities lend themselves to end state-activity assessment, which provides performance information to the learner profile. The learning goal of each activity in Metis will be directly linked to KSAs in the content map. For non-interactive activities, like video or texts, data can be collected about events such as time on task, the learning goal of the activity (though, without really knowing if it was achieved), and genre. Watching a video will give the learner the equivalent of a checkmark for the goal KSA. However, the proficiency level of the learner can be updated only when using an interactive activity like a game or simulation. Proficiency level can be based on a final score, speed, correctness, as well as such things as number of times to pass a level or to reach a certain score, depending on the nature of the activity.

## Metis Recommendations

The recommender module uses information from the learner profile and the content map to determine what KSAs the student is ready for, whether for remediation or continued learning. Metis peruses the content map and associated activities for relevance to the learner, and recommends to the learner a set of activities that are appropriate. The recommender algorithm can be supplemented with information about preferred genre, demographic information about the learner, and self-selected learner preferences.

A learner then chooses an activity from the recommended activity list, and can base the selection on any desired attributes, for example, genre or popularity. Learners can also ignore the list entirely and choose any desired activity. One reason to provide choice is that students prefer to have control over their learning environments, and advice, direction, and choice are perceived well, but complete control over what to work on is perceived as controlling and may be met with resistance (Underwood, 2008). Through activity selection from the set of recommended activities, individualized learning paths are created, where learners interact with activities they are ready for. Working with such activities that challenge a learner the right amount will improve interest and self-efficacy in math, which may lead to improved performance.

We now demonstrate the types of information that gets collected and how Metis selects activities to recommend.

## A Metis Scenario

For our example, we will be using the following publicly accessible digital activities: New Mexico State University (http://mathsnacks.org) has developed games for learners to practice math facts, and animations and comic books that present math concepts in engaging ways; Khan Academy (http://khanacademy.org) contains videos that clearly explain math concepts and procedures for many levels of math; Explore Learning (http://explorelearning.com) contains simulation tools, or "gizmos", that let learners explore mathematical concepts; and the Math Forum @ Drexel (http://mathforum.org/escotpow/) contains math simulations that learners work with to solve specific problems. Each of the selected activities is shown connected to its associated learning goal KSA in our math content map (see Figure 2).

Mrs. Ruby has Charlie's 6th grade class watch a Math Snack animation called Atlantean Dodgeball. In Atlantean Dodgeball, ratio errors confuse one of the coaches in an "epic" dodgeball tournament. Mrs. Ruby chose this activity because she's recently taught the concept of ratios, and her class understands how to compare and order numbers, which are the two prerequisite KSAs that Metis's math map lists for *using ratios for comparison*. After watching this engaging video, each student in the class is asked to complete some associated activities. When the class shares their work with each other, Mrs. Ruby notices that Charlie is rather quiet and looks uncomfortable. Charlie had transferred into her class just a couple of weeks ago, and she's noticed that he isn't picking up the material as quickly as the other students.

Mrs. Ruby wonders if Metis can help him catch up. She indicates to Metis that Charlie didn't understand the Atlantean Dodgeball animation, and then logs Charlie into MygameIQ, where many of the learning activities are stored.

Metis presents Charlie with four recommended activities from the two prerequisite KSAs: Fish Farm (game), Number Rights (animation), Pearl Diver (game), and a "gizmo" called "Ordering percents, fractions, and decimals" (simulation). Of course, Charlie can choose any of the activities on the MygameIQ site if he chooses. Charlie chooses Fish Farm, since it's a game and it has fish, and he likes fish. It turns out that it's an exploratory simulation, and Charlie has fun exploring how to set the fish up in the proper ratios according to the game's goals. He does pretty well, and that information is stored in his profile. He rates the game highly, which is also stored.

Metis then asks Charlie to answer a couple of questions to help it recommend suitable activities for him, and Charlie obliges. Metis now knows that Charlie likes to play video games and doesn't think he's good at math.

Metis then recommends three new games, in addition to the remaining three activities from the previous recommendation set: Overruled (animation), "Beams to Moon" (simulation), and "Understanding Proportions" (video). The games and simulations are listed first, since Charlie has shown preference for those genres. This time, Charlie chooses Pearl Diver, a game in which he has to order numbers and fractions quickly to win the game. When fractions are involved, Charlie has a hard time getting them right. He rated the game as "okay", and the relevance as low.

Metis then suggests to Charlie that he watch Number Rights, explaining that it might help him get over his problems in Pearl Diver. It's a fun animation that explains how certain fractions and decimals are equivalent and belong in the same place on the number line. Then Metis suggests using the simulation gizmo for "Ordering percents, fractions, and decimals", saying that it will help him practice the concepts he just saw in the Number Rights video. Something in there seems to click for him, and he whizzes his way through it, performing well. He goes back to Pearl Diver, and now he seems to do well there, too.

Metis then asks Charlie to answer a couple more questions to help it recommend even more suitable activities for him. In addition to some new questions, Charlie now says that he likes math better.

Charlie's profile has been updated after each activity, and it will remember both the difficulties and the successes that Charlie had with the activities. He is now listed as *understanding the concept of ratios and proportions* (thanks to Fish Farm) and knowing how to *compare and order numbers* (thanks to Number Rights, Pearl Diver, and Ordering Percents, Fractions, and Decimals). Games, animation videos, and simulations all seem to work well for Charlie, though it could have gone otherwise. Based on determining the math concepts Charlie understood in the math map, combined with his preferences and experiences with these types of activities, Metis recommended appropriate activities to improve Charlie's learning.

Next time, if he continues using Metis, he can play the games linked to *Solve a proportion*. But now it's time to rejoin the class in the Atlantean Dodgeball activities, which he is probably ready for now.

## DISCUSSION

The design of Metis as described in this chapter is based on the idea that having a content map based on prerequisites will improve learners' interest and hence their achievement because only activities that the learner is ready for will be recommended. However, since Metis is still in the design phase, this hypothesis has not yet been tested.

In Metis, learners select an initial activity with which to interact, at which point Metis tries to figure out what knowledge the learner already has. A teacher or mentor can also choose a starting point for the learner so they do not flounder trying to find appropriate activities to interact with. It may be more useful, or at least efficient, for learners to take a pretest to estimate the knowledge they start with, for the system to "locate" them in the content map. We like the metaphor of location, since it is hard to give directions to someone if you don't know where they are. ALEKS (Falmagne, 2004) uses this pretest method for this precise purpose. We would design our pretest to sample the content map and to adaptively figure out where a learner is.

The approach we outline in the chapter for using demographic data to improve recommendations can be improved. To find correlations between demographic data and activity use and performance, it would be worthwhile to run a large study to collect a lot of data. We would then use a content map as the primary form of contextual and individualized recommendations, and then reliably use usage and demographic data as a secondary mechanism to guide a more traditional approach to recommendations.

Metis is currently designed to use only end states of activities for an indication of how learners perform. Activities can also be designed to facilitate the measurement of within-activity problem-solving. Activities can be instrumented to collect within-activity events, for example, about decisions, actions, or teamwork. One way these data can be used is to compare them to known or expected patterns to see where learners are having difficulties. More importantly, learners will often come up with approaches not considered by the activity designer or subject matter experts. The ultimate goal of using within-activity embedded assessments, then, would be to address this "long tail" of learners – that is, the many individuals who do not fall into statistical groups. Research in this area is just beginning.

One area we did not address in this chapter is how Metis will address the case of learners forgetting – for example, if in a later session, learners show less knowledge for a KSA than was previously displayed. This is an open question, of course. One way to address this would be to weight the current session more highly than stored data. There is certainly research in this area (e.g., Abadzi, 2003) that could be used to inform the cognitive representation of forgetting in the learning process.

We outlined the types of data that can be analyzed to determine proficiency in a KSA, but more research needs to be done in this area. For example, statistics or data mining approaches can be used in creative ways to facilitate the analysis.

Our plan is to expand the content map in math as we identify other activities that can be used. We would also be interested in expanding it to other areas including science. The key to determining what areas to expand it to will be based on the availability of digital learning activities and resources. One of the reasons we decided to go the route of developing a centralized repository for math games and activities is that there are so many sites that contain games and no easy way for learners to figure out which ones to use. The math map can help by itself, with links to learning activities anywhere on the web. This raises the issue of the quality of the activities. After an initial screening for relevance, it would be costly to evaluate all the new activities for quality, since quality means different things to different people. It would be better to have learners and other users (e.g., parents, teachers) try them and rate them, using algorithms from more standard approaches to recommender systems. In this way, quality is determined by the eyes and fingers of the learner, and the good ones rise to the top.

How can we learn more about the prerequisites to make the map as objective as possible? As we take a learner down through the map, determining what KSAs they have, we may find that some links are incorrectly connected for some learners. That is, they may show proficiency in one node, and be missing some of its prerequisites. How would this be detected in Metis? It could be that as a learner moves forward in the map, suddenly there is a gap that was previously unexplained. That it the time to check those interconnected relationships. In addition, how can we build out the map based on data? Hitting a leaf node (one without prerequisites) without good performance will indicate that something is missing. It could be that a human tutor needs to get involved. Perhaps that will be a service offered by the Metis system, especially during research and development.

The math map can also be used as a guide for determining what activities need to be developed. As part of a public learning network, people interested in developing content can see what parts of the map need activities. They can not only find KSAs that have no activities (see Figure 2 for an example), but can also find KSAs that can use additional activity genres to allow learners to choose the approach that best suits them.

Our approach, as shown in the example above, makes recommendations in two different ways. It recommends a set of all activities from all prerequisite KSAs and also recommends a single activity and gives an explanation about why Metis thinks it would be effective for a particular learner. Perhaps it would be better to have mouse rollovers, or some other metaphor, that explains why each activity in the larger set is suggested. Or perhaps it would be better to just let the learner choose from the entire set of recommended activities. Tintarev & Masthoff (2007) document effective approaches to recommendation explanations that we will consider.

After Metis is developed, we will run research studies to see if students are more engaged with Metis than by just interacting with the digital activities. Since they will be interacting with the same set of activities, we hope to be able to conclude that their interest is due to first achieving the prerequisites before being given material that those prerequisites are based on. Then, if those studies show promise, we will run studies to see if achievement is directly affected.

It is interesting that most educational researchers who have designed tutoring systems take a procedural approach (i.e., have students demonstrate a procedure and make corrections along the way) rather than probing for prior knowledge. In some sense, continually correcting students may give students the idea that they are always wrong. The Metis approach tries to find a good place to start rather than try to fix where they are. There is at least one case of an intelligent tutoring system research team that explains why they took a procedural approach (Sleeman, Ward, Kelly, Martinak, & Moore, 1991), namely because it was the approach of just about all the teachers they interviewed – except for one teacher, they report, who used a probing approach to figure out the sources of her students' problems. They found this point worth mentioning, but did not investigate which approach would be more effective in an automated tutoring environment. It could be that probing for prior knowledge is more effectively done by a computer even though it is not commonly done by people. We aim to find out.

## CONCLUSION

The Metis approach to recommender systems stands out from other recommender systems because of its reliance on a content map structured by prerequisite relations between knowledge, skills, and abilities. This approach is built on Cognitively Guided Instruction, which has only been carried out by humans, and has not to date been implemented in an automated system. Metis is designed to assess in real-time how students are performing and to use this information, along with a content map, as a basis for recommending a set of activities that the learner is ready for. It is also designed to pool together all the digital learning content that is available on the web so it is easy to find quality educational activities. Though not developed yet, we are painting a picture of what might be available in the future. We envision it being used in after school centers, informal learning environments, by adults brushing up on math, and last but not least, in classrooms. Metis is currently being designed, and research is just beginning.

## ACKNOWLEDGMENT

The author would like to thank Ian Underwood of the Math Forum @ Drexel for his help in constructing the prerequisite math content map,

Stacy Kruse for her unending support while I was writing this chapter including her graphical artistry for the figures, and anonymous reviewers for their insightful comments and suggestions.

## REFERENCES

Abadzi, H. (2003). *Improving adult literacy outcomes: Lessons from cognitive research for developing countries*. World Bank Publications.

Anderson, C. (2008). *The long tail: Why the future of business is selling less of more*. New York, NY: Hyperion.

Anderson, J. R., Corbett, A. T., Koedinger, K., & Pelletier, R. (1995). Cognitive tutors: Lessons learned. *The Journal of Learning Sciences, 4*, 167–207. Retrieved March 2, 2006, from http://act-r.psy.cmu.edu/papers/129/CogTut_Lessons.pdf

Bangert-Drowns, R. L., Kulik, J. A., & Morgan, M. T. (1991). The instructional effect of feedback in test-like events. *Review of Educational Research, 61*, 213–238.

Barab, S. A., Arici, A., & Jackson, C. (2005). Eat your vegetables and do your homework: A design based investigation of enjoyment and meaning in learning. *Educational Technology, 65*(1), 15–21.

Bloom, B. (1983). *Human characteristics and school learning*. McGraw-Hill.

Burke, R. (2000). Knowledge-based recommender systems. In A. Kent (Ed.), *Encyclopedia of library and information science*, volume 69, (pp. 180-201). CRC Press.

Carpenter, T. P., Fennema, E., & Franke, M. L. (1996). Cognitively guided instruction: A knowledge base for reform in primary mathematics instruction. *The Elementary School Journal, 97*(1), 3–20. doi:10.1086/461846

Chamberlin, B. (2003). *Creating entertaining games with educational content: Case studies of user experiences with the children's website: The Food Detectives Fight BAC!* Dissertation, University of Virginia, Charlottesville, VA.

Chen, S., & Michael, D. (2005). *Proof of learning: Assessment in serious games*. Retrieved on December 10, 2008, from http://www.gamasutra.com/features/20051019/chen_01.shtml

Chi, M. T. H., Glaser, R., & Rees, E. (1982). Expertise in problem solving. In R. Sternberg (Ed.), *Advances in the Psychology of Human Intelligence, 1*, 7–75. Hillsdale, NJ: Erlbaum.

Csikszentmihalyi, M. (1990). *Flow: The psychology of optimal experience*. New York, NY: Harper Perennial.

Drachsler, H., Hummel, H. G. K., & Koper, R. (2008). Personal recommender systems for learners in lifelong learning networks: the requirements, techniques and model. *Int. J. Learning Technology, 3*(4), 404-423. Retrieved October 11, 2010, from http://dspace.ou.nl/bitstream/1820/937/5/2008%20Drachsler%20IJLT.pdf

Falmagne, J.-C., Cosyn, E., Doignon, J.-P., & Thiery, N. (2004). *The assessment of knowledge, in theory and in practice.* Retrieved February 20, 2006, from http://www.business.aleks.com/about/Science_Behind_ALEKS.pdf

Gee, J. P. (2003). *What video games have to teach us about learning and literacy*. New York, NY: Palgrave Macmillan.

Geyer-Schulz, A., Hahsler, M., & Jahn, M. (2001). Educational and scientific recommender systems: Designing the information channels of the virtual university. *Journal of Engineering Education, 17*(2), 153–163.

Hickey, D. T. (2009). *Designing assessments and assessing designs in educational videogames.* Presentation at AERA 2009, San Diego, CA.

Ketelhut, D. J., Nelson, B., & Schifter, C. (2009). *Situated assessment using virtual environments of science content and inquiry*. San Diego, CA: Presentation at AERA.

Kluger, A. N., & DeNisi, A. (1996). The effects of feedback interventions on performance: Historical review, a meta-analysis and a preliminary feedback intervention theory. *Psychological Bulletin, 119*, 254–284. doi:10.1037/0033-2909.119.2.254

Martinez, J. G. R., & Martinez, N. C. (1999). Teacher effectiveness and learning for mastery. *The Journal of Educational Research, 92*(5), 279–285. doi:10.1080/00220679909597607

Miller, G. A. (1956). The magical number seven, plus or minus two: Some limits on our capacity for processing information. *Psychological Review, 63*, 81–97. doi:10.1037/h0043158

Plass, J. L., Underwood, J. S., Homer, B. D., Frye, J., Hendee, C., Case, J., & Perlin, K. (2010). *Defining and measuring engagement in educational games*. Presented at Games Learning + Society Conference, Madison, WI.

Razzaq, L., Feng, M., Nuzzo-Jones, G., Heffernan, N. T., Koedinger, K. R., Junker, B., et al. (2005). The Assistment project: Blending assessment and assisting. In C.K. Looi, G. McCalla, B. Bredeweg, & J. Breuker (Eds.), *Proceedings of the 12th Artificial Intelligence in Education Conference* (pp. 555–562). Amsterdam, The Netherlands: ISO Press. Retrieved March 7, 2006, from http://www.assistment.org/project/papers/AIED2005/mainAIED.pdf

Recker, M., Walker, M., & Lawless, K. (2003). What do you recommend? Implementation and analyses of collaborative information filtering of web resources for education. *Instructional Science, 31*, 299–316. doi:10.1023/A:1024686010318

Schoenfeld, A. (2002). Making mathematics work for all children: Issues of standards, testing, and equity. *Educational Researcher, 31*, 13–25. doi:10.3102/0013189X031001013

Shute, V. J. (1994). Learning processes and learning outcomes. In Husen, T., & Postlethwaite, T. N. (Eds.), *International encyclopedia of education* (2nd ed., pp. 3315–3325). New York, NY: Pergamon Press.

Shute, V. J., Hansen, E. G., & Almond, R. G. (2007). *An assessment for learning system called ACED: Designing for learning effectiveness and accessibility,* (ETS Research Report RR-07-26). Princeton, NJ: ETS.

Shute, V. J., Lajoie, S. P., & Gluck, K. A. (2000). Individualized and group approaches to training. In Tobias, S., & Fletcher, J. D. (Eds.), *Training and retraining: A handbook for business, industry, government, and the military* (pp. 171–207). New York, NY: Macmillan.

Shute, V. J., & Psotka, J. (1996). Intelligent tutoring systems: Past, present and future. In Jonassen, D. (Ed.), *Handbook of research on educational communications and technology*. New York, NY: Scholastic Publications.

Shute, V. J., Ventura, M., Bauer, M. I., & Zapata-Rivera, D. (2008). Melding the power of serious games and embedded assessment to monitor and foster learning: Flow and grow. In Ritterfeld, U., Cody, M. J., & Vorderer, P. (Eds.), *The social science of serious games: Theories and applications*. Philadelphia, PA: Routledge/LEA.

Sleeman, D., Ward, R. D., Kelly, A. E., Martinak, R., & Moore, J. L. (1991). An overview of recent studies with PIXIE. In Goodyear, P. (Ed.), *Teaching knowledge and intelligent tutoring*. Norwood, NJ: Ablex Publishing.

Sweller, J. (1988). Cognitive load during problem solving: Effects on learning. *Cognitive Science, 12*, 257–285. doi:10.1207/s15516709cog1202_4

Tintarev, N., & Masthoff, J. (2007). Effective explanations of recommendations: User-centered design. In *Proceedings of the 2007 ACM conference on Recommender Systems*.

Tobias, S. (1989). Another look at research on the adaptation of instruction to student characteristics. *Educational Psychologist*, *24*(3), 213–227. doi:10.1207/s15326985ep2403_1

Tobias, S. (1994). Interest, prior knowledge, and learning. *Review of Educational Research*, *64*(1), 37–54.

Underwood, J. S. (2005). *What am I learning? Performance feedback in an open learning environment.* Presented at the Conference on Advancing the Effectiveness and Sustainability of Open Education, Logan, UT.

Underwood, J. S. (2007). *Evaluation of automated diagnosis and instruction for mathematics problem-solving*. (ETS Research Report RR-07-28). Princeton, NJ: ETS.

Underwood, J. S. (2008). Effective feedback: Guidelines for improving performance. *Proceedings of the International Conference of the Learning Sciences*, Utrecht, The Netherlands.

Underwood, J. S., Kruse, S., & Jakl, P. (2010). Moving to the next level: Designing embedded assessments into educational games. In Zemliansky, P., & Wilcox, D. (Eds.), *Design and implementation of educational games: Theoretical and practical perspectives*. Hershey, PA: IGI Global. doi:10.4018/978-1-61520-781-7.ch009

Vygotsky, L. S. (1978). *Mind and society: The development of higher mental processes*. Cambridge, MA: Harvard University Press.

White, B. Y., & Frederiksen, J. R. (1986). *Progressions of quantitative models as a foundation for intelligent learning environments* (Technical Report No. 6277). Cambridge, MA: Bolt, Beranek, and Newman

Zapata-Rivera, D. (2009). *Assessment-based gaming environments*. San Diego, CA: Presentation at AERA.

## KEY TERMS AND DEFINITIONS

**Digital Learning Activity:** Any activity designed specifically for learning in a computer (digital) environment, such as videos, animations, games, simulations, and text.

**Prerequisite Content Map:** As used in this chapter, a prerequisite content map is a particular ordering of concepts such that each concept is linked to all the concepts that are its prerequisites and to all of the concepts for which it is a prerequisite. The structure is not a hierarchy or tree, since any concept can point to (i.e., be a prerequisite for) many other concepts.

**Embedded Assessment:** This type of assessment is embedded into the fabric of a digital activity so that in addition to content knowledge, process and problem-solving can also be measured. Its counterpart in real life is when one person is teaching another and they can witness progress and areas of weakness in learners as they are in the process of learning.

**Individualized Learning Paths:** The actions taken in response to a particular learner's activity. Embedded assessments in a digital learning environment that are linked to prerequisite content maps can foster individualized learning paths.

## APPENDIX A: DEMOGRAPHICS SURVEY

1. How old are you?
2. What is your ethnicity?
3. What is your gender?
    a. boy
    b. girl
4. Is English your first language?
5. How often do you use a computer?
    a. every day
    b. once a week
    c. once a month
    d. almost never
6. If you use a computer, where do you use it most often?
    a. at home or a friend's house
    b. at school
    c. at the Boys & Girls Club
7. How often do you play video games?
    a. every day
    b. once a week
    c. once a month
    d. almost never
8. If you play video games, where do you play most often?
    a. on a computer
    b. on a Wii / Xbox / Playstation
    c. on a phone
    d. through Facebook
9. If you play games, what kind do you most enjoy?
    a. virtual worlds like Habbo Hotel or Club Penguin
    b. puzzle games like Bejeweled
    c. strategy games like Starcraft
    d. casual games like Facebook Farmville or Mafia Wars
    e. action games like Halo or Counterstrike
10. Do you like math?
11. Do you feel like you are good at math?
12. Do you like school?
13. Do you feel you are a good student?

# Chapter 3
# Context-Aware Recommendations using Topic Maps Technology for the Enhancement of the Creativity Process

**George A. Sielis**
*University of Cyprus, Cyprus*

**Christos Mettouris**
*University of Cyprus, Cyprus*

**Aimilia Tzanavari**
*University of Cyprus, Cyprus*

**George A. Papadopoulos**
*University of Cyprus, Cyprus*

## ABSTRACT

*Learning can be observed in the creativity process. When this process is supported by a Creativity Support Tool (CST), considering the context in which ideas are developed, as well as the context around the user himself and the task he is carrying out can potentially enhance creativity.The tool's awareness of such context can be exploited in the offering of useful context-aware recommendations to the users on topics such as relevant resources, people, ideas, projects, et cetera. These recommendations can help users during the creativity process and the learning involved, by providing productive stimuli. In the work presented in this chapter we focus on describing a method for enhancing the creativity process through context-aware recommendations. The method uses ontologies for the knowledge representation of context and the topic maps technology for storing, managing, and delivering content used as recommendations. Furthermore we present the software system that has been developed to support this method in a particular collaborative CST, as well as its evaluation.*

DOI: 10.4018/978-1-61350-489-5.ch003

## INTRODUCTION

Creativity is recognized as a psychological term and is usually measured using psychological methods. The transition of creativity from a psychological term to a computer related term was achieved by modelling it through several creativity techniques and simulating these techniques in Creativity Support Tools (CSTs). A creativity process on the other hand is a sequence of steps, during which context dynamically changes: different contextual factors can influence the process according to the stage of the process.

The current work aims to facilitate the creativity process through the integration of a context aware recommender system within a CST. It is in our belief that the use of context awareness within CSTs will be able to enhance the creativity process by offering the user useful recommendations. A first step towards the establishment of this task is the definition of the context awareness ontology related to creativity. Defining the contextual elements of creativity and modelling them as an individual ontology offers the flexibility to use the Topic Maps technology. The ontology that has been designed for a specific CST is described in detail.

The context of a CST was modelled by defining and describing the most important contextual entities and their role in the creative process. Following context modelling, the context reasoning procedure is described, a method that reasons upon context in order to provide the most relevant recommendations based on the user and the task he is carrying out at that point in time. In the next section we will introduce areas and background work relevant to our work.

## BACKGROUND

According to Dey's definition (Dey, Abowd, & Salber, 2001), "context is any information that can be used to characterize the situation of an entity. An entity is a person, place, or object that is considered relevant to the interaction between a user and an application including the user and applications themselves". (Jun-Zhao & Sauvola, 2003) mentions that context entities can be structured into three domains: the user domain, the computer domain and the environment domain. Modeling the context considering these three domains, it is important to ensure that they interact with each other. In this way it is ensured that the context data can be collected as an ensemble of the context data for an entity. According to (Jun-Zhao & Sauvola, 2003) the representation of context is a description of the internal and external features that constitute the context information. Internal features describe characteristics that exist inside an entity or its domain. External features are those which describe the context information that can be retrieved from the interaction of an entity with other entities. (Brown, Bovey & Chen, 1997) use the Standard Generic Markup Language (SGML) for the representation of context information, aiming to prove that the representation of context information can be achieved as easy as the development of a web page in HTML. In the same work they give emphasis on the syntax of the languages that are commonly used for context representation.

In the existing literature several methods and techniques for modelling context can be found (Key-value models, Mark-up schemes, Graphical models, Object oriented models, Logic Based models and Ontological based models). Based on an evaluation of context modeling in the work of Strang and Linnhoff-Popien (2004), ontologies are the most expressive models and fulfill most of the requirements for context modeling such as simplicity, flexibility, extensibility, generality and expressiveness. For the purpose of the work presented in this chapter, ontological modelling is assumed to be the most suitable method for context modelling of creativity. The proposed context model constitutes an ontology schema supported by the Topic Maps concepts.

The development of context aware applications dictates the use of combined technologies for modelling the context, as well as for the design and development of context reasoning techniques. Topic Maps technology is one of the well known methods used for the representation of context. It is part of the ISO standards of the Semantic Web Technologies. The ISO standard of Topic Maps is formally known as ISO 13250. In general, Topic Maps are used in semantic web applications for finding and exchanging information using topics. Topic Maps are designed for the enhancement of navigation and information retrieval. This is achieved by the addition of semantics into the resources and their representation as context data sets (Hatzigaidas, Papastergiou, Tryfon & Maritsa, 2004). Topic Maps technology consists of frameworks which support the design of topic maps ontologies and also include Topic Maps Query Languages for data retrieval and reasoning. An example is the Ontopia Knowledge Suite (OKS) (Anonymous, 2010) and Tolog Topic Maps Query Engine (Anonymous, 2010).

Creativity on the other hand, which is a term difficult to define, can be simply explained as "the ability to create". The conceptualization of creativity process is seen as a sequence of steps, in which the context changes dynamically: different contextual factors can influence the process according to the stage of the process.

In the literature however, a contextual model for the creativity process has not yet been proposed. Foreseeing the benefits that context awareness may offer in such a process justifies that context aware applications are able to operate upon contextual data and provide services that will enhance the creativity process. An example is a recommender system utilizing the context for recommending resources to inspire the user during the creative process.

The usage of a recommender system in a learning platform aims to the facilitation in finding resources and learning material (Shen & Shen 2005; Simon, Mikls, Nejdl, Sintek & Salvachua 2003). In the same way an e-commerce recommender system aims to stimulate the curiosity of the user to view products that belongs in the area of his interests. Research work presented by Tintarev & Masthoff (2007), presents seven advantages of the usage of recommender systems. The usage of a recommender system for the enhancement of creative process highlights two of the advantages identified by Tintarev & Masthoff (2007): Effectiveness and efficiency. For the aims of this article it is necessary to make an overview on creativity in order to define its context and model it.

For the better understanding of the meaning of Creativity Support Tools and their usage, we use some examples of relevant research articles that can be found in the existing literature. For the research topic of computational creativity we can find CSTs implemented for domain specific purposes as well as commercial CSTs. Examples of domain specific research CSTs are related to topics such as the interactive music creation, the collaborative media creation and exploration and the creative writing. In particular an interactive music CST is MySong (Simon, 2008). MySong uses a Hidden Markov Model and a music database for the automatic selection of chords in order to produce melodies automatically. RiTa Toolkit (Howe, 2008) is a CST which is used specifically for the examination of the Computational Literature. RiTa is a suite of open source components, tutorials and examples providing support for a range of tasks related to the practice of creative writing and programmable media. A story generating CST, presented by Riedl (2008) uses artificial intelligence to model the story generation as a model. The application views the story generation as problem-solving activity where the problem is to create an artifact that achieves particular desired effects on an audience.

In addition to the above research based CSTs several commercial CSTs can be found too. Examples of such tools are the Comapping (http://

www.comapping.com), Mind Meister (http://www.mindmeister.com), MindManager 8 (http://www.mindjet.com), Thinkature (http://thinkature.com/) and TRIZ (http://en.wikipedia.org/wiki/TRIZ). In contrast to the research based CSTs that we mentioned these tools do not use any AI algorithm during their process neither they have a specific domain of use. In general these tools are used as aiding tools that guide the users to shape a problem during a creativity process. Therefore we can define Creativity Support Tools as the software tools that support users during all stages of a creativity process.

The aim of this work is the design and development of the contextual model for the creativity process within CSTs and the usage of this model for producing recommendations which are most relevant to the user and the particular creativity process. Our main focus is not to compare recommender systems and algorithms to prove that our proposed method excels, but to show that the traditional creativity process supported in CSTs lacks of contextual usage and support and that this can be compensated by using context-aware recommendations. In particular, this chapter includes the following sections: a description of a use case scenario to illustrate the usefulness of the proposed recommender in a creativity process; an overview of the most well known context modelling and reasoning techniques; a description of Topic Maps technology; further elaboration on the topic of creativity and an attempt to identify its contextual elements and finally a description of the proposed model for creativity focusing on its application in the idSpace platform. We describe a preliminary evaluation that has been setup for the extraction of conclusions regarding the usefulness and usability of a context aware recommender system in CSTs. We conclude this work with a discussion of the present work and the future directions it may take.

## A USE CASE SCENARIO

We will depict the importance of a context aware recommender system in a CST through a use case scenario.

A large company, specialized in environmental fuel production, is consisted of several branches (in the US, Europe and Asia). The company assigns to the engineering department in Europe a new project regarding the design and production of a new type of fuel that will be environmental friendly for future use on aircrafts. As a first step, the biology engineering team in Paris produces a chart representing all the scientific domain fields related to the task. Next, Tom, the project leader, must organize a team by finding the most suitable experts of each scientific field among all company branches, who will be able to contribute to the project with new ideas. Formulating a team is not an easy task, since hundreds of people work for the company in many different branches in many different countries and in various fields. Tom will need to work with a multidisciplinary expert group, the company's best of the best, to ensure that the outcomes of this project will be the anticipated. Through creativity sessions, he expects to hear different opinions and thoughts, initiate fruitful discussions, collect valuable resources and eventually select the best solution for the task at hand. Tom decides to use a Collaborative Support Tool (CST) to collaborate. The first task is to prepare the project by carefully stating the problem. To help Tom with the problem stating procedure, the tool's context aware recommender system provides him with solutions of past projects that are most relevant to the current project, so that Tom gets informed of the related work in his company and how this work had been accomplished. This will help him clarify what needs to be done further by his current project and consequently assist him in choosing a good, solid problem statement. Then, he needs to formulate the expert group of users to collaborate with during the creativity session.

He thinks that explicitly searching one by one his colleagues' profiles to find those with most expertise in every related to the project domain to collaborate with would be time consuming, so he decides to use the tool's recommender system to get recommendations for users. The system automatically recommends 5 people to Tom, but prior to selecting any one of them he checks out their profiles and decides that the last two recommended users in the list are not so relevant to the subject. He selects only the top three users in the list and uses again the recommender system, but only after inputting additional relevant information to guide the system towards his needs. The recommender system takes into account the context as well as Tom's criteria to recommend more people. This time, Tom selects all 5 recommended experts. After forming the experts group, the collaborative creative session starts. At this point, the recommender system provides recommendations of relevant to the topic ideas, thoughts and recourses formulated and produced in past projects. In this way the group is able to discover more easily and effectively the correct path that leads to a good solution for the problem at hand.

The above scenario depicts the usefulness of a recommender system in a Collaborative Support Tool. In the example described, if Tom wasn't able to use the recommender system he would not be able to easily find people to collaborate with, he would spend time in searching for resources to study and no inspiration stimuli would be offered to him and his team during the ideation process. The scenario described consists of a problem solving creativity process. Problem Solving is a mental process and is part of the larger problem process that includes problem finding and problem shaping. Considered the most complex of all intellectual functions, problem solving has been defined as higher-order cognitive process that requires the modulation and control of more routine or fundamental skills. Problem solving occurs when an organism or an artificial intelligence system needs to move from a given state to a desired goal state. This move makes problem solving part of creativity process where the participants are called to shape a problem and then use the utilities that a CST supports, in order to find the solution approaches through collaboration. The creativity process in idSpace CST includes the process of problem shaping (called "problem definition and problem statement"), which is a part of the more general "problem solving" area. However, the creativity process in idSpace is not just about shaping the problem, it is also about facilitating collaboration between users, enable resource sharing among them, and as the focus of this paper is, provide recommendations that will stimulate even more their creativity".

## CONTEXT MODELING AND REASONING TECHNIQUES

The importance of context awareness focuses on the automated services that can be offered from computing systems to users. In a common dictionary such as the one found in http://www.thefreedictionary.com, the word "context" is defined as the set of facts or circumstances surrounding a situation or event. Being aware of the context means "knowing" the circumstances or the facts that surround an event, in order to activate that event.

After conducting a comprehensive research in the area of creativity, we note that very little work exists in modeling the context of creativity. None of the most well known and used CSTs supports any context aware recommendation mechanism that takes into account the creativity context attributes (i.e *Comapping*http://www.comapping.com, *Mind Meister*http://www.mindmeister.com and *MindManager 8*http://www.mindjet.com). In (Sielis, Tzanavari, Papadopoulos, 2008) it was argued that the creative process can be enhanced with the use of context awareness within the

CSTs. In this paper we try to take a step further and propose a contextual model for creativity that will be used for the implementation of a context awareness tool, specifically for CSTs. A review of the most important context modeling methods and context reasoning techniques follows.

## Methods of Modeling Context

### Key-Values Models

Key-value coding is a mechanism for accessing an object's properties indirectly, using strings to identify properties, rather than through invocation of an access method or accessing them directly through instance variables. Key-Values models are the simplest data structure for context modeling and they are frequently used in various service frameworks, where the key-value pairs are used to describe the capabilities of a service. (Schilit, Adams & Want, 1994) used the key values for modeling context. Key-value coding supports properties that are objects and non-object parameters and return types are detected and automatically wrapped, and unwrapped, as required. Key-Values Modeling is simple but not very efficient for more sophisticated data structuring purposes, because it needs exact matching to support retrieval context algorithms and it does not support inheritance. For better understanding, a coding example using key-values is shown in Table 1 that demonstrates the method of modeling the social news in a project described by Reddit (2010).

*Table 1. Example of key-values supporting lists*

```
id = incr NextId => 1
set news_url_<id> "http>//foobar.org"
set news_title_<id> "My foobar story"
push myList 1
id = incr NextId => 2
set news_url_<id> "http>//antirez.net"
set news_title_<id> "The blog you reading now"
push myList 2
```

### Markup Scheme Models

All mark-up based models use a hierarchical data structure consisting of mark-up tags with attributes and content. The content of the mark-up tags are defined in other mark-up tags. The mark-up schemes are usually used to collect information for profiles. The context information profile building usually uses the SGML which is the Standard Mark-up Language the super class of all the mark-up languages like XML. There are multiple examples of such profiles given by (Strang & Linnhoff-Popien, 2004) like the Composite Capabilities / Preferences Profile (CC/PP) and User Agent Profile (UAProf).

### Graphical Models

UML (Unified Modeling Language) is a modeling context language which is structuring the context modeling based on UML diagrams. A Context graphical model is also introduced by (Henricksen, Indulska & Rakotonirainy, 2003), which is an ORM extension (Object Role Extension) which differs from the classic ORM. In the classic ORM model, an entity describes a domain, and an entity which can be a concept, a fact or a set of facts, can serve as a model for the domain. (Henricksen, Indulska & Rakotonirainy, 2003) extended the ORM to allow fact types to be categorized, according their persistence and source, either as static or as dynamic. The latter ones are further distinguished depending on the source of the facts as either profiled, sensed or derived types (Strang & Linnhoff-Popien, 2004).

### Object Oriented Models

Object oriented context modeling approaches are using the benefits of the object oriented programming possibilities, the encapsulation and reusability. With these characteristics of object oriented programming, problems raised with the dynamic context in ubiquitous environments are covered and the details of context processing are encapsulated on an object level and hence hidden to other components. In OO models the data are modelled as object types. An object represents a class with associated attributes and its meta-data as relationships, constraints, etc. Every object inherits the parent object type. The inheritance of the object types allows the evolution of types easier and increase the application scalability.

### Logic-Based Models

Logic-based models have a high degree of formality. Typically, facts, expressions and rules are used to define a context model. A logic based system is then used to manage the aforementioned terms and allows adding, updating or removing new facts. In these systems the context is defined as facts expressions and rules. The contextual information is usually added to, updated in and deleted from a logic based system in terms of facts.

### Ontology-Based Models

According to Gruber (1993) an Ontology is a specification of a conceptualization. Hendler & Heflin (2000) defines ontology as a set of knowledge terms, including the vocabulary, the semantic interconnections and some simple rules of inference and logic for some particular topic. In a more general definition, ontology is the representation of the knowledge over a specific domain using the concepts that describe the domain and associations between the concepts with the use of semantics. Ontologies provide a number of useful features for intelligent systems, as well as for knowledge representation in general and for the knowledge engineering process such as *vocabulary, taxonomy, content theory* and *knowledge sharing and reuse*. *Vocabulary* is the list of terms in a subject area. A vocabulary in ontologies contains a finite list of terms that they are denoted with the same identifier. Hence the terms of a vocabulary can easily be processed by a machine. Part of a vocabulary in ontologies is the *thesauri* which provide additional semantics in the form of synonym relationships between the terms. *Taxonomy* is a hierarchical categorization or classification of entities within a domain based on common ontological characteristics. Ontologies provide taxonomy in a machine readable and machine process-able form (Gaaevic, Djuric, Devedzic & Selic, 2006). *Content theory* is the identification of classes of objects, their relations and concept hierarchies in an elaborative way using ontology representation languages. *Knowledge sharing and Reuse* refers to the ability of the ontologies to be reused in several applications. Every ontology provides a description of the concepts and relationships that can exist in a domain and that can be shared and reused among intelligent agents and applications (Gaaevic, Djuric, Devedzic & Selic, 2006). Therefore, ontologies are a very promising instrument for modeling contextual information due to their high and formal expressiveness and the possibilities for applying ontology reasoning techniques. Due to the evaluation of the context model made by Strang & Linnhoff-Popien (2004), ontologies are characterized as expressive models that fulfill most of their requirements. Some of these requirements are simplicity, flexibility, extensibility, generality, and expressiveness.

## Context Reasoning Techniques

When taking a formal approach to context modelling, context can be processed with logical reasoning mechanisms and has two approaches: checking the consistency of context, and deducing high-level, implicit context from low-level, explicit context (Wang, Zhang, Gu & Pung, 2004). Modelling context as an individual ontology offers the possibility to declare and control the reasoning mechanisms. Contextual reasoning refers to the creation of relations and associations that contribute as the reasoning rules for the extraction of the contextual information. Giunchiglia (Giunchiglia, 1993) gives the meaning of contextual reasoning by describing the difference between *context* and *situation*. According to (Giunchiglia, 1993) contexts are not situations. A situation records the state of the world as it is, independently of how it is represented in the mind of the reasoner. On the other hand context is inside the reasoning individual. It is part of the state and it is responsible for the subjective view of the captured information. In computing systems the formal representation of context helps to capture the information, which is characterized by a situation, and then set the reasoning mechanism for the creation of the context.

In order to make the context reasoning tasks achievable, researchers deployed context reasoning techniques such as *Ontological Reasoning, Rule Based Reasoning, Distributed Reasoning, Case Based Reasoning, Offline Reasoning* and *Probabilistic Reasoning*. These techniques are distinguished in *Non-Symbolic* reasoning techniques and *Symbolic* techniques. The classification of these techniques to Symbolic or Non-Symbolic is depended on the methods of representation of the reasoning *events* and *situations*. The methods of representation might be deterministic by using symbols and regular expressions (Symbolic) or non deterministic using probabilistic methods (Non-Symbolic). A third reasoning method is the Hybrid which is a combination of the other two:

- Non-symbolic reasoning techniques use probabilistic methods and machine learning algorithms for the prediction of data to be recommended. The architecture requirements of systems supporting learning algorithms for reasoning are not only determined by algorithms; they are also determined by data sets and the interaction of algorithms within a larger system (Crago et al., 2006).
- Symbolic reasoning techniques are expressed with symbols. A very simple form of symbolic reasoning can be expressed as a single-case based simulation where each variable can only have a single constant value and the association of an expression with each variable at each point of execution (Blank, Eveking, Levihn & Ritter, 2001).
- Hybrid reasoning techniques combine two or more of the presented Symbolic or non-Symbolic Techniques. A very common combination of techniques is the integration of rule based and case based reasoning.

## TOPIC MAPS AND CONTEXTUAL REASONING

Topic Maps are used in semantic web applications for finding and exchanging information using topics. Wrightson (2001) in his description of Topic Maps mentions the distinguished differences between topic maps and ontologies. Ontologies are used for the description of shared common understanding aspects, like objects or relations between them. A topic map is used for the representation of an ontology by linking its entities. In other words, a topic map is the collection of topics, associations and scopes (Anonymous, 2001).

We follow an ontological reasoning approach, which belongs to the category of symbolic reasoning techniques. Modeling the context requires the definition of the context elements that constitute the ontology. Thus, the contextual elements can be represented as entities which can be exalted to symbols. By using a context awareness ontology, the context data are collected and managed by certain entities and are expressed by means of references to ontological classes and relations. The classes and the relations-associations within the ontology can be represented using Topic Maps technology for the integration of reasoning. In other words, Topic Maps can depict the ontology that describes the entities as topics, as well as the associations between them. The result is a transformation of the ontology in a topic maps suitable format, such as XTM or LTM. For the retrieval of data contained in the topic map, various query languages and engines can be used such as TOLOG. More information on Topic Maps technology and tools can be found in (Hatzigaidas, Papastergiou, Tryfon & Maritsa, 2004).

## CONTEXT AWARENESS ONTOLOGY FOR CREATIVITY: THE CASE OF THE *IDSPACE* PLATFORM

The current work refers to the idSpace platform (Dols, 2009), a web based collaborative creativity support platform that aims to support creativity and facilitate teams effectively to design innovative products. The idSpace platform enhances the creativity process by providing modular guidance and advice scenarios that can be adapted and applied by the users. It also includes tools to articulate, process and store new ideas resulting from the elaboration of ideas from related creativity sessions. The advice that is offered in the form of recommendations, is given by a context awareness tool, whose modelling and reasoning we describe here.

### Creativity Overview: Definition of the Creativity Contextual Elements

As already mentioned, creativity has not a standard definition since it can be used in many disciplines. However, many have attempted to allocate a meaning to the creative process and its potential outcomes. Plucker & Beghetto (2004) define creativity as the interplay between ability and process by which an individual or a group produces an outcome or product that is both novel and useful as defined within some social context. (Shneiderman *et al.* 2006) support that creativity is the development of a novel product that has some value to the individual and to a social group. Cougar (1995) perceives creativity at three levels: as discovery method through the idea generation, as invention with the development of ideas, and as innovation with the transformation of ideas into services (Karapidis, Kienle & Schneider, 2005). (Atman, Turns, Cardella & Adams, 2003) and (Shneiderman, 2000) conceptualize creativity as a sequence of steps with variants. Simulating the creativity steps along with applying creativity techniques produce the software tools known as CSTs.

In (Sielis, Tzanavari & Papadopoulos, 2008) creativity process perceived as a two stages process: "preparation" and "ideation". This two-stage process highlights the steps of creativity defined in (Shneiderman, 2000) in a more concrete way. This grouping of the steps into the two stages facilitates the specification of each step's context attributes and therefore their grouping in "primary" and "secondary" entities, following the transformation proposed by (Haya, Montoro & Alaman, 2004). This transformation has actual value for the design of context awareness ontology.

From the existing studies in the area of creativity, it is possible to identify the context of creativity. From the definition given for creativity, the significance of the user (or group of users), social environment and task as contextual elements in formulating a creativity process is transparent. Each one of these elements constitutes information and includes attributes that can be perceived as individual entities. The combination of these entities builds the overall context of the creativity process. We consider those entities as "primary" and a description for each "primary" context entity is given as follows:

#### User

This may include someone's competences, preferences, etc. This information defines the profile of a user. This profile can for example be used in creating balanced teams or in establishing the qualification to perform a task. User modeling follows an approach of standard based modeling suggested in (Dolog & Schaefer, 2006) based on combination of open specifications for learner profiles such as IEEE PAPI and IMS LIP where the user's learning activities are recorded in her performance and portfolios. User modeling is mainly used to formulate a profile. The profile defines the user's role in the creative process and thereby the context in which someone functions. The context for the user in idspace platform is a combination of the user's actions, attributes as well as their associations with the other context entities that are subsets of the contextual elements. For example a user portfolio in idSpace depends on the performance, since the user's performance is defined based on the ideas generated or elaborated. At the same time the participation of a user in a creative session, collaborative or individual, depends on user's competences, knowledge background or social background

### Social Environment

The social background of the users and the social environment in which the learning takes place. This possibly includes information such as group composition, roles played in the group, etc. The generation of an idea is usually an individual process followed by knowledge transfer to other people, or knowledge received by others. The collaborative process is often used as an internal process in team-groups, companies or organizations. Therefore the conceptualization of Social Environment in terms of the idSpace project, demands the formulation of the appropriate associations between other entities in regards to the social background of the user. The social background of a user can be constructed based on her knowledge background, in domain specific subjects/areas, the social role, the expertise and social attributes such as the language and the location. The importance of the Social Environment in idSpace platform as a context element is traced in its necessity for the formulation of social groups and the assignment of social roles to the participants. The social role and the social background of a user constitute important context factors that influence the final recommendation of a user for her participation in a team's creative session.

### System

This may include information such as the software or platform used at a given time. The idSpace platform strives not to be a one-size-fits-all model. Instead, mixing tools and automatically tweaking system functions should result in a platform which can be used in various settings. Some settings require a more formalized environment and other settings require an informal environment. In both cases, a creative process will be facilitated. One way to make a difference between the two options is to offer a set of concepts and associations as a starting point and delimiter for the creative session for formalized and restricted sessions and in the case of a more informal session, to offer a blank slate to be filled in by the users. The system context element can be defined by the following discrete attributes:

- **Connection Speed:** the connection speed influences the collaborative procedure, and is important to the proposed resources type. (E.g. multimedia, real time Skype conversations, etc.)
- **Type of device accessing:** The user may access the idSpace platform from a PC, PDA, and Pocket PC. The interface and supported modules of idSpace must be adapted
- **3rd Party applications:** The system must search on the client's PC for the necessary 3rd Party applications which are used in idSpace and if they are not installed, the idSpace must propose Links for Download (e.g. Skype).
- **Operating System Used:** Different plug-ins and 3rd party applications compatible with the OS.

### Task (Also Referred to as Ideation)

Information about a task including which project it concerns, the specific activity, the objective, the owner and the stakeholders of a task. Ideation is the most important element of the creative process. The overall model of contextualization of creativity aims to facilitate successful ideation. The task can be defined through the associations of the aforementioned context elements with contextual entities which are influencing the "ideation". With respect to the idSpace project the "ideation" session depends on the selected creativity technique, which supports the creative process and the creative team that includes the participants of a session. The enhancement of the creative process with the use of the context awareness of the creative process converges to the *Task*. The design of an ontology schema constructed by the described context elements aims to the implementation of a context aware recommender tool that will maximize effectiveness of innovation through its recommendations.

Based on the above contextual elements we have specified all possible contextual entities that are most relevant to the process of creativity. More particular, we defined the context within a collaborative creativity support tool, as described in the next section.

### Topic Maps Context Awareness Ontology for idSpace

The design and representation of the context awareness ontology schema for creativity was made using the Topic Maps technology. The context elements described earlier, and their subset entities, are represented as topics. These topics are connected through associations. Entities, associations and occurrences are creating a semantic network which is represented as a topic map.

More specifically for the idSpace project the conceptual model of creativity has been represented as a Topic Map (Figure 1). Figure 1 shows all the topic types (called contextual entities) of the context aware creativity ontology. Keywords and domains characterize users, ideas, solutions and problems and can be used as metadata to search for content to be recommended. Depending on the recommendation type, several other entities are used in the recommendation process, e.g. for recommending users, the system uses Social Role, Social Group, Competence etc.

## SYSTEM DESCRIPTION AND EVALUATION

Based on the above conceptual model, we have designed, implemented and evaluated a context aware recommender system for the idSpace platform, aiming at recommending: i) people to collaborate with, ii) related solutions of past projects, iii) related ideas conceived in past projects, iv) related recourses used in past projects and v) the best pedagogical pattern to be followed for solving the problem at hand. All these recommendations aim at assisting the user during the creativity session.

Each recommendation type is based on a set of factors. These factors are ontology entity types, for example "keywords", "problems", "domains", etc. Depending on the recommendation type, the recommender examines all instances within the appropriate entity types and measures their relevance to the given problem to be solved, in order to opine which are the most relevant to be recommended. The relevance is being measured by using ontology associations. If an instance of such an entity type is highly associated with the current creativity session at hand, then it is highly recommended by the system. The instance and the creativity session at hand are highly associated if they have common keywords and domains (amongst other things). The more common data they have, the more associated they are considered to be. In the following section the different recommendation types are briefly explained.

*Figure 1. Topic map ontology for idSpace*

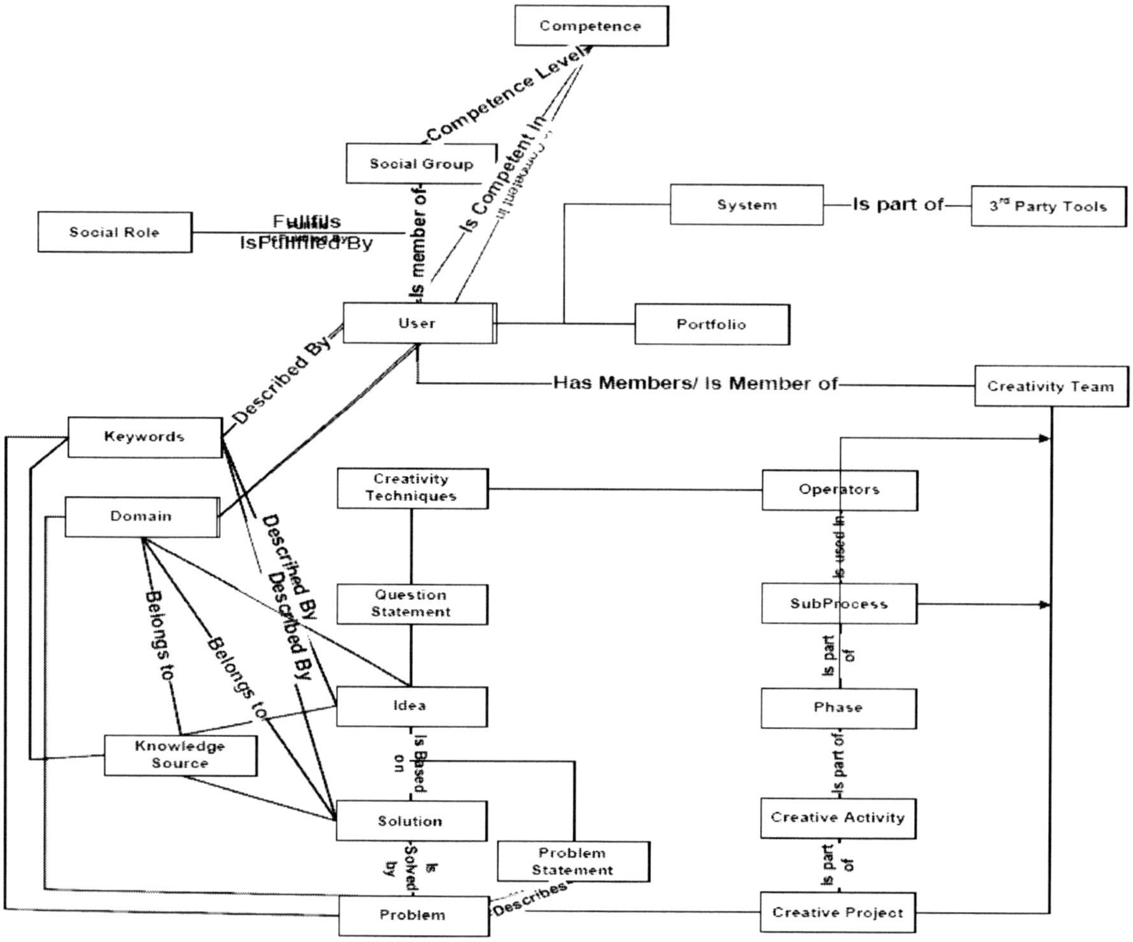


## Recommend Users

The recommender system provides recommendations of users that are most relevant to the particular idSpace session (problem solved), in terms of their competence, expertise in various relevant domains, as well as relevance based on the keywords in the user's profile. "User Recommendations" will help the user in forming a proper user group, which will have the best potentials to solve the session's problem. The purpose of user recommendations is to recommend, not only the users who are experts in the project's thematic area, but also users that may have experience in related fields or may have solved relevant problems in the past. Based on the idSpace main process diagram, the recommendation of users will be used in the stages indicated in Figure 2.

User recommendations will initially be needed at the stage of composing a new group of users. At this point, the user wants to add to his/her team the most expert users in certain domains, the most experienced, as well as the most competent ones. The system helps by recommending a list of ranked users, those with higher relevance shown first, according to the previously stated factors.

*Figure 2. idSpace main processes diagram. The large arrows indicate where the recommendations of users will be provided (adapted from Sielis, Mettouris, Tzanavari & Papadopoulos (2009)).*

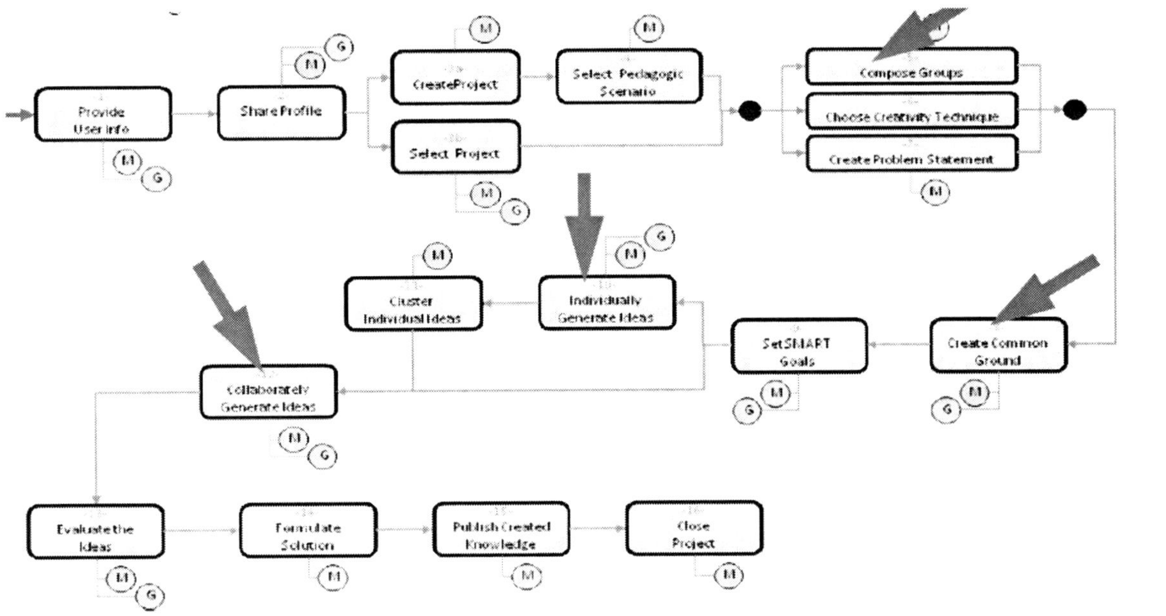


Recommendation of users will also be needed in the "create common ground" stage. During this procedure, the user may eventually decide that some of the selected users in his group were not a good choice, so a new set of user recommendations would be very helpful.

Last but not least, user recommendations would be beneficial when a user asks for help or guidance during the ideation procedure. The system should then be able to recommend other users that are experts in a certain field or have experience in a certain technique or procedure.

Figures 3.a, b and c depict the recommender's interface for recommending users. In Figure 3.a the user may specify the parameters he would like to be more significant in the recommendation procedure (keywords in the user's profile, domains in the user's profile, user's previews work and/or user's competence) by specifying a weight for each parameter (high, medium or low). Next, he can choose the role that recommended users should have (the system supports users and moderators – users with more abilities such as creating projects and organizing teams to collaborate). Finally, he is provided with the option to input more keywords and by that to specify particular attributes he prefers the people constituting his collaborative user group to have. The *"tip"* links provide tips as to how to use the weights to receive more effective recommendations (Figure 3.b.). Figure 3.c. depicts a list of ranked recommended users as the result. The link *"Options for more recommendations"* takes the user in the beginning of the recommendation process to re-adjust his input and receive more tailored to his needs recommendations.

## Recommend Solutions

The recommender provides recommendations of relevant solutions to the problem being solved. The recommended solutions will indicate to the user how related projects were solved in the past. Based on the main process diagram of idSpace

*Figure 3. a. The recommender system's interface for recommending users. b. The "tip" links provide tips as to how to use the interface to receive more effective recommendations. c. Recommended users ranked*

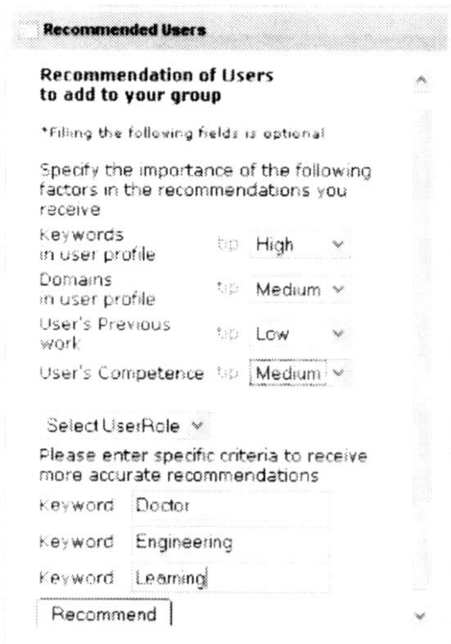


Figure 3.a The recommender system's interface for recommending users

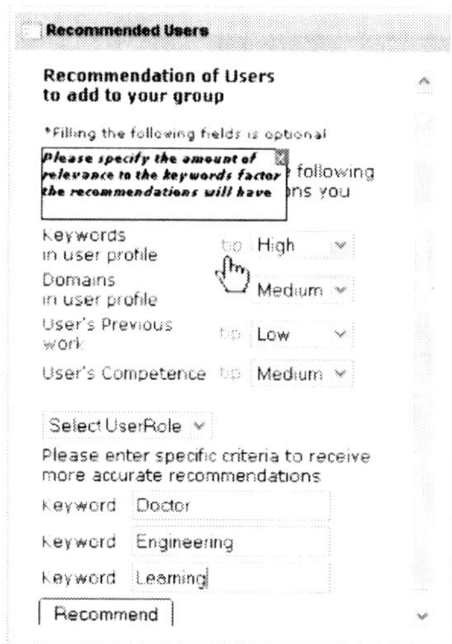


Figure 3.b . The "tip" links provide tips as to how to use the interface to receive more effective recommendations

Figure 3.c Recommended users ranked

*Figure 4. idSpace main processes diagram. The large arrows indicate where the recommendations of solutions will be provided (adapted from Sielis, Mettouris, Tzanavari & Papadopoulos (2009)).*

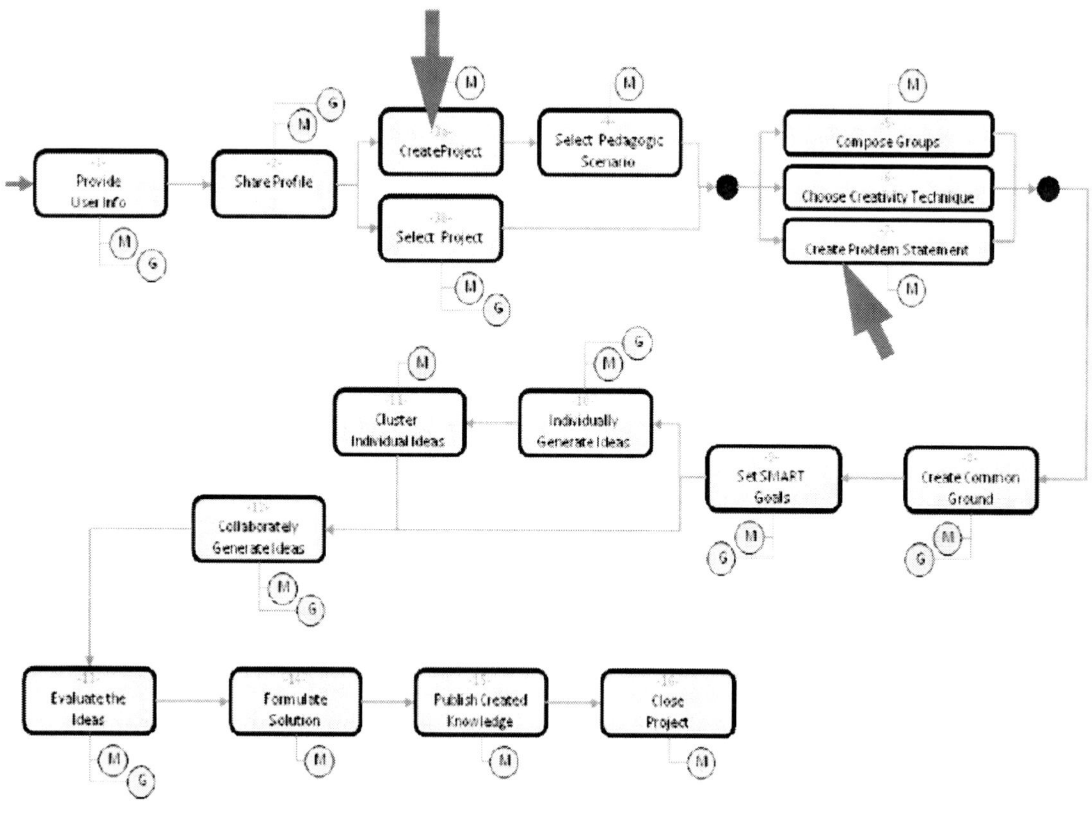

(Figure 4), the recommendation of solutions will be used in the stages indicated with red arrows in Figure 4. The recommendations of solutions will be provided in the phase of starting a new project. At this point, the user is thinking of how to correctly state a problem in the IdSpace platform, in order to use the platform to find a solution. Thus, in the stages "Create a Project" and "Create a Problem statement", the system will provide relevant solutions.

## Recommend Ideas

The recommender provides recommendations regarding relevant ideas. The purpose of these recommendations is to inspire the user during the "ideation session" stage and provide him with motives to become more creative. Based on the idSpace main process diagram, the recommendation of ideas will be used in the stages indicated in Figure 5.

## Recommend Resources

The recommender supports the recommendation of relevant resources. These recommendations will guide the user to creating new ideas during the "ideation" stage. A resource might be a web page, a document, a picture etc. that users used to support their ideas. The recommendation of resources is a helpful tool for the user, because it may initiate his thinking towards directions he would not normally explore. Moreover, this kind of recommendations could stimulate one's imagination, thus, making him or her more creative. Based on the idSpace main process diagram, the recommendation of resources will be used in the stages indicated in Figure 6.

Apart from the "Ideation Session" stage, recommendations of resources may be provided at the "Idea Evaluation" stage as well. During this procedure, the user is attempting to evaluate the ideas that resulted from the ideation session. One way of doing so, is by finding tangible evidence that support the idea (e.g. resources that document

*Figure 5. idSpace main processes diagram. The large arrows indicate where the recommendations of ideas will be provided (adapted from Sielis, Mettouris, Tzanavari & Papadopoulos (2009)).*

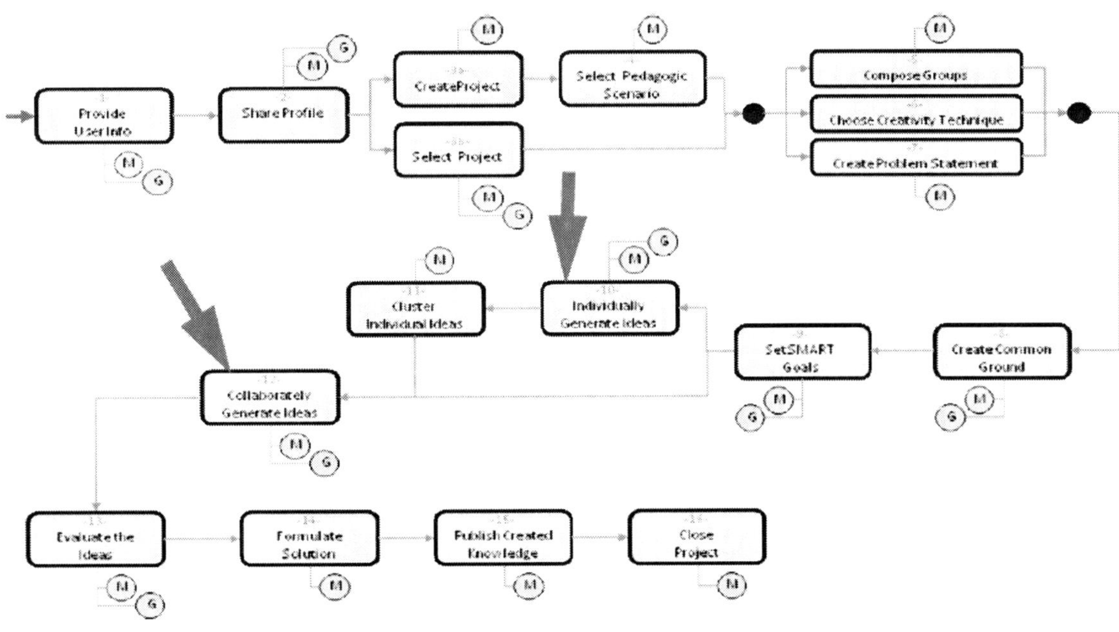

*Figure 6. idSpace main processes diagram. The large arrows indicate where the recommendations of resources will be provided (adapted from Sielis, Mettouris, Tzanavari & Papadopoulos (2009)).*

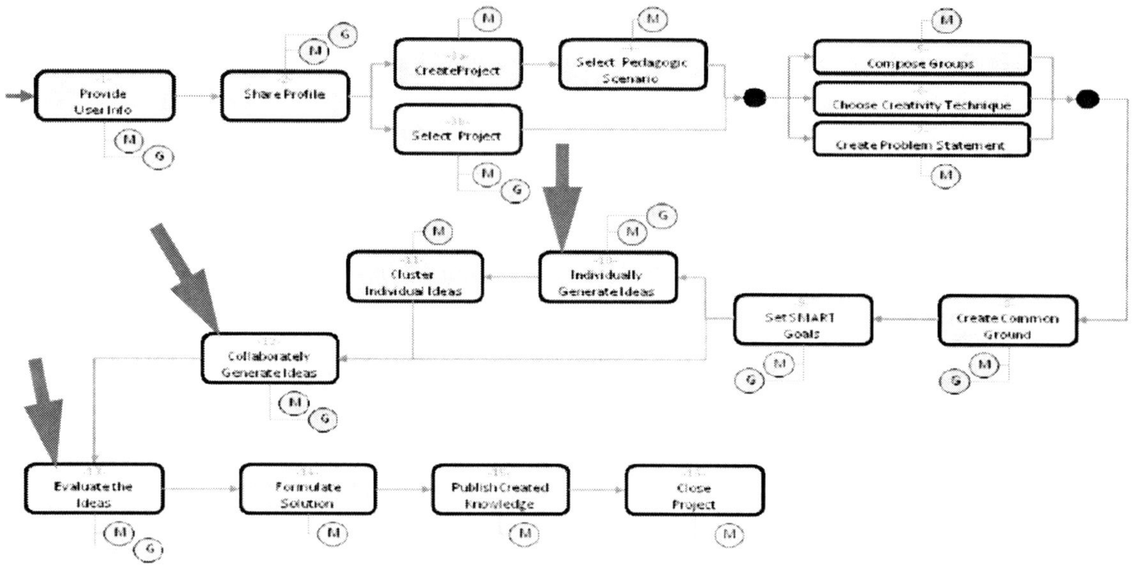


it) and/or identify it in previous projects. The recommender system could provide the user with such evidence in the form of resource recommendations.

## Recommend Pedagogical Pattern

"A pattern describes a problem which occurs over and over again in our environment, and then describes the core of the solution to that problem, in such a way that you can use this solution a million times over, without ever doing it the same way twice" (Alexander et al., 1977). A pattern language is a set of related patterns (in a patterns' hierarchy) that work together in some context, towards a bigger problem's solution. Design Patterns express the accumulated knowledge with respect to a specific problem and propose how this problem can be solved when someone deals with it. Within Design Patterns the acquired experience from previous circumstances facing the specific problem, is concentrated and the way dealing with it is documented. This is especially useful for problems that occur repeatedly and have been assessed worth been documented, so that everybody dealing with that problem can apply the pattern in order to solve it.

The recommender provides recommendations regarding the best suited pedagogical pattern to be used in the current idSpace session. A pedagogical pattern is a set of steps to be followed in the idSpace platform aiming at solving the specific problem at hand. A pedagogical pattern can be correlated with one or more creativity techniques. The selection of a pedagogical pattern influences the sequence of the steps of the creativity process which can be followed during the process. The selected pedagogical pattern is a result of the consideration of several context parameters that the system must be aware of. The recommended pedagogical pattern aims to aid the users in solving creative problems more efficiently and effectively. Thus, the goal of our system in this case is to recommend the most suitable pattern for the current problem and its context. The recommendation of the pattern is ontology independent and it is based on parameters regarding the specific problem the user is trying to solve (e.g. type of the problem, problem definition, problem complexity, if the problem is divisible, objectives, if expert knowledge required etc.). These parameters are inputted by the user during the preparation of an idSpace session, in order to facilitate the creativity process regarding the usage scenario of the session.

Each pedagogical pattern on the other hand has a combination of characteristics, which differentiate it from the others. The selection of the best pattern to be used is the result of a scoring method based on the values of these characteristics, and on the values of the aforementioned parameters provided by the user that regard the problem at hand.

The recommendation of the Pedagogical Pattern takes place during the "Create Project" stage of the overall creativity process as it is shown in Figure 7.

Considering a usage scenario, the moderator defines the following attributes: problem type, problem definition, problem complexity, divisible problem, employees, moderator, objectives, co-operation and expert knowledge required (Bitter, 2009). For instance, for the attribute values below, the most suitable pattern is in this example the Pyramid pattern, as presented in Table 2.

Attribute 1. Problem type: **open**
Attribute 2. Problem definition: **ill-defined**
Attribute 3. Problem complexity: **medium**
Attribute 4. Divisible problem: **yes**
Attribute 5. Employees: **7**
Attribute 6. Moderator: **yes**
Attribute 7. Objectives: **positive interdependence**
Attribute 8. Co-operation: **yes**
Attribute 9. Expert knowledge required: **yes**

Based on the example above, the CA component processes the moderator's data and results in the pedagogical pattern which is the most ap-

*Figure 7. idSpace main processes diagram. The large arrow indicates where the recommendation of the pedagogical pattern will be provided (adapted from Sielis, Mettouris, Tzanavari & Papadopoulos (2009)).*

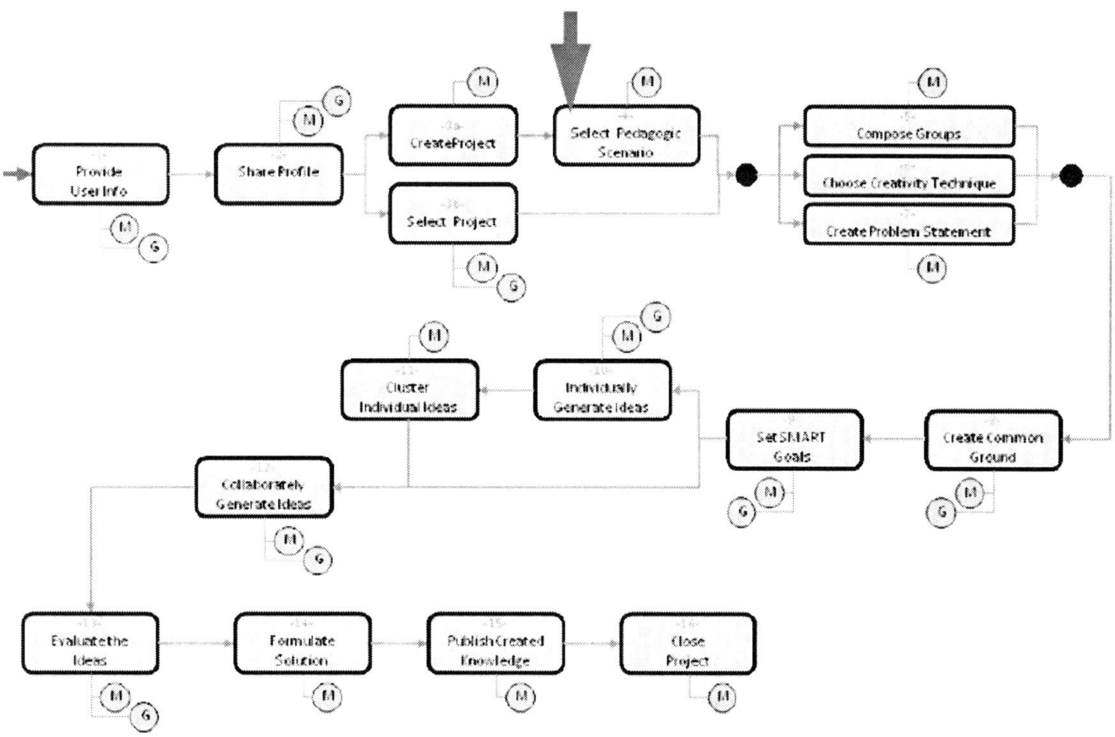

*Table 2. Pedagogical pattern scoring example*

| Patterns / attributes | Attribute 1 | Attribute 2 | Attribute 3 | Attribute 4 | Attribute 5 | Attribute 6 | Attribute 7 | Attribute 8 | Attribute 9 | score |
|---|---|---|---|---|---|---|---|---|---|---|
| Jigsaw | | | ✓ | ✓ | | ✓ | ✓ | ✓ | ✓ | 6 |
| Pyramid | ✓ | | ✓ | | ✓ | ✓ | ✓ | ✓ | | 7 |
| Think Pair Share | ✓ | | ✓ | | ✓ | ✓ | ✓ | ✓ | | 6 |
| Six Hats | ✓ | | | | ✓ | ✓ | | ✓ | | 5 |
| Progres-sive Inquiry | | ✓ | | | ✓ | ✓ | | ✓ | | 4 |
| Disney | ✓ | | | | ✓ | ✓ | | ✓ | | 4 |

propriate to be used for the current session (seen in Table 2 as the pattern with the highest score).

## Evaluation

The context aware recommender system was formally evaluated with respect to its perceived usefulness, as well as its usability. The evaluation method of user testing was chosen as the most appropriate. Two well known questionnaires by Lewis (1995) and Davis (1989), were adapted for our purpose and were used as instruments for our testing. Our users were postgraduate students from the Computer Science Department of the University of Cyprus with work experience in the IT sector. They were asked to voluntarily participate in the evaluation session for the context aware recommender system of the idSpace platform. The aim of this evaluation was currently not to measure the influence of context awareness usage in the creativity process, but only to collect opinions regarding the perception of usefulness and the usability of the context aware recommender system within the specific CST. Measuring or estimating the influence that the use of a context aware recommender may have in the creativity process is far more complicated and it cannot be achieved in a short period of time.

The goal was for the participants to carry out three tasks during the evaluation session and complete a post-task questionnaire after each task. They began by creating a profile, and then were asked to login as moderators (to gain additional user rights) and use the recommender system for completing the following three tasks:

**Task 1**: "Use the Context Awareness Recommender System to receive recommendations on solutions to related problems. You want to find out whether there existed similar problems and how they were solved, to use that knowledge and perhaps build on that".

**Task 2:** "Use the Context Awareness Recommender System to receive recommendations on suitable users to add to your team. Suitable users are users who have expertise related to the problem you want to solve".

**Task 3:** "Use the Context Awareness Recommender System to receive recommendations on ideas that may be useful/relevant for solving the particular problem. Ideas are used to build up a solution".

The post-task questionnaire included 4 7-level Likert items and was based on Lewis (1995):

1. Overall, I am satisfied with the ease of completing this task

2. Overall, I am satisfied with the amount of time it took to complete the task
3. Overall, I am satisfied with the support information (recommender system's explanation guidelines, documentation) when completing the task
4. The presented recommendations were useful

The data was analyzed and the results indicated that the mean for answers for all tasks were close to 5. In particular the mean for Task 1 was 5.14, for Task 2 it was 5.11 and for Task 3 it was 4.86. The average standard deviation was 1.54 for Task 1 answers, 1.86 for Task 2 answers and 1.63 for Task 3 answers. Task 3 had the lowest mean, probably because the recommender system had a small delay in presenting the results and users sometimes had to refresh the page to avoid this.

In general, the satisfaction regarding the recommendation results was high (close to 5). Recommendation of solutions (task 1) received the highest results. A possible reason for this is that the recommender system, by providing recommendation of solutions, helped significantly the users to better understand the current problem they were working on. Moreover, through the recommendation of other existing related projects' solutions, users could more easily understand what the expected outcome of the current project was, and by that, formulate the problem at hand more clearly in their minds.

After completing the tasks and the post-task questionnaire, the participants were asked to fill a *post-test questionnaire*. The questionnaire, retrieved from (Davis, 1989) and adjusted accordingly, included six 7-level Likert items and was designed to test the Perceived Usefulness and the Perceived Ease of Use. From the post-test questionnaire it was noticed that the participants' opinions about how they perceived the usefulness and the ease of use both of the individual tasks, as well as the recommender system as a whole, were generally positive. The highest results received, were about the recommender system's usefulness for effectively solving a problem during the creative process. The lowest results received, were observed in questions related to the interface and the interaction with it. Through this test, the users confirmed the significance of the existence of a recommender system in a CST such as idSpace.

## FUTURE RESEARCH DIRECTIONS

The existing creativity support tools are not supported by any context aware mechanism. This is a verification that we concluded from previous work (Sielis et al, 2008). The implementation of context aware systems that will be able to support creativity is a topic that generates several research questions such as, what is the impact of context awareness in the creativity of a user; how context awareness influences the creativity process; which are the proper contextual elements for creativity and how these can be modeled; and finally, issues regarding the evaluation methods that can be used to prove the aforementioned.

A very important and challenging task is the knowledge representation of creativity's context. As it was mentioned before, creativity has a multidimensional perspective. This generates two research challenges that need to be proved. The first is the definition of the contextual elements of creativity. For many years this was a subject of research for many psychologists and theorists. Therefore in the existing literature it is possible to find several approaches in defining which of those elements are the most important, to be taken into account, in order to model creativity. The second challenge is the modeling and representation of creativity using knowledge representation methods. The importance of modeling creativity considering all sub-models that influence it is a step forward from the existing creativity support tools. The existing tools are used to simulate a creativity technique and deliver it to the user as a substitute of a whiteboard, paper or pencil. The enhancement offered by these tools in relation to the whiteboard or the paper is consisted of the memory and the visualization tools included in the tools. However, modeling the context of creativity and implementing creativity support tools aiming at adaptation and personalization can enhance the support of the user during the creative process. Therefore, we identify as the most important and challenging issues the definition of the creativity model, the user model and the domain model and implement a collaborative creativity support tool based on these models. In addition, the evaluation of a collaborative creativity support tool which uses context awareness supportive mechanisms is also necessary. It is important to examine the impact such a tool can have to the user or to the creativity process by using evaluation methods and creativity metrics.

## CONCLUSION

After observing that the existing literature lacks a conceptual model for context awareness in creativity, we designed and developed a model that constitutes a first step towards that direction. The implementation of the ontology for creativity using Topic Maps offers the developers the ability to trace the users' actions and monitor the context changes during the creative process. The presented model for creativity is partly used in the architecture of the idSpace platform. The idSpace platform uses Topic Maps and Tolog Query engine in its overall architecture. The described model is already designed and implemented and has been tested using specific queries. The queries provided a successful and accurate retrieval mechanism for the necessary data used by the context reasoning and context adaptation mechanisms for implementing the context aware recommender for the idSpace platform.

The system has been formally evaluated through user testing leading to very optimistic findings. The duration of the project was not sufficient to organize a larger scale evaluation to measure also the real usefulness of the recommendations, in real life creative problem solving scenarios. This however is something highly sought after, because of the inherent complexity of offering meaningful recommendations and because of the lack of other similar recommender systems to compare against. CSTs design is a relatively newly explored area for recommendations. Further evaluation in this sense will also help towards the improvement and calibration of the model itself, which might be demonstrated as corrected or new associations of the topics, or even entirely new topics.

## ACKNOWLEDGMENT

The present work was carried out as part of the idSpace project http://idspace-project.org. The idSpace project was funded in part by the European Commission FP7-IST-2007-1-41, project number 216799. This document does not represent the opinion of the European Union, and the European Union is not responsible for any use that might be made of its content.

## REFERENCES

Alexander, C., Ishikawa, S., Silverstein, M., Jacobson, M., Fiksdahl-King, I., & Angel, S. (1977). *A pattern language*. New York, NY: Oxford University Press.

Anonymous. (2001). *XML topic maps (XTM) 1.0*. Retrieved October 10, 2010, from http://www.topicmaps.org/xtm/index.html#desc-intro

Anonymous. (2010). *Ontopia solutions – Navigator framework*. Retrieved from http://www.ontopia.net

Atman, C. J., Turns, J., Cardella, M. E., & Adams, R. S. (2003). The design processes of engineering educators: Thick descriptions and potential implications. *Expertise in Design: Proceedings of the Design Thinking Research Symposium*, vol. 6.

Bitter, M. (2009). *idSpace D1.3 – Templates V2*. Retrieved September 10, 2010, from http://dspace.ou.nl/bitstream/1820/2156/1/idSpace%20D1.3%20final%20EC%2012-11-2009.pdf

Blank, C., Eveking, H., Levihn, J., & Ritter, G. (2001). Symbolic simulation techniques - State-of-the-art and applications. *HLDVT '01: Proceedings of the Sixth IEEE International High-Level Design Validation and Test Workshop* (HLDVT'01), (p. 45).

Brown, J., P., Bovey, J. D., & Chen, X. (1997). Context-aware applications: From the laboratory to marketplace. *IEEE Personal Communications, 4*(5), 58-64

Cougar, J. D. (1995). *Creative problem solving and opportunity finding*. Boyd & Fraser Publishing Co.

Crago, S. P., McMahon, J. O., Archer, C., Asanovic, K., Chaung, R., Goolsbey, K., et al. (2006). CEARCH: Cognition enabled architecture. *Proceedings of the Tenth Annual High Performance Embedded Computing Workshop,* Lexington, MA.

Davis, F. D. (1989). Perceived usefulness, perceived ease of use, and user acceptance of Information Technology. *Management Information Systems Quarterly, 13*(3), 319–340. doi:10.2307/249008

Dey, A. K., Abowd, G., & Salber, D. (2001). A conceptual framework and a toolkit for supporting the rapid prototyping of context-aware applications. *Human-Computer Interaction, 16*(2), 97–166. doi:10.1207/S15327051HCI16234_02

Dolog, P., & Schaefer, M. (2005). A framework for browsing, manipulating and maintaining interoperable learner profiles. *Proceedings of UM2005 - 10th International Conference on User Modeling.*

Dols, R. (2009). *idSpace D4.4 – idSpace platform & user guide v2.* Retrieved January 10, 2010, from http://hdl.handle.net/1820/2159

Gaaevic, D., Djuric, D., Devedzic, V., & Selic, B. (2001). *Model driven architecture and ontology development.* New York, NY: Springer-Verlag, Inc.

Garshol, L. M. (2010). *Tolog: A topic map query language.* Retrieved October 22, 2010, from http://www.ontopia.net/topicmaps/materials/tolog.html

Giunchiglia, F. L. (1993). Contextual reasoning. *Epistemologia, Special Issue on I Linguaggie le Macchine, 345,* 345-364.

Gruber, T. R. (1993). Toward principles for the design of ontologies used for knowledge sharing. In Guarino, N., & Poli, R. (Eds.), *Formal ontology in conceptual analysis and knowledge representation.*

Hatzigaidas, A., Papastergiou, A., Tryfon, G., & Maritsa, D. (2004). *Topic map existing tools: A brief review.* ICTAMI 2004 (International Conference on Theory and Applications of Mathematics and Informatics).

Haya, A. P., Montoro, G., & Alaman, X. (2004). *A prototype of a context-based architecture for intelligent home environments.* On the Move to Meaningful Internet Systems.

Hendler, J., & Heflin, J. (2000). Dynamic ontologies on the Web. *Proceedings of the Seventeenth National Conference on Artificial Intelligence* (AAAI-2000). Menlo Park, CA: AAAI/MIT Press.

Henricksen, K. Indulska., J., & Rakotonirainy., A. (2003). *Generating context management infrastructure from high-level context models.* Industrial Track Proceedings of the 4th International Conference on Mobile Data Management (MDM2003), (pp. 1–6).

Howe, D. C. (2008). RiTa: Creativity support for generative literature. *Proceedings of Gerative Art Intl. Conference.*

Jun-Zhao, S., & Sauvola, J. (2003). Towards a conceptual model for context-aware adaptive services. *The 4th International Conference on Parallel and Distributed Computing, Applications and Technologies* PDCAT'2003, (pp. 90-94).

Karapidis, A., Kienle, A., & Schneider, H. (2005). *Creativity, learning and knowledge management in the process of service development*. Results from a Survey of Experts, Proceedings of I-Know ´05.

Lewis, J. R. (1995). IBM computer usability satisfaction questionnaires: Psychometric evaluation and instructions for use. *International Journal of Human-Computer Interaction*, 7(1), 57–78. doi:10.1080/10447319509526110

Plucker, J. A., & Beghetto, R. A. (2004). Why creativity is domain general, why it looks domain specific, and why the distinction does not matter. In Sternberg, R. J., Grigorenko, E. G., & Singer, J. L. (Eds.), *Creativity: From potential to realization* (pp. 153–167). Washington, DC: American Psychological Association. doi:10.1037/10692-009

Reddit. (n.d.). *Home*. Retrieved September 14, 2010, from http://www.reddit.com/

Riedl, M. O. (2008). *Vignette-based story planning: Creativity through exploration and retrieval*. Joint Workshop on Computational Creativity.

Schilit, B., Adams, N., & Want, R. (1994). *Context-aware computing applications*. 1st International Workshop on Mobile Computing Systems and Applications, (pp. 85-90).

Shen, L., & Shen, R. (2005). Ontology-based learning content recommendation. *International Journal of Continuing Engineering Education and Life-Long Learning, 15*(3/4/5/6), 308–317.

Shneiderman, B. (2000). Creating creativity: User interfaces for supporting innovation. *ACM TOCHI*, 7(1), 114–138. doi:10.1145/344949.345077

Shneiderman, B., Fischer, G., Czerwinski, M., Resnick, M., Myers, B., & Candy, L. (2006). Creativity support tools: Report from a U.S. National Science Foundation sponsored workshop. *International Journal of Human-Computer Interaction, 20*(2), 61–77. doi:10.1207/s15327590ijhc2002_1

Sielis, A. G., Mettouris, C., Tzanavari, A., & Papadopoulos, G. (2009). *idSpace D3.3 – Definition and implementation of context awareness*, v2. Retrieved January 18, 2010, from http://hdl.handle.net/1820/2158

Sielis, A. G., Tzanavari, A., & Papadopoulos, A. G. (2008). *Enhancing the creativity process by adding context awareness in creativity support tools*. HCI International 2009, San Diego, USA.

Simon, B., Mikls, Z., Nejdl, W., Sintek, M., & Salvachua, J. (2003). *Smart space for learning: A mediation infrastructure for learning services*. In WWW 2003, May 2003, Hungary.

Simon, I., Morris, D., & Basu, S. (2008). MySong: Automatic accompaniment generation for vocal melodies. In *Proceeding of the Twenty-Sixth Annual SIGCHI Conference on Human Factors in Computing Systems* (Florence, Italy, April 05 - 10, 2008), (pp. 725-734). New York, NY: ACM. DOI= http://doi.acm.org/10.1145/1357054.1357169

Strang, T., & Linnhoff-Popien, C. (2004). *A context modelling survey*. First International Workshop on Advanced Context Modeling, Reasoning And Management (UbiComp '04), Nottingham England.

Tintarev, N., & Masthoff, J. (2007). A survey of explanations in recommender systems. *Proceedings of the 2007 IEEE 23rd International Conference on Data Engineering Workshop*, (pp. 801-810). IEEE Computer Society.

Wang, X. H., Zhang, D. Q., Gu, T., & Pung, H. K. (2004). *Ontology based context modeling and reasoning using OWL*. Proceedings of the Second IEEE Annual Conference Pervasive Computing and Communications Workshops, (pp. 18-22). ISBN: 0-7695-2106-1

Wrightson, A. (2001). *Topic maps and knowledge representation*. Retrieved September 14, 2010, from http://www.ontopia.net/topicmaps/materials/kr-tm.html

## ADDITIONAL READING

Atman, C. J., Turns, J., Cardella, M. E., & Adams, R. S. The Design Processes of Engineering Educators: Thick Descriptions and Potential Implications, Expertise in Design: Proceedings of the Design Thinking Research Symposium 6, 2003

Chuan, C. H., Chew, E.: "Evaluating and Visualizing Effectiveness of Style Emulation in Musical accompaniment", Proc. Intl. Symposium on Music Information Retrieval (ISMIR), 2008

Cougar, J. (1995). *D: Creative Problem Solving and Opportunity Finding*. Boyd & Fraser Publishing Co.

Durkin, J.: "Expert Systems: Design and Development", Macmillan, New York.

Howe, D. C.: "RiTa: Creativity Support for Generative Literature", Proceedings of Gerative Art Intl. Conference, 2008

Joonhee, K., & Sungrim, K. (2005). Context-aware Recommendation using Pattern Discovery in Ubiquitous Computing. *Key Engineering Materials*, *277-279*, 278–286. doi:10.4028/www.scientific.net/KEM.277-279.278

Karapidis, A., Kienle, A., & Schneider, H. Creativity, Learning and Knowledge Management in the Process of Service Development – Results from a Survey of Experts, Proceedings of I-Know ′05, 2005

Kirton, M. "Kirton KAI Inventory Tool" http://pubs.acs.org/subscribe/archive/ci/31/i11/html/11hipple_box3.ci.html, Accessed: Jannuary, 2010

McCarthy. J.: "Concepts of logical AI": http://www-formal.stanford.edu/jmc/concepts-ai/concepts-ai.html, 1999

Pascal, G., Schmid, K.: "idSpace D2.1 State of the Art in Tools for Creativity", idSpace Project, 2008

Plucker, J. A., & Beghetto, R. A. "Why creativity is domain general, why it looks domain specific, and why the distinction does not matter", In: Sternberg, R.J., Grigorenko. E.G., Singer, J.L. (Eds.), Creativity: From Potential to Realization. American Psychological Association, Washington, DC, pp. 153-167.

Riedl, M. O.: "Vignette-Based Story Planning: Creativity Through Exploration and Retrieval", Joint Workshop on Computational Creativity, 2008

Schmidt, "Management of Dynamic and Imperfect User Context Information," On the Move to Meaningful Internet Systems 2004: OTM 2004 Workshops, 2004, pp. 779-786.

Sharma, P. (2002). Teaching Creativity- a Systematic viewpoint. In *Enhancing curricula* (pp. 330–342). London: Exploring Effective Curricula Practices in Art, Design and Communication.

Shneiderman, B. (2000). Creating creativity: User interfaces for supporting innovation. *ACM TOCHI*, *7*(1), 114–138. doi:10.1145/344949.345077

Shneiderman, B., Fischer, G., Czerwinski, M., Resnick, M., Myers, B., & Candy, L. (2006, May). Creativity Support Tools: Report From a U.S. National Science Foundation Sponsored Workshop. *International Journal of Human-Computer Interaction*, *20*(Issue 2), 61–77. doi:10.1207/s15327590ijhc2002_1

Simon, I., Morris, D., & Basu, S. "MySong: automatic accompaniment generation for vocal melodies", In Proceeding of the Twenty-Sixth Annual SIGCHI Conference on Human Factors in Computing Systems (Florence, Italy, April 05 - 10, 2008). CHI '08. ACM, New York, NY, 725-734. DOI= http://doi.acm.org/10.1145/1357054.1357169, 2008

Sowa, J. F. (2005). *"Knowledge Representation: Logical, Philosophical and Computational foundations", Brooks Cole, Pacific Grove, CA, 2000 Creativity in the Classroom: Schools of Curious Delight. Contributors: Alane Jordan Starko - author. Publisher: Lawrence Erlbaum Associates. Place of Publication.* Mahwah, NJ: Publication Year.

Sternberg, R. (2006). J.: "The Nature of Creativity. *Creativity Research Journal*, *18*(1), 87–98. doi:10.1207/s15326934crj1801_10

Truong, H., L., Dustdar, S.: „A survey on Context-aware Web Service Systems", International Journal of Web Information Systems, 5(1):5-31, Emerald, 2009

Unsworth, K. (2001). L.: "Unpacking creativity. *Academy of Management Review*, *26*(2), 286–297.

Williams, R. "Integrating Distributed Learning with just-in-context Knowledge Management", Electronic Journal of e-Learning, Volume 1 Issue 1, pp. 45-50, 2003

## KEY TERMS AND DEFINITIONS

**Context (of an Application):** Any information relevant to the application, its users and its/their environment.

**Context-Awareness:** The ability of an entity (e.g. a system) to be aware of its context.

**Context Modeling:** The process of modeling the context.

**Context Reasoning:** The process where the context is used in order to obtain meaningful information.

**Creativity:** The process of creating something new and novel that has value.

**CST:** Creativity Support Tool is a software tool that supports the user in being creative.

**Ontology:** A complete organization of a knowledge domain in a hierarchical way. It contains all relevant entities as well as their relations.

**Recommender System:** A system that recommends items to users according to several criteria such as the user preferences, user history information and the context.

**Topic-Maps:** XML-like Context Representation Technology.

# Chapter 4
# An Ontology Network for Educational Recommender Systems

**Alicia Díaz**
*Universidad Nacional de La Plata, Argentina*

**Regina Motz**
*Universidad de la República, Uruguay*

**Edelweis Rohrer**
*Universidad de la República, Uruguay*

**Libertad Tansini**
*Universidad de la República, Uruguay*

## ABSTRACT

*This chapter presents how an ontology network can be used to explicitly specify the relevant features of Semantic Educational Recommender Systems. This ontology network conceptualizes the different domains and features involved in these kind of systems in a set of interrelated ontologies. Basically, this chapter presents a detailed study of the semantic relationships that exist among the ontologies in the network considering learners and educators goals and taking also into account relevance feedback by users. One important contribution of this work is to show how the ontology-based reasoning mechanism can be used to validate the recommendation criteria and to assure flexibility for tailoring the educational resource adequacy features (called Educational Resource Quality).*

## INTRODUCTION

The large number of educational material currently available through the Web requires the presence of Educational Recommender Systems which not only reflect the most appropriate educational resource provision for a student, taking into account their preferences and personal characteristics, but also considering the educator point of view. The resource and student properties are generally modeled by corresponding ontologies. Nowadays, autonomously developed ontologies emerge quite

DOI: 10.4018/978-1-61350-489-5.ch004

naturally in different domains (health, tourism, learning, quality of services, etc.). These ontologies, each one built for different purposes, are used together in complex applications. However, how they are combined is usually hidden in the application code. Particularly, the modeling of educational recommender systems involves the combination of many features: specific educational domain, quality assurance domain, and user context domain, among others. Therefore, when specifying an educational recommendation system, the proper interrelationship of all these features must be ensured. In this sense, this chapter focuses on showing how the different ontologies involved in an educational recommender system can be modeled as an ontology network in order to explicitly specify the recommendation system. One of the main contributions of this chapter is the specification of an ontology-network and the use of ontology reasoning mechanisms on that network to validate the recommendation criteria.

The remainder of the chapter is organized as follows. The next section describes background notions on semantic recommendation systems, ontology networks and ontology validations. In the following section, the desired aspects of a recommender system within the educational environment are discussed. After that, details about educational resource quality, user goals and relevance feedback are given. These aspects help to identify the component ontologies of the framework. Then, it is described the role of the ontology-network within a Semantic Educational Recommender System. Finally, some future research directions and conclusions are discussed.

## BACKGROUND

This section presents background material on semantic recommender systems, ontology-networks and ontology validation.

### Semantic Recommendation Systems Background

Previous works on semantic recommendation systems, specially tailored for the e-commerce and digital libraries area, use ontologies to determine semantically similar items following the widely known content-based recommendation technique. Porcel, Moreno and Herrera-Viedma (2010) present four different classes of recommendation techniques: (1) *content-based systems*, based on the terms used about resources (2) *collaborative systems* that consider the user preferences, (3) *Demographic systems* that represent the different user profiles and (4) *knowledge-based systems*, based on inferences about resources that satisfy the users. These authors proposed a hybrid approach that combines content-based and collaborative techniques. Recently, in (Bellogín, Cantador, Castells, & Ortigosa, 2010), the construction of a recommender system is presented, which is described as an iterative process where at each iteration a model representing the preferential characteristics for the recommendation is obtained. That system is an ontology-based recommendation process that produces semantic recommendations by applying content-based, context-aware and collaborative criteria.

Even though the idea of semantic recommender systems for the e-learning domain has been employed for around a decade, there are only few approaches that use the full reasoning capabilities of the ontology model. It is common that for semantic educational recommender systems the ontology is used for the point of view of a vocabulary-based recommender system, to specify semantic content either for the educational resources and for the learner profile, model hierarchical classification of items or to enhance semantic descriptions. Some works in this direction are those from Yu, Nakamura, Jang, Kajita, and Mase (2007), Oufaida & Nouali (2009) and Zhuhadar, Nasraoui, Wyatt & Romero (2009).

On the other hand, Intelligent Tutorial Systems (Aleven, McLarren, Sewall, & Koedinger, 2009; Stanko, Rosic, Zitko, & Grubisic, 2008), Web Based Educational Systems (Brusilovsky & Peyl, 2003) are developed on the basis of an Educational Recommender System (ERS) that provide the learner with the educational resources she/he needs together with a pedagogic strategy and an instructional design. Related with these systems, but with emphasis on the personalization features of the social web environments are the so called personal Learner Environments (Soylu, Wild, Modritscher, & De Causmaecker, 2010) (Mödritsche, 2010). Learning services, content, and functions that best fit their requirements will be recommended to the learners. The services can be integrated into learning-management systems and social networks like Facebook so that the technologies can connect optimally. However, in this chapter we restrict ourselves to perform information retrieval from educational resources.

## Ontology-Network Background

Currently, the development of ontologies to the Semantic Web is based on the integration of existing ontologies favoring the modularization, reuse of ontologies and re-engineering of knowledge resources as well as the collaborative and argumentative ontology development. This paradigm is being increasingly applied, instead of custom-building new ontologies from scratch. Therefore, ontologies are not studied as isolated artifacts, but they are seen as a set of ontologies that are explicitly or implicitly related with each other. In the context the concept of *ontology network* emerges.

An *ontology network* is a collection of ontologies related together through a variety of different relationships such as mapping, modularization and versioning among others (Allocca, d'Aquin, & Motta, 2009).

Distributed and collaborative methodologies of ontology design, such as Diligent (Vrandečić, Pinto, Sure, & Tempich, 2005) and the Neon project approach (Suárez-Figueroa et al., 2009), enable to design local models based on the core model. From the point of view of model integration, in a ontology network each ontology conceptualizes a specific domain and play a particular role. An ontology network differs from a set of interconnected single ontologies, because of in an ontology network the meta-relationships among the networked ontologies are explicitly expressed. Intuitively, defining an ontology network involves the following tasks: to select a set of networked ontologies, to express the role of each networked ontology and finally, to specify how each one relates to others. Especially important it is the problem of identifying the different kinds of relationships between networked ontologies.

There are some models that cover both the syntactic and semantic aspects of dealing with ontology relationships in networked ontologies. For instance, the Ontology Metadata Vocabulary (OMV) (Hartmann et al., 2005) uses classes and relations to talk about authoring aspects, ontology type, purpose, etc. On the other hand, the Collaborative Ontology Design Ontology (C-ODO) (Gangemi & Presutti, 2007) is an ontology network that enables designers to talk about design entities (ontologies, modules, ontology elements, requirements, activities, tools, reusable knowledge, teams, people, etc.). Allocca et al. (2009) present general relations between ontologies. These relationships are *includedIn*, *equivalentTo*, *similarTo*, *versioning* among others. These relationships were conceptualized in the DOOR (Descriptive Ontology of Ontology Relations) ontology that defines ontology relations using ontological primitives and rules.

There are other works that use ontologies networks. In the context of web searching, Cremades, Rodriguez, Costilla and Pena (2007) present mapping techniques to build ontology networks. Jung and Euzenat (2007) show the usefulness of ontology networks in social networks. This work describes a three-layered architecture for constructing semantic social networks, composed of a social layer, an ontology layer and a concept layer. The ontology layer is an ontology network in which the authors identify two relationships: *import*, when an ontology include another ontology and *refer*, when an ontology uses some concept of another ontology. The approach focuses on obtaining a measure of similarity between ontologies, and to infer a measure of affinity among users of the social network.

The work presented in this chapter addresses the main problem of specifying the semantic relationships between independent ontologies. One important contribution of this work is the specification of these semantic relationships inters networked ontologies for the conceptualization of a ERS.

## Ontology Validation Background

One of the main advantages of using ontologies as a formalism to represent the learning resources metadata is the possibility to validate the developed knowledge specifications. To express this validation is needed to understand some theoretical concepts in the field of knowledge representation and deduction mechanism. This chapter focuses in the use of ontologies as the knowledge representation formalism, and particularly, in OWL as ontology language. However, it is not always enough to do some deductions and then, it is needed to combine OWL with other representation formalism as rules. In the following, it give some light in this topics.

The integration of rules and the OWL formalism has been object of a lot of research, in order to take advantage of the benefits of Description Logics (DL) and Logical Programming (LP) (Baader, Horrocks, & Sattler, 2009; Drabent, 2010). Before OWL, F-Logic was an alternative approach of expressing ontologies based on rules and the logic programming paradigm. The main reason for combining these paradigms is to retain both the modeling and computational properties of the respective components (Baader et al., 2009).

On one hand, *rules* in logical programming enable *non-monotonic reasoning*, which means the possibility of inferring negative knowledge. This is the idea of the *closed world assumption*, that allows concluding $\neg A$ when $A$ cannot be concluded. On the other hand, in DL, the reasoning is *monotonic* (Drabent, 2010). Achieving a conceptually integration of OWL and rules is a difficult task because OWL (based on first-order predicate logic) adheres to the *open-world assumption*, while rules generally follow the *closed-world assumption* (Baader et al., 2009).

Within the approaches of integration of both paradigms, there exist some approaches that allows non-monotonic reasoning and other which only permit monotonic reasoning. There also exist approaches called *homogeneous* in contrast with the *heterogeneous* ones. In a homogeneous approach there is no distinction between the rule predicates and DL predicates, in contrast with a heterogeneous approach (Drabent, 2010).

One of the integration approaches is the Semantic Web Rule language (SWRL), which aims to be the standard rule language of the Semantic Web. It provides the ability to write Horn-like rules expressed in terms of OWL concepts (O'Connor, Knublauch, Tu, and Musen, 2005). Then, it is an homogeneous approach, where the union of an ontology and a set of rules is considered as a single first order theory. Thus, non-monotonic reasoning is no supported (Drabent, 2010).

SWRL is a rule extension of OWL DL which adheres to the opn-world assumption and it is enterily in the sprit of the OWL DL language. It is unrestricted union of OWL DL (DL SHOI(D)) and (binary) function-free Horn logic. The result is a very expressive formalism, which is undecidable. Then, existing implementations include a subset of "DL-safe rules", which have a safety condition where the possible values of (explicit) variables in SWRL rules are restricted to named individuals only which confines the direct effects of such rules to the ABox (Baader et al., 2009). SWRL allows users to write rules that can be expressed in terms of OWL concepts and that can reason about OWL individuals (O'Connor, Shankar, Nyulas, Tu, & Das, 2008). This combination of features, that arises from the integration of DL and rules paradigms with the benefits of a homogeneous approach, is very valuable at the moment of doing the ontology validation. When it is necessary to verify the correct classification of instances, OWL is not sufficient if validations implying individuals comparison are required.

## DESIRED ASPECTS OF THE RECOMMENDER SYSTEM

As is was pointed out at the First Workshop on Recommender Systems for Technology Enhanced Learning (Manouselis, Drachsler, Verbert, & Santos, 2010), Educational Recommender Systems differ from traditional ones that they must consider educational objectives, and not only the users' preferences. However, there exist some common aspects with the recommender systems used in commercial fields. Considering the classification of recommendation techniques given in (Porcel, Moreno & Herrera-Viedma, 2009), our proposal also matches user profiles and resources, although we rather combine content-based (educational resource 's properties) and demographic (student profiles) approaches. Furthermore, some aspects faced by Bellogín, Cantador, Castells, and Ortigosa (2011), like considering context issues (i.e. the task and role at the moment the user makes a query) and the exploitation of query goal, are also considered in our work. In this sense, important features of our proposal are increase classical user goals from meta topics in education and consider the relevance feedback given by both learners and educators. Besides, we consider relevant to explicitly model the education resource adequacy properties (called Education Resource Quality), to explicitly say the reason for the recommendation and to allow the validation of the recommendation criteria. We use the ontology-network model to enable these features. The ontology-network not only provides the structure to model the Educational Resource Quality but also to model the relations among User Goals and Relevance Feedback.

The following subsections describe our approach to Educational Resource Quality, User Goals and Relevance Feedback.

### Educational Resource Quality

We consider educational resource quality as a specific type of data quality. There are, basically, two ways of defining data quality: the first one uses a scientific approach and defines data quality dimensions rigorously, classifying them as dimensions that are or are not intrinsic to an information system (Wang & Strong, 1996). The second one is a pragmatic approach aimed at defining data quality in an operational fashion (Wand and Wang, 1996). Wang and Strong (1996) identified four data quality dimensions: (i) intrinsic data quality; (ii) contextual data quality, which defines the quality of the information within the context of the task; (iii) data quality for data representation, which determines if the system presents the information in a concise, consistent, understandable way; (iv) data quality regarding data access, which defines quality in terms of the role of the information system in the provision of the data.

Within each dimension, it is possible to identify several factors, including: for intrinsic data quality dimension: believability, accuracy, objectivity and for context dimension: value-added, relevancy, timeliness, completeness, among others. The domain expert is the one who decides which of these factors are relevant for a specific domain and she/he is who defines the appropriate metrics to measure these factors.

Regarding believability, two definitions are introduced in (Wand & Wang, 1996): *Believability,* which is *the extent to which data is regarded as true and credible* and *Reputation,* which is *the extent to which data is highly regarded in terms of its source or content*. For the readability factor, in (DuBay, 2004), it is introduced different readability metrics that were created for different domains and user profiles. It sets the following definition: *Readability is what makes some texts easier to read than others*. There are a lot of readability formulas created for different authors, like FOG[1] and SMOG[2] grade levels. Here also, the decision on which formula have to be used must be taken by a domain expert. The first step is to specify a formal model that represents the factors involved in the acquisition of the quality of educational resources as well as the different metrics that can be applied. The main intention of measuring the educational resource quality is to provide a quantitative meaning of quality dimensions. Metrics are these quantitative or categorical representations of one or more attributes.

Our approach to face this challenge is the design of an ontological model inspired in our previous work (Llambías, Motz, Toledo & de Uvarow, 2008) on web data warehouse quality, by modeling a generic ontology for educational quality factors, independent from the specific domain and the different types of educational resources. It is easily tailored to different user domains and different types of data through its connection in the proposed ontology-network.

## User Goals

A better representation of what material is likely to be relevant for the learner may be found by allowing the learner and the educator more control over the selection process, paying more attention to the tasks the user is trying to achieve through the system. Most researchers in the field (Rose, 2006; Carbonaro & Ferrini, 2008) agree that it is very important to capitalize goal–awareness in order to improve the search experience of users and search results, helping users to select the most appropriate item when there is abundance of information.

The goal of the users is not in the final search result but is an intermediate step in the information retrieval process. Knowledge about the goal of the queries may improve the search experience of the users through some kind of personalization, for instance, the search interface. The search results may be improved by exploiting the user goal to present the results to the user in, for example, the relevance–ranking algorithm, answer presentation and result clustering.

Some authors claim that this can be achieved by using ontologies to extract the different purposes (specificity or exhaustivity) of context for a given query to retrieve based on a user's goal (Tao, 2006). Their results indicate that while performing a specificity search for the goal of information search the results are with better precision, whereas while performing an exhaustivity search for navigational search the results are with better recall.

Characterization of user goals is largely based on Broder's influential classification of queries by user intent into *informational*, *navigational*, and *transactional*.

There are mainly two types of user goal data collection systems: explicit data collection systems, where the users are asked to voluntarily provide their preferences, and implicit data collection systems, where the system users are monitored and their preferences are inferred. Because there are mainly active users in the educational environment, it is possible and advantageous to explicitly ask users about their goal for each specific query to aid in the recommendation process. This will be done at three levels:

- Type of query - *informational*, *navigational* and *transactional*
- Meta topic in education - *analyze, evaluate, create, apply, understand* and *remember*

- Topic – *extracted from the Educational Resource domain ontology*

The type of query will be reflected in the *Context Domain ontology* (detailed in the next section). The possible intentions of a user may be *informational, navigational* or *transactional.* An informational query seeks information about a topic or question. A navigational query aims at finding a specific site such as the web page of a University or a company: many of these queries include part of a URL or the name of a company such as "google.com" or "www.ucla". Finally the transactional queries have the purpose of doing some transaction, and therefore the search is for pages to download items or service providers.

The proposed information retrieval system is ontology-based and hence a search may be performed using the query type given by the user to select the level of the ontology in the *Educational Resource ontology* (detailed in the next section) depending on the user's goal. If the user performs an informational query, the process may be a specificity retrieval. For example, for a query of "Foundations on databases book", the specific concept may be "foundations on databases". Because the user has a precise idea about the information need, the query is supposed to be served with results as precise as possible. Whereas, if the user wants a navigational search (e.g. the user wants materials on "databases"), the search might lead to an exhaustivity retrieval. This time the general concept of "database" rather than " foundations on databases book" covers a broader semantic area, and the user will have more exhaustive results relevant to the query. In this sense, the ontology helps to find synonymous or multilingual concepts (i.e. "bases de datos", "databases", etc.) or related concepts as database products, or user guides (i.e. "Postgres user guides"), or a book on query language for databases (i.e. "SQL").

Meta-topics are inspired by Bloom's Taxonomy and its later revision (Krathwohl & Anderson, 2001), which are classifications of learning objectives within education. They can serve as means to guide the recommendations not only by the usual user preference but also by educational criteria. The proposal is to use *analyze, evaluate, create, apply, understand* and *remember* as the possible pedagogical objectives for the resource the user is looking for. Meta topics will be defined in the *Context Ontology*.

Some of the important topics in understanding, capturing and exploiting the context of the learner are: the discovery and modeling of personal, social and contextual information to support the recommendation of resources and applications for learning; context-aware data management and processing; semi-automatic identification and evolution of semantic structures underlying the collaboration behavior of the users; semi-automatic identification of user profile data and their interconnectivity; reputation and trust management; as well as privacy preservation issues.

Because the proposed system is ontology-based it is composed of semantic knowledge structures that can provide valuable domain insight as well as user information. It is effortless and valuable to automatically extract the relevant topics from the specific ontologies once they are built, not only reducing the effect of cold-start problems where no initial information is available early on upon which to base recommendations, but in general allowing for a natural set of topics for the user to select from.

Similar approaches have been used in the system designed by Wang and Kong (2007) that uses semantic information from the categorical characteristics of items and where similarities between user pairs is calculated by a weighted mean method that calculates three similarity measures: the similarity of user evaluation histories (using the Pearson correlation coefficient on usage information of the system in terms of a user-item evaluation data matrix); the similarity of these user's demographic data (calculated with a weighted mean); and the users similarity in interest or preference based on the semantic similarities of the items retrieved and/or evaluated (Harman, 1988). Similar semantic recommendations for students is presented by Yu, Nakamura, Jang, Kajita and Mase (2007).

## Relevance Feedback

Although searchers may not be able to convert their need for information into a request, once the system had presented the user with an initial set of documents the user can usually indicate those documents that contain useful information. Relevance feedback takes advantage of the results to a query that is initially returned to the user to obtain information about whether those results are relevant to that query or not.

Once the users have indicated which documents are *relevant* to their needs, the Information Retrieval system may use this information quantitatively - retrieving more documents like the relevant documents - and qualitatively – retrieving documents similar to the relevant ones before other documents by producing a modified version of the query. The modified query is then used to retrieve a new set of documents for presentation to the users. Users only have to *identify* relevant material not *describe* it perfectly.

Relevance feedback is frequently used for *interactive query expansion* (IQE), allowing users to select the terms to be added to the new query - in the believe that the users can select better query expansion terms than the system can do automatically (AQE).

Harman, (1988), demonstrated that selecting terms could improve retrieval effectiveness in a simulated case. Magennis and Van Rijsbergen (1997) extended this study in two ways: by studying the degree to which IQE can theoretically improve performance over AQE and whether this theoretical improvement can be realized with actual users.

In the network ontology system the feedback of the user will be used as input to the Recommendation Module through the recommendation rules/criteria to improve the current query and to be used in future searches. Therefore the information that will be stored is a tupple made of the user profile, user context, query goal and resource characteristics along with their classification.

The recommendation process is greatly based on the *isInterestedIn* property in the *User Profile Ontology* which conceptualizes the topics the user is interested in. This property is changed every time the user classifies a resource as relevant, if the resource is within a topic which was not registered previously as being of interest for the user. The *User Profile Ontology* is part of the *Context Ontology* which are user properties, query properties and user action properties. Topics are taken from the *Educational Domain ontology*.

Topic interest is stored as a value in the range [0,1] and a time decay function may be used to weigh recently seen resources as being more important than older ones. User feedback also adjusts the interest of topics within the profile. Ontological relationships between topics of interest are used to infer other topics of interest, which might not have been browsed explicitly.

The *hasEducationalObjective* property that corresponds to a resource in the *Educational Resource Ontology* (see next section) may also be populated from the user feedback together with the user goal information regarding the Meta Topic in education. A relevant classification of a resource after a search with a specific Meta Topic in education indicates at least one of the pedagogical objectives of the resource.

The current topics of interest are taken from the users profile, and a list of similar people is computed in the function *who isSimilar()* for example by applying Pearson-r correlation to all user profiles. Recommendations are thus resources on the current topics of interest that have also been retrieved by similar people to the current user.

Recommendation rules/criteria are specified by indicating which context resources and quality dimensions will be taken into account for the recommendations, see section *Correctness Checking by the ERS Ontology Network* for further explanation. For a given user *Paul* and a resource *LO1*, such rules may be instantiated as follows (Exhibit 1).

For a complete definition of the process and validation of the ERS as well as more examples see next two sections.

In the long run the user feedback may also be exploited to modify the recommendation criteria and even the Recommendation ontology.

## Role of an Ontology Network for ERS

The ontology network is a model that helps to represent in a formal way the main features of the ERS. Specifically, it conceptualizes the different knowledge domains that are involved in a recommendation system and validate the recommendation criteria. Moreover, the ontology network makes explicit the reasons for the recommendation and allows to easily set up metrics for measure the adequacy of the educational resources to the learner and educator goals.

Currently, the development of ontologies to the Semantic Web is based on the integrations of existing ontologies favoring the modularization and reuse of ontologies. As side effect, it proposes the ontology development as a collaborative activity. In this context, ontologies should not be studied as isolated artifacts, but they should be seen as a set of ontologies that are explicitly or implicitly related with each other (Kleshchev & Artemjeva, 2005).

In this context, the semantic of an ERS is specified as a set of interrelated ontologies. It joins in an only one ontology network all the different ontologies involved in an ERS in order to explicitly specify the recommender system. Particularly, the modeling of a ERS involves the combination of many domains: educational topic domain, educational resource domain, quality assurance domain, user context domain and recommendation domain. Therefore, the *ERS ontology network* integrates a set of ontologies, one for each of these domains. In turn, each domain ontology is represented by one or more interrelated ontologies, and thus, it is conceptualized as an ontology network too. Accordingly, the *ERS ontology network* is a network of ontology networks.

These ontology networks are: the *Topic Domain* ontology network, the *Educational Resource* ontology network, the *Quality Assurance* ontology network, the *Recommendation* ontology network, and the *Context* ontology network. Figure 1 broadly outlines this approach; the different ontology networks are arranged by columns and the relation inter-ontology networks are shown by arrows crossing columns.

Having an ontology-based recommender system is advantageous at least for the following two reasons:

- at the moment of configuring this kind of systems, it is useful for instance to discover knowledge domain units since it is pos-

*Exhibit 1.*

```
if exists another user who isSimilar(Paul) and
that user performs the same task than Paul and
that user made the same query than Paul and
that user assigned "high" relevance level to LO1 then
     LO1 is "highly recommended"
```

*Figure 1. The ERS ontology network*

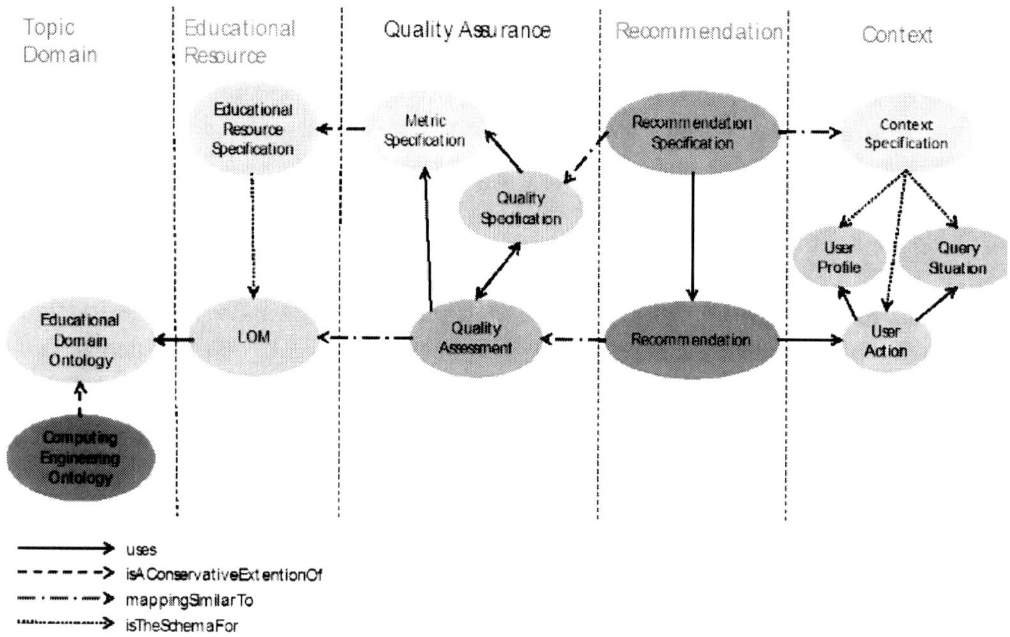


sible to index learning resources based on the specific learning domain ontology

- it is helpful to validate the resulting configuration of the systems. The ERS ontology network helps to check the validity of the resulting system and thus, to guarantee its correctness. Combining the ERS ontology with a validation process will be the strategy that we will introduce in section *Correctness Checking by the ERS Ontology Network*.

In order to preserve the benefits of having a ERS semantically specified by an ontology network during the development of a ontology network, it must be ensure the proper interrelationship of all participating ontologies. Next, the relationships that can arise between ontologies to shape an ontology network will be conceptually introduced; then, these relationships will be applied to describe the specific-domain ontology networks and the ERS ontology as a network of ontology networks respectively.

As depicted in Figure 1, the *ERS* ontology network is modeled by four different relationships: one relationship named *Uses* and three relationships taken from the DOOR ontology (Allocca et al., 2009): *isAConservativeExtentionOf*, *mappingSimilarTo* and *isTheSchemaFor*.

- The *Uses* relationship describes an extension of a given ontology by importing a number of individuals from a different ontology.
- The *isAConservativeExtentionOf* relationship describes an extension of an ontology by a number of additional axioms that describe that was not covered yet by an existing ontology.
- The *mappingSimilarTo* relationship relies on the existence of an alignment between two ontologies.

- The *isTheShemaFor* relationship keeps the link between a model and its meta-model.

These relationships are used in the specification of the ontology network composing the ERS ontology network. Bellow, the networked ontologies for each domain are briefly described, as well as the above defined relationships among them.

The *Educational Domain ontology network* conceptualizes the educational topic domain. The core ontology may be an already existing ontology (i.e. Education in postgraduate course), which can be extended in terms of a specific educational area (i.e. Literature or Architecture). Both ontologies are related by the *isAConservativeExtentionOf* relationship.

The *Educational Resource ontology network* conceptualizes the domain of educational contents and particularly describes the learning resources that will be considered to participate in a quality assessment. Among the properties of an educational resource, there is a particular one, the "keyword" property that relates concepts (learning objects) from the existing *LOM* ontology with concepts in the *Educational Domain Ontology*. LOM is a widely accepted metadata standard for learning object (LO). The *keyword* property describes what a learning object is talking about. An interesting feature of the *Educational Resource* ontology network is the use of the *isTheSchemaFor* relationship.

The *Educational Resource Specification* ontology plays the role of metamodel for the *LOM* ontology (depicted in Figure 2). The main concepts of this ontology are *Educational Resource* and *Educational Resource property*. An *Educational resource* is for instance a learning object. On the other hand, *Educational Resource properties* model the properties that can be attached to an *Educational Resource*. For instance, possible properties of a LO could be *hasLOMGeneral*, *hasSource*, etc.

The *Quality Assurance ontology network* conceptualizes metrics, quality assurance specifications and quality assessments. *Metrics* are formulas defined based on the properties of resources, such as learning objects. For example, a metric can measure or calculate if an educational resource has an author, or count its number of words, etc. Metrics can be simple formulas or complex, based on other metrics. A *quality assurance specification* describes the different *quality dimensions*; for instance, some of them are readability, precision, believability, completeness or timeliness. In order to make a quality assessment, one or more suitable metrics must be applied. For example a metric to evaluate the believability dimension of an educational resource can be based on the extraction of the name of the resource's author. The definition of what metrics to use is, in general, a decision of an domain expert. A *quality assessment* models the evaluation of a particular educational resource (i.e. a learning object) for a particular quality dimension through a specific metric, which is based on educational resource properties. As a result it is obtained a quality level, which represents the result of the quality assessment, for example, "high believability" or "low believability" can be quality levels for the believability dimension. As it is shown in Figure 3, in the *Quality Assurance ontology network*, the *Quality Specification Ontology* is related with the *Metric Specification* one through the *uses* relationship; since a dimension of quality is always based on a metric. In this case, the occurrence of the *uses* relation is given by the *assessedBy* property that associates to each quality dimension the corresponding metric. The *mappingSimilarTo* relationship appears between the *Metric Specification* and *Educational Resource Specification* ontologies. It was defined an alignment between the *Feature* and *Educational Resource Property* concepts. Thus, it is possible to specify that a metric is based on some property of an educational resource. Here, it is possible to appreciate the convenience of having some ontologies that plays the role of metamodel for others. The *mappingSimilarTo* relationship also

*Figure 2. The educational resource ontology network*

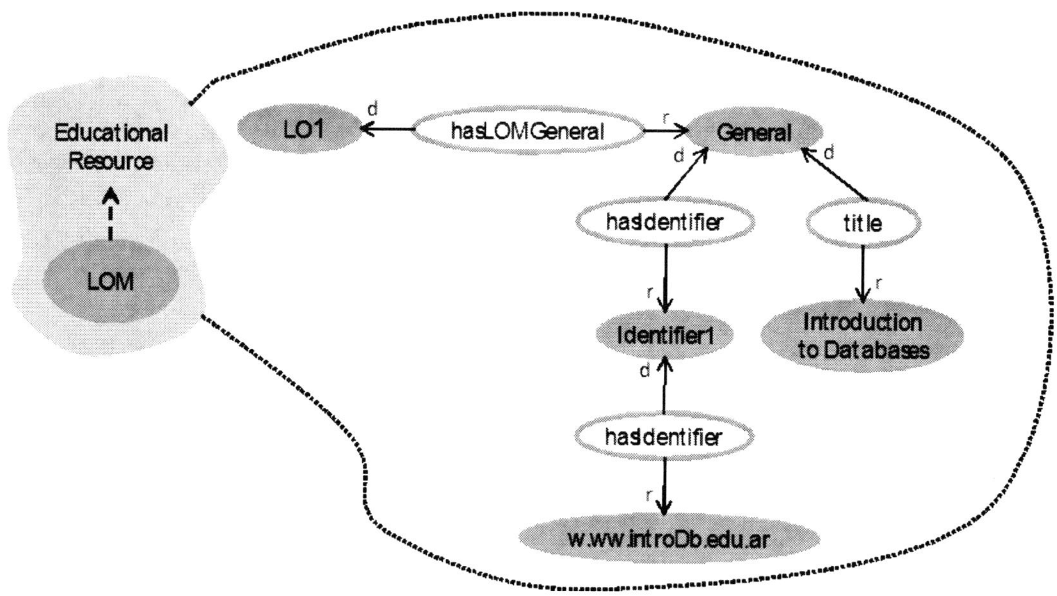


links the *QualityAssessment* and *LOM* ontologies, because it was defined an alignment between the *Resource* and *LO* concepts. This alignment allows expressing that a quality assessment is done for an educational content.

The *Context ontology network* describes user profiles, query situations and user actions. Thus, in the *Context ontology network,* depicted graphically in Figure 4, three ontologies interact: *User Profile Ontology*, *Query Situation Ontology* and

*Figure 3. The quality assurance ontology network*

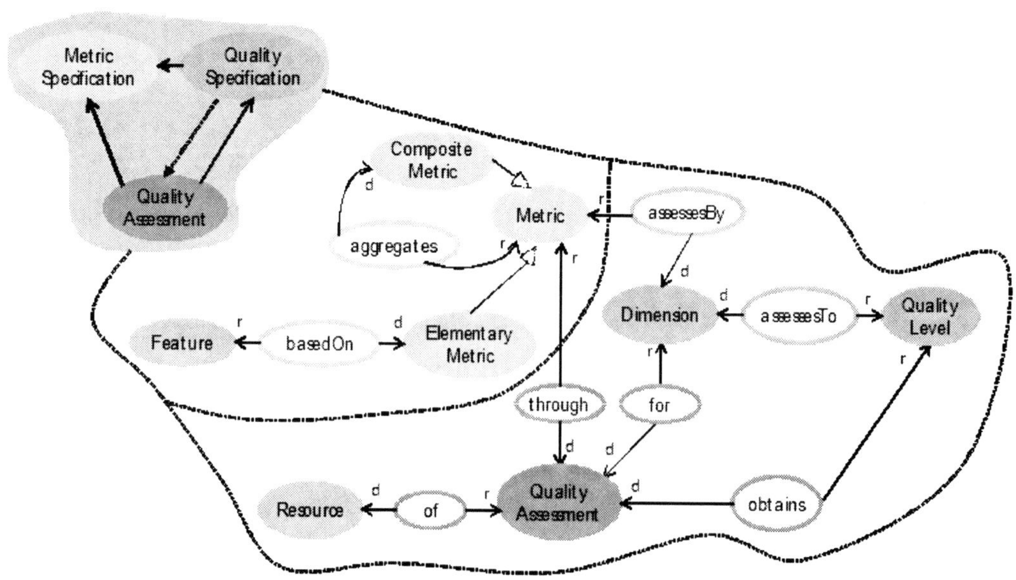

*User Action Ontology*. The *User Profile Ontology* conceptualizes all user properties. Some of them are more static than others. For instance, the property *plays* a *LearningRole (*where the role can be student or tutor), is less dynamic than the properties *performs* (a Task) or *isMemberOf* (a *Group*), which can suffer various changes in the immediate future for a given user. Nevertheless, independently of the dynamic nature of these properties, their values may be captured and kept up-to-date. We do not focus on this issue but there are a widely current studies in (Tchuente, Canut, Jessel, Péninou & El Haddadi, 2010; Ma, Silver & Shakshuki, 2010; Castellano et al., 2010). The *Query Situation Ontology* models the type of a query (concept *QueryGoal*), which can be informational, navigational or transactional and the contents returned by a specific query. The *User Action Ontology* relates the *User Profile* ontology and the *Query Situation* ontology. It represents the action of the user when he/she makes a query in the context of a specific task, graphically depicted in Figure 4. Once the query returns a set of educational resources, the user gives his/her relevance feedback. The concept *UserAction* is related to the concept *Task* through the relationship *performing*. In the same way, the relationship *playing* represents the instance in which the user is playing the role. The relationship *makes,* with range *Query*, models the query the user executes in order to be able to perform the task. The relationship *inA*, with range *Group,* is another property of the user action, it models that the user is performing the task as a member of a group. The concept *UserAction* is also the domain of the relationship *produces*, with the range the concept *RelevanceFeedback* represent the feedback given by the user to the educational resources returned by the query, when he/she executes the action. Then, the concept *RelevanceLevel* (for instance,

*Figure 4. The context ontology network*

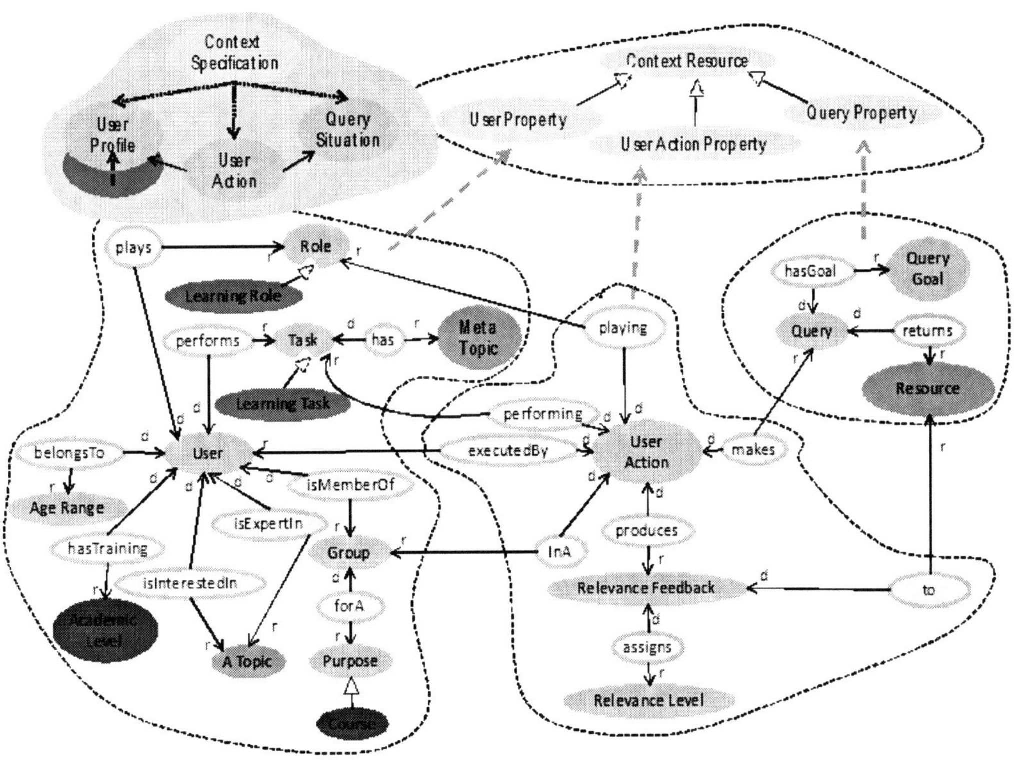

"high", "medium" or "low" relevance) represents the relevance degree assigned by the user. The concept *UserAction* is taken from (Ermolayev et al., 2010), where a context model is described using different specialization levels. The first level corresponds to foundational ontologies, the second level models a general ontology of context domain, while in the lowest leve,l different ontologies specialize the general one. Among them, the PSI E2H Core Ontology describes events (*UserAction*) perceived by observers (*User*) in a context. In our *User Profile ontology*, a *User* in the educational context *plays* a *LearningRole*, *performs* a *LearningTask* and *is member of* a *Group*, for a specific purpose: a *Query Goal*.

The *Recommendation ontology network* describes the different criteria of recommendation for a particular context (user profile, query situation and user action), some quality dimensions, and the obtained recommendation level. It has two related ontologies: *Recommendation Specification* and *Recommendation* (Figure 5). The former specifies the recommendation definition concept, which describes the criterion upon which it relies to make a recommendation (i.e, a quality dimension), the context feature to take into account and the possible recommendation levels. The *Recommendation Ontology* models concrete recommendation assessments. Here, the relationship *uses* is identified between this ontology and the *Recommendation Specification Ontology* in order to define that a recommendation is done through a recommendation definition, for a *criteria* and assesses to a *recommendation level*. As is showed in Figures 1 and in Figure 5, the *mappingSimilarTo* relationship relates the *RecommendationSpecification* and *QualitySpecification* ontologies, because it was defined an alignment between the *criteria* and *dimension* concepts.

## The Semantic Educational Recommender System

The *Recommendation Process* covers the different moment and tasks that take place when a ERS is action. This process comprises the entire task that have to be considered in order to recommend educational resource to a particular user. These tasks are organized in three different phases: the start up of the ERS, the adequacy assessment and the execution of recommendation assessments. The *ERS start-up phase* is in charge of preparing the

*Figure 5. The networked recommendation ontology*

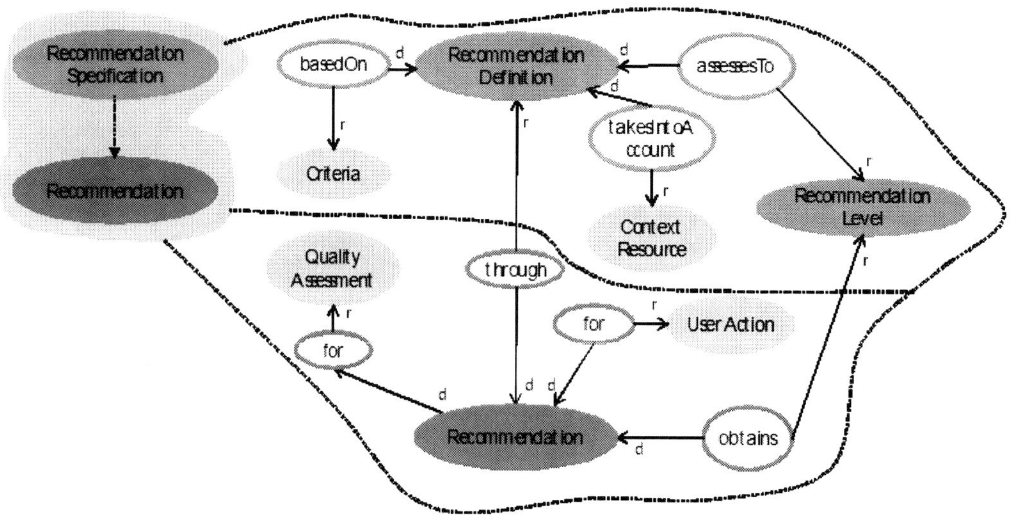

requested information, user properties and learning goal, and recommendation criteria, what means the configuration of the system. In the *adequacy assessment phase*, a set of educational resources from federated repositories are assessed and it is determined their adequacy level according the learning goals and user context. This phase takes place after the stat-up phase. Finally, the *recommendation assessment phase* is in charge of generating a set of recommended educational resources to particular user goal and take place in real time when a user query the ERS to retrieve some educational material.

During the execution of the recommendation process, the ERS ontology network plays different roles: in some cases it helps to discover knowledge domain units from the educational resource repositories (i.e. based on the educational domain ontology and the specific educational ontology, for instance, the Computing Engineering ontology, the learning resources are indexed*)*. In other cases, it helps to support quality and recommendation assessments by both, assisting in the modeling and specification of the ERS, and checking the correctness of the resulting system specification.

The following subsection will discuss each recommendation process phase in deep, detailing how the ERS ontology network is populated in each phase. The population of the ERS ontology network results in the knowledge base that later can be used to make semantic queries. Later, it will discuss how the ontology network can be used to validate the appropriateness of the ERS configuration from the formal point of view, validating the resulting specification in terms of ontologies by using OWL[3] and SWRL[4] .

## An ERS Ontology Network Population Example

We introduce an example scenario in order to get a better comprehension of the manipulation of the ERS ontology network. Figure 6 represents the resulting knowledge base when the *"LO1"* learning object was assessed to be recommended to the *user Paul.* In this example the recommendation assessment took into account the *Believability* quality dimension, which was assessed by *Provenance*, which uses the *hasSource* property of the *"LO1"* learning object. The recommendation assessment also considers the fact the user *Paul* is member of a group, the *DB Course Group*, as well as the user *Peter*, and both perform the *DB Design* task, whose meta topic is *Create a DB*. In order to carry out this task, *Paul makes* a query, with the *Looks for Design Patterns* goal. The fact that the *Peter* returned relevance levels when he made the same query than *Paul*, is also considered in the recommendation assessment.

This scenario involves a lot of information that has to set to the ERS in the start-up phase, as for instance the *Believability* quality dimension. This means that the ERS is configured to be able to assess the *Believability* quality dimension. Other information have to be retrieve in the adequacy assessment phase, as the *hasSource* property of the *"LO1"* learning object, that is recovery when the the learning resources are indexed. Finally, in the recommendation assessment phase, which is tigger by a user query, is when the *Looks for Design Patterns* is recovery as the goal of the user query. Below, It will be detailed where, when and how the *ERS ontology network* is populated.

## Recommendation Start-up Phase

The start-up phase is in charge of preparing the information about properties of educational resources, user properties, quality criteria and recommendation criteria, which is needed in order to configure the ERS. This phase takes place at the moment the ERS is configured This phase is made up of the tasks: *educational resource definition*, *quality criteria definition* and *recommendation criteria definition*. Each task is responsible of populating different ontologies as it is detailed below and have to be carried out by expert in

*Figure 6. A population example of the ERS ontology network*

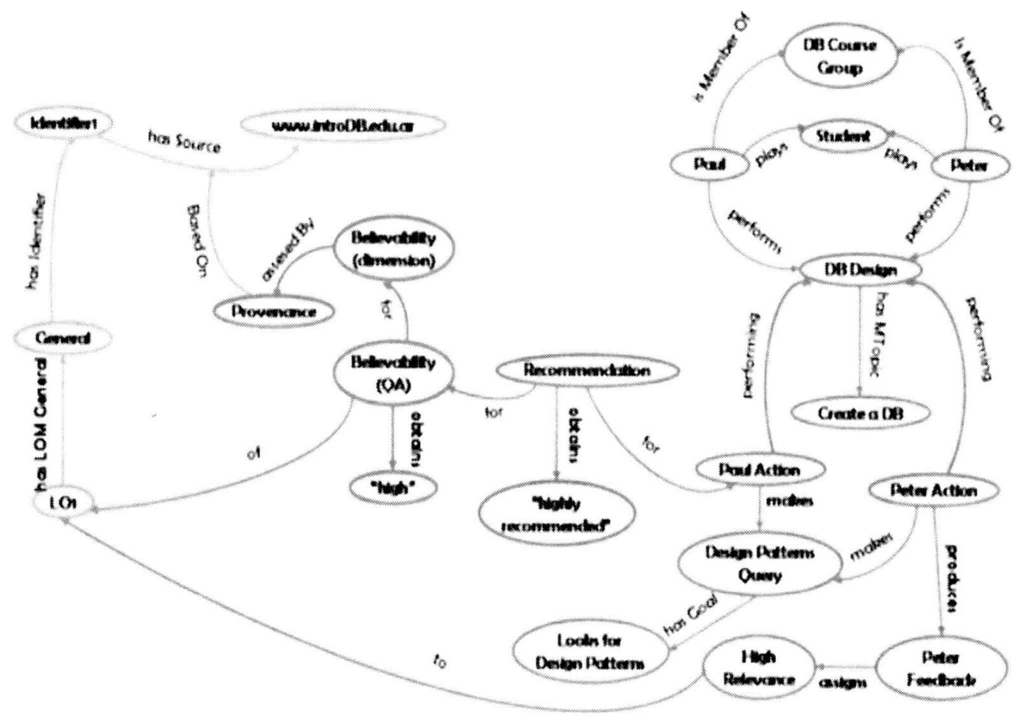


educational resources, educational resources quality assurance and recommendation criteria.

The *Educational Resource Definition* task refers to the population of the *LOM* ontology according to a given set of educational resources and their indexation based on the specific domain ontology. Consequently, after the execution of this task, the ERS is tailored to an educational specific domain. The *Educational Resource* ontology network is populated with educational concepts (one for each given learning object) and with their associated properties; for example the *hasLOMGeneral* property. Later, these learning objects are indexed according to the specific domain ontology; in the case of the *ERS ontology,* it can correspond, for instance, to the *Computing Engineering* ontology. As result, the *keyword* property is specified between learning objects and Computing Engineering concepts. Regarding the example of the Figure 6, the *keyword* property is specified between the "LO1" learning object and the *DBDesign* concept. There are other properties that should be defined, but they will be specified later in the Quality Criteria definition task.

The *Quality Criteria Definition* task refers to the definition of metrics and quality dimensions that will be supported by the ERS. Based on a repertoire of metrics, the definition of quality criteria involves specifying what metric assesses each quality dimension and what the possible obtained quality levels are. First of all, the repertoire of metrics has to be specified. The specification of metrics can not be done in isolation because metric features are based on concepts that were defined in the *Educational Resource* ontology network. For instance, to instantiate the *provenanceMetric*, the *basedOn* property has to be instantiated, in order to link the *provenanceMetric* with the *hasSource* property; being the *hasSource* property an instance of the *property* concept from *Educational Resource* ontology. From this, the *Quality Specification* ontology has to be populated, i.e.

*dimension* concepts have to be instantiated. The resulting specified dimensions will be those supported by the ERS. Each dimension has defined at least once the *assesedBy* property applied to a metric, whic is used to asses the dimension. Dimensions have also defined the *assessesTo* property, which links a dimension to its possible *quality levels*. For instance, *assesedBy* property links the *Believability* quality dimension with the *provenance* concept and the *assessesTo* property to the set of strings: "high", "medium", "low".

Based on the quality criteria definition, the *Recommendation Criteria Definition* task implies to configure recommendation criteria of the ERS based on quality dimensions and context resources. *Context resources* are *user properties*, *query properties* and *user action properties*. The output of this task is a set of recommendation rules which specify the *recommendation level* for each assessed educational resource. These rules are like:

if *recommendation definition(thisEducationalResource)*
then *recommendationLevel(thisEducationalResource)*

where *thisEducationalResource* is the currently processed resource and the *recommendation definition(thisEducationalResource)* is described in terms of quality assurance and context ontology networks. The *recommendationLevel* for an educational resource is one of the values of the scale of recommendation levels that were configure in the ERS (for example, "highly recommended", "stronger recommended"). Then, by following the aforementioned scenario, the above rule is instantiated as follows (Exhibit 2).

In this rule the recommendation definition is based on the "Believability" dimension, Paul's profile, the query goal and the relevance feedback.

The *Context Resource Definition* task is in charge of defining those context resources that have to be taken into account to make recommendations. These context resources will be identified in the recommendation criteria definition. Mainly, they are: the user properties, the user action properties and the query properties. The *user properties* are those that were already relieved at the recommendation criteria definition task and will be populated at the moment of registering a user to the recommender system. For example, if at the recommendation criteria definition was specified the *isMemberOf* property, when the user Paul is registered at the system, this property is populated by creating an instance of this property that links *Paul* and *DBCourseGroup* concepts. Regarding the *user action properties*, the most important is the *relevance feedback* given by the user. This feedback links the retrieved learning contents with a specific *query*, performing a *task*. The *relevance feedback* can be provided by the user both explicitly or implicitly. The query properties refer to query attributes like *query goal*.

*Exhibit 2.*

```
        if BelievabilityQA(LO1) assesTo "high" and
            exists another user who isMemberOf some of the groups Paul isMem-
berOf and
            user performs the same task than Paul and
            user made the same query than Paul and
             user assigned "high" relevance level to LO1 and
            the task meta topic is "Create aDB"
             then LO1 is "highly recommended"
```

Once the ERS is configured, the learning content has to be pre-processed to complete the population of the *LOM* ontology which specializes the *Educational Resource* ontology. This task is known as *Indexing Educational Resources.* Particularly, the indexing of the educational resources consists in completing them by associating learning object properties. The metrics, which are involved in a quality definition, determine the learning object properties to be considered. For example, in the quality definition of the *Believability* dimension is used the *provenance* metric which refers to the source of the learning object. This means that the learning object should have associated the *hasSource* property. Therefore, it has to be determined which information retrieval processes have to be performed in order to discover these new learning object properties. The retrieved information will be used to complete the population of the *Learning Object Metadata* by extending the *Educational Resource* ontology. For instance, by using a specific information retrieval process that retrieves the source of a learning content, the *hasSource* property can be defined between the "LO1" learning object and the concepts in "www.introDb.edu.ar".

## Quality Assessment Phase

The Quality Assessment phase is in charge of collecting information about the quality of the learning content according to the quality dimension supported by the ERS. Once the learning object metadata is collected by indexing the educational material, the *quality assessment* itself is performed. The quality assessment execution calculates the *quality level* of each learning object for each *quality dimension*. For that, the corresponding *metric* is executed to determine the *quality level* of such learning object. In this step, the *QualityAssurance ontology* is populated, mainly, by adding creating *Quality Assessment* concepts and linking them to the assessed learning object and the obtained *quality level*. Regarding the followed example, in this moment, the "Believability" is instantiated as an individual of the *Quality Assessment* concept and the *obtains* property is defined between "Believability" and the "high" *quality level.*

## Recommendation Assessment Phase

The Recommendation Assessment phase is in charge of generating a set of recommended learning objects to a particular *query,* executed by the user when he/she is performing a task. This phase take place when the ERS system is in-use. A user *query* is the trigger of this recommendation assessment phase. When a *user* makes a query, the recommender system evaluates the recommendation rules, which were set in the recommendation criteria definition task, in in order to determine the *recommendation level.* All of those learning objects, which assess to an appropriated level, are recommended. The assessment is done by evaluating the recommendation rules.

The evaluation of the recommendation rules is based on the *user profile*, the *quality level* of the indexed learning objects, the *query properties* and the *user action properties*, such as the *relevance feedback*, which have been determined in the previous two phases. *Query properties* have to be discovered at this moment, a query property type could be a *query goal*. The *user feedback* to the resources has to be collected from previous queries in order to be taken into account in the recommendation rules. Those relevance feedback evaluations can correspond both to similar learning objects or learning objects recommended to other users related to the user who is making the query. Both, the similarity degree of learning objects and who are the users related to the current user, are determined by the recommendation rules. The output of this phase is a set of recommended educational resources.

## Correctness Checking by the ERS Ontology Network

During the configuration and execution of the recommendation process, non-expected situations can arrive. For example, during the quality assessment phase, someone might try to assess a quality dimension with a inappropriate metric. Having an ontology-based recommendation system is not only advantageous at the moment of configuring this kind of systems (for instance to discover knowledge domain units), but also it is helpful to validate the resulting configuration of the systems. In the last case, the ERS ontology network can be also used to check the validity of the resulting system and thus, to guarantee its correctness. Combining the *ERS Ontology Network* with a validation process will be the strategy that we will introduce in this section.

The potential of this validation process depends on the potential of the tools which are used to express the ontology network. Ontology languages, like OWL and their combination with rules like SWRL (W3C Semantic Web Rule Language) are potential tools to express the ERS Ontology Network. OWL allows implementing each networked ontology and gives facility to describe the relationships between them; for instance, the *isAConservativeExtentionOf* and *uses* relationships can be implemented with OWL resources such as owl: subclasses or owl:import. However, OWL does not provide facilities to draw inferences about individuals. This drawback can be mitigated by combining OWL with SWRL, since it is possible to write Hornlike rules expressed in terms of OWL concepts. Besides, the OWL query language SQWRL[5], based on SWRL, provides the chance of querying OWL ontologies and also provides with a very useful array of set operators to perform closure operations like counting and aggregation, among others. SWRL is used to describe the recommendation rules. An OWL-SWRL based ERS Ontology, can take advantages of these two paradigms.

Following, it is illustrated the utility of OWL, SWRL and SQWRL in model checking of inconsistencies through some examples. First OWL restrictions examples are presented to complete the specification of a class. Then, SWRL and SQWRL examples are showed to detect specification anomalies.

As it was explained before, the quality criteria definition task involves the definition of quality dimensions and their possible obtained quality levels. Within the *Quality Assurance* ontology network, a *quality dimension* assesses to a *quality level*. Considering *believability* as an individual of the *Dimension* concept, in order to the assessment makes sense, there must be at least two individuals of the *QualityLevel* concept related to the *believability* individual, for example "high believability" and "low believability". This requirement can be guarantee by attaching a contraint to the Dimension concept. This constraint can be expressed in OWL as the conjunction of the following two restrictions to represent (It is used a description logic-style notation for simplicity).

$$assessesTo.QualityLevel \qquad (1)$$

$$>= 2assessTo.QualityLevel \qquad (2)$$

These axioms express an existential restriction and a cardinality restriction respectively. The first one, says: for each individual of the *Dimension* concept that has defined the relationship *assessTo* must exist at least an individual of the *QualityLevel* class linked to it. The last one says: each individual of the *Dimension* concept that has defined the relationship *assessTo* will be related with a minimum of two individuals of the *QualityLevel* class.

Continuing in the scenario of the *Quality Criteria Definition*, we can define for example a metric called *BasicPropertiesMetric*, to measure whether an educational resource has certain basic properties like author and source. It is a composite metric that uses two elementary metrics: the *authorMetric*, that measures if the educational resource has an author, and the *sourceMetric,* that measures if it has a source. An expert working in the ERS can define that to assess the *Believability* dimension the *BasicPropertiesMetric* metric must be applied.

Then, the *Believability* individual, which is an instance of the *Dimension* class, will be related to the *BasicPropertiesMetric* individual, which is an instance of the *Metric* concept, through the property *assessedBy*. At the moment of carrying out the quality assessment of an educational resource for the *Believability* dimension, the *BasicPropertiesMetric* metric must be used. But, the hypothetical situation where the dimension assessment was executed through another metric, for example *authorMetric*, would be a mistake; it is not a right metric to assess the *Believability* dimension. Therefore, before populating the ERS knowledge base, it is necessary to guarantee that the input of new information does not leave the knowledge base in a inconsistent state. In the example, there should be a mechanism to detect that *authorMetric* is not a right metric to assess *Believability* dimension.

For instance, to identify invalid quality assessments, the *InvalidQualityAssessment* class could be added as a subclass of the *QualityAssessment* class. This new class will contain inconsistent quality assessments. Then, before executing the assessment itself, a validation process can be run.

This validation process will classify a quality assessment into the InvalidQualityAssessment class when assessment has some inconsistency.

The implementation of that validation process can be done using SWRL rules with SQWRL operations and queries. The following rule implements the validation of the example (Exhibit 3):

In this rule, for each individual *?a* of the *QualityAssessment* concept, it is retrieved:

- those *?m* related to *?a* by the object property *through* and those *?d* related to *?a* by the object property *for*, by *(3)* and *(4)*. They are the *metric* and the *dimension* that were used in the *quality assessment.*
- those *?mD* related to the *?d* by the object property *assesedBy*, by *(5)*. These are all metrics that can be selected to assess current dimension.
- A set *?s1* is constructed containing the *?m*, grouped by *quality assessments* by *(6)*. Each set has the metric associated to the *quality assessment.*
- A set *?s2* is constructed containing all *?mD*, grouped by *quality assessment* and *dimension* by *(7)*. Each set has the *metrics* associated to the *quality assessment* and the *dimension.*
- The built-in *notIntersects* guarantee that there is no common individuals between *?s1* and *?s2 (8)*.

In case of the intersection set is empty, the instance *?a* is classified into the *InvalidQualityAssessment* class, by *(9)*. Therefore, this rule infers that an *BelievabilityQA* assessment for *Believ-*

*Exhibit 3.*

```
QualityAssessment(?a) Λ Metric(?m) Λ through(?a; ?m)            (3)
    Λ Dimension(?d) Λ for(?a; ?d)                               (4)
    Λ Metric(?mD) Λ assesedBy(?d; ?mD)                          (5)
    Λ sqwrl: makeSet(?s1; ?m) Λ sqwrl: groupBy(?s1; ?a)         (6)
    Λ sqwrl: makeSet(?s2; ?mD) Λ sqwrl: groupBy(?s2; ?a; ?d     (7)
    Λ sqwrl: notIntersects(?s1; ?s2)                            (8)
  => InvalidQualityAssessment(?a)                               (9)
```

*ability* dimension with the *authorMetric* is invalid, and then, it will be included as an individual of the *InvalidQualityAssessment* class.

## FUTURE RESEARCH DIRECTIONS

The conceptualization of a semantic ERS gives us a rich experience in the development of ontologies networks that should be profit to future works. Therefore, one of the next steps in this research direction should be to take advantage of this work and review the design and implementation activities carried out, in order to formalize a design and development methodology of ontology networks. The proposed methodology will continue analyzing in depth the different ontology integration methods, taking into account the network ontology relationships presented in this paper, as well as new ones that could arise.

Furthermore, starting from the presented design, good practices on ontology engineering lead to evaluate the model in an interaction between ontology engineers and domain experts, in particular for ERS with educators and pedagogues. From this evaluation, it is expected to obtain a feedback to reach a final refinement of the structures which compose the ontology network.

Another interesting feature to take into account in the near future is the validation of the resulting recommendation. After receiving a recommendation, the user is able to give some feedback to the system in order the ERS system improve future recommendations. However, it is not evident how to consider opposite feedback, i.e. two different users can have contradictory opinion about the same learning resources. This can happens due to the different users' profile, context and needs, but also because of user belong to different social context. Therefore, one interesting approach to face this issue is to consider the user's social context as another item to consider in the recommendation. A first step in this direction is to validate feedback in the context of the user's social network. Because, it is highly probable that individual that are "closer" in the social network have similar feedback than those more distant. Currently, the research activity in the field of social network and recommendation systems based on "crowsourcing" is very active and there are a lot high quality results. Therefore, it will be an interesting approach to combine both the approach described in this chapter with results in the social network field, and explore how it is the better way to mix both.

## CONCLUSION

In this chapter, we have introduced a novel approach which uses an ontology network to assist the modeling and execution of a educational resource recommender system. It is a quality-based approach to get the more adequate educational resource for a given user and context.

Mainly, the chapter focused on describing the ontology network that models the different domains related to a recommender system. Moreover, we showed how this ontology network can be tailored, to specific domains and user profiles. The main aim of this design was to obtain a flexible model that was not dependent on any particular mechanism of content evaluation, such as a specific quality metric or educational domain. Whenever it is required to assess a different quality dimension or to consider another educational domain, new extensions of learning object metadata, educational resources quality and recommendation criteria ontologies might be added, keeping up the core model intact.

On the other hand, the ontology network is a conceptual model which is a first step in the development of an ERS. In practice, there are two important challenges: one is the cold-start problem of recommender systems and the other one is the acquisition of learning resources metadata.

The former can be handled by semantic knowledge structures, such as ontologies. They can provide valuable domain knowledge and user information for the cold-start problem of recommender systems. This is a crucial problem since not good enough initial user profiles lead to poor recommendations and hence users will not use the recommender system and it will never get a chance to improve. The ontology-based user model can be constructed automatically by monitoring user web browsing habits and analyzing feedback on recommendations.

In particular, for the acquisition of learning resources metadata, in previous work reported in (Motz, Badell, Barrosa, Sum, Díaz & Castro, 2009), we present a system that is capable of extracting learning objects with their metadata from XML and HTML files, Word documents, Power Point slides and PDF files, as well as from SCORM packages. The proposed architecture is based on the use of the GATE# natural language processing tool, which is guided by domain ontology and the LOM ontology.

In addition, a valuable feature of driving the recommendation process by ontologies is the property of checking the consistency among concepts and relationships that allows one to detect inconsistencies at the design phase. Based on the intrinsic properties of ontologies, the model provides a high level abstraction that allows specifying in simple way relations between dimension and metrics for defining quality assurance. Besides, it is worth to mention that having an ontology-based recommendation system implemented using OWL language and SWRL rules, is helpful to validate the resulting configuration of the recommender system. These tools offers the possibility of defining restrictions and Horn-like rules that have to be hold in order to achieve consistent specifications of quality or recommendation assessments, detecting anomalous specifications.

Starting from the presented design, good practices on Ontology Engineering lead to evaluate the model in an interaction between ontology engineers and pedagogues or domain experts. From this evaluation, it is expected to obtain a feedback to reach a final refinement of the structures which compose the ontology network.

## ACKNOWLEDGMENT

This work was partially funded by: the SALUS/CYTED and PROSUL projects which are sponsored by the CnPq, Brazil and the CyTED, Spain; the PAE 37279-PICT 02203 which is sponsored by the ANPCyT, Argentina; and by Laccir R1210LAC007R1210LAC007.

## REFERENCES

Aleven, V., McLarren, B. M., Sewall, J., & Koedinger, K. R. (2009). A new paradigm for intelligent tutoring systems: Example-tracing tutors. *International Journal of Artificial Intelligence in Education, 19*, 105–154.

Allocca, C., d'Aquin, M., & Motta, E. (2009). Door - Towards a formalization of ontology relations. In J. L. G. Dietz (Ed.), *International Conference on Knowledge Engineering and Ontology Development* (pp. 13-20). INSTICC Press.

Baader, F., Horrocks, I., & Sattler, U. (2009). Description logics. In S. Staab & R. Studer (Eds.), *Handbook on ontologies*, (pp. 3-28). Berlin, Germany: Springer-Verlag. doi I 10.1007/978-3

Bellogín, A., Cantador, I., Castells, P., & Ortigosa, A. (2011). Discerning relevant model features in a content-based collaborative recommender system. preference learning. In J. Fürnkrans & E. Hüllermeier, (Eds.), *Preference learning*, (pp 429-455). Springer-Verlag. doi:10.1007/978-3-642-14125-6_20

Brusilovsky, P., & Peyl, C. (2003). Adaptive and intelligent Web-based educational systems. *International Journal of Artificial Intelligence in Education Computer & Communiation Science, 13*(2-4), 1560–4306.

Carbonaro, A., & Ferrini, R. (2008). Personalized information retrieval in a semantic-based learning environment. In Goh, D., & Foo, S. (Eds.), *Social information retrieval systems: Emerging technologies and applications for searching the Web effectively* (pp. 270–288). Hershey, PA: Idea Group Inc.

Castellano, G., Castiello, C., DellAngello, D., Fanelli, A., Mencar, C., & Tosello, M. (2010). Learning fuzzy user profiles for resource recommendation. *International Journal of Uncertainty. Fuzziness and Knowledge-Based Systems, 18*(4), 389–410. doi:10.1142/S0218488510006611

Cremades, J., Rodriguez, M., Costilla, C., & Pena, A. (2007). Mapping techniques for an ontology network. In *Proceedings of the International Multi-Conference on Computing in the Global Information Technology* (ICCGI '07). IEEE Computer Society. doi=10.1109/ICCGI.2007.37

Drabent, W. (2010). Hybrid reasoning with non-monotonic rules. In Aßmann, U., Bartho, A., & Wende, C. (Eds.), *Reasoning Web. Semantic technologies for software engineering. 6th International Summer School*. Dresden, Germany: Tutorial Lectures. doi:10.1007/978-3-642-15543-7_2

DuBay, W. H. (2004). *The principles of readability*. Costa Mesa, CA.

Ermolayev, V., Ruiz, C., Tilly, M., Jentzsch, E., Gomez-Perez, J., & Ekkehard Matzke, W. (2010). A context model for knowledge workers. In *2nd International Workshop on Context, Information and Ontologies (CIAO 2010), LNCS 4227*, (pp. 525-530). doi: 10.1007/11876663_47

Gangemi, A., & Presutti, V. (2007). C-ODO: An OWL meta-model for collaborative ontology design. In *Proceedings of CKC Workshop at WWW2007,* Banff, Canada. Berlin, Germany: Springer.

Harman, D. (1988). *Towards interactive query expansion* (pp. 321–331). SIGIR Proceedings.

Hartmann, J., Palma, R., Sure, Y., Suarez-Figueroa, M., Haase, P., Gomez-Perez, A., & Studer, R. (2005). Ontology metadata vocabulary and applications. In Meersman, R., Tari, Z., & Herrero, P. (Eds.), *OTM Workshops, LNCS 3762* (pp. 906–915). Berlin, Germany: Springer-Verlag.

Jung, J. J., & Euzenat, J. (2007). Towards semantic social networks. In E. Franconi, M. Kifer, & W. May (Eds.), *ESWC, LNCS 4519*, (pp. 267-280). Springer. doi: 10.1007/978-3-540-72667-8_20

Kleshchev, A., & Artemjeva, I. (2005). An analysis of some relations among domain ontologies. *International Journal on Information Theories and Applications*, *12*, 85–93.

Krathwohl, D., & Anderson, L. (2001). *Taxonomy for learning, teaching, and assessing. A Revision of Bloom's Taxonomy of Educational Objectives, complete edition*. New York, NY: Longman.

Llambías, G., Motz, R., Toledo, F., & de Uvarow, S. (2008). Learning to get the value of quality from web data. In Meersman, R., Tari, Z., & Herrero, P. (Eds.), *OTM Workshops, LNCS 5333* (pp. 1018–1025). Springer.

Ma, Z., Silver, D., & Shakshuki, E. (2010). User profile management: reference model and web services implementation. [IJWGS]. *International Journal of Web and Grid Services*, *6*(1), 1–34. .doi:10.1504/IJWGS.2010.032189

Magennis, M., & van Rijsbergen, A. J. (1997). The potential and actual effectiveness of interactive query expansion. In *Proceedings of the 20th Annual International ACM SIGIR Conference on Research and Development in Information Retrieval*, (pp. 324-332).

Manouselis, N., Drachsler, H., Verbert, K., & Santos, O. (2010). Proceedings of the 1st Workshop on Recommender Systems for Technology Enhanced Learning (RecSysTEL 2010). *Elsevier's Procedia Computer Science, 1*(2), 2773-2998

Mödritscher, F. (2010). Towards a recommender strategy for personal learning environments. 1st Workshop on Recommender Systems for Technology Enhanced Learning. In *RecSysTEL, Elsevier's Procedia Computer Science, 1*(2), 175-18.

Motz, R., Badell, C., Barrosa, M., Sum, R., Díaz, G., & Castro, M. (2009). LooKIng4LO: Sistema Informático para la Extracción Automática de Objetos de Aprendizaje: Caso de Estudio. *IEEE-RITA, 4*(3), 223–229.

O'Connor, M., Knublauch, H., Tu, S., & Musen, M. (2005). Writing rules for the Semantic Web using SWRL and Jess. In *Proceeding of the 8th International Protege Conference, Protege with Rules Workshop.*

O'Connor, M., Shankar, R., Nyulas, C., Tu, S., & Das, A. (2008). Developing a Web-based application using OWL and SWRL. In *Proceedings of the AAAI Spring Symposium*, Stanford, CA.

Oufaida, H., & Nouali, O. (2009, July). Exploiting Semantic Web technologies for recommender systems. A multi view recommendation engine. In *Proceedings of the 7th Workshop on Intelligent Techniques for Web Personalization Recommender Systems* (ITWP'09), Pasadena, California, USA.

Porcel, C., Moreno, J. M., & Herrera-Viedma, E. (2009). A multi-disciplinary recommender system to advice research resources in university digital libraries. *Expert Systems with Applications, 36*(10), 12520–12528. doi:10.1016/j.eswa.2009.04.038

Recker, M., & Wiley, D. A. (2001). A non-authoritative educational metadata ontology for filtering and recommending learning objects. *Journal of Interactive Learning Environments, 9*(3), 255–271. doi:10.1076/ilee.9.3.255.3568

Rose, D. (2006). Reconciling information-seeking behavior with search user interfaces for the web. *Journal of the American Society for Information Science and Technology, 57*(6), 797–799. doi:10.1002/asi.20295

Soylu, A., Wild, F., Mödritscher, F., & De Causmaecker, P. (2010). Semantic mash-up personal and pervasive learning environments (SMupple). In *Symposium of the WG HCI in Work and Learning Life and Leisure USAB*, (pp. 501-504).

Stanko, S., Rosic, M., Zitko, B., & Grubisic, A. (2008). Tex-Sysmodel for building intelligent tutoring systems. *Computers & Education, 51*, 1017–1036. doi:10.1016/j.compedu.2007.10.002

Suárez-Figueroa, M., Blomqvist, E., D'Aquin, M., Espinoza, M., Gómez-Pérez, A., & Lewen, H. ... Dzbor, M. (2009). *Neon deliverable d5.4.2. Revision and extension of the Neon methodology for building contextualized ontology networks.* Technical report, NeOn Project. Retrieved February 10th, 2011, from http://www.neon-project.org/web-content/images/Publications/neon_2009_d542.pdf

Tao, X. (2006). Associate a user's goal: Exhaustivity and specificity information retrieval using ontology. *In Proceedings of the Fourth International Conference on Active Media Technology*, (pp. 448-450).

Tchuente, D., Canut, M.-F., & Jessel, N. B. Péninou, A., & El Haddadi, A. (2010). Visualizing the evolution of users' profiles from online social networks. In *International Conference on Advances in Social Networks Analysis and Mining (ASONAM)*, (pp. 370-374). doi: 10.1109/ASONAM.2010.79

Vrandečić, D., Pinto, H. S., Sure, Y., & Tempich, C. (2005). The diligent knowledge processes. *Journal of Knowledge Management, 9*(5). doi:10.1108/13673270510622474

Wand, Y., & Wang, R. Y. (1996). Anchoring data quality dimensions in ontological foundations. *Communications of the ACM, 39*(11), 86–95. doi:10.1145/240455.240479

Wang, R., & Kong, F. (2007). Semantic-enhanced personalized recommender system. Machine learning and cybernetics. In *Proc. of the Int. Conference on Machine Learning and Cybernetics, 7*(19-22), 4069-4074.

Wang, R., & Strong, D. (1996). Beyond accuracy: What data quality means to data consumers. *Journal of Management Information Systems, 12*(4), 5–33.

## ADDITIONAL READING

Agichtein, E., Brill, E., & Dumais, S. (2006a). Improving Web search ranking by incorporating user behavior information. In *Proceedings of the 29th Annual International ACM SIGIR Conference on Research and Development in Information Retrieval*, 19–26.

Agichtein, E., Brill, E., Dumais, S., & Ragno, R. (2006b). Learning user interaction models for predicting Web search result preferences. In *Proceedings of the 29th Annual International ACM SIGIR Conference on Research and Development in Information Retrieval*, 3–10.

Arazy, O., Kumar, N., & Shapira, B. (2010). A Theory-Driven Design Framework for Social Recommender Systems. In *Journal of the Association for Information Systems*. 11(9), Article 2.

Baeza-Yates, R. A., & Ribeiro-Neto, B. (2010). *Modern Information Retrieval* (2nd ed.). Reading, Massachusetts: Addison-Wesley.

Balabanovi'c, M., & Shoham, Y. (1997). Fab-Content-based, collaborative recommendation. *Communications of the ACM, 40*(3), 66–72. doi:10.1145/245108.245124

Beliakov, G., Calvo, T., & James, S. (2011) Aggregation of Preferences in Recommender Systems. In *Recommender Systems Handbook 2011*, 705-734.

Burke, R. D. (2008). *(2080). Robust recommender systems* (pp. 331–332). RecSys.

Büttcher, S. Clarke C. L. A. &Cormack, G.V. (2010) *Information Retrieval: Implementing and Evaluating Search Engines*, MIT Press.

De Marsico, M., Sterbini, A., & Temperini, M. (2010). Tunneling Model Between Adaptive e-Learning and Reputation-based Social Activities. In *DEXA Workshops*, 69-73.

Dery, L. N., Kalech, M., Rokach, L., & Shapira, B. (2010). *Iterative voting under uncertainty for group recommender systems* (pp. 265–268). RecSys.

Gemmell, J., Schimoler, T., Mobasher, B., & Burke, R. D. (2010). *Hybrid tag recommendation for social annotation systems* (pp. 829–838). CIKM.

Gemmell, J., Schimoler, T., Mobasher, B., & Burke, R. D. (2010). Resource Recommendation in Collaborative Tagging Applications. *EC-Web, 2010*, 1–12.

Ghauth, K. H., & Abdullah, N. A. (2010). Measuring learner's performance in e-learning recommender systems. In *Australasian Journal of Educational Technology*, 26(6), 764-774

Ghidini, C., Pammer, V., Scheir, P., Serafini, L., & Lindstaedt, S. (2007). Learn@work with semantic web technology. In *I-Know '07*. Graz, Austria: APOSDLE.

Gruber, T. R. (1993). A translation approach to portable ontology specifications. *Knowledge Acquisition, 5*, 199–220. doi:10.1006/knac.1993.1008

Hunyadi, J. P. (2008). Ontology used in an e-learning multi-agent architecture. In WSEAS *Transactions on Information Science and Applications*, 5.

Maidel, V., & Shoval, P. Shapira & B., Taieb-Maimon, M. (2008). Evaluation of an ontology-content based filtering method for a personalized newspaper. In *RecSys 2008*, 91-98.

Manouselis, N., Drachsler, H., Vuorikari, R., Hummel, H. G. K., & Koper, R. (2011). Recommender Systems in Technology Enhanced Learning. In Recommender Systems Handbook 387-415 Ricci, F, Rokach L., Shapira, B. & Paul B. Kantor. Springer, ISBN 978-0-387-85819-7

Marinho, L. B., Nanopoulos, A., Schmidt-Thieme, L., Jäschke, R., Hotho, A., Stumme, G., & Symeonidis, P. (2011). Social Tagging Recommender Systems. In *Recommender Systems Handbook 2011*: 615-644.

Middleton, S., Alani, H., Shadbolt, N., & De Roure, D. (2002). Exploiting synergy between ontologies and recommender systems. In *Proceedings of the WWW2002 International Workshop on the Semantic Web*, Workshop Proceedings, Maui, HW, USA, 55

Nadolski, R. J., van den Berg, B., Berlanga, A. J., Drachsler, H., Hummel, H. G. K., Koper, R., & Sloep, P. B. (2009). Simulating Light-Weight Personalised Recommender Systems in Learning Networks: a Case for Pedagogy-Oriented and Rating-Based Hybrid Recommendation Strategies. *Journal of Artificial Societies and Social Simulation*, *12*(14).

Ruthven, I., & Lalmas, M. (2003). A survey on the use of relevance feedback for information access systems. *The Knowledge Engineering Review*, *18*(2), 95–145. doi:10.1017/S0269888903000638

Sieg, A., Mobasher, B., & Burke, R. D. (2007). Web search personalization with ontological user profiles. In *CIKM 2007*, 33, 525-534

Sieg, A., Mobasher, B., & Burke, R. D. (2007). *Representing Context in Web Search with Ontological User Profiles* (pp. 439–452). CONTEXT.

Torniai, C., Jovanović, J., Gašević, D., Bateman, S., & Hatala, M. (2008). E-learning meets the Social Semantic Web. In *Proc. of the 8th IEEE Int'l Conference on Advanced Learning Technologies (ICALT 2008)*, Santander, Cantabria, Spain, 389-393

Vu, D. T., & Plumbaum, T. (2010). Semantic DaiKnow - Development of an enterprise ontology for adaptive recommendations in a social tagging system. In Technsiche Universität Berlin.

Wan, X., Anma, F., Ninomiya, T., & Okamoto, T. (2008). Collabo-eNOTE: A Hybrid Recommender System for Group Learning Support. In *IJCSNS International Journal of Computer Science and Network Security*, 8(9).

Wang, X., Fang, H., & Zhai, C. (2008). A study of methods for negative relevance feedback. In *Proceedings of the 31st Annual International ACM SIGIR Conference on Research and Development in Information Retrieval*, 219–226.

Yu, Z., Nakamura, Y., Jang, S., Kajita, S., & Mase, K. (2007). Ontology-Based Semantic Recommendation for Context-Aware E-Learning. In *Proc. of the 4th Conference on Ubiquitous Intelligence and Computing*, LNCS 4611, 898-907, Springer, Berlin, Heidelberg.

Zhu, F., Ip, H. H. S., Fok, A. W. P., & Cao, J. (2007). PeRES: A Personalized Recommendation Education System Based on Multi-agents & SCORM. In *Advances in Web Based Learning*. ICWL.

## KEY TERMS AND DEFINITIONS

**ERS:** Educational Recommender Systems, recommender systems in educational scenarios.

**LO:** Learning object.

**LOM:** widely accepted metadata standard for learning object.

**Ontology:** A formal representation of knowledge as a set of concepts within a domain, and the relationships between those concepts.

**Ontology Network:** a set of interrelated ontologies.

**Recommender System:** Systems that attempt to recommend information items (movies, music, books, news, images, web pages, scientific literature such as research papers etc.) that are likely to be of interest to the user, usually based on some kind of information filtering system technique.

**Relevance Feedback:** Indication of the usefulness of documents presented to the user.

**User Goal:** Characterization of the tasks the user is trying to achieve trough the recommendation system.

## ENDNOTES

1 FOG grade level = 0.4 (average sentence length + hard words)

2 SMOG grade level = 3 + ?polysyllable count

3 http://www.w3.org/TR/owl-features/

4 http://www.w3.org/Submission/SWRL/

5 http://protege.cim3.net/cgi-bin/wiki.pl?SQWRL

# Section 2
# Techniques, Algorithms and Architectures to Support the Recommendation Process

# Chapter 5
# Reputation in Peer-Based Learning Environments

**Thieme Hennis**
*Delft University of Technology, The Netherlands*

**Stephan Lukosch**
*Delft University of Technology, The Netherlands*

**Wim Veen**
*Delft University of Technology, The Netherlands*

## ABSTRACT

*This chapter proposes a reputation model to support peer-based learning in online communities. Based on literature on quality, trust, and learning, we argue that a reputation system for peer-based learning environments must at least address quality, context, and sustainability issues. We analyzed a number of successful online reputation systems with these issues, and developed a reputation model to support knowledge management, quality assurance, and increase user engagement in peer-based online learning communities. The description of the model includes a conceptual and mathematical representation, a process description to support implementation, and an evaluation framework. A simple example shows how the model can be applied.*

## INTRODUCTION

The Internet is a platform that offers new possibilities to learn and build knowledge with others. The decentralized aspect of the network allows anyone with an Internet connection to participate in this process, but this poses challenges to the way we judge about information, provide learning support, and evaluate learning results. Online learning requires new mechanisms through which support, guidance and evaluation can take place to optimize learning effects for participants involved. Considering learning environments that provide access to all, new socio-technical systems are needed in order to bring these new learning environments to maturity. A critical issue in getting there is how to create sustainable learning processes where participants can rely on each other and

DOI: 10.4018/978-1-61350-489-5.ch005

available content. Trust is an underlying concept for individuals to learn from and with each other in an online community. Implementing systems fostering trust through reputation can enhance the learning effectiveness, and provide alternatives for the traditional pedagogical approaches still in place in current e-learning courses. Formal education could profit from such new learning environments adopting these pedagogical approaches and related technical systems.

Forums, online communities, and professional networks are these new learning environments, where people find and share information, collaborate and learn on demand. A significant challenge is to motivate people to participate in the knowledge-sharing and learning process. Especially in peer-based learning environments, where learning depends on the effort of all participants, it is essential to provide enough incentives to participate and share information with others. This chapter will focus on how data analysis and reputation technologies can improve engagement and learning in online communities.

In this chapter, we describe the need for an online reputation system for peer-based learning environments, present a model with design requirements, and propose an evaluation framework to evaluate a prototype in a community.

## Organization of the Chapter

The background section is divided into two parts. First, it elaborates on changes in the learning landscape, with a focus on self-organized and peer-based learning systems. In this context we focus on the relevance of reputation to increase trust in people and content in online learning communities. We then examine a number of successful online reputation systems in order to elicit design requirements for a reputation model to support peer-based learning in online communities. The model can be used to develop reputation systems in peer-based learning environments. In addition, we propose a method to implement and develop of the reputation model in an organizational context, and an evaluation framework to evaluate and improve the reputation system. The concluding section focuses on relevant research directions and relevant domains in the context of the proposed model.

## BACKGROUND

In 2008, George Siemens and Stephen Downes organized an online course on Connectivism and Connective Knowledge (CCK08). Over 2200 persons worldwide actively participated in an online, peer-based learning network. Because the organizers were unable to assess and give individual feedback to each of the students, called the teacher-bandwidth problem, they motivated students to give peer-feedback, using technologies of all kind: virtual worlds, blogging, commenting, RSS feed-readers, Moodle CMS, and much more (Downes, 2008). The course was a so-called Massive Open Online Course, given for free, as part of a research project by the two organizers (Mackness, Mak, & Williams, 2010).

Open education has grown from sharing repositories containing courseware, to a variety of online initiatives, including full-fledged online e-learning courses, open source learning environments, and self-organized online courses. All these initiatives have the objective of providing better access to learning through the provision of free learning resources on the Internet (Brown & Adler, 2008).

The kinds of open, online courses given by Siemens and Downes rely in part on peer-guidance support. Connectivist and networked learning approaches focus on the ability of the network as a whole to learn, and to learn from the network using a variety of technologies. Connectivism describes a form of knowledge and a pedagogy based on the idea that knowledge is distributed across a network of connections and that learning consists of the ability to construct and traverse those networks. It implies a pedagogy that seeks to describe 'successful' networks (as identified by their properties diversity, autonomy, openness, and connectivity). Also, it seeks to describe the practices that lead to such networks, both in the individual and in society (Downes, 2008; Siemens, 2005).

CCK08 shows how open education is evolving from the provision of static courseware, to interactive and dynamic learning networks. Rather than focusing on automating learning tasks, and providing automatic feedback through intelligent systems, a more feasible and sustainable approach to overcome the "teacher-bandwidth" problem seems to be self-organization (Wiley & Edwards, 2002). Hence, the challenge for future online learning is to focus on creating sustainable self-organizing online learning networks, in particular the mechanisms by which learners engage in connecting, sharing and collaborating. We propose a strategy how to achieve such learning networks based on the concepts of trust and reputation. The approach we describe in this paper could also apply for knowledge-based organizations aiming at facilitating networked learning for their employees, customers and business-to-business relationships.

## Learning on the Web

The Internet and the numerous online communities of practice and professional networks provide opportunities for informal, self-regulated and networked learning. Above all, the Internet offers relatively cheap access for individual learners worldwide to connect with people and find relevant content. The Internet is an environment in which skills can be developed that are needed in a technology driven, and rapidly changing society (Brown & Adler, 2008). The skills that learners develop in regular education systems are different from those developed in peer-based communities, most importantly pro-active learning behavior and responsibility (Soekijad, Huis in 't Veld, & Enserink, 2004; Stahl, 2003; Wenger, 2000).

## The Social Nature of Learning

A popular psychological theory is constructivism, which argues that humans construct knowledge and meaning from their experiences (Bruner, 1991; Piaget & Cook, 1952; Vygotsky, 1978). Constructivist educational theory focuses on concept development and deep understanding, rather than behaviors or skills, as the goals of instruction (Amory & Seagram, 2003). Personal development and deep understanding happens through the construction of meaning by the learner himself, not through transmission from one person (the teacher) to another (the learner). The fundamental principle of constructivism is that learners actively construct knowledge through interactions with their environment (Hout-Wolters, Simons, & Volet, 2000). Learners are viewed as constructing their own knowledge of the world in a social context (Vygotsky, 1978). Learning as a social practice is well established and dialogue is one of the cornerstones of social constructivism. Forums and online communities could therefore be effective places for learning. George Siemens and Stephen Downes explain learning in a digital age by combining and enhancing different learning views, and developed Connectivism (Downes, 2005; Siemens, 2005; 2006). An important distinction from social constructivism is the emphasis on learning that happens outside a person's mind (i.e., teaching your computer to think for you). In the Information Age the learning process concerns activities such as synthesizing and recognizing patterns, meaning making, and forming connections between specialized communities. Know-how and know-what is supplemented with *know-where* as the understanding of where to find the knowledge or person needed. Recommender systems are becoming increasingly important in that process.

## Recommender and Reputation Systems in Education

Historically, education has focused more on memory than understanding. An emphasis on understanding leads to one of the primary characteristics of current theories of learning: its focus on the processes of knowing (Piaget & Cook, 1952; Vygotsky, 1978). Humans are viewed as goal-directed agents who actively seek information. They enter a learning process with a range of prior knowledge, skills, beliefs, and concepts that significantly influence what they notice about the environment and how they organize and interpret it (Lave, 1988; Lave & Wenger, 1991). This, clearly, can have both positive and negative consequences for the learning process and their abilities to remember, reason, solve problems, and acquire new knowledge. Effective learning environments, effective support systems for learning, and effective teachers therefore take into account the background of a learner. The effectiveness in learning environments can be enhanced when there is substantive information about the learners and the information (McCalla, 2004). Recommender systems and standards have been be developed that take into account the background, needs, and level of a learner, and see if there are matching characteristics with information or other learners (Drachsler, 2009). Several technologies have been proposed that automatically produce recommendations based on interest and interactions in online learning environments (Lemire, Downes, & Paquet, 2008; Vuorikari, Manouselis, & Duval, 2006; Wolpers, Najjar, Verbert, & Duval, 2007). Recommender systems use either collaborative filtering techniques or content filtering techniques (Drachsler, Hummel, & Koper, 2008). Both techniques become more powerful when learners and content in an online network are described in detail, and reputation management, rating, and tagging can be used for that.

## Potential of Reputation Management in Professional Online Communities

Tuomi (2007) describes that the social importance of formal educational certificates is now declining, as the capabilities, interests, and reputations of people can be directly evaluated online. Even, in some expertise areas, such as computer programming, employment opportunities sometimes depend on a track record that can be reconstructed by search engines and personal blogs. The digital identities of persons now consist of their own representations of achievements and experiences, as well as reputations that accumulate through the comments of others. Formal educational certificates may be components in such digital representations of capabilities, but their relative importance will diminish (Tuomi, 2007).

Online communities and networks provide a potentially effective place for learners to engage in meaningful interactions with peers and experts. A learner's past is relevant and influences the learning experience. Therefore, recommender systems often focus on the allocation of human and information resources more effectively (and automatically) based on a learner's past (Drachsler, 2009). The past of a learner in online environments can be seen as the sum of its interactions, actions, and contributions in that environment. Reputation management systems can therefore benefit learners in online communities in multiple ways:

- Effective learning environments consider the background of an individual learner. Reputation systems could be used to capture and store the actions and contributions of individuals in order to make a contextualized picture of their interests and capability to solve problems.
- Learners must be activated and engaged to participate in the process of knowledge construction and sharing. Reputation is becoming a strong motivator for people to share knowledge in online communities

(Burke, Marlow, & Lento, 2009; Hoisl, Aigner, & Miksch, 2007; Kollock, 1997; Meiszner, Glott, & Sowe, 2008; Moore & Serva, 2007). This aspect could be beneficiary for those learners who feel they have nothing to contribute, because there is a reason for people to support them and answer their questions.

- We lack models and systems that support recognition of learning activities in peer-to-peer communities (Schmidt, Geith, Håklev, & Thierstein, 2009). In the future, online reputation could become a substitute for or complementary to formal certificates, to which a large part of the world does not have access to.

Reputation management is a promising approach to support learning in online communities. In the next section, we discuss some background information below.

## Reputation Management in Online Communities

Several researchers have investigated the field of trust and reputation systems (Farmer & Glass, 2010; Jøsang, 2007; Jøsang, Ismail, & Boyd, 2007; Lim, Keung, & Griffiths, 2010; Noorian & Ulieru, 2010; Sabater & Sierra, 2005; Wang, 2005). In this chapter, we are concerned with the structured aggregation of reputation information, rather than the interpretation of that information in trust-metrics or recommendations. Most trust and collaborative filtering techniques are aimed towards this, and reputation information can be a useful input for these systems.

Trust is the confidence in or reliance on some quality or attribute of a person or thing, or the truth of a statement. In fact, trust is often used interchangeably with related words like credibility, confidence or reliability (Wang, 2005). Trust is the basis for interpersonal interaction and especially for cooperation in a social network. Merriam-Websters Collegiate Dictionary states that trust is *"... the assured reliance on the character, ability, strength, or truth of someone or something."*[1] Kinateder and Rothermel (2003), from an Artificial Intelligence perspective, define trust in an entity as the belief that under certain circumstances, the entity will perform in a certain way (Kinateder & Rothermel, 2003). Another definition of trust commonly found is trust as a particular level of subjective probability with which agent can assess if another agent will perform a certain action (Gambetta, 2000). Mui et al. emphasize the importance of expectation an agent has about another's future based on the history of encounters, instead of working with probability (Mui, Mohtashemi, & Halberstadt, 2002). The history of encounters is what one could call reputation. Reputation is information used to make a value judgment about an object or person (Farmer & Glass, 2010). Usually, reputation is based on actions or achievements done by individuals or groups. Whereas trust in between agents can be defined as a subjective expectation an agent has about future behavior, reputation has more global characteristics (Jøsang, 2007). When people interact with one another over time, the history of past interactions informs them about their abilities and dispositions. The expectation of reciprocity or retaliation in future interactions creates an incentive for good behavior. An expectation that people will consider one another's pasts in future interactions constrains behavior in the present (Resnick, Zeckhauser, Friedman, & Kuwabara, 2000).

### Reputation in Knowledge-Based Communities

Especially in knowledge-based communities, with a range of expertise domains, inferring reputation from online interactions is challenging (Vu, Papaioannou, & Aberer, 2009). Learning implies that people are continuously constructing new knowledge (Vygotsky, 1978). It implies that an explicit a-priori representation of information is not possible and that subjectivist and objectivist approaches must complement each other in information management (Huizing, 2007). Rather than providing a 'global' trust value (Golbeck & Hendler, 2004; Jøsang, 2007; Kamvar, Schlosser, & Garcia-Molina, 2003), reputation systems for knowledge-based communities must address the dynamic nature of shared information. There are different approaches to model reputation. Game theoretic approaches assume interactions and transactions as games and monitor the result of those games in terms of agents being honest or cheating (Ba, 2001). This results in systems that are likely to give good results in scenarios that concern simple interaction patterns between human beings, such as those in online marketplaces. However, when the complexity of the scenario increases, these models are less suitable. Game theoretic and Bayesian reputation systems reduce trust and reputation to a probability or perceived risk in decision-making (Sabater & Sierra, 2005). This seems to be too restrictive in more complex processes such as knowledge sharing. Reputation cannot be understood as a *"static attribute, rigidly codified as footprints of social hierarchy"* (Squazzoni, 2004). On the contrary, it has dynamic properties, because reputation attribution is a socio-cognitive mechanism that takes root in communication processes. Both the "reputed agent" and the "reputing agent" should be taken into consideration, and the context and relevant processes in which trust is established (Squazzoni, 2004).

## Transitivity and Cross-Community Reputation

The argument that reputation is less a global characteristic can be explained from the perspective of transitivity of trust: If X trusts Y and Y trusts Z, does not imply that X would automatically trust Z. The problem is usually one of context (Abdul-Rahman & Hailes, 2000). So X cannot be sure in which context Y trusts Z. For this, approaches have been suggested to incorporate context or categories into trust systems (Tan & Thoen, 2000). We have argued above that in order to make reputation a useful element in knowledge-based environments, there needs to be some kind of contextualization. To translate too rigidly or literally from the sociological and psychological domains can be difficult and would lead to high dimensionality. Therefore, a set of categories or contexts would need to be chosen, for which the trust between peers could be transitive for individual categories and could be applied inter-categorically where possible. But, as we described above, the context cannot always be known in advance, because new knowledge and topics emerge from interactions. A more dynamic approach to contextualization might be needed to increase trust in knowledge-based systems. On the other hand, this might also impede cross-community reputation, because that relies on agreement about trust and reputation values and contexts. The less is known about the context in which reputation is established, the more difficult it may be to reuse reputation across communities. Reuse of reputation does not happen often, despite the considerable advantages (Vu, Papaioannou, & Aberer, 2009). They include (i) leverage of reputation data from multiple communities; (ii) producing more accurate recommendations; (iii) reputation accumulation: a user does not have to build a reputation from scratch; (iv) users are able to maintain (global or community-specific) offline reputation certificates; and (v) faster establishment of new virtual communities by importing reputation data from related communities (Gal-Oz, Grinshpoun, Gudes, & Meisels, 2008). Also, the trade of reputations may lead to new opportunities for communities as a reputation provider. For example, a reputation provider for experts in solar energy may offer communities and their members to share reputations across a network of solar energy companies, researchers, and institutes. For this to happen, reputations need to be constructed in a way that allows for interoperability and synchronization between communities. Kinateder & Rothermel propose a directed graph of categories to support mapping of dependencies and relationships in different reputation systems (Kinateder & Rothermel, 2003). Related context increases the likeliness of having similar incentives and ranking between communities, improving compatibility and thus the possibility of reputation mapping. Berlanga et al. warn for privacy issues that will arise when participants' online identity and reputation are transferred from one community to another (Berlanga, Rusman, Bitter-Rijpkema, & Sloep, 2009).

### Aim of the Research

Learning is a creative process in which knowledge is constructed. Online communities have the potential to support that, and reputation systems can support the process in different ways, most importantly with regard to motivation and quality concerns, and the provision of data to be used in recommender systems. Knowledge is constructed, used, and interpreted in online communities, and its usefulness is contextual. The dynamic character of context of information objects has not been addressed by reputation systems so far. We therefore propose that the objective of a reputation system for knowledge-based communities should be to model the specific value (or expertise) of an individual based on his/her shared and created knowledge. In this chapter, we want to find out how this can be done:

*How can we Model Reputation of an Object Based on its Interactions with the Environment and How Can Reputation be Inferred Through the Network?*

The aim of the research is to develop a standard for aggregating, not interpreting, relevant interactions with contributed information objects in order to give insight into the perception of people about the value of these objects and their authors. Many trust systems are advanced systems in which agents make decisions based on the information they retrieve from a central database or in a decentralized manner, In this chapter, we take one step back, and look at how perceptions and usage can be aggregated so useful recommendations can be made. In this chapter, we are not concerned with trust or recommender systems, we focus on the reputation of individuals and their contributions in online communities.

## EXAMINATION OF REPUTATION SYSTEMS

We can learn from existing systems to see how they address the trust and motivation issues. Based on the analysis of different reputation systems, we will propose a reputation model, including a conceptual and mathematical representation, an implementation process description, example, and an evaluation framework. For the evaluation of online reputation systems, we use the ontology on Web reputation systems proposed by Farmer and Glass (Farmer & Glass, 2010). They propose that the basic entity of a reputation system is a 'reputation statement', see Figure 1.

The above statement is an elementary particle of every reputation system. Simple reputation systems calculate a reputation based on one type of claim, from a small number of sources, to a small number of targets. For example, on eBay, the source is usually the buyer, the claim consists of 4 elements (price, quality, communication, and delivery), and the target is the seller. The system merely aggregates all the claims by buyers, and shows the (weighted) average.

In addition to a generic description of reputation, we want to focus on three important aspects of the system. Reputation concerns the mapping and aggregation of interactions and ratings by users, because this means something in terms of value or quality. The first aspect thus concerns a specific description of how quality is perceived and determined by the system. Secondly, we

*Figure 1. Reputation model (Farmer & Glass, 2010)*

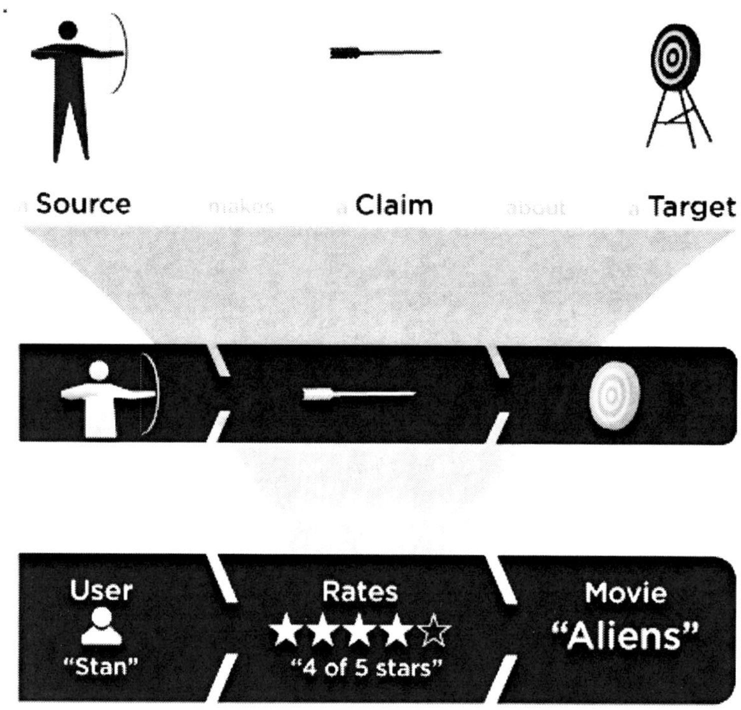


focus on the way the system addresses context of reputed objects, because that seems a required element for reputation systems concerned with knowledge sharing. As explained in the learning section, we lack systems that recognize and assess learning activities and interactions between peers in online communities. In addition, online reputation could lead to opportunities on the labor market or within an organization. The third aspect we intend to look at is the business model or in more generic terms, the sustainability of the system, because we argue that peer-based learning could be supported by reputation if it is recognized in a professional context. These three aspects form the major challenges for reputation systems to support peer-based learning in online communities.

Following the above structure, we now discuss several successful online reputation systems. In choosing the systems, we had several objectives in mind. First of all, the systems needed to be mutually different, because we wanted to learn from the different approaches. Secondly, we intended to include systems that have a specific approach to at least on of the mentioned aspects context, quality and sustainability. In addition, we chose Guru.com and StackOverflow, because they have specific relevance in the context of learning and professional development.

## Google PageRank

Google PageRank (and the other algorithms that followed) has proven to be one of the most successful reputation systems online. The main reason for choosing this example is that it is fully automated and is based on regular 'behavior' and structure of the Web and its users, and therefore relatively little resources (except for cheap computing power) are needed to sustain the system.

*Figure 2. Google PageRank*

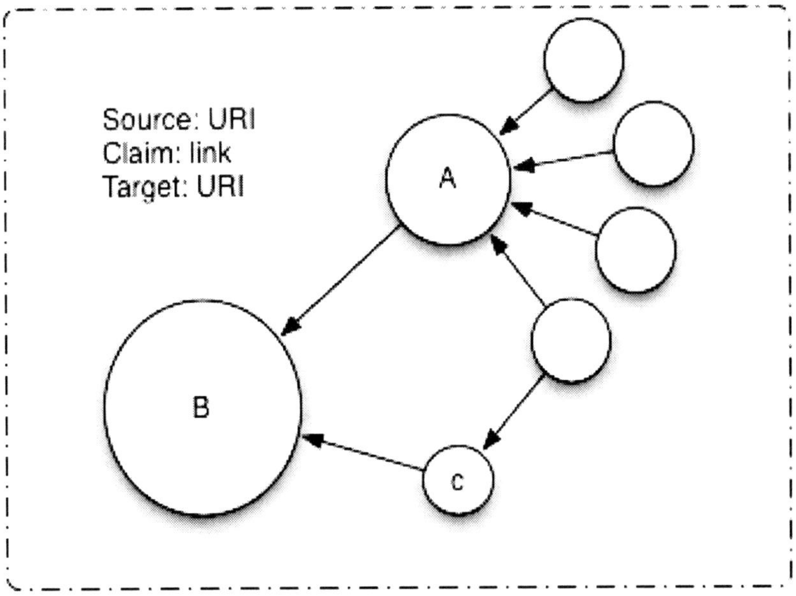


Various approaches have followed the PageRank system proposed in 1998 (Brin & Page, 1998), including BrowseRank (Y. Liu et al., 2008) and BlogRank (Lin & Kao, 2010).

Google's PageRank system calculates relevance of a web resource by looking at its relation with other web resources. PageRank and other similar technologies such as HITS, use the Web's vast link structure as an indicator of an individual page's value (Brin & Page, 1998; Lewandowski & Höchstötter, 2008). In essence, Google interprets a link from page A to page B as a vote, by page A, for page B. In addition to the PageRank, Google introduced the TrustRank, to give more weight to links coming from trusted and more popular sources (sources with a high PageRank). The image below makes clear how this works, in a simplified form: A's link to B is assigned more weight than c's link to B, because of differences in popularity (PageRank). Next to popularity Google analyzes contextual factors of webpages and their relations to allow semantic searching.

In the PageRank algorithm, sources and targets are URI's, or Internet 'things'. All things that can be found by typing in a link can be a source as well as a target. The claim is a vote from one link to another.

## Quality

Quality relates with the number of incoming links. This notion of quality can be improved through the incorporation of relevant user-behavior, such as number of clicks, time spent on the website, etc (Y. Liu et al., 2008). In addition, links from "trusted web sources (such as the BBC website)" get extra weight.

## Context

Quality is derived from measuring static and dynamic relationships between URIs. Based on these relationships and their connection value, Google is able to define a notion of relevance of a webpage and knows how to connect this notion to specific contexts. If a search query corresponds to a context, Google shows the most relevant and highest valued results for that context. This information is also being used to know more about the Internet user, in order to provide better contextualized advertisements (in addition to search results). Google also uses something called TrustRank to define the trustworthiness of websites and uses this TrustRank to add more or less weight to a vote/outgoing link. Other proposed extensions to the algorithm have been proposed, including the PopRank and AuthorRank, but these methods perform ranking only by using the link information between web-pages, and do not consider the topic information (Tang et al., 2010).

### Sustainability

PageRank is an automated system: it does not rely on specialized committees who analyze and evaluate the relevance of a webpage, but uses available data of the Internet's interconnected websites to determine relevance and quality. Computation power is much cheaper than human power, so Google has been able to scale its system exponentially. Google provides a range of services, making users of those services more dependent on Google. There is an incentive for website owners and content contributors to behave according to the rules set by Google (adding keywords to your website, for example). Bad behavior can be detected, and rules and algorithms are in place to counter that (such as removing from search results). Jøsang argues that there is still an untapped potential for integrating reputation systems with search engines (Jøsang, 2007).

### Conclusions

Google shows that giving away services for free can be highly profitable and sustainable. In the context of peer-based learning environments, this means that you can profit from sharing your knowledge if that leads to more traffic (and opportunities) to you as a person. The reputation system is interesting, because it interprets available data about behavior and connections, and translates the authority of source objects into weights influencing a vote.

## eBay Seller Reputation

eBay's success depends on its reputation system, despite the fact that the high percentage of positive ratings seem unrealistic (Resnick, Zeckhauser, Swanson, & Lockwood, 2006). The possible explanation they provided for the positive rating bias was that positive ratings are a sort of exchange of courtesies, whereas negative ratings are avoided because of fear of retaliation from the other party. The choice for eBay has been the straightforwardness of the approach, and the explicit trust factors, On eBay, sources are buyers and sellers are targets. The claims are structured in four categories: "Item as described", "Communication", "Shipping time", and "Handling charges". Buyers give a 5-star rating for each of the categories after purchasing. The evaluation is linked to a specific purchase.

### Quality

After a sale, a buyer can rate the seller using a 5-star scale. Untrustworthy sellers are removed from the system. In addition to the explicit ratings, there are implicit parameters, such as "Number of transactions" and "Years active". Also, the whole transaction history is publicly shown. As such, eBay approaches trust and reputation from different angles.

### Context

The eBay system is a straightforward reputation system that concerns four factors for which quality is rated: a seller must not ask an unreasonable price, must ship fast, must not add unreasonable extra costs, and must reply on emails fast. Still, these categories are very generic. Such a generic contextualization of quality seems inappropriate for knowledge sharing in online communities.

*Figure 3. eBay reputation*

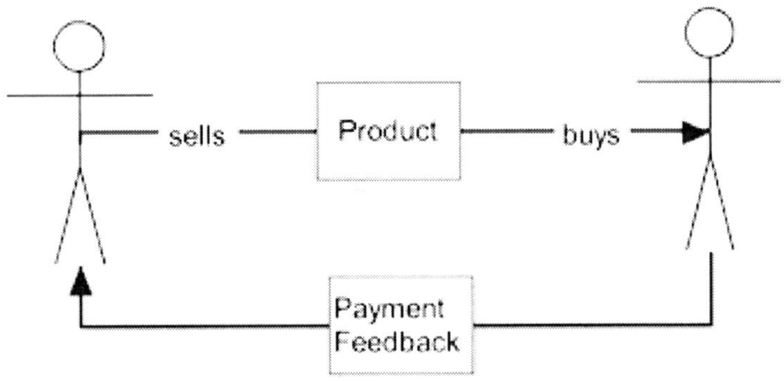


## Sustainability

Rating happens in a very decentralized way. Even though human resources are needed to settle cases (this cannot be automated), it seems like the business generated by the system outweighs the resources needed to maintain it. The desired behavior is clearly defined by the factors for which a buyer must rate. Sellers who behave as such are more likely to be trusted and will be able to sell more. The eBay trust system has proven to be scalable, hosting millions of transactions per day.

## Conclusions

eBay is very clear about desired behavior (setting price/quality, communication, handling charges, etc.). This explicitly guides sellers' behavior, and also motivates them to conduct as many transactions as possible. As shown by Resnick et al., direct feedback can be ambiguous (Resnick, Zeckhauser, Swanson, & Lockwood, 2006). Therefore, eBay adopts different angles to reputation, including rating, but also years active, and number of transactions.

# Guru Professional Reputation

Malone & Laubacher (1998) coined the term 'e-lance economy', meaning an economy largely based on temporary organizations of individuals that emerge and dissolve when business opportunities arise and disappear, and where IT serves to link individual nodes (Malone & Laubacher, 1998). Online marketplaces, such as Guru.com provide a place for individuals and organizations to find each other and employ or be employed. Reputation consists of implicit parameters (including amount of money earned), and direct feedback by employers. Freelancers can also provide a resume, portfolio of work, and do standardized tests to prove certain basic skills. Another way to increase reputation is to answer questions on the forum. The image below shows how freelancers are presented in Guru, showing the most important trust parameters, including badges (community accreditation).

The objective of the reputation system is to match employers and freelancers. For employers, the reputation system has the objective of providing a level of trust in freelancers. For freelancers it is an instrument to show accomplishments, become distinguishable, and increase in value. An employer is the source making a claim (rating and comment) about a freelancer after the freelancer has done a job. As with eBay, people are needed to solve disputes. Payment is also a strong indicator of value-transfer, and thus taken as an indicator of a freelancer's value.

*Figure 4. Guru.com reputation*

## Quality

Various indicators define the quality, or value, of a freelancer: accumulated earnings, ratings and recommendations, and other indicators as badges. In addition, a freelancer can add credentials and diplomas to support claims of expertise or skills. The quality of a freelancer is equal to the perceived quality of his work for others. As with eBay, this is a very direct way of rating and the validity of ratings could therefore be questionable.

## Context

Expertise or skills are (by definition) limited, which makes a personal reputation always contextualized to an expertise domain. It is likely that a freelancer does jobs within a single arena, and a reputation is therefore valuable within that same arena. Guru defines those arenas, so software companies can find programmers and a movie director can find a scriptwriter.

A reputation on Guru relates to activity generated on Guru, but it is not unthinkable that a freelancer uses his Guru reputation in another professional context.

## Sustainability

Case-settlement is one of the few centrally organized processes. All ratings happen entirely decentralized. Guru is comparable with eBay. Sellers on eBay depend on their reputation as freelancers on theirs on Guru. Contrary to eBay, the context in which reputation is earned does matter: you don't want to hire a financial consultant to solve an IT issue. Guru freelancers are motivated to do a good job. Employers are motivated to support freelancers and pay in time.

## Conclusions

Reputation is approached from different angles. In addition to employer feedback and rating, history of transactions and a portfolio is visible which makes it more difficult to 'game' the system. As with eBay, the feedback by employers is structured (i.e. price, quality, communication, etc.). Similarly, freelancers rate employers (i.e. ability to pay in time). Employers and freelancers find each other within a given, explicit context: the industry expertise area. Designers are rated on the quality of their designs, not anything else. Finally, internal and external accreditation possibilities improve trust in the system.

## StackOverflow Question & Answering Community

StackOverflow is an online community for people discussing IT-related issues. There are now numerous websites using the original StackOverflow reputation system, collectively named the Stack-Exchange. On the forum community members can ask questions and/or provide answers and comments. The answers receive votes by community, and the answer with the highest amount of votes is chosen as the best answer. In addition to votes and answers, members can add tags to questions and answers. These tags play an important role in the reputation of users. Part of member profiles is dynamically updated with the tags of Q&A topics they participate in, as shown in the picture below.

StackOverflow wants to keep the quality of questions and answers high. On the forum, people are the *sources*, who vote (*claim*) and tag (contextualize) *targets* such as answers, questions, and comments.

### Quality

Quality is measured in terms of votes for answers, questions, and comments. Answers are assessed on quality and are contextualized using tags. This makes it easy for Search engines as Google to use the content on the community and for people to find the content they need. "Good" behavior, or in other words: giving the right answers, earns points, expertise tags, and badges. Each person has a personal profile showing their reputation and history of questions and answers on the site.

### Context

StackOverflow is a very interesting example from the perspective of context. Because every question is contextualized with keywords, an individual contributor develops a list with keywords representing the topics of the questions in which they have shown their expertise. These keywords each have an individual score, depending on the votes for the answer (or question). It therefore becomes a very contextualized profile. The community itself maintains the list of keywords (a domain ontology).

### Sustainability

StackOverflow reputation can lead to job opportunities, because you can allow it to be published on http://careers.stackoverflow.com/. The reputation system also motivates members to specify keywords for a question, to formulate questions well, and to provide high quality answers. Additionally, it motivates them to scrutinize answers on their quality. There is no danger of excessive use of tags, because it is useless from the perspective of members to have a reputation on a keyword that no one uses. As such, the reputation is specific and uses a commonly agreed and maintained ontology defining the topics and domains.

### Conclusions

StackOverflow shows how in the modeling of reputation, context and quality are combined through the involvement of the community. At the same time, the community is motivated to maintain and agree upon topical keywords representing the knowledge and subjects dealt with by the community. Unlike more static representations of context (i.e. eBay: "communication", "price", "delivery time", etc.), StackOverflow is able to combine

Figure 5. StackOverflow

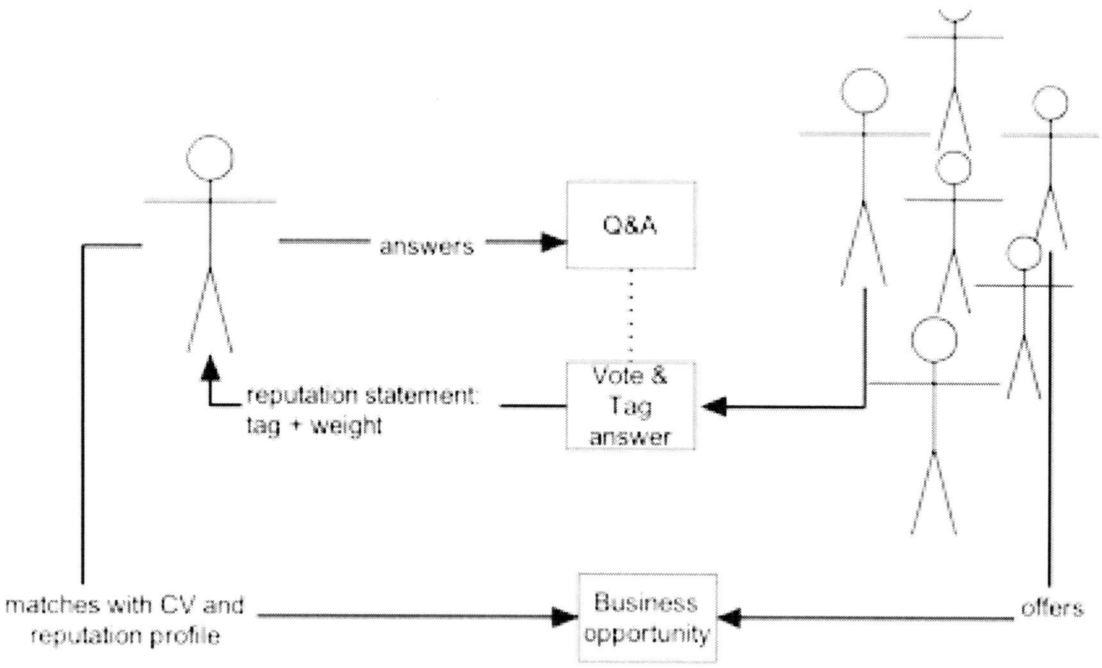


the contextual factors (tags assigned to questions) with votes to make a dynamic representation of the quality of a person based on his/her contributions. It is self-organized contextualization. There is no imposing of taxonomy or structure for all questions and answers.

Another relevant conclusion is that, if a member wants it, reputation can be shown to 3rd parties. These potential employers can search the database and get software experts from the community. Their Q&A reputation is important, and forms an important incentive for the members to answer questions (and show-off/share expertise). Sharing expertise for free can lead to employment and improve professional reputation. Active and self-directed learning is possible and sustained in decentralized communities, if the right tools and mechanisms are in place. Reputation, which is crucial for the electronic freelancer, depends on contributions. It is an important incentive to collaborate in order to get business opportunities.

## Summary of Examination

A reputation model can be used to develop a community specific reputation system. Based on the above examination of successful reputation systems, we provide a model that is relevant for peer-based learning communities. A peer-based learning community can be any forum or professional network where people exchange information and learn from each other. The context is problem-based and active learning. There is no pressure on anyone to engage in the learning or teaching processes, and motivation must come from interest, need, or visibility/reputation. A model to describe the most relevant information exchange and assessment processes is needed to develop an effective reputation system. Such a system can stimulate learners to consult peers or be consulted by peers who have a question or request. Below we summarize the outcomes of the various reputation systems and describe implications for the design of a reputation system for peer-based learning environments.

## General Remarks

All systems have the objective of recommending people or information, to provide information about how an object or person can be trusted. eBay shows the aggregated information and allows an individual to make his or her own choice. The PageRank algorithm, on the other hand, accumulates so much information about websites that it would be impossible for any human being to interpret, so their interpretation algorithms do that. Individuals only get a list of recommended websites for their search query. The nature and complexity of the system either allows or disallows interpretation by users. In addition, if the exact calculation of reputation is disclosed, then website owners could find loopholes in order to become more relevant.

The design of a reputation system for peer-based learning environments should start with the description of relevant knowledge-sharing and evaluation processes of a community or organization. The description contains processes and contributions that could benefit from a reputation system, the claims that relate to a type of quality, and the source objects that make these claims. These processes could be interrelated and form a complex network of targets. In a human-based community, the objective is to motivate people to produce high-quality target objects. The reputation of *a person* depends on quality of his/her produced target objects.

## Quality

In the analysis we saw that in the aggregation of information about quality or trust, the systems address both implicit and explicit *claims*. Implicit claims are retrieved by means of logging and interpreting the structure or behavior in the system, such as number of links and page-visits (Google PageRank). Explicit rating requires the input of users, and could therefore include bias. They also depend on the willingness of users to provide the explicit input. Implicit statements and cues, embedded in the normal process of knowledge sharing, can be more difficult to interpret if they are not expressive. A large number of statements is then needed to infer a notion of quality. It can be challenging to determine and rank the implicit statements and cues. Google PageRank is an example of how simple, implicit statements can be used to structure the Web. Google does not ask users to rate websites, because it knows that it will be used strategically. The size of the web makes it impossible to control, but this is usually not the case of communities, where social control could be possible.

## What Does This Mean For Peer-Based Learning Environments?

Reputation should be approached from different angles. All relevant statements and their meaning (check with stakeholders) should be described that are implicit and already part of the system. In addition, find out if people are willing to provide explicit feedback and how this can be organized and embedded into the system. The result is an overview of all the implicit and explicit statements (claims), and describes how they are interrelated, and how they should be interpreted. If the interpretation is difficult, contextual information might be needed to make the right interpretation. Reputation statements can be bundled if they have similar meaning, and ranked based on their expressiveness and importance. These interpretation rules need to be verified with the user community, and calibrated with through use.

## Context

The context of information exchange in a knowledge-based system is complex. On eBay, reputation statements are structured according to four elements (quality, communication, delivery, price). This simplicity is highly effective if the interactions are simple, because the desired behavior is also simple. If the context of a target object is more complex, contextualization of a reputation statement becomes more important. For example, on StackOverflow the context of an answer (target object) is more contextualized by keywords (added by users). People on the platform add these keywords. The result is that on eBay, your reputation is generic, and can be simply represented by a number ("99% Positive Feedback"). On StackOverflow, your reputation is specified by keywords. On knowledge-based communities, capturing the field of expertise and relevant domain for each reputation statement (claim) is necessary to add relevancy.

### What Does This Mean for Peer-Based Learning Environments?

The topics of expertise dealt with in a community should be made explicit and made part of the reputation system. It is possible that the community itself maintains the ontology, which can be used to contextualize reputation statements. The context of a reputation statement cannot fully be known in advance. On a forum on mathematics, you know in advance that each question will be related with mathematics, but specific context (i.e. "Bayes theorem") is added in a more dynamic and bottom-up way (for instance through tagging or content analysis techniques).

We have seen with Google's PageRank principle that the source website's PageRank rating influences the vote (claim) to another website. We propose a similar principle here, which is to address expertise in a reputation statement, because expertise matters in evaluating the value of knowledge. Comparing reputation profiles of source and target can result in higher or lower weight to the statement. In other words, if someone has a high reputation for "Bronchitis", he/she is able to answer questions about Lung diseases than someone who has a high reputation for "Semantic Web".

## Sustainability

Sustainability is the ongoing ability to meet the objectives of an organization, project, or system. The sustainability of a reputation system is highly related with its acceptance and the trust it generates. The sustainability of a system is related to the effort needed from people and whether or not they are willing to make this effort. On different platforms (eBay, Guru), we saw that dispute settlement is needed. Manual, human intervention may be needed to check or maintain the quality of reputation profiles and recommendations, but it may also inhibit the scalability and growth of the system, especially when the resources required for this, are not available.

Motivation is a central element in any reputation system. The aggregation of behavioral data, of personal history and transactions, and its publication, influences the behavior of people in the system. We saw that reputation acquired on the web is used professionally and to earn money. Therefore, gaming the reputation system might have benefits. Most systems use information from different sources and angles to validate data. As we saw, human intervention is sometimes needed to detect and signal wrong behavior.

### What Does This Mean for Peer-Based Learning Environments?

The sustainability of a learning system is its ability to provide high-quality resources and support for each learner. Because we are talking about peer-support, we should evaluate the level of participation and willingness to engage in peer-support processes, and the quality and availability of learning resources.

Capturing implicit statements is an approach the lowers the reliance on explicit ratings from the community and adds viability to the reputation system. When explicit ratings by people are needed, it should be clear why they would be willing to do this. With the StackOverflow example, we saw that the community is willing to maintain the topic ontology, because their reputations would become *more useful* with a standardized grammar.

The way knowledge and skills are represented, should be understandable and searchable for 'reputation consumers', such as peers and potential future employers. Obviously, they relate with core-processes of the community. Check if and how good behavior can be reinforced and put effort in embedding a wider (professional or societal) context into the reputation system.

When a system is implemented, it should be evaluated on its merits and costs (above), and on its quality: Does the system produce relevant reputation profiles that express knowledge, expertise, or value? Can the calculated reputation be relied on? Do they relate with the core community processes of peer-based learning and knowledge-exchange? Does it really motivate people to engage in these processes?

Finally, in what way will the system be able to adapt to changes and/or wrong assumptions? How will it implement necessary changes in the rule system and use feedback? Can the system be gamed?

## DESCRIPTION OF THE MODEL

Below, we conceptualize the above conclusions in a graphical and mathematical representation, and use simple examples with each step. We propose a unique approach to model reputation adopting several lessons learned:

- The utilization of keywords to infer a very specific (contextualized) reputation;
- The translation of several context factors into weights, including the automatic calculation of authority weight based on the source-object's topic expertise.

In the description, we use the simple definition of a reputation statement proposed by Farmer and Glass (2010):

- A target $T = \{t_1,\ldots,t_n\}$
- A claim $C = \{c_1,\ldots,t_m\}$
- A source $S = \{s_1,\ldots,s_r\}$

We will use these definitions in our proposed reputation model. We propose a model that specifies reputation per keyword, rather than provides a generic measure of trust.

First of all, we define our understanding of targets and sources. They are both objects (see formula (1)). Objects have a reputation consisting of keywords *k* and a corresponding keyword value *kv* (see formula (2)). All keywords form the set *K*. This means that the reputation of an object (which can be a person) is defined by keywords and that each of the keywords has a value.

$$O = T \cup S \qquad (1)$$

$$R_o = \{(k,kv_o) \mid k \in K \wedge kv_o \in \mathrm{R}_0 \wedge o \in O \qquad (2)$$

*Figure 6. Example of sources, claims, and targets*

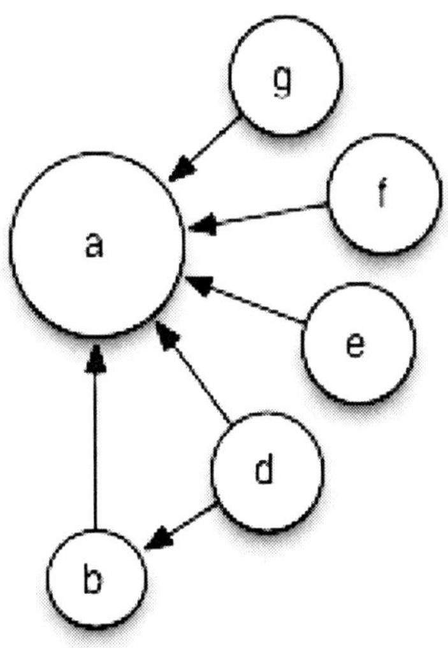

*Figure 7. Meta-object and its contributed objects*

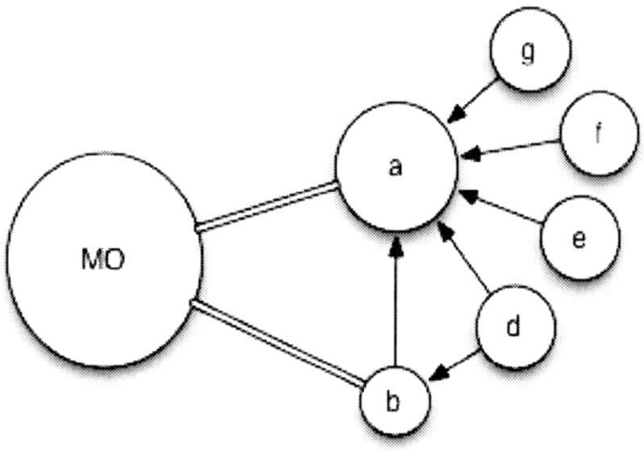


In the scenario below, a and b are target objects, and all except a is a source object. The arrows are claims.

We now introduce the concept of a meta-object *MO*. A meta-object is the creator of target objects. For example, in a scientific community a researcher is the meta-object of his/her contributions (papers, articles, etc.). In human communities, meta-objects are people. A person's reputation $R_{MO}$ is an aggregation of the reputation of his/her contributions (all the target-objects produced by this person).

$$MO \subseteq O \quad (3)$$

Obviously, these meta-objects can also be normal source or target objects. We have seen that direct rating can be ambiguous (Resnick, Zeckhauser, Swanson, & Lockwood, 2006). Despite that, direct rating is a normal practice in communities and we must not exclude that.

To summarize, we look at reputation of *target-objects*. These objects are creates or produced by *meta-objects*. The *meta-object* inherits the reputation of its produced target objects. We then explained that these meta-objects could be source and target objects as well (Algorithm 1).

The example below shows how meta-object MO has contributed a and b. It means that every claim made about a and b will be *inferred* by MO.

When we take the above example, we see that MO is the creator of target objects *a* and *b*. All reputation statements directed at *a* and *b* will become part of the reputation of MO.

## What is a Reputation Statement?

The reputation of an object is determined by the reputation statements directed at it. A reputation statement is defined in terms of a claim, a source, and a target. We specify this picture by adding context.

- *k*: affiliated keywords describe the context of a target object. The affiliated keywords can be "passed on" to the object to become part of its reputation. They are discovered or added by people, but not yet part of the reputation. Something can only become part of the reputation through a claim. Affiliated keywords are those keywords in a community that represent the topics and knowledge domains.
- • $rv^k_{avg.}$ : each keyword has an average reputation value, which is the total reputation value for that keyword of all target-objects (not the meta-objects: that would be double-counting) divided by the number of target-objects.

*Algorithm 1.*

Algorithm $R_{MO}$
  Forall $o \in MO$
    Forall $(k, kv_o) \in R_o$
      If $k \notin R_{MO}$
        $R_{MO} = R_{MO} \cup (k,\ kv_o)$
      Else
        $kv_{MO} = kv_{MO} + kv_o$
      endif
    endfor
  endfor

$$rv_{avg.}^{k} = \frac{\sum_{i=0}^{n} kv_{o_i}}{n} \quad (4)$$

- $w_t^k$: Affiliated keyword weight is the weight of a single affiliated keyword in relation to the other affiliated keywords of a target object o. Sometimes, the weights are equally divided, if both affiliated keywords have similar importance in representing the target. If one keyword describes the target better than the other, this can be shown by the affiliated keyword weight. Affiliated keyword weight could be calculated in different ways, depending on the way they are added in the first place (either the result of content analysis or through tagging).
- $w_t$: Target weight depends on the type and location of the target, or maybe even the popularity. For example, in a community, an answer to a question can be considered more important than posting a comment, even though both are considered targets that should be monitored. This difference in importance is reflected by the target weight.
- $w_c$: Claim weight addresses the differences in claims. Some claims, such as official endorsements, may carry more weight than others (like a page visit).
- $v_c$: Claim value is the actual rating itself, which can be positive or negative.
- $w_s^k$: Source weight is another word for "authority of a source object to make a claim about an affiliated keyword". Hence, it is the source object's reputation value, specified per affiliated keyword. If the source object has a value higher than the average value, the claim will be reinforced by the source weight. A lower than average reputation score for an affiliated keyword will weaken the claim for that keyword. Source weight can be calculation in many ways, it includes at least some comparison between the source reputation value for a keyword and the average reputation value for that keyword. We add one in order to make claims valid even if the source does not have reputation for that keyword. We propose to calculate the source weight as follows:

$$w_s^k = \frac{rv_s^k + 1}{rv_{avg.}^k} \quad (5)$$

In order to calculate reputation per keyword, we must split each reputation statement into individual claims containing one of the affiliated keywords. This is important, because sources have reputations consisting of keywords with values. The actual source object weight for an affiliated keyword is calculated by comparing its reputation score for the affiliated keyword with the average score for that keyword.

So, how does a reputation statement look like then? For each of the affiliated keywords, the reputation value for the target is calculated as the product of (i) Affiliated keyword weight, (ii) Target weight, (iii) Claim weight, (iv) Claim value, and (v) Source weight (authority).

$$c_t^k = w_t^k w_t w_c v_c w_s^k \quad (6)$$

An example is shown in the picture below. The first step in a reputation statement is to determine the affiliated keywords. These can be added manually by the source object, or are already available. Then, for each of the affiliated keywords, a claim is made. In the example, we see that there are only two affiliated keywords, and that the source only has reputation on one of them (Skin diseases). The source weight is calculated for each of the keywords, and as can be seen, the statement (3 stars) weighs 3 times as much for the keyword "Skin diseases" than for the keyword "Sexually Transmitted Diseases".

This example makes clear that the source object's reputation influences the weight of a claim *per affiliated keyword*. If a target has 100 affiliated keywords, a reputation statement will be divided into 100 separate claims and for each of the claims, a unique source weight will be calculated.

## Calculation of Weights

The weights regarding target-types and claim-types are really community concerns. Each community has its own values and norms about what is desired behavior, which should be reflected by the weights assigned to specific targets and claims.

- With regard to *target weights*, we can think of this example: a reputation system of a research institution that supports Open Access establishes lower weights for articles that are published in journals that are not open access. The higher target weight for articles (target objects) that are published in Open Access journals motivates the research institution's researchers to publish there.
- With regard to *claim type weights*, we follow the above example: the institution finds Google PageRank of a Journal more relevant than the impact factor. Google's PageRank (claim type & value) impacts the relative value of a journal (in this scenario *a target object*) more than the claim-type and value of the impact factor. The weight for PageRank is therefore higher than for "impact factor".

These weights are either defined in advance (in agreement with the community), or the result of a calculation (with parameters defined by the community).

We have already discussed the affiliated keyword weight and authority. In the section about further research, we mention the retrieval and management of affiliated keywords as key challenges. Also, trust systems are very relevant with respect to calculating trust of an agent (or person) in a system. This information could be useful as another weight influencing the rating of a source object.

*Figure 8. Reputation statement & calculation of authority*

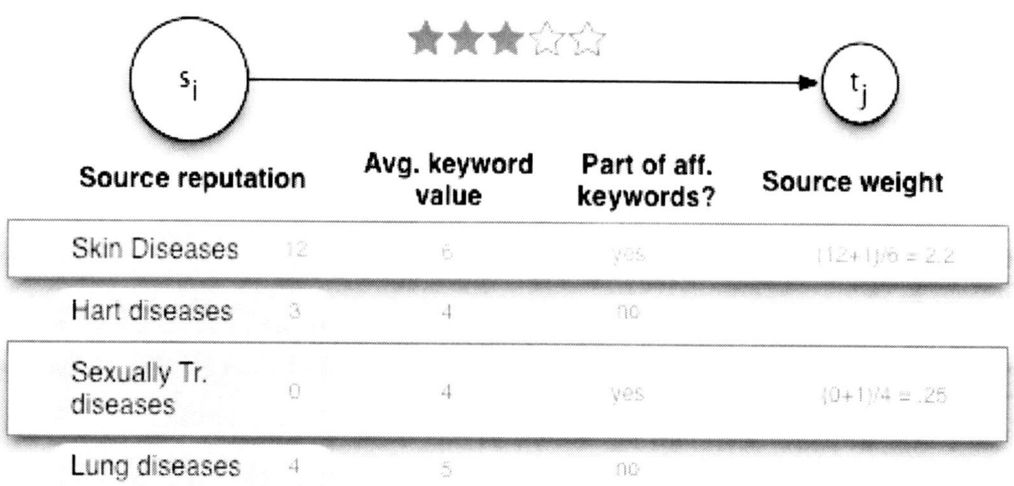

## DESIGN AND IMPLEMENTATION PROCESS

In order to make a design and develop a reputation system according to the proposed model, we have defined a number of steps below.

### Step I: Define the Target Objects, Source Objects and the Claims

The model shows that reputation statements consist of a target, source and claim. In order to make a model, one should understand and model all *relevant* targets, sources, and claims in a system, community, or organization. Relevant targets, sources, and claims are those that are related with core knowledge management and learning processes in the organization or community. The focus should be on processes and objects that are reusable and digital.

- Create overview of knowledge exchange processes and contributions in the community.
  - KM processes. How do people manage/share/create knowledge?
  - Learning processes. How do people learn with and from each other?
- Set boundaries: motivation & technology
  - Motivation. Which processes and contributions would be enhanced by a reputation system?
  - Technology. Which of these processes and results of processes can be monitored online?

### Step II: Establishing Rules for the Weights

Secondly, the weights must be defined (or the rules to calculate them). Each claim directed at a target will be divided into separate claims containing for each of the target's affiliated keywords. This means that each of the separate claims is a value-keyword combination. As defined in formula (6), the actual claim for an affiliated keyword is the product of (i) affiliated keyword weight, (ii) target weight, (iii) claim weight, (iv) claim value, (v) source weight. The rules and or static values of these weights are the result of discussions or calculation.

## Example: LiLa

The example we use is the EU project Library of Labs, an existing EU-funded initiative for the mutual exchange of and access to virtual laboratories (simulation environments) and remote experiments (real laboratories which are remotely controlled via the internet). The portal includes technology like scheduling systems, library resources, and social tools such as a forum and peer-reviewed assessments. At the moment of writing, the portal is not fully functional, so the example does not use real data.

In LiLa, the main objective of a reputation system is to support and motivate students and teachers to support each other and answer questions, when they are asked about a specific theory or experiment. As defined above, we define the relevant source and target objects, and all claims.

- Source objects are users: registered and non-registered users.
- Target objects are answers on the forum and assessment reviews.
- Claims are different for the target objects: answers and reviews are not evaluated by the same claims. The table below shows the different claims per target object (Table 1).

Most knowledge systems are more complex than this, and the list will likely be more extensive.

Experiments are explicitly contextualized with keywords (they are part of the metadata set), and each assessment belongs to one experiment. Hence, each assessment review will get the key-

*Table 1.*

| Claim type | Description | Target(s) |
|---|---|---|
| Favorite | People can add a review to their Favorites for future reference. | Review |
| Rating | People can rate a review on a three-point scale: Very helpful – Ok – Not helpful | Review<br>Answer |
| Clicks | The page visits on the forum topic or review page. This claim type influences the reputation of the target as a whole. | Review<br>Answer |

words of the experiment it belongs to. In LiLa, keywords affiliated to a target get an equal weight, so if there are two affiliated keywords to a target, each gets a weight of 0,5. If keywords are hierarchically related, the lowest level keywords are the only ones being included, because the target will inherit the higher-level keywords.

There are different target weights for answers and reviews in LiLa, because reviews are considered more important than answers. Similarly, there are different weights for the different claims. The table below shows all the different weights, and the calculation of the reputation value for a reputation statement by user "userID_321" by "userID_426". The keywords affiliated to the target "Review#456" is "carbon-dating" and "radio-metric dating", and the claim is a "Favorite". Below only the part of the claim concerned with affiliated keyword "carbon-dating" (Table 2).

Target object "Review#456" has two affiliated keywords. Each time a source object makes a claim, two reputation statements are issued (one for each keyword), because the source-weight will be different for each keyword. For the keyword "carbon-dating" the claim results in a value of 2.17. It means that the reputation value of target "Review#456", and therefore also its author's reputation value, will increase with 2.17 for that keyword.

## LINKING THE MODEL WITH THE BACKGROUND AND ANALYSIS SECTIONS

The first sections of this chapter focused on learning and education in the 21st century. In this section we connect the reputation model of the previous section with the background and analysis sections on learning, trust, and reputation. First, we argued that learning increasingly happens in open and closed online communities, and that there is a need for quality assurance and insight into people's contributions in these communities by peers as well as potential employers. Recommender and reputation modeling could help in creating trust and motivation, and increase insight in the quality of online contributions. We identified several factors that should be addressed when designing and implementing a reputation system for such communities. These are motivation, quality, context, scalability, and sustainability. Based on lessons

*Table 2.*

| Affiliated keyword | Carbon-dating | Target | Review#456 | Claim | Favorite | Source | userID_426 |
|---|---|---|---|---|---|---|---|
| Aff. keyword weight | 0,5 | Target weight | 0,7 | Claim weight | 2 | Weight | 3,1 |
| | | | | Claim value | 1 | | |

learned from existing reputation systems about each of these factors, we developed a reputation model. Below, we describe how our reputation model addresses these factors.

### Quality

Quality is a perception, but some people (or objects) are better in perceiving quality than others. The model calculates authority for each keyword and uses this to assign (extra) weight on claims. Someone's reputation is therefore not only communicative, but instrumental in the evaluation process as well.

### Context

Context concerns those factors and issues that directly influence the reputation process. Although not extensively, we have proposed numerous ways to include context, most importantly by means of *affiliated keywords*. In addition, we have proposed the inclusion of weights in order to address differences between affiliated keywords, target objects, claim types, and authority. We proposed a model that can be set up rather simply, but can be extended, as the complexity of the system requires that.

### Sustainability

Sustainability is defined as the ongoing ability to meet the objectives of a system, organization, or project. In our process description, we describe how from the analysis of core-processes and community objectives, we define what could be part of the reputation system. A well-designed reputation system is able to motivate people, increase trust, and gives insight into the quality of a community as a whole or a single entity in specific. Motivation is concerned with the individuals and their willingness to participate as well as the intention of the system to motivate certain (preferential) behavior. The various weights we introduced allow for configuration of the model to support or counter certain behavior. Scalability was defined as the ability of a system to grow when needed or to handle growing amounts of interactions. In our analysis, we relate this with the level of dependence on people to maintain a system. A central element of the reputation model is its emphasis on the utilization of logs and available information about processes and interactions, not on asking people to do something extra.

## EVALUATION FRAMEWORK

Evaluation must be part of the design of a system from the beginning. It is impossible to design a perfect system. Feedback and analysis is the basis for each new design phase. We suggest a number of issues and questions for framing the evaluation of the system, aimed at improvement and further implementation (rather than initial design requirements). The evaluation framework is structured according to the earlier quality/context/sustainability framework.

### Quality and Context

- **Quality of the system:** the quality of the system and the reputation profiles it produces can be evaluated in different ways. First the produced profiles should be analyzed using historical data, the perceptions of the users themselves, and validated using other reputation approaches. Because there is little interpretation in the proposed system, and mainly the aggregation, the only way to influence the results are by establishing different weights. As said, these can be the result of content analysis, collaborative filtering or trust techniques, or just agreed upon by the users.
- **Context and transitivity:** how specific are the generated reputation profiles, and how does this influence the transitivity?

This depends on the quality of how well the context is defined of digital objects and users and relates to the keyword management system.

- **Gaming the system:** is the system easy to game, and how can this be countered?
- **Learning:** the quality of the system clearly depends on the benefits it brings to the learning process. Therefore, we must measure the quality and availability of information and information producers. Hence, this includes the willingness of individuals to answer questions or publish their experiences.
- **Professional benefits:** this concerns the trust and acceptance by employers, coworkers, and third parties. Also, increased visibility of useful content and people can be measured.

### Sustainability

Sustainability of a peer-based learning community depends on the motivation or engagement of its members to contribute. Evaluation should focus on the measurement of motivation of individuals to contribute and to be engaged in the main processes of knowledge sharing and learning processes. Also, a cost-benefit analysis can be made to estimate the potential of the system. This can be divided into initial and ongoing costs:

- **Initial costs**
  - Analysis of the existing organizational structures and processes concerned with knowledge sharing (within the boundaries of the prospected system).
  - Describing design requirements and functional design of the reputation system based on the analysis.
  - Evaluation of the design requirements amongst stakeholders, and development of the actual technical system and algorithms.
  - Implementation and support.
- **Ongoing costs**
  - Development and implementation of changes in the technical system (based on feedback or changes in the environment).
  - Communication about the benefits of the system and promoting it to various stakeholders.
  - Costs for dispute settlement, updating the reputation ontology, algorithms, etc.

For the development of a reputation system, it is wise to start small, test, and improve in various sequential phases. In addition to retrieving information about the usefulness, quality or failure of a system, this also engages a core group of people to make use of the system. This group of people may be very useful in a further stage. Communicating the potential and long-term benefits of the system to stakeholders is also very important. They decide about the social, financial and technical support for the system and must therefore know about its potential (i.e. motivation of employees, self-organization, peer-based learning, etc.).

## FUTURE RESEARCH DIRECTIONS

Centralized approaches in knowledge management usually fail (Benbya & Van Alstyne, 2010) and centralized approaches in education are unable to cope with the increasing demand for high-quality education worldwide (Schmidt, Geith, Håklev, & Thierstein, 2009). Self-organization of knowledge management and learning is a promising approach to tackle problems in centralized environments, but is only possible with supporting technologies. Recommender systems play an essential role in supporting learners and matching people with others and with relevant content. Reputation information and profiles can be used as an input for recommender systems, and as an alternative for traditional methods of recognition, such as diplomas. In the context of this book, we propose a reputation system that monitors and aggregates the interactions and contributions of individuals in online communities to get an idea of where knowledge resides in the network. The proposed reputation model is a generic model that can be made community-specific. Through observation and interviewing community members, processes, weights, and objects can be defined that represent the reputation and knowledge management processes. This process of designing, implementing, calibrating, and improving a reputation system based on the model brings up many interesting research topics. The model itself provides a good way to structure and research these questions. We define a number of relevant topics below.

## Target and Source Objects

Popular frameworks and models that describe knowledge and learning, such as Bloom's taxonomy or more recent descriptions (Furst, 1981; Illeris, 2003; Siemens, 2005), or learning and knowledge processes in organizations (N. K. Kakabadse, A. Kakabadse, & Kouzmin, 2003; Ley, Kump, & Albert, 2010; Savery & Duffy, 2001; Schreiber, Wielinga, de Hoog, Akkermans, & Van de Velde, 2002), can be used to guide the initial structure for describing the set of source and target objects. If the objects are described using such a framework, there is more insight into the meaning of interactions in terms of learning, sharing expertise or acquiring competencies. Importantly, it will also enable the separation of knowledge and skills, which could influence the character of the proposed model. It will also give insight into ways to evaluate the learning.

Collaborative Filtering (CF) techniques can be used to further interpret the data generated by the proposed reputation model. The specific information about people and their contributed objects, contextualized using keywords and rated by users (implicitly and explicitly), can be used as input in various user-based and content-based CF techniques (X. Su & Khoshgoftaar, 2009). Effective recommender systems for learning take into account the context of the learner and the context of use (Drachsler, Hummel, & Koper, 2008). Literature on educational recommender systems can be used to improve the description of the set of source and target objects, such that it can become useful for recommender systems using collaborative filtering techniques.

If we look at target objects, the group, community or organization itself and the system can be considered targets as well. If we look at a group or organization, belonging to that group has significance as well in terms of reputation (Tadelis, 2003). Just as we now consider students from Harvard as being exceptional gifted (because of Harvard's reputation), we will have similar considerations for people having a reputation in highly esteemed online communities. The interesting topic is how to evaluate the reputation of a group as a whole, because individual reputations are derived from that. Possibly, reputation systems will emerge that focus on the reputation of communities as a whole (and their reputation system).

## Claims

Much related to the above is the topic of defining claims and their meaning. As we have proposed, implicit claims should be addressed as well as explicit ones. Whereas the explicit claims are usually expressive, the meaning of implicit claims is not always as clear. Several approaches can be taken to assure the validness of interpretation, including a qualitative approach (asking people about their behavior), or a mathematical approach, where correlation between behavior and more explicit ratings is tested.

Research into the (voting) behavior of people from different backgrounds and cultures is relevant, especially in internationally oriented, large communities (Ardichvili, 2008). Another interesting topic concerns false claims (either too positive or too negative), and many researchers have addressed this in different domains. Yu & Singh for example, propose a deception model that takes false claims into account in the calculation of trust (Yu & Singh, 2003a). Other ways to game the system can be addressed with game-based trust systems (Mui, Mohtashemi, & Halberstadt, 2002).

In the background we discussed trust systems, and explained that they are distinct from our approach. Trust systems can be of use in three ways:

- For evaluating our model, we can compare results from our model with results from a trust model on the same data set. Using Bayesian classifiers or collaborative filtering techniques, it might be possible to locate expertise in a network in another way than according to our proposed model (i.e. based on connections, something that is not included in our model);
- Also, we can use trust metrics to improve or set the weights in the model. The weights can be set manually, but if they relate to dynamic factors, it might be better to establish rules to set them. These rules can be based on trust metrics, as we gave the example above about the deception model.
- The results of our model can be used as an input for collaborative filtering and trust measurement techniques. We do not propose any way to handle the data generated by the model, and there are many opportunities to interpret data for expertise location, trend analysis, and more.

Vector space model, especially the approach suggested by Yu and Singh (Yu & Singh, 2003b), is a classical information retrieval technique that results in similar representations of knowledge/expertise as we have proposed (using weights for expertise). It can therefore be used to evaluate our proposed model.

## Affiliated Keywords

The ability to add keywords (tagging) to online content sparks the discussion about representing and management of knowledge. In our model, we have proposed the term affiliated keyword. Context and content analysis techniques can support the generation and management of affiliated keywords, and thereby our model. Affiliated keywords can be part of a topic-ontology, developed and maintained by the community. Semantic web research provides with tools and standards to develop and even infer ontologies, and expert systems usually adopt context and content based approaches to locate expertise in an organization or online (P. Liu, Curson, & Dew, 2006; Reichling & Wulf, 2009; Stankovic, Wagner, Laublet, & Jovanovic, 2010; Won & Pipek, 2003; Yimam-Seid & Kobsa, 2003). A large amount of work has been done in Natural Language Processing and Information Retrieval techniques, such as Latent Semantic Indexing, term frequency, etc. Such techniques cannot only help the location of domains of expertise in a network, but might even be used to set the affiliated keyword weights. Interesting topics are the discovery or retrieval of affiliated keywords, the semantics of keywords and relationships, and the different approaches of manual versus automatic tagging.

Additional research must be done to model the reputation flow between connected keywords? In other words: if you have a high reputation for keyword 'x', which is part of domain X, what are ways to infer your reputation for A? Hierarchical modeling techniques could be useful here.

## Additional Research Topics

There are more relevant topics that need to be addressed. First of all, there is a large variety of technical implementations for expert recommender systems, based on text, structured data (program code, scientific references or social networks), or different sources of personal data (Reichling &

Wulf, 2009). The model we propose need to be implemented and evaluated, and a comparison of results from different approaches will shed light on the various benefits and drawbacks.

Another relevant and interesting topic is the influence on time on reputation. This is relevant in real life, but how can that be represented in the system? Standards such as e-foaf and weighted interest ontology propose ways to recalculate reputation after each time period based on reinforcement (Aroyo & Houben, 2010).

Obviously, within the context of learning, the relevance of reputation must be analyzed. Things like acceptance, learning effectiveness and motivation, and organizational structure are relevant. Also the characteristics of the groups where the proposed model is deployed should be measured, because group size, number of interactions, offline reputation, organizational embedding, and heterogeneity possibly influence the usefulness and acceptance of the proposed model.

## CONCLUSION

First, it elaborates on changes in the learning landscape, and describes the need for self-organized and peer-based learning environments to overcome problems intrinsic to centralized learning environments concerning knowledge management, access, and flexibility. In this context we focus on the relevance of reputation to recognize and increase trust in people and quality of content. Based on literature analysis, we argue that a successful reputation system in a learning environment must address at least challenges of quality, context, and sustainability. Using these three elements, we examine a number of successful online reputation systems and mechanisms. Based on these systems, we elicit basic design requirements for a reputation system to support peer-based learning in online communities. The proposed reputation model can be used to develop custom reputation systems in peer-based learning environments, and includes the algorithms needed to automatically generate reputation profiles. In addition, we propose a method to implement and develop of the reputation model in an organizational context, and an evaluation framework to evaluate and improve the reputation system. Finally, using constituents of the proposed reputation model, we formulated a number of relevant research issues and questions.

The proposed reputation model must be tested to prove its value. We prepared this phase in this chapter, by not only providing the algorithms, but also the design, implementation, and evaluation processes. Further research will focus on testing the applicability and quality of the model.

## ACKNOWLEDGMENT

The lead author would like to thank Job Timmermans (Delft University of Technology) for all inspiring conversations about the concept of quality and knowledge sharing in online communities. His ideas were essential for the development of the reputation model proposed in this chapter.

## REFERENCES

Abdul-Rahman, A., & Hailes, S. (2000). Supporting trust in virtual communities. *Proceedings of the 33rd Annual Hawaii International Conference on System Sciences*, (p. 9). IEEE Comput. Soc. doi: 10.1109/HICSS.2000.926814.

Amory, A., & Seagram, R. (2003). Educational game models: Conceptualization and evaluation. *South African Journal of Higher Education*, *17*(2), 206–217.

Ardichvili, A. (2008). Learning and knowledge sharing in virtual communities of practice: Motivators, barriers, and enablers. *Advances in Developing Human Resources*, *10*(4), 541–554. .doi:10.1177/1523422308319536

Aroyo, L., & Houben, G. J. (2010). User modeling and adaptive Semantic Web. *Semantic Web, 1*(1), 105–110. IOS Press. doi: 10.3233/SW-2010-0006

Ba, S. (2001). Establishing online trust through a community responsibility system. *Decision Support Systems, 31*(3), 323–336. .doi:10.1016/S0167-9236(00)00144-5

Benbya, H., & Van Alstyne, A. (2010). How to find answers within your company. *MIT Sloan Management Review, 52*(2), 65–75.

Berlanga, A., Rusman, E., Bitter-Rijpkema, M., & Sloep, P. (2009). Guidelines to foster interaction in online communities. In R. Koper (Ed.), *Learning network services for professional development* (pp. 27-42). Berlin, Germany: Springer. doi: 10.1007/978-3-642-00978-5_3

Brin, S., & Page, L. (1998). The anatomy of a large-scale hypertextual Web search engine. *Computer Networks and ISDN Systems, 30*(1-7), 107-117. Elsevier. doi: 10.1.1.109.4049

Brown, J. S., & Adler, R. P. (2008). Minds on fire: Open education, the long tail, and learning 2.0. [Educause.]. *EDUCAUSE Review, 43*(1), 16.

Bruner, J. (1991). The narrative construction of reality. [JSTOR.]. *Critical Inquiry, 18*(1), 1–21. doi:10.1086/448619

Burke, M., Marlow, C., & Lento, T. (2009). Feed me: Motivating newcomer contribution in social network sites. *Proceedings of the 27th International Conference on Human Factors in Computing Systems* (pp. 945–954). ACM.

Downes, S. (2005). E-learning 2.0. *eLearn, 2005*(10), 1. doi: 10.1145/1104966.1104968.

Downes, S. (2008). Places to go: Connectivism & connective knowledge. *Innovate, 5*(1), 6.

Drachsler, H. (2009). *Navigation support for learners in informal learning networks*. SIKS Dissertation Series.

Drachsler, H., Hummel, H. G. K., & Koper, R. (2008). Personal recommender systems for learners in lifelong learning networks: The requirements, techniques and model. [Inderscience.]. *International Journal of Learning Technology, 3*(4), 404–423. doi:10.1504/IJLT.2008.019376

Farmer, F. R., & Glass, B. (2010). *Building Web reputation systems* (Treseler, M. E., & Dimant, L., Eds.). O'Reilly Media.

Furst, E. J. (1981). Bloom's taxonomy of educational objectives for the cognitive domain: Philosophical and educational issues. *Review of Educational Research, 51*(4), 441–453. doi:. doi:10.3102/00346543051004441

Gal-Oz, N., Grinshpoun, T., Gudes, E., & Meisels, A. (2008). Cross-community reputation: Policies and alternatives. *IADIS Int. Conf. on Web Based Communities (WBC2008)* (pp. 197-201).

Gambetta, D. (2000). Can we trust trust? In D. Gambetta (Ed.), *Trust: Making and breaking cooperative relations* (pp. 213-237). doi: 10.1.1.24.5695.

Golbeck, J., & Hendler, J. (2004). Accuracy of metrics for inferring trust and reputation in Semantic Web-based social networks. *Lecture Notes in Computer Science*.

Hoisl, B., Aigner, W., & Miksch, S. (2007). Social rewarding in Wiki systems – Motivating the community. In Schuler, D. (Ed.), *Online communities and social computing* (pp. 362–371). Berlin, Germany: Springer. doi:10.1007/978-3-540-73257-0_40

Hout-Wolters, B. V., Simons, R., & Volet, S. (2000). *Active learning: Self-directed learning and independent work* (pp. 21–36). Kluwer Academic Publishers.

Huizing, A. (2007). The value of a rose: Rising above objectivism and subjectivism. *Working Papers on Information Systems, 7*(11), 25. Amsterdam.

Illeris, K. (2003). Towards a contemporary and comprehensive theory of learning. [Routledge.]. *International Journal of Lifelong Education, 22*(4), 396–406. doi:10.1080/02601370304837

Jøsang, A. (2007). Trust and reputation systems. In Aldini, R., & Gorrieri, R. (Eds.), *Foundations of security analysis and design 2006/2007* (*Vol. 2006*, pp. 209–245). Berlin, Germany: Springer-Verlag.

Jøsang, A., Ismail, R., & Boyd, C. (2007). A survey of trust and reputation systems for online service provision. *Decision Support Systems, 43*(2). doi:10.1016/j.dss.2005.05.019

Kakabadse, N. K., Kakabadse, A., & Kouzmin, A. (2003). Reviewing the knowledge management literature: Towards a taxonomy. *Journal of Knowledge Management*, 7(4), 75–91. .doi:10.1108/13673270310492967

Kamvar, S. D., Schlosser, M. T., & Garcia-Molina, H. (2003). The Eigentrust algorithm for reputation management in P2P networks. *Proceedings of the Twelfth International Conference on World Wide Web - WWW '03*, (p. 640). New York, NY: ACM Press. doi: 10.1145/775152.775242

Kinateder, M., & Rothermel, K. (2003). Architecture and algorithms for a distributed reputation system. [Springer.]. *Lecture Notes in Computer Science*, 1–16. doi:10.1007/3-540-44875-6_1

Kollock, P. (1997). The economies of online cooperation: Gifts and public goods in cyberspace. In Smith, M. A., & Kollock, P. (Eds.), *Communities in cyberspace* (pp. 220–239). New York, NY: Routledge.

Lave, J. (1988). *Cognition in practice: Mind, mathematics, and culture in everyday life*. Cambridge Univ Pr. doi:10.1017/CBO9780511609268

Lave, J., & Wenger, E. (1991). *Situated learning: Legitimate peripheral participation*. Cambridge Univ Pr.

Lemire, D., Downes, S., & Paquet, S. (2008). *Diversity in open social networks*. Retrieved February 15, 2011, from http://www.daniel-lemire.com/fr/documents/publications/DiversityTechReport_October2008.pdf

Lewandowski, D., & Höchstötter, N. (2008). *Web searching: A quality measurement perspective. Web Search* (pp. 309–340). Springer.

Ley, T., Kump, B., & Albert, D. (2010). A methodology for eliciting, modelling, and evaluating expert knowledge for an adaptive work-integrated learning system. *International Journal of Human-Computer Studies, 68*(4), 185-208. Elsevier. doi: 10.1016/j.ijhcs.2009.12.001

Lim, S. N., Keung, C., & Griffiths, N. (2010). Trust and reputation. In N. Griffiths & K.-M. Chao (Eds.), *Agent-based service-oriented computing* (pp. 189-224). London, UK: Springer. doi: 10.1007/978-1-84996-041-0

Lin, C.-L., & Kao, H.-Y. (2010). Blog popularity mining using social interconnection analysis. *IEEE Internet Computing, 14*(4), 41–49. doi:. doi:10.1109/MIC.2010.51

Liu, P., Curson, J., & Dew, P. (2006). *Exploring RDF for expertise matching within an organizational memory. Advanced Information Systems Engineering* (pp. 100–116). Springer.

Liu, Y., Gao, B., Liu, T. Y., Zhang, Y., Ma, Z., He, S., et al. (2008). BrowseRank: Letting web users vote for page importance. *Proceedings of the 31st Annual International ACM SIGIR Conference on Research and Development in Information Retrieval* (p. 451–458). ACM.

Mackness, J., Mak, S. F. J., & Williams, R. (2010). The ideals and reality of participating in a MOOC. In L. Dirckinck-Holmfeld, V. Hodgson, C. Jones, M. de Laat, D. McConnell, & T. Ryberg (Eds.), *Proceedings of the 7th International Conference on Networked Learning* (pp. 266-274).

Malone, T., & Laubacher, R. (1998). The E-lance economy. *Harvard Business Review*, *76*(September - October), 145–152.

McCalla, G. (2004). The ecological approach to the design of e-learning environments: Purpose-based capture and use of information about learners. *Journal of Interactive Media in Education*, *7*(May), 1–23.

Meiszner, A., Glott, R., & Sowe, S. (2008). Free/Libre open source software (FLOSS) communities as an example of open participatory learning ecosystems. *UPGRADE*, *9*(3), 62–69.

Moore, T. D., & Serva, M. A. (2007). Understanding member motivation for contributing to different types of virtual communities: A proposed framework. *Proceedings of the 2007 ACM SIGMIS CPR Conference on Computer Personnel Research: The global Information Technology Workforce* (p. 153–158). New York, NY: ACM. doi: http://doi.acm.org/10.1145/1235000.1235035

Mui, L., Mohtashemi, M., & Halberstadt, A. (2002). Notions of reputation in multi-agents systems. *Proceedings of the First International Joint Conference on Autonomous Agents and Multiagent Systems Part 1 - AAMAS '02* (pp. 280-287). New York, NY: ACM Press. doi: 10.1145/544741.544807

Noorian, Z., & Ulieru, M. (2010). The state of the art in trust and reputation systems: A framework for comparison. *Electronic Commerce Research*, *5*(2), 1–22.

Piaget, J., & Cook, M. (1952). *The origins of intelligence in children*. New York, NY: International Universities Press. doi:10.1037/11494-000

Reichling, T., & Wulf, V. (2009). Expert recommender systems in practice: Evaluating semi-automatic profile generation. *Conference on Human Factors in Computing Systems* (pp. 59-68). Boston, MA.

Resnick, P., Zeckhauser, R., Friedman, E., & Kuwabara, K. (2000). Reputation systems. *Communications of the ACM*, *43*(12), 45–48. doi:10.1145/355112.355122

Resnick, P., Zeckhauser, R., Swanson, J., & Lockwood, K. (2006). The value of reputation on eBay: A controlled experiment. [Springer.]. *Experimental Economics*, *9*(2), 79–101. doi:10.1007/s10683-006-4309-2

Sabater, J., & Sierra, C. (2005). Review on computational trust and reputation models. *Artificial Intelligence Review*, *24*(1), 33–60. .doi:10.1007/s10462-004-0041-5

Savery, J. R., & Duffy, T. M. (2001). Problem based learning: An instructional model and its constructivist framework. In Wilson, B. G. (Ed.), *Constructivist learning environments: Case studies in instructional design* (pp. 135–151).

Schmidt, J., Geith, C., Håklev, S., & Thierstein, J. (2009). Peer-to-peer recognition of learning in open education. *International Review of Research in Open and Distance Learning*, *10*(5).

Schreiber, G., Wielinga, B., de Hoog, R., Akkermans, H., & Van de Velde, W. (2002). CommonKADS: A comprehensive methodology for KBS development. [IEEE.]. *IEEE Expert*, *9*(6), 28–37. doi:10.1109/64.363263

Siemens, G. (2005). Connectivism - A learning theory for the digital age. [Citeseer.]. *International Journal of Instructional Technology and Distance Learning*, *2*(1), 3–10.

Siemens, G. (2006). *Knowing knowledge*. Lulu.com.

Soekijad, M., & Huis in 't Veld, M. a a, & Enserink, B. (2004). Learning and knowledge processes in inter-organizational communities of practice. *Knowledge and Process Management*, *11*(1), 3–12. .doi:10.1002/kpm.191

Squazzoni, F. (2004). Review of reputation in artificial societies: Social beliefs for social order. *Journal of Artificial Societies and Social Simulation, 7*(3). Retrieved October 28, 2010, from http://jasss.soc.surrey.ac.uk/7/3/reviews/squazzoni.html

Stahl, G. (2003). Meaning and interpretation in collaboration. In B. Wasson, S. Ludvigsen, & U. Hoppe (Eds.), *Designing for Change in Networked Learning Environments: Proceedings of the International Conference on Computer Support for Collaborative Learning (CSCL '03)* (pp. 523-532). Bergen, Norway: Kluwer Academic Publishers.

Stankovic, M., Wagner, C., Laublet, P., & Jovanovic, J. (2010). *Looking for experts? What can linked data do for you?* LDOW2010. Raleigh, USA.

Su, X., & Khoshgoftaar, T. M. (2009). A survey of collaborative filtering techniques. *Advances in Artificial Intelligence, 2009*(Section 3), 1-20. doi: 10.1155/2009/421425

Tadelis, S. (2003). Firm reputation with hidden information. [Springer.]. *Economic Theory, 21*(2), 635–651. doi:10.1007/s00199-002-0257-z

Tan, Y.-H., & Thoen, W. (2000). Towards a generic model of trust in electronic commerce. *International Journal of Electronic Commerce, 5*(2), 61–74.

Tang, J., Zhang, J., Jin, R., Yang, Z., Cai, K., & Zhang, L. (2010). Topic level expertise search over heterogeneous networks. *Machine Learning, 82*(2), 211–237. .doi:10.1007/s10994-010-5212-9

Tuomi, I. (2007). Learning in the age of networked intelligence. *European Journal of Education, 42*(2), 235–254. .doi:10.1111/j.1465-3435.2007.00297.x

Vu, L.-H., Papaioannou, T. G., & Aberer, K. (2009). Synergies of different reputation systems: Challenges and opportunities. *2009 World Congress on Privacy, Security, Trust and the Management of e-Business* (pp. 218-226). Saint John, Canada: IEEE Computer Society. doi: http://doi.ieeecomputersociety.org/10.1109/CONGRESS.2009.8

Vuorikari, R., Manouselis, N., & Duval, E. (2006). Using metadata for storing, sharing, and reusing evaluations in social recommendation: The case of learning resources. In Go, D. H., & Foo, S. (Eds.), *Social information retrieval systems: Emerging technologies and applications for searching the web effectively*. Hershey, PA: Idea Group Publishing.

Vygotsky, L. S. (1978). In Cole, M., John-Steiner, V., Scribner, S., & Souberman, E. (Eds.), *Mind in society: The development of higher psychological processes* (p. 91). Cambridge, MA: Harvard University Press.

Wang, Y. (2005). An overview of online trust: Concepts, elements, and implications. *Computers in Human Behavior, 21*(1), 105–125. .doi:10.1016/j.chb.2003.11.008

Wenger, E. (2000). Communities of practice and social learning systems. *Organization, 7*(2), 225–246. doi:10.1177/135050840072002

Wiley, D. A., & Edwards, E. K. (2002). Online self-organizing social systems: The decentralized future of online learning. *Quarterly Review of Distance Education, 3*(1), 33.

Wolpers, M., Najjar, J., Verbert, K., & Duval, E. (2007). Tracking actual usage: The attention metadata approach. *Journal of Educational Technology & Society, 10*(3), 106–121.

Won, M., & Pipek, V. (2003). Sharing knowledge on knowledge - The eXact peripheral expertise awareness system. *Journal of Universal Computer Science, 9*(12), 1388–1397. doi:.doi:10.3217/jucs-009-12-1388

Yimam-Seid, D., & Kobsa, A. (2003). Expert-finding systems for organizations: Problem and domain analysis and the DEMOIR approach. *Journal of Organizational Computing and Electronic Commerce*, *13*(1), 1–24. doi:10.1207/S15327744JOCE1301_1

Yu, B., & Singh, M. P. (2003a). Detecting deception in reputation management. *Proceedings of the Second International Joint Conference on Autonomous Agents and Multiagent Systems - AAMAS '03* (p. 73). New York, NY: ACM Press. doi: 10.1145/860575.860588

Yu, B., & Singh, M. P. (2003b). Searching social networks. *Proceedings of the Second International Joint Conference on Autonomous Agents and Multiagent Systems* (p. 72). New York, NY: ACM. doi: 10.1145/860586.860587

## ADDITIONAL READING

Berlanga, A., Bitter-Rijpkema, M., Brouns, F., & Sloep, Pb. (2008). On the importance of personal profiles to enhance social interaction in Learning Networks. In P. Kommers (Ed.), *Proceedings of Web Based Communities Conference (WEBC 2008)* (pp. 55-62). Amsterdam: IADIS Press.

Bollen, J., Rodriguez, M. A., & Van de Sompel, H. (2006). Journal status. *Scientometrics*, *69*(3), 669–687. .doi:10.1007/s11192-006-0176-z

Breslin, J., & Decker, S. (2007). The Future of Social Networks on the Internet: The Need for Semantics. *IEEE Internet Computing, 11*(6), 86-90. IEEE Computer Society. doi: 10.1109/MIC.2007.138.

Brown, J. (2002). The Social Life of Learning: How can Continuing Education be Reconfigured in the Future? *Continuing Higher Education Review*, *66*, 50–69.

Carter, J., Bitting, E., & Ghorbani, A. (2002). Reputation formalization within information sharing multiagent architectures. *Computational Intelligence*, 1-21. doi: doi://10.1.1.16.1665.

Casare, S., & Sichman, J. (2005). Towards a functional ontology of reputation. [ACM.]. *AAMAS, 05*, 505–511. doi:10.1145/1082473.1082550

Conte, R., & Paolucci, M. (Eds.). (2002). *Reputation in artificial societies: social beliefs for social order* (p. 208). Dordrecht: Kluwer Academic Publishers.

Dörner, C., Pipek, V., & Won, M. (2007). *Supporting expertise awareness: finding out what others know. CHIMIT'07*. ACM.

Downes, S. (2004). Resource profiles. *Journal of Interactive Media in Education*, (May): 1–32. Retrieved from http://www-jime.open.ac.uk/2004/5/downes-2004-5.pdf.

Downes, S. (2005). Semantic networks and social networks. *The Learning Organization*, *12*(5), 411–417. .doi:10.1108/09696470510700394

Farmer, F. R., & Glass, B. (2010). *Building Web Reputation Systems*. O'Reilly Media.

Gal-Oz, N., Grinshpoun, T., Gudes, E., & Meisels, A. (2008). Cross-Community Reputation: Policies and alternatives. *IADIS Int. Conf. on Web Based*, 197-201.

Golbeck, Jennifer, & Hendler, James. (2004). Accuracy of Metrics for Inferring Trust and Reputation in Semantic Web-based Social Networks. *Lecture Notes in Computer Science*.

Golbeck, J., Parsia, B., & Hendler, J. (2003). Trust networks on the semantic web. [Springer.]. *Cooperative Information Agents, VII*, 238–249.

Halpin, H. (2006). Identity, reference, and meaning on the web. *Proceedings of the Workshop on Identity, Meaning and the Web (IMW06) at WWW2006*. Edinburgh, Scotland: Citeseer.

Harel, D., & Rumpe, B. (2004). Meaningful Modeling: What's the Semantics of "Semantics"?. *Computer*, (October), 64-72. doi: 0018-9162/04.

Josang, A. (2007). Trust and Reputation Systems. In Aldini, R., & Gorrieri, R. (Eds.), *FOSAD 2006/2007* (pp. 209–245). Heidelberg: Springer-Verlag.

Kollock, P. (1998). Social Dilemmas: The Anatomy of Cooperation. *Annual Review of Sociology*, *24*(1), 183–214. .doi:10.1146/annurev.soc.24.1.183

McAlpine, M. (2005). E-portfolios and Digital Identity: some issues for discussion. *E-learning*, *2*(4), 378. .doi:10.2304/elea.2005.2.4.378

McLure-Wasko, M., & Faraj, S. (2005). Why Should I Share? Examining Social Capital and Knowledge Contribution in Electronic Networks of Practice. *Management Information Systems Quarterly*, *29*(1).

Neylon, C., & Wu, S. (2009). Article-level metrics and the evolution of scientific impact. *PLoS Biol.*

Ochoa, X., & Duval, E. (2006). Use of contextualized attention metadata for ranking and recommending learning objects. *Workshop on Contextualized Attention Metadata.*

Preece, J., & Maloney-Krichmar, D. (2003). Online communities: focusing on sociability and usability. In Jacko, J., & Sears, A. (Eds.), *Handbook of human-computer interaction* (pp. 596–620). Mahwah, New Jersey: Lawrence Erlbaum Associates Inc. Publishers.

Rusman, E., Bruggen, J. V., Sloep, P., & Valcke, M. (2010). The Mind's Eye on Personal Profiles; How to Inform Initial Trustworthiness Assessments in Virtual Project Teams. *CRIWG'10*. Maastricht, the Netherlands.

Schmidt, J., Geith, C., Håklev, S., & Thierstein, J. (2009). Peer-To-Peer Recognition of Learning in Open Education. *International Review of Research in Open and Distance Learning*, *10*(5).

Shadbolt, N., Berners-Lee, T., & Hall, W. (2006). The Semantic Web Revisited. *IEEE Intelligent Systems*, *21*(3), 96–101. .doi:10.1109/MIS.2006.62

Vu, L.-H., Papaioannou, T. G., & Aberer, K. (2009). Synergies of Different Reputation Systems: Challenges and Opportunities. *2009 World Congress on Privacy, Security, Trust and the Management of e-Business* (pp. 218-226). Saint John, Canada: IEEE Computer Society. doi: http://doi.ieeecomputersociety.org/10.1109/CONGRESS.2009.8.

Wiley, D. A., & Edwards, E. K. (2002). Online self-organizing social systems: The decentralized future of online learning. *Quarterly Review of Distance Education*, *3*(1), 33.

Zimmerman, B. (2000). Attaining self-regulation: A social cognitive perspective. In Boekaerts, M., Pintrich, P., & Zeidner, M. (Eds.), *Handbook of self-regulation* (pp. 13–40).

## KEY TERMS AND DEFINITIONS

**Context:** Is infinite. In this chapter, we have two types of context. The first type is defined as the factors that influence the reputation statement, such as authority, location or time. The other type concerns the topical analysis of an information object or person: what is it about or what is his/her expertise?

**Peer-Based Learning:** Active, self-directed, and self-organized learning in online communities. There is no top-down structure or extrinsic incentive for members of communities to participate in the learning process and help each other. Therefore, they rely on intrinsic motivations, such as interest, recognition, and reputation.

**Quality:** Like beauty, is in the eye of the beholder, but some beholders have better eyes. In knowledge-based systems, the quality, impact, or usefulness of an information object can be better assessed by someone who has expertise about topics of the object than a layman. In this chapter, we focus on the quality of a person or object to support peer-based learning (such as by sharing knowledge). The quality is contextualized to specific areas of expertise and skills.

**Reputation:** Information used to make a value judgment about an object or person. In this chapter, reputation of an object (or person) is the contextual value as perceived by the community or organization where the object is used.

**Sustainability:** The ongoing ability to meet the objectives of an organization, project, or system. In peer-based learning environments it concerns the ability to motivate and support learners to maintain meaningful interactions and develop high-quality content in a decentralized fashion.

## ENDNOTE

1 http://www.merriam-webster.com/netdict/trust

# Chapter 6
# Factorization Techniques for Predicting Student Performance

**Nguyen Thai-Nghe**
*University of Hildesheim, Germany*

**Lucas Drumond**
*University of Hildesheim, Germany*

**Tomáš Horváth**
*University of Hildesheim, Germany*

**Artus Krohn-Grimberghe**
*University of Hildesheim, Germany*

**Alexandros Nanopoulos**
*University of Hildesheim, Germany*

**Lars Schmidt-Thieme**
*University of Hildesheim, Germany*

## ABSTRACT

*Recommender systems are widely used in many areas, especially in e-commerce. Recently, they are also applied in e-learning for recommending learning objects (e.g. papers) to students. This chapter introduces state-of-the-art recommender system techniques which can be used not only for recommending objects like tasks/exercises to the students, but also for predicting student performance. We formulate the problem of predicting student performance as a recommender system problem and present matrix factorization methods, which are currently known as the most effective recommendation approaches, to implicitly take into account the prevailing latent factors (e.g. "slip" and "guess") for predicting student performance. As a learner's knowledge improves over time, too, we propose tensor factorization methods to take the temporal effect into account. Finally, some experimental results and discussions are provided to validate the proposed approach.*

DOI: 10.4018/978-1-61350-489-5.ch006

## INTRODUCTION

Recommender systems are widely used in many areas, especially in e-commerce (Rendle, Freudenthaler, and Schmidt-Thieme, 2010). One of their main aims is to make vast catalogs of products consumable by learning user preferences and to apply them to items formerly unknown to the user. Thus they can learn which products have a high likelihood of being interesting to the target user. Recently, recommender systems have also been applied to e-learning, especially in technology enhanced learning (Manouselis, Drachsler, Vuorikari, Hummel, and Koper, 2010).

On the other hand, educational data mining has also been taken into account recently to assist the students in the learning process. One of the main educational data mining tasks, for instance, is to predict student performance. It is applicable when we would like to know how the students learn (e.g. generally or narrowly), how quickly or slowly they adapt to new problems or if it is possible to infer the knowledge requirements to solve the problems directly from student performance data (Feng, Heffernan, and Koedinge, 2009). Generally speaking, the prediction of student performance is the problem of predicting the student's ability (e.g., estimated by a score metric) in solving tasks when interacting with a tutoring system. Cen, Koedinger, and Junker (2006) have shown that an improved model for predicting student performance could save millions of hours of students' time and effort in learning algebra that they could otherwise have spent on other subjects or leisure. Moreover, many universities are extremely focused on assessment, thus, the pressure on teaching and learning for examinations leads to a significant amount of time spent for preparing and taking standardized tests. Any move away from standardized and non-personalized tests holds promise for increasing deep learning (Feng et al., 2009). From an educational data mining point of view, *a good model which accurately predicts student performance could replace some current standardized tests and yield truly personalized, adaptive test.*

To address the student performance prediction problem, many works have been published. Most of them rely on traditional methods such as neural networks (Romero, Ventura, Espejo, and Hervs, 2008), Bayesian networks (Bekele and Menzel, 2005), logistic regression (Cen et al., 2006), support vector machines (Thai-Nghe, Busche, and Schmidt-Thieme, 2009) and so on.

In the recommender system context, predicting student performance can be considered as a rating prediction problem since student, task, and performance information could be treated as user, item, and rating, respectively, which are the main objects recommender systems learn from, nowadays. Recently, Thai-Nghe, Drumond, Krohn-Grimberghe, and Schmidt-Thieme (2010) and Toscher and Jahrer (2010) have proposed the use of recommendation techniques, especially matrix factorization, for predicting student performance. The authors have shown that using recommendation techniques could improve prediction results compared to regression methods (Thai-Nghe et al., 2010) but they have not taken the temporal effect into account. Obviously, in the educational point of view, we always expect that the students (or generally, the learners) can improve their knowledge over time, so temporal information is an important factor for such prediction tasks.

Furthermore, in predicting student performance, two crucial user-dependent aspects need to be taken into account:

1. The probability of a student to guess correctly while not knowing how to solve the problem at hand or not having the required skills related to the problem (which we call "guess" for short); and the probability of a student to fail while knowing how to solve the problem or having all of the required skills related to the problem (which we call "slip" for short);

2. The increase in knowledge over time obviously has an effect on a student's performance, e.g. the second time a student does his exercises, the performance gets better on average, and therefore, the sequential effect is important information.

Factorization techniques are a promising approach for this problem since they *i)* implicitly take into account the latent factors such as "slip" and "guess", and *ii)* incorporate the sequential (time) aspect to their models. Moreover, the importance of the proposed approach is that besides predicting student performance, we can also recommend the similar tasks (exercises) to the students and can determine which tasks are notoriously difficult for a given student. The predicted student performance represents the estimation of a student's performance on a given exercise. For example, there is a huge database of exercises where students lose a lot of time solving problems which are too easy or too hard for them. When a system is able to predict their performance, it could recommend more appropriate exercises for them. Thus, we could filter out the tasks with predicted high performance / confidence since these tasks are too easy for them, or filter out the tasks with predicted low performance (too hard for them) or both, depending on the goals of the e-learning system. As mentioned in the literature, recommender systems for educational purposes are a complex and challenging research direction (Drachsler, Hummel, and Koper, 2009). The preferred learning activities of students might pedagogically not be the most adequate (Tang and McCalla, 2004) and recommendations in e-learning should be guided by educational objectives, and not only by the user's preferences (Santos and Boticario, 2010). *Our approach which uses student performance prediction for the recommendation of e-learning tasks would be a promising approach to tackle the above problems since we can recommend the tasks for students based on their performance but not on their preferences.*

Please note that in this chapter we have not focused on building a real system, e.g. how the system interface looks like or which particular objects are recommended, but on how to apply the state-of-the-art recommender system techniques to generate the most accurate performance estimation.

More precisely, the purposes of this chapter are to

- formulate the problem of predicting student performance in the context of recommender systems;
- propose matrix factorization models for predicting student performance, which are extended from previous works (Thai-Nghe et al., 2010; Toscher and Jahrer, 2010) and presented in a formalized and detailed way that can be helpful for the researchers who come from educational domains. We can empirically show that these factorization techniques can implicitly encode the "slip" and "guess" factors as well as "student effect" (e.g. how clever/good the student is in performing the task) and the "task effect" (e.g. how hard/easy the task is in general) in predicting student performance;
- propose tensor factorization techniques to take into account the temporal effect, e.g. how the knowledge of the learners improves over time;
- map the student performance data from two real data sets to recommender system context;
- experiment with the proposed approach and compare with some other baselines.

## BACKGROUND

In the area of recommender systems for technology enhanced learning (Manouselis et al., 2010), almost all the works are focused on the construction of recommender systems for recommendation of learning resources (materials/ resources) or learning activities to the learners (Ghauth and Abdullah, 2010; Manouselis et al., 2010) in both formal and informal learning environments (Drachsler et al., 2009). More precisely, Garcia, Romero, Ventura, and Castro (2009) use association rule mining to discover interesting information through student performance data in the form of IF-THEN rules, followed by generating recommendations based on those rules; Bobadilla, Serradilla, and Hernando (2009) proposed an equation for collaborative filtering which incorporated the test score from the learners into the item prediction function; Ge, Kong, and Luo (2006) combined the content-based filtering and collaborative filtering to personalize the recommendations for a courseware selection module; Soonthornphisaj, Rojsattarat, and Yim-Ngam (2006) applied collaborative filtering to predict the most suitable documents for the learners; while Khribi, Jemni, and Nasraoui (2008) employed web mining techniques with content-based and collaborative filtering to compute the relevant links for recommending to the learners. This use of recommender systems corresponds to the so-called item recommendation (or item prediction) task in the recommender literature. But what so far is missing in e-learning systems is the exploitation of the recommender systems capability to predict scores – a task called rating prediction.

On the student performance prediction problem, many works have been published, too. Most of them rely on traditional methods. E.g., Romero et al. (2008) compared different data mining methods and techniques (like neural networks, decision trees, etc.) to classify students based on their Moodle usage data and the final marks obtained in their respective courses; Bekele and Menzel (2005) used Bayesian networks to predict student results; Cen et al. (2006) proposed a method for improving a cognitive model, which is a set of rules/skills encoded in intelligent tutors to model how students solve problems, using logistic regression; Thai-Nghe, Janecek, and Haddawy (2007) analyzed and compared some classification methods (e.g. decision trees and Bayesian networks) for predicting academic performance; while Thai-Nghe et al. (2009) proposed to improve the student performance prediction by dealing with the class imbalance problem using support vector machines (i.e., the ratio between passing and failing students is usually skewed).

Although some novel approaches have been proposed for predicting student performance recently, there are still several open issues. So far, the works have just focus on explicit modeling of the "slip" and "guess" latent factors, e.g. using Hidden Markov Models as Pardos and Heffernan (2010) did. Or they deal with thousands of features using feature engineering and hundreds of models stacked together in large ensembles as Yu et al. (2010) proposed. Thus, those suggested approaches need tremendous computational resources and human effort for data pre-processing. Yet, they do not take the temporal effect of the underlying process into account as in Thai-Nghe et al. (2010) and Toscher and Jahrer (2010).

Usually, the mentioned approaches work well when sufficient information is available about the students as well as tasks or learning resources. However, in real-world applications we face the problem of information acquisition as the collection of attributes and metadata about users, tasks and resources is often very expensive or even not possible at all. The information easily obtainable is the results the students yielded on the various tasks they previously worked on. This information could be captured by the {student, task, score} tuple. Interestingly, this is exactly the kind of information, current recommender systems rely on, though in the recommender terminology the above mentioned tuple would be rephrased as {user, item, rating}. This perspective allows two distinct kinds of treatment. First, the so-called "implicit feedback" view where only the information that a specific user (student) as interacted with a given item (task). This can nicely be represented by a binary or even unary matrix on users and items storing those interactions. Second, the "explicit feedback" view where a numerical (preference) value can be obtained as the result of the interaction between user and item. This, too, can be represented as an interaction matrix on users and items. In both cases, however, the resulting matrix will be sparse, as most of the students will tackle only a (small) subset of the tasks / exercises available in the e-learning system.

For recommender systems, the so called collaborative filtering approach prevails since the late nineties. Collaborative filtering is based on the assumption that similar users like similar things and, being content-agnostic, focuses only on the past ratings assigned. Factorization techniques are the most popular collaborative filtering techniques (Koren, Bell, and Volinsky, 2009), used for both item and rating recommendations. Moreover, it has been shown that even a few ratings are often more valuable than metadata (Pilaszy and Tikk, 2009), thus, the use of factorization techniques are in place for recommendation task. In case of sparse data with no additional metadata, the use of collaborative filtering techniques has been shown to be very effective.

Factorization techniques outperform other state-of-the-art collaborative filtering techniques. They belong to the family of latent factor models which aim at mapping users and items to a common latent space by representing them as vectors in that space. The dimensions of this space are called the factors. Here we should mention, that we usually don't now the exact "meaning" of these factors, we are just interested in the correlation between the vectors in that space. For example, imagine a well-known simplified movie rating example where users and movies are mapped to a two-dimensional latent space (Koren et al., 2009). Here, each user and each movie is represented by two factors. These factors can represent genre, seriousness, amount of action, quality of actors or any other concept. Even if we don't know what exactly the given two factors (dimensions of the latent space) represent, the "closeness" of particular user and movie vectors in that space expresses the preference of a given user on the given movie. Thus, we can expect with high certainty that the before mentioned slip and guess factors are somehow encoded in the latent factors of the computed factorization models and we do not need to explicitly take care of them as in case of other methods, e.g. Hidden Markov Models (Pardos and Heffernan, 2010). Other latent characteristics of students and tasks could also be implicitly encoded in the models such as how good the performance of a student is, how hard/easy the task is, etc. Furthermore, by using a tensor with three or more dimensions instead of a matrix we can represent the sequential (time) aspect or any other additional context such as students' skills. As also mentioned Pilaszy and Tikk (2009), the performance of these techniques are very good in case of using just two or three features such as student ID, task ID and/or time. Thus, memory consumption and the human effort in pre-processing can be reduced significantly while the prediction quality is reasonable.

With the recommendation of learning resources, recommender systems already address an important problem in technology enhanced learning. Nonetheless, with rating prediction a highly appreciated capability of recommender systems is so far underexplored in e-learning environments. As we have already seen, all information necessary for recommender systems for both item and rating prediction is available in these systems and could be exploited. Furthermore, we have highlighted the power of recommender systems in addressing latent factors and their excellent runtime characteristics. The remainder of this chapter will proceed to show, how rating prediction can be mapped to predicting student performance.

## PREDICTING STUDENT PERFORMANCE

Figure 1a presents an example (Koedinger et al., 2010) of the task in predicting student performance. Given the circle and the square as in this figure, the task for students could be "What is the remaining area of the square after removing the circular area?"

To solve this task (question), students could do some smaller subtasks which we call a "step". Each step may require one or more skills (or "knowledge components"), for example:

- Step 1: Calculate the circle area ($area_1 = \pi * (OE)^2$)
- Step 2: Calculate the square area ($area_2 = (AB)^2$)
- Step 3: Calculate the remaining ($area_2 - area_1$)

Each solving-step is recorded as a transaction. Figure 1b presents a snapshot of transactions. Based on the past performance, we would like to predict students' next performance (e.g. correct/incorrect) in solving the tasks. To do this we first need to consider the amount and the quality of information we have collected about the students and tasks as well as their interactions. Such data can be collected from some Student Information Systems (SIS) or from the Computer-Aided Tutoring Systems (CATS).

*Figure 1. Predicting student performance - A scenario. (Adapted from PSLCDatashop.web.cmu.edu/KDDCup).*

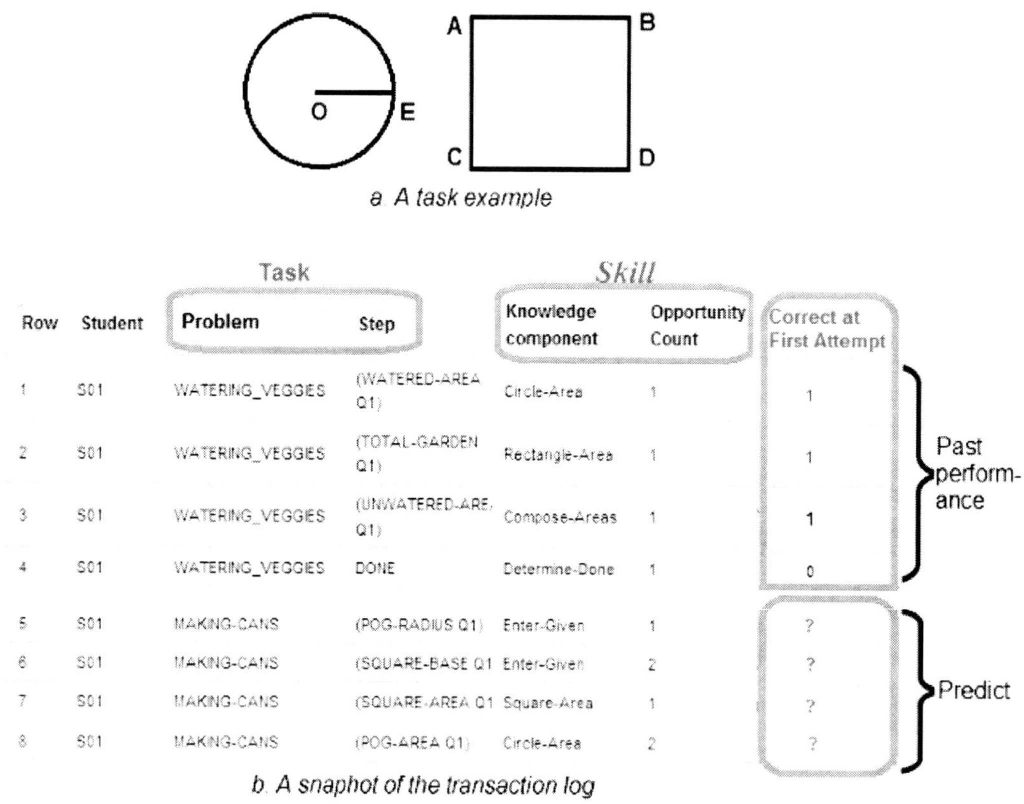

Computer-aided tutoring systems (CATS) allow students to solve some exercises with a graphical front-end that can automate some tedious tasks, provide some hints and provide feedback to the student (Massey, Psotka, and Mutter, 1988). Such systems can profit from anticipating student performance in many ways, e.g., in selecting the right mix of exercises, choosing an appropriate level of difficulty and deciding about possible interventions such as hints. Thus, CATS are valuable environments for collecting data for prediction and for interacting with students in an intelligent way.

## Problem Formulation in the Context of Computer-Aided Tutoring Systems (CATS)

The problem of student performance prediction in CATS is to predict the likely performance of a student for some exercises (or part thereof such as for some particular steps) which we call the tasks. The task could be to solve a particular step in a problem, to solve a whole problem or to solve problems in a section or unit, etc. In CATS, tasks usually are described in two different ways: First, tasks can be located in a topic hierarchy, for example

unit $\supseteq$ section $\supseteq$ problem $\supseteq$ step

Second, tasks can be described by additional meta data such as the skills that are required to solve the problem:

$\text{skill}_1, \text{skill}_2, \ldots, \text{skill}_n$

All this information, the topic hierarchy, skills and other task meta data can be described as attributes of the tasks. In the same way, also attributes about the student may be available.

CATS allow collecting a rich amount of information about how a student interacts with the tutoring system and about his past successes and failures. Usually, such information is collected in a click-stream log with an entry for every action the student takes. The click-stream log may contain many useful information, e.g. about the time, student, context, action.

For performance prediction, such click streams can be aggregated to the task for which the performance should be predicted and eventually be enriched with additional information. For example, if the aim is to predict the performance for each single step in a problem, then all actions in the click-stream log belonging to the same student and problem step will be aggregated to a single transaction and enriched, for example with some performance metrics.

More formally, let $S$ be a set of students, $T$ be a set of tasks, and $P \subseteq \mathbf{R}$ be a range of possible performance scores. Let $M_S$ be a set of student meta data descriptions and $m_S: S \rightarrow M_S$ be the meta data for each student. Let $M_T$ be a set of task meta data descriptions and $m_T: T \rightarrow M_T$ be the meta data for each task. Finally, let $D^{train} \subseteq (S \times T \times P)^*$ be a sequence of observed student performances and $D^{test} \subseteq (S \times T \times P)^*$ be a sequence of unobserved student performances. Furthermore, let

$$\pi_p: S \times T \times P \rightarrow P, (s, t, p) \rightarrow p$$

and

$$\pi_{s,t}: S \times T \times P \rightarrow S \times T, (s, t, p) \rightarrow (s, t)$$

be the projections to the performance measure and to the student/task pair. Then the problem of student performance prediction is, given $D^{train}$, $\pi_{s,t} D^{test}$, $m_S$, and $m_T$ to find

$$\hat{p} = \hat{p}_1, \hat{p}_2, \ldots \hat{p}_{|D^{test}|}$$

such that

$$err(p,\hat{p}) = \sum_{i=1}^{|D^{test}|}(p_i - \hat{p}_i)^2$$

is minimal with $p := \pi_p D^{test}$. Some other error measures could also be considered.

In principle, this is a regression or classification problem (depending on the error measure). Specifically, we have to treat *(i)* two variables, e.g. the student ID and the task ID, both being nominal with many levels (1,000-100,000s), which can be considered as *rating prediction* in recommender systems since *s, t*, and *p* would be user, item and rating, respectively (Thai-Nghe et al., 2010), as illustrated in Figure 2. *Thus, we could apply factorization techniques or other collaborative filtering techniques for this problem*; and (ii) potentially sequential effects which describes how students gain experience over time.

## FACTORIZATION TECHNIQUES

The two most common tasks in recommender systems are Top-N item recommendation where the recommender suggests a ranked list of (at most) N items $i \in I$ to a user $u \in U$ and rating prediction where the aim is predicting the preference score (rating) $r \in \mathbf{R}$ for a given user-item combination.

In this work, we make use of matrix factorization (Rendle and Schmidt-Thieme, 2008; Koren et al., 2009), which is known to be one of the most successful methods for rating prediction, outperforming other state-of-the-art methods (Bell and Koren, 2007) and tensor factorization (Kolda and Bader, 2009; Dunlavy, Kolda, and Acar, 2010) to take the sequential effect into account.

Please note that the techniques presented in this chapter compute the prediction as a linear combination of factors. Although it may happen that in some cases linear combination of factors can be insufficient. In such cases, we can use non-linear extensions of factorization techniques (Lawrence and Urtasun, 2009). However, as showed in Takacs, Pilaszy, Nemeth, and Tikk (2009), using the standard factorization models is enough to reach good prediction accuracy in an efficient and scalable way. The results of this approach in our experiments (provided later in this chapter) as well as the results of experiments in other domains (Koren et al., 2009) constitute some empirical evidence that assuming a linear interaction between the factors is a reasonable approach. The connection of factorization techniques to other methods, such as Neural Networks, can be seen e.g. in Takacs et al. (2009). We will describe the basic matrix and tensor factorization techniques to present the idea behind these approaches. Discus-

*Figure 2. An illustration of casting student/task/performance in PSP as user/item/rating in RecSys*

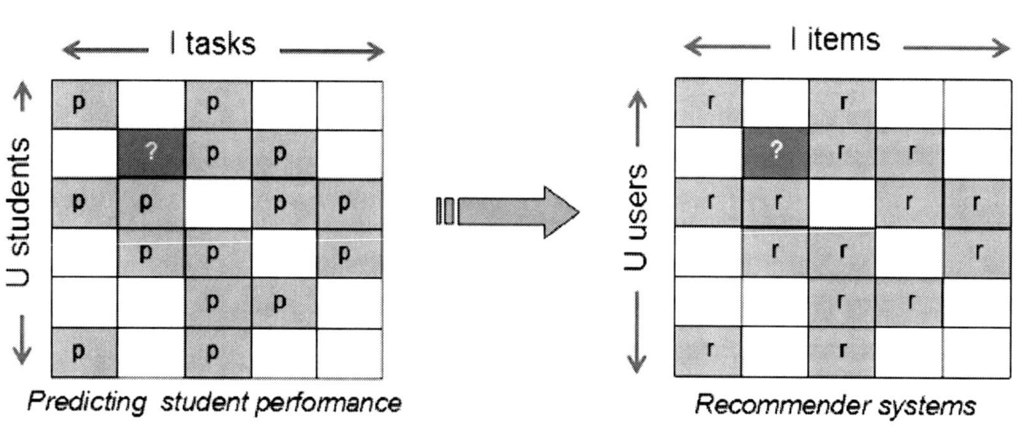

sion of other advanced factorization techniques is out of the scope of this chapter.

*Notation*: A matrix is denoted by a capital italic letter, e.g. $X$; A tensor is denoted by a capital bold letter, e.g. $\mathbf{Z}$; $w_k$ denotes a vector (one index); $w_{uk}$ is the element of a vector (two indices); and $\circ$ denotes an outer product. We denote $p$ as the actual value and $\hat{p}$ as the prediction value. From here to the end of the chapter, we will call *student, task*, and *performance* instead of *user, item*, and *rating*, respectively.

## Matrix Factorization

Matrix factorization is the task of approximating a matrix $X$ by the product of two smaller matrices $W$ and $H$, i.e. $X \sim WH^T$ (Koren et al., 2009). $W \in \mathbf{R}^{U \times K}$ is a matrix where each row $u$ is a vector containing the $K$ latent factors describing the student $u$ and $H \in \mathbf{R}^{I \times K}$ is a matrix where each row $i$ is a vector containing the $K$ factors describing the task $i$. Let $w_{uk}$ and $h_{ik}$ be the elements of $W$ and $H$, respectively, then the performance $p$ given by a student $u$ to a task $i$ is predicted by:

$$\hat{p}_{ui} = \sum_{k=1}^{K} w_{uk} h_{ik} = (WH^T)_{u,i} \tag{1}$$

The main issue of this technique is how to find the optimal parameters $W$ and $H$ (the elements of $W$ and $H$) given a criterion such as root mean squared error (RMSE):

$$RMSE = \sqrt{\frac{\sum_{ui \in D^{test}} (p_{ui} - \hat{p}_{ui})^2}{|D_{test}|}} \tag{2}$$

### Training Phase

In this approach, training the model is finding the optimal parameters $W$ and $H$. One approach is that we first initialize these two matrices with some random values (e.g. from the normal distribution $N(0, \sigma^2)$ with mean is 0 and standard deviation $\sigma^2 = 0.01$), and compute the error function

$$err = \sum_{u,i \in D^{train}} e_{ui}^2 \tag{3}$$

where

$$e_{ui}^2 = (p_{ui} - \hat{p}_{ui})^2 = (p_{ui} - \sum_{k=1}^{K} w_{uk} h_{ik})^2 \tag{4}$$

then try to minimize this error by updating the values of $W$ and $H$ iteratively. Such a method is called gradient descent (Koren et al., 2009). To minimize equation (3), we need to know for each data point in which direction to update the value of $w_{uk}$ and $h_{ik}$. Thus, we compute the gradient of the function (4):

$$\frac{\partial e_{ui}^2}{\partial w_{uk}} = -2e_{ui} h_{ik} = -2(p_{ui} - \hat{p}_{ui}) h_{ik} \tag{5}$$

$$\frac{\partial e_{ui}^2}{\partial h_{ik}} = -2e_{ui} w_{uk} = -2(p_{ui} - \hat{p}_{ui}) w_{uk} \tag{6}$$

After having the gradient, we update the values of $w_{uk}$ and $h_{ik}$ in the direction opposite to the gradient:

$$w'_{uk} = w_{uk} - \beta \frac{\partial e_{ui}^2}{\partial w_{uk}} = w_{uk} + 2\beta e_{ui} h_{ik} \tag{7}$$

$$h'_{ik} = h_{ik} - \beta \frac{\partial e_{ui}^2}{\partial h_{ik}} = h_{ik} + 2\beta e_{ui} w_{uk} \tag{8}$$

where $\beta$ is the learning rate. We iteratively update the values of $W$ and $H$ until the error converges to its minimum or reaching a predefined number of iterations.

*Regularization*: To prevent overfitting, we modify the error function (4) by adding a term which controls the magnitudes of the factor vectors such that $W$ and $H$ would give a good approximation of $X$ without having to contain large numbers. The function (4) now becomes:

$$(p_{ui} - \sum_{k=1}^{K} w_{uk} h_{ik})^2 + \lambda(\|W\|_F^2 + \|H\|_F^2) \qquad (9)$$

where $\lambda$ is a regularization term and $\|\cdot\|_F^2$ is Frobenius norm. With this new error function, the values of $w_{uk}$ and $h_{ik}$ are updated by

$$w'_{uk} = w_{uk} + \beta(2e_{ui}h_{ik} - \lambda w_{uk}) \qquad (10)$$

$$h'_{ik} = h_{ik} + \beta(2e_{ui}w_{uk} - \lambda h_{ik}) \qquad (11)$$

Recall that there are 2 issues that should be taken into account when predicting student performance, namely the "guess" and "slip" factors expressing the probabilities that the students will guess correctly or make a mistake. Matrix factorization techniques are appropriate for handling these issues because these two factors could be implicitly encoded in the latent factors of $W$ and $H$.

Algorithm 1 describes details of training a matrix factorization model using stochastic gradient descent (we use stochastic gradient descent for all algorithms in this chapter since it has been shown that the computing cost of stochastic gradient descent has a huge advantage for large-scale problems (Bottou, 2004)). This method factorizes the student and the task that student wants to solve. First, the parameters W and H are initialized randomly from the normal distribution $\mathbf{N}(0,\sigma^2)$ with mean is 0 and standard deviation $\sigma^2 = 0.01$, as in lines 2-3. For each iteration, we

*Algorithm 1. A matrix factorization for factorizing student and task using stochastic gradient descent with Iter iterations, K factors, $\beta$ learning rate, and $\lambda$ regularization*

```
1: procedure Student-Task-MatrixFactorization(D^Train, Iter, K, β, λ)
Let u ∈ S be a student, i ∈ T a task, p ∈ P a performance score
Let W[|S|][K] and H[|T|][K] be latent factors of students and tasks
2: W:= N(0,σ^2)
3: H:= N(0,σ^2)
4: for (iter:=1; iter <= Iter*D^Train; iter++)
5:          Draw randomly (u, i, p) from D^Train
6:          p^:= 0
7:          for (k:=1; k<=K; k++)
8:                    p^:= p^ + W[u][k]*H[i][k]
9:          end for
10:          e_ui = p - p^
11:          for (k:=1; k<=K; k++)
12:                   W[u][k]:= W[u][k] + β(e_ui * H[i][k] - λ * W[u][k])
13:                   H[i][k]:= H[i][k] + β(e_ui * W[u][k] - λ * H[i][k])
14:          end for
15: end for
16: return {W, H}
17: end procedure
```

randomly select an instance in the training set *(u, i, p)*, then compute the prediction for this student and task, as in lines 5-9. We estimate the error in this iteration and update the values of *W* and *H* as in lines 11-14 (Algorithm 2).

## Prediction Phase

After having the optimal *W* and *H*, the performance of a student *u* for a given task *i* is predicted easily by

*Algorithm 2. A biased matrix factorization for factorizing student and task using stochastic gradient descent with Iter iterations, K factors, β learning rate, and λ regularization*

```
1: procedure Student-Task-Biased-MatrixFactorization(D^Train, Iter, K, β, λ)
          Let u ∈ S be a student, i ∈ T a task, p ∈ P a performance score
          Let W[|S|][K] and H[|T|][K] be latent factors of students and tasks
          Let b_u[|S|] and b_i[|T|] be student bias and task bias
```

2: $\mu := \sum_{p \in \pi_p(D^{Train})} \frac{p}{|D^{Train}|}$

```
3: for each student u do
```

4: $b_u[u] := \frac{\sum_{i \in D^{Train}} (p_{ui} - \mu)}{|D_u^{Train}|}$

```
5: end for
6: for each task i do
```

7: $b_i[i] := \frac{\sum_{u \in D^{Train}} (p_{ui} - \mu)}{|D_i^{Train}|}$

```
8: end for
9:  W:= N(0,σ²)
10: H:= N(0,σ²)
11: for (iter:=1; iter <= Iter*D^Train; iter++)
12:         Draw randomly (u, i, p) from D^Train
```

13: $\hat{p}_{ui} := \mu + b_u[u] + b_i[i] + \sum_{k=1}^{K} (W[u][k] * H[i][k])$

```
14:         e_ui := p_ui - p^_ui
15:         μ:= μ + β*e_ui
16:         b_u[u]:= b_u[u] + β*(e_ui - λ*b_u[u])
17:         b_i[i]:= b_i[i] + β*(e_ui - λ*b_i[i])
18:         for (k:=1; k<=K; k++)
19:                 W[u][k]:= W[u][k] + β(e_ui * H[i][k] - λ * W[u][k])
20:                 H[i][k]:= H[i][k] + β(e_ui * W[u][k] - λ * H[i][k])
21:         end for
22: end for
23: return {W, H, b_u, b_i, μ}
24: end procedure
```

$$\hat{p}_{ui} = \sum_{k=1}^{K} w_{uk} h_{ik} \qquad (12)$$

For the students or tasks in the test set but not in the train set, we return the average performance on the training set (we will discuss more about this later).

## An Example

Figure 3 shows an example of how we can factorize the students and tasks. Suppose that we have 6 students and 5 exercises (tasks) which are presented in matrix *X*. Each task is to compute the values of *y*, e.g. $y = -2x$, given a specific value of *x*. These students have performed some tasks which are measured by correct (1) and incorrect (0) performance. Our problem is to predict the other tasks that they have not done (the empty values in *X*).

Please note that the presented techniques do not depend on specific tasks. Importance is that the matrix represents a relation between two types of objects, which are in our case students and math tasks but any other types of objects can also be used, e.g. students and courses, students and learning objects (books, multimedia..) as well as tasks in other disciplines.

After the training phase with $K = 2$ latent factors, we get the optimized parameters *W* and *H* as in Figure 3. Now, suppose that we would like to predict Mary's performance for the task $y = -x-1$ (the cell with question mark). We can easily compute the prediction using equation (12)

$$\hat{p}_{ui} = \sum_{k=1}^{K} w_{uk} h_{ik} = 0.7 * 0.36 + 0.69 * 0.96 = 0.91$$

From this prediction result, we can see that Mary can correctly answer her task with high confidence (0.91). In a similar way, we can predict the performance of other students in tasks which they have not done yet. Moreover, using this approach, besides predicting student performance, we can also recommend the similar tasks (exercises) to the students. For example, there is a huge database of exercises and that students lose most of their time solving problems which are too easy or too hard for them. By being able to predict their performance, the system could recommend just the appropriate exercises for them. The student performance represents how good the student will perform in a given exercise. Thus, we could filter out the tasks with high performance/confidence since these tasks are too easy for them, or filter out the tasks with low performance (too hard for them) or both, depending on the system goal.

## Biased Matrix Factorization

Besides the basic matrix factorization model, we also employ the biased matrix factorization model to deal with the problem of "user effect" and "item effect", or we can call "user bias" and

*Figure 3. An example of factorizing on students and tasks*

| | y=3x-4 | y=-2x | y=1/x | y=-x-1 | y=x |
|---|---|---|---|---|---|
| Bob | 1 | 0 | | | 1 |
| Alice | | | 1 | 0 | |
| Mary | | 0 | 1 | ? | 1 |
| John | 0 | 1 | | 0 | |
| Tutu | 0 | | | 1 | |
| Susan | 1 | 0 | | | 1 |

X

| | | |
|---|---|---|
| Bob | 0.64 | 0.75 |
| Alice | 0.66 | 0.75 |
| Mary | 0.70 | 0.69 |
| John | 0.90 | 0.94 |
| Tutu | 0.27 | 0.93 |
| Susan | 0.75 | 0.64 |

W

•

| y=3x-4 | y=-2x | y=1/x | y=-x-1 | y=x |
|---|---|---|---|---|
| 0.71 | 0.51 | 1.02 | 0.36 | 0.72 |
| 0.70 | 0.56 | 0.41 | 0.96 | 0.69 |

$H^T$

"item bias", respectively (Koren et al., 2009). On the educational setting, the user and item bias are, respectively, the student and task biases. They model how good a student is (i.e. how likely is the student to perform a task correctly) and how difficult/easy the task is (i.e. how likely is the task in general to be performed correctly). The performance prediction function for student $u$ and task $i$ is now determined by

$$\hat{p}_{ui} = \mu + b_u + b_i + \sum_{k=1}^{K} w_{uk} h_{ik} \quad (13)$$

where $\mu$, $b_u$, and $b_i$ are global average, student bias and task bias, respectively. With these biases, the error function now becomes:

$$(p_{ui} - \sum_{k=1}^{K} w_{uk} h_{ik})^2 + \lambda(\|W\|_F^2 + \|H\|_F^2 + b_u^2 + b_i^2)$$

Algorithm 2 describes more details about this method. First, we compute the global average, student bias and task bias as in lines 2-8. Parameters $W$ and $H$ are again initialized randomly from the normal distribution $\mathbf{N}(0,\sigma^2)$ with mean is 0 and standard deviation $\sigma^2 = 0.01$. Then, we update the value of $\mu$, $b_u$, $b_i$, $W$, and $H$ at each iteration as in lines 11-21 (Algorithm 2).

After having these parameters, we can easily compute the prediction in the test set for any existing student and task with the same formula in line 13.

## Tensor Factorization

In previous section, we used matrix factorization models to take into account the latent factors "slip" and "guess" but not the temporal effect. Obviously, from the education point of view, "The more the learners study the better the performance they get". Moreover, the knowledge of the learners will be cumulated over the time, thus, the temporal effect is an important factor to predict the student performance. We adopt the idea from Dunlavy et al. (2010) which applies tensor factorization for link prediction. Instead of using only two-mode tensor (a matrix) as in the previous section, we now add one more mode to the models - the time mode, thus, this method is a general form of matrix factorization.

Given a three-mode tensor $\mathbf{Z}$ of size $U \times I \times T$, where the first and the second mode describe the student and task as in previous section; the third mode describes the context, e.g. time, with size $T$. Then $\mathbf{Z}$ can be written as a sum of rank-1 tensors by using Tucker decomposition (Tucker, 1966):

$$Z = \sum_{r=1}^{R} \sum_{s=1}^{S} \sum_{p=1}^{P} C_{rsp} w_r \circ h_s \circ q_p \quad (14)$$

or by using CANDECOM-PARAFAC (Harshman, 1970):

$$Z = \sum_{k=1}^{K} w_k \circ h_k \circ q_k \quad (15)$$

where $\mathbf{C}_{rsp}$ is a core tensor, $\circ$ is the outer product, and the vector $w_k \in \mathbf{R}^U$, $h_k \in \mathbf{R}^I$, and $q_k \in \mathbf{R}^T$ describe the latent factors of student, task, and time, respectively. Please refer to specialized articles (Kolda and Bader, 2009; Dunlavy et al., 2010) for more details.

To take into account the "student bias" and "task bias", the prediction function now becomes:

$$\hat{p}_{ui} = \mu + b_u + b_i + \left( \sum_{k=1}^{K} w_k h_k^T \varphi_k \right)_{u,i} \quad (16)$$

$$\varphi_k = \frac{\sum_{t=T-T_{\max}+1}^{T} q_k(t)}{T_{\max}} \quad (17)$$

where $q_k$ is a latent factor vector representing the time, and $T_{max}$ is the number of solving-steps in the history that we want to go back. This simple method averages $T_{max}$ performance steps in the past to predict the current step. We will call this approach TFA (Tensor Factorization - Averaging).

Another important factor is that "memory of human is limited", so the students could forget what they have studied in the past, e.g., they could perform better on the lessons they learn recently than the one they learn from last year or even longer. Moreover, we recognize that the second time the students do their exercises and have more chances to learn the skills, their performance on average gets better (we will explain more about this in Figure 5). Thus, we could use a decay function which reduces the weight θ when going back to the history. We call this approach TFW (Tensor Factorization - Weighting). The $\phi_k$ now becomes:

$$\varphi_k = \frac{\sum_{t=T-T_{\max}+1}^{T} q_k(t) \cdot e^{t \cdot \theta}}{T_{\max}} \tag{18}$$

An open issue for this is that we can use forecasting techniques instead of weighting or averaging. We leave this solution for future work.

## Dealing with the Cold-Start Problem

One of the challenging problem of collaborative filtering approaches like matrix factorization is to deal with the "new user" (new student) and/or "new item" (new task), e.g., those that are in the test set but not in the train set. We treat this problem with a simple strategy: providing the global average score for the new users or new items. Of course, more sophisticated methods can improve the prediction results (Preisach, Marinho, & Schmidt-Thieme, 2010; Gantner, Drumond, Freudenthaler, Rendle, & Schmidt-Thieme, 2010), but we leave these solutions for future work.

Moreover, in the educational data mining scenario, the cold-start problem is not as harmful as in the e-commerce environment where the new users and new items appear every day or even hour. In educational environment, the new students and new tasks (or courses) appear only in every term/semester, and thus, the models need not to be re-trained continuously.

# EMPIRICAL EVALUATION

An important problem in using recommender systems for predicting student performance is that which task to be considered as item. This section will discuss about this problem. At first, we will look in details 2 real world data sets which are collected from the Knowledge Discovery and Data Mining Challenge 2010 (KDD Cup, 2010). These data sets, originally labeled "Algebra 2008-2009" and "Bridge to Algebra 2008-2009", will be denoted "Algebra" and "Bridge" in the remainder of this chapter. The Algebra (Bridge) data set has 23 (21) attributes, 8,918,054 (20,012,498) records for training, and 508,912 (756,386) records for testing. These data represent the log files of interactions between students and CATS. While students solve math related problems in the tutoring system, their activities, success and progress indicators are logged as individual rows in the data sets.

The central element of interaction between the students and the tutoring system is the problem. Every problem belongs into a hierarchy of unit and section. Furthermore, a problem consists of many individual steps such as calculating a circle's area, solving a given equation, entering the result and alike. The field problem view tracks how many times the student already saw this problem. Additionally, a different number of knowledge components (KC) and associated opportunity counts are provided. Knowledge components represent specific skills used for solving the problem (where available) and opportunity counts encode the number of times the respective knowledge component has been encountered before.

Target of the prediction task is the correct first attempt (CFA) information which encodes whether the student successfully completed the given step on the first attempt (CFA = 1 indicates correct, and CFA = 0 indicates incorrect). The prediction would then encode the certainty that the student will succeed on the first try.

There is an obvious mapping of users and ratings in the student performance prediction problem:

student → user

performance (correct first attempt) → rating

The student becomes the user, and the correct first attempt (CFA) indicator would become the rating, bounded between 0 and 1. With this setting there are no users in the test set that are not present in the training set which simplifies predictions.

For mapping the item, several options seemed to be available to us. From the official KDD Challenge dataset description it was immanent that an item was supposed to be the combination (concatenation) of problem hierarchy (PH), problem name (PN), step name (SN), and problem view (PV). Choosing PH-PN-SN-PV as the item had the drawback of incurring the new-item problem into our recommendation task: in the test sets, instances of PH-PN-SN-PV would occur that are unavailable in the training set, thus our models would not be able to learn much about them. Another problem with this approach is that it leads to huge sparsity and to a high number of new items on the test set. For instance, for the algebra dataset this configuration would lead to a total of 1,416,473 items (see Table 1). Since there are 8,918,054 examples on the training set for this dataset one could expect to see, on average, 6 observations per item (99.78% sparsity). Indeed, as shown in (Thai-Nghe et al., 2010) the different mappings yield different results. Table 1 presents the information of user-item-rating which are used for experimenting in this chapter. Other candidates of "items" can be found in Thai-Nghe et al. (2010).

Generally speaking, there are three important factors for the evaluation of the candidate items:

- the percentage of new users or new items in the test set
- the overall sparsity of the resulting matrix
- the percentage of missing values

*Table 1. Mapping student performance data to user/item in recommender systems. Solving-step is a combination of problem hierarchy (PH), problem name (PN), problem group (PG) extracted from PN, step name (SN), and problem view (PV). Skill is also called knowledge component (KC).*

| | **Algebra** | **Bridge** |
|---|---|---|
| *User* | *#User* | *#User* |
| Student | 3,310 | 6,043 |
| *Item* | *#Item* | *#Item* |
| Solving-Step (PH, PN, SN, PV) | 1,416,473 | 887,740 |
| Skill (KC) | 8,197 | 7,550 |
| *Rating* | *#Rating* | *#Rating* |
| Correct first attempt (CFA) | 8,918,054 | 20,012,498 |

*Table 2. Hyperparameters and approximation of the running-time*

| Method | Data set | Hyperparameters | Train time (min.) | Test time (sec.) |
|---|---|---|---|---|
| MF | Algebra | β=0.005, #iter=120, K=16, λ=0.015 | 16.83 | 0.15 |
| Biased MF | Algebra | β=0.001, #iter=80, K=128, λ=0.0015 | 19.12 | 0.23 |
| MF | Bridge | β=0.01, #iter=80, K=64, λ=0.015 | 40.15 | 0.34 |
| TFA | Bridge | β=0.01, #iter=30, K=32, λ=0.015, $T_{max}$=8 | 296.25 | 2.84 |
| TFW | Bridge | β=0.01, #iter=30, K=32, λ=0.015, $T_{max}$=8, θ= 0.4 | 904.40 | 22.56 |

## Baselines and Model Setting

### Baselines

We use the global average as a baseline method, i.e. predicting the average of the target variable from the training set. The proposed methods are compared with other methods such as user average, biased-user-item (Koren, 2010). Please note that, as shown in Thai-Nghe et al. (2010), matrix factorization already outperforms the traditional regression methods such as linear/logistic regression. Thus, in this chapter we have not considered these algorithms for the evaluation.

### Hyper Parameter Setting

We do the hyper parameter search to determine the best hyper parameters for all methods, by optimizing the RMSE (Root mean squared error) on a holdout set. We will later report the hyper parameters for some typical methods (in Table 2). Please also note that we have not performed a significance test (t-test) because the real target variables of two data sets from KDD Challenge 2010 have not been published yet. In order to obtain the RMSE on the two data sets we have to submit the generated predictions to the KDD Challenge 2010 website. Thus, all the results reported in this study are the RMSE score from this website (it still opens for submission after the challenge). Of course, we could use an internal split (e.g. splitting the training set to sub-train and sub-test) but we wanted compared to the other KDD cup participants' approaches on the given datasets for better comparability (we will report later in the discussion section).

*Figure 4. RMSE of matrix and biased matrix factorization which factorize on a) student and the solving-step (task) and b) student and the required skills (KC) in solving the step. Algebra data set.*

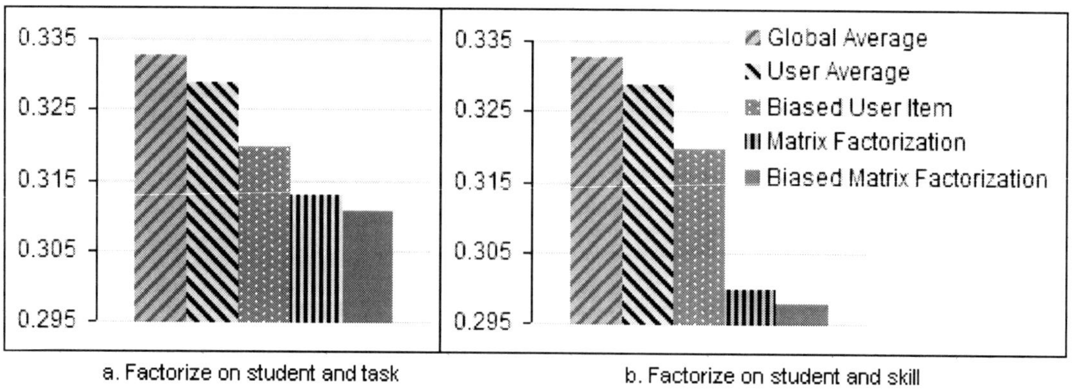

## Implicitly Encoding Latent Factors Using Matrix Factorization

Figure 4 presents the comparison of root mean squared error for Algebra data set. In Figure 4a, we factorize on the student and the task, which is the solving-step. The result significantly outperforms any baseline method.

Moreover, if we have more metadata, e.g., the required skills in solving the step, we see an additional improvement. Figure 4b clearly shows that when using both matrix factorization and biased matrix factorization on the student (as user) and the required skills (as item) to solve the step, the result is again improved compare to other methods and increases the gap between the baseline methods and the best factor model. These results somehow reflect that the proposed approach can deal with the "slip" and "guess" factors by implicitly encoding them as the latent factors of the model. The reason for the improvement of factorizing on the student/skill could be that, in this setting, there are less (tasks) items (8,197) and the same number of (performance) ratings, thus, on average, each (student) user has more ratings (8,918,054/8,197 ~ 1,088 ratings/user), which means that the algorithms have more data to learn from.

*Figure 5. The effect of the time on the knowledge of the learners. The x-axis presents the number of times the student learns the knowledge components. The y-axis is the probability of solving the problem correctly.*

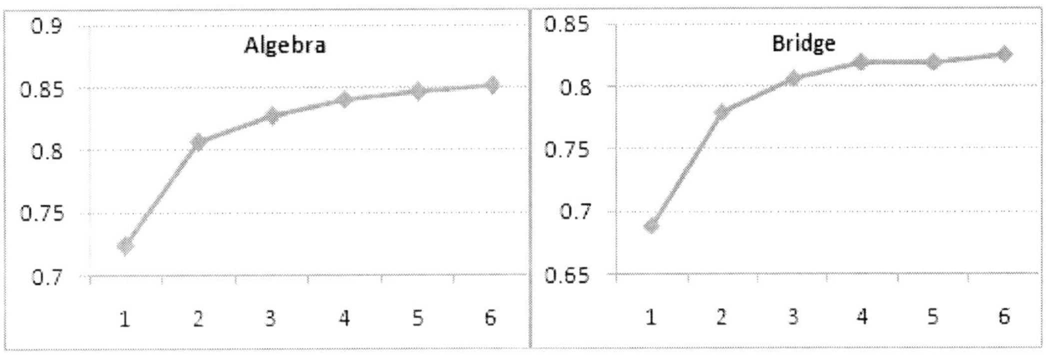


*Figure 6. RMSE of taken into account the temporal effect using tensor factorization which factorize on student, solving-step, and time*

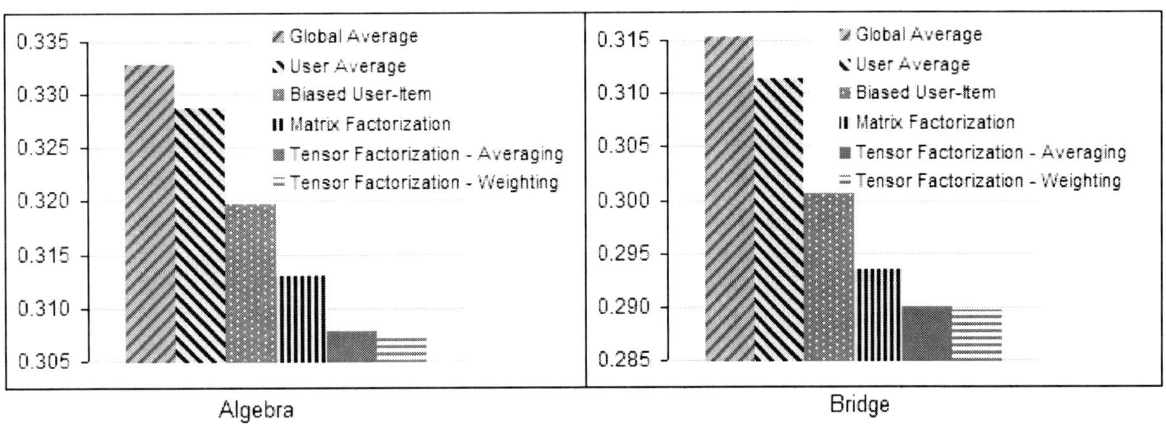

## Tensor Factorization for Exploring Temporal Effects

The previous section shows that the "slip" and "guess" factors could be implicitly encoded in the models. In this section, we present the result of taking into account the temporal information. Figure 5 describes the effect of the time on knowledge of the learners for both Algebra and Bridge data sets. In this figure, the x-axis is the number of times that the students have chances to learn the skills (the "opportunity count" column in the data set), and the y-axis is the ratio of the number of students solving the problem correctly. Clearly, we can see that their performance has been improved when they have additional approaches to learn the skills. This trend also reflects the educational factor that "the more the students learn, the better their performance gets".

Figure 6 presents the RMSE of tensor factorization methods which factorize on the student (as user), solving-step (as item), and the sequence of solving-step (as time) on both data sets. The results of the proposed methods are also improved compared to those already presented. Compared with a vanilla matrix factorization which does not take the temporal effect into account, the tensor factorization methods perform better. This result somehow reflects the natural fact that we mentioned before: "the knowledge of the student is improved over the time and human memory is limited". However, the result of tensor factorization by weighting with a decay function (TFW) has a small improvement compared to the method of averaging on the time mode (TFA).

For referencing, we report the best hyper parameters found via cross validation and approximation of the running-time in Table 2, which produce the results in Figure 6. Please note that although the training time of TFW is high, e.g. ~15 hours for Bridge data set, in educational environment where the models need to be retrained on each term/semester/year, run times in this order of magnitude are not an issue, as we already discussed in the cold-start subsection.

## DISCUSSION

To this end, one would raise the following question: *"How do the delivered recommendations look like?"*

The delivered recommendations depend on the goal of the system. Let's discuss the recommendation for a single student:

- In case of rating prediction, which is the problem approached in this chapter, we are interested in student's performance for a given item. In our case, it means that we compute the expected performance on all tasks not solved by the student in the past. Then, we have several choices: we can provide the student with tasks she will be more likely to solve successfully or we can let the teacher decide about the right mix of tasks or simply present the prediction as a measure of estimated difficulty of that task for the student at hand.
- If we are most interested in those items the students is expected to have problems with and which we therefore want to present to him for further learning (*item prediction* is the recommender systems task at hand), we compute the expected score for each item the student has not tackled in the past. We sort these items according to the predicted score and deliver the student the top-k scored items as those have the highest likelihood of him failing this task.
- Furthermore, we can of course tackle classic problems such as providing the student with the top-k learning resources (courses, materials, tasks...) he/she would be more likely interested in.

As shown above, there is a plethora of areas of application for recommender systems in learning environments. For instance, in the example of Figure 3, we could recommend to the students some similar exercises which are neither too hard nor too easy for them, thus, the system can help the student improve their knowledge by learning/doing similar tasks. Moreover, from the scenario of Figure 1, when the students solve a problem, we could also recommend them some similar problems which may help them consolidate and expand their knowledge. Another example is the recommendation of similar grammar structures, vocabularies, or even a similar problem/section when the student is learning or doing exercises in an English course, etc.

Another important question could be raised is that *"How good our approach is compared to the others competitors on KDD Challenge data?"* The RMSE score of the best student teams is summarized from the leader-board as the following:

- First place: RMSE = 0.27295, National Taiwan University team (Yu et al., 2010)
- Second place: RMSE = 0.27659, Zach A. Pardos team (Pardos and Heffernan, 2010)
- Third place: RMSE = 0.28048, SCUT Data Mining team (Shen et al., 2010)
- *Our approach: RMSE = 0.29519 (not submitted)*
- Fourth place: RMSE = 0.29801, Y10 team

Please note that the focus of this work is not producing a system for the KDD Challenge but on getting the real datasets from an e-learning system and applying recommender systems, especially factorization techniques for predicting student performance. Although the other methods reached lower RMSE, they are more complex and require much effort on data preprocessing (e.g. feature engineering) as well as generating hundred of models and ensembling these together. On the other hand, factorization methods like those presented in this work are simple to implement and need not so much human effort and computer memory to deal with large datasets (e.g., we just need 2 and 3 features for matrix and tensor factorization, respectively). More complex models using matrix factorization can also produce the better results as shown in Toscher and Jahrer (2010). This means that factorization techniques are promising for the problem of predicting student performance.

One more issue should also be discussed is that *"what does the presented RMSE reduction mean in practical? E.g., in helping the education managers, students..."* As in the Netflix Prize (netflixprize.com) it has been shown that a 10% of improvement on RMSE could bring million of dollars for recommender systems of a company. In this work, we are on educational environment, and of course, the benefit is not as explicit as in e-commerce but the trend is very similar. Moreover, in Cen et al. (2006) it has been shown that an improved model (e.g. lower RMSE) for predicting student performance could save millions of hours of students' time and effort since they can learn other courses or do some useful activities. The better a model captures the student's skills, the lower will be its error in predicting the student's performance, thus, an improvement on RMSE would show that our models are better capable of capturing how much the student has learned; and finally, a good model which accurately predicts student performance could replace some current standardized tests.

## FUTURE RESEARCH DIRECTIONS

An open issue is that recommender systems for educational purposes are more complex and challenging research direction (Drachsler et al., 2009) compared to the case of e-commerce in which recommender systems are widely being used. The reasons are that learners have specific learning goals that they want to achieve within a specified competence in a certain time, and that the preferred learning activities of learners might not be the pedagogically the most adequate (Tang and McCalla, 2004). As discussed in Santos and Boticario (2010), recommendations for technology enhanced learning scenarios have differences from those in other domains because recommendations in e-learning should be guided by educational objectives, and not only by the user's preferences. Thus, in future work, the proposed approach which uses student performance for recommendation would be promising to tackle the above problems since we can recommend the tasks for students based on their performance but not on their preferences.

Moreover, to improve the prediction results, one can apply more sophisticated methods to deal with the cold-start problems. Also, using ensemble methods on different models generated from matrix and tensor factorization can be investigated. Moreover, to take into account the sequential effect, instead of using averaging or weighting methods on the third mode of tensor, one could use forecasting techniques such as single exponential smoothing or Holt-Winter methods (Chatfield and Yar, 1988).

Another open issue is that each solving-step relates to one or many skills, thus, use multi-relational matrix factorization (Singh and Gordon, 2008; Lippert et al., 2008) could be developed to deal with this problem.

## CONCLUSION

In this chapter, we have discussed on the problem of predicting student performance as well as personalized recommending tasks/exercises to students. We introduce state-of-the-art factorization techniques for predicting student performance. These techniques are useful in case of sparse data, and even in the case that we have no background knowledge about the students and the tasks. After introducing and formulating this problem in the context of recommender systems, we present factorization methods, which are currently known as the most effective recommendation approaches, by a formalized and detailed way that can be helpful for the researchers who come from educational domains.

Factorization techniques belong to the family of latent factor models, thus, they can implicitly take into account the important latent factors in predicting student performance such as "slip" (student knows the solution but making a mistake) and "guess" (student does not know the right solution but guessing correctly) as well as "student effect" (e.g. how clever/good the student is, in performing the task) and "task effect" (e.g. how hard/easy the task is). Moreover, as a natural fact, the knowledge of the learners improves over the time, thus, we propose tensor factorization methods to take the temporal effect into account. Finally, some experimental results and discussions are provided to validate the proposed approach.

## ACKNOWLEDGMENT

The first author was funded by the "Teaching and Research Innovation Grant" project of Cantho University, Vietnam. The second author was funded by the CNPq, an institute of the Brazilian government for scientific and technological development. Tomáš Horváth is also supported by the grant VEGA 1/0131/09.

A simple implementation of Matrix Factorization (in Java) is available at http://www.ismll.de/personen/nguyen.html. Several other methods can be found in MyMediaLite, a recommender system library (http://ismll.de/mymedialite).

## REFERENCES

Bekele, R., & Menzel, W. (2005). A Bayesian approach to predict performance of a student (BAPPS): A case with Ethiopian students. In *Artificial Intelligence and Applications*, (pp. 189-194). Vienna, Austria.

Bell, R. M., & Koren, Y. (2007). Scalable collaborative filtering with jointly derived neighborhood interpolation weights. In *Proceedings of the 7th IEEE International Conference on Data Mining* (ICDM 2007), (pp. 43-52). Washington, USA. IEEE CS.

Bobadilla, J., Serradilla, F., & Hernando, A. (2009). Collaborative filtering adapted to recommender systems of e-learning. *Knowledge-Based Systems, 22*(4), 261–265. doi:10.1016/j.knosys.2009.01.008

Bottou, L. (2004). Stochastic learning. In Bousquet, O., & von Luxburg, U. (Eds.), *Advanced Lectures on Machine Learning, Lecture Notes in Artificial Intelligence, LNAI 3176* (pp. 146–168). Berlin, Germany: Springer Verlag.

Cen, H., Koedinger, K., & Junker, B. (2006). Learning factors analysis: A general method for cognitive model evaluation and improvement. In *Intelligent Tutoring Systems* (*Vol. 4053*, pp. 164–175). Berlin, Germany: Springer. doi:10.1007/11774303_17

Chatfield, C., & Yar, M. (1988). Holt-winters forecasting: Some practical issues. Special Issue: Statistical Forecasting and Decision-Making. [The Statistician]. *Journal of the Royal Statistical Society Series D, 37*(2), 129–140.

Drachsler, H., Hummel, H. G. K., & Koper, R. (2009). Identifying the goal, user model and conditions of recommender systems for formal and informal learning. *Journal of Digital Information, 10*(2).

Dunlavy, D. M., Kolda, T. G., & Acar, E. (2010). (in press). Temporal link prediction using matrix and tensor factorizations. *ACM Transactions on Knowledge Discovery from Data.*

Feng, M., Heffernan, N., & Koedinger, K. (2009). Addressing the assessment challenge with an online system that tutors as it assesses. *User Modeling and User-Adapted Interaction, 19*(3), 243–266. doi:10.1007/s11257-009-9063-7

Gantner, Z., Drumond, L., Freudenthaler, C., Rendle, S., & Schmidt-Thieme, L. (2010). Learning attribute-to-feature mappings for cold-start recommendations. In *Proceedings of the 10th IEEE International Conference on Data Mining* (ICDM 2010). IEEE Computer Society.

Garcia, E., Romero, C., Ventura, S., & Castro, C. D. (2009). An architecture for making recommendations to courseware authors using association rule mining and collaborative filtering. *User Modeling and User-Adapted Interaction, 19*(1-2). doi:10.1007/s11257-008-9047-z

Ge, L., Kong, W., & Luo, J. (2006). Courseware recommendation in e-learning system. In *International Conference on Web-based Learning* (ICWL 2006), (pp. 10-24).

Ghauth, K., & Abdullah, N. (2010). *Learning materials recommendation using good learners' ratings and content-based filtering. Educational Technology Research and Development* (pp. 1042–1629). Boston, MA: Springer.

Harshman, R. A. (1970). Foundations of the PARAFAC procedure: Models and conditions for an "explanatory" multi-modal factor analysis. *UCLA Working Papers in Phonetics, 16*(1), 84.

Khribi, M. K., Jemni, M., & Nasraoui, O. (2008). Automatic recommendations for e-learning personalization based on web usage mining techniques and information retrieval. In *Proceedings of the 8th IEEE International Conference on Advanced Learning Technologies*, (pp. 241-245). IEEE Computer Society.

Koedinger, K. R., Baker, R. S. J. d., Cunningham, K., Skogsholm, A., Leber, B., & Stamper, J. (2010). A data repository for the EDM community: The PSLC DataShop. In Romero, C., Ventura, S., Pechenizkiy, M., & Baker, R. S. J. d. (Eds.), *Handbook of educational data mining*. Boca Raton, FL: CRC Press. doi:10.1201/b10274-6

Kolda, T. G., & Bader, B. W. (2009). Tensor decompositions and applications. *SIAM Review, 1*(3), 455–500. doi:10.1137/07070111X

Koren, Y. (2010). Factor in the neighbors: Scalable and accurate collaborative filtering. *ACM Transaction Knowledge Discovery Data, 4*(1), 1–24. doi:10.1145/1644873.1644874

Koren, Y., Bell, R., & Volinsky, C. (2009). Matrix factorization techniques for recommender systems. *IEEE Computer Society Press, 42*(8), 30–37.

Lawrence, N. D., & Urtasun, R. (2009). Non-linear matrix factorization with Gaussian processes. In *Proceedings of the 26th Annual International Conference on Machine Learning* (ICML 2009), (pp. 601-608). New York, NY: ACM.

Lippert, C., Weber, S. H., Huang, Y., Tresp, V., Schubert, M., & Kriegel, H.-P. (2008). *Relation prediction in multi-relational domains using matrix factorization*. In NIPS 2008 Workshop: Structured Input - Structured Output.

Manouselis, N., Drachsler, H., Vuorikari, R., Hummel, H., & Koper, R. (2010). Recommender systems in technology enhanced learning. In P. B. Kantor, F. Ricci, L. Rokach, & B. Shapira (Eds.), *1st Recommender Systems Handbook*, (pp. 1-29). Berlin, Germany: Springer.

Massey, L. D., Psotka, J., & Mutter, S. A. (1988). *Intelligent tutoring systems: lessons learned* (Psotka, J., Massey, L. D., Mutter, S. A., & Seely Brown, J., Eds.). Hillsdale, NJ: L. Erlbaum Associates.

Pardos, Z. A. & Heernan, N. T. (2010). *Using HMMS and bagged decision trees to leverage rich features of user and skill from an intelligent tutoring system dataset*. KDD Cup 2010: Improving Cognitive Models with Educational Data Mining.

Pilaszy, I., & Tikk, D. (2009). Recommending new movies: Even a few ratings are more valuable than metadata. In *Proceedings of the Third ACM Conference on Recommender Systems* (RecSys 2009), (pp. 93-100). New York, NY: ACM.

Preisach, C., Marinho, L. B., & Schmidt-Thieme, L. (2010). Semi-supervised tag recommendation using untagged resources to mitigate cold-start problems. In *14th Pacific-Asia Conference on Knowledge Discovery and Data Mining (PAKDD 2010), LNCS 6118*, (pp. 348-357). Springer.

Rendle, S., Freudenthaler, C., & Schmidt-Thieme, L. (2010). Factorizing personalized Markov chains for next-basket recommendation. In *Proceedings of the 19th International Conference on World Wide Web* (WWW 2010), (pp. 811-820). New York, NY: ACM.

Rendle, S., & Schmidt-Thieme, L. (2008). Online-updating regularized kernel matrix factorization models for large-scale recommender systems. In *Proceedings of the ACM conference on Recommender Systems* (RecSys 2008), (pp. 251-258). New York, NY: ACM.

Romero, C., Ventura, S., Espejo, P. G., & Hervs, C. (2008). Data mining algorithms to classify students. In *1st International Conference on Educational Data Mining* (EDM 2008), (pp. 8-17). Montral, Canada.

Santos, O. C., & Boticario, J. G. (2010). Modeling recommendations for the educational domain. *Proceedings of the 1st Workshop on Recommender Systems for Technology Enhanced Learning (RecSysTEL 2010). Procedia Computer Science, 1*(2), 2793-2800.

Shen, Y., Chen, Q., Fang, M., Yang, Q., Wu, T., Zheng, L., & Cai, Z. (2010). *Predicting student performance: A solution for the KDD Cup 2010 challenge*. KDD Cup 2010: Improving Cognitive Models with Educational Data Mining.

Singh, A. P., & Gordon, G. J. (2008). Relational learning via collective matrix factorization. In *Proceeding of the 14th ACM SIGKDD International Conference on Knowledge Discovery and Data Mining* (KDD 2008), KDD '08, (pp. 650-658). New York, NY: ACM.

Soonthornphisaj, N., Rojsattarat, E., & Yim-Ngam, S. (2006). Smart e-learning using recommender system. In *International Conference on Intelligent Computing*, (pp. 518-523).

Stamper, J., Niculescu-Mizil, A., Cunningham, K., Demi, S., Leber, B., & Rankin, J. … Yu, S. (Organizers). (2010). *KDD Cup: Improving Cognitive Models with Educational Data Mining*. Retrieved from https://pslcdatashop.web.cmu.edu/KDDCup/

Takacs, G., Pilaszy, I., Nemeth, B., & Tikk, D. (2009). Scalable collaborative filtering approaches for large recommender systems (special topic on mining and learning with graphs and relations). *Journal of Machine Learning Research*, *10*, 623–656.

Tang, T., & McCalla, G. (2004). Beyond learners interest: Personalized paper recommendation based on their pedagogical features for an e-learning system. In Zhang, C. W., Guesgen, H., & Yeap, W. K. (Eds.), *PRICAI2004: Trends in Artificial Intelligence, LNCS 3157* (pp. 301–310). Berlin, Germany: Springer. doi:10.1007/978-3-540-28633-2_33

Thai-Nghe, N., Busche, A., & Schmidt-Thieme, L. (2009). Improving academic performance prediction by dealing with class imbalance. In *Proceeding of 9th IEEE International Conference on Intelligent Systems Design and Applications* (ISDA'09), (pp. 878-883). Pisa, Italy, IEEE Computer Society.

Thai-Nghe, N., Drumond, L., Krohn-Grimberghe, A., & Schmidt-Thieme, L. (2010). Recommender system for predicting student performance. In *Proceedings of the 1st Workshop on Recommender Systems for Technology Enhanced Learning* (RecSysTEL 2010), (volume 1, pp. 2811-2819). Elsevier's Procedia CS.

Thai-Nghe, N., Janecek, P., & Haddawy, P. (2007). A comparative analysis of techniques for predicting academic performance. In *Proceeding of 37th IEEE Frontiers in Education Conference* (FIE'07), (pp. T2G7-T2G12). Milwaukee, USA, IEEE Xplore.

Toscher, A., & Jahrer, M. (2010). *Collaborative filtering applied to educational data mining*. KDD Cup 2010: Improving Cognitive Models with Educational Data Mining.

Tucker, L. (1966). Some mathematical notes on three-mode factor analysis. *Psychometrika*, 279–311. doi:10.1007/BF02289464

Yu, H.-F., Lo, H.-Y., Hsieh, H.-P., Lou, J.-K., McKenzie, T., Chou, J.-W., … Lin, C.-J. (2010). *Feature engineering and classifier ensemble for KDD Cup 2010*. KDD Cup 2010: Improving Cognitive Models with Educational Data Mining.

## ADDITIONAL READING

Adomavicius, G., & Tuzhilin, A. (2005). Toward the next generation of recommender systems: A survey of the State-of-the-Art and possible extensions. *Knowledge and Data Engineering. IEEE Transactions on*, *17*(6), 734–749.

Baker, R. S., & Yacef, K. (2009). The state of educational data mining in 2009: A review and future visions. [JEDM]. *Journal of Educational Data Mining*, *1*(1), 3–17.

Bishop, C. M. (2007). *Pattern Recognition and Machine Learning (Information Science and Statistics)* (2nd ed.). Springer.

Castro, F., & Vellido, A. Nebot, n., and Mugica, F. (2007). Applying data mining techniques to e-learning problems. In Kacprzyk, J., Jain, L., Tedman, R., and Tedman, D., editors, Evolution of Teaching and Learning Paradigms in Intelligent Environment, volume 62 of Studies in *Computational Intelligence*, pages 183-221. Springer Berlin Heidelberg.

Cichocki, A., Morup, M., Smaragdis, P., Wang, W., and Zdunek, R. (2008). *Editorial: advances in nonnegative matrix and tensor factorization.* Intelligent Neuroscience, 2008:2:1-2:3.

Cichocki, A., & Zdunek, R. (2007). *Regularized alternating least squares algorithms for non-negative Matrix/Tensor factorization* (pp. 793–802). Advances in Neural Networks.

Cichocki, A., Zdunek, R., Phan, A. H., & Amari, S.-i. (2009). *Nonnegative Matrix and Tensor Factorizations: Applications to Exploratory Multi-way Data Analysis and Blind Source Separation*. Wiley Publishing.

Duda, R. O., Hart, P. E., & Stork, D. G. (2001). *Pattern Classification* (2nd Edition). Wiley-Interscience, 2 edition.

Ghauth, K. I., & Abdullah, N. A. (2010). Measuring learner's performance in e-learning recommender systems. *Australasian Journal of Educational Technology*, *26*(6), 764–774.

Gunawardana, A., & Shani, G. (2009). A survey of accuracy evaluation metrics of recommendation tasks. *Journal of Machine Learning Research*, *10*, 2935–2962.

Hastie, T., Tibshirani, R., & Friedman, J. (2009). *The Elements of Statistical Learning: Data Mining, Inference, and Prediction*. Second Edition (Springer Series in Statistics). Springer.

Herlocker, J. L., Konstan, J. A., Terveen, L. G., & Riedl, J. T. (2004). Evaluating collaborative filtering recommender systems. *ACM Transactions on Information Systems*, *22*(1), 5–53. doi:10.1145/963770.963772

Kumar, V., Nesbit, J., Winne, P., Hadwin, A., Jamieson-Noel, D., & Han, K. (2007). Quality rating and recommendation of learning objects. In Jain, L., Wu, X., & Pierre, S. (Eds.), *E-Learning Networked Environments and Architectures, Advanced Information and Knowledge Processing* (pp. 337–373). Springer London. doi:10.1007/978-1-84628-758-9_12

Luo, J., Dong, F., Cao, J., & Song, A. (2010). A context-aware personalized resource recommendation for pervasive learning. *Cluster Computing. Springer-Netherlands*, *13*(2), 213–239.

Mairal, J., Bach, F., Ponce, J., & Sapiro, G. (2010). Online learning for matrix factorization and sparse coding. *Journal of Machine Learning Research*, *11*, 19–60.

Manouselis, N., Vuorikari, R., & Van Assche, F. (2010). Collaborative recommendation of e-learning resources: an experimental investigation. *Journal of Computer Assisted Learning*, *26*(4), 227–242. doi:10.1111/j.1365-2729.2010.00362.x

Markowska-Kaczmar, U., Kwasnicka, H., & Paradowski, M. (2010). Intelligent techniques in personalization of learning in e-learning systems. In Xhafa, F., Caball, S., Abraham, A., Daradoumis, T., and Juan Perez, A., editors, Computational Intelligence for Technology Enhanced Learning, volume 273 of Studies in *Computational Intelligence*, pages 1-23. Springer Berlin / Heidelberg.

Mcsherry, D. (2005). Explanation in recommender systems. *Artificial Intelligence Review*, *24*(2), 179–197. doi:10.1007/s10462-005-4612-x

Morup, M. (2011). Applications of tensor (multiway array) factorizations and decompositions in data mining. Wiley Interdisciplinary Reviews. *Data Mining and Knowledge Discovery*, *1*(1), 24–40. doi:10.1002/widm.1

Nishino, K., Shimoda, T., Iribe, Y., Mizuno, S., Aoki, K., & Fukumura, Y. (2010). Predicting e-learning course adaptability and changes in learning preferences after taking e-learning courses. In Setchi, R., Jordanov, I., Howlett, R., and Jain, L., editors, *Knowledge-Based and Intelligent Information and Engineering Systems*, volume 6277 of Lecture Notes in Computer Science, pages 143-152. Springer Berlin / Heidelberg.

Pardos, Z., Heffernan, N., Anderson, B., & Heffernan, C. (2007). The effect of model granularity on student performance prediction using bayesian networks. In Conati, C., McCoy, K., and Paliouras, G., editors, *User Modeling*, pages 435-439. Springer Berlin / Heidelberg.

Peter, J. B., & Richard, A. D. (2002). *Introduction to Time Series and Forecasting*. Springer.

Rendle, S. (2010). *Context-aware Ranking with Factorization Models*. Springer.

Ricci, F., Rokach, L., Shapira, B., & Kantor, P. B. (Eds.). (2011). *Recommender Systems Handbook*. Springer. doi:10.1007/978-0-387-85820-3

Romero, C., & Ventura, S. (2005). *Data Mining in E-Learning. (Advances in Management Information)*. WIT Press.

Romero, C., Ventura, S., Pechenizkiy, M., & Baker, R. S. (2010). *Handbook of Educational Data Mining*. Chapman and Hall/CRC, Data Mining and Knowledge Discovery Series.

Schafer, J. B., Konstan, J. A., & Riedi, J. (1999). Recommender systems in e-commerce. In Proceedings of 1st *ACM Conference on Electronic Commerce*, pages 158–166.

Shen, Y., Chen, Q., Fang, M., Yang, Q., Wu, T., Zheng, L., and Cai, Z. (2010). Predicting student performance: A solution for the kdd cup 2010 challenge. *KDD Cup 2010: Improving Cognitive Models with Educational Data Mining*.

Skillicorn, D. (2007). *Understanding Complex Datasets: Data Mining with Matrix Decompositions*. Chapman and Hall/CRC, Data Mining and Knowledge Discovery Series.

Su, X. and Khoshgoftaar, T. M. (2009). A survey of collaborative filtering techniques. *Advance in Artificial Intelligence*, 2009.

Tan, P.-N., Steinbach, M., & Kumar, V. (2005). *Introduction to Data Mining* (1st ed.). Boston: Addison-Wesley Longman Publishing Co., Inc.

Yu, Z., Nakamura, Y., Jang, S., Kajita, S., & Mase, K. (2007). Ontology-based semantic recommendation for context-aware e-learning. In Indulska, J., Ma, J., Yang, L., Ungerer, T., and Cao, J., editors, *Ubiquitous Intelligence and Computing*, volume 4611 of Lecture Notes in Computer Science, pages 898-907. Springer Berlin/Heidelberg.

## KEY TERMS AND DEFINITIONS

**Collaborative Filtering (CF):** CF filters the information or patterns based on the collaboration among users, items, etc. CF generates the recommendations based on the ideas that "similar users like similar things".

**Cold-Start Problem:** A user/item has not been known by the models (new user/item)

**Computer-Aided Tutoring System (CATS):** CATS is any computer system that provides direct customized instruction or feedback to students (Wikipedia.org).

**Educational Data Mining (EDM):** EDM is concerned with developing methods for exploring data that come from educational settings (Educationaldatamining.org).

**Matrix Factorization (MF):** MF is an approximation of a matrix by two (or more) low-rank matrices.

**Predicting Student Performance (PSP):** PSP is the problem of predicting student's ability (e.g., estimated by a score metric) in solving the tasks when interacting with the tutoring system.

**Rating Prediction:** The prediction of the rating values (scores) for items (e.g. movies, books) that a user may like.

**Tensor:** Tensor is a three (or more) dimensional matrix

**Tensor Factorization (TF):** TF is a generalization of MF.

# Chapter 7
# Clustering of the Web Search Results in Educational Recommender Systems

**Constanta-Nicoleta Bodea**
*Academy of Economic Studies, Romania*

**Maria-Iuliana Dascalu**
*Academy of Economic Studies, Romania*

**Adina Lipai**
*Academy of Economic Studies, Romania*

## ABSTRACT

*This chapter presents a meta-search approach, meant to deliver bibliography from the internet, according to trainees' results obtained at an e-assessment task. The bibliography consists of web pages related to the knowledge gaps of the trainees. The meta-search engine is part of an education recommender system, attached to an e-assessment application for project management knowledge. Meta-search means that, for a specific query (or mistake made by the trainee), several search mechanisms for suitable bibliography (further reading) could be applied. The lists of results delivered by the standard search mechanisms are used to build thematically homogenous groups using an ontology-based clustering algorithm. The clustering process uses an educational ontology and WordNet lexical database to create its categories. The research is presented in the context of recommender systems and their various applications to the education domain.*

## INTRODUCTION

Learners are asking for intelligent services in order to discover and access the content they need. The mechanism for discovering Web documents are powerful search engines, with specialized discovery services, indexes, and databases. But, a simple query can produce hundreds or thousands of results, making it practically impossible for the trainee to check the relevance of each of them. .This chapter argues that grouping the results into relevant clusters might make the learner to use them more efficiently. The chapter describes

DOI: 10.4018/978-1-61350-489-5.ch007

a meta-search engine of an education recommender system, attached to an e-assessment application for project management knowledge. The meta-search engine is meant to deliver bibliography (web pages) from the internet according to trainees' results obtained at an e-assessment task. Meta-search means that, for a specific query (or mistake made by the trainee), several search mechanisms for suitable bibliography (further reading) could be applied. The lists of results delivered by the standard search mechanisms are used to build thematically homogenous groups using an ontology-based clustering algorithm. The clustering process uses an educational ontology and WordNet lexical database to create its categories. Organizing search results in clusters is not meant to replace the classical way of presenting results in ranked lists. Its purpose is to provide supplementary organization for those results. The clustering method will provide a series of search results clusters, with the properties that the pages inside one cluster are similar to each other, and the pages belonging to different clusters differ from one another. Inside each cluster, the initial ranking order provided will be preserved.

The chapter demonstrates that a meta-search approach using an ontology-based clustering algorithm for results' presentation produces high quality recommendations for the students who want to use the e-assessment tool in project management and, thus, sharpen their knowledge. Exploiting the clustering technologies improves the performance issues of the educational recommender system attached to the e-assessment application, which gains a formative value and becomes a learning tool. The issue of educational recommender systems, closely related to web search applications, is a common concern in Technology Enhanced Learning (TEL) domain: "Since information retrieval (in terms of searching for relevant learning resources to support teachers or learners) is a pivotal activity in TEL, the deployment of recommender systems has attracted increased interest." (Manouselis, Drachsler, Vuorikari, Hummel, & Koper, 2010) An insight of other researches regarding ontology-based clustering of web-meta search in recommender systemsis also presented, before describing the original solution. Experimentation results are presented and the efficiency of the proposed solution is discussed in the context of similar applications.

## ONTOLOGY-BASED CLUSTERING OF THE WEB-META SEARCH RESULTS IN EDUCATIONAL RECOMMENDER SYSTEMS

A recommender system guides the user to interesting objects (concepts) in a large space of possible options (Burke, 2002). Usually, recommender systems (RS) must choose which of the items should be shown to the user or when and how the recommendations must be shown (Hernandez del Olmo & Gaudioso, 2008). A RS is different from an information retrieval system, as it offers options worthy of considerations, not only matches to the user's query (Burke, 2007). The results offered by RS are customized to particular users. RS evolved over the years: at the beginning, people provided recommendations and RS just aggregated and directed them to the users, now RS can generate suggestions (interactive RS) or filter them (non-interactive RS), by rating (Hernandez del Olmo & Gaudioso, 2008). Researchers groups RS into three categories: collaborative filtering RS, content-based filtering RS (Adomavicius & Tuzhilin, 2005) and hybrids (Balabanovic & Shoham, 1997). Content-based filtering RS suggest items similar to the ones considered useful in the past by the user. Collaborative filtering RS use the ranking of items given by a wide variety of users. Hybrid RS use data mining techniques to guide and filter the results for the user. Cho, Kim, and Kim (2002) present a personalized recommender system based on Web usage mining and decision tree induction. Hsu (2008) presents a RS which incorporates two data mining techniques—clustering and association rules algorithm. IJntema, Goossen, Frasincar, and Hogenboom (2010) use an ontology to recommend concepts of interests from a certain domain. Middleton (2003) uses ontology for user profiling. Weng and Chang (2008) use it for knowledge domain description. Burke (2007) argues that recommendation techniques differ one from another on the basis of their knowledge sources: "where does the knowledge needed to make recommendations come from? In some systems, this knowledge is the knowledge of other users' preferences. In others, it is ontological or inferential knowledge about the domain, added by a human knowledge engineer."(Burke, 2007) We consider that both the knowledge sources and the algorithms used to work with those sources have an impact on RS architecture and applications.

Finding useful information from web is critical, but hybrid RS can make smart decisions in complex information systems (Göksedef & Gündüz-Ögüdücü, 2010). Recommendation systems became a promising area in academia and industry (Zhen, Huang, & Jiang, 2010). They are used from helping online buyers and customers to helping students to find suitable lessons (Hsu M.-H., 2008). In educational area, RS started to spread more and more (Yang, 2010), (Kardan, Abbaspour, & Hendijanifard, 2009): some assist students to plan their semester schedule, by checking courses that comply with constraint regulation and with students' preferences (Hsu I.-C., 2009), others are used to give proper knowledge to proper members in collaborative team contexts, by respecting role, tasks, members' level of knowledge (Zhen, Huang, & Jiang, 2010), give books recommendations (Mooney & Roy, 2000) or help ESL (English as a Second Language) students to learn English (Hsu M.-H., 2008).

The chapter argues that including a RS into an e-assessment application makes that application a useful tool in educational area. At the end, the students who took the e-test can fill their knowledge gaps, by consulting the recommended web documents. This kind of e-assessment has an important role in learning and teaching (Delcea & Dascalu, 2009). It is well-used in organizational learning (Bodea & Dascalu, 2010), (Frey & Fisher, 2009), being known as "assessment for learning" (Birenbaum, Kimron, Shilton, & Shahaf-Barzilay, 2009). To increase the educational effect of the e-assessment, the recommendations are given to the trainees into a clustered form, using an educational ontology.

The clustering issue has been used before in RS, but not for intelligent grouping of the final results. Martin-Guerrero, Palomares, Balaguer-Ballester, Soria-Olivas, Gomez-Sanchis and Soriano-Asensi (2006) use it for user modeling. Users of a web-portal are clustered, thus enabling the study of future success of RS by means of prediction strategy. New users are recommended according to the cluster in which they have been classified. Five clustering algorithms are used: k-means, fuzzy k-means, hirerarchical clustering, expectation-maximization algorithm and self-organizing MAP (SOM), which uses artificial neutral nets for clusters. The last two algorithms prouved to be more efficient,from the interpretability point of view. The researchers considered that those two clustering algorithms are suitable for classifying the logical behaviour of people. Choosing the right clustering algorithm for each research problem might influence the quality of the final research results. Niwa, Doi and Honiden (2006) uses clustering for tag grouping, though solving the problem of "tag redundancy in Folksonomy". The issue addressed by these three researchers is also the problem of web pages recommendations, based on previous user profiles. They noticed that, in certain cases, there are no previous preferences for web pages: in these cases, social bookmarks are used. Social bookmarks are web services on which users can share their bookmarks, these bookmarks being put through "folksonomy" – a method through which keywords called "tags" are established for each web page, feely and subjectively, based on users' sense of value. Because the tags set by users are sometimes redundant, clustering those tags for suitable recommendations seems to be a valid solution (Niwa, Doi, & Honiden, 2006). In educational recommender systems, clustering are used to empower the students to choose proper tools, artifacts, learning materials, for their activities. A good example for choosing the best instrument to find literature in a Personal Learning Environment (PLE) setup is given by Mödritscher (2010): the researcher made an experiment in which he discovered that 33 out of 99 activities in a PLE could be assigned to 9 tools, through clustering. Google Scholar turned out to be the most used tool for bibliography search.

In educational area, combining the strength of clustering recommendations with an ontological approach of a learning domain is a valuable solution, as this chapter wants to prove. Ontologies are used for increasing the interoperability quality in education RS. Domain models can be implemented as ontologies, so two applications with the same domain model, can share the same ontology: "Ontologies express the shared view on domain semantics and come with a full package of technologies developed within the framework of the Semantic Web initiative" (Sosnovsky, Brusilovsky, Yudelson, Mitrovic, Mathews, & Kumar, 2009). If different ontologies are used for the same domain, researchers recommend using at least common reference ontology: this reference ontology can act as a "meta-translator for the shared concepts" (Sosnovsky, Brusilovsky, Yudelson, Mitrovic, Mathews, & Kumar, 2009). Ontologies are also used when software information agents are transformed into recommender systems: IAOM (information agent ontology model) is used in RS to "explicitly represents each object and each group of objects contained in the environment of an agent, using a unique name of a common vocabulary" (Rosaci, 2007). Ontologies increase the personalization capabilities in RS. Blanco-Fernández, et al. (2008) used the reasoning based strategy to discover the semantic relationships between users' preferences and the items available in a domain ontology. In this way, the system obtained extra knowledge about the users' interests and, consequently, the personalization process became more accurate. Zheng, Kang and Kim (2008) suggest exploiting ontologies when searching for relevant web documents. We propose using this kind of ontology-based web search within a recommender system. Zheng, Kang and Kim (2008) advice using an artificial neural network based on a domain-specific ontology and applied to the classification of web pages.

Adopting an ontology approach is a common way of dealing with semantics of the web search results. Most of the existing ontology-based clustering methods identify the conceptual features (or concepts) to be used on the clustering process, instead of the index words occurring in web documents (Hotho, Staab & Stumme, 2003). The corresponding concepts are identified with the aid of ontology class labels and the WordNet lexical database. In WordNet the terms are organized in synsets, which are sets of synonyms. Using concepts instead index words could reduce the clustering dimensionality, considering that we can have multiple index words replaced by the same concept. Some methods recommend adding the identified concepts to the index words list, and increasing the process dimensionality. As consequence, it is not possible to consider the concept-based clustering as an implicit solution for the dimensionality issue. The clustering solution proposed in this chapter is based on the concepts identification, via WordNet and the replacement of the index words by the corresponding concepts.

For clustering purpose, a document is represented as a vector of index words in a vector space model. The vector components are weights of the correspondent index words showing their relative importance in the document and the entire set of documents. Having the vector collection (all documents represented as vectors), some distance measures could be used in order to compute the distance or similarity between documents, as part of clustering algorithms, such as k-means. In order to take into consideration the document semantic, different ontology-based measure were defined (Hotho, Maedche & Staab, 2001). Considering the semantic relationship between each pair of words, as mutual information between terms, the extension of the vector space model can be made with a mutual information matrix and an Euclidian distance measure considering the correlation between each pair of terms. Using this modeling framework a clustering method, named FW-Kmeans, was defined, performing better than classical methods.

Hotho, Maedche, and Staab (2001) proposed the *COSA (Concept selection and aggregation)* clustering method. The COSA approach uses a core ontology for restricting the document features used by aggregation process. The aggregation result is exploited by K-means algotrithm, in order to produce a set of clustering results, considered as a set of views.

An ontology-based clustering framework is proposed by Lula and Paliwoda-Pekosz (2008), giving the possibility of incorporating various kinds of measure to determine similarity between objects and set of objects in the following three dimensions: taxonomic, relationship and attribute. Kogilavani and Balasubramanie (2009) developed a system which revise the user query by mapping it with synonyms and semantically related concepts using MeSH ontology knowledge source. The system first cluster terms using a term semantic similarity measure. Then the term is re-weighting to increase the weight of the terms which are more semantically similar. The similarity measures are defined based on information content.

The chapter recommends the relative semantic relevance of a concept with respect to its prerequisites, named the *self weight of the concept,* to be used in the clustering process. The concept's self weight is combined with the weight of the corresponding term obtaining the final *concept's weight.* This measure is used in order to compute the distance or similarity between documents, as part of clustering algorithms, such as k-means. The measure is used also for the space graph projections, in order to select the concepts, for clustering dimensionality reduction. The self weight of the concept is defined based on expert opinions.

The educational recommender mechanism which uses the ontology-based clustering web search reveals a novel aspect regarding the application of RS: they can assist learners in a formative e-assessment process. This reliance is further underlined, together with the RS mechanism itself. Then, details about the web search are carefully provided.

## AN EDUCATIONAL RECOMMENDER ENGINE

The proposed educational recommender engine is geared when an e-assessment is finished. Although the engine can be used as a stand-alone system, its value as a learning tool is increased when is exploited in the context of formative e-assessment.

### E-Assessment Application Used to Fire the Recommender Engine

As project management knowledge has a tremendous impact on economical well-being, various efforts have been made to fill knowledge gaps in project management domain (Zhen, Huang, & Jiang, 2010), (Delcea & Dascalu, 2009). Among these efforts, there are the ones made by the Romanian Association of Project Management, which provides an e-assessment application for certification exam preparation: www.pm.org.ro/certexam. The test items are multiple-choice questions. The score sheet has incorporated an automated feedback mechanism: the user can return to the incorrectly answered questions (which are marked with red in Figure 1) or to the correctly answered questions (which are marked with green), if he considers that he guessed the answer. The user can also ask for an exam report, which will give him a "pdf" document (see Figure 1) with the correct

*Figure 1. Automated included feedback in a project management e-assessment application*

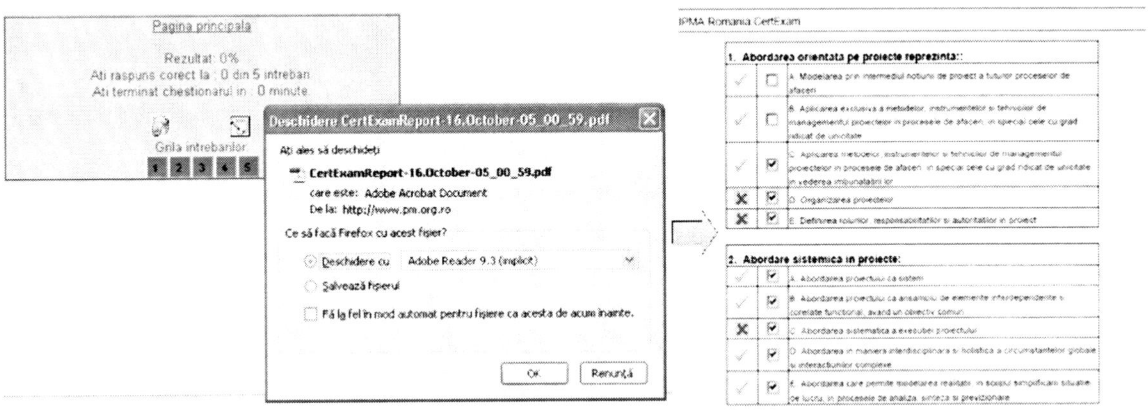


answers. The formative dimension of the test can be increased by pressing the "Search on WEB" button from Figure 1: a recommender engine will be called and the users will obtain a set of web documents related to the knowledge checked by the questions which were incorrectly answered. The algorithm standing behind this recommender-based feedback is an ontology-based clustering algorithm. The project management e-assessment is a client-server application: the client part is developed in javascript, using Ajax technologies and the server part is developed in C#. Net.

## Mechanism of the Recommender Engine

Each question of an e-assessment session checks a certain number of concepts from the knowledge domain in project management. This knowledge domain is represented by an educational ontology. The recommender engine should search for web documents related to the concept of the incorrectly answered question, but also for web documents related to the parent node of the concept in the domain ontology and other child nodes of that parent. The lexical instances of these concepts are the entry points for the clustering algorithm. The concepts are converted to their lexical instances, using the educational ontology. The recommender engine is a C# web-service. The mechanism of the recommender engine is presented in Figure 2.

According to Figure 2, the following steps are available in the recommender engine mechanism:

1. The user takes the test.
2. The user finishes the test and the 'user profile' is built: a set of concepts related to the incorrectly answered questions.
3. The user profile is mapped in the domain ontology, taking account a $\lambda$ parameter used as an entry data: according to that parameter, child nodes from the initial set of concepts might be chosen. For all chosen concepts, lexical instances are extracted and further used for web-search.
4. The web search is processed for the lexical instances from Step 3 and for the following admin parameters: the set of search engines to be used (the administrator of the e-assessment application can choose the available engines from a combo-box), the number of links per page, the number of clusters.
5. A clustering algorithm is applied. Clustering will be realized after a predefined number of iterations. This number will be determined experimentally in order to find a compromise between computing time and quality of clusters obtained. By default, we

*Figure 2. Recommender engine mechanism*

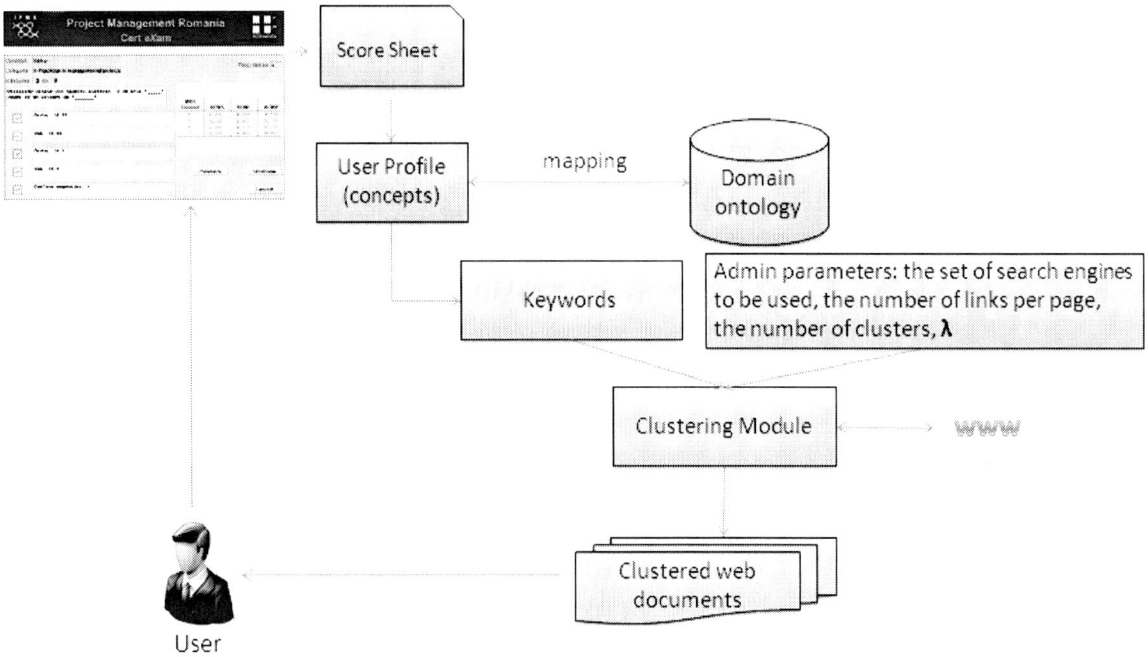


make 6 clusters, the 7th cluster representing unclassified documents and we use a threshold value of 0.3 for classification of instances in clusters. After each clustering, we recalculate the centroids and we reset the clusters' components. The new centroids are calculated using the average weigh of words reached in that cluster.

## ONTOLOGY-BASED CLUSTERING PROCEDURE FOR THE WEB META-SEARCH

Clustering the search results means grouping them into object classes which are developed using the search results characteristics, with the purpose of simplifying the user work to retrieve the relevant results. Meta-search means the use of more search tools simultaneously for the same query. Organizing search results in clusters is not meant to replace the classical way of presenting results in ranked lists (Brin & Page, 1998), but to provide supplementary organization for those results. Clustering is applied after the query results are provided by the search engines. The user interface provides the user's query to different search engines, and takes the list of results offered by traditional web search. When the meta-search is integrated in a recommender system, this user interface might be replaced by an internal mechanism of the recommender system, like in our case.

Generally, the list of results provided by a search engine is composed of link to the site that meet the query criteria, brief description of the page (usually the selection of page) and the page title.

Using this information, the user usually goes through the entire list of results to find relevant pages. The recommender system has the role to provide the user the perfect list of pages, according to his current level of knowledge. Even if the results list is sorted by a rank which gives a score of importance of the site, there are cases where the user will have to go through a high number of results (20 to 100 sites) in order to find the desired pages, or because a query poorly supplied, with sufficient detail or because the desired pages have a low share in the search.

In order to make the user's job easier, the clustering algorithm will divide the list of results in homogenous groups. The user will have to identify the cluster in which his pages are most likely to be and only search through that cluster, ignoring the other clusters.

The search results clustering module of a crawler has to meet the following requests:

- It has to simplify the user's work in finding the results
- The module must not overcrowd the search tool's resources
- It must not over extend the time needed to find the proper web page: e.g. if Google offers results for a query in few milliseconds, a clustering process that will take tens of seconds will be unsatisfactory (Leouski & Croft, 1996).

The results clustering module takes over the search keywords for querying different search engines (Google, Yahoo, MSN search, and so on). The search module will send keywords to different search engines which will retrieve the results and send them to the clustering module. The clustering algorithm is run on the local machine. The clustering results are presented to the user, together with all web documents (the link and description) included in those clusters.

Being integrated in a recommender system, the clustering model has to receive a set of parameters from its parent system:

- The set of search engines to be used;
- The number of links per page;
- The choice of the number of clusters;
- Various filters, such as filters for blogs, adult sites

## Ontology Used in the Clustering Procedure

The ontology used for results clustering is an educational one. An educational ontology is an explicit formal specification of how to represent learning concepts, learning objects, and other entities and the relationships among them (Kanellopoulos, Kotsiantis, & Pintelas, 2006). For these ontologies, an important relationship type is *requires(Ci, Cj)*, meaning "Ci requires Cj as prerequisite", where Ci and Cj are two learning concepts. Each concept class of the ontology has its self-weight as class attribute. The attribute value is set using expert opinions.

The *space graph* of concept Ci is the graph which has Ci as the root node and all other concepts directly or indirectly connected to Ci with "requires" links as graph nodes. The relevance of the concept Ci with respect to its prerequisites is measure by $W_s(i)$, *the self weight* of the concept. The *prerequisite weight* of concept Ci, $W_p(i)$ is the relative semantic relevance of the prerequisite topics and *the link weight l(i,j)* represents the relative importance of learning concept Cj for learning Ci. For all nodes of the concept space graph, the sum of self-weight and prerequisite weight is 1. The sum of all prerequisite link weights to the child nodes is also 1.

$$W_s(i)+W_p(i) = 1, \forall i \quad (1)$$

$$\sum_{j=1}^{n} l(C_0, C_j) = 1 \quad (2)$$

Figure 3 shows an example of concept space graph (for concept C1.02), with $W_p(i)$ shown on the right side of node and $W_s(i)$ on the left side.

Given a root concept $C_0$ and a projection threshold coefficient $\lambda$, *a projection graph* is defined as a sub-graph with root $C_0$ and all nodes $C_t$, where there is at least one path from $C_0$ to $C_t$ such that node path weight $\eta(C_0, C_t)$ satisfies the

*Figure 3. The projection graphs for different values of the λ parameter*

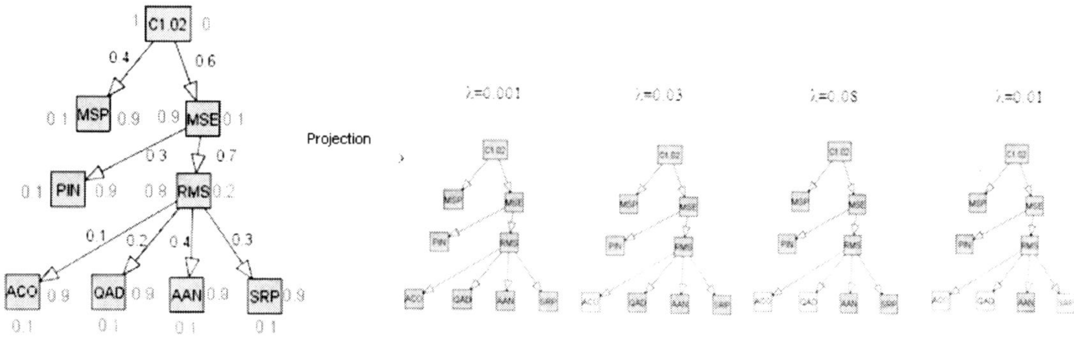


condition: $\eta(C_0, C_t) >= \lambda$, where node path weight between $C_0$ and $C_t$ for the path $[C_0, C_1, \ldots, C_t]$ is:

$$\eta(C_0, C_t) = W_s(t) \prod_{m=n}^{1} l(C_{m-1}, C_m) * W_p(m-1) \tag{3}$$

We consider as an example the concept space graph shown on the left side of Figure 3. A small value for λ parameter has as result a larger projection graph than bigger one, as shown in Table 1.

The results from Table 1 are also presented graphical format in the right side of Figure 3. The white nodes of the concept space graph are not included in the projection graphs.

The projection graphs are used during the concept selection process, in order to reduce the dimension of the extended index concept vector.

The result of the concept selection process is the reduced index vector list, so useful in the process of web documents search.

Each concept class has lexical instances, in addition to usual concept instances. The lexical instances are created using the synonym classes of the WordNet and represent synonyms for the concept label. The number of lexical instances is related to the concept self-weight measure. In our experiments, we applied relation (4) to set the lexical instance number for each ontology concept.

$$Li_i = \gamma \cdot e^{w_s(i)} \tag{4}$$

where: $Li_i$ is the number of lexical instances for concept class i, $\gamma$ is a positive parameter, greater than 1 (we used $\gamma$=10), and $W_s(i)$ is the self-weight

*Table 1. The projection results for different values of the λ parameter*

| R (Root) | N (Node) | η(R,N) | η(R,N) >= (λ=0.001) | η(R,N) >= (λ=0.03) | η(R,N) >= (λ=0.08) | η(R,N) >= (λ=0.01) |
|---|---|---|---|---|---|---|
| C1.02 | MSP | 0.36000 | √ | √ | √ | √ |
| | MSE | 0.06000 | √ | √ | √ | X |
| | PIN | 0.14580 | √ | √ | √ | √ |
| | RMS | 0.07560 | √ | √ | X | X |
| | ACO | 0.02722 | √ | X | X | X |
| | QAD | 0.05443 | √ | √ | X | X |
| | AAN | 0.10886 | √ | √ | √ | √ |
| | SRP | 0.08165 | √ | √ | √ | X |

of the concept Ci. The optimal value for parameter $\gamma$ was determined experimentally and the number of lexical instances is obtained using formula 4, through truncation.

The synonyms of ontology concepts are used on the concept mapping process, to find the corresponding ontological class for each index word. A direct matching between the concept labels and index words is not recommended, because most of the ontologies have a very limited lexicon, comparing to the web content, so there is a small chance to find concept labels in the index word list.

## The Search Results Clustering Procedure

The main steps of the search results clustering are the following:

1. Obtaining the web page list
2. Pre-processing of the documents
3. Transforming the documents into vector representation
4. K-means clustering, with adequate adaptations for web pages
5. Designing the cluster representation for final results

### Obtaining the Web Page List

The initial web page list is obtained putting all results delivered by all search tools in a single list. This list will be used to cluster the results. In order to obtain the web page list the next steps have to be done:

a. Performing simultaneous queries on multiple search engines.
b. Elimination of the multiple links: because the results are obtained from more search tools it's more than likely the same site will be returned by more than one tool.

Calculating the new rank: the formula below will be used.

$$Rank_{new} = I_M * NrRez + I_{Rez} \quad (5)$$

Where:

$Rank_{new}$: the new rank calculated for each web page

$I_M$ : the index of the search engine which provided this page

NrRez: total number of results after the duplicates were eliminated

$I_{Rez}$: the index of the page in the $I_M$ search tool

d) Duplicate web pages will receive the rank from the search tool with the lowest index

### Pre-Processing of the Documents

The clustering algorithm uses information from the pages in order to determine its subject or characteristics. Most document clustering algorithms use the whole document for this process, but such approach would slow our web page clustering algorithm too much. Therefore the algorithm will only use the snippets provided by the initial search tools. Previous work has showed that snippets provide good quality description of web pages, so justifying their use (Leuski & Allan, 2000). The title of the web page will also be used, if there is one. Title words will become then more important for classification than snippet words. Web pages processing is made up by the following operations.

a. **The tag cleaning:** It will eliminate the portions of the web document which are strictly related to the text formatting. The main processes are the following:
b. **The lexical analysis:** the purpose of the analyses is to identify distinct words. The process implies eliminating useless char-

acters such as comma, punctuation marks, sometimes numbers, or characters like: #, $...

c. **The word root extraction:** the goal is to obtain a homogenous one-word description of similar but not identical words. The word obtain in the end doesn't have to have a meaning, nor be grammatically correct, but it will contain the description and similarity with all the other words that it represents. For example: *implementing, implementation, implemented* will be described by the root word *implement*.
d. **The stop word elimination:** a stop word is a word that does not have an informational value. In all languages there are a series of words which are considered stop words. For example: "on", "and", "the", "in", etc.
e. **Establishing the index words:** an index word, is a word that is representative in the context of the document.

## Transforming the Documents into a Concept Vector Representation

In order to use the k-means clustering algorithm we need to transform each document into a concept vector. The vectors will have the same size, turning our result list into an M*N matrix. A line represents one web page and each column represents a concept. The N dimension represents the total number of concepts that will be used for document clustering, from all documents. The dimension M represents the remaining number of web pages after the duplicate eliminations, the final search result list.

Supposing we have:

M web pages: $d_1$, $d_2$,..., $d_M$ and

N indexed concepts from 1 to N

a web page will be represented in concept vector space using the following formula:

$$d_i = [W'_{i1}, W'_{i2}, ..., W'_{iN}] \quad (6)$$

where $W'_{ij}$ represents the weight of concept j for document $d_i$

Transforming the documents into concept vector space representation requires the following steps:

a. **Index word vector identification and vector space representation:** It implies joining together in one vector all the index word from all the documents. For each document and each index word we will count the number of times one word appears in the same page.
b. **Word weight calculation for each document:** In order to calculate each word weight, the frequency of word in document and the inverted document frequency are used.

**The concept mapping**: each index word is checked against the lexical instances, for all ontology concept classes, starting with those having the greatest $W_s$. The first successful matching will indicate the parent class as the concept to be assigned to the index word. Having the index word list as input data of the concept mapping process, an extended index concept list will be produce as result of this process

c. **The concept selection:** projection graphs of the concepts included in the extended index concept list are used to reduce the dimension of the extended index concept vector during the concept selection process. The result is a reduced index concept vector list.
d. **Concept weight calculation for each document and the concept-based representation of documents:** the concept weight for a document is the weight of the corresponding word adjusted with the concept's self weight.

*Table 2. Vector space representation of the search results*

| Document / Words | course | Risk | Management | ... | Project |
|---|---|---|---|---|---|
| d1 | 2 | 3 | 3 | | 0 |
| d2 | 0 | 2 | 2 | | 1 |
| d3 | 1 | 3 | 3 | | 0 |

We start the concept vector space representation of documents with the index word vector identification. For example, using as search query "risk management" we will have the vector space representation presented by Table 2.

The words 1..L are usually the index words, and they are obtained after the pre-processing the documents. Assigning each word a weight it's crucial in order to distinguish the more relevant words from the less important ones. In the end we will quantify the importance that each concept has for a given web page.

The weight of word $t_j$ for a specific document $d_i$ is calculated using the formula (7):

$$w_{ij} = fT_{ij} * \log(n / fd_j) \tag{7}$$

where:

$w_{ij}$ is the weight of word $t_j$ for document $d_i$

$fT_{ij}$ is the frequency of word $t_j$ in $d_i$ document

$fd_i$ is the total number of web pages in which the word $t_j$ appears.

The term $\log(n/fd_j)$ is also called *inverted document frequency*. The words that have a higher frequency in a page will most likely be a better description than the words that have low frequency. But also, the terms that have high frequency in all documents, will not make good description for differences that appear between pages. The term inverted document frequency intends to minimize the importance of the words that appear frequently in all documents (Chi, 2003).

*The weight of concept $C_k$ for the document $d_i$,* $W'_{ik}$ is calculated using the following formula (8):

$$W'_{ik} = W_{ik} * \log\left(\frac{1}{W_s(k)}\right) \tag{8}$$

where:

$W_{ik}$ is the weight of corresponding word for document $d_i$

$W_s(k)$ is the self weight of the concept k.

The Table 3 presents the weights concept-based representation for the previous example.

## K-Means Clustering, With Adequate Adaptations for Web Pages

Classical K-means clustering algorithm uses numerical input to build up distinct clusters. It splits the total data set into exclusive clusters using a measure called "distance". The distance can be calculated using many formulas, but basically having the meaning of metric distance. Just as in traditional k-means clustering, a cluster K will be represented by its centre or centroid (Baeza-Yates

*Table 3. Concept-based representation of documents*

| Document / Concepts | Risk | ... | Project |
|---|---|---|---|
| d1 | 0.176 | ... | 0 |
| d2 | 0 | ... | 0.477 |
| d3 | 0.176 | ... | 0 |

& Ribeiro-Neto, 1999). For web page clustering this centroid will represent a weighted concept document within the vector space documents. This centroid will be called "the representative of cluster $K_k$" noted $R_k$.

In order for $R_k$ to be equivalent with the centre of clusters from the traditional k-means clustering, it must meet the following conditions:

- Each document $d_i$ from $K_k$ has joined concepts with $R_k$
- The concepts in $R_k$ also appear in the most documents in $K_k$
- Not all the concepts from $R_k$ have to also appear in all the documents from $K_k$
- The weight of concept $C_j$ from $R_k$ is calculated as an average weight of all the concepts present in all documents of $K_k$ (Chi, 2003).

After determining the representatives of the cluster, the web meta-search results clustering algorithm is as follows:

- ***Input data:*** *Di* are the web pages/documents provided by the initial search.
  - l is the number of clusters, accordingly to k-means traditional algorithm.
- ***Output data:***
  - l clusters with documents (the clusters can overlap, meaning the same page can be assigned to more than just one cluster, for each distribution there will be a weight assigned to the document)

**Step 1:** *l documents from the web page list are randomly selected.* These l documents will form the starting representatives of the clusters. We have $K_1, K_2, \ldots, K_l$ clusters and $R_1, R_2, \ldots, R_k$ as clusters representatives.

**Step 2:** *For each web page from $D$:$d_i \in D$ and each cluster $K_k$, $k = 1, \ldots, l$* we calculate the similarity between the web page and the representative of the cluster $S(d_i, R_k(K_k))$.

**Step 3:** *If the similarity is bigger than a given threshold* $S(d_i, R_k(K_k)) > \delta$, than the document $d_i$ will be assigned to cluster $K_k$ with a weight attached, the weight being calculated based upon the similarity value:

$$m(d_i, K_k) = S(d_i, R_k(K_k)) \tag{9}$$

**Step 4:** For each cluster the representative is re-calculated taking into account the new documents that were assigned to that particular cluster

**Step 5:** The process is re-started from step 2 until new modifications are below a given threshold.

**Step 6:** *For each web page $d_n$ which is not assigned to any cluster* the closest neighborhood will be calculated $V(d_u)$. The neighborhood must not contain documents that have similarity measure zero. The $d_n$ web page will be assigned to the cluster to which the neighborhood $V(d_u)$ belongs to. The weight for $d_n$ assignation to $K_k$ is calculated:

$$m(d_n, K_k) = m(V(d_u), K_k) * S(d_n, (V(d_u))) \tag{10}$$

**Step 7:** For each cluster $K_k$ the representative of the cluster $R_k$ is recalculated.

Similarity is calculated using the following formula, also named as Salton's cosine coefficient (Salton, 1989):

$$S(x, y) = \frac{\sum_{i=1}^{t} x_i y_i}{\sqrt{\sum_{i=1}^{t} x_i^2 + \sum_{i=1}^{t} y_i^2}} \tag{11}$$

In Figure 4, the logical scheme of the clustering process is presented, starting with calculating the frequency of documents.

*Figure 4. Logical scheme of clustering process*

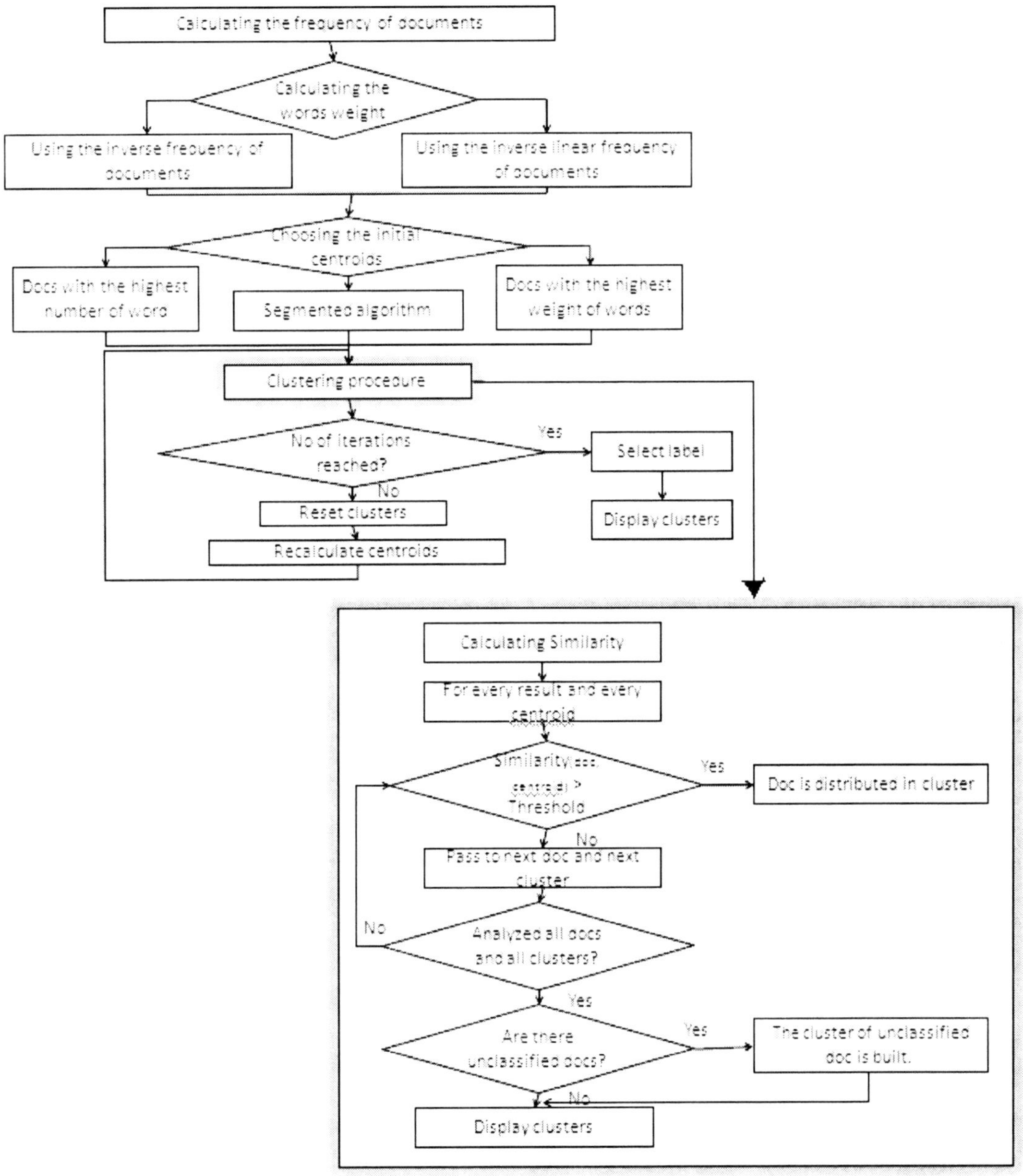


## Developing the Cluster-Like Representation for the Final Results

a. **Label extraction:** For each clusters the sequence of words with the highest frequency will be assigned as label for that class. If a sequence of words is not found than a single word will be used instead.

b. **Creating the cluster structure:** It will be done using both the size of the clusters and the weight of the pages inside the cluster. A measure of the cluster quality will be calculated.

c. **Results delivery:** During the pre-processing phase, we extracted the root for the similar words and we eliminated the stop words, and some other modifications took place in order to make the document suitable for clustering. In order for the user to understand what a page is about it must be presented with a short relevant description of that web page. In almost all cases the initial search result list provides a short description (the snippet). That description can be kept, and delivered to the user after clusters are developed, but it can also be enhanced with particular characteristics of the cluster.

Clustering solutions for web documents which queries search engines must meet the following

*Figure 5. Scenario for constructing the query "Mediul social extern al proiectulu" (External social environment of the project)*

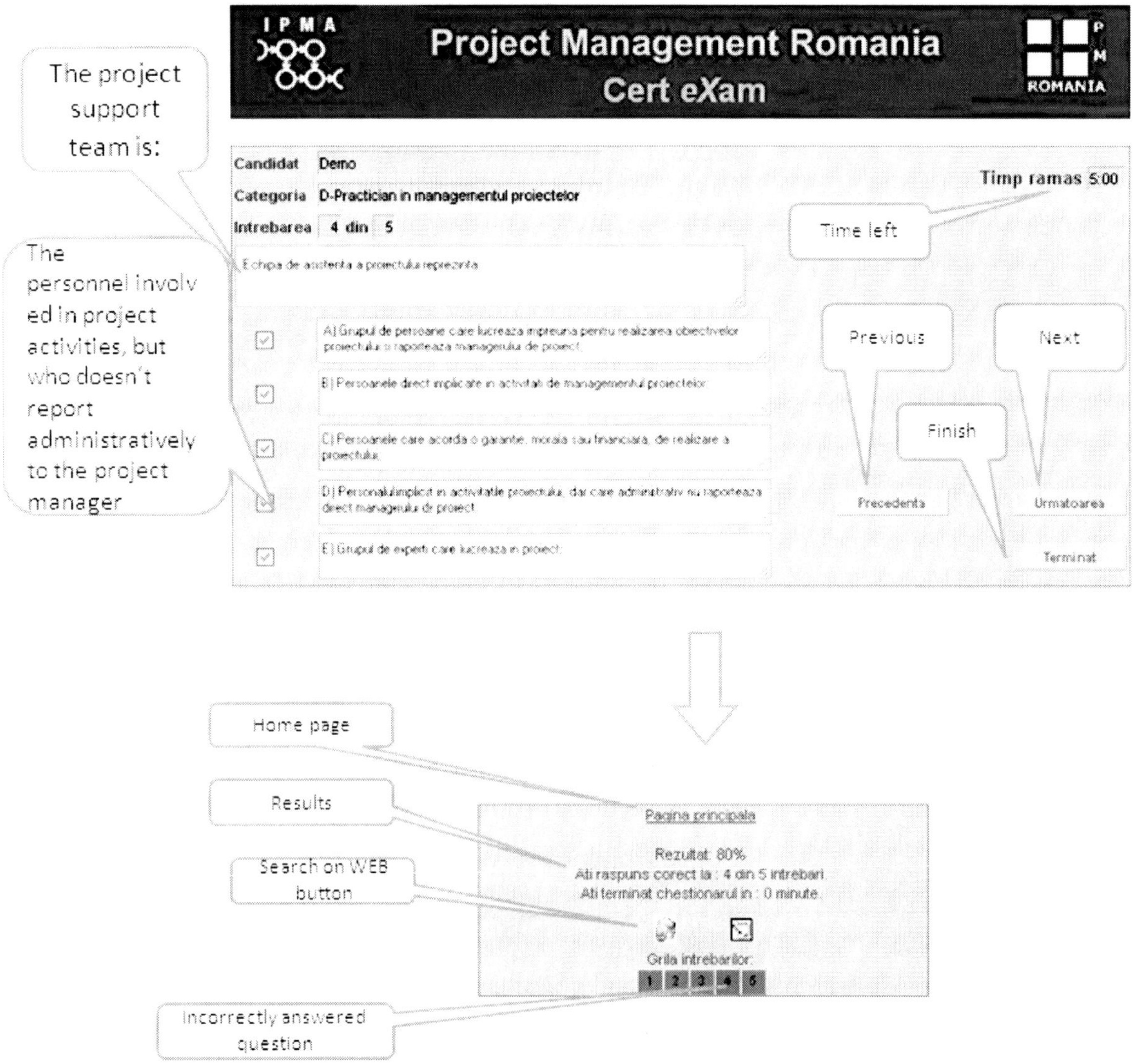

functions: acquisition of queries from the user, providing one or more query search engines, results acquisition, processing of web documents, web documents clustering and results display. In order to better understand the workflow of recommendations for an e-assessment user, we further describe a possible scenario.

## SCENARIO FOR RECOMMANDATIONS USING THE ONTOLOGY-BASED CLUSTERING PROCEDURE

### Scenario Description

#### Build-Up Query Process

A demo version of the e-assessment application is used by *UserDemo*. The session contains 5 multiple-choice questions. The user answers correctly to all questions, except question 4, as seen in the second part of the Figure 5: question 4 is marked with red. The incorrectly answered question is depicted in the first part of the Figure 5.

Incorrectly answered question: "The project support team is:"

The correct answer: "The personnel involved in project activities, but who doesn't report administratively to the project manager."

The answers given by the user: all available choices.

When going to the score sheet (second part of the Figure 5), the user click on "Search on Web" button. Because the only incorrect answer was the one given to question 4, the matches between question 4 and educational ontology is made. The "MSE" concept is found as the matching concept (see Figure 3 for the place of "MSE" concept in the ontology). The lexical instance of "MSE" was found to be "Mediul social extern al proiectulu"(in English "External social environment of the project"), which became the query given to the RS search engine.

### Parameters used in Query "Mediul Social Extern al Proiectulu":

- Search engines: Google, Yahoo!
- Number of used results: maximum
- Language preferences: Romanian
- Similarity threshold: 0,3
- Number of clusters: 4
- Method of calculating the weight: inverted document frequency
- Method of calculating the initial centroids: documents with the highest number of word

### Results of Clustering Process

Figure 6 presents the results of the query **Mediul social extern al proiectulu"** delivered as clusters. On the left side, there are mentioned four clusters induced for this search. On the right side, we can see the links and the related snippets for the cluster with the label "Partile interesate" (in English, "Stakeholders").

## EXPERIMENTATION RESULTS

In this section, we propose some methods for evaluating the results clustering (user method of evaluating the clustering performance and expert method of evaluating the clustering performance) and methods to evaluate the utility of the recommended web documents with respect to the users' needs.

### Methods for Evaluating the Results Clustering

Clustering of Web searches is intended to facilitate the work of a user in retrieving desired web pages, by ordering the results in groups with different topics. The quality of a clustering can be defined taking account its usefulness. Such a measure is subjective because different users will have differ-

*Figure 6. Search results delivered as clusters for the query "Mediul social extern al proiectului" (External social environment of the project)*

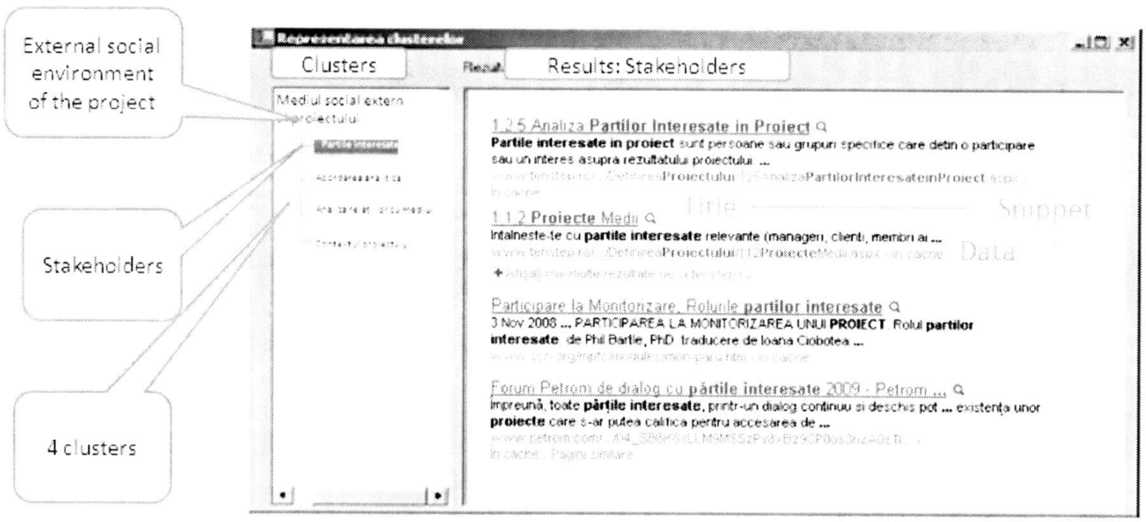


ent requirements, making the evaluation process difficult. We propose two methods of assessing the results of clustering. The first one evaluates the usefulness of clustering, from a normal user perspective. Its disadvantage is that it requires a long testing time, with a large number of distinct users to provide statistically accurate results. The expert method of evaluating the usefulness of clustering is the second provided method of evaluation. Its main disadvantage is that it requires a set of data which is hard to find, because a manual clustering can lead to different results if made by different individuals (Osinski, 2003).

## Methodology

### User Method of Evaluating the Clustering Performance

There are two ways of evaluating the clustering performance by user methods: first is the observation of navigation patterns of clusters in the logs and the second is interrogating the users through specific forms. We used the second method: we defined some quantitative indicators for evaluating the clustering utility, in our users' perspective (Osinski, 2003).The utility of a cluster is defined by the need for that cluster and the proper allocation of an instance in that cluster. We consider the following questions to be valuable for finding out whether a cluster is useful or not for a user:

- Do you consider the cluster k to be useful in classifying the set of results returned? (Yes/No)
- Does the document Dk correspond to the description of k cluster label? (Yes/No/Partial)

After collecting the users' responses, one can define the following metrics (Wróblewski, 2003):

- number of useful clusters of all clusters;
- number of documents correctly and incorrectly classified in each cluster environment;

We also consider important the following indicators:

- the quality of cluster label, measured as the ratio of the number of existing relevant clusters and total clusters (Wróblewski, 2003);
- the quality of document distribution within a cluster, measured by the number of documents correctly classified in the cluster, the number of documents incorrectly classified and the number of documents probably classified correctly; quality distribution of the documents will be better when the number of correctly classified documents is higher and the other two indicators are lower;
- the coverage degree of clustering, which measures the number of classified instances from the total number of instances; we have to take into account that there are instances which remain unclassified (Wróblewski, 2003);
- the overlapping degree of clusters, which can be measured through the total number of documents classified in more than one cluster;

### Expert Method of Evaluating the Clustering Performance

The export method can be performed though:

- evaluating the clustering on a set of documents from different domains, by applying the „merge than cluster" algorithm (Cho, 2001);
- the hypothesis of true base set or „ground truth hypothesis" (Cho, 2001): a set of data which was manually clustered is used by the application and, after processing, the results are compared;

## Experimental Results

### Experiment Description

For testing the clustering algorithms, we use four queries, with the following features:

- **Query 1:** query string: "Controlul financiar al proiectului", query specificity: low, number of tested results: 90;
- **Query 1:** query string: "Auditarea proiectului", query specificity: high, number of tested results: 100;
- **Query 1:** query string: "Terminarea proiectului", query specificity: high, number of tested results: 82;
- **Query 1:** query string: "Excelenţa în managementul proiectului", query specificity: medium, number of tested results: 90;

It should be noted that the evaluation was made using a low number of users, which is not enough to provide statistically plausible results, but enough to give an overview of operating performance. The parameters used in queries are the following:

- Search engines: Google, Yahoo!
- Number of used results: maximum
- Similarity threshold: 0,3
- Number of clusters: 4
- Method of calculating the weight: inverted document frequency
- Method of calculating the initial centroids: documents with the highest number of word

### Results Obtained in Evaluating the Quality of the Cluster Label

In our tests, the quality of the cluster label range between 0.6 and 0.95, with the observation that the quality is higher for queries with low specificity. This aspect is also intuitive, because when queries have low specificity, there are less lexical instances for them, though the results are more related with what the user wants. The average number of useful clusters range between 2.4 and 3.8, which is a very good result, considering the fact that we had only 4 clusters.

## Results Obtained in Evaluating the Quality of Documents' Distribution

The coverage degree for the four queries is:

- **Query 1:** 0.96;
- **Query 2:** 0.88;
- **Query 3:** 0.89;
- **Query 4:** 0.84;

Taking into account the above results and the charts from Figure 7, one can draw the following conclusions:

- The number of incorrectly classified instances is less than the number of correctly classified instances, in all cases;
- The number of partial/medium classified instances is less than the number of correctly classified instances, in all cases;
- Correctly classified instances dominate the clusters;

*Figure 7. Indicators of documents classification: empirical results*

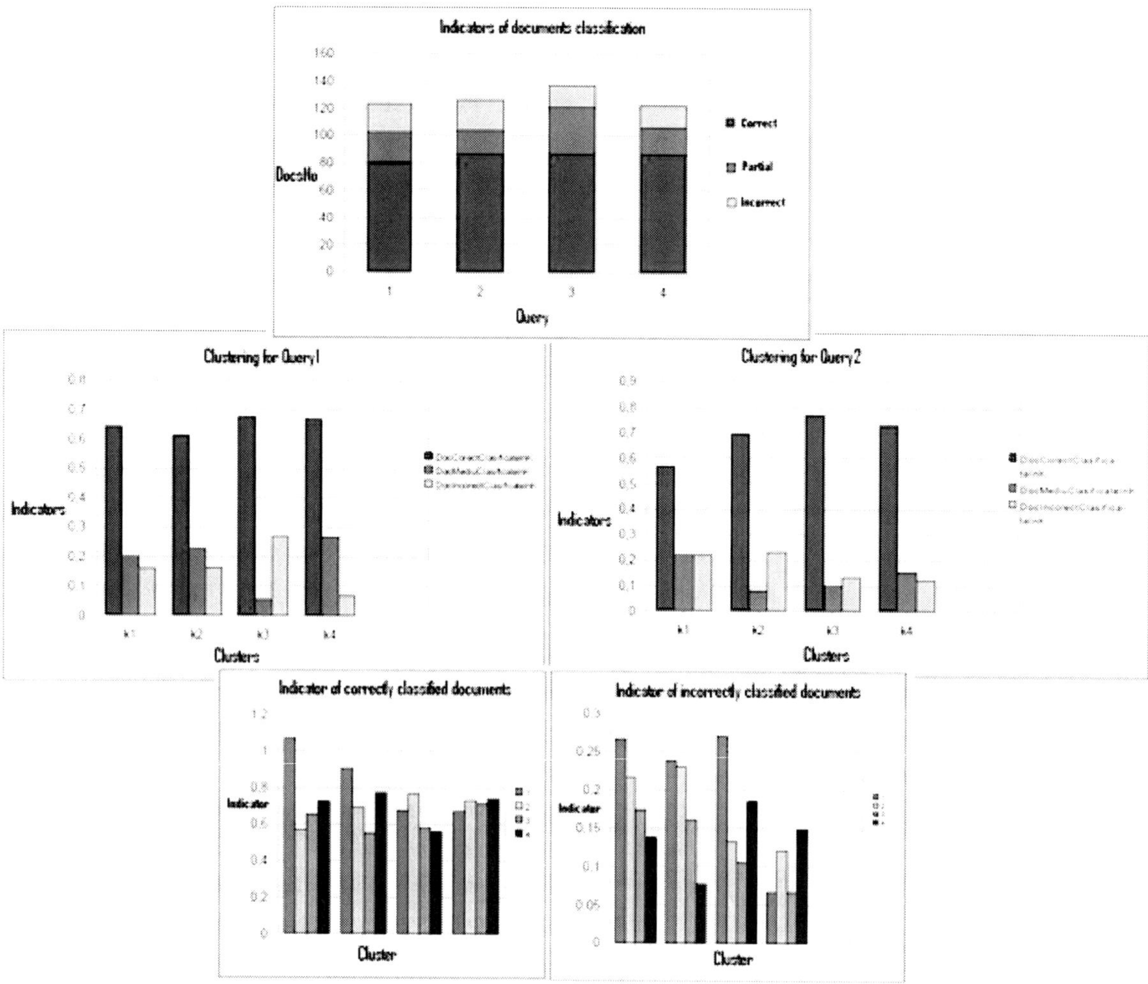

## Determining the Optimal Combination of Preferences

Resuming testing on the same set of four queries, an expert test was performed on various combinations available in the program. The following parameters were tested:

- the ideal number of clusters to achieve quality;
- the clustering quality when using the three types of initial choice of centroids;
- preferences which have the lowest speed of clustering;

In addition to the above aims, another target was to find the weight that would provide a high degree of clustering purity.

The tests revealed the following:

- the best clustering in terms of the usefulness of clusters, will be obtained for a number of 4 clusters;
- the most efficient choice of initial centroids is segmented algorithm;
- the two formulas for calculating the weights are the same performing;
- the clustering average speed is 10 seconds, for 50 results;
- the components that have the greatest effect on clustering are the root extraction modules and replacement of stop words;

## Comparison with Other Similar Applications

After comparing the performance of our ontology-based clustering solution to other three clustering applications, available on the market (Carrot – see Table 5, Clusty – see Table 6 and WebClust – see Table 7), we came to these conclusions:

- our application has the highest average number of clusters for a query in Romarnian language;
- the quality of cluster label is higher than the one from other implementations for the Romanian language;
- for queries in Romanian we will get the largest number of correctly classified documents and the lowest number of incorrectly classified documents;

*Table 5. Estimation of performances obtained by Carrot (http://search.carrot2.org/stable/search)*

| Query No | Average no of useful clusters | Quality of cluster label | Indicator of correctly classified docs (avg) | Indicator of incorrectly classified docs (avg) | Coverage degree |
|---|---|---|---|---|---|
| 1 | 4.3 | 0.86 | 0.66 | 0.22 | 0.98 |
| 2 | 6.1 | 0.92 | 0.87 | 0.1 | 0.87 |
| 3 | 2 | 0.56 | 0.33 | 0.2 | 0.78 |
| 4 | 3 | 0.6 | 0.45 | 0.5 | 0.77 |
| 5 | 3 | 0.6 | 0.51 | 0.45 | 0.81 |
| 6 | 2 | 0.55 | 0.53 | 0.4 | 0.83 |
| 7 | 4 | 0.7 | 0.55 | 0.53 | 0.87 |
| 8 | 5 | 0.6 | 0.57 | 0.34 | 0.78 |
| 9 | 6.1 | 0.61 | 0.62 | 0.3 | 0.79 |
| 10 | 4.3 | 0.63 | 0.64 | 0.23 | 0.78 |

*Table 6. Estimation of performances obtained by Clusty (http://search.yippy.com/)*

| Query No | Average no of useful clusters | Quality of cluster label | Indicator of correctly classified docs (avg) | Indicator of incorrectly classified docs (avg) | Coverage degree |
|---|---|---|---|---|---|
| 1 | 4.1 | 0.78 | 0.59 | 0.33 | 0.68 |
| 2 | 5.5 | 0.77 | 0.7 | 0.12 | 0.88 |
| 3 | 2.1 | 0.55 | 0.25 | 0.66 | 0.78 |
| 4 | 2.2 | 0.45 | 0.31 | 0.42 | 0.82 |
| 5 | 2.6 | 0.6 | 0.51 | 0.45 | 0.81 |
| 6 | 2.8 | 0.78 | 0.53 | 0.12 | 0.88 |
| 7 | 2.9 | 0.77 | 0.59 | 0.66 | 0.78 |
| 8 | 4.1 | 0.55 | 0.7 | 0.34 | 0.82 |
| 9 | 3.9 | 0.45 | 0.25 | 0.12 | 0.79 |
| 10 | 4.3 | 0.63 | 0.31 | 0.66 | 0.78 |

*Table 7. Estimation of performances obtained by WebClust (http://www.webclust.com/)*

| Query No | Average no of useful clusters | Quality of cluster label | Indicator of correctly classified docs (avg) | Indicator of incorrectly classified docs (avg) | Coverage degree |
|---|---|---|---|---|---|
| 1 | 3.3 | 0.67 | 0.45 | 0.43 | 0.83 |
| 2 | 1 | 0.8 | 0.79 | 0.12 | 0.75 |
| 3 | 1.9 | 0.5 | 0.22 | 0.52 | 0.78 |
| 4 | 2.4 | 0.55 | 0.23 | 0.43 | 0.6 |
| 5 | 3 | 0.67 | 0.79 | 0.45 | 0.81 |
| 6 | 2 | 0.8 | 0.22 | 0.4 | 0.83 |
| 7 | 1.9 | 0.5 | 0.23 | 0.43 | 0.75 |
| 8 | 2.4 | 0.55 | 0.45 | 0.12 | 0.78 |
| 9 | 1 | 0.61 | 0.79 | 0.52 | 0.6 |
| 10 | 1.9 | 0.63 | 0.64 | 0.41 | 0.78 |

- the coverage degree is lower than at Carrot system, being higher in one example out of four queries;

In order to make the above observations, we inserted in Carrot, Clusty and WebClust the same lexical instances used as queries in our application.

## Methods for Evaluating the Utility of the Recommended Web Documents

### Methodology

According to Hernandez and Gaudioso (2008), the utility of the recommended web documents can be calculated using the following formula:

$$Utility_u = \frac{\sum_{i=0}^{n} P(u,i)}{n}, P(u,i) \in \{0,1\} \quad (12)$$

Where

u = an user;

P(u,i) = the utility of the document *i* to the user *u*;

P(u,i)=0, if document *i* is considered useless by the user;

P(u,i)=1, if document *i* is considered useful by the user;

n = the total number of recommended documents;

## Experimental Results

### Experiment Description

35 users of the e-assessment application were asked to grade the utility of the recommended web documents, using the Formula 12. All the users were students in the second year of a project management master and were preparing themselves for taking the same type of certification in project management.

### Results

According to Figure 8, 48% of them consider that the utility of the documents is greater than 75% and 37% consider the utility between 50% and 75%. These are very good scores, which prove the recommended engine gives a good feed-back to the trainees.

Because of the novelty of the application (RS for an e-assessment tool), we couldn't compare it with other RS but we tried to whole the evaluation by a qualitative analysis made by the 35

*Figure 8. Utility of the recommended documents*

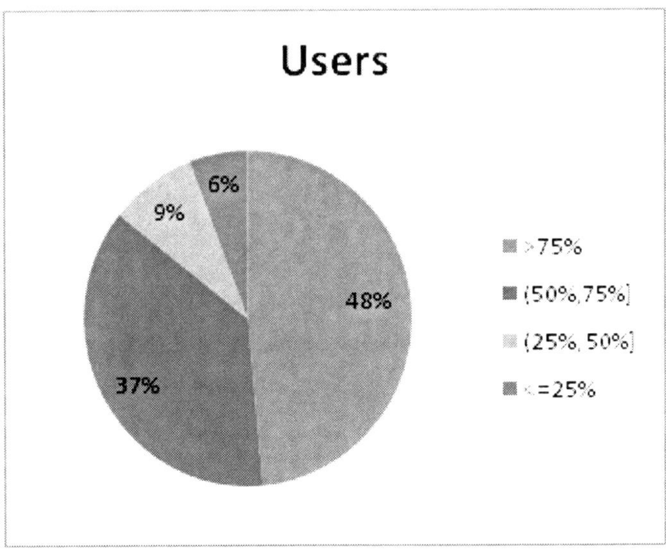

users. 27 of them considered the toolset to be useful especially when preparing for the project management certification exam. The rest of them acknowledged the formative value of the toolset for their general training in project management. All of them said they browsed the recommendations, after being influenced by the cluster label.

## FUTURE RESEARCH DIRECTIONS

The recommendation mechanism can be further refined. The user profile can be enriched by adding information about his type of certification (level A, B, C, D) and, in this way, association rules can be attached to recommendations. For example, all D level users can receive some specific web documents, as recommended bibliography. A more detailed profile user (which contains information about his previous studies or experience in project management) can be used to recommend documents which were recommended to the same type of user, in the past and considered useful by that type of user. In order to increase the usability of the solution, we should migrate the clustering process on the web and go for a distributed architecture: the ontology can stay on a machine, the clustering process on other machine and so on. For the moment, the recommender engine works only for Romanian language. In the future, it should be extended to other languages, too.

## CONCLUSION

The chapter presents a procedure for clustering web-based results, using an educational ontology. The procedure is included in a recommender engine, which is fired each time an e-assessment application is used, this fact being the core contribution of the current research work. The clustering algorithm applied is the k-means one, as it is the most exploited algorithm in RS researches. Schafer, Frankowski, Herlocker and Sen (2007) identified 40 such researches, while the hierarchical divisive was applied in 31 studies and agglomerative clustering to 35 studies. By using the RS engine, the e-assessment application gets formative features: it gives proper knowledge (through reading recommendations) to proper users (users receive these recommendations, depending on their mistakes). The feedback mechanism is generally considered to be highly important for the formative dimension of an e-test (Biggam, 2010), but some researchers argue that it does not increase the students' performance (Wieling and Hofman, 2010). The chapter states that, if included in a recommender system, it efficiently adjusts learning: experimentation results are also provided. The clusters of recommendations were evaluated via a survey on the users of the e-assessment application: special interest was given to the documents' distribution in clusters, the clusters' labels, comparison with other clustering applications and the utility of the recommended web documents to the users. The analysis of the results reveals that the recommendations offered are efficiently clustered and satisfactory enough for the users to continue their learning process.

## REFERENCES

Adomavicius, G., & Tuzhilin, A. (2005). Toward the next generation of recommender systems: A survey of the state-of-the-art and possible extensions. *IEEE Transactions on Knowledge and Data Engineering*, *17*(6), 734–749. doi:10.1109/TKDE.2005.99

Baeza-Yates, R., & Ribeiro-Neto, B. (1999). *Modern information retrieval*. New York, NY: Addison Wesley & ACM Press.

Balabanovic, M., & Shoham, Y. (1997). Content-based collaborative recommendation. *Communications of the ACM*, *40*(3), 66–72. doi:10.1145/245108.245124

Biggam, J. (2010). *Using automated assessment feedback to enhance the quality of student learning in universities: A case study*. In Technology Enhanced Learning. Quality of Teaching and Educational Reform. Athens, 2010. Springer.

Birenbaum, M., Kimron, H., Shilton, H., & Shahaf-Barzilay, R. (2009). Cycles of inquiry: Formative assessment in service of learning in classrooms and in school-based professional communities. *Studies in Educational Evaluation*, *35*, 130–149. doi:10.1016/j.stueduc.2010.01.001

Blanco-Fernández, Y., Pazos-Arias, J. J., Gil-Solla, A., Ramos-Cabrer, M., López-Nores, M., & García-Duque, J. (2008). Exploiting synergies between semantic reasoning and personalization strategies in intelligent recommender systems: A case study. *Journal of Systems and Software*, *81*, 2371–2385. doi:10.1016/j.jss.2008.05.009

Bodea, C.-N., & Dascalu, M. (2010). Competency-based e-assessment in project management and firm performance: A case study. *Proceedings of the 4th Conference on European Computing Conference* (pp. 76-81). Bucharest, Romania: WSEAS.

Brin, S., & Page, L. (1998). The anatomy of a large-scale hypertextual Web search engine. *Proceedings of the Seventh International World Wide Web Conference* (pp. 107--117). Brisbane, Australia: Elsevier Science Publishers.

Burke, R. (2002). Hybrid recommender systems. *User Modeling and User-Adapted Interaction*, *12*(4), 331–370. doi:10.1023/A:1021240730564

Burke, R. (2007). Hybrid Web recommender systems. In Brusilovsky, P., Kobsa, A., & Nejdl, W. (Eds.), *The Adaptive Web, LNCS 4321* (pp. 377–408). Berlin, Germany: Springer-Verlag. doi:10.1007/978-3-540-72079-9_12

Chi, N. L. (2003). *A tolerance rough set approach to clustering web search results*. Master thesis, Warsaw, Poland: Faculty of Mathematics, Informatics and Mechanics, Warsaw University.

Cho, J. (2001). *Crawling the web: Discovery and maintenance of large-scale web data*. PhD thesis, Stanford University.

Cho, Y., Kim, J., & Kim, S. H. (2002). A personalized recommender system based on web usage mining and decision tree induction. *Systems with Applications*, *23*, 329–342. doi:10.1016/S0957-4174(02)00052-0

Delcea, C., & Dascalu, M.-I. (2009). Knowledge strategies tools for managing enterprise crisis. *Knowledge Management: Projects, Systems and Technologies, Proceedings of the 4th International Conference on Knowledge Management* (pp. 115-119). Bucharest, Romania: UNAP.

Frey, N., & Fisher, D. (2009). Using common formative assessments as a source of professional development in an urban American elementary school. *Teaching and Teacher Education*, *25*, 674–680. doi:10.1016/j.tate.2008.11.006

Göksedef, M., & Gündüz-Ögüdücü, S. (2010). Combination of Web page recommender systems. *Expert Systems with Applications*, *37*, 2911–2922. doi:10.1016/j.eswa.2009.09.046

Hernandez del Olmo, F., & Gaudioso, E. (2008). Evaluation of recommender systems: A new approach. *Expert Systems with Applications*, *35*, 790–804. doi:10.1016/j.eswa.2007.07.047

Hotho, A., Staab, S., & Stumme, G. (2003). WordNet improves text document clustering. *Proceedings of the Semantic Web Workshop at 26th Annual International ACM SIGIR Conference*. Toronto, Canada.

Hsu, I.-C. (2009). SXRS: An XLink-based recommender system using Semantic Web technologies. *Expert Systems with Applications*, *36*, 3795–3804. doi:10.1016/j.eswa.2008.02.062

Hsu, M.-H. (2008). A personalized English learning recommender system for ESL students. *Expert Systems with Applications, 34*, 683–688. doi:10.1016/j.eswa.2006.10.004

IJntema. W., Goossen, F., Frasincar, F., & Hogenboom, F. (2010). Ontology-based news recommendation. *Proceedings of the 2010 EDBT/ICDT Workshops.* Lausanne, Switzerland: ACM.

Kanellopoulos, D., Kotsiantis, S., & Pintelas, P. (2006). Ontology-based learning applications: A development methodology. *Proceedings of the 24th IASTED International Multi-Conference Software Engineering* (pp. 27-32). Innsbruck, Austria: IASTED.

Kardan, A. A., Abbaspour, S., & Hendijanifard, F. (2009). A hybrid recommender system for e-learning environments based on concept maps and collaborative tagging. *The 4th International Conference on Virtual Learning* (pp. 200-207). Iasi, Romania: ICVL.

Kogilavani, A., & Balasubramanie, P. (2009). Ontology enhaced clustering based summarization of medical documents. *International Journal of Recent Trends in Engineering, 1*. Academy Publisher.

Leouski, A., & Croft, W. (1996). *An evaluation of techniques for clustering search results*. Amherst, MA: Department of Computer Science, University of Massachusetts.

Leuski, A., & Allan, J. (2000). Improving interactive retrieval by combining ranked list and clustering. *Proceedings of RIAO, College de France*, (pp. 665-681). Paris.

Lula, P., & Paliwoda-Pekosz, G. (2008). An ontology-based cluster analysis framework. *Proceedings of the First International workshop on Ontology-supported business inteligence*, (pp. 1-6). Karlsruhe, Germany.

Manouselis, N., Drachsler, H., Vuorikari, R., Hummel, H., & Koper, R. (2010). Recommender systems in technology enhanced learning. In Ricci, F., Rokach, L., Shapira, B., & Kantor, P. B. (Eds.), *Recommender systems handbook* (pp. 387–420). London, UK: Springer.

Martin-Guerrero, J. D., Palomares, A., Balaguer-Ballester, E., Soria-Olivas, E., Gomez-Sanchis, J., & Soriano-Asensi, A. (2006). Studying the feasibility of a recommender in a citizen web portal based on user modeling and clustering algorithms. *Expert Systems with Applications, 30*, 299–312. doi:10.1016/j.eswa.2005.07.025

Micarelli, A., Gasparetti, F., Sciarrone, F., & Gauch, S. (2007). Personalized search on the World Wide Web. In Brusilovsky, P., Kobsa, A., & Nejdl, W. (Eds.), *The Adaptive Web, LNCS 4321* (pp. 195–230). Berlin, Germany: Springer-Verlag. doi:10.1007/978-3-540-72079-9_6

Middleton, S. E. (2003). *Capturing knowledge of user preferences with recommender systems.* Southampton, UK: Doctoral thesis, Univ. Southampton.

Mödritscher, F. (2010). Towards a recommender strategy for personal learning environments. *Procedia Computer Science, 1*, 2775–2782. doi:10.1016/j.procs.2010.08.002

Mooney, R., & Roy, L. (2000). Content-based book recommending using learning for text categorization. *Proceedings of the ACM International Conference on Digital Libraries* (pp. 195–204). San Antonio, TX: ACM.

Niwa, S., Doi, T., & Honiden, S. (2006). Web page recommender system based on folksonomy mining. *Proceedings of the Third International Conference on Information Technology: New Generations* (pp. 388-393). Las Vegas, NV: IEEE.

Osiński, S. (2003). *An algorithm for clustering of Web search results.* Master thesis, Poznań University of Technology.

Rosaci, D. (2007). CILIOS: Connectionist inductive learning and inter-ontology similarities for recommending information agents. *Information Systems*, *32*, 793–825. doi:10.1016/j.is.2006.06.003

Schafer, J. B., Frankowski, D., Herlocker, J., & Sen, S. (2007). Collaborative filtering recommender systems. In Brusilovsky, P., Kobsa, A., & Nejdl, W. (Eds.), *The Adaptive Web, LNCS 4321* (pp. 291–324). Berlin, Germany: Springer-Verlag. doi:10.1007/978-3-540-72079-9_9

Sosnovsky, S., Brusilovsky, P., Yudelson, M., Mitrovic, A., Mathews, M., & Kumar, A. (2009). Semantic integration of adaptive educational systems. In Kuflik, T., Berkovsky, S., Carmagnola, F., Heckmann, D., & Krüger, A. (Eds.), *Advances in ubiquitous user modelling* (pp. 134–158). Berlin, Germany: Springer-Verlag. doi:10.1007/978-3-642-05039-8_8

Weng, S.-S., & Chang, H.-L. (2008). Using ontology network analysis for research document recommendation. *Expert Systems with Applications*, *34*, 1857–1869. doi:10.1016/j.eswa.2007.02.023

Wieling, M., & Hofman, W. (2010). The impact of online video lecture recordings and automated feedback on student performance. *Computers & Education*, *2010*, 992–998. doi:10.1016/j.compedu.2009.10.002

Wróblewski, M. (2003). *A hierarchical WWW pages clustering algorithm based on the vector space model.* Master thesis, Department of Computing Science, Poznań University of Technology.

Yang, S.-Y. (2010). Developing an ontology-supported information integration and recommendation system for scholars. *Expert Systems with Applications*, *37*, 7065–7079. doi:10.1016/j.eswa.2010.03.011

Zhen, L., Huang, G. Q., & Jiang, Z. (2010). An inner-enterprise knowledge recommender system. *Expert Systems with Applications*, *37*, 1703–1712. doi:10.1016/j.eswa.2009.06.057

Zheng, H.-T., Kang, B.-Y., & Kim, H.-G. (2008). An ontology-based approach to learnable focused crawling. *Information Sciences*, *178*, 4512–4522. doi:10.1016/j.ins.2008.07.030


## ADDITIONAL READING


Blanco-Fernandez, Y., Pazos-Arias, J., Gil-Solla, A., Ramos-Cabrer, M., Lopez-Nores, M., & Garcıa-Duque, J. (2008). A flexible semantic inference methodology to reason about user preferences in knowledge-based recommender systems. *Knowledge-Based Systems*, *21*, 305–320. doi:10.1016/j.knosys.2007.07.004

Blochdorn, S., & Hotho, A. (2004). Text classification by boosting weak learners based on terms and concepts. *Proceedings of the 4th IEEE International Conference in Data Mining* (pp. 331-334). Brighton, UK: IEEE.

Bobadilla, J., Serradilla, F., & Hernando, A. (2009). Collaborative filtering adapted to recommender systems of e-learning. *Knowledge-Based Systems*, *22*, 261–265. doi:10.1016/j.knosys.2009.01.008

Bodea, C., & Dascalu, M. (2009a). Designing project management tests based on semantic nets and concept space graphs, *Proceedings of the 12nd International Business Information Management Association Conference (IBIMA)* (pp. 1232-1236), Kuala Lumpur, Malaysia.

Bodea, C., & Dascalu, M. (2009b). A parameterized web-based testing model for project management, *Proceedings of the* 8th International Conference Aachen, Germany.

Bodea, C., & Lipai, A. (2009). Development of a meta-search tool for the web using a clustering algorithm, *Proceedings of the 12nd International Business Information Management Association Conference (IBIMA)* (pp. 729-733), Kuala Lumpur, Malaysia.

Bodea, C., Trandafir, I., & Borozan, A. M. (2008). Assessment of project management knowledge using semantic networks in the SinPers system, Proceedings of the 22rd IPMA World Congress on Project Management, Rome, Italy.

Cutting, D. R., Karger, D. R., Pedersen, J. O., & Tukey, J. W. (1992). Scatter/Gather: a cluster-based approach to browsing large document collections. *Proceedings of the 15th International Conference on Research and Development of Information Retrieval (SIGIR)* (pp. 318-329). Copenhagen: ACM.

Franstrom, F., & Lewis, J. (2000). *CiteSeer.* Retrieved December 27, 2009, from Fast, single-pass K-means algorithms: http://citeseerx.ist.psu.edu/viewdoc/summary?doi=10.1.1.36.7008

Funk, M., Rozinat, A., Karapanos, E., Alves de Medeiros, A., & Koca, A. (2010). In site evaluation of recommender systems: Frameworkandinstrumentation. *International Journal of Human-Computer Studies*, *68*, 525–547. doi:10.1016/j.ijhcs.2010.01.002

Hotho, A., Maedche, A., & Staab, S. (2001). *Ontology-based text clustering. Text Learning: Beyond Supervision*. Seattle, USA: IJCAI.

Hsu, J.-L., Chou, H.-W. & Chang, H.-H., 2010. EduMiner: Using text mining for automatic formative assessment. *Expert Systems with Applications*.

Osiński, S. (2003). *An Algorithm for Clustering of Web Search Results (master thesis).* Poznań: University of Technology.

Price, G. (2004, September 30). *Reducing Information Overkill.* Retrieved January 28, 2010, from Reducing Information Overkill: http://searchenginewatch.com/showPage.html?page=3415071

Stefanowski, J., & Weiss, D. (2003). Carrot2 and Language Properties in Web Search Results Clustering. *Proceedings of the First International Web Intelligence Conference* (pp. 240-249). Madrid: Springer.

Thai-Nghe, N., Drumond, L., Krohn-Grimberghe, A., & Schmidt-Thieme, L. (2010). Recommender System for Predicting Student Performance. *Procedia Computer Science*, *1*, 2811–2819. doi:10.1016/j.procs.2010.08.006

Wang, Y.-F., Chuang, Y.-L., Hsu, M.-H., & Keh, H.-C. (2004). A personalized recommender system for the cosmetic business. *Expert Systems with Applications*, *26*, 427–434. doi:10.1016/j.eswa.2003.10.001

Weiss, D. (2001). *A clustering interface for web search results in polish and english (master's thesis).* Poznan: University of Technology.

Wróblewski, M. (2003). *A Hierarchical WWW Pages Clustering Algorithm Based on the Vector Space Model (master thesis).* Poznań: Department of Computing Science, University of Technology.

Yang, H.-L., & Wang, C.-S. (2009). Recommender system for software project planning one application of revised CBR algorithm. *Expert Systems with Applications*, *36*, 8938–8945. doi:10.1016/j.eswa.2008.11.050

Yuan, S.-T., & Cheng, C. (2006). Ontology-based personalized couple clustering for heterogeneous product recommendation in mobile marketing. *Expert Systems with Applications*, *26*, 461–476. doi:10.1016/j.eswa.2003.10.006

Zamir, O. (1999). *Clustering Web Documents: A Phrase-Based Method (PhD thesis).* Washington: University of Washington.

Zamir, O., & Etzioni, O. (1998). Web Document Clustering: A Feasibility Demonstration. *Proceedings of the 19th International Computer Research and Development of Information Retrieval (SIGIR)* (pp. 46-54). Melbourne: ACM.

Zenebe, A., & Norcio, A. (2009). Representation, similarity measures and aggregation methods using fuzzy sets for content-based recommender systems. *Fuzzy Sets and Systems*, *160*, 76–94. doi:10.1016/j.fss.2008.03.017

## KEY TERMS AND DEFINITIONS

**Cluster Centroid:** The concept or word which appears in all the documents from the same cluster. The cluster centroid is the most specific concept or word for the cluster and, usually, provides the cluster label.

**Clustering Search Results:** Grouping the results into object classes which are developed using the search results characteristics, with the purpose of simplifying the user work to retrieve the relevant results. Clustering is applied after the query results are provided by the search engines. The user interfaces send queries to different search engines, then take the list of results offered by traditional web search and divide it into relevant sub lists, using clustering algorithms, such as k-means, hierarchical divisive clustering or agglomerative clustering.

**Documents Vectoring:** The method by which numerical vectors are built for each document, according to the frequency of each word in a document; stop words (such as "and", "or", "in)" and characters are not included. Document vectoring is a method of word-weight calculation for each document, which can be applied after preprocessing the documents (the tag cleaning, the word root extraction, the stop word elimination) and establishing the index words (the most representative words in the context of each document).

**Formative e-Assessment:** A type of e-assessment, which places much more emphasis on the role of feedback, giving the students the possibility to revise their mistakes. Formative e-assessment is different from diagnostic e-assessment (which takes place before the learning process) and from summative assessment (which takes place at the end learning process). It is present during the learning process, being more than an evaluation tool: it is a learning tool, which shows the users where their knowledge gaps are and how these gaps can be filled. Formative e-assessment is known as the assessment for learning.

**Meta-Search:** The use of more search tools simultaneously for the same query. A meta-search engine sends the same request to several other search engines (such as Google, Bing, Ask), then aggregates the results into the same list, taking into account the users' criteria.

**Ontology:** A formal representation of the knowledge by a set of concepts within a domain and the relationships between those concepts. Ontology is a structural framework for organizing knowledge, used in artificial intelligence, system engineering, software engineering and so on. Usually, the components of ontology are: classes (collections, concepts), instances or objects, relationships (the way in which classes relates one to each other), rules, restrictions.

**Recommender System:** An intelligent system, used for guiding the user to interesting objects (concepts) in a large space of possible options. Recommender systems must choose which of the items should be shown to the user or when and how the recommendations must be shown. Recommender can generate suggestions or filter them, by rating. They have a wide range of applications, including educational domain.

# Chapter 8
# A Recommender System for Learning Objects Personalized Retrieval

**Ana Casali**
*Universidad Nacional de Rosario, Argentina*

**Valeria Gerling**
*Universidad Nacional de Rosario, Argentina*

**Claudia Deco**
*Universidad Nacional de Rosario, Argentina*

**Cristina Bender**
*Universidad Nacional de Rosario, Argentina*

## ABSTRACT

*This chapter describes the development of a recommender system of learning objects. This system helps a user to find educational resources that are most appropriate to his/her needs and preferences. The search is performed in different repositories of learning objects, where each object has descriptive metadata. Metadata is used to retrieve objects that satisfy not only the subject of the query, but also the user profile, taking into account his/her characteristics and preferences. A multi-agent architecture that includes several types of agents with different functionalities is used. In this chapter, we describe the modelization of the Personalized Search Agent (PS-Agent) as a graded BDI (Belief-Desire-Intention) agent. This agent is responsible for making a flexible content-based retrieval and provides an ordered list of the resources that better meet the user profile data. A prototype was implemented, and experimentation results are presented.*

DOI: 10.4018/978-1-61350-489-5.ch008

## INTRODUCTION

Nowadays, there is a large number and diversity of resources that can contribute to the educational process. In the last years, repositories of different resources have arisen to gather materials for educational purpose. A Learning Object (LO) is any digital self-contained and reusable entity, with a clear educational purpose, with at least three internal and editable components: content, learning activities and elements of context. Learning objects must have an external structure of information to facilitate their identification, storage and retrieval: the metadata (Chiappe, 2007). LOs may be useful for a student who wants to learn a subject, or for a teacher who is trying to prepare didactic material for his/her class. LOs are stored in online repositories. Here are a few examples: the Ariadne Foundation for the Knowledge Pool (European Association open to the World, for Knowledge Sharing and Reuse), the OERCommons (Open Educational Resources initiative, created by ISKME, the Institute for the Study of Knowledge Management in Education as part of the Foundation's worldwide OER initiative) and FLOR (Federación Latinoamericana de Repositorios, created by the Latin-American Community of Learning Objects). These LO repositories store useful and interesting resources about different subjects and most of them have a search engine to retrieve LOs according to a particular topic.

When a student or a teacher needs to find educational resources, he/she could submit a query to these repositories. But different users get the same list of objects for a given search. In general, users check only the top results, but in many cases, these top results are not the most suitable if the search is performed considering only subject keywords. This is because users have different personal characteristics and preferences, which should be also considered in the search. Recommender systems arise to help in this kind of problem. Then, they can be used to automatically select LOs that are more appropriate to each user.

For example, suppose that two Argentinean students at the university, José and María, need to study on Java language, and they decide to search a repository looking for a course about Java. But José and María are different. José is studying an informatics career and María studies industrial engineering. José handles English fluently, and he prefers to solve problems in a practical way to understand what he needs to learn. María has not knowledge of English, and she prefers a theoretical knowledge of the subject to understand. Furthermore, José has previous knowledge on programming languages but María has not it. Both made the search for Java programming language in the repository, and both get the same list of courses as a result. When José scrolls the list of results, he discards the top ten because they are theoretical or very basic, and he chooses to use the eleventh. María discards the first four items of the list because she does not have prior knowledge to understand them or are in English. She chooses to use the sixth item, which is theoretical and no prior knowledge is needed. Both José and María have spent time and effort to evaluate the retrieved list of courses, and they discard several of them for various reasons unrelated to the topic of interest. So, taking into account language, difficulty and learning style, etc. that the user prefers, the recommender system can make a ranking of the best LOs for that user, and it puts them as top results.

Agent based architecture seems to be a promising approach for recommender systems design. Agents are autonomous and intelligent software entities that are able to handle specific tasks with little or no human supervision. The aim of these agents is to explore and filter the best options from a user profile (personal data, preferences, characteristics, etc.) considering a large number of different possibilities. This requires a user profile extracted in an implicitly or explicitly way. One of the most remarkable agent architectures is the BDI agent proposed by Rao and Georgeff (Rao, 1995). This model is based on the explicit representation of the agent's beliefs (B), desires (D) and intentions (I). Its beliefs (B) represent the information related to the state of the environment; its desires (D) represent the states of the world the agent wants to reach; its intentions (I) model their goals (the states of the world that it is committed to). This architecture has evolved over time and has had important applications in multi-agent systems. In order to make the BDI architecture more flexible, Casali et al. (2009) have proposed a general model for designing graded BDI agents (g-BDI). This model allows to specify architectures for dealing with an uncertainty environment and with graded mental attitudes in order to design and develop agents that may have a better performance in uncertain and dynamic environments. This agent model is suitable for the design of a Personalized Search Agent. The g-BDI agent model allows the representation of graded users' preferences and the uncertainty of reaching the different pedagogical goals through a particular LO.

We present in this chapter a recommender system that selects the best learning objects from a federation of repositories taking into account not only the subject, but also the user characteristics and preferences, modelled in personal profiles. Learning objects are described using metadata with semantic descriptions. This multi-agent system includes several types of agents according to different roles and functionalities.

To show the feasibility of the system and to evaluate preliminary results, a prototype was implemented, by using the SWI-Prolog language and Ruby on Rails, an open source framework to develop web applications. Experimentation was performed in Ariadne (http://www.ariadne-eu.org/) because this repository stores a great amount of LOs in different languages and has educational metadata. Experimentation results show that the proposed system is feasible and useful. The main characteristic of the recommender system of LOs presented in this chapter was stated in (Casali, 2010). In that paper we proposed the same general architecture for the recommender system, but in this chapter we added the rules used by the PS-Agent to compute the degree of satisfaction of the user preferences and restrictions for each LO, and also new experimentation is presented.

We organize the chapter in the following way. In the next section, we describe basic concepts such as learning objects, standards and repositories, agent architectures and recommender agents. After that, a general Recommender System Architecture is described. Then, the Personalized Search Agent design is presented. This agent is modelled as a graded BDI agent and its contexts and rules are described. Next sections present a prototype implementation, experimentation, and related work respectively. Finally, we present some discussions of our proposal and future work.

## BACKGROUND

### Learning Objects and Repositories

The concept of learning objects is useful to store, classify and reuse educational resources. A Learning Object (LO) is any digital resource that can be reused to support learning (Wiley, 2002). LOs can be used by a student who wants to learn a subject, or may be used by a teacher who wants to prepare materials for his/her class. LOs are described with metadata. The standard LOM (http://www.ieee.org) specifies the syntax and semantics of learning object metadata. This standard was developed by the IEEE working group with contributions of the IMS Global Learning Consortium together with the ARIADNE Foundation. Other metadata specification is the Dublin Core (http://dublincore.org), standardized as ANSI/NISO Z39.85, which provides a simpler, more loosely-defined set of elements with some overlap with LOM, and which is useful for sharing metadata across a wide range of services. The Dublin Education Working Group aims to provide refinements of Dublin Core for the specific needs of the education community. We chose LOM standard because it is used by LO repositories to describe their learning objects. This is because relevant attributes of LOM standard include pedagogical attributes, such as teaching or interaction style, besides the classical attributes of documents.

Recker & Wiley (2001) analyze metadata to support the discovery and the instructional reuse of learning objects. They make a distinction between authoritative and non-authoritative metadata. Differences are based on the persistent (authoritative) aspects of a LO (e.g., file size) and the (non-authoritative) context of learning object use and re-use (e.g., its value or usefulness within a particular instructional situation). Authoritative metadata is generally contributed by the author or authorized cataloguers. Non-authoritative metadata is more likely to be contributed by users of LOs, who also describe and discuss the application of collaborative filtering techniques within a non-authoritative metadata structure in order to support automatic filtering and automatic recommendation of relevant LOs.

In relation to finding appropriate courses in e-learning, Michael Sonntag (2004) analyzes the importance of metadata for learning objects, as these resources may often and possibly be reused in different contexts. One of the problems he points out is the diversity of standards and search engine supports. As preparing learning resources with suitable metadata is a labour-intensive activity, there is consequently a lack of quality information in metadata.

Users can retrieve LOs through searches in web repositories. These repositories have educational metadata for each resource. Examples of such repositories are: FLOR (http://www.laclo.org), Ariadne (http://www.ariadne-eu.org), and OER Commons (http://www.oercommons.org). FLOR is a federation of repositories of learning objects from different educational institutions in Latin America. Every institution concerned can share their learning objects in FLOR. Objects metadata are specified by using the LOM standard and can be retrieved through SQI (Simple Query Interface). ARIADNE is a European Association for Knowledge Sharing and Reuse. It promotes international cooperation in education, open to everyone, and allows federated searches. Some of the repositories of the federation it works with are: CGIAR, EducaNext, LACLO-FLOR, Merlot and OER Commons. OER Commons is the first open network for learning. For metadata transmission, it uses OAI-PMH (Open Archives Initiative - Protocol for Metadata Harvesting). Ariadne and OER Commons also use LOM standard to specify learning object metadata.

## Recommender Systems

In recent years, the Artificial Intelligence community has developed a great deal of work on recommender systems (Resnick, 1997). This type of systems can help people to find out what they want, especially *from* the Internet, by taking into account their personal preferences. Recommender systems are the technical response to the fact that we often rely on other people's experience and recommendations when confronted with a new field of expertise, when we do not have a broad knowledge of all facts, or when such knowledge exceeds the amount of information human beings can cognitively deal with. The main task of a recommender system is to locate items - educational resources in this case - considering user's preferences. This involves the construction of user models and the ability to anticipate and predict user preferences. When building the user's profile a distinction is made between explicit and implicit forms of data collection.

By looking at definitions of the design space of recommender systems (Resnick, 1997; Terveen, 2001), there seems to be some basic items common to most of them (Niinivara, 2004):

- *Resources:* The targets of the recommendation process.
- *Recommenders:* Those entities that give out opinions about resources. In practice,

recommenders are actors and they could also be artificial agents.

- *Descriptions:* Information about resources that include opinions.
- *Preferences:* Recommendation seeker's position towards resources.
- *Techniques for Computing Recommendation*: The system means to evaluate resources automatically by using descriptions and preference information.
- *Recommendations:* The concrete results of the evaluation process for the recommendation seeker. The recommendations may be presented in different ways (e.g. by filtering out resources, ordering resources).

One possibility for designing this kind of systems is to use agent architectures. Agents are software entities that have sufficient autonomy and intelligence to be able to handle specific tasks with little or no human supervision. The aim of these agents is to explore and filter the best options from a user profile considering a large number of different possibilities. This involves building a user model or a user profile that can be obtained implicitly or explicitly. A detailed taxonomy of recommender systems can be seen in (Montaner, 2003) and the main techniques for their development can be grouped into collaborative filtering systems, content-based filtering, knowledge-based filtering and hybrid systems.

Collaborative filtering techniques focus on the behaviour of users towards items -which are to be recommended- rather than on the internal nature of the items. These techniques work better when there is a broad user community and each user has already rated a significant number of items.

Content-based filtering focuses on the internal nature of items or on the content of description files. These systems use two main classes of algorithms: information retrieval or attribute-based filtering algorithms. This approach prefers content semantics to social interactions or user behaviour.

There are other types of products that are less frequently acceded to use collaborative filtering and for recommending such items. Consequently, the system must support a more detailed elicitation of user requirements and domain description. In these cases, deep domain knowledge has to be exploited in order to be able to make more precise and reliable recommendations. Knowledge-based (KB) recommender technologies (Burke, 2000) are suitable for this.

A recommender system provides a user search close to his/her information needs (Niinivara, 2004). The education domain appears to be a good candidate for recommender systems application because educational resources offers are constantly growing.

In our recommender system, the items are learning objects, which are not frequently accessed, then we consider that a hybrid approach combining a content-based filtering with knowledge based-filtering is a good alternative for the our recommender.

## Agents and Multi-Agent Systems

In recent years, the design and implementation of multi-agent systems have increased in order to develop complex distributed systems, and in particular, they have been used for the development of recommender systems. Agent technology allows these systems to generate and use user profiles, to infer and add information from heterogeneous and distributed sources, to obtain scalable, open and secure systems, and to perform tasks requiring less user intervention. With respect to agent technology, several architectures have been proposed to provide agents with a formal support (Wooldridge, 1995; Wooldridge 2009). Among them, a well-known intentional formal approach is the BDI architecture (Rao, 1995). This model is based on the explicit representation of the agent's beliefs (B), desires (D), and intentions (I). The agent´s beliefs represent all the information the agent has about the environment, the agent's desires are the states of the world the agent wants to reach (the agent's desires may be ideal and sometimes unattainable). Some of these states are the goals the agent is committed to achieve, i.e. the agent's intentions. Indeed, this architecture has evolved over time and to some extent has been used for several of the most significant multiagent applications developed up to now (Georgeff, 1999; Wooldridge, 2009). However, the importance of BDI models is not limited to the theoretical field. In the last years, there have been different developments of particulars BDI architectures. One of the specific BDI agent architectures is IRMA (Bratman, 1988) and the best-known implementation of the BDI model is the Procedural Reasoning System (PRS). PRS has been implemented in different platforms, as for example JACK (Howden, 2001) and JASON (Bordini, 2007).

A more flexible BDI architecture for the design and development of agents potentially capable of having a better performance in uncertain and dynamic environments has been proposed in (Casali, 2009). In this work, the authors have proposed a general model for graded BDI (g-BDI) agents specifying an architecture able to deal with the environment uncertainty and with graded mental attitudes. In this agent model, *belief degrees* represent to what extent the agent believes a formula is true. *Degrees of positive or negative desires* enable the agent to set different levels of preference or rejection respectively. *Intention degrees* give also a preference measure but, in this case they model the cost/benefit trade off of reaching an agent's goal. Consequently, agents having different kinds of behaviour can be modelled by the representation and interaction of these three attitudes. This agent architecture has solid logic formalization (Casali, 2009) and it has been used to model and implement a tourism recommender agent (Casali, 2008).

This g-BDI agent model is specified using multi-context systems (MCS) introduced by Ghidini and Giunchiglia (2001). This approach is suitable to represent complex logical systems for it allows to represent local logical aspects in different contexts and then to combine them by inter-context rules. The MCS specification contains three basic components: units or contexts, logics, and bridge rules, which channel the propagation of consequences among theories. Thus, an agent is defined as a group of interconnected units: $\langle\{C_i\}_{i\in I}, \Delta_{br}\rangle$, where each context $C_i \in \{C_i\}_{i\in I}$ is the tuple $C_i = \langle L_i, A_i, \Delta_i\rangle$ where $L_i$, $A_i$ and $\Delta_i$ are the language, axioms, and inference rules respectively. When a theory $T_i \in L_i$ is associated with each unit, the specification of a particular MCS is complete. The deduction mechanism of these systems is based on two kinds of inference rules, internal rules $\Delta_i$, and bridge rules $\Delta_{br}$, which allow to embed formulae into a context whenever the conditions of the bridge rule are satisfied.

In the g-BDI agent model, we have at least mental contexts to represent *beliefs* (BC), *desires* (DC) and *intentions* (IC). The purpose of the BC is to model the agent's beliefs about the environment. In the DC, the agent's desires are represented. Desires represent the ideal agent's preferences regardless of the agent's current perception of the environment and regardless of the cost involved in actually achieving them. This model allows a bipolar representation of preferences that formalizes agent's positive and negative desires. Positive desires represent what the agent would like to be. Negative desires correspond to what the agent rejects or do not want to occur. Both, positive and negative desires can be graded. The IC unit is used to represent the agent's intentions. Together with desires, they represent the agent's preferences. However, we consider that intentions cannot depend just on the benefit of reaching a goal, but also on the cost of transforming the world into one where the goal is satisfied. By setting degrees in intentions we represent a measure of the cost/benefit relation involved in the agent's actions towards the goal. This agent model also considers two functional contexts for Planning (PC) and Communication

(CC). The Planner Context (PC) has to look for feasible plans in a repository and the Communication unit (CC) makes it possible to encapsulate the agent's internal structure and have a unique and well-defined interface with the environment.

Formally, a g-BDI agent model is defined as:

$$A_g = (\{BC, DC, IC, PC, CC\}, \Delta_{br}).$$

The overall behaviour of the system will depend on the logic representation of each intentional notion in the different contexts *and the bridge rules*. In order to represent graded notions of beliefs, desires and intentions, and reason about them, the agent model uses a modal many-valued approach. For instance, let us consider a Belief context where belief degrees are to be modelled as probabilities. Then, for each classical formula $\varphi$, we consider a modal formula $B\varphi$ that is interpreted as "$\varphi$ is probable". This modal formula $B\varphi$ is then a fuzzy formula, which may be more or less true, depending on the probability of $\varphi$. In particular, we can take the probability of $\varphi$ as a truth-value of $B\varphi$. Moreover, using a many-valued logic, it can express the governing axioms of probability theory as logical axioms involving modal formulae. Then, the many-valued logic machinery can be used to reason about the modal formulae $B\varphi$, which faithfully respect the uncertainty model chosen to represent the degrees of belief. It has been set up an adequate axiomatization for the belief context logic by combining axioms for the different formulae. The same many-valued logic approach is used to represent graded attitudes in the other mental contexts, and reason about them.

## Related Work

In the last years agent technology has proved to be a promising approach to engineering recommender systems by appreciating the facts that we want the systems to take personal preferences into account and to infer and to aggregate intelligently relationships from heterogeneous and distributed sources and data. Relevant uses of software agent technology in achieving tasks related to recommendation are analyzed in (Niinivaara, 2004) and a complete taxonomy of recommender agents can be seen in (Montaner, 2003).

Respect to the use of BDI model of agents in recommender systems, the Seta2000 infrastructure (Ardissono, 2005) offers a built-in recommendation engine, based on a multi-agent architecture. Moreover, the infrastructure supports the integration of heterogeneous software and the development of agents (particularly BDI agents) that can be configured to offer specialized facilities within a recommender system, but also to dynamically enable and disable such facilities, depending on the requirements of the application domain. In (Carbó, 2001) a BDI agent architecture is presented where the reputation of a potential recommender agent is evaluated. In a multiagent recommender system, for shopping centres (Bajo, 2006) a recommender agent is implemented as a Case-Based Reasoning (CBR) approach to the implementation of BDI agents (implementing cases as beliefs). Besides, a tourism recommender agent in a multiagent platform using the graded BDI agent model can be seen in (Casali, 2008). The system goal is to recommend the best tourist packages on Argentinean destination according to the user's preferences and restrictions.

Respect to recommender systems in education, Zhu (2008) proposes a multi-agent architecture of personalized recommendation system, which can provide personalized services for learners and instructors. Six software agents coordinate work hierarchy with each other to offer a range of primary functions that include static and dynamic users modelling, learning plan generation and adjustment, personalized content search, personalized recommendation, as well as real-time evaluation of learning progress.

Wang (2007) presents an adaptive personalized recommendation model in order to recommend SCORM-compliant learning objects from repositories in the Internet. They adopt an ontological approach to perform semantic discovery and preference-based and correlation-based approaches to rank the degree of relevance of LOs to a learner's intension and preference. In addition, their proposal infer a learner's preference periodically and can predict the suitability of a LO by referencing the history of usages of other similar learners.

Lu (2004) proposes a framework of a personalized learning recommender system, which aims to help students find learning materials they would need to read. Two key research issues involved in the study are how to identify a student's need, and how to find accurately the learning materials, which match the student's need. For this, he develops two related technologies: a multi-attribute evaluation method to justify a student's need, and a fuzzy matching method to find suitable learning materials to best meet each student need. Once a resource is retrieved and a student's personal information is obtained, the system uses a computational analysis model to identify the student's learning requirement, and then uses matching rules to generate the recommendation.

García Salcines (2008) presents a recommender system oriented to suggest the most appropriate modifications to the teacher in order to improve the effectiveness of a course. They propose to use a cyclical methodology to develop and carry out the maintenance of web-based courses in which they have added a specific data-mining step. They have developed a distributed rule mining system in order to discover information in the form of IFTHEN recommendation rules. They use an iterative and interactive association rule algorithm without parameters and with a weight-based evaluation measure of the rule interest. They present a collaborative recommender system that uses distributed data mining that allows teachers with similar profiles to share and score their research results because of applying data mining locally on their own courses.

Soonthornphisaj (2006) proposes a system to integrate recommended resources before giving it to the user. They develop an e-learning web application that integrates the materials recommender system to facilitate the learners during the learning process. The system evaluates each learner via the quiz generator by randomly selecting a set of questions that are created by the instructor. Their smart e-learning system helps instructors to create and maintain both compulsory materials and questions. They implemented the system at the faculty of Resource and Environment, Kasetsart University at Sri-racha campus and found that their system got a very good response from the instructors and learners. Furthermore, they propose the global e-learning framework using web service that has an ability to aggregate the recommended materials from other e-learning web sites and predicts suitable materials to learners.

Ghauth (2009) proposes a framework to recommend learning materials based on the similarity of content items, using Vector Space Model, and based on good learners' average rating strategy. They propose two types of recommendations: a content-based recommendation and a recommendation based on good learners' average ratings. The first recommends additional learning resources that are similar to those of the viewing item. The second recommendation aims to guide learners in selecting good learning resources in order to improve their learning process. Their proposal also ensures that the current learning sequence is not interrupted and recommended items always remain within the learning context. This paper presents the overall architecture of the proposed system and its potential implementation via a prototype design.

Our proposal differs from most of these works because we use a multiagent system including a graded BDI agent that uses the user preferences and restrictions in a content-based approach, while Wang utilizes statistic approaches, Lu uses a fuzzy matching method, García Salcines applies data mining techniques and Ghauth works with Vector Space Model for ranking purposes. Multiagent systems are used also by Zhu, but they do not use graded BDI agents in their architecture as we do.

A good survey of systems proposed for recommending learning objects has recently been presented in (Manouselis et al., 2011). In this survey, twenty systems were briefly described and analyzed. Twelve of them still remain at a prototyping stage of development and only ten systems have been reported to be evaluated through trials that involved human users. Following the analysis made by these authors, our recommender system, as most of the reported systems in their work, is in a prototype stage and the system usage has been evaluated by human users.

## GENERAL ARCHITECTURE OF THE RECOMMENDER SYSTEM

We present a general system architecture to recommend Learning Objects (LOs) from a federation of repositories, according to user's characteristics and preferences. We found very suitable to design this system using a multi-agent architecture because it can manage heterogeneous and distributed information, such as LOs Repositories, and have a high degree of modularity and autonomy. Furthermore, these systems are highly scalable and open.

Many different Agent Oriented Software Engineering (AOSE) approaches have been proposed, a survey of them can be seen in (Bengenti, 2004). More recently, some proposals have been presented for BDI Agent Software Development Process (Jo, 2005; Zhang, 2003) as a specialization of traditional and Object Oriented software engineering methodologies. Based on these previous works, Casali et al. (2006) have presented a methodological framework to engineer graded BDI agents, working up those approaches, adapting and extending them, to engineer agents with a more complex internal architecture. In this work, the authors emphasized in the separation of the system design from the agent design phase, and considered important to include some social aspects in the system design phase and to add some steps to support the agent detailed design. Following this methodology, we design first the types of agents that might compose the recommender system and then, we model the architecture for its main agent, the *Personalized Search Agent.*

The architecture for the system proposed may include several types of agents according to their different roles. The *Interface Agent* (*I-Agent*) captures user input data. The *Semantic Refining Agent (SR-Agent)* is in charge of generating the search strategy associated with the user interest. A *User Profile Agent (UP-Agent)* builds and maintains the user profile. Several *Searchers Agents ($S_i$-Agent)* find LOs that satisfy the subject and constraints of user interest in repository $R_i$. A *Mediator Agent (M-Agent)* integrates results of each $S_i$-Agent. Finally, the *Personalized Search Agent (PS-Agent)* is responsible for making a flexible retrieval and it gives as result an ordered list with the best resources according to the user profile. The system architecture, showing these component agents and their interactions, is shown in Figure 1 and some details of the agents' functionalities are described next.

The *Interface Agent (I-Agent)* interacts with the user through a graphical interface. It captures data submitted by the user, and displays search results. This agent provides user preferences and restrictions to the *UP-Agent*. In addition, it provides the search topic to *SR-Agent*. Then, it receives from *PS-Agent* the recommendation (ranking of LOs) that it will be given to the user and finally, receives the user feedback.

The *Semantic Refiner Agent (SR-Agent)* uses information retrieval techniques to produce the search strategy associated to the user interest (Deco, 2005). When a user asks a query, he/she gives as input a set of concepts that describes his/her search topic. The result given by the *SR-Agent* is a search strategy associated to these concepts. A search strategy is a logical expression composed by different concepts combined with logical connectors, and it consists on the disjunction of

*Figure 1. General multiagent system architecture*

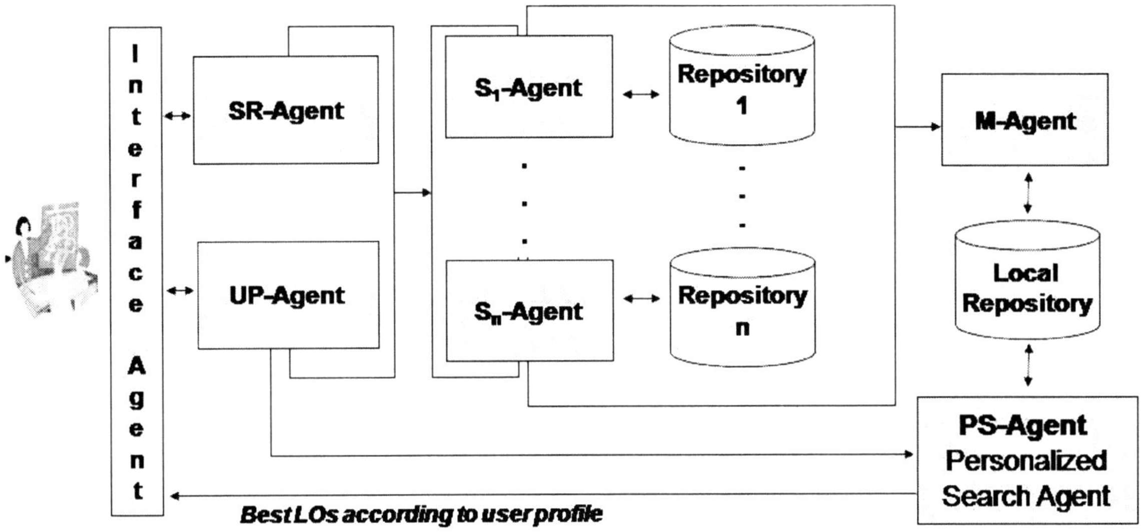


the expansions of each concept, and then, the conjunction of these expansions. In this process, this agent uses linguistic resources such as thesauri, dictionaries, multilingual dictionaries and ontologies. Therefore, the *SR-Agent* uses as input the set of terms that describe the topic of interest, disambiguating them and expanding each term by incorporating synonyms and semantically related terms. The output of this agent is a search strategy that will be provided to each search agent.

The *User Profile Agent (UP-Agent)* receives user data, user preferences and restrictions from the *Interface Agent*, in order to build his/her profile. This agent provides to the *Search Agents* (*$S_i$-Agent*) some restrictions (called primary restrictions) that can collaborate to filter LOs; for example, if the materials have or have not cost. In addition, this agent provides to the *Personalized Search Agent* preferences and remaining restrictions of the user, so that the objects are properly sorted.

Each *Search Agent ($S_i$-Agent)* searches, in a LO repository, objects that match user search strategy and some of the primary restrictions (e.g. be costless). For this, it adapts the search strategy to the query language syntax of the repository to which it accesses and then it establishes a communication with the repository through a communication protocol. Each result is parsed, transformed into a common format (e.g. XML), and sent to the *Mediator Agent* which stores this result in a local repository.

The *Mediator Agent (M-Agent)* integrates these results and solves conflicts in order to have consistent data. It stores the information in the local repository. For example, if the *M-Agent* receives from different *$S_i$-Agents* metadata information related to the same object, it complements/integrates these metadata describing it in the local repository.

The *Personalized Search Agent (PS-Agent)* takes this information and produces an ordered list of recommended objects. The *PS-Agent*, which is responsible for the retrieval of the best learning objects according to the user profile, has been developed following a content-based approach. It has been modelled as a g-BDI agent and we focus on the design of this agent. In the *PS-Agent*, beliefs represent the information the agent has about the educational environment and particularly, about

*Figure 2. Sequence diagram of the recommender system*

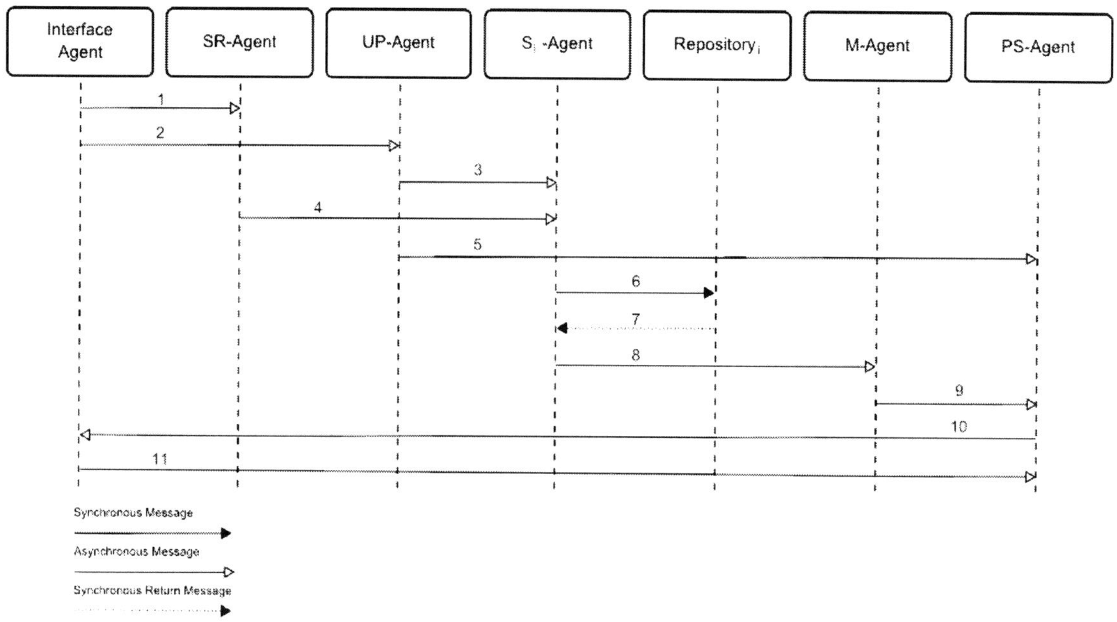


the LOs (described by the metadata). This context is also in charge of determining the degree of satisfaction of the different user's preferences by a set of proposed LOs. This estimation is inferred by a set of suitable rules. The positive and negative desires represent respectively the preferences and restrictions a user has respect to LO characteristics. Degrees of desires enable the agent to set different levels of preference or rejection respectively. Intentions are the final educative goals we want to reach with the retrieved resource, degrees give also a preference measure but, in this case, modelling the cost/benefit trade off, of reaching an agent's educational goal using an educational resource. In this agent the intentions degrees are computed by taking into account the degree of the agent's desires (modelling the users preferences and restrictions), the expected satisfaction of the desires by a LO, the cost and duration of the LO, among others factors. This agent is described in some detail in the following section.

To represent the agent's interaction in the multi-agent system we use a sequence diagram, which is shown in Figure 2, where the information flow between agents is described in a time line. In the diagram the information interchanged is the following: (1) Subject of interest, (2) User information (preferences and restrictions), (3) Primary user restrictions, (4) Query strategy, (5) User preferences and additional restrictions, (6) Query for Repository-i, (7) Retrieved LOs, (8) Retrieved LOs, (9) LOs with integrated metadata, (10) Recommendation (Order list of LOs) and (11) User feedback.

## DESIGN OF THE PERSONALIZED SEARCH AGENT

The Personalized Search Agent (*PS-Agent*) has been specified using the g-BDI model presented in a previous section. This agent model is suitable for the *PS-Agent*, since it allows to represent in an explicit way graded positive and negative preferences (i.e. as the agent's desires) and uses them to conduct the agent to the best intention (i.e. the

LO more suitable for the educational goal). The g-BDI agent model has contexts to represent the agent beliefs (BC), the agent desires (DC) and the agent intentions (IC), and we have chosen an appropriate reasoning model to deal with graded attitudes in the different contexts. We describe the principal characteristics of these contexts and give an example of a bridge rule in the *PS-Agent*. Particularly, we focus on the rules used in the Belief Context to compute the expected satisfaction of the different kinds of preferences.

## PS-Agent Contexts

### Belief Context (BC)

This context represents the information the *PS-Agent* has about education environment, including characteristics of the LOs. These characteristics are described by metadata according to LOM standard and encoded in XML. From the LOM metadata set, we have selected the most relevant to the recommender agent, such as Language, Learning Resource Type, Interactivity Level, Intended End User Role, Context, Difficulty, Typical Learning Time and Cost.

These metadata will be considered by the agent to infer the degree of preferences satisfaction, namely, to compute the belief degree $b_{ik}$ with that an object $O_i$ is expected to satisfy a particular user preference $p_k$. This is represented by the formula $B(O_i, p_k, b_{ik})$. For example, the belief degree with that the object $O_i$ satisfies the user's preference that the resource would be "practical", considering that its Learning Resource Type is specified as [exercise, lecture], is computed as 0.6 in the BC and is represented by $B(O_i$,style=practical,0.6).

A set of rules have been established for each kind of preferences (e.g. interaction, role, learning style, language) and an adequate distance is used for each case, some of them are described in the next subsection Rule base.

### Desire Context (DC)

The global desire of the *PS-Agent* is to find the LO that best fits the user profile, taking into account his/her selected subject, restrictions and preferences. In this context, we represent the user preferences and the restrictions that he/she wants for the LOs. The preferences considered in this approach are: language, role of the user (e.g. learner, teacher), interaction, learning style (e.g. theoretical, practical), academic context (e.g. high school, university) and knowledge level (e.g. initial, medium, high). Besides, the restrictions taking into account are maximum duration and cost. In turn, preferences and restrictions may be graded (with values, called priorities, in [0, 1]) expressing respectively different levels of preference and rejection. An extract of an example of user profile is shown in Table 1.

This table shows that the user strongly prefers that the LO language should be Spanish (degree equal 1); also he is satisfied with a resource in English (degree equal 1) and may be in French with a lower degree of preference (0.6). Furthermore, the user desires, with degree 0.7, that the interactivity with the LO should be low. Regarding restrictions, the user indicates with priority 0.7, that he/she does not want objects which duration exceeding 60 minutes.

Formally, this is represented by $D^{\pm}$ (*Preference/Characteristic=value, priority degree*). For example:

$D^+$ (*language*=Spanish, 1)

$D^+$ (*language*=English, 1)

$D^+$ (*language*=French, 0.6)

$D^+$ (*interaction*=low, 0.7)

$D^-$ (*Max-duration*=60, 0.7)

*Table 1. Extract from a user profile*

| Preference/Characteristic | Priority |
|---|---|
| Mother language="Spanish" | |
| Language="Spanish" | 1.0 |
| Language="English" | 1.0 |
| Language="French" | 0.6 |
| Role="learner"' | 1.0 |
| Interaction="low" | 0.7 |
| Learning style="practical'" | 1.0 |
| Academic context="university" | 1.0 |
| Knowledge level ="initial" | 1.0 |
| **Restriction** | **Priority** |
| Max-duration ="60" | 0.7 |
| Cost="no" | |

## Intention Context (IC)

Intentions are the educational goals that the user will try to reach through the best object (or objects) selected. It is expected that the user's learning process will be improved by the LOs that fit best his/her profile.

The intention to reach the goal (of satisfying a set of preferences $P=\{p_k \mid k = 1\ldots n\}$) by a particular $O_i$, has a degree $r_i$ and is represented by the formula $I(P, O_i, r_i)$. To compute $r_i$ the agent considers each preference $p_k$ with a degree $d_k$ and the expected satisfaction of this preference through an educational resource $O_i$, represented by $b_{ik}$. These variables are combined through an appropriate bridge rule (see rule (1)) that using belief and desire formulas, determines the degree of intention $r_i$ of each $O_i$ to satisfy all the preferences.

$$\frac{DC:(D^{+}p_1,d_1),\ldots,(D^{+}p_n,d_n);BC:B(O_i,p_1,b_{i1}),\ldots,B(O_i,p_n,b_{in})}{IC:I(P,O_i,r_i)} \qquad (1)$$

This degree of intention is then used to rank the LOs in the agent final recommendation.

The function $f$ to compute the degree of intention $r_i$ associated with each $O_i$, $f(d_1, \ldots, d_n, b_{i1}, \ldots, b_{in})$, may be defined in different ways. For example, in our prototype implementation we have defined it as the average of the expected satisfactions of all the user's preferences.

$$r_i = \frac{\sum_{j=1}^{n} d_j \times b_{ij}}{n} \qquad (2)$$

Other factors may be included in the bridge rule (1) as for example, the cost of the resource (if there is any) or the reliance on the source of the learning object (e.g. institution, author). Also, different functions can be used to compute the intention degree, modelling in this way different behaviours of the *PS-Agent*.

## Rule Base

In order to compute the degree of expected satisfaction of different kinds of preferences, we have design a set of rules in the belief context. This rules represents different functions used to estimate the belief degree in which a LO labelled

*Table 2. Degrees of belief for interaction*

| Metadata<br>Preference | *very low* | *low* | *medium* | *high* | *very high* | *unknown* |
|---|---|---|---|---|---|---|
| *low* | 1 | 1 | 0.6 | 0.2 | 0.1 | 0.5 |
| *medium* | 0.4 | 0.6 | 1 | 0.6 | 0.4 | 0.7 |
| *high* | 0.1 | 0.2 | 0.6 | 1 | 1 | 0.5 |

with metadata is expected to satisfy the user's preferences. Considering the nature of the diverse preferences and the value they can take, we have defined different sets of rules. These rules may be improved with the system experimentation. Below we describe some of these types of rules, a more complete description can be found in (Gerling, 2009).

## Interaction

The value of Interaction may be low, medium, high or ignore. The associated metadata is InteractivityLevel and it can take the values: very low, low, medium, high or very high. We have define a set of rules that associate to these five possible values the satisfaction of the three possible instances the user may choose, assigning degrees of belief in each case. The values used are shown in Table 2 and next we present an example of one of these rules:

(R1) IF InteractivityLevel($O_i$)=medium THEN B($O_i$, interaction=low, 0.6)

*"If the interactivity degree (represented by InteractivityLevel metadata) of the object $O_i$ is medium, Then the agent's belief respect to the satisfaction of the user's preference interaction=low takes an intermediate value (equal to 0.6)".*

## Role

The possible values for this preference are student or teacher (also may be ignore if the user did not set a value). For this preference, the corresponding metadata is IntendedEndUserRole. This metadata have a list of values (L). To specify the degrees of belief, we considered the position of a relevant metadata in the list of roles of these metadata and diverse similarities degrees to other roles (author, manager, etc.) correspond to learner or teacher roles. Table 3 resume the degrees used for the different situations.

As an example, we have the following rule in this category:

(R4) IF IntendedEndUserRole($O_i$)=[a,b,c, teacher,... ] and a,b,c $\in$ {learner, author, manager}

THEN B($O_i$, role=teacher, 0.4)

*"If the intended user role of the object $O_i$ is a list where Teacher is in the 4th place, Then the agent's belief respect to the satisfaction of the user's preference role=teacher takes a intermediate value (equal to 0.4)".*

## Academic Context and Knowledge Level

These two preferences specify the type of audience for which the object has been sought and their association establishes the level expected of the resource. The corresponding metadata are Context

*Table 3. Degrees of belief for role*

| | Values | Degree |
|---|---|---|
| | [learner,...] | 1 |
| | [a,learner,.. . ] and a ∈ {teacher, author, manager} | 0.8 |
| | [a,b,learner,.. . ] and a,b ∈ {teacher, author, manager} | 0.6 |
| learner | [a,b,c,learner,.. . ] and a,b,c ∈ {teacher, author, manager} | 0.4 |
| | [teacher,.. . ] and learner ∉ L | 0.3 |
| | ([author,.. . ] or [manager,.. . ]) and learner ∉ L | 0.1 |
| | [unknown] | 0.8 |
| | [teacher,...] | 1 |
| | [a, teacher,.. . ] and a ∈ {learner, author, manager} | 0.8 |
| | [a,b, teacher,.. . ] and a,b ∈ {learner, author, manager} | 0.6 |
| teacher | [a,b,c, teacher,.. . ] and a,b,c ∈ {learner, author, manager} | 0.4 |
| | ([learner,.. . ] or [author,.. . ]) and teacher ∉ L | 0.3 |
| | [manager,.. . ] and teacher ∉ L | 0.1 |
| | [unknown] | 0.2 |

and Difficulty. The Academic context can take the values: primary school, secondary school and third level/university. In turn, Knowledge level may be state as initial, medium and advanced. On the other hand, considering the LO metadata, Context values are school, higher education, training, other; and the values for Difficulty are very easy, easy, medium, difficult and very difficult.

Both topics contribute to focus on the audience of a LO, thus we have considered appropriate to deal with the combination of preferences and the corresponding pair of metadata. For this purpose we have defined first two functions *f* and *g*, where $f$: $Context \times Level \rightarrow N$ and $g$: $Context \times Difficulty \rightarrow N$.

These functions respectively translate the pair of preferences and metadata into natural scales in [1,9] and [1,13] and their definition can be seen in Table 4. Then, a distance between these functions is defined to compute the belief degree of satisfaction of the user's preferences related to Academic context and Knowledge level by a LO (with Context and Difficulty metadata).

From these two functions we can define the belief degree that the object with a particular pair of metadata (c2,n2) can satisfied the values of preferences (c1,n1). This degree is computed by a heuristic function from distance between the functions *f* and *g* assigned to each pair. Formally:

$$b((c1,n1),(c2,n2)) = \begin{cases} 1-(2\,h/10) & \text{if } h \leq 4, \text{ where } h = h((c1,n1),(c2,n2)) = |\,g(c2,n2) - f(c1,n1)\,| \\ 0.1 & \text{otherwise} \end{cases}$$

If the metadata Context is *unknown*, the belief degree is set as 0.5 (i.e. the average of the belief degrees).

For instance, we present the following rule:

(R5) IF Context($O_1$)=higher education and Difficulty($O_1$)=difficult

THEN B($O_1$,(context=third level/universitary) and (level=initial), 0.6)

*Table 4. Definition of the functions f and g*

| *f* | *g* |
|---|---|
| *f*(primary school, initial) = 1<br>*f*(primary school, medium) = 2<br>*f*(primary school, advanced) = 3<br>*f*(secondary school, initial) = 4<br>*f*(secondary school, medium) = 5<br>*f*(secondary school, advanced) = 6<br>*f*(third level/universitary, initial) = 7<br>*f*(third level/universitary, medium) = 8<br>*f*(third level/universitary, advanced) = 9 | *g*(school, very easy) = 3<br>*g*(school, easy) = 4<br>*g*(school, medium) = 5<br>*g*(school, difficult) = 6<br>*g*(*x*) = 7, (*x*=(school, very difficult) or<br>*x*=(higher education, very easy) or<br>*x*=(higher education, easy))<br>*g*(higher education, medium) = 8<br>*g*(*x*) = 9, (*x*= (higher education, difficult) or<br>*x*=(higher education, very difficult) or<br>*x*=(training, very easy))<br>*g*(training, easy) = 10<br>*g*(training, medium) = 11<br>*g*(training, difficult) = 12<br>*g*(training, very difficult) = 13 |

### Restriction of Maximum Duration

The agent determines which object satisfies this restriction imposed by the user. For the objects that violate this constraint the agent computes a negative weight that depends on the priority assigned to this restriction and the distance to the maximum value assigned by the user (expressed in minutes).

Let MO be the LO associated metadata TypicalLearningTime and let MU be the user´s selected maximum time. The agent compares the value of MO with MU plus a percentage of this value to make this interval more flexible.

Namely:

If MO $\leq$ 1.2 * MU

- then the constraint is satisfied.
- else the agent computes the negative weight $p_n$ corresponding to an object (with time MO): $p_n = [MO/(2 * (1.2 * MU)) - 0.5] * Pr$

where Pr is the priority assigned by the user to this preference.

In the following section, we present a simple example to illustrate the different features and interactions of the agents in the multiagent system.

## Example

Suppose that José is an engineering student who is looking for documents with information about Matrix as he is studying a first course of Algebra. On the other hand, he has great knowledge of English, and understands some French. José wishes that the learning style should be practical. He wants that the time that takes the development of the material will not exceed 60 minutes and also, that the selected object will has no cost.

When José performs the search via the Interface Agent, he provides as input the word *matrix* and his preferences. The Semantic Refiner Agent interacts with the user and constructs the associated search strategy. Then, the User Profile Agent builds the profile of José through the input form. From this interaction, his profile contains among other data, the information shown in Table 1.

Suppose now that the Search Agents, based on the resulting search strategy and the primary restrictions (Cost="no"), retrieved from the repositories a set of four learning objects ($O_1$, $O_2$, $O_3$, $O_4$) with their metadata. After the Mediator Agent solves potential conflicts and integrate data,

*Table 5. Relevant metadata of retrieved objects*

| LO Id | $O_1$ | $O_2$ | $O_3$ | $O_4$ |
|---|---|---|---|---|
| **Language** | English | Spanish | French | English |
| **Learning Resource Type** | lecture | [exercise, lecture] | slide | exercise |
| **Interactivity Level** | low | low | very low | high |
| **Intended End User Role** | learner | learner | learner | teacher |
| **Context** | higher education | higher education | school | higher education |
| **Difficulty** | medium | easy | medium | difficult |
| **Typical Learning Time (min)** | 40 | 50 | 20 | 50 |
| **Cost** | no | no | no | no |

these LOs are stored into a local repository. Table 5 shows the most relevant metadata (according to LOM standard) of these retrieved objects $O_i$, $i \in \{1 \ldots 4\}$.

All these objects satisfy the user's selected subject and the restriction of having no cost. Now the *PS-Agent* starting from the remaining restrictions and preferences will select those that are most appropriate for José. First, the agent applies the rule of maximum duration restriction. As each $O_i$, $i \in \{1 \ldots 4\}$ satisfies this condition and also the language of each one is selected by the user (at different level of priority), then the four LOs are considered for the ranking.

The *PS-Agent* using the rules in the Context Belief (defined previously) calculates the expected satisfaction of each user's preferences (e.g., interaction=low, language=Spanish) through the different characteristics of each $O_i$. From these rules, the *PS-Agent* computes the belief degree $b_{ij}$ to which an object $O_i$ is expected to satisfy a particular user preference $p_j$, $B(O_i, p_j, b_{ij})$.

Then, *PS-Agent* calculates the intentions to reach their goal by applying the bridge rule (1) and the function defined by the equation (2). Computing these values for the four objects selected, the following degrees of intention are obtained:

$r_1 = 0.72$ $r_2 = 0.86$ $r_3 = 0.6$ $r_4 = 0.608$

Finally, the *PS-Agent* sorts the objects by decreasing the value of the degree obtained: $O_2$, $O_1$, $O_4$, $O_3$. Then the system recommends to José the course $O_2$ as the most suitable and also gives an ordered list of the other alternatives.

## PROTOTYPE IMPLEMENTATION

A preliminary prototype of the Recommender System composed by the Personalized Search Agent (*PS-Agent*), the Interface Agent (*I-Agent*) and one Search Agent (*S-Agent*) has been implemented. For the development of this prototype it was used the languages SWI-Prolog (www.swi-prolog.org) and Ruby on Rails (rubyonrails.org). The *PS-Agent* is implemented using SWI-Prolog because it is an open source logical programming language. Moreover, it is multithread allowing representing in a suitable way the agent logical architecture and deductions. Ruby is used to implement the *I-Agent* and the *S-Agent*, since it supports the ability to consume Web Services with SOAP, which is necessary to communicate with the repositories using the SQI protocol.

Through a graphic interface, the user introduces the current preferences and restrictions in his/her profile. Figure 3 shows the prototype user interface (it is in Spanish language as it was develop for regional purpose).

*Figure 3. User interface; subject, preferences and restrictions of the LO*

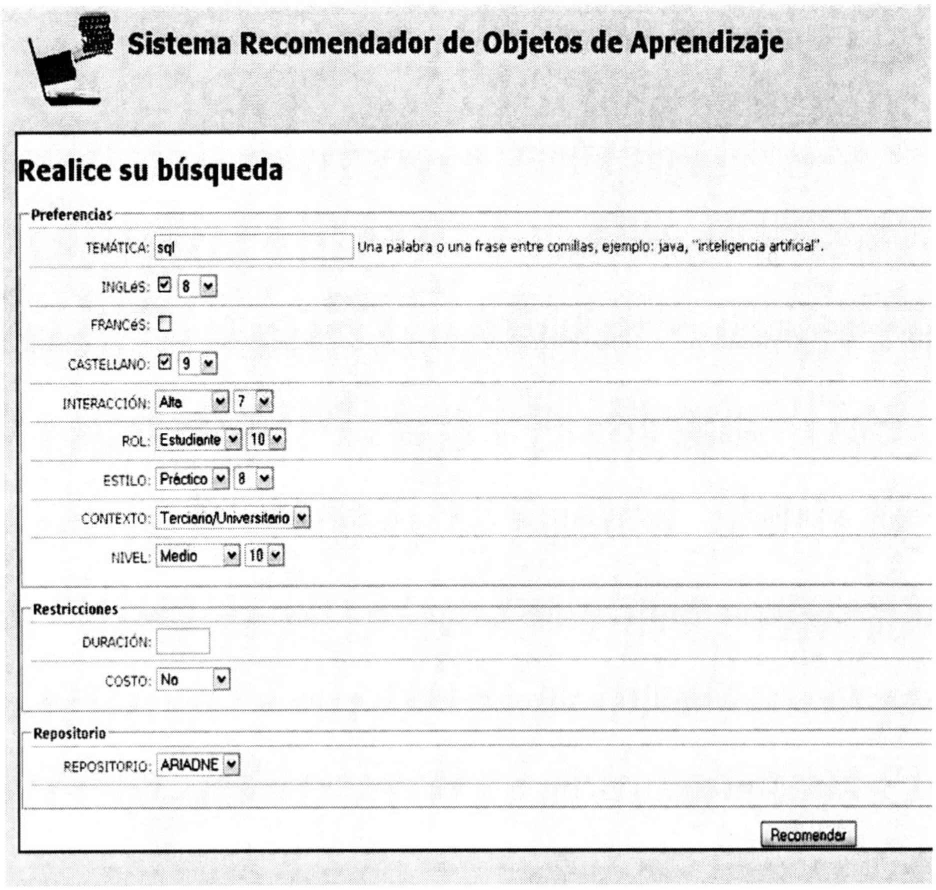


The Interface Agent (*I-Agent*) acquires and saves in a data file the information of the user's search. This data file stores also the user search history, keeping the chosen subject and his/her preferences (languages, role, interaction, etc.), for statistical post processing. Then, the *I-Agent* communicates the subject of interest to the Search Agent (*S-Agent*) and the information related to preferences and restrictions to the Personalized Search Agent (*PS-Agent*).

The first search of LO (i.e. a subject search) is made by the *S-Agent*. The *S-Agent* sends a query according to the selected subject to a repository (or federation of repositories) and waits for a response. In this first prototype, we use the repositories Ariadne and FLOR. The *S-Agent* can communicate with these repositories through the SQI protocol and the query language VSQL. As response, the *S-Agent* receives an XML file containing the metadata, according to the LOM standard, of each of the LOs that satisfy the selected subject. Furthermore, the *S-Agent* creates an XML file for each of these objects, and stores them in the local repository. Also, it creates a file with the number of objects and the name of each XML file describing each object. Then, this file is communicated and used by the *PS-Agent* to generate the ordered list that the Interface Agent presents to the user. From the resulting LOs retrieved from the repositories, the *PS-Agent* selects the more suitable ones and provides them to the *I-Agent*. For achieving this, the *PS-Agent* generates a file with the ranked results and displays the top 10 (this is a system parameter and may be change).

*Figure 4. Illustrates the results of a recommendation together with the details of one of the selected LO*

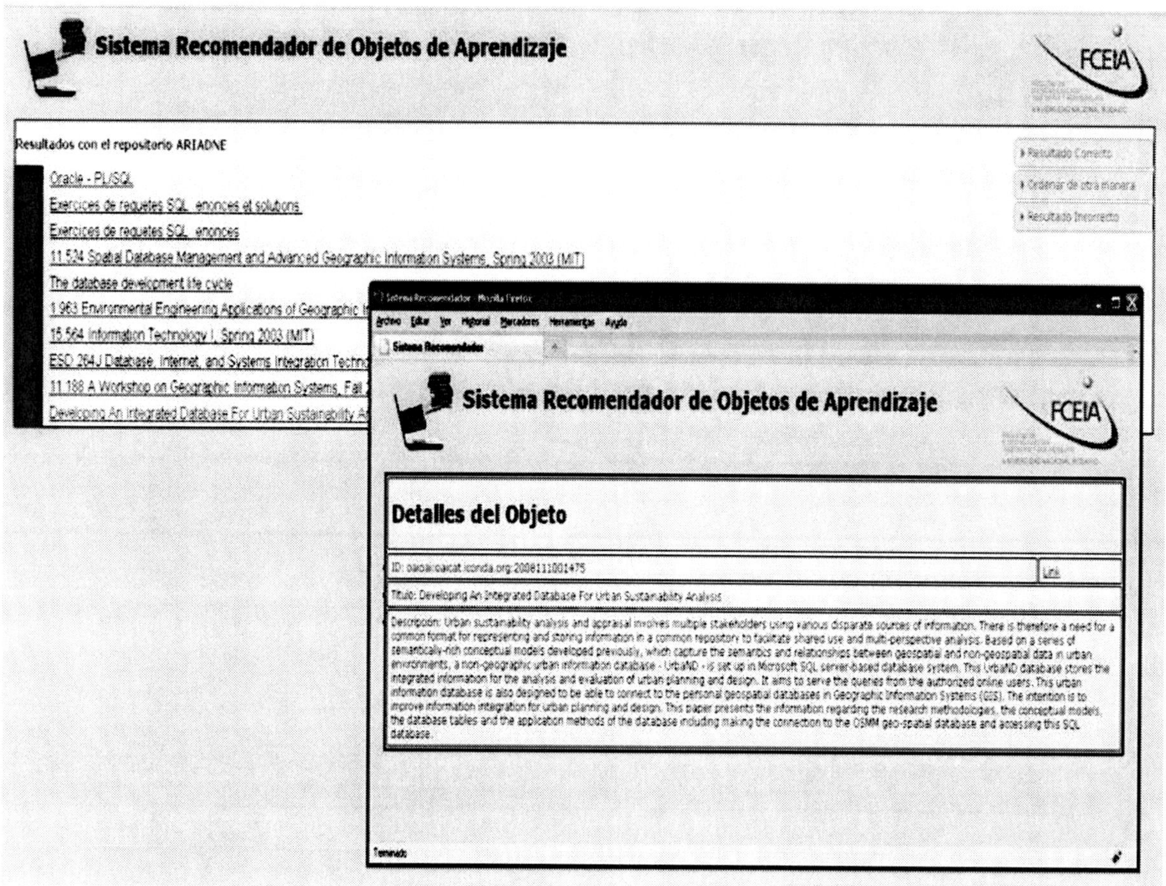


For each of the selected LO, it is shown its identification (ID) and the following characteristics: title, description and location.

After receiving the recommendation, the user can analyze it and can express its opinion through the interface selecting one of the following three options:

- *Correct*: when the ranked list of objects satisfies the user.
- *Different order*: when the user is in accordance with the selected objects but the order does not match his preferences. Then, the user can indicate which he/she considers the best top five.
- *Incorrect*: when the user is not satisfied with the list of recommended objects. Then, the interface enables him to introduce a textual comment.

In this prototype, there exists a user with an administrator profile. This administrator can view the search history of all users and their personal data and, in order to evaluate the system performance, he/she can access to different statistics obtained from the stored data. Example of the use of these data will be seen in the experiments presented in next section.

## EXPERIMENTATION

There are several ways to evaluate recommender systems. As Herlocker et al. (2004) say, effective and meaningful evaluation of recommender systems is challenging. In their work, they have attempted to overview the factors that have been considered in evaluations. Classic metrics in information retrieval are precision and recall. Precision is defined as the number of relevant documents retrieved by a search divided by the total number of documents retrieved by that search, while Recall is defined as the number of relevant documents retrieved by a search divided by the total number of existing relevant documents. In our general architecture, the Semantic Refiner agent resolves precision and recall. Results of this are shown in (Deco, 2005). An improvement of search results is to show them sorted according to the user characteristics and preferences. As in this chapter we describe the PS-Agent, which is in charge of showing the retrieved items in the correct order, we want to evaluate the proximity between *PS-Agent* recommended ranking and the user's own ranking. That is to say, how close the recommender system's ranking is to the user's raking. In this direction, to measure distances between positions we decided to use Manhattan distance (Block distance), which is suitable for this.

Two experiments are presented. The first one, allows us to evaluate the recommendation ranking using the same search topic submitted by users with different profiles. In the second experiment, we analyze different queries made by users with different profiles.

## Experimentation Using the Same Subject

For this experimentation Ariadne repository was used, since it has a high percentage of loaded LO educational metadata and this information is fundamental to allow the recommender system to have a good result (building an ordered list of LOs that satisfy the user profile). For this analysis, users were students and professors of the Computer Science career of our University, and the selected subject was *Java*. We decided to search this topic, because it is well known for these users and also, Ariadne has free accessible material on this topic. As the different users have diverse characteristics and have different purposes, their preferences and restrictions are different. This is shown in Table 6, according to the information captured by the Interface Agent.

The Interface Agent captures user's characteristics of interest, such as his/her Mother Language and user`s preferences with its priorities. The preferences considered in this prototype are different languages (French, English and Spanish),

*Table 6. User profiles*

| Profile | User1 | User2 | User3 | User4 | User5 | User6 |
|---|---|---|---|---|---|---|
| Mother language | Spanish | Spanish | Spanish | Spanish | Spanish | Spanish |
| Subject | java | java | java | java | java | java |
| Language Spanish Pr | 10 | 10 | 10 | 10 | 10 | 10 |
| Language English Pr | 9 | 10 | 10 | 10 | 10 | 10 |
| Language French Pr | 0 | 9 | 9 | 9 | 9 | 9 |
| (Role,Pr) | (l,10) | (l,10) | (l,10) | (t,8) | (t,8) | (t,7) |
| (Interaction,Pr) | (medium,5) | (ignore,-) | (ignore,-) | (ignore,-) | (high,7) | (ignore,-) |
| (Style,Pr) | (theo,9) | (theo,9) | (p,9) | (theo,10) | (theo,10) | (p,10) |
| (Context,Level,Pr) | (u,i,9) | (u,i,10) | (u,m,10) | (u,i,9) | (u,a,9) | (u,i,7) |
| (Max-duration,Pr) | (0,-) | (0,-) | (0,-) | (0,-) | (0,-) | (90,9) |
| Cost | no | no | no | no | no | no |

Role, Interaction, Style, Context, Max-duration. It also captures if the user wants LO with or without Cost. The value for Role may be teacher (t) or learner (l). Interaction refers to the level of interaction the user prefers (i.e. low, medium, high) expressing his preference about the LO. Style value may be theoretical (theo) or practical (p). The Context may be university (u), school (sch), etc., and its associated Level may be advanced (a), medium (m) or initial (i). All these different kinds of preferences may have a Priority (Pr), represented by an integer number in [0, 10], expressing different level of the user′s preferences.

In the experimentation, the Ariadne repository had 263 objects related to Java. Then, the search filtered 27 of these objects, whose language was English, French or Spanish. The recommender system offers to each user an ordered list of objects according to his/her preferences. For example, for User2 (see Table 6) the system recommends the following ordered list of the ten first LOs:

$\{Id_{12}, Id_{11}, Id_{13}, Id_{7}, Id_{6}, Id_{8}, Id_{4}, Id_{15}, Id_{26}, Id_{2}\}$

Table 7 shows the most relevant metadata of some of these retrieved objects: Language, Learning Resource Type (i.e. the kind of LO), Interactivity Level (the degree of interactivity characterizing this LO), Intended End User Role (principal role for which this LO was designed), Context (the principal environment within the use of this LO is intended to take place), Difficulty (how hard it is to work with or through this LO for the typical intended target audience), and Typical Learning Time (in minutes). The notation we use is as follows: French (fr), English (en), and education (educ). A value unknown in a metadata represents that this metadata value is absent in the LO description.

After receiving the ranked list, the user can give his/her opinion about the recommendation results. User2 was satisfied with the objects but the order does not match exactly his preferences and suggests as feedback *Different Order*, proposing that the first three objects should be:

$\{Id_{7}, Id_{6}, Id_{8}\}$.

To evaluate the proximity between *PS-Agent* recommended ranking and the user's own ranking we used an algorithm based in Manhattan distance (Block distance), which is suitable to capture distances between positions. We use Manhattan distance between groups of LOs with the same intention degree. This distance was calculated between positions of the first items ordered by the user with the corresponding positions in the ten LOs recommended list.

*Table 7. Relevant metadata of some of the objects retrieved*

| LO | $Id_6$ | $Id_7$ | $Id_8$ | $Id_{11}$ | $Id_{12}$ | $Id_{13}$ |
|---|---|---|---|---|---|---|
| **Language** | fr | fr | fr | en | en | en |
| **Learning Resource Type** | slide | slide | slide | slide | slide | narrative text |
| **Interactivity Level** | unknown | unknown | unknown | medium | high | unknown |
| **Intended End User Role** | learner | learner | learner | learner | learner | learner |
| **Context** | higher educ. | higher educ. | higher educ. | higher educ. | higher educ. | higher educ. |
| **Difficulty** | unknown | unknown | unknown | medium | medium | unknown |
| **Typical Learning Time (min)** | 90 | 135 | 90 | 60 | 90 | 3 |

The algorithm to compute this distance is the following:

Let be $LOR = [OR_1, OR_2, OR_3, ..., OR_n]$ the recommended ranked list, where $OR_n$ is the n-th object of $LOR$, and let be $GI = [G_1, G_2, G_3; ..., G_n]$ the list of the intention degrees of the recommended LO, where $G_i$ is the intention degree of object $OR_i$, and let be $LOU = [OU_1, OU_2, OU_3, ..., OU_N]$ the user ranked list.

If $OU_1 = OR_i$, $OU_2 = OR_j$, $OU_3 = OR_k$, ..., $OU_N = OR_m$ then distance between the recommender system ranking and the user ranking is:

$$Dist(LOR;LOU) = s_1 + s_2 + s_3 + _{...} + s_N$$

Taking into account that $OU_r = OR_p$ , $s_r$ is calculated as follows:

$$s_r = \sum_{n=p}^{r} x_n \ where\ x_n = \begin{cases} 0 & if\ G_n = G_p \\ 1 & if\ G_n \neq G_p \end{cases}$$

This represents the distance between the object in position $p$ ($OR_p$) with $G_p$ intention degree, and the user desired object in position $r$ ($OU_r$).

For example, if the LO recommended list is $LOR = [OR_1, OR_2, OR_3, ..., OR_{10}]$ with its intention degrees $GI = [6.7, 6.5, 6.2, 6.0, 6.0, 5.96, 5.28, 5.28, 5.1, 5.1]$, and the user suggests the following order $LOU = [OR_2, OR_1, OR_5, OR_3, OR_9]$, the distance is calculated as follows:

$$Dist(LOR;LOU) = s_1 + s_2 + s_3 + s_4 + s_5 = 1 + 1 + 1 + 1 + 4 = 8$$

The distance for this first experiment was calculated between positions of the first three items ordered by the user with the corresponding positions in the LOs recommended list, composed by 27 elements, and taking into account the degree of intention of each object in the list.

The Agent may compute distance values between zero (in the case of *Correct* answer, meaning that the user agrees with the proposed order) to 65.2, which is the average of the worst case. To compute this value we suppose that the three first LOs are in the more distant position. Considering this scale and considering that we have obtained a distance average of 13.6, we can say that in most cases the list of recommended objects is not so far from the user´s one. Thus, we can claim that the preliminary performance of the *PS-Agent* gave us promising results. However, results may not satisfy a user since there are subjective factors that are difficult to capture and model.

*PS-Agent* performance depends mainly that all the LO in the repository has quality information in all metadata. During this experimentation, we found some difficulties associated with metadata information. For example, in Table 7 we can see that some of the LOs metadata (Interaction level and Difficulty) have an unknown value. This is a common situation in many of repositories. The lack of information in these metadata implies that the agent cannot compute the preferences satisfaction of the LO respect to the user selection in these characteristics. In some cases, an incorrect metadata was found. For example, a document had metadata Language=English, but it had only the title in English and the document body was in French. In addition, we found metadata that classified correctly a document from the point of view of the file type, but they did not adequately describe the document contents. For example, a document had metadata LearningResourceType=narrative text, but it was actually a Java program to solve the travelling salesman problem; so it should be better classified as an exercise or example. This classification of the resource as narrative text makes that the agent infers that the object best satisfies the theoretical style, which is not true. These problems with metadata information have been also pointed in (Sonntag, 2004) and it is a challenge for future work oriented to automatic metadata extraction.

## Experimentation Using Different Subjects

In this second experimentation, we also evaluate proximity between *PS-Agent* recommended ranking and the user's own ranking. We used the same algorithm based in the Manhattan distance as in the previous experiment.

FLOR and Ariadne repositories were used. Users were students and professors of the Computer Science career of our University. A total of 25 searches were submitted by six users. For each search, the user provides his/her preferences using the Interface Agent. Some subjects were: "sql", "intelligent agent", "haskell", and "inteligencia artificial" (in Spanish). For each search, the recommender system offers to each user an ordered list of objects according to his/her preferences. Then, each user evaluates the recommendation results. In order to standardize the user's evaluation, we decided to limit the list of results to the top ten.

We observed that 64% of the searches were successfully evaluated. 24% of the searches were considered incorrect, and in some few searches (12%), the Personalized Search Agent does not recommend documents because although these documents satisfy the subject search, they do not satisfy some restriction imposed by the user.

Computing these distances over successful cases (with feedback *Correct or Different Order*), discarding incorrect results and empty recommendations, we obtained an average distance of 1.75. The range of distance values is between 0 and 7.81. The value 0 corresponds to the best case (Correct recommendation) and the value 7.81 was obtained from the average of the worst cases.

As we have previously pointed, *PS-Agent* performance depends mainly on the completeness of LO metadata in the repository and on the quality of this information. In this second experimentation, we also found problems with the lack of information in some metadata. For example, Interactivity Level, Difficulty and Typical Learning Time metadata are absent in many cases, and generally the metadata Intended End User Role contains the value "learner". The same occurs with Learning Resource Type, which is set as "narrative text" or "slide", but in some cases, it could be set with more detail as "exercise" or "figure". Consequently, objects have the same intention degree and distance is zero independently of their order.

Considering this problem, the distances average obtained shows that the list of recommended objects is not so distant from the user's one. Thus, we can claim that the preliminary performance of this recommender system gave us promising results. However, results may not satisfy a user since, although a document satisfies his/her preferences set in the interface, this specification may not fit what really the user wants, because there are subjective factors that are difficult to capture and model.

## FUTURE RESEARCH DIRECTIONS

There are several future research directions to follow. On the one hand, the proposed prototype could be extended by incorporating the rest of the agents in the architecture. Particularly, we will integrate the SR-Agent to the system. The UP-Agent can be improved by using the history of the user's queries and feedbacks. In addition, new Search Agents (Si Agents) can be added in order to increase the retrieval from other LO repositories. Different behaviours of the PS-Agent may be experimented by modifying the function that computes the intention degrees, which are used to order the LOs.

On the other hand, until now, we do not consider in the recommendation, information about the use of each LO and his/her qualifications after its use. Further experimentation could be important to evaluate the pedagogical results after the user applies each retrieved object for teaching or learning. This evaluation is difficult to execute because it requires the compromise of a user to give his/her feedback after its use and this requires a long time of evaluation. In this line of work, we are planning to add new metadata in the local repository to compute users' qualifications in order to improve the proposed approach including collaborative aspects.

In addition, we are working in a Latin-American Project, to integrate the proposed recommender system as part of an assistant to help teachers to assemble learning objects according to an instructional design, considering their students characteristics and preferences.

Furthermore, related to the lack of information on many of educational metadata of the learning objects in the repositories, we are working in automatic metadata extraction to bridge this gap.

## CONCLUSION

In this chapter, we have presented the architecture and implementation of a general recommender system for Learning Objects personalized retrieval. This architecture is based on a multiagent system, which allows to present a scalable framework that is able to work with heterogeneous and distributed information from different LO repositories. In this general architecture, we have proposed different agents for the relevant roles in the system.

We have implemented a first prototype including some of these agents and we focus on the design, implementation and evaluation of the Personalized Search Agent. This prototype will be extended by incorporating the rest of the agents in the architecture. In addition, new Search Agents (Si Agents) can be added to the system in order to increase the retrieval from other LO repositories. Each search agent will be in charge of the communication and it will adapt the search strategy to the repository query language syntax.

In particular, we designed the Personalized Search Agent (*PS-Agent*) as a graded BDI agent since it is suitable to deal with user's graded preferences and restrictions. This recommender agent is designed as a hybrid approach using content- and knowledge-based techniques. These techniques are suitable for items, which are less frequently acceded (e.g. LOs) and that must support a more detailed elicitation of user requirement (e.g. user preferences and restrictions) and domain description (e.g. metadata and rules to infer the satisfaction degree of preferences). A distinctive characteristic of this model of agent is that it can deal with graded user preferences and/or restrictions that represent different levels of preferences and/or restrictions. In our system, on the one hand, restrictions (e.g. no cost) are considered strict and then, the system discards objects that do not satisfy these conditions. On the other hand, preferences are used to find those items that satisfy most of them and in a higher degree. This is weighted in the intention degree evaluation for each candidate LO. We have proposed to compute it as the average of the expected satisfaction of all user preferences, but this function can be modified to obtain different agent's behaviour and can be improved with further experimentation. This implies a flexible behaviour of the PS-Agent since it does not discard those objects that do not satisfy some of the user's preferences and it orders them in the recommended ranking list. This agent model has been used to design and implement a tourism recommender agent with good results. Therefore, we can say that this approach is adequate to engineer recommender systems in different domains.

A prototype of the recommender system was implemented using Ruby on Rails for Interface Agent and Search Agents, and SWI-Prolog for the *PS-Agent*. This prototype allows us to make some experimentation in order to show that the system architecture is feasible and can help people to find suitable objects giving promising results. Two experimentations were done to evaluate the system results. For this, users evaluated whether the retrieved objects were interesting for them and if the recommended order was correct, according to his/her opinion, after browsing the retrieved resources.

The lack of information on many of educational metadata of the learning objects in the repositories was one problem that emerged in the experimentation. This problem has been previously pointed by other authors, this is because preparing learning resources with suitable metadata is labour-intensive, it needs expertise and consequently there is also a lack of quality information in metadata. Therefore, to improve the content-based recommender system results, an important challenge is automatic quality metadata extraction.

## ACKNOWLEDGMENT

The authors thank the anonymous reviewers for their useful comments that have helped to improve the paper and acknowledge partial support by the projects Jardin LACCIR-RFP2008 and Project 219308 SECTEL, Gobierno de Santa Fe.

## REFERENCES

Ardissono, L., Goy, A., Petrone, G., & Segnan, M. (2005). A multi-agent infrastructure for developing personalized web-based systems. *ACM Transactions on Internet Technology, 5*(1). New York, NY: ACM.

Bajo, J., Corchado, J. M., de Paz, Y., de Paz, J. F., & Martín, Q. (2006). A multiagent recommending system for shopping centres. In *Proceedings of the ECAI 2006 Workshop on Recommender Systems*, August 28-29, 2006, Riva del Garda, Italy, (pp. 92-96).

Bergenti, F., Gleizes, M. P., & Zambonelli, F. (Eds.). (2004). *Methodologies and software engineering for agent systems: The handbook of agent-oriented software engineering*. New York, NY: Kluwer Academic Publishing. doi:10.1007/b116049

Bordini, R. H., Hübner, J. F., & Wooldridge, M. (2007). *Programming multi-agent systems in agentspeak using Jason*. John Wiley and Sons. doi:10.1002/9780470061848

Bratman, M. E., Israel, D. J., & Pollack, M. E. (1988). Plans and resource-bounded practical reasoning. *Computational Intelligence, 4*, 349–355. doi:10.1111/j.1467-8640.1988.tb00284.x

Burke, R. (2000). Knowledge-based recommender systems. In A. Kent (Ed.), *Encyclopedia of library and information systems*, (p. 69).

Carbo, J., Molina, M., & Davila, J. (2001). A BDI agent architecture for reasoning about reputation. In *Proceedings of the 2001 IEEE Systems, Man, and Cybernetics Conference.*

Casali, A., Gerling, V., Deco, C., & Bender, C. (2010). A multiagent system for personalized recommendation of learning objects. In *Proceedings Congreso Iberoamericano de Informática Educativa*. IE 2010, Santiago de Chile (pp. 503-510).

Casali, A., Godo, L., & Sierra, C. (2006). A methodology to engineering graded BDI agents. In *Proceedings WASI-CACIC 2006*. Potrero de Funes, Argentina.

Casali, A., Godo, L., & Sierra, C. (2009). g-BDI: A graded intensional agent model for practical reasoning. In V. Torra, Y. Narukawa, & M. Inuiguchi, (Eds.), *Modeling Decisions for Artificial Intelligence, 6th International Conference, MDAI 2009. Lecture Notes in Artificial Intelligence, 5861*, Awaji Island, Japan, Springer, (November 30, 2009) (pp. 5-20).

Casali, A., Von Furth, A., Godo, L., & Sierra, C. (2008). A tourism recommender agent: From theory to practice. *Revista Iberoamericana de Inteligencia Artificial, 12*(40), 23–38.

Chiappe, A., Segovia, Y., & Rincon, Y. (2007). Toward an instructional design model based on learning objects. In *Educational Technology Research and Development* (pp. 671–681). Boston, MA: Springer.

Deco, C., Bender, C., Saer, J., Chiari, M., & Motz, R. (2005). Semantic refinement for web information retrieval. In *Proceedings of the 3rd Latin American Web Congress* (pp. 106-110). IEEE Press.

García Salcines, E., Romero, C., Ventura, S., & de Castro Lozano, C. (2008). Sistema recomendador colaborativo usando minería de datos distribuida para la mejora continua de cursos e-learning. *IEEE-RITA*, *3*(1), 19–30.

Georgeff, M., Pell, B., Pollack, M., Tambe, M., & Wooldridge, M. (1999). The belief-desire-intention model of agency. In Muller, J. P., Singh, M., & Rao, A. (Eds.), *Intelligent Agents V, LNAI 1365*. Springer-Verlag.

Gerling, V. (2009). *Un Sistema Inteligente para Asistir la Búsqueda Personalizada de Objetos de Aprendizaje*. Degree Thesis on Computer Science. National University of Rosario. DOI=www.fceia.unr.edu.ar/lcc/t523/tesina.php?campo1=21

Ghauth, K. I. B., & Abdullah, N. A. (2009). Building an e-learning recommender system using vector space model and good learners average rating. In *Ninth IEEE International Conference on Advanced Learning Technologies* –IEEE (pp. 194-196)

Ghidini, C., & Giunchiglia, F. (2001). Local model semantics, or contextual reasoning = locality + compatibility. *Artificial Intelligence*, *127*(2), 221–259. doi:10.1016/S0004-3702(01)00064-9

Herlocker, J. L., Konstan, J. A., Terveen, L. G., & Riedl, J. T. (2004). Evaluating collaborative filtering recommender systems. *ACM Transactions on Information Systems*, *22*(1), 5–53. doi:10.1145/963770.963772

Howden, N., Rönnquist, R., Hodgson, A., & Lucas, A. (2001). JACK summary of an agent infrastructure. In *Proceedings of the 5th International Conference on Autonomous Agents*.

Jo, C. H., & Einhorn, J. M. (2005). A BDI agent-based software process. *Journal of Object Technology*, *4*(9). doi:10.5381/jot.2005.4.9.a3

Lu, J. (2004). A personalized e-learning material recommender system. In *Proceedings of the 2nd International Conference on Information Technology for Application (ICITA 2004)* China, (pp. 374-379).

Manouselis, N., Drachsler, H., Vuorikari, R., Hummel, H. G. K., & Koper, R. (2011). Recommender systems in technology enhanced learning. In Kantor, P. B., Ricci, F., Rokach, L., & Shapira, B. (Eds.), *Recommender systems handbook* (pp. 387–415). Berlin, Germany: Springer. doi:10.1007/978-0-387-85820-3_12

Montaner, M., López, B., & de la Rosa, L. (2003). A taxonomy of recommender agents on the Internet. [Kluwer.]. *Artificial Intelligence Review*, *19*, 285–330. doi:10.1023/A:1022850703159

Niinivaara, O. (2004). *Agent-based recommender systems*. Technical Report, University of Helsinki, Dept. of Sciences.

Rao, A., & Georgeff, M. (1995). BDI agents: From theory to practice. In *Proceedings of the 1st International Conference on Multi-Agents Systems*, (pp. 312-319).

Recker, M., & Wiley, D. A. (2001). A non-authoritative educational metadata ontology for filtering and recommending learning objects. *Journal of Interactive Learning Environments*, *9*(3), 255–271. doi:10.1076/ilee.9.3.255.3568

Resnick, P., & Varian, H. (1997). Recommender systems. *Communications of the ACM*, *40*(3), 56–58. doi:10.1145/245108.245121

Sonntag, M. (2004). Metadata in e-learning applications: Automatic extraction and reuse. In Hofer, C., & Chroust, G. (Eds.), *IDIMT-2004, 12th Interdisciplinary Information Management Talks* (pp. 219–231). Linz, Austria: Universitätsverlag Rudolf Trauner.

Soonthornphisaj, N., Rojsattarat, E., & Yimngam, S. (2006). Smart e-learning using recommender system. In *LNCS 4114* (pp. 518–523). Berlin, Germany: Springer.

Terveen, L. G., & Hill, W. (2001). Beyond recommender systems: Helping people help each other. In Carroll, J. (Ed.), *HCI in the new millennium*. Addison Wesley.

Wang, T. I., Tsai, K. H., Lee, M. C., & Chiu, T. K. (2007). Personalized learning objects recommendation based on the semantic-aware discovery and the learner preference pattern. *Journal of Educational Technology & Society*, *10*(3), 84–105.

Wiley, D. (2002). Connecting learning objects to instructional design theory: A definition, a metaphor, and a taxonomy. In Wiley, D. A. (Ed.), *Instructional use of learning objects*. Association for Instructional Technology.

Wooldridge, M. (2009). *Introduction to multiagent systems*. John Wiley and Sons, Ltd.

Wooldridge, M., & Jennings, N. R. (1995). Intelligent agents: Theory and practice. *The Knowledge Engineering Review*, *10*(2), 115–152. doi:10.1017/S0269888900008122

Zhang, T., Kendall, E., & Jiang, H. (2003). A software engineering process for BDI agent-based systems. In *Proceedings of the IEEE/WIC International Conference on Intelligent Agent Technology* (IAT'03).

Zhu, F., Ip, H., & Cao, J. (2008). PeRES: A personalized recommendation education system based on multi-agents & SCORM. In *Advances in Web Based Learning (ICWL 2007), LNCS 4823*, (pp. 31-42).

## ADDITIONAL READING

Readers interested in personalization could refer to the following publications: Abidi, S. S. R., & Zeng, Y. (2006). Intelligent Information Personalization Leveraging Constraint Satisfaction and Association Rule Methods. In Lamontagne, L., & Marchand, M. (Eds.), Proc. of Canadian AI 2006, LNAI 4013, 134-145.

Association of College and Research Libraries Information Literacy Competency Standards for Higher Education. http://www.ala.org

Casali, A., Godo, L., & Sierra, C. (2011). (2011). A graded BDI agent model to represent and reason about preferentes. *Artificial Intelligence*. .doi:10.1016/j.artint.2010.12.006

Dolog, P., Henze, N., Nejdl, W., & Sintek, M. (2004). Personalization in Distributed e-Learning Environments. In *Proceedings of the 13th International World Wide Web Conference*, Track on Education. ISBN:1-58113-912-8. ACM, New York, USA, pp 179-179.

EduCa Project. Educación con Calidad Cultural. www.fing.edu.uy/inco/grupos/csi/esp/Proyectos/Educa.

Georgeff, M., Pell, B., Pollack, M., Tambe, M., & Wooldridge, M. (1999). The Belief-Desire-Intention Model of Agency. In Muller, J. P., Singh, M., & Rao, A. (Eds.), *Intelligent Agents V - LNAI (Vol. 1365)*. Springer-Verlag.

Guzmán, J., & Motz, R. (2005). Towards an Adaptive Cultural Web-based Educational System. In *Proceedings of the 3rd Latin American Web Congress*. La Web 2005. IEEE Press. pp 183-186. Buenos Aires, Argentina.

IMS Meta-Data Best Practice and Implementation Guide, Final Specification, Version 1.1. IMS Global Learning Consortium, Inc. http://www.imsproject.org/metadata/index.html

Jennings, N., Sycara, K., & Wooldridge, M. (1998). A Roadmap of Agent Research and Development. *Autonomous Agents and Multi-Agent Systems*, *42*(1), 7–38. doi:10.1023/A:1010090405266

Readers interested in agent systems could refer to the following publications: Jennings, N., & Wooldridge, M. (1996). Software agents. *IEEE Review*, *42*(1), 17–20. doi:10.1049/ir:19960101

Learning Technology Standards Committe, I. E. E. E. LOM specification. http://ltsc.ieee.org/wg12

Merlot Project. http://www.merlot.org/Home.po

Nwana, H. S. (1996). Software Agents: An overview. *The Knowledge Engineering Review*, *11*(3), 205–244. doi:10.1017/S026988890000789X

Parsons, S., Sierra, C., & Jennings, N. R. (1998). Agents that reason and negotiate by arguing. *Journal of Logic and Computation*, *8*(3), 261–292. doi:10.1093/logcom/8.3.261

Perugini, S., & Ramakrishnan, N. (2003). Personalizing Interactions with Information Systems. in Zelkowitz, M. (Eds.), Advances in Computers, 57, Academic Press, 323-382.

Ramakrishnan, N., Rosson, M. B., & Carroll, J. M. (2007). Explaining Scenarios for Information Personalization. arXiv:cs/0111007v1 [cs.HC]. http://arxiv.org/pdf/cs/0111007v1.

Rao, A., & Georgeff, M. (1995). BDI agents: From theory to practice. In proceedings of the 1st International Conference on Multi-Agents Systems, pp 312-319.

Rao, A. S., & Georgeff, M. (1998). Decision procedures of BDI logics. *Journal of Logic and Computation*, *8*(3), 293344. doi:10.1093/logcom/8.3.293

Readers interested in learning objects metadata and repositories could refer to the following publications: Ariadne: Alliance of Remote Instructional Authoring and Distribution Networks for Europe. http://www.ariadne-eu.org

Russell, D., & Norvig, P. (2003). *Artificial Intelligence: A Modern Approach* (2nd ed.). Upper Saddle River, New Jersey: Pearson Education, Inc.

SMETE Digital Library. http://smete.org

Souto, M. A. M., Verdin, R., & de Oliveira, P. M. J. Discovering Web Usage Patterns for Modeling Learner's Cognitive Abilities. In: 3rd Latin American Web Congress - LA- Web, 2005, Buenos Aires. Proceedings. Los Alamitos, CA 90720, USA: IEEE Computer Society Press. V. 1. p. 279-285.

Weiss, G. (1999). Modern Approach to Distributed Artificial Intelligence. In Weiss, G. (Ed.), *Multiagent Systems*. The MIT Press.

Wiley, D. Selected publications and researches from http://davidwiley.org/

Wooldridge, M. (2009). Introduction to Multiagent Systems, John Wiley and Sons, Ltd. Readers interested in BDI agents could refer to the following publications: Aïmeur, E., Burke, R., & Mouaddib, A. (2005). Multi-Agent Information Retrieval and Recommender Systems, (IJCAI 2005), Edimburgh. http://www.iro.umontreal.ca/~aimeur/publications/Workshop20.pdf

Wooldridge, M. (2009). *Introduction to Multiagent Systems*. John Wiley and Sons, Ltd.

Wooldridge, M., & Jennings, N. (1995). Intelligent Agents: Theory and Practice. *The Knowledge Engineering Review*, *10*(2), 115–152. doi:10.1017/S0269888900008122

## KEY TERMS AND DEFINITIONS

**BDI Agent:** A notorious agent architecture. This model is based on the explicit representation of the agent's beliefs (B), desires (D) and intentions (I). Agents having different kinds of behaviour can be modelled by the representation and interaction of these three attitudes. This agent architecture has solid logic formalization.

A Graded BDI (g-BDI) is a more flexible BDI architecture capable of representing and reasoning with graded attitudes (i.e. B, D, I).

**Learning Object:** A digital or non-digital entity, which can be used, reused or referenced for learning, education or training purposes. These objects have learning objectives. In order to identify and retrieve these objects, they are described with metadata (structure of external information).

**LOM (Learning Object Metadata):** The standard for learning objects metadata developed by the IEEE LTSC, which allows specifying syntax and semantics of learning object metadata. In LOM, the metadata is organized hierarchically, grouping them into categories. Its purpose is to support reusability of learning objects, to aid discoverability, and to facilitate their interoperability.

**Metadata:** Descriptive information of learning objects, information on its structure, how they are organized, and to who is targeted. It provides information that can identify and retrieve objects.

**Multiagent System:** A system composed of several intelligent agents that interact with each other to solve problems. Each agent plays a role and performs different system functions. Agents in a multiagent system are autonomous, heterogeneous and potentially independent.

**Repository:** Storage of learning objects and its metadata. Repositories allow users to share, manage and use educational resources.

**User Profile:** Contains information on personal data and preferences with respect to a particular topic of interest associated to a specific user. This information can be exploited by different systems (e.g. recommender systems) that personalize search results.

# Chapter 9
# Meta-Rule Based Recommender Systems for Educational Applications

**Vicente Arturo Romero Zaldivar**
*Atos Origin SAE, Spain*

**Daniel Burgos**
*Atos Origin SAE, Spain & International University of La Rioja, Spain*

**Abelardo Pardo**
*University Carlos III of Madrid, Spain*

## ABSTRACT

*Recommendation Systems are central in current applications to help the user find relevant information spread in large amounts of data. Most Recommendation Systems are more effective when huge amounts of user data are available. Educational applications are not popular enough to generate large amount of data. In this context, rule-based Recommendation Systems seem a better solution. Rules can offer specific recommendations with even no usage information. However, large rule-sets are hard to maintain, reengineer, and adapt to user preferences. Meta-rules can generalize a rule-set which provides bases for adaptation. In this chapter, the authors present the benefits of meta-rules, implemented as part of Meta-Mender, a meta-rule based Recommendation System. This is an effective solution to provide a personalized recommendation to the learner, and constitutes a new approach to Recommendation Systems.*

## INTRODUCTION

Nowadays, when the amount of information is becoming over-exceeding, Recommendation Systems emerge as the right solution to find the best fit. In i.e. electronic commerce, knowledge management systems, social networks, and other fields and markets, recommendation systems help users to find products, lessons, and contributions, convenient for them. There are many inputs which can be used as information sources like, i.e. user similarities with other users, user profile, and user preferences. All these inputs provide the system with valuable data to suggest the user the best

DOI: 10.4018/978-1-61350-489-5.ch009

way to follow up or the most appropriate choice. There are other information sources, for instance, people ratings (Rocchio, 1971), user interests, goals, and objectives; they all look useful for educational applications.

However, educational applications lack of enough amounts of data to establish user similarities in a precise way. In this case, recommendations are based on information stored in a user model which is extended explicitly or implicitly. There are also hybrid approaches which ask some minimum information to the user, while the rest is achieved in an implicit way. At present, ontologies are one of the most often used approaches for the implementation of user models; a good example of this is the ontology GUMO (Heckmann, Schwarzkopf, Mori, Dengler, & Kröner, 2007).

To this extent, for educational applications *rule-based Recommendation Systems* have proved as more useful than other systems (Abel, Bittencourt, Henze, Krause, & Vassileva, 2008). In general, acceptable recommendations can be obtained with a small amount of information. However, when the system achieves a better knowledge of the user, recommendations increase precision since rules evolve in parallel or new ones are included to the rule-set. However, expressing user preferences, goals and interest with rules can be difficult, in general (Anderson, Ball, Boley, Greene, Howse, Lemire, & McGrath, 2003). Large amounts of data are required to narrow down the recommendation, although this solution comes along with an additional problem: the size and complexity of the rule-set can be unaffordable, and inconsistencies may appear. Last, recommendations are more accurate when rules are generated out of a database, or out of the user's interaction, which increases the adaptability to the specific user.

In this chapter, we present a solution to this problem by the introduction of a new abstraction level, *meta-rules*, which provide the common ground for an effective personalization process in a number of fields like, e.g. learning. This approach has been implemented in the context of Meta-Mender (Romero & Burgos, 2010), a meta-rule-based Recommendation System. In addition, the Meta-Mender architecture and its implementation to contextualize the meta-rules approach, is presented.

## THEORETICAL BACKGROUND

In the field of educational recommendations, there are approaches which use a modified page ranking algorithm for the generation of recommendations (El Helou, Salzmann, Sire, & Gillet, 2009). This algorithm takes into account a number of actors, activities, and resources, as main entities. The user's activity is used to create a directed graph representing the entities and links between them are generated. After that, a rank is assigned to nodes, and finally, this information is used to generate recommendations for a user query. This work is valuable to us because meta-rules take the user's activity for the automatic generation of rules, as an input.

In addition, in the field of rule-based recommenders, there are some relevant reports in the literature (Abel, Bittencourt, Henze, Krause, & Vassileva, 2008), which describe a rule based Recommendation System for online discussion forums for the educational online board Comtella-D. Actually, the system is able to call several encapsulated recommenders, collaborative filtering or content-based recommenders, and the rules decide according to the amount and type of user data which recommender should be called. In doing so, the rules define a meta-recommender which is very interesting but tangential to this work, mostly because the obtained rule-set is very simple. The rules just decide which recommender system to pass the control to and the actual recommendation is provided by the attached recommender systems.

An advantage of rule-based recommenders against other approaches is how easy it is to generate explanations for these systems. In many cases, it is almost impossible to explain to the user how a Recommendation System has derived a conclusion. If the user is not sure of a given recommendation and-or prefers to receive some logic-supported arguments which help him to choose a given solution, rules-based systems are the best ones prepared to solve this issue. This problem is usual in automated collaborative filtering systems (Herlocker, 1999), where the lack of explanations decreases the system acceptance and affects user trust.

The Recommender System RACOFI (Anderson, Ball, Boley, Greene, Howse, Lemire, & McGrath, 2003) is defined by its authors as a rule-applying collaborative filtering system. This system is a hybrid conformed by a collaborative filtering recommender plus a rule-based recommender. It was designed for recommending Canadian music but its authors argue that the system is content independent. RACOFI uses rules to modify, for example, ratings of items based on item similarity. This means that if a user rates an album as highly original, other albums' originality of the same author will be incremented.

With regards to meta-rules, we have not found anything similar to our proposal in the Recommender Systems field. Initially used by LISP (McCarthy, Abrahams, Edwards, Hart, & Levin, 1985) and other languages, the closest concept in rule systems is rule templates, followed by OpenRules, see references, and the Object Oriented RuleML (OO RuleML, see references). This approach allows handling rules as data, thus generating entire rules from its component parts. These approaches are very valuable. However, our approach of producing rules using imperative programming comprises these two approaches and, at the same time, it seems to be more powerful. For instance, Meta-Mender can generate meta-rules, or other supplementary features, easily. In addition, as it will be shown in the next sections, using meta-rules in Rule-based Recommender Systems is not common, and it provides other benefits like maintainability, reengineering and on-the-fly generation. Finally, the introduction of another level of abstraction is very valuable for adaptation.

For the implementation of a rule or meta-rule based recommender using a rule-management system can be of great help. In this respect, Meta-Mender makes use of DROOLS, see references, as rule engine. DROOLS is a business rule management system (BRMS) with a forward chaining inference-based rules engine (the so-called rule system). This system makes use of an enhanced implementation of the Rete algorithm (Forgy, 1982). DROOLS has been designed to allow plug-able language implementations. Currently, rules can be written in Java, MVEL, Python, and Groovy, see references. It is also possible to write functions to be executed as the consequence of any rule; this feature has been used to generate rules from meta-rules. It is also possible to assign a priority to rules, which is a way to address the execution order by the rule designer.

As mentioned in the introduction rule-based recommender systems are suitable when a small amount of user data is available. But if it is the case that a dataset is available it is very important to know how to build the best-fit rule set for the existing data. In this chapter we will show this process through a real example.

An additional issue related to Educational Recommendation Systems is the user model, which is the main repository of input data. Adaptive hypermedia systems have been supporting user models since the very first times. Several authors have defined the essential parts such a system must have (De Bra, Aroyo, & Chepegin, 2004; Benyon, 1993; Martins, Faria, Vaz de Carvalho, & Carrapatoso, 2008): the user model, the domain model, and the interaction model.

The last issue to take into consideration in Recommendation Systems is the interaction between peers. Social networks have shown the potential for knowledge sharing and thus, they should be incorporated in the learning process as a first class component.

There are three main general classifications for user models:

- Regarding the amount of users modeled by the system (canonical vs. individual)
- Regarding information acquisition approach (explicit vs. implicit)
- Regarding information persistence (long term vs. short term)

The first classification (canonical versus individual models) seems more appropriate to Meta-Mender. It comes from the classical software tradeoff between a multipurpose and easy to maintain model and a flexible but more demanding one. Even when user models are not the main focus of this chapter, we will expose the approach we follow to implement the user model in real applications, since this topic is strongly related with Educational Recommendation Systems.

## RECOMMENDER SYSTEMS IN THE CLASSROOM

In this section we describe a real situation in which Meta-Rule Based Recommender Systems can be used in the classroom. This example is interesting because several tools are used and because the recommender can be used not only to provide feedback to the student but also as a warning system for the professor.

The scenario is an undergraduate course on C Programming. The instructors provide students with a pre-configured production environment, similar to a real environment at a corporation. The environment is deployed in personal computers through the use of a virtual machine. This virtual machine has all the tools the student need: compiler, debugger, memory profiler, browser, and the Version Control System Subversion to upload the code to a server. Also a Learning Management System (LMS) is available for the students to access supplementary information. Assignments should be uploaded to a server in a daily basis but students are free to do it at any point in time. As long as the virtual machine is installed at their personal computers students can work at any place. Furthermore, students are advised to work on the course material in pairs. They are informed that, unless disabled, the given environment includes a recording mechanism where certain events are recorded. The environment is downloaded only if the user agrees with the terms described in a document. In the described scenario, a total of 89% of the students agreed to participate.

Similar scenarios have been reported in the literature but using the data stored in the LMS (Macfadyen, & Dawson, 2010), (Romero, Ventura, & García, 2008). In the first referred paper, the authors identified three variables obtained from the information about the student activities in the LMS that are used to predict success or not of a student in a course. These variables are: the number of discussion messages posted, the number of assessments finished and the email messages sent. There are other variables which have some influence in the final score for example total number of online sessions, total time online, etc. In our case, the system records events that take place outside of the LMS. That is why we tried to identify which of the non-LMS variables could help in predicting student achievement.

The following tools are installed in the virtual machine: a C compiler (GCC), Mozilla Firefox, the editor Kate, and KDeveloper an IDE for C. They are free to use these tools or any other. We collected the following variables: number of times the compiler has been executed, number of compiling errors, number of warnings, total working time (with GCC in seconds), number of accesses to educational Web pages (these pages include an LMS provided for the subject, shared resources, etc), and final scores (from 0 to 110).

As mentioned before students can work in pairs or alone, so data should be handled differently for a pair than for a single student. In the case of a single student the process is straightforward all the student related data is assigned to himself. In the case of a pair the numerical information is added up to obtain a total. In the case of the final score we calculated the average.

As it will be discussed in the following sections events generated by users with the mentioned tools can be analyzed and useful information can be extracted from it. Our study will try to answer the following research questions:

- Is it possible to predict the final score from usage data?

If this research question can be answered then two recommenders can be developed. Firstly, a professor oriented recommender which will work as a warning system. This recommender will recommend the professor which students to work more with. If it is possible to detect at initial stages which users are likely to obtain a low score then the professor can pay a greater attention to those students. Secondly, a student oriented recommender can also be generated. This recommender will receive as input student's usage data and supporting material. Supporting material may include solved examples, exercises, Web pages, between others. The material should include metadata in order to determine the target students: students with low programming abilities, students with logical reasoning difficulties, etc. Latter the recommender should recommend to every student the material that fits better for her, according to her preferences, usage data, past actions, results, etc.

## DATA COLLECTION PROCESS

The row data was represented in text files. A software was created to analyze these files and extract the information. The particular scenario described here should be taken into account in order to interpret the obtained data. First it should be taken into account that students were working in a real production scenario with all the tools necessary for accomplishing theirs assignments. Also as long as the related subject had a heavy practical component, the performance of the students should be related with their performance with tools like GCC, the C compiler, see references.

Each time the student executed a GCC command, several text lines were written into a log file. The first line included the date of the event, the command executed and below the result of the command, errors and warnings in the case of a compilation, the commonest event. See Listing 1 for an example of the events users generates while compiling the code with the GCC compiler. In this example the user has done a compilation. This compilation has been unsuccessful, the code has some errors. And after modifying the code the second compilation has some warnings but no errors.

In the case of the browser, every time the user accessed to a link a new line was added to a log file. Main site names were sought. See Listing 2 for an example of the navigation user generated events. Web addresses have been cut showing the site high level structure only. As it can be seen, navigational events contain detailed information of user interests.

The information extracted from the log files was inserted into a database in order to organize the information and to make the information process easier. See Figure 1 for a simplified representation of the described scenario.

Once the usage is stored in the database a lot of relations can be established. In this case it is possible to estimate the working time with the GCC compiler, number of errors per student or per pair, high activity periods, what links were visited during active working periods. This information is very useful because it can be used to recommend links with a high usefulness probability.

*Listing 1. GCC user generated events*

```
-BEGIN 2010-09-15 13:41:56 /usr/bin/gcc -g -Wall -o file1 file1.c
file1.c: In function 'main':
file1.c:6: warning: statement with no effect
file1.c:6: error: 'i' undeclared (first use in this function)
file1.c:6: error: (Each undeclared identifier is reported only once
file1.c:6: error: for each function it appears in.)
file1.c:7: warning: implicit declaration of function 'square'
file1.c:7: warning: format '%p' expects type 'void *', but argument 4 has type
'int'
-END
-BEGIN 2010-09-15 13:48:48 /usr/bin/gcc -g -Wall -o file1 file1.c
file1.c: In function 'main':
file1.c:7: warning: implicit declaration of function 'square'
file1.c:7: warning: format '%p' expects type 'void *', but argument 4 has type
'int'
file1.c:9: warning: control reaches end of non-void function
-END
```

*Listing 2. Firefox user generated events*

```
2010-09-21 18:52:57 http://www.it.uc3m.es/labas/info/
2010-09-21 18:53:08 http://www.it.uc3m.es/labas/DataStructuresPointer/
2010-09-21 18:54:03 http://www.it.uc3m.es/labas/DataStructuresPointer/
2010-09-21 18:58:25 http://www.it.uc3m.es/labas/DataStructuresPointer/
2010-09-21 18:58:40 https://aulaglobal2.uc3m.es/
2010-09-21 18:58:41 https://aulaglobal2.uc3m.es/login/index.php
2010-09-21 18:58:56 http://aulaglobal2.uc3m.es/
2010-09-21 19:45:18 http://www.it.uc3m.es/labas/info/
2010-09-21 19:45:26 http://www.it.uc3m.es/labas/DataStructuresPointer/
2010-09-21 19:48:53 http://www.it.uc3m.es/labas/DataStructuresPointer/
2010-09-21 19:49:04 http://www.it.uc3m.es/labas/DataStructuresPointer/
2010-09-21 19:49:08 http://www.it.uc3m.es/labas/DataStructuresPointer/
2010-09-21 20:03:29 http://www.it.uc3m.es/labas/DataStructuresPointer/
2010-09-21 20:45:01 http://www.it.uc3m.es/labas/info/
2010-09-21 20:45:13 http://www.it.uc3m.es/labas/DataStructuresPointer/
2010-09-21 20:45:47 http://www.it.uc3m.es/labas/DataStructuresPointer/
```

*Figure 1. The scenario described in this section*

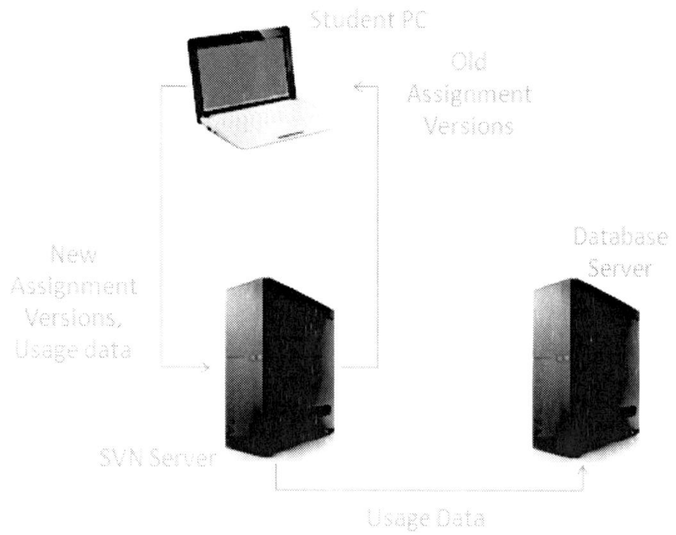


## OBTAINING A RECOMMENDER SYSTEM FROM PREVIOUS RESULTS

As we mentioned before several variables can be obtained analyzing the user generated events. Between them active working time with the GCC compiler, number of errors, links visited, number of warnings, between others. All these variables were correlated with the final score and the more promising ones were used to obtain a linear regression. After analyzing the data with SPSS version 17.0, see references, we obtained that two variables can predict the final score: total working time and error count. With this result we have really important information of how student's performance is related with final score. Also even when a variable like educational Web pages visited is not so important in determining the final score; Web pages are an important way to provide the student with useful information. In order to build a recommender system first it is important to determine what resources to recommend. In this case programming exercises, solved problems, Web pages and documents are strong candidates. Then it is needed to determine which of the existing recommender systems could be more suitable for this situation.

Collaborative filtering recommender systems are not a suitable solution here. Analyzing the Mozilla Firefox logs it was determined that a several of students accessed Web applications like YouTube, Facebook and Twitter.

A collaborative filtering recommender system would recommend these pages to a student and it can be argued their usefulness for the educational process. Also some pages are recurrently accessed during the course and during active working periods even when the total number of accesses is not significant. Nevertheless these pages are important and should be recommended in certain situations.

Another important issue with collaborative filtering recommenders is self explanation (Herlocker, 1999). They are a black box and it is very hard to explain why it recommended a given item to a given student. It is really important that the professor can understand why and how the recommender achieved to a given conclusion because he is the final valuator of the recommender. If you fail recommending a movie maybe you will lose a client but if you fail recommending resources to some students maybe they will lose a year.

For these reasons we consider that rule based recommender systems are more suitable for this problem. With the obtained information it is possible to generate a rule based recommender system. The recommender system will handle the following information: total working time, error count and scores. The score is necessary to determine if we are dealing with a high profile student or no. The recommendation should be different depending on that. The recommender will recommend the following items: exercises, solved problems, Web pages, and documents. The rules obtained from previous results have the following form in pseudo code, see Listing 3.

Rules similar to those at Listing 3 can be executed with high performance giving the recommendation to the user in a short time. But there is a problem they are fixed to specific and, very likely, changing information:

- Thresholds, they are not static. In general thresholds should augment as the course advances.
- Current time, rule sets are a picture of the current moment and in general are valid for a short period of time: an hour, during a class, for the current day, for a week, and so on.

Nevertheless, the concepts behind a rule set has a greater persistence, so if it is possible to represent a rule set in a more abstract and reusable way it will be possible to use this representation several times no matter changing conditions. In order to solve the problem of the low reusability and validity of rule sets used for defining rule based recommender systems we have developed the Meta-Rule Recommender System concept. The implementation of this concept is our Meta-Mender recommender system which architecture and implementation is discussed in the next section.

*Listing 3. Pseudo code of a rule subset for generating the recommendations*

```
if user has a poor academic performance and
   working time < threshold for working time and
   current unit is introduction to programming
then recommend a solved problem for first unit
if user has a poor academic performance and
   error count < threshold for error count and
   current unit is introduction to programming
then recommend an exercise for first unit
if user has a high academic performance and
   working time < threshold for working time and
   current unit is introduction to programming
then recommend a difficult exercise for first unit
if user has a high academic performance and
   error count < threshold for error count and
   current unit is introduction to programming
then recommend an a code with errors to find them within a time
     interval
```

*Figure 2. The Meta-Mender architecture*

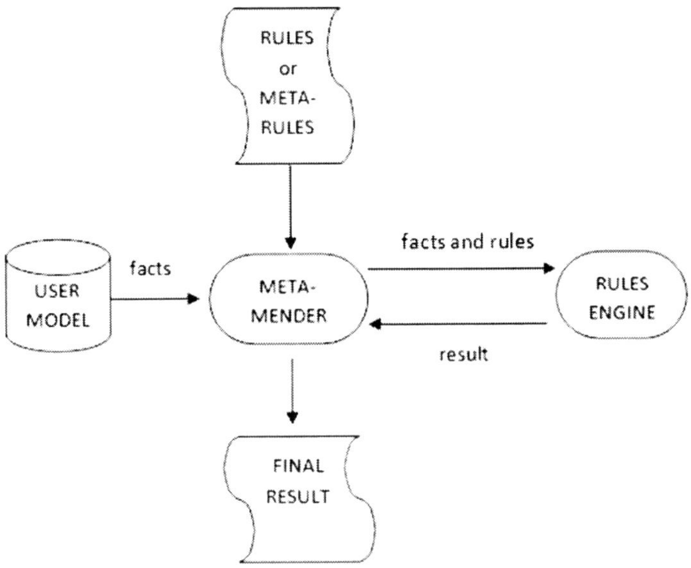


## THE META-MENDER ARCHITECTURE AND IMPLEMENTATION

As previously mentioned, the Meta-Mender Recommendation System uses DROOLS as the rule engine. This rule system works as follows, first it is required to feed the engine with a set of rules (or meta-rules in this case); these meta-rules are defined by the professor or by the technical team, or derived from a rule set, according to the application requirements. Later some facts should be added to the engine. These facts are extracted commonly from a database, be it relational or ontological. As the facts are added to the rule engine, rules antecedents are checked for completeness and once the engine is started, rules that fulfill its antecedents are fired and the corresponding consequences are executed. The order of execution is arbitrary, so rule priority must be stated if the order of execution is important for the final result. In our case the order is important because the output of this iteration will be a file of rules and these files have a structure, so the rules that generate the header must be executed before the rules that generate the body. The output, the rule-set, is used for a second iteration from which the final recommendations are obtained. See Figure 2 for a simplified representation of the Meta-Mender architecture and Listing 4 for an example of a meta-rules file. This file can generate the set of rules showed at Listing 3.

It is worth mentioning that in DROOLS, rule conditions cannot contain functions, this is a common issue in rule systems and the behind reason is performance. The condition is formed by a conjunction of patterns that must be matched by the inference algorithm.

In Meta-Mender rules and meta-rules get input from the user model. This information may come from a table, if the user model is represented in a relational database or from an ontology class if it is represented using ontologies. It is important to note that there is a tradeoff here. The more variables you use in the condition the more queries you need to execute over the data repository and the more it will take the recommender system to give an answer.

As stated before rules are in a way fixed and must be defined statically, it is not possible to add

*Listing 4. Pseudo code of a meta-rule file*

```
moduleName
declarations
rule MetaRuleI
        when ConditionI
        then ActionI
end
rule MetaRuleII
        when ConditionII
        then ActionII
end
...
```

new conditions to a rule dynamically or to change the value a given field. The only way to adapt a rule-set to changing conditions, as we already commented, is by generating rules dynamically. These changing conditions can be:

- Changes in the application architecture, this includes the addition of a new unit to a given course..
- Changes in membership conditions, access restrictions, or similar.
- Changes in user model and others.

It is clear that a static defined condition cannot cope with all these changes. So if there is a way for generating rules according to current user needs, it could save time and effort as long as increase adaptation.

In the other hand meta-rules can handle with changing conditions. Different rules can be generated depending on user preferences, course characteristics, etc.; also rules priority can be different which may imply different recommendations. Rule output can be related with rule priority since it will be possible to order the results and give the user a list of recommendations ordered by priorities.

This way the generated rule will be adapted to the information stored in the data repository and next time if there are new conditions they will be generated on the fly according to the current information available in the user model.

It is important to note that this rule generation approach is actually more powerful than it may appear. A meta-rule set is a kind of meta-program, a program able to generate another program, and all the benefits of meta-programming apply also to meta-rules, for more information on meta-programming see (Abrahams, & Gurtovoy, 2005). The direct implication of this is that it is possible to generate rules for a language different to the original meta-rule language. This meta-programming feature allows using the Meta-Mender Recommender System for a wide range of applications: business rules systems, decision support systems, complex code generation, etc.

## PRACTICAL IMPLEMENTATIONS OF THE META-MENDER RECOMMENDER SYSTEM

Apart from the recommender system created for the C programming course mentioned before, the Meta-Mender recommender is been used at present as part of two projects, in development at present. The first one, TELMA, see references, is focused on the application of Communications and Information Technologies in lifelong training of surgeons of Minimally Invasive Surgery (MIS).

TELMA develops an online learning environment which manages the content and knowledge generated by users in an efficient way. TELMA creates a new training strategy based on knowledge management, cooperative work and communications and information technologies aiming to the improvement of the formation process of the surgeons of MIS.

In order to cover all these needs and to achieve its goals, TELMA develops a cooperative and adaptable learning platform. This platform is composed of a training system which integrates a tool for the authoring of didactic multimedia content, a Recommendation System and a social network. The Recommendation System, Meta-Mender, manages the knowledge generated by the users creating the foundations for adaptive learning. The learning platform allows the construction of a complete knowledge base thanks to the reuse and sharing of the knowledge generated for the professionals who access the learning system.

The second project, GAME·TEL, see references, is focused on the creation of a system for the design, development, execution and evaluation of educational games and simulations, adapted to student preferences, educational goals, profile, (Burgos, Tattersall, & Koper, 2007) .

The games and simulations are conversational adventures which are both usable and understandable. These characteristics benefit to the content creator, the professor in most cases, as long as to the final user, usually the student (Moreno-Ger, Burgos, Martínez-Ortiz, Sierra, & Fernández-Manjón, 2008; Torrente, Moreno-Ger, & Fernández-Manjón, 2008).

The software system is composed of several interconnected modules which allow the integration and intercommunication between games and simulations and several tools widely used for communities of professors. Initially these tools are the learning management systems Moodle and .LRN, and the authoring and learning units execution system LAMS (Burgos, Tattersall, & Koper, 2006; Moreno-Ger, Martínez-Ortiz, Sierra, & Fernández-Manjón, 2006). In this context the Meta-Mender Recommendation System will suggest to users the best learning path according with their preferences, goals and objectives and will help with the game adaptation problem.

## AUTOMATIC META-RULE GENERATION

Meta-Mender is a Meta-rule Based Recommender System this implies that it works with meta-rules which are in general harder to obtain than simple rules. That is why we have developed a tool called Dyme for automatic meta-rule generation. Dyme and its functionality are described in this section.

There are several candidate approaches to develop an automatic tool for meta-rule obtention. Genetic Programming (GP) is a strong one (Banzhaf, Nordin, Keller, & Francone, 1998), but it is not a direct method and not always a suitable solution is obtained. Another option is to notice that a compiler can be written for any rule language. This is a very interesting option because a compiler can not only generate automatically the meta-rule set but also can be used to test if the meta-rule set so obtained is valid after changing the original rule set. But there is an important fact to take into account: the scenario in which an automatic meta-rule generation tool is supposed to be used is the following: there is no previous knowledge of the rule set, and every structure of the rule language should be learned from scratch and the compiler should also be generated automatically which is not a trivial task.

Finally we selected the compiler option because of our previous experience in the compilers field and because of the inherent simplicity of a rule language this method is enough to find suitable solutions. Next, the architecture of Dyme will be described. The method followed can be named Dynamic Compiler Generation (DCG) the tool has been developed in Java and two Open Source projects have been used for the scanner and parser generation, JFlex for the scanner and CUP for the parser, see references. The architecture can be seen at Figure 3.

The input for Dyme is a rule set and the output is the corresponding meta-rule set. Also a compiler able to generate automatically the meta-rules is obtained. This compiler can be used to check that after the inclusion of new rules in the initial rule set the meta-rules are still valid. This way an automatic validation method has been developed. This method allows verifying that a rule set can be generated by a meta-rule set. Another final product that can be obtained from Dyme is a facts base that can be used for future tests. This facts base is obtained automatically during the dynamic compiler generation process. These facts can be stored in a database and can be used as the initial test set for the recommender.

Dyme follows an iterative process in which after every iteration a new compiler is obtained, this compiler is able to compile the input analyzed in each iteration. Every iteration takes as input a rule from the rule set and this rule is added to the compiler input. This way after n iterations the compiler input will have n rules. The process can be described as follows:

1. Initialization, the first rule is read from the input and a scanner and a parser able to compile it are generated. The generation is done using JFlex and CUP.
2. Read next rule, if there are no more rules then exit the process successfully.
3. Try to compile the input, all previous rules plus the current one, using the current compiler.
4. If the previous step was successful go to step 2.
5. Generalize the scanner and the parser; the generalization process will be described below.
6. Generate a new scanner and a new parser using JFlex and CUP.
7. Go to step 2.

The generalization process commented in step five above consist actually of two processes: one to generalize the scanner and another one to generalize the parser. The main idea behind the generalization processes is to assume at every

*Figure 3. Architecture of Dyme, an automatic meta-rule generation tool*

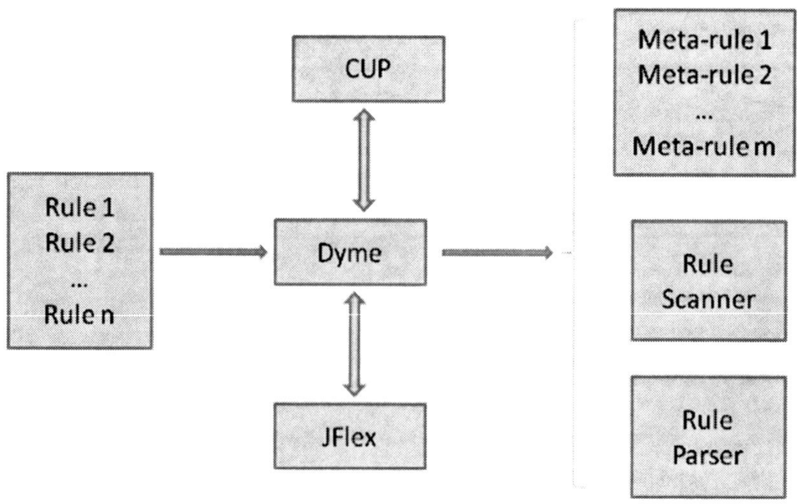

stage the most restrictive production rule. Later if this assumption does not hold the rule is modified. After the final rule from the input set has been processed the parser contains the most restrictive production rules able to parse the rule set.

After the last iteration we have the compiler, but this compiler does nothing. It can parse the rule set but it is not able to generate the meta-rule set. The main reason for this is that in most cases rules contain literal values and meta-rules should abstract this information in order to be able to generate not only the input provided but also new rules depending on the data provided. So at each iteration a facts base is built which will contain the data extracted from every rule. This facts base will later be useful to test the meta-rule set obtained.

After the final iteration we have a compiler able to compile the rule set, recall that it is not still able to produce the meta-rule set, and a facts base. Analyzing the semantic of the productions obtained at the last iteration it is possible to produce meta-rules. It is even possible to modify the parser in order for it to be able to generate the meta-rules for us. With this information the meta-rules can be written, in our case using a DROOLS rule language, but the information is general enough to be useful for any technology or language.

The methodology proposed here is useful for automatic meta-rule generation and at the same time for helping in the implementation of Meta-rule based Recommendation Systems from existing Rule-based Recommender Systems. Also the compiler obtained can be used as a test for proving that a given rule set can be generated from a meta-rule set. If the compiler is not able to compile a given rule set, then a new meta-rule set should be generated. As the proposed method is a direct one, it will find a suitable solution for any input.

## SOME ISSUES ON PRACTICAL USER MODEL IMPLEMENTATION

At present, one of the commonest approaches used to implement user models is the definition of one or several ontologies which define the user characteristics and its relations with each other and with the host application. The common approach is to reuse existing ontologies like FOAF or SIOC, see references, and reasoning is applied in order to obtain new knowledge. This approach useful and actually on the top of the wave has nevertheless some practical drawbacks. Firstly sometimes the database available to work with is a relational one and it is possible that for compatibility with other parts of the application it should remain as is. Secondly even when the design can be ontology based from the very beginning, for some practical issues it is a better idea to use a relational model instead of an ontology based one. These practical issues may include time constraint, huge data sets, and others. Anyway the advantages of ontologies are so worthy that a workaround, if it exists, is more than desirable. It is important to note that the duplication of the whole database in an ontological repository, e.g. Jena or Sesame, see references, is not an option in these cases, because of the added difficulty and added risk of having to maintain two data repositories.

The solution we propose for the mentioned issues consist of two parts: first to maintain the relational database as is and second to create a mapping between the database and one or several ontologies, trying to reuse existing ones whenever possible. There are several open source projects suitable for this kind of solution, e.g. OpenLink Virtuoso, Triplify and D2R, see references. OpenLink Virtuoso is a very powerful tool more intended for large applications and offers in general more power than needed for most educational applications. It has two versions a professional and an open source one; both have a long list of features. For small and medium applications D2R is a good option: simple to install and to use and it is the one we are using in real applications.

In order to create the mapping a text file should be provided which maps from table columns to triples. Every triple will be defined by the table key, the column name and the column value. It is not necessary to map the entire database, but only what it is necessary to extract ontological information and can be defined incrementally as needed. A mapping file can be large enough to include a whole example here, nevertheless there is a small example below, but what is really important is to realize the advantages of this approach. These advantages include:

- It is possible to provide a data repository with all the advantages of relational databases, fast response time, scalability, consistency checking, etc.
- An ontology view of the data repository can be implemented which can be queried using SPARQL, see references. The information retrieved can be used to do some reasoning on it obtaining new knowledge.

In our projects we are using this approach, user interactions are read and stored using a relational database connection and information useful for the Meta-Mender Recommendation System is extracted using the mapping between relational and ontological data.

The proposed approach does not imply that an ontology design could be skipped. We consider that a flexible, generic and at the same time powerful ontology design is the first step before starting the construction of a map with a relational database. Several authors have proposed generic ontology designs for formal learning, the set of ontologies LOCO (Learning Objects Context Ontologies) is a good example (Jovanovic, Gaševic, & Devedžic, 2006; Stokić, Pata, Devedžić, Jovanović, Urošević, Gašević, Kieslinger, & Wild, 2008), but there is a gap in the literature for informal learning applications. That is why we have developed the ONAIL ontology network (Ontology Network for Adaptive and Informal Learning), the conceptual model defined in this paper is a fully open and flexible logical model based on the composition of different vocabularies. The power of this ontology network allows to:

- Develop a conceptual model independent of the application,
- Reuse public vocabularies,
- Extend the conceptual model with new vocabularies,
- Achieve interoperability concerns between the descriptions of different contents,
- Search information using semantic criteria,
- Enlarge the knowledge base with a reasoning feature e.g. using the semantic rules, and
- Manage system information and make recommendations using the semantic rules too.

The approach we have followed for the definition of ONAIL consist of some basic steps. The first step consists on the development of an ontology network to represent the diversity of data and content. In order to organize the ontology network, the network kernel must be formed by generic concepts and most important relations between them. This approach allows focusing in the main concepts, the user for example, and extends them by adding specialized ontologies, a knowledge domain ontology for example.

There are also other criteria to assure the quality of the defined ontologies and the semantic coherence of the model.

The ONAIL model has been defined for its use in several applications which need to model the user experience, interrelations between users, professors, media, etc. The main ontologies that compound the ontology network and its interrelations are shown at Figure 4.

*Figure 4. Ontologies of the ONAIL ontology network and theirs interrelations*

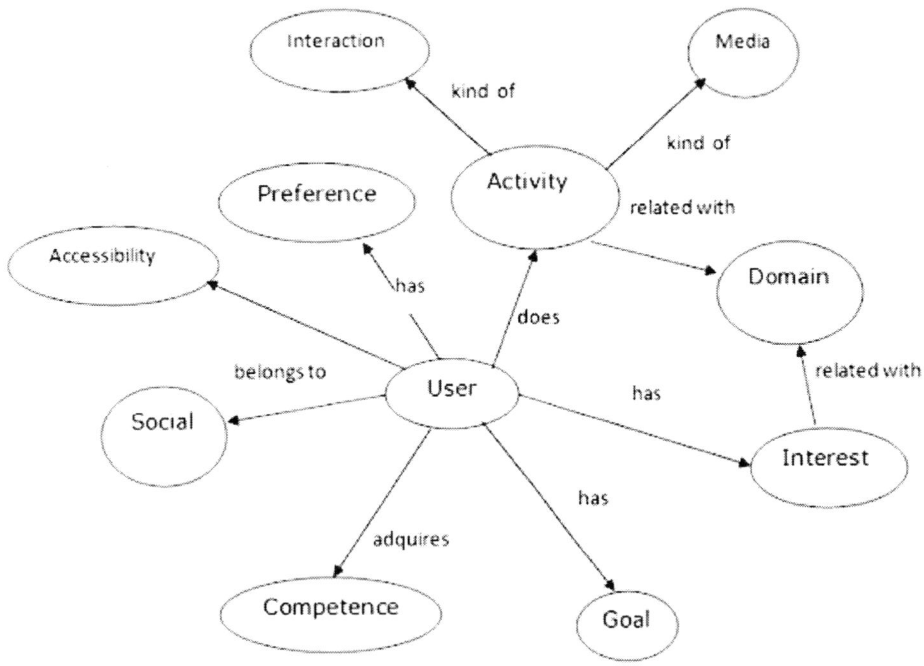


## DESCRIPTION OF THE ONAIL ONTOLOGIES

First, the User ontology will be described; it represents the application user and its main properties: demographic and personal data, education, etc. It contains the User class which inherits from the foaf:Person class. Some new properties have been added, between them: hasActivity, hasCompetence, hasGoal, hasGroup, hasInterest, hasPreference. These are object properties which reference instances of other classes. It can be inferred that these properties relate the User ontology with the ontologies of Figure 4.

The Social ontology models user communities, it represents user membership, the goals associated with a user community and provides an identity to the community as a whole. This ontology has the class Team which inherits from the foaf:Group class.

Regarding the Competence ontology it is important to note that an actual implementation of it depends a lot on the target application. In consequence a simple definition of the main classes has been made. First, the Competence class has been defined which is the parent class of the CognitiveCompetence, PhysicalCompetence and TechnicalCompetence classes. These classes are very simple; the idea is that annotations are related to acquired competences be generated with semantic rules which depend on the characteristics of the given application.

The Goal ontology models personal and professional objectives that motivate a person to use a software application. Here it can be found the Goal class which is the parent of the EducationalGoal, SocialGoal and ThematicGoal classes. User goals can determine which educational resource should be recommended to the student. In fact a change in user goals could imply a modification in the recommendation strategy from that moment on. This characteristic is also common to the Interest ontology which focus on professional and / or education interest of the user. This ontology models the interest in function of, between other characteristics, the knowledge the user has of the domain. It is clear that an expert and a beginner will not have the same interests and this difference should be considered by the user model.

The Domain ontology models the knowledge domain. It can be incremented with references to ontologies specific to a given domain. This means that this ontology is a kind of connector and its definition will depend on the application and available domain ontologies.

The Activity ontology models the activities performed by the user. These activities can include: social interactions, media interaction, etc. This ontology is also related with the domain ontology, a media ontology (if necessary) and in an ontology related with user interaction. The goal is to annotate any activity performed by the user and to achieve it any number of ontologies which models the user activities can be connected.

The Preference ontology has been defined to model all user preferences but those related with accessibility. The Preference class has been defined; it is the parent class of classes like CognitivePreference and LearningPreference. The Accessibility ontology contains the AccessibilityPreference class which inherits from Preference and is the parent of the classes ContentAccessibility, ContextAccessibility, ControlAccessibility and DisplayAccessibility.

AudioAccessibility, VideoAccessibility, KeyboardAccessibility, etc., inherit from ContentAccessibility. Other classes could be added and existing ones incremented according to applications needs and requirements. It does not make sense to define a complete accessibility ontology with the associated effort and then to use a minimal part of it. So a simple ontology should define basic concepts and create the frame for future additions and modifications.

The modular definition of ONAIL permits to disconnect any ontology in case it is not useful for a given application. This should not affect the rest of the network. This flexibility should boost its applicability to several software projects.

## FUTURE RESEARCH DIRECTIONS

Recommender systems applied to the context of learning experiences are still in their initial steps. Although the technology has proven effective in other context, there is still much work needed to prove its benefits in a learning experience. The direction toward learning experiences are evolving seems to suggest that recommender systems could potentially become a decisive technology. Students tend to increase their learning activities aside from the given material. Efforts to design and enact detailed scripts to choreograph the different actions taking place in a learning experience are confronted with a sense of freedom when searching and using educational resources derived from current Internet technologies.

As a first future direction for recommender systems we believe they may provide a powerful compromise between totally unsupervised learning and tightly controlled learning environments. Recommender systems have three aspects that may have a profound effect on learning. The first one is complexity. Although these systems require a set of rules to operate, these rules can be significantly simpler that user models already present in sophisticated tutoring systems. This feature may significantly lower the adoption threshold of these tools for instructors with basic computer skills.

The second aspect with a potentially large impact is the potential to easily capture already existing instructor experience. With the right approach, part of the know-how that a instructor acquires over the years can be formulated in terms of rules or meta-rules suitable to be used by a recommender system. Instructors are, to some extent, already performing such tasks. When preparing material for a course, the teaching staff selects certain resources as the most appropriate for the students. Typically, the collection of considered resources is larger than what students might use. When gathering these resources, instructors may have different type of students in mind. Capturing these different profiles and formulating them in terms of simple rules may pave the way to an intuitive recommendation system.

And the third aspect where recommender systems may have an impact on learning is to fill an existing gap between the high complexity, highly specialized, individualized tutoring systems, and the highly interactive, face-to-face., collaborative interaction. A recommender system based on meta-rules may provide a platform simpler than an specialized intelligent tutor, may require much less design time, and may provide appropriate actions, resources, or interactions, to learning experiences ranging from pure face-to-face, to asynchronous virtual experiences.

With this landscape, we strongly believe that there is a fertile research area ahead of us. Recommender systems are already used in an ever increasing set of areas and learning has all the ingredients suggesting the potential for these applications plus a need for simpler yet effective systems to boost the performance of students.

## CONCLUSION

In this chapter, we presented a meta-rule based approach Recommender Systems. Meta-rules are rules that generate rules, and are able to generalize a rule-set providing bases for adaptation, reengineering and on the fly generation. In this chapter, the benefits of meta-rules have been exposed. As an implementation example some details of Meta-Mender a meta-rule based Recommendation System have been also presented. The concept the Meta-Mender is based on, meta-rules for adaptation starts a new branch in the recommendation field and broadens the scope for new solutions in the field.

Also meta-rules are an effective solution to provide a personalized recommendation to the learner, and constitute a new approach in rule-based Recommendation Systems.

Meta-rules constitute a new abstraction level, which provides foundations for effective adaptive and personalized processes, such as in, e.g. learning. This abstraction level is also highly valuable for adaptation. The rules obtained can be different for different users or for the same user at different periods of time. Meta-Mender is a recommendation system that implements this approach.

In this chapter it is shown the process of creating a recommender for a real situation. The process is described in detail from the data collection stage to the recommender definition.

At present, we use Meta-Mender in two R&D projects. In both, the next step is an evaluation phase with real data from actual users (in fact, two different, separate target groups). These two evaluation processes will provide a first-hand feedback of the implementation of Meta-Mender. Out of these results, we will refine the engine and we will design a visual authoring tool for meta-rules.

Because of the strong relation between user models and Recommender Systems in educational applications, some practical issues and solutions have also been considered by the authors. With the content provided in this chapter it is possible to define and implement a Meta-rule based Recommender System useful for educational or general purpose applications.

## REFERENCES

D2R. (n.d.). *The D2R server*. Retrieved from http://www4.wiwiss.fu-berlin.de/bizer/d2r-server/

Abel, F., Bittencourt, I. I., Henze, N., Krause, D., & Vassileva, J. (2008). A rule-based recommender system for online discussion forums. *Proceedings of the 5th International Conference on Adaptive Hypermedia and Adaptive Web-Based Systems*, Hannover, Germany.

Abrahams, D., & Gurtovoy, A. (2005). *C++ template metaprogramming: Concepts, tools, and techniques from boost and beyond*. Addison-Wesley.

Anderson, M., Ball, M., Boley, H., Greene, S., Howse, N., Lemire, D., & McGrath, S. (2003). RACOFI: A rule-applying collaborative filtering system. *In Proceedings of the IEEE/WIC COLA'03*, Halifax, Canada.

Banzhaf, W., Nordin, P., Keller, R. E., & Francone, F. D. (1998). *Genetic programming: An Introduction: On the automatic evolution of computer programs and its applications*. Morgan Kaufmann.

Benyon, D. (1993). Adaptive systems: A solution to usability problems. *Journal of User Modeling and User Adapted Interaction*, *3*(1), 1–22.

Burgos, D., Tattersall, C., & Koper, R. (2006). Repurposing existing generic games and simulations for e-learning. *Special Issue on Education and Pedagogy with Learning Objects and Learning Designs*: *Computers in Human Behavior*.

Burgos, D., Tattersall, C., & Koper, R. (2007). How to represent adaptation in eLearning with IMS learning design. *Interactive Learning Environments*, *15*(2), 161–170. doi:10.1080/10494820701343736

CUP. (n.d.). *LALR parser generator in Java*. Retrieved from http://www2.cs.tum.edu/projects/cup/

De Bra, P., Aroyo, L., & Chepegin, V. (2004). The next big thing: Adaptive Web-based systems. *Journal of Digital Information*, *5*(1).

DROOLS. (n.d.). *The business logic integration platform*. Retrieved from http://www.jboss.org/drools

El Helou, S., Salzmann, C., Sire, S., & Gillet, D. (2009). The 3A contextual ranking system: Simultaneously recommending actors, assets, and group activities. *In Proceedings of the Third ACM Conference on Recommender Systems RecSys '09*, (pp. 373-376). New York, NY: ACM.

Firefox. (n.d.). The Mozilla open source browser. Retrieved from http://www.mozilla.org/

FOAF. (2010). *Friend of a Friend Ontology*. Retrieved from http://xmlns.com/foaf/spec/20100101.rdf

Forgy, C. (1982). Rete: A fast algorithm for the many pattern/many object pattern match problem. *Artificial Intelligence*, *19*, 17–37. doi:10.1016/0004-3702(82)90020-0

GAMETEL. (n.d.). *The GAMETEL Project*. Retrieved from www.ines.org.es/gametel

GCC. (n.d.). *The GNU compiler collection*. Retrieved from http://gcc.gnu.org/

Groovy. (n.d.). *The Groovy programming language*. Retrieved from http://groovy.codehaus.org/

Heckmann, D., Schwarzkopf, E., Mori, J., Dengler, D., & Kröner, A. (2007). *The user model and context ontology GUMO revisited for future Web 2.0 extensions*. Retrieved March 16, 2010, from http://citeseerx.ist.psu.edu/viewdoc/download?doi=10.1.1.142.9981&rep=rep1&type=pdf

Herlocker, J. L. (1999). Position statement - Explanations in recommender systems. *In Proceedings of the CHI'99 Workshop*, Pittsburgh, USA.

IBM SPSS Statistics 17. (n.d.). *Statistics software*. Retrieved from http://www.spss.com/

Java. (n.d.). *Java technology*. Retrieved from http://www.oracle.com/us/technologies/java/index.html

Jena. (n.d.). *A Semantic Web framework for Java*. Retrieved from http://jena.sourceforge.net/

JFlex. (n.d.). *The fast scanner generator for Java*. Retrieved from http://jflex.de/

Jovanovic, J., Gaševic, D., & Devedžic, V. (2006). Ontology-based automatic annotation of learning content. *International Journal on Semantic Web and Information Systems*, *2*(2), 91–119. doi:10.4018/jswis.2006040103

Macfadyen, L. P., & Dawson, S. (2010). Mining LMS data to develop an early warning system for educators: A proof of concept. *Computers & Education*, *54*, 588–599. doi:10.1016/j.compedu.2009.09.008

Martins, A. C., Faria, L., Vaz de Carvalho, C., & Carrapatoso, E. (2008). User modeling in adaptive hypermedia educational systems. *Journal of Educational Technology & Society*, *11*(1), 194–207.

McCarthy, J., Abrahams, P. W., Edwards, D. J., Hart, T. P., & Levin, M. I. (1985). *LISP 1.5 programmer's manual*. MIT Press.

Moreno-Ger, P., Burgos, D., Martínez-Ortiz, I., Sierra, J., & Fernández-Manjón, B. (2008). Educational game design for online education. *Computers in Human Behavior*, *24*(6), 2530–2540. doi:10.1016/j.chb.2008.03.012

Moreno-Ger, P., Martínez-Ortiz, I., Sierra, J., & Fernández-Manjón, B. (2006). A descriptive markup approach to facilitate the production of e learning contents. *In Proceedings of 6th International Conference on Advanced Learning Technologies* (ICALT 2006), (pp. 19-21). Kerkrade, The Netherlands, (IEEE Computer Society).

MVEL. (n.d.). *The MVEL expression language*. Retrieved from http://mvel.codehaus.org/

OO RuleML. (n.d.). *Object-oriented RuleML*. Retrieved from http://ruleml.org/indoo/indoo.html

OpenLink Virtuoso. (n.d.). *Virtuoso universal server*. Retrieved from http://virtuoso.openlinksw.com/

OpenRules. (n.d.). *Business rules management system*. Retrieved from0 http://openrules.com/index.htm

Python. (n.d.). *The Python programming language*. Retrieved from http://www.python.org/

Rocchio, J. J. (1971). *Relevance feedback in information retrieval, in the SMART Retrieval System. Experiments in automatic document processing* (pp. 313–323). Englewood Cliffs, NJ: Prentice Hall, Inc.

Romero, C., Ventura, S., & García, E. (2008). Data mining in course management systems: Moodle case study and tutorial. *Computers & Education*, *51*, 368–384. doi:10.1016/j.compedu.2007.05.016

Romero, V. A., & Burgos, D. (2010). Meta-Mender: A meta-rule based recommendation system for educational applications. *Procedia Computer Science*, *1*(2), 2877–2882. doi:10.1016/j.procs.2010.08.014

Sesame. (n.d.). *Sesame repository*. Retrieved from http://www.openrdf.org/related.jsp

SIOC. (n.d.). *Semantically-interlinked online communities ontology*. Retrieved from http://sioc-project.org/

SPARQL. (n.d.). *Query language for RDF*. Retrieved from http://www.w3.org/TR/rdf-sparql-query/

Stokić, D., Pata, K., Devedžić, V., Jovanović, J., Urošević, L., & Gašević, D. … Wild, J. (2008). *Intelligent learning extended organizations*. TE-Learn Conference, Hanoi.

TELMA. (n.d.). *The TELMA project*. Retrieved from www.ines.org.es/telma

Torrente, J., Moreno-Ger, P., & Fernández-Manjón, B. (2008). Learning models for the integration of adaptive educational games in virtual learning environments. *In Proceedings of the 3rd International Conference on E-learning and Games, Lecture Notes in Computer Science 5093*, Nanjing, China (pp. 463–474).

Triplify. (n.d.). *The Triplify project.* Retrieved from http://triplify.org/

## ADDITIONAL READING

Balabanovi, M., & Shoham, Y. (1997). Fab: content-based, collaborative recommendation, *Communications of the ACM Volume 40, No. 3.*

Bollacker, K.D., Lawrence, S., & Giles, C.L. (1998). CiteSeer: An Autonomous Web Agent for Automatic Retrieval and Identification of Interesting Publications, *Proceedings of the Second International Conference on Autonomous Agents, Minneapolis MN, USA.*

Breslin, J., Harth, A., Bojars, U., & Decker, S. (2005). Towards semantically-interlinked online communities. *In Proceedings of the 2nd European Semantic Web Conference.*

Cook, R., & Kay, J. (1994). The justified user model: a viewable, explained user model. *In Proceedings of the Fourth International Conference on User Modeling, Hyannis, Cape Cod, MA, USA, 145-150.*

Denaux, R., Dimitrova, V., & Aroyo, L. (2004). Interactive Ontology-Based User Modeling for Personalized Learning Content Management. *In AH 2004: Workshop Proceedings Part II, 338 – 347.*

Deshpande, M., & Karypis, G. (2004). Item-based top-n recommendation algorithms. *ACM Transactions on Information Systems*, *22*, 143–177. doi:10.1145/963770.963776

Dolog, P., & Nejdl, W. (2003). Challenges and Benefits of the Semantic Web for User Modelling, retrieved April 14, 2010, from http://wwwis.win.tue.nl/ah2003/proceedings/paper9.pdf.

Heckmann, D., Schwarzkopf, E., Mori, J., Dengler, D., & Kröner, A. (2007). The User Model and Context Ontology GUMO revisited for future Web 2.0 Extensions, retrieved March 16, 2010, from http://citeseerx.ist.psu.edu/viewdoc/download?doi=10.1.1.142.9981&rep=rep1&type=pdf.

Konstan, J. A., Miller, B. N., Maltz, D., Herlocker, J. L., Gordon, L. R., & Riedl, J. (1997). GroupLens: applying collaborative filtering to Usenet news. *Communications of the ACM*, *40*(3). doi:10.1145/245108.245126

Kulles, B. (2000). User Modeling for Adaptive and Adaptable Software Systems. Retrieved March 5, 2010, from http://otal.umd.edu/uuguide/wmk/.

Manouselis, N., Drachsler, H., Vuorikari, R., Hummel, H., & Koper, R. (2010). Recommender Systems in Technology Enhanced Learning. In Kantor, P., Ricci, F., Rokach, L., & Shapira, B. (Eds.), *Recommender Systems Handbook: A Complete Guide for Research Scientists & Practitioners.*

Middleton, S.E., Shadbolt, N.R., & De Roure, D.C. (2004). Ontological user profiling in recommender systems. *ACM Transactions on Information Systems (TOIS) Volume 22, Issue 1, 54 – 88 13.*

Mödritscher, F. (2010). Towards a recommender strategy for personal learning environments. Procedia Computer Science Volume 1, Issue 2, *2010, 2775-2782. Proceedings of the 1st Workshop on Recommender Systems for Technology Enhanced Learning (RecSysTEL 2010).*

Razmerita, L., Angehrn, A., & Maedche, A. (2003). Ontology-based User Modeling for Knowledge Management Systems. Lecture Notes in Computer Science *Vol. 2702 / 2003, 148-152.*

Razmerita, L., Angehrn, A., & Nabeth, T. (2003). On the Role of User Models and User Modeling in Knowledge Management Systems, retrieved April, 14, 2010, from http://www.calt.insead.edu/project/Ontologging/documents/2003-HCI-On_the_role_of_user_models_anduser_modeling_in_Knowledge_Management_Systems.pdf.

Resnick, P., & Varian, H. R. (1997). Recommender systems. *Communications of the ACM*, *40*, 56–58. doi:10.1145/245108.245121

Santos, O. C., & Boticario, J. G. (2010). Modeling recommendations for the educational domain. Procedia Computer Science Volume 1, Issue 2, *2793-2800. Proceedings of the 1st Workshop on Recommender Systems for Technology Enhanced Learning (RecSysTEL 2010).*

Schwab, I., Pohl, W., & Koychev, I. (2000). Learning to Recommend from Positive Evidence, *In Proceedings of Intelligent User Interfaces, ACM Press, 241-247.*

Terveen, L., Hill, W., & Amento, B. McDonald, & D., Creter, J.(1997). PHOAKS: a system for sharing recommendations, *Communications of the ACM Volume 40, No. 3.*

## KEY TERMS AND DEFINITIONS

**Compiler:** a computer program that transforms source code written in a programming language into another computer language.

**Meta-Rule:** a rule which generates one or several rules.

**Meta-Rule Based Recommender Systems:** Recommender Systems which abstract a rule set in a meta-rule set. One of its advantages is that meta-rules are more flexible than rules and can adapt better to changes in the user related data.

**Recommender Systems:** A system which attempts to recommend the user information useful for him based on user preferences, past actions or decisions, etc.

**Rule:** A rule in computer science is a programming construction which has a condition and a consequence. The consequence executed if the condition is valid.

**Rule-Based Recommender Systems:** Recommender Systems which use rules for deciding what items to recommend to the user.

**Virtual Machine:** a software implementation of a machine (i.e. a computer) that executes programs like a physical machine.

# Chapter 10
# A Systematic Approach for Designing Educational Recommender Systems

**Patrick H. S. Brito**
*Federal University of Alagoas, Brazil*

**Ig Ibert Bittencourt**
*Federal University of Alagoas, Brazil*

**Aydano Pamponet Machado**
*Federal University of Alagoas, Brazil*

**Evandro Costa**
*Federal University of Alagoas, Brazil*

**Olavo Holanda**
*Federal University of Alagoas, Brazil*

**Rafael Ferreira**
*Federal University of Pernambuco, Brazil*

**Thiago Ribeiro**
*Federal University of Alagoas, Brazil*

## ABSTRACT

*The construction of Educational Recommender System (ERS) demands the incorporation of quality attributes at the software design, such as availability for preventing the service to be unavailable for a long time, and scalability for preventing the system from going offline due to a large number of simultaneous requests. The incorporation of such characteristics makes ERS more complex and expensive, but existing strategies for designing ERS do not consider quality attributes in an explicit way. This chapter presents an architecture-centered solution, which is partially supported by tools and considers quality attributes as early as possible in the software development process in a systematic way, from requirements to the source code. The feasibility of the proposed process is showed in terms of a case study executed in a "step-by-step" fashion, presenting how the software architecture can be designed and gradually refined until it achieves the level of object-oriented classes generated based on design patterns.*

DOI: 10.4018/978-1-61350-489-5.ch010

## INTRODUCTION

Recommender Systems are systems that typically compare a user profile to some reference characteristics, aiming to rate the items according to the particular needs of the user.

In the context of education, Educational Recommender Systems (ERS) are used for recommending content to learners according to their needs and knowledge levels. ERS are particularly important to the learning process since they allow teachers and learners to find content in a more appropriate way, according to their educational profile and needs. The importance of ERS is even greater in the context of distance education, in which the average number of learners per teacher is usually higher than in traditional face-to-face education. In a scenario of a high number of learners, the recommendation of personalized content is impracticable for a human teacher, so there is a natural tendency to generalize the recommended educational content, such as exercises and reading material, according to the average profile of the class. The recommendation of general learning objects may discourage learners that need special attention thus increasing the dropout rate.

Due to its importance for distance education, ERS should be integrated to Virtual Learning Environment (VLE), in order to allow learners to access specific learning content, according to their profiles at the time that suits them. Knowing the importance of ERS and the fact that the VLEs should be online in a 24x7, ERS can be considered a critical system with which we must take special care throughout their life cycle, especially during its design and development.

Despite its importance to the learning process, the construction of ERS is considered a complex task, which demands the incorporation of quality attributes (Sommerville, 1995) usually related to critical software systems, such as scalability and security (privacy-protecting). Scalability property means that the system should be able of recommending content to a large number of users at the same time; while the security property aims to protect the personal data into the system profile from unauthorized access.

Although the aforementioned characteristics are very important in the context of ERS, their incorporation causes software to be more complex, and consequently makes the development process more error prone and the final software more expensive. To cope with the inherent complexity related to quality attributes, it has been claimed that quality requirements should be systematically incorporated as early as possible in the software development process, especially during the requirements engineering and the architectural design (Rubira, de-Lemos, Ferreira, & Castor-Filho, 2005), (Brito, Rocha, Castor-Filho, Martins, & Rubira, 2005). Software architectures explicitly represent the structure of systems, and it is one of the earliest artifacts that permits the analysis of system quality attributes, such as, adaptability, performance and reliability (Bass, Clements, & Kazman, 2003).

Although the addition of quality attributes in complex software systems has received considerable attention (Bass, Clements, & Kazman, 2003), (Brito, de-Lemos, Rubira, & Martins, 2009), (Bradbury, 2004), in the context of ERS it is not considered in an explicit way. Regarding the design of ERS, some authors have proposed multi-agent architectures that can provide personalized services for learners and teachers (Zhu, Ip, & Cao, 2008), (Casili, Gerling, Deco, & Bender, 2010). In such solutions, software agents coordinate work for offering recommendation services including personalized recommendation. (Wang, Tsai, Lee, & Chiu, 2007) propose an adaptive personalized model for learning objects recommendation. They propose to combination of two algorithms for recommending leaning objects: preference-based and correlation-based. (Lu, 2004) presents a framework for recommending learning content by using a multi-attribute evaluation method combined with a fuzzy matching method. A common characteristic of these approaches concerns the fact that in terms of quality attributes, the ERS are developed in an ad-hoc manner, by focusing only on the system functionality (e.g., recommendation algorithm, learner profile management, and domain management), but they do not consider different design decisions according to quality attributes derived from non-functional requirements as part of the development process. This ad-hoc way of dealing with quality attributes can impair the recommendation accuracy or even derail its use in a real environment with, for example, a critical requirement of scalability.

Regarding the quality of ERS, Intelligent Tutoring Systems (ITS) can be seen as an important ally for improving the quality of the ERS, as it offers a large number of data related to both learners and teachers. Moreover, combined with ITS, ERS may use not only the learner profile, but also the educational objectives (Santos & Boticario, 2010) of the course, which are also available in the pedagogical model.

The aim of this paper is to define an architecture-centric approach for designing ERS in such a way that their quality attributes are considered in a systematic manner. The underpinning of our approach is a simple process which touches two levels of software design: (i) architectural design, which deals with quality attributes in a high-level way; and (ii) detailed design, which deals with lower level modeling strategies for realizing the software architecture at the source code. The proposed approach relies on architectural styles (Bass, Clements, & Kazman, 2003) and good practices for allowing the structural definition of the system, and design patterns for allowing the implementation of quality attributes related to ERS (e.g., adaptability, performance and reliability) by using object-oriented programming languages.

The rest of this paper is organized as follows. The next section provides some background to the paper. Section 3 describes a case study of an ERS for an Intelligent Tutoring System (ITS), which will be used throughout the paper for exemplifying and evaluating the feasibility of the proposed solution. Section 4 presents how to design ERS by means of a systematic process in which important design decisions should be taken. Finally, Section 5 provides some concluding remarks and future directions of research.

## BACKGROUND

### Component-Based Software Architectures

The *software architecture* of a program or computing system is the structure or structures of the system, which comprises software elements, the externally visible properties of those elements (architectural components and connectors), and the relationships among them (architectural configuration) (Bass, Clements, & Kazman, 2003). Since the software architecture represents the structure of the software system, it is a set of significant decisions about the organization of software. Those decisions concern the selection of the structural elements and their interfaces by which the system is composed, together with their behavior as specified in the collaborations among those elements (Kruchten, Obbink, & Stafford, 2006). Moreover, since software architecture deals with the design and implementation of the high-level structure of the software, its decisions have a decisive impact into the quality attributes of the whole system, such as availability, reliability, and testability.

Figure 1 presents an example of an architectural configuration involving two components and a connector. *Architectural components* (e.g., A and B) are primary computational elements or data stores of a system and are defined through the list of operations that they provide (provided interfaces), as well as the operations necessary for executing their functionalities (required interfaces). To exemplify the concept of provided

*Figure 1. Example of an architectural configuration in UML*

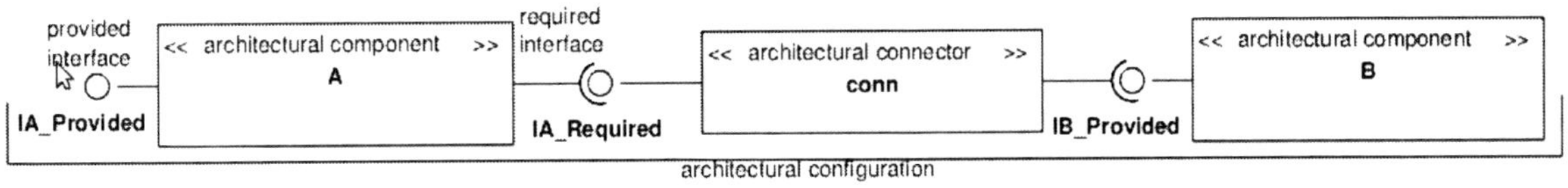


and required interfaces, component A of Figure 1 has a provided interface called IA_Provided, and a required interface called IA_Required. *Architectural connectors* (e.g., conn) are mediators of the communication and coordination activities among components. That is, they define the rules governing component interaction and specify any auxiliary implementation mechanism required. The way that components and connectors are connected together is defined by the *architectural configuration*.

Besides representing the structure of a software system, the software architecture can also represent its behavior through architectural scenarios. A scenario is a sequence of incidents expected during the system operation, which includes environment conditions, expected stimuli and responses (Schneider & Winters, 1998). Basically, scenarios focus on how the system behaves to implement its functionalities. Since *architectural scenarios* represent high-level interactions amongst the architectural elements, they allow to verify and assess properties regarding important non-functional requirements, such as, reliability, availability, and scalability (Fu, Bultan, & Su., 2002), (Gillmann, Weissenfels, Weikum, & Kraiss, 2000), (Paul, Tsai, & Mikell, 2004). Scenarios can be used to guide the software development during the different phases since they permit multiple views of an interaction at different levels of abstraction (Carroll, 2000). In particular, they are relevant at the architectural level because they enhance the structural representation of the system with an abstract representation of its behavior.

## The COSMOS* Component Model

The COSMOS* component implementation model (Gayard, Rubira, & Guerra, 2008) is a generic and platform-independent implementation model, which uses object-oriented structures, such as interfaces, classes and packages, to implement component-based software architectures. The main objectives of the COSMOS* model are: (i) to provide traceability between the software architecture and the source code of the application; and thus (ii) to facilitate the evolution of its implementation.

Figure 2 illustrates the internal structure of the A_int component following the COSMOS* model. COSMOS* defines five sub-models, which address different aspects of component-based software systems: (i) the *specification model*, presented in Figure 2 (a), specifies the components using UML; (ii) the *implementation model* (Figure 2 (b)) explicitly separates the specification of provided and required interfaces (spec package) and also defines how the services provided by the component are implemented (impl package); (iii) the *connector model* (not illustrated) specifies the connections between components using connectors, thus enabling two or more components to be connected in a configuration; (iv) *composite component model* (not illustrated) specifies the implementation of high-granularity components, which are composed by smaller COSMOS* components; and (v) *system model* (not illustrated) defines a software component which can be deployed and executed, including reference to external dependencies, such as libraries and frameworks. Each of these models is implemented as a set of

*Figure 2. Structure of the COSMOS* implementation model in UML*

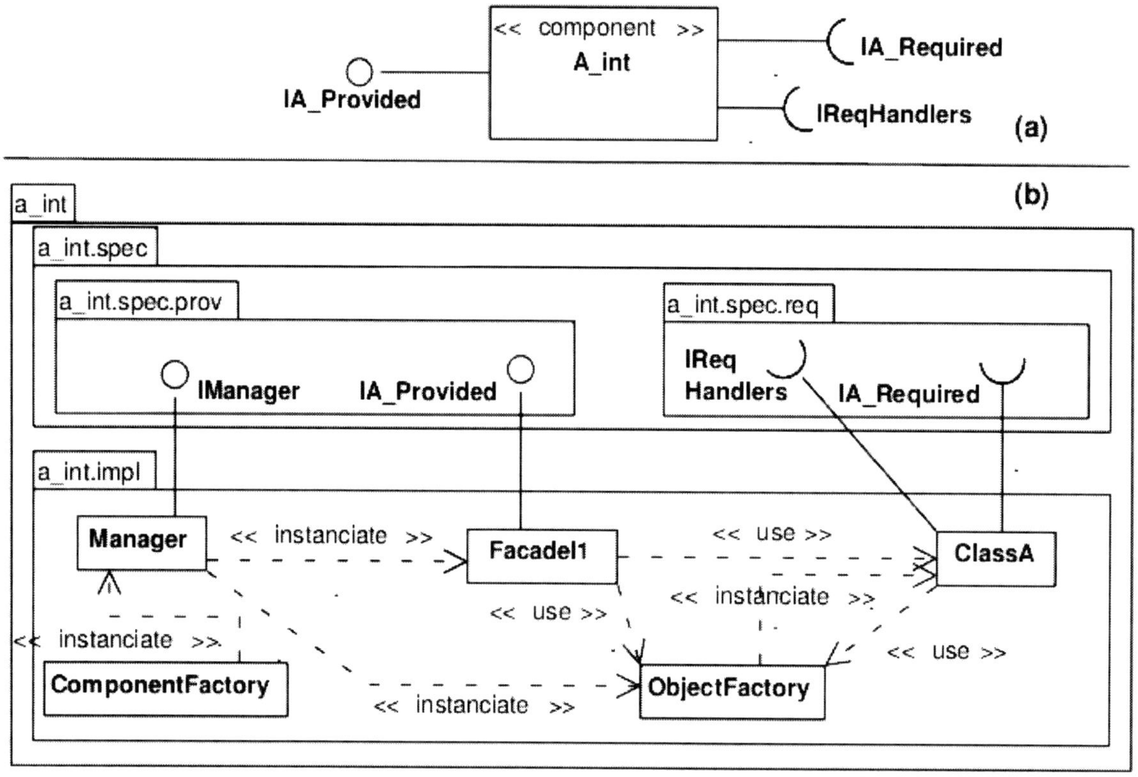


well-defined patterns which can be automatically translated to source code (Tomita, Castor-Filho, Guerra, & Rubira, 2004).

## Architecture-Centered Software Development

The software architecture is an artifact that is essential in the software lifecycle and should support the phases of software development (Chen, Wang, Mei, & Yang, 2002). Part of such importance is due to the architecture structural representation in a high level of abstraction it provides, which makes the system easier to analyze and understand.

An architecture-centered software development process, besides boasting of architectural abstraction in all phases of development, should provide a means of specifying the system architecture, following the requirements imposed by their non-functional requirements (You-Sheng & Yu-Yun, 2003). Furthermore, while traditional processes consider the composition of the system as an implementation activity (Cheesman & Daniels, 2000), architecture-centered processes consider the components composition should be considered at different stages of development. In other words, the composition must be designed in different levels of abstraction (abstract model, detailed specification and implementation) (Chen, Wang, Mei, & Yang, 2002).

The main advantages of adopting an architecture-centered process are: (i) It provides an explicit structural representation of the system; (ii) it is easier to specify non-functional properties of the system; (iii) it allows reuse in a higher level of granularity; (iv) it reduces the time to market; (v) it improves the system understandability and maintainability.

Motivated mainly by the chance of a large scale reuse of software, an increasing number of companies are being using architecture-centered development techniques (Koskimies, 2001).

## The UML Components Process

The UML Components process is a software development process which focuses on the construction of component-based systems (Cheesman & Daniels, 2000). In order to simplify the development, it adopts the layered architectural style (Bass, Clements, & Kazman, 2003), focusing attention on two layers: a *system layer*, which comprises components related to the particularities of the software system, and a *business layer*, comprising components that can be reused across different applications. This process is divided into six phases. The first phase is the *requirements specification* where the developer specifies the functional requirements of the system as a set of *use cases* (Schneider & Winters, 1998), as well as the *business concept model*, representing the basic entities of the conceptual domain which the system belongs to. The second phase is called *specification*, and it is divided into three sub-phases: (i) *component identification*, when the developer identifies system layer interfaces and their respective operations based on use case descriptions and also business layer interfaces, defined from the core entities (or *core types*) of the business concept model; (ii) *component interaction*, when the operations of the business layer, which are required by the system layer, are defined; and (iii) *component specification*, when the interfaces are refactored and operation execution contracts are formalized through pre and post-conditions (Meyer, 1988).

The third phase is called *provisioning*, when components are either built from scratch or acquired from third-parties. In the fourth phase, called *assembling*, these components are combined in order to realize the architectural configuration of the system. The fifth and sixth phases of UML Components are respectively *testing* and *deployment*, but they are not detailed by UML Components.

## Intelligent Tutoring Systems

According to (Sleeman & Brown, 1982), an Intelligent Tutoring System (ITS) is a computer program which uses Artificial Intelligence techniques to represent the knowledge and to reproduce the behavior of the teacher in the teaching process. Thus, an ITS must have characteristics in its basic structure that involving the following issues: (i) What to teach? (ii) How to teach? and (iii) Whom to teach?

Several methods and tools of computer science, psychology, and education are complementary and collectively cover almost completely the area of artificial intelligence and education. (i) Artificial intelligence handles arguing about intelligence, and therefore learning, (ii) psychology, particularly the subfield of cognitive science, this is how people think and learn, and (iii) education focuses on how to support the teaching of a better way.

The first goal of the Intelligent Tutoring Systems is to provide an adapted teaching to each learner, trying to approximate the behavior of a human teacher in the classroom. However, to enable its construction, it is necessary that tutoring system has embedded inside of it, a large quantity of code related to various distinct aspects. These, as previously described, search to answer the three basic questions: what to teach, how to teach and whom to teach. Such questions flow into models as next described (Domain Model, Student Model and Pedagogical Strategies) (Woolf, 2009).

**Domain Model**: This model is responsible to model the content which the tutor is enabled to teach, answering the question what to teach. It must be a representation of specialized knowledge in a specific domain. Therefore, it should represent the facts, procedures, or methods that specialists use to perform tasks or solve problems.

Figure 3. Pedagogical strategies

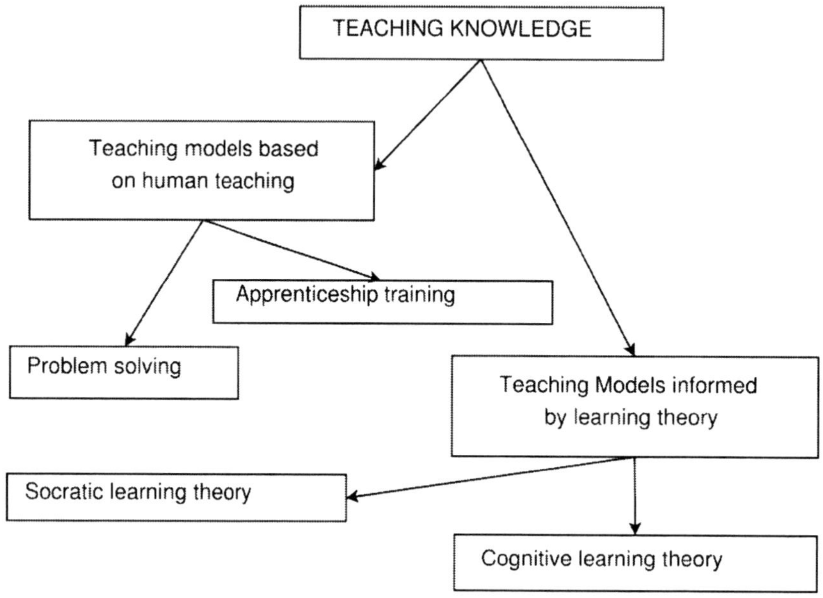


**Student Model**: This one is responsible for modeling the behavior of the student who will undergo the process of teaching by a tutor in any area, so there may be an automated reasoning over the same. Student models typically represent the student behavior, including student answers, actions, results of actions and intermediate results. The student behavior reflects his knowledge, as well as the most common errors.

**Pedagogical Strategies**: Represents the strategies and tactics of teaching, answering the question how to teach, it holds the knowledge of how it will be taught, that is, it produces the sequence of activities that will be passed to the student based on information obtained by the student and domain model. As can be seen in Figure 3, the pedagogical strategies can be implemented through learning theories, teaching strategies empirically acquired in experience with real situations or through the development of computational resources that provide different mechanisms of teaching.

Therefore, Figure 4 illustrates the classic architecture of an ITS. As it can be seen, the Learner interacts to the system via a User Interface that presents information regarding the learner (from Student Model) and the learning subject (from the Tutor model). Both Student Model and Tutor Model should be contextualized by domain-specific information (Domain Model). It is also known as the tripartite role or traditional archi-

Figure 4. Classic architecture of an ITS

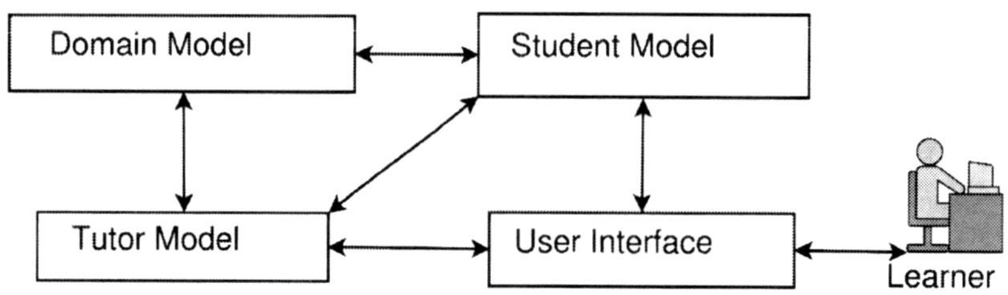

tecture of an ITS. The term refers to the functions associated with the models of the tutor (pedagogical), student (learner) and the domain.

## Educational Recommender Systems

Recommender systems aim to offer relevant guidance to users who have to make choices in daily life situations. This guidance is especially important in the context where the users lack sufficient experience or knowledge to support their decisions.

Educational Recommender Systems (ERS) (Santos & Boticario, 2010), (Casili, Gerling, Deco, & Bender, 2010), (Lu, 2004) are systems that aim to support people on finding out relevant content, especially on the Internet. These systems usually consider personal preferences in order to infer the user ranking about heterogeneous sources of data. Among recommender systems, ERS concentrate on recommending content of the educational domain, and are considered important tools for improving the teaching-learning process and reducing truancy.

Although ERS share come common key objectives of general recommenders, in the context of education there are some particularities that does not allow the directly use of existing solutions from general domains. For example, recommendations in the educational domain should also be guided according to pedagogical strategies, plus the learners' preferences. In this context, Intelligent Tutoring Systems (ITS) (Section 2.5) are considered a potential ally of ERS, since they explicitly define models for representing the learning state of the student (Student Model), the pedagogical criteria (Pedagogical Strategies), the domain information (Domain Model), as well as the relationship among these three models.

In order to perform specific recommendations for each user, which considerably speeds the search process involving large amounts of information, the user profile should be up to date and reflect its real need and will. The user profile can be defined in at least two complementary ways: explicit and implicit. The explicit definition consists on asking the user for filling data forms in order to express his/her specific preferences. Despite its effectiveness, this method often leads to dissatisfaction by the users due to the time required for filling the forms. Therefore, the filling is often overlooked, which harms the accuracy of the profile data. The implicit definition consists on automatically infer profile data, such as schooling, affinity and preferences by using automatic analysis techniques based on how the user interacts with the system. The implicit definition is normally used to refine the user profile by using artificial intelligence techniques such as natural language processing over the artifacts produced by the user.

Despite their complexity, these systems should also have some quality attributes, which are important to use them in real environments. The main properties desirable for ERS are availability, scalability, security (privacy-protecting), reliability, adaptability and performance. Availability is important for preventing the recommender service to be unavailable for a long time; the scalability property means that the system should be able of recommending content to a large number of users at the same time; the security (privacy-protecting) property aims to protect the personal data into the system profile from unauthorized access; the reliability property means that the provided recommendation should supply the user needs whenever possible; adaptability is important for working with different algorithms; while performance is desirable for recommending timely.

# CASE STUDY DESCRIPTION

To illustrate the solution proposed in this paper, we shall use a recommender system for educational content in the context of an Intelligent Tutoring System (ITS). In order to improve the system efficacy, the proposed recommender system should recommend based on the usage history of each

*Figure 5. Overview of the case study*

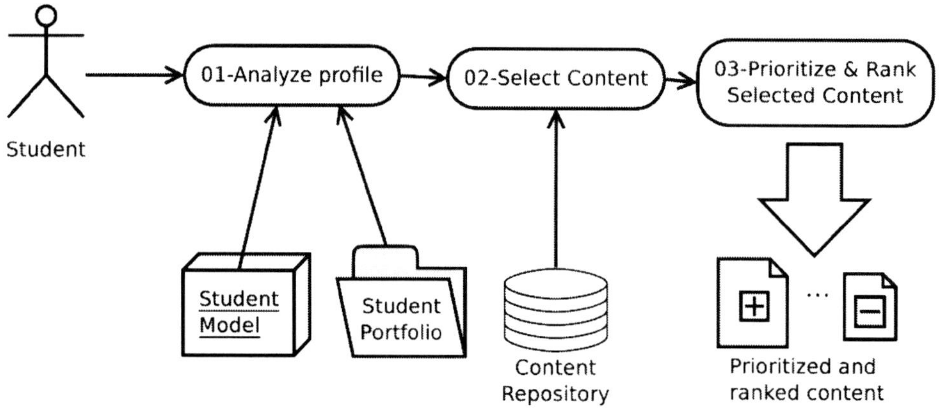


learner (Student Model), as well as the content of his/her personal portfolio.

Figure 5 illustrates the general idea of the proposed recommender system. First, after receiving the request of a user for a list of content, the recommender system analyzes the student model and the learner portfolio (Activity 1). Based on the usage history of the learner (student model) and on the content of the learner personal profile, the recommender system searches the repository in order to identify contents related to the learner interests (Activity 2). Finally, the contents related to the learner must be prioritized and ranked, according to its importance to the student learning (Activity 3). Notice that although it is a relatively simple process, the recommender system involves complex algorithms and technologies, such as natural language processing in order to analyze the learner's profile, as well as pedagogical rules for ranking the content according its relative importance to the student's learning.

This case study will be used as an illustrating example throughout the paper.

## PROCESS FOR DESIGNING ERS

Since ERS is considered a complex software system, which can deal with different challenges in terms of algorithms and technology, we have proposed an architecture-centered process for guiding the development based on the software architecture and architectural scenarios. The focus on the software architecture allows controlling the system complexity by abstracting away from lower-level details, when designing structural concerns, such as quality attributes. Moreover, this approach allows a clear separation of concerns between functional requirements (architectural components) and non-functional requirements (architectural connectors). This separation is preserved from the analysis level, passing through the design and implementation levels of abstraction.

Figure 6 presents the general process of the proposed approach for designing ERS. First, the system requirements should be specified, which is done in two parallel steps: (i) Specify the functional requirements of the ERS (Activity 1a); and (ii) Select quality attributes and resolve tradeoffs among them (Activity 1b). Then, following an architecture-centered approach (Section 2.3), the software architecture should be designed (Activity 2) in order to guide the further phases of the software development.

The following subsections detail each activity of the proposed process, presenting examples when appropriate.

*Figure 6. General process for designing ERS*

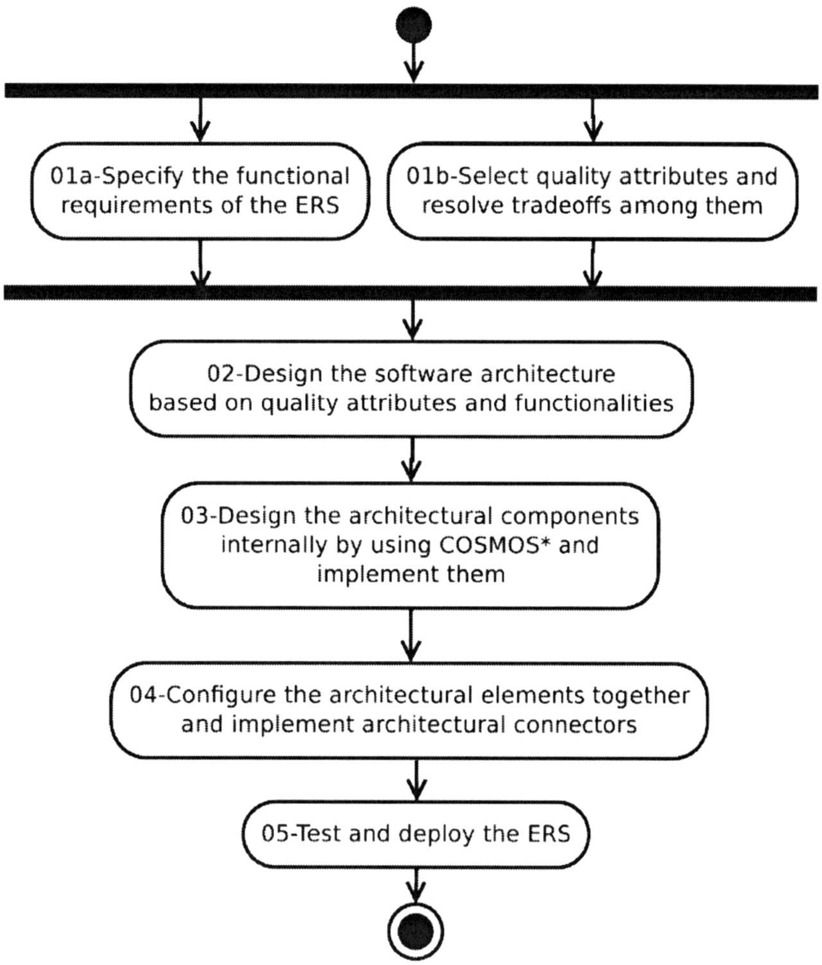


## Specify the Functional Requirements of the ERS

The specification of the functional requirements of the ERS (Activity 1a) consists on the production of two artifacts: (i) a Conceptual Model, which should represent general characteristics of ERS; and (ii) a UML Use Case Diagram containing the systems functionalities and the relationship among them.

Figure 7 presents the conceptual model of the case study. Notice that this model makes it explicit that the recommendation should be done in a customized way, according to the leaner needs. This diagram also shows that in order to evaluate content, might be necessary to use natural language processing techniques. Moreover, the proposed approach suggests the use of semantic notations, such as ontology (Mizoguchi, 2004) for annotating the contents to be recommended, as well as for describing the pedagogical rules used to rank them according to the student needs and learning strategy.

A simplified list of the system functionalities is presented in Figure 8, through a use case diagram. Notice that the diagram also presents the relationships among functionalities, which will support the definition of the architectural con-

Figure 7. Conceptual model of the ERS case study

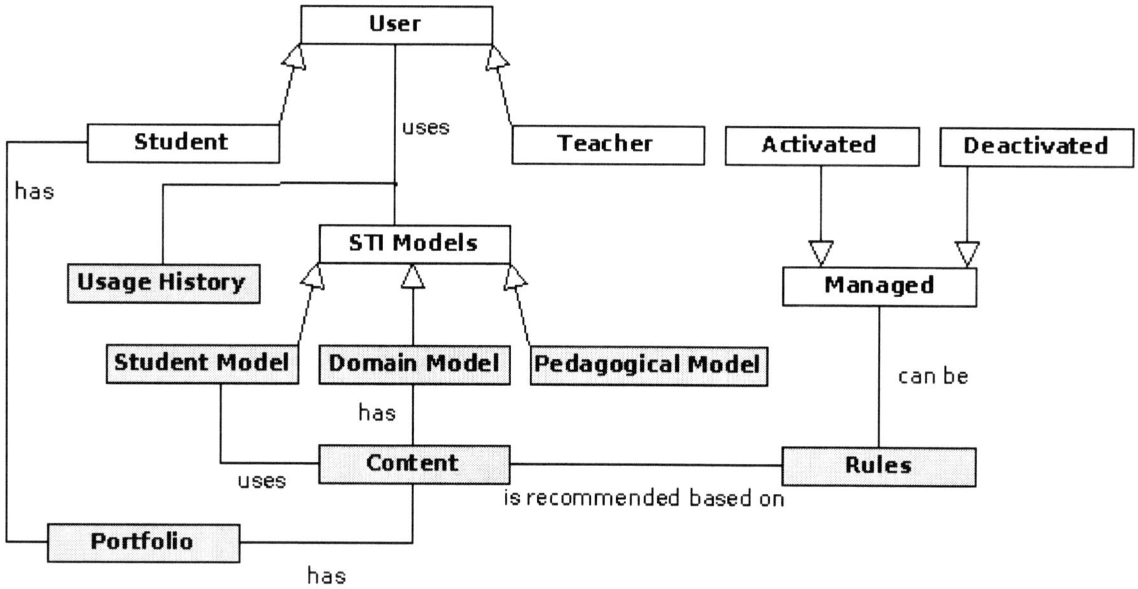


figuration in further phased of the software development. Moreover, as presented in Section 4.3.3, the use case diagram is a key artifact for identifying architectural components based on functionality. This strategy of identifying components aims to improve the cohesion of the system and consequently its understandability and maintainability.

## Select Quality Attributes and Resolve Tradeoffs Among Them

The quality attributes of a system, which are realized as non-functional requirements, describe *how* the system performs its functionalities. For this reason, the quality attributes should be specified at the beginning of the development process, since they define the structure of the system and the way the system components interact each other.

In this paper, we suggests the use of a precedence tree that represents the priorities related to quality attributes in a top-down hierarchical way. The first step in the non-functional analysis of the system is to stipulate the evaluation criteria, ie, the priority of each quality attribute, based on the tradeoff between them. Following the ATAM method (Kazman, Klein, & Clements, 2000), the client together with the software architect must establish a precedence tree that represents the priority of each non-functional requirement in the context of the ERS under development. Thus, as shown in Figure 9, the higher is the level, the more general is the requirement; and in the context of this example, the adaptability, availability, maintainability and performance requirements are considered general requirements. The proposed approach suggests that the developer must distribute a total of 100 points among the non-functional requirements listed; the higher the number, the greater the importance of the requirement. For example, in the same tree of Figure 9, the ranking of quality attributes is as follows: 1st - adaptability; 2nd - availability; 3rd - maintainability, and 4th - performance.

Then, from the use cases descriptions and scenarios, we should identify statements that il-

Figure 8. Use case diagram of the ERS case study

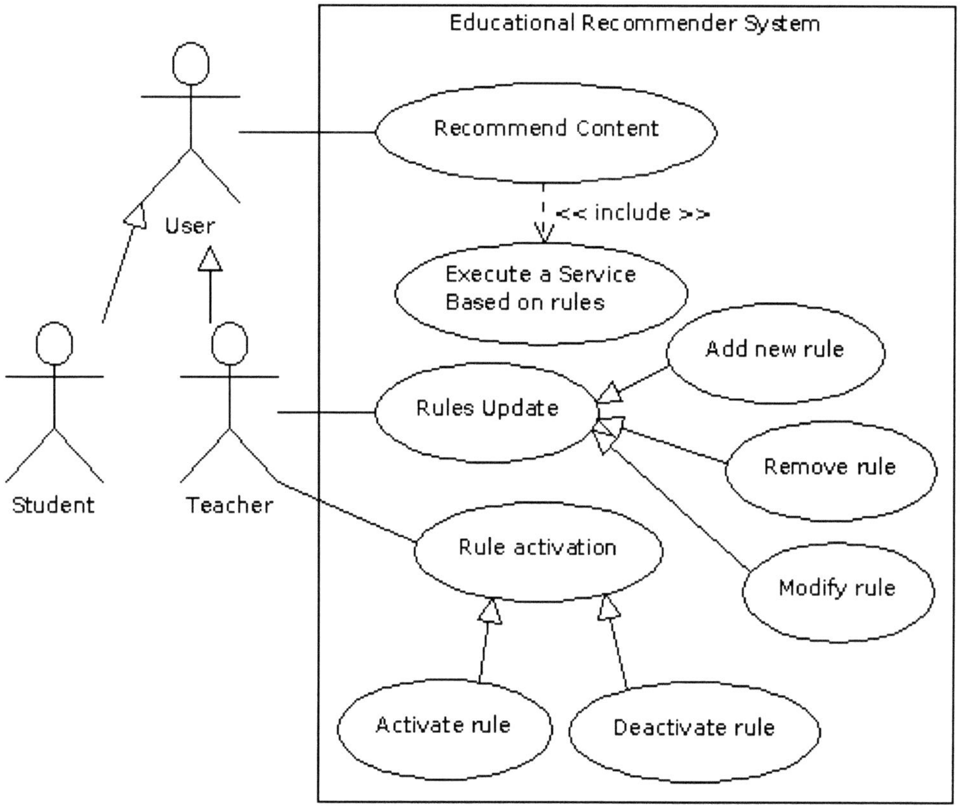


lustrate the real need of the non-functional requirements. These phrases are used to highlight the interests of stakeholders and could be used to refine the importance rank among the non-functional attributes. For example, attributes required for some critical functionality typically have a higher priority. The UML notes present in Figure

Figure 9. Precedence tree involving the non-functional requirements of the ERS (with scenarios)

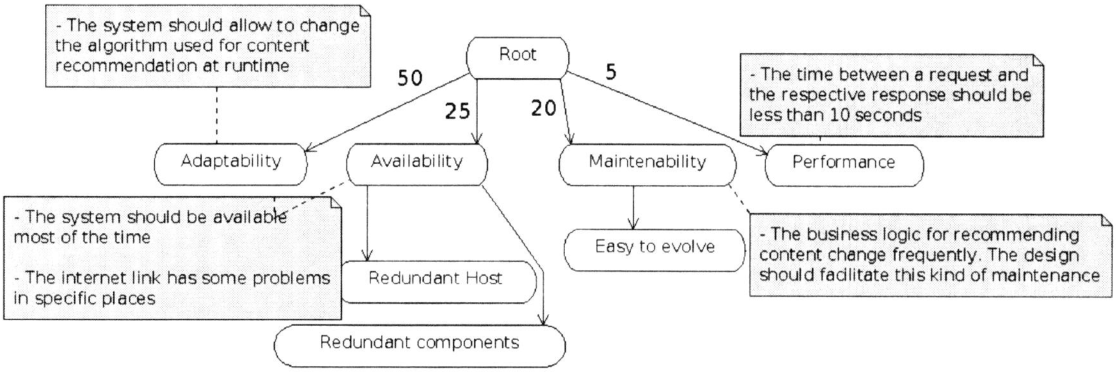

9 show some scenarios that illustrate the need of non-functional requirements.

## Design the Software Architecture Based on Quality Attributes and Functionalities

The architectural design consists on identifying the system modules (architectural elements) and structuring them in such a way that the quality attributes previously specified be satisfied. Figure 10 presents the activities proposed for designing the software architecture of ERSs. The architectural design is considered the most important activity of an architecture-centered process, and then the activities presented in Figure 10 are detailed in the following.

*Figure 10. Architectural design of ERS*

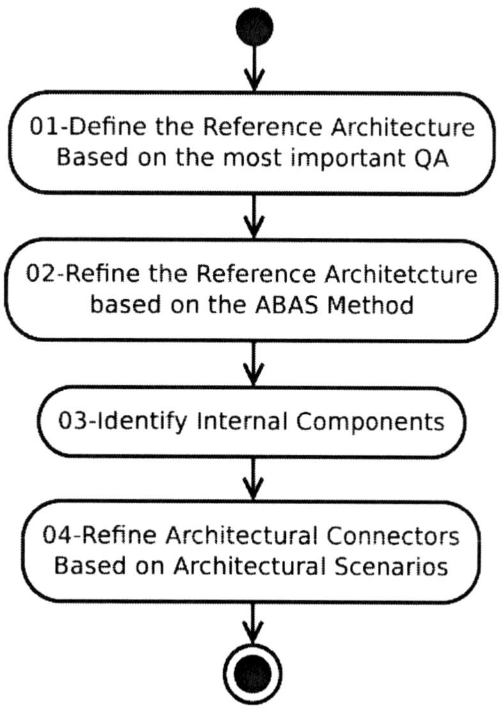


## Define the Reference Architecture Based on the Most Important Quality Attributes

Based on the definition of priorities among the quality attributes of the system, the architect should do a screening of the architectural styles candidate to reference architecture. Examples of possible reference architectures in the context of ERS systems are: (i) pipes and filters, which is recommended to ERS that execute a sequence of preprocessing actions, when the output of an activity is input to the next one; (ii) Model-View-Controller, which is recommended when the preprocessing actions are performed in a mode complex way and then has to be controlled by a central module (the controller); and (iii) virtual machine, which is recommended when the preprocessing activities are dynamically defined and can be constantly updated. In the context of the case study, we have selected the virtual machine architectural style as a reference architecture, since the rules for recommending a content in an ITS can constantly change according to the pedagogical strategy being used and the current state of the student model. Figure 11 presents the reference architecture of the system. The Inference Engine layer is responsible for implementing the virtual machine, which executes actions of the Basic Services layer based on the rules defined in the Recommendation Rules layer. Then the Inference Engine receives a service request, it looks at the respective rules to know what Basic Services should be executed, as well as the respective sequence. In the context of the case study, the algorithms used for executing the three activities presented in Figure 5 and the respective data collection could be dynamically changed. Besides, different rules could be activated depending on a specific Student Model.

But it is also necessary to analyze the consequences of choosing the virtual machine architectural style: once these rules are verified each time a recommendation is requested (for allowing

Figure 11. Reference architecture of the ERS

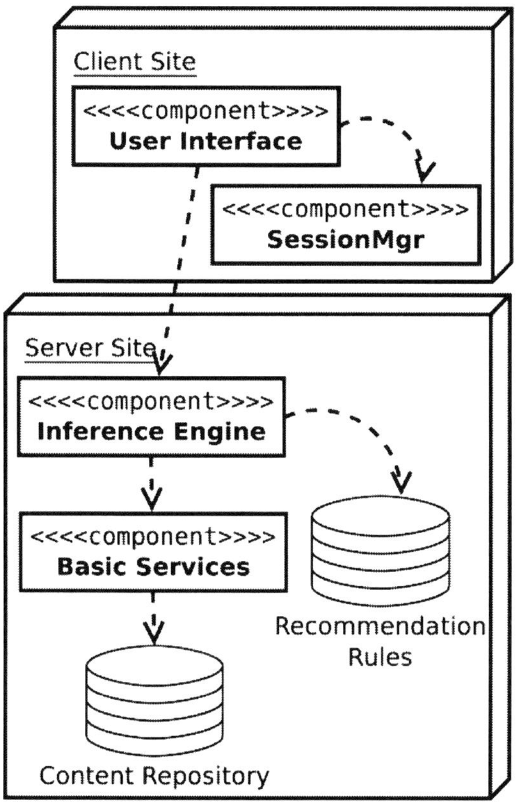


dynamic update) the architecture should have a negative impact on performance. Even with this negative impact, the choice of the architect can be justified, since adaptability is much more important than performance (Figure 9).

In order to support the architect for choosing reference architecture, it is possible to use a rule-based case tool, which should reflect the expertise of the company based on previous experiences. We have designed a CASE tool with this specific purpose (Figure 12), which works as a wizard. First, the user must distribute weights, according to his/her preferences related to the desired ranking of non-functional requirements (a). Then, the system consults the knowledge rules, which should reflect the expertise of the company with previous projects, and then suggests a set of architectural styles that have been identified as possible reference architectures, followed by the percentage reliability of each choice. The final decision should be taken by the software architect (b).

## Refine the Reference Architecture Based on the ABAS Method

Since in most cases a single architectural style is not able to satisfy every quality attribute of an ERS, it is necessary to consider a systematic way to combine different styles together not forgetting the tradeoff between the quality attributes. For this, the proposed approach suggests the use of the Attribute-Based Architectural Styles (ABAS) method (Klein & Kazman, 1999), combined with a set of guidelines provided for architecting ERS based on its most common quality attributes. An important artifact used in this activity is the Precedence Tree involving the non-functional requirements of the ERS presented in Section 4.2 (Figure 9). As presented in Table 1, for each quality attribute, a refinement might be done, depending on the tradeoff among the requirements. For example, the availability requirement (2nd most important in Figure 9) could be achieved by replicating the Server Site of the architecture in different locations, as presented in Figure 13.

## Identify Internal Components

This activity consists on detailing the internal structure of the modules defined at the reference architecture (Figure 11). With this progressive reduction of the components granularity, the proposed process allows a mapping between an architectural component and an implementation component, used in the context of component-based development (Szyperski, 2002). The guidelines to execute this activity are based on the UML Components process presented in Section 2.4, but many changes have been proposed.

Figure 14 presents the guidelines proposed for identifying implementation components from the system requirements. First, the process takes two artifacts as input: (i) conceptual model; and (ii)

*Figure 12. Rule-based CASE tool for supporting the definition of a reference architecture*

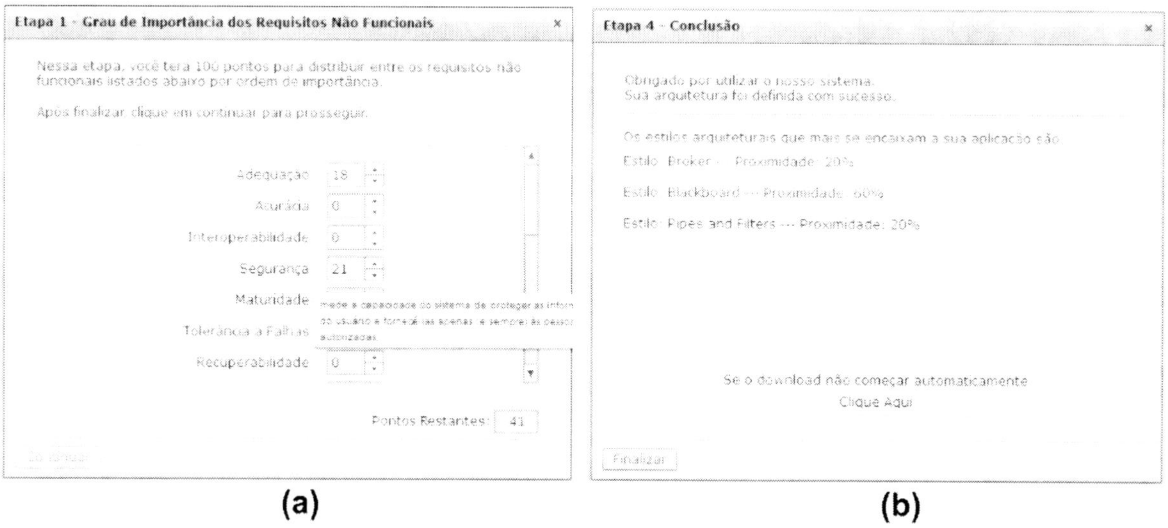


*Figure 13. Refined reference architecture of the ERS*

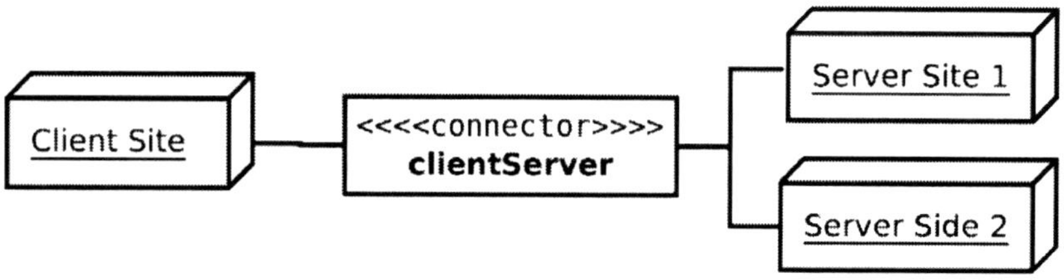


UML use case diagram. Then, seven activities should be performed in order to gradually identify implementation components: (i) Identify provided interfaces; (ii) Identify internal components; (iii) Identify "basic" components; (iv) Create components to other modules of the reference architecture; (v) Identify dependencies between the internal components; (vi) Define required interfaces; and (vii) Realize architectural configuration. In the following, these activities are previously described.

## Identify Provided Interfaces

Initially, a provided interface should be created for each use case. Then, it is necessary to identify the core entities of the conceptual model, according to the expected scope for the system. A useful guideline to identify such entities is to ask a simple question for each entity: "*if it does not exist, do the entities associated with it still make sense (even partially)?*" If the answer is Yes, this entity should not be so important; otherwise, if the answer is No, that entity is a serious candidate to be considered core. But it is worth remembering that this is just a guideline and the final decision should be made by the software architect. Then, for each core entity of the conceptual model, a provided interface should be defined. In the context of the case study, we have considered only the gray entities of Figure 7 as core entities. The white entities where considered either out of scope (User, Student and Teacher), or representing a state of a rule (Managed, Activated and Deactivated).

*Figure 14. Identify internal components of the reference architecture*

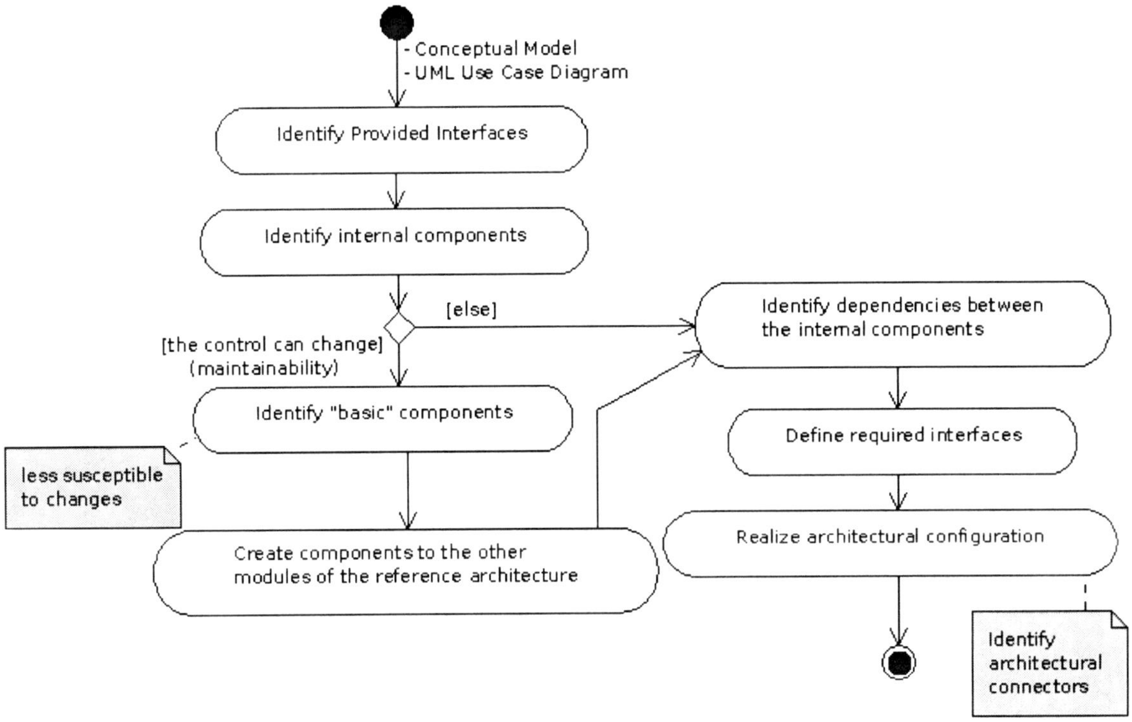


## Identify Internal Components

This activity consists on selecting the component that will implement each of the interfaces identified. For each interface, the developer must define a component to be responsible for its implementation. A component can provide as many interfaces as the architect consider cohesive enough.

## Identify Basic Components

If the software architect has defined maintainability as a required quality attribute, it is necessary to separate the internal components according to the origin of their provided interfaces: (i) control components, which should provide the interfaces derived from the use cases; and (ii) basic components, which should provide the interfaces derived from the conceptual model. The basic components are less susceptible to changes, since they are used as building blocks by the control components.

In the context of the case study, the control components were placed in the Inference Engine layer of the reference architecture presented in Figure 11, while the basic components were placed in the Basic Services layer.

## Create Components to Other Modules of the Reference Architecture

Since each module of the software architecture should have at least a single implementation component, this activity guarantees that if the reference architecture has other modules, such as the Recommendation Rules layer, they will also be implemented.

## Identify Dependencies Between the Internal Components

The dependencies between the internal components are identifying by analyzing the interaction

*Table 1. Guidelines for architecting ERS*

| Quality Attribute | Scenario Description | Refinement Action Guideline |
|---|---|---|
| Availability | The system should be online all the time, even in cases of server maintenance and electrical faults. | The architecture should use a Client-Server architectural style in which the Server component is replicated in at least two different physical locations. Depending on the criticality of availability and the resources available, more replicas should be specified. It is important to highlight that the connector between client and server should consider the switching activity among the available Servers. |
| Reliability | The recommendation should be as precise as possible. The recommended content should meet user's expectations, with no false positives (recommend unwanted content) and false negatives (fail to recommend the desired content). | The architecture should combine a Client-Server architectural style with an Event-Based architectural style. In this heterogeneous architecture, the Server component should be redundant (with design diversity, not only replicated) in at least three different sites (can be in a single physical location). Depending on the criticality of reliability and the availability of resources, more redundancies should be specified. It is important to highlight that the connector between client and server should execute all the Servers in parallel (event-based architecture) and implement a deciding algorithm (e.g., majority election and average ranking) based on the results provided by the Servers. |
| Performance | The recommendation should be provided as soon as possible for the client. The client cannot wait for a long time for the recommended content. The time between the request and the response should not be more than # seconds. (the # should be specified according to the user needs). | The architecture should combine a Client-Server architectural style with an Event-Based architectural style. In this heterogeneous architecture, the Server component should be replicated in at least two different sites (can be in a single physical location). Depending on the criticality of performance and the availability of resources, more replicas should be specified. It is important to highlight that the connector between client and server should execute all the Servers in parallel (event-based architecture) and consider the first recommendation provided. |
| Adaptability | The recommendation can be done by using different algorithms, depending on the configuration of the system, which can be changed by the system administrator. | The architecture should use an Independent Components architectural style in which the Components should be derived based on the system's functionalities (use cases). Besides, components related to different recommendation algorithms should provide a similar interface, in order to facilitate the switching by the connector, according to the desired algorithm. |
| Maintainability | The system should be structured in such a way that new recommendation algorithms could be easily added after the system is deployed. The changes to add extra algorithms should be ideally concentrated in at most a single architectural element. | The architecture should be structured in the same way as in the case of Adaptability. There are only two differences: first, a façade connector should be specified for connecting to every recommendation algorithm; the second difference concerns the way this architectural connector should be implemented. For facilitating the addition of other algorithms without restarting the server, the connector should instantiate the recommender components by using computational reflection based on a configuration file. |
| Scalability | The system should be prepared to attend a high number of recommendation requests. Besides, in case of an increase in the number of users, the system architecture should allow the increase of its throughput. | The architecture should be structured in the same way as in the case of Availability. The difference concerns the behavior of the architectural connector between client and server layers. For achieving scalability, the connector should implement a load balance algorithm for choosing a server which is not congested. The connector should allow a hot configuration in order to inform the number of servers, as well as their locations. |
| Security | The personal data on the system profile should be kept private, protected from unauthorized access. | The architecture should implement a Demilitarized Zone (DMZ) for the data (Brenton, 1999). That is, it is recommended to have a server specifically for the database. The access to this server should be done exclusively through a connector which implements an authentication algorithm. |
| Availability & Reliability | See the two scenarios of availability and reliability | These attributes are not in conflict each other and can be combined directly. |
| Availability & Performance | See the two scenarios of availability and performance | These attributes are not in conflict each other and can be combined directly. |

*continued on next page*

*Table 1. continued*

| Quality Attribute | Scenario Description | Refinement Action Guideline |
|---|---|---|
| Availability & Adaptability | See the two scenarios of availability and adaptability | These attributes are not in conflict each other and can be combined directly. |
| Availability & Maintainability | See the two scenarios of availability and maintainability | These attributes are not in conflict each other and can be combined directly. |
| Reliability & Performance | See the two scenarios of reliability and performance | Although these attributes adopt the same architectural style they are considered in conflict each other. The incompatibility occurs in terms of scenarios, since while performance is implemented by accepting the first recommendation received, reliability expects all the recommendations to compare and provide a more reliable result. To combine both requirements, it is possible to define some criteria, such as receiving three recommendations in a set of six replicated components. But this combination is considered much expensive. |
| Reliability & Adaptability | See the two scenarios of reliability and adaptability | Although these attributes are not in conflict each other and can be combined directly, it considerably increases the system cost. So, this combination should be considered only in cases when both attributes are considered critical and there are resources available. |
| Reliability & Maintainability | See the two scenarios of reliability and maintainability | Although these attributes are not in conflict each other and can be combined directly, it considerably increases the system cost. So, this combination should be considered only in cases when both attributes are considered critical and there are resources available. |
| Performance & Adaptability | See the two scenarios of performance and adaptability | These attributes are considered in conflict each other, since the definition of many components (for adaptability) implies in a high cost for making them redundant. Moreover, the more components defined, the more binding has to occur, which can hinder the performance. The combination of both requirements can be done by making the many "small and cohesive" components redundant, but this combination is considered much expensive. |
| Performance & Maintainability | See the two scenarios of performance and maintainability | These attributes are considered in conflict each other, but can be combined each other in the same way used for "Performance & Adaptability". |
| Adaptability & Maintainability | See the two scenarios of adaptability and maintainability | These attributes are not in conflict each other and can be combined directly. |

defined as use case scenarios. Usually, control components request services to the basic components, but it can also request services to other control components, depending on the existence of dependencies between different use cases (<<include>> and <<extend>>).

## Define Required Interfaces

Based on the dependencies between internal components, it is possible to design sequence diagrams for identifying operations. The set of operations a component requests to others represents its required interfaces. The proposed approach suggests that dependencies involving different modules of the reference architecture should generate different required interfaces.

## Realize Architectural Configuration

Finally, for each required interface, a connector must be defined in order to link the requester component to its respective providers.

Figure 15 presents the internal components of the Inference Engine and Basic Services layers, as well as their configuration.

*Figure 15. Reference architecture refined with internal components*

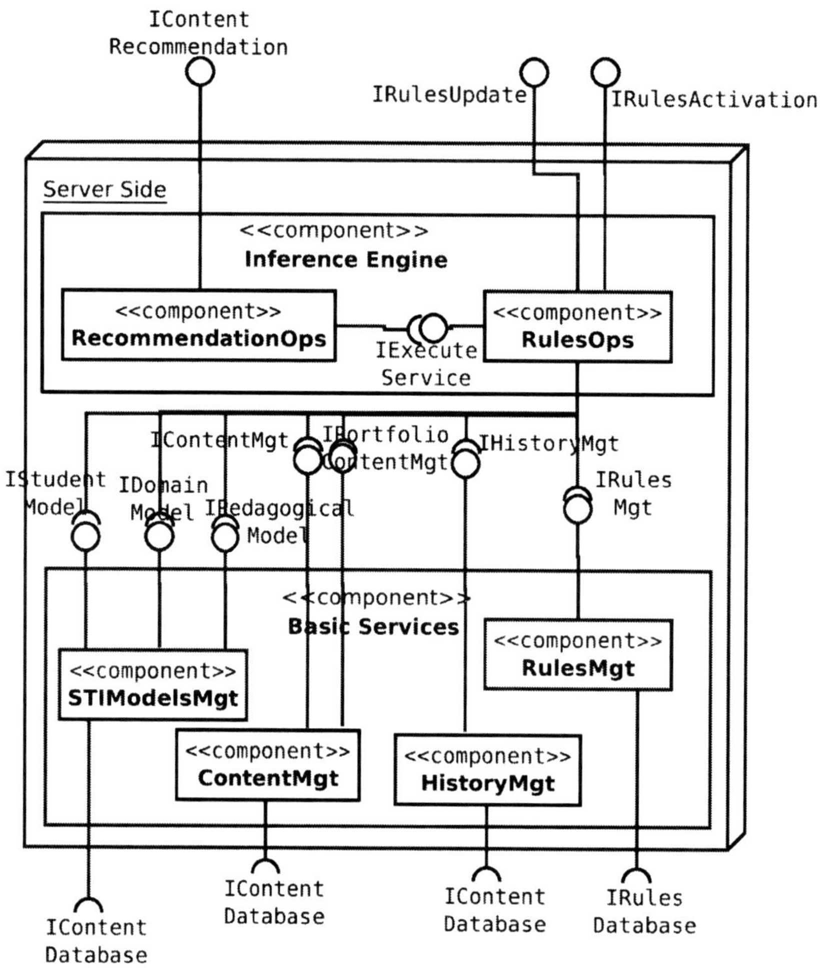


## Refine Architectural Connectors Based on Architectural Scenarios

This activity consists on refining the reference architectural, in order to make the interaction scenarios involving the system components explicit. Since the architectural connectors have a privileged location at the software architecture (knows both the requirer and the provider components), they are considered the main elements to implement non-functional requirements.

In the context of the case study, in order to implement the availability non-functional requirement, the clientServer connector was made explicit in the architectural refinement (Figure 13). This connector must implement distribution (HTTP protocol) and switching between servers. In other words, to take advantage of the redundant servers defined in Section 4.3.1, the clientServer connector must be capable of detecting when the main server is off-line to then, redirect the request in a redundant location. Such error detection and switching scenarios should be specified in this activity.

### Design the Architectural Components Internally by Using COSMOS*

For designing the object-oriented model of each component, the proposed approach suggests the adoption of the COSMOS* component implementation model, presented in Section 2.2. The reason for adopting COSMOS* is because it is based on three design patterns (Gamma, Helm, Johnson, & Vlisside, 1995) and thus be independent of programming languages.

The three design patterns used by COSMOS* are: (i) Factory Method, which is used for instantiating the component; (ii) Façade, which is used for implementing the provided interfaces and delegate the execution to internal controllers; and (iii) Object Factory, which reduces the internal coupling between classes and improves the component evolvability.

Besides the three design patterns considered mandatory by COSMOS*, it is possible to use any other design pattern during the component implementation.

The next step consists on choosing a programming language and implementing the systems components. Notice that although COSMOS* defines the structure of the source-code in terms of classes and interfaces, the methods of the provided operations should be implemented manually.

### Configure Architectural Elements Together and Implement Architectural Connectors

After the components have been provisioned in the previous activity, they should be putted together in an architectural configuration. Since COSMOS* defines explicit required interfaces, it is necessary to define a connector for each pair of components interact each other.

For this, the proposed approach suggests the use of the Adapter design pattern, which consists on a class that realizes a set of required interfaces and uses a set of provided interfaces. Besides adapting the operations' signatures, this connector is able to add any processing between the requests of the required and provided interfaces, such as to open a remote connection, and to switch from a server to another.

### Test and Deploy the ERS

Although test is outside the scope of this paper, the proposed approach suggests the use of graybox test cases (Moraes, Durães, Barbosa, Martins, & Madeira, 2007), by means of considering information related to the provided and required interfaces of the components. Complementary testing strategies could be used (Binder, 1999): (i) component testing for testing the provided interfaces of the components; (ii) integration testing for testing the required interfaces of the components; (iii) system testing for testing the architectural configuration; and (iv) robustness testing for testing the non-functional requirements realized by the connectors.

Finally, the deployment of the system should consider the environment preparation into the client site, as well as the execution of the acceptance testing for assessing if the user is satisfied with the consistency between the requirements specified and actually implemented.

## FUTURE RESEARCH DIRECTIONS

The main problem to build recommender system is the creation and updating of user profile. There is a large amount of features that may be acquired through registration forms. However, these features do not always guarantee a good recommendation, it is necessary to monitor the user to create a more detailed profile.

For example, in an education environment the user (student) interacts with the teacher, tutors and other students, through tools such as: blog, forum, chat. All these interactions may help create a more detailed profile of the student, thus ensuring a better recommendation.

Considering this above arguments, it is necessary to use mechanisms to improve the description of users. In the context of the Web, using semantic web techniques may help to increase the description and consistency of the description.

Another problem is the changing data. The recommendation system may suggest the best, sometimes old, and new have difficulty. For example, in the domain of fashion, past trends may be better classified in the system, but there are no longer interesting for users. Finally, another difficulty is the design decisions, such as: the recommendation is spontaneous or requested; collaborative or individual; recommending only what is new; is a necessity or preference.

## CONCLUSION AND FUTURE WORK

The construction of Educational Recommender System (ERS) demands the incorporation of complex requirements at the software design, e.g., adaptability for working with different algorithms, performance for recommending timely, and availability for preventing the service to be unavailable for a long time. The incorporation of such characteristics makes ERS more complex, and consequently makes the development process more error prone and the final software more expensive. Although software architectures is one of the earliest artifacts that permits the analysis of system quality attributes, such as, adaptability, performance and reliability (Bass, Clements, & Kazman, 2003), existing strategies for designing ERS do not consider the software architectures in an explicit way.

To cope with the inherent complexity related to quality attributes, we have presented an architecture-centered solution that incorporates such characteristics as early as possible in the software development process in a systematic way. The underpinning of our approach is a simple process which touches two levels of software design: (i) architectural design, which deals with quality attributes in a high-level way; and (ii) detailed design, which deals with lower level modeling strategies for realizing the software architecture at the source code. The proposed approach relies on architectural styles (Bass, Clements, & Kazman, 2003) and good practices for allowing the structural definition of the system, and design patterns for allowing the implementation of quality attributes related to ERS (e.g., adaptability, performance and reliability) by using object-oriented programming languages.

The case study has showed in a "step-by-step" fashion how the software architecture can be designed and gradually refined until achieve the level of object-oriented classes generated based on design patterns.

Although the entire process has showed to be effective for constructing ERS with complex quality attributes, most of the process has been conducted manually, except the identification of the reference architecture that is supported by a case tool presented in Section 4.3.1 (Figure 12). As a current work, we intend to automate other activities of the process: (i) Refinement of the Reference Architecture (Section 4.3.2), (ii) Identification of internal (lower-level) components (Section 4.3.3); (iii) Internal design of the components using COSMOS* (Section 4.4); and (iv) Generation of test cases (Section 4.6).

## REFERENCES

Bass, L., Clements, P. C., & Kazman, R. (2003). *Software architecture in practice* (2nd ed.). Addison-Wesley.

Binder, R. V. (1999). *Testing object-oriented systems: Models, patterns, and tools*. Boston, MA: Addison-Wesley Longman Publishing Co., Inc.

Bradbury, J. S. (2004). *Organizing definitions and formalisms for dynamic software architectures*. School of Computing, Queen's University.

Brenton, C. (1999). *Mastering network security*. Network Press.

Brito, P. H., de-Lemos, R., Rubira, C. M., & Martins, E. B. (2009). Architecting fault tolerance with exception handling: Verification and validation. [JCST]. *Journal on Computer Science & Technology*, *24*(2), 212–237. doi:10.1007/s11390-009-9219-2

Brito, P. H., Rocha, C. R., Castor-Filho, F., Martins, E., & Rubira, C. M. (2005). A method for modeling and testing exceptions in component-based software development. In *Proc. of the 2nd Latin American Symposium on Dependable Computing (LADC 2005), LNCS 3747* (pp. 61-79). Salvador, Brazil: Springer.

Carroll, J. M. (2000). Making use: Scenarios and scenario-based design. *Proc. of the Conference on Designing Interactive Systems (DIS '00)* (pp. 4-20). New York, NY: ACM Press.

Casili, A., Gerling, V., Deco, C., & Bender, C. (2010). *Congreso Iberoamericano de Informática Educativa, Volume I*, (pp. 503-510). Santiago, Chile.

Cheesman, J., & Daniels, J. (2000). *UML components*. Addison-Wesley.

Chen, F., Wang, Q., Mei, H., & Yang, F. (2002). *An architecture-based approach for component-oriented development*. 26th Annual International Computer Software and Applications Conference.

Fu, X., Bultan, T., & Su, J. (2002). Formal verification of e-services and workflows. *Proc. of the International Workshop on Web Services, E-Business, and the Semantic Web (WES'02)* (pp. 188–202). London, UK: Springer-Verlag.

Gamma, E., Helm, R., Johnson, R., & Vlisside, J. (1995). *Design patterns: Elements of reusable object-oriented software*. Reading, MA: Addison-Wesley.

Gayard, L. A., Rubira, C. M., & Guerra, P. A. (2008). *COSMOS*: A component system model for software architectures*. Technical Report.

Gillmann, M., Weissenfels, J., Weikum, G., & Kraiss, A. (2000). Performance and availability assessment for the configuration of distributed workflow management systems. *Proc. of the 7th International Conference on Extending Database Technology (EDBT '00)* (pp. 183–201). London, UK: Springer-Verlag.

Kazman, R., Klein, M., & Clements, P. (2000). *ATAM: Method for architecture evaluation*. Pittsburgh, PA: CMU/SEI.

Klein, M., & Kazman, R. (1999). *Attribute-based architectural styles*. Pittsburgh, PA: CMU/SEI.

Koskimies, K. (2001). Towards architecture-oriented programming environments. *Proc. of the First ASERC Workshop on Software Architecture.*

Kruchten, P., Obbink, J. H., & Stafford, J. A. (2006). The past, present, and future for software architecture. *IEEE Software*, *2*(23), 22–30. doi:10.1109/MS.2006.59

Lu, J. (2004). A personalized e-learning material recommender system. *Proceedings of the 2nd International Conference on Information Technology for Application (ICITA 2004)*, (pp. 374-379). China.

Meyer, B. (1988). *Object-oriented software construction* (1st ed.). Prentice-Hall.

Mizoguchi, R. (2004). Tutorial on ontological engineering - part 2: Ontology development, tools and language. *New Generation Computing*, *1*(22), 61–96. doi:10.1007/BF03037281

Moraes, R. L., Durães, J., Barbosa, R., Martins, E., & Madeira, H. M. (2007). Experimental risk assessment and comparison using software fault injection. *Proc. of the 37th Annual IEEE/IFIP International Conference on Dependable Systems and Networks (DSN'2007)*, (pp. 512–521). Edinburgh, UK.

Paul, R. A., Tsai, W. T., & Mikell, J. S. (2004). *Rapid simulation evaluation from scenario specifications for command and control systems*. Washington, DC: Department of Defense.

Rubira, C. M., de-Lemos, R., Ferreira, G., & Castor-Filho, F. (2005, March). Exception handling in the development of dependable component-based systems. *Software, Practice & Experience*, *35*(5), 195–236. doi:10.1002/spe.632

Santos, O. C., & Boticario, J. G. (2010). Modeling recommendations for the educational domain. *1st Workshop on Recommender Systems for Technology Enhanced Learning* (pp. 2793-2800). (RecSysTEL 2010): Elsevier.

Schneider, G., & Winters, J. P. (1998). *Applying use cases: A practical guide* (1st ed.). Addison-Wesley.

Sleeman, D., & Brown, J. (1982). *Intelligent tutoring systems*. London, UK: Academic Press.

Sommerville, I. (1995). *Software engineering* (6th ed.). Addison-Wesley.

Szyperski, C. (2002). *Component software: Beyond object-oriented programming*. Boston, MA: Addison-Wesley Longman Publishing Co., Inc.

Tomita, R. T., Castor-Filho, F., Guerra, P. A., & Rubira, C. M. (2004). *Bellatrix: An environment with architectural support for component-based development* (in Portuguese), (pp. 43–48).

Wang, T., Tsai, K., Lee, M., & Chiu, T. (2007). Personalized learning objects recommendation based on the semantic-aware discovery and the learner preference pattern. *Journal of Educational Technology & Society*, *3*, 84–105.

Woolf, B. P. (2009). *Building intelligent interactive tutors: Student-centered strategies for revolutionizing e-learning*. Amsterdam, The Netherlands: Morgan Kaufmann Publishers/Elsevier.

You-Sheng, Z., & Yu-Yun, H. (2003, March). Architecture-based software process model. *Software Engineering Notes, 2*(28).

Zhu, F., Ip, H., & Cao, J. (2008). PeRES: A personalized recommendation education system based on multi-agents & SCORM. *Advances in Web Based Learning (ICWL 2007), LNCS 4823*, (pp. 31-42).

## ADDITIONAL READING

Badrul Sarwar, G. K. (2000). Analysis of recommendation algorithms for e-commerce. *EC '00: Proceedings of the 2nd ACM conference on Electronic commerce* (pp. 158-167). ACM.

Buschmann, F. R. M. (1996). *Pattern-oriented Software Architecture: A system of patterns*. England: John Wiley & Sons Ltd.

Dietmar Jannach, M. Z. (2010). *Recommender Systems: An Introduction*. Cambridge University Press.

Erich Gamma, R. H. (1994). *Design Patterns: Elements of Reusable Object-Oriented Software*. Addison-Wesley Professional.

Gündüz-Ögüdücü, Ş. (2010). *Web Page Recommendation Models: Theory and Algorithms*. Synthesis Lectures on Data Management.

Herlocker, J. L. (January de 2004). Evaluating collaborative filtering recommender systems. *ACM Transactions on Information Systems*, pp. 5-53.

Huang, D. a. (2008). The Research of Web Page Recommendation Model Based on FCA and Enterprise Ontology. *Proceedings of the 2008 IEEE Pacific-Asia Workshop on Computational Intelligence and Industrial Application* (pp. 232--236). Washington, DC, USA: IEEE Computer Society.

Ingo Schwab, W. P. (2000). Learning to recommend from positive evidence. [ACM.]. *Proceedings of Intelligent User Interfaces, 2000*, 241–247.

James Rumbaugh, G. B. (1999). *The Unified Modeling Language Reference Manual*. Addison-Wesley Professional.

John Cheesman, J. D. (2000). *UML Components: A Simple Process for Specifying Component-Based Software*. Addison-Wesley Professional.

Khoshgoftaar, X. S. (2009). A survey of collaborative filtering techniques. *Advances in Artificial Intelligence* .

Len Bass, P. C. (2003). *Software Architecture in Practice*. Boston, MA, USA: Addison-Wesley Longman Publishing Co.

Obradovic, S. V. (2000). *A regression-based approach for scaling-up personalized recommender systems in e-commerce. ACM WebKDD 2000 Web Mining for E-Commerce Workshop*. ACM.

Pazzani, M. J. (2007). Content-based recommendation systems. In *P. a. Brusilovsky, The adaptive web* (pp. 325–341). Berlin, Heidelberg: Springer-Verlag. doi:10.1007/978-3-540-72079-9_10

Peter Brusilovsky, A. K. (June de 2007). The Adaptive Web: Methods and Strategies of Web Personalization. *Lecture Notes in Computer Science*.

Resnick, P. a. (March de 1997). Recommender systems. *Commun. ACM*, pp. 56--58.

Rong Pan, Y. Z. (2008). One-class collaborative filtering. *IEEE International Conference on Data Mining* (pp. 502-511). Los Alamitos, CA, USA: IEEE Computer Society.

Sandvig, J. J. B. M. (2007). Robustness of collaborative recommendation based on association rule mining. *RecSys '07: Proceedings of the 2007 ACM conference on Recommendersystems* (pp. 105-112). ACM.

Sarwar, B. a. (2001). Item-based collaborative filtering recommendation algorithms. *Proceedings of the 10th international conference on World Wide Web* (pp. 285-295). New York, NY, USA: ACM.

Sommerville, I. (2004). *Software Engineering*. Pearson Education Ltd.

Tao Zhou, Z. K.-g.-c. (2010). Solving the apparent diversity-accuracy dilemma of recommender systems. *PNAS*.

Tuzhilin, G. A. (June de 2005). Toward the next generation of recommender systems: A survey of the state-of-the-art and possible extensions. *IEEE Transactions on Knowledge and Data Engineering*, pp. 734-749.

W-S. H. S.-Y.-C. (2003). Content-Independent Task-Focused Recommendation. *Online Information Review*, pp. 169-182.

Yunhong Zhou, D. W. (2008). Large-scale parallel collaborative filtering for the netflix prize. *AAIM '08: Proceedings of the 4th international conference on Algorithmic Aspects in Information and Management* (pp. 337-348). Berlin, Heidelberg: Springer-Verlag.

Zhang, T. a. (March de 2002). Recommender systems using linear classifiers. *Journal of Machine Learning Research*, pp. 313-334.

## KEY TERMS AND DEFINITIONS

**Design Patterns:** Describes general reusable solutions to a common problem on the development of software systems.

**Intelligent Tutoring Systems:** Computer program which uses Artificial Intelligence techniques to represent the knowledge and to reproduce the behavior of the teacher in the teaching process.

**Quality Attributes:** Non-functional requirements with the purpose to evaluate the performance of a system.

**Recommender Systems:** Systems that typically compare a user profile to some reference characteristics, aiming to rate the items according to the particular needs of the user.

**Software Architecture:** Structure or structures of the system, which comprises software elements, the externally visible properties of those elements, and the relationships among them.

**Software Development Process:** Methodology or structure introduced on the development of a software product.

**Software Components:** Primary computational elements or data stores of a system and are defined through the list of provided interfaces and required interfaces.

# Section 3
# Real World E-Learning Scenarios

# Chapter 11
# Case Study:
## Material Additions, Ratings, and Comments in a Course Setting

**Juha Leino**
*University of Tampere, Finland*

## ABSTRACT

*As recommender systems are making inroads to e-learning, the new ecosystem is placing new challenges on them. This Chapter discusses the author's experiences of adding recommender features to additional reading materials listing page in an undergraduate-level course. Discussion is based on use-log and student questionnaire data. Students could both add materials to lecture readings and peer-evaluate the pertinence of the materials by rating and commenting them. Students were required to add one material and rate five as part of the course requirements. Overall, students perceived the system as useful and did not resent compulsoriness. In addition, perceived social presence promoted social behavior in many students. However, many students rated materials without viewing them, thus undermining the reliability of aggregated ratings. Consequently, while recommenders can enhance the e-learner experience, they need to be robust against some students trying to get points without earning them.*

## INTRODUCTION

Internet offers students access to a vast array of materials of varying quality, ranging from specialist columns, expert articles, and scientific papers to presentation slides and video interviews.

DOI: 10.4018/978-1-61350-489-5.ch011

In fact, a large majority of students already use online resources to augment course materials at the college/university level and are ready to share these with fellow students (Hage & Aïmeur, 2008). Since students are already filtering a mass of potential materials down to the pertinent ones for themselves, the question is how to make use of and share the fruits of all this labor with others.

The author of this Chapter lectures a course on User-Centered Design (UCD) at undergraduate level. He decided to harness the collective intelligence and efforts of the students to collect additional materials to complement his selection and to allow students to determine the pertinence of the materials as a community. Consequently, the Lecture Slides and Reading Materials page (LSRM) on the course's website was designed to allow adding materials to lectures and rating and commenting the added materials. The purpose was twofold, 1) to help students find high-quality materials to read, and 2) to encourage students to read more widely on UCD (in part by lowering the cost of finding pertinent materials with LSRM). The importance of the second point is underlined by the fact that information literacy, the ability to find, access, evaluate, and use information from various sources, is seen as a survival skill in the information-intensive age and as crucial for professional success after graduation (Kiliç-Çakmak, 2010).

Recommending thus took place at two levels, 1) adding materials one had found useful, and 2) rating and commenting the added materials. At both levels, the purpose of the recommender was to help students *find good items* (Herlocker, Konstan, Terveen, & Riedl, 2004).

Adding a material to a lecture is an act of implicit recommending, as it implies prior selection from the multitude of materials available on the Internet—users filtering materials for other users. The second level, rating and commenting, allowed students to help each other decide which materials were worth reading, thus aggregating knowledge (Neumann, 2007). Again, this goes back to the idea of collective intelligence: A community can best determine what materials are interesting, useful, and at correct level of complexity for its members. In a sense, the system enabled a kind of peer-reviewing process. As accessing LSRM required logging in, the community here was a closed one.

The fact that both the recommending approaches were non-algorithmic makes them no less recommendations, as for instance such non-algorithmic approaches as ratings and comments/reviews are widely considered bona fide recommendations (Leino & Räihä, 2007; Neumann, 2007; Schafer, Konstan, & Riedl, 1999).

In 2009, students were required to add at least one material and five ratings as part of the course requirements due to the lackluster levels of contributions in 2007 and 2008 when all contributing was voluntary. While compulsoriness brought the number of contributions to a sufficiently high level that students found the system useful, it also brought out the problem of significant number of students rating materials without reading them.

In this Chapter, we first briefly discuss recommenders in e-learning in general and then turn to the case study at hand. After describing LSRM, we look at the use statistics (collected automatically) and student views (collected with a questionnaire) to describe the use of the systems and to evaluate its usefulness. As the design decisions related to LSRM and student perceptions of ratings and commenting features have already been discussed in Leino (2010), we only recap them briefly where relevant, focusing instead on previously unreported aspects. In particular, we look at using compulsoriness to elicit contributions in e-learning and discuss the problem of dishonest ratings.

This Chapter makes two major contributions to the field. First, there is a dire need of studies of real-life application, as most systems are at design or prototype level, and only very few systems have been evaluated with trials involving human users (Manouselis, Drachsler, Vuorikari, Hummel, & Koper, 2011). Thus, the real-life, actual use scenario of this case study provides much-needed experiences to the field. Second, while hostile attacks on e-commerce recommenders have been widely discussed, this is to the author's knowledge the first time that gaming recommenders is discussed in the context of e-learning. The likely reason for this omission is the lack of real-life experiences. In addition, the study sheds light on using compulsoriness in the e-learning context.

## BACKGROUND

### Recommender Systems and E-Learning

Recommender systems (RS) help us deal with information overload in two somewhat overlapping ways: They help us in finding salient items (e.g. books we might be interested in) and in making decisions (e.g. which book to buy) (Leino & Räihä, 2007; Santos & Boticario, 2008; Schafer et al., 1999). The wide breadth of recommender features spans from comments (often shown as entered) through ratings (shown individually, as aggregates, or used to calculate predictions) to prediction-computing with content-based filtering and collaborative filtering (CF) (Leino & Räihä, 2007; Schafer et al., 1999). A recommender system might consist of one or more recommender features. In addition, RS are widely used to personalize the interface and use experience although not all recommenders are personalizing (Schafer et al., 1999).

Originally, the typical application areas of RS, such as e-commerce, news, and movies, were not related e-learning (Tang & McCalla, 2004a). Lately, however, RS have made inroads into e-learning and their potential in e-learning has attracted increasing research interest (see e.g. Ghauth & Abdullah, 2010; Hage & Aïmeur, 2008; Tang & McCalla, 2004a). Although recommenders in e-learning serve similar purposes as in e-commerce, there are also differences that make transferring RS from other domains to e-learning challenging (Drachsler, Hummel, & Koper, 2009).

For one, pedagogical aspects are an important consideration in e-learning, and so the user interest is not alone the determining factor (Santos & Boticario, 2008; Tang & McCalla, 2004a). Instead, in e-learning recommendations should also consider such factors as what a certain learner needs to learn at certain point (Santos & Boticario, 2008; Tang & McCalla, 2004a), thus taking into account such aspects as the learner's background knowledge, suitability of the material (e.g. not recommending highly technical papers to beginners), and recommending materials in the right order so that they build on each other (Tang & McCalla, 2004a). Thus, RS in e-learning may also have to support learners sequentially in the learning process and over a longer timeframe than is typical in e-commerce (Drachsler et al., 2009).

Importantly, Tang & McCalla (2004a) found that in the learning context learners are also ready to read papers that are not so interesting but are pedagogically grounded. This underlines that user goals also differ in the e-learning and e-commerce contexts (Stefani, Vassiliadis, & Xenos, 2006). Also, while in e-commerce, the objective is to support and maximize selling, in e-learning, the goal is to enhance learning through information transfer and engagement (Granić & Adams, 2010; Stefani et al., 2006).

There are no one-size-fits-all RS solutions in e-learning any more than in e-commerce. The learning contexts where recommenders are employed vary (Ghauth & Abdullah, 2010). For example, what is recommended varies (e.g. courses or course materials) as does the learning context (e.g. diversity of teaching/learning settings and whether the system aims to replace or support the tutor), and so the RS strategy needs to be adjusted accordingly (Ghauth & Abdullah, 2010; Granić & Adams, 2010).

Overall, adaptive, personalized systems in e-learning have enjoyed rather limited success thus far (Granić & Adams, 2010; Stefani et al., 2006). Compared to many other RS scenarios, in e-learning the number of users tends to be limited and there may not be time to initiate the user model, which typically requires time and often also explicit user activity (Granić & Adams, 2010). Since the accuracy and amount of data in the model are crucial to the quality of recommendations, the inherent bootstrapping problems (Granić & Adams, 2010) have forced researchers to consider such solutions as generating artificial learners to provide recommendations (e.g. Tang and McCalla, 2004b). Obtaining sufficient modeling data remains challenging in e-learning (Granić & Adams, 2010).

## Rating Interfaces and Their Effects on Ratings

As many RS make recommendations based on user actions and preferences, without sufficient data they cannot produce reliable recommendations (Granić & Adams, 2010; Harper, Chen, & Konstan, 2005; Neumann, 2007). Data can be collected implicitly or explicitly, implicit referring to collecting behavioral usage data (e.g. items purchased or time spent) and explicit to directly asking users their opinion (e.g. evaluating an item with a five-star scale) (Amatriain, Pujol, Tintarev, & Oliver, 2009; Neumann, 2007). Although it imposes an extra task on users, explicit collecting is often perceived to provide more reliable data (Amatriain et al., 2009; Ghauth & Abdullah, 2010) although implicit data collected over time can also provide high-quality recommendations (Gadanho & Lhuillier, 2007).

Ratings are a typical method of collecting explicit preference data. The granularity (level of precision) of rating scales varies widely (Cena, Vernero, & Gena, 2010), ranging from a simple unary (e.g. *Like* button—only positive ratings) and binary (e.g. *thumbs up/down* buttons—both positive and negative ratings) scales to Likert-style scales (e.g. five-star rating) and larger rating scales that may also include negative values (Cosley, Lam, Albert, Konstan, & Riedl, 2003; Lang, Spear, & Wu, 2010). Interface implementations, for instance a button, a line of (typically five) stars, a slider or a continuous bar, also vary (Cosley et al., 2003). Rating scales may also have emotional connotations, for instance sliders appearing technical and precise but detached and thumbs up/down youthful but potentially impolite (Cena et al, 2010).

People's voting behavior appears to depend to some extent on the scale used. Cena et al. (2010) compared user ratings on three different scales and found that when trying to map different scales in mathematical proportion, 40% of ratings departed considerably from it.

The prediction shown on the interface also affects how the user rates an item and even the user's opinion (Cosley et al., 2003). Cosley et al. (2003) showed participants deliberately incorrect predictions (off by one star on a five-star scale) and the effect on the ratings was statistically significant. Cosley et al. (2003) also believe that showing predictions can actually changes people's opinions at least temporarily. Talwar, Jurca, and Faltings (2007) found that past reviews and ratings can influence the future ones by creating expectations to which reviewers react based on their actual experiences, and so sequential reviews can become discussion threads where reviewers comment on the earlier reviews, either by agreeing with them or contradicting them.

## E-Word-of-Mouth vs. the True Item Quality

While user-contributed ratings, reviews and comments, considered electronic version of Word-of-mouth (eWOM), have become an important source of information for judging products and services in e-commerce, their ability to reflect the real quality of products and services has been questioned (Hu, Pavlou, & Zhang, 2006; Talwar et al., 2007). While controlled experiments produce normal distributions on items, rating for the same items in actual services are often bimodal; most ratings are either very positive or very negative (Talwar et al., 2007). It appears that users with moderate views choose not to voice their views, resulting in unrepresentative samples of views (Talwar et al., 2007). Consequently, the rating averages online may rather reflect the balance point between the two extreme opinions than the true product quality, and thus lead consumers to erroneous decisions (Hu et al., 2006).

As a rating depends on the aspect being rated, reviews and comments can help understand the reasoning behind the rating but reading them requires time and they typically contain repetitious information (Talwar et al., 2007).

Another problematic aspect is that while reviews are expected to represent true views of the reviewers, for instance in case of Amazon, some reviews have been recognized to be strategic posts by interested parties, such as book authors and their competitors (Talwar et al., 2007).

While reviews and ratings at such sites as Amazon tend to be overwhelmingly positive (Chevalier & Mayzin, 2006; Talwar et al., 2007), negative votes appear to have stronger effect than positive ones (Chevalier & Mayzin, 2006).

## Motivation and Contributing

Motivating users to contribute is crucial for most RS (Harper et al., 2005; Nov & Ye, 2010) even if RS entirely based on implicit data constitute an exception (Neumann, 2007). As new items need ratings and new user need to rate items in user-based RS, the struggle to keep ratings coming is constant (Harper et al., 2005; Neumann, 2007).

In e-commerce, contributions appear to come mainly from highly opinionated users and users who believe they have something distinctive to contribute, thus resulting in bimodal distributions (Talwar et al., 2007). Hu et al. (2006) suggest that due to the incentive problem (benefits of reviewing not being clear), contributions are motivated by brag and moan model that explains bimodal distributions at least partially. Hennig-Thurau, Gwinner, Walsh, & Gremler's (2004) concept of *homeostate utility* similarly suggests that a strongly negative or positive consumption experience may result in imbalance and that balance can be restored by *expressing positive emotions* or *venting negative feelings*.

Hennig-Thurau et al. (2004) further suggest that eWOM providers can be grouped by what motivates them into four segments that may need different encouragement strategies. The segments are 1) *self-interested helpers* (driven by economic incentives in addition to concern for other consumers), 2) *multiple-motive consumers* (motivated by many factors but not by economic incentives), 3) *consumer advocates* (motivated primarily by concern for other consumers), and 4) *true altruists* (motivated by helping other consumers and companies). For all four groups, however, the primary motivator was concern for other customers. Multiple-motive consumers engaged most in eWOM while true altruists and consumer advocates made the fewest contributions.

In addition, Harper et al. (2005) found that power users in MovieLens rated movies to keep a list of movies they had seen, to influence others, and because rating movies was fun, and Nov & Ye (2010) confirmed that perceived social presence encouraged contributing tags in Flickr. Regrettably, there are also more sinister motives, such as shilling in e-commerce (Lam & Riedl, 2004; Lang et al., 2010).

In learning, motivation is a complex, multifaceted construct (Rienties, Tempelaar, Van den Bossche, Gijselaers, & Segers, 2009; Ruohotie & Nokelainen, 2003) that has proven difficult to quantify by measuring (Neumann, 2007). While motivation has a positive impact on learning and developing effective learning-strategies also in e-learning (Kiliç-Çakmak, 2010; Ruohotie & Nokelainen, 2003), not considering its various dimensions can be misleading (Rienties et al., 2009). Little, however, is known about the type or number of effective motivators (Kiliç-Çakmak, 2010). Nevertheless, self-rated motivation has been shown to have a positive relationship to the number and quality of comments and newsgroup messages the learner contributes (Ruohotie & Nokelainen, 2003).

As different learners contribute different amounts and types of discourse in e-learning setting, Rienties et al. (2009) studied the difference between *intrinsically motivated, extrinsically motivated*, and *a-motivated* e-learners. Intrinsically motivated e-learners (IML) derive satisfaction and pleasure from the activity of learning while extrinsically motivated e-learners (EML) see learning as a means to an end. A-motivation can result from meaning barriers, lack of relatedness, and lack of perceived competence. Rienties et al.'s (2009) results show that the type of motivation is one of the determining factors for the amount and quality of contributions. Specifically, IML contribute more especially to *higher cognitive discourse* (theoretical ideas and explication as opposed to facts and opinions that constitute *lower cognitive discourse*) and make more social contributions. They are also more central in the social networks of discourse and have more connections to other learners. Thus, motivating contributing in e-learning may require a mix of different approaches.

## Evaluating Recommender Systems

While accuracy metrics are still an important measure of algorithmic RS, user experience is increasingly seen as the decisive factor (Herlocker et al, 2004; McNee, Riedl, & Konstan, 2006; Santos & Boticario, 2008). The most accurate recommenders are not necessarily the most useful, and at least sometimes users prefer results that are less accurate but provide more serendipitous recommendations (McNee et al., 2006). Users come to RS with a purpose, and judge it in terms of that need being met (McNee et al., 2006). In addition to providing accuracy and usefulness, recommenders need to be pleasurable to use (McNee et al., 2006). Moreover, accuracy metrics can typically only be applied to algorithmic recommenders, and for instance reviews cannot be evaluated by them.

In evaluating recommenders, Herlocker et al. (2004) recommend combining explicit and implicit data to see all the sides of the equation. Furthermore, as in non-commercial contexts performance cannot be measured by such measures as number of items sold and not returned, they consider user satisfaction data the best approach.

In e-learning, meeting pedagogical goals is also important and it can be measured by various means in addition to examination results and grades. Common learner-based measures in e-learning include effectiveness, efficiency, satisfaction and drop-out rate (Manouselis et al., 2011). Especially satisfaction is an important measure as it is closely related to motivation (Drachsler et al., 2009). As satisfaction in e-learning is based on mastered competencies that develop over time, RS in e-learning often need to be evaluated also in terms of the support they give to the whole learning process rather than just to selecting an item, as often is the case in e-commerce (Drachsler et al., 2009). Naturally, when deciding the evaluation metrics, the purpose of the particular RS in a particular e-learning context needs to be considered.

## LSRM in E-Learning Terms

One important dimension in e-learning is that of *formal* and *informal* learning (Manouselis et al., 2011). Formal learning takes place on formal educational settings, such as universities and schools, leading typically to accreditation, while informal learning is self-directed and depends on information from various providers, some of which are non-institutional (Drachsler et al., 2009; Manouselis et al., 2011). Consequently, *top-down* approach, where domain professionals provide structure/curriculum and learning materials, is seen as suitable for recommenders in formal learning and *bottom-up* approach, where e-learners provide information (tags, ratings, behavioral data etc.) on which recommendations are based, is seen as more fitting for informal learning (Drachsler et al., 2009; Santos & Boticario, 2010).

The setting of this study is a combination of formal and informal; as a university course with face-to-face lectures and clear curriculum, it represents formal learning, but at the same time the online learning section represents a combination of informal and formal elements, and consequently top-down and bottom-up approaches to recommending, although heavily slanting toward informal/bottom-up. While both the lecturer and students provided materials, students provided the information (ratings and comments) on which the recommending was based. However, the lecturer also provided comments, thus injecting some top-down approach to LSRM. The informality of LSRM can also be seen in that the students were not tested on the material and were only expected to read more on topics that interested them.

In fact, the purpose of e-learning in the course was as much to instill a good habit of keeping up with the developments in the field as to fulfill any academic requirement, as information literacy is considered crucial for professional success after graduation in the information age (Kiliç-Çakmak, 2010).

LSRM can also be characterized as a learning network as it connected learners (asynchronously), its recommendations—and even half the content—were based on student contributions, and it used Web 2.0 approach and technologies as enablers (Manouselis et al., 2011). Like LSRM, learning networks, while combining formal and informal, tend to support informal learning in particular (Drachsler, et al., 2009). Users in learning networks typically need support in finding and selecting suitable information (Drachsler et al., 2009), something LSRM was designed to provide.

By combining online and face-to-face learning, the course setting also represented *blended learning* (Garrison & Kanuka, 2004). Blended learning has been found to have a positive effect on student performance, to provide a more flexible learning environment and student autonomy, and to develop capacity for reflection, resulting in a deeper understanding of the subject matter (López-Pérez, Pérez-López, & Rodríguez-Ariza, 2011). As such, it is seen as a paradigm shift from teacher-centered learning toward learner-centered learning and from teaching to learning, thus providing learners with real-life skills (López-Pérez et al., 2011; Ruohotie & Nokelainen, 2003). Blended learning is seen as the wave of the future (Garrison & Kanuka, 2004), as e-learning is seen to complement face-to-face learning but unable to replace it in the formal education setting (López-Pérez et al., 2011).

## CASE STUDY SETTING

### Student Community and Use Context

The learner community consisted of 32 students (10 females) who took the UCD course taught at the University of Tampere in the fall, 2009. All 32 completed the course successfully. (Originally, 44 students enrolled in the course but 12 dropped out almost immediately, mainly due the heavy workload. As the 12 used LSRM very little and did not add anything to it, filtering their use data out was straightforward.)

Most were undergraduate students, as the course is usually taken on the 2nd or 3rd year of studies. Twenty-nine were computer science majors, two information science majors, and one statistics major. Four students had prior work experience in designing interfaces.

The course consisted of seven lectures (Sept.-Oct.) and fourteen weekly assignment meetings (Sept.-Nov.), all taking place in a classroom. The course website required logging in, and in addition to the LSRM page, it had pages for describing the weekly assignments and the design assignment. Design assignments, due Nov. 30, were presented Dec. 2-4. All work was done as small-groups of mostly three members.

There was no examination as students were graded based on the weekly assignments (20% of the grade) and the design assignment (80% of the grade) with extra points awarded for attendance (non-compulsory). Consequently, reading materials attached to lectures was voluntary (apart from the fact that each student needed to add one material and rate five).

## Data Collecting

Study data was collected in two ways: 1) log data and 2) online questionnaire. All activity on the LSRM page—viewing materials or comments, adding materials, rating and commenting materials, and opening links inside comments—was logged. This log data gives almost a click-by-click picture of the activity taking place on the LSRM page.

The online questionnaire was filled out by 23 students (72%). The male-female ratio in the course and among the respondents was practically the same, 31% to 30% respectively. The questionnaire consisted of both open-ended and multiple choice questions. Most multiple choice questions allowed commenting. The questionnaire surveyed six areas: Materials, ratings, commenting, adding materials, implementation, and general impressions. The questionnaire answers could be connected to student's use data. Students were told this but assured that their replies would in no way affect their grade.

LSRM has been used in the course since 2007, but previously the system did not record opening materials on a tab with right-click or ctrl+click. This feature was only added to the 2009 version to enable recording detailed use data. In addition, previously making contributions to the system was voluntary. In 2007, contributions were non-anonymous.

## LSRM Interface

LSRM design was strongly affected by the fact that it has low number of users and items, and it is used only for one semester at a time. This contrasts with many other e-learning and most e-commerce contexts, and effectively ruled out CF-based approaches. The goal was to make adding materials, ratings and comments as effortless as possible and to make every explicit contribution immediately useful. As mentioned, the design logic is discussed in Leino (2010) in detail.

LSRM was implemented with HTML, JavaScript, AJAX, and PHP. All activity, adding materials, rating, commenting, and viewing comments, took place without reloading the page. All material additions, comments and reviews were anonymous.

Figure 1 shows the LSRM interface. Materials were added under lectures by clicking *Add a reading material* (Figure 1:1). The form opened on the page with input fields only for material title and URL (both compulsory). After submitting, the success/failure message (in red) was displayed in the place of the form and the material was added on top of the lecture's materials. Added materials could be modified but not deleted. When a material title was clicked, the link opened in another browser window.

Materials could be rated on a binary scale (*Yes* and *No* buttons) in response to the question *Did you find this material useful?* (Figure 1:2). The goal was to provide a quick-and-easy interface while still supporting both promoting and demoting an item in response to a clearly stated evaluation criterion. After rating an item, the user was given a *Change your vote* button with the current vote visible as text (Figure 1:3). The rating of a material (*all positive votes/all votes*) was shown on the top-left corner of the material (Figure1:4) to make ratings scannable. Users could only rate materials added by others. Deleting ratings was not possible.

Students could rate materials without commenting them and vice versa. Users could comment items they had added and commenting one material more than once was possible to allow discussing. To lower the barrier for contributing, the word *comment* was used instead of *review* to emphasize that even shorter and less formal

*Figure 1. LSRM interface (Interface translated into English from Finnish. Material order changed for illustrative purposes but otherwise the content is real. Student comments blurred.)*

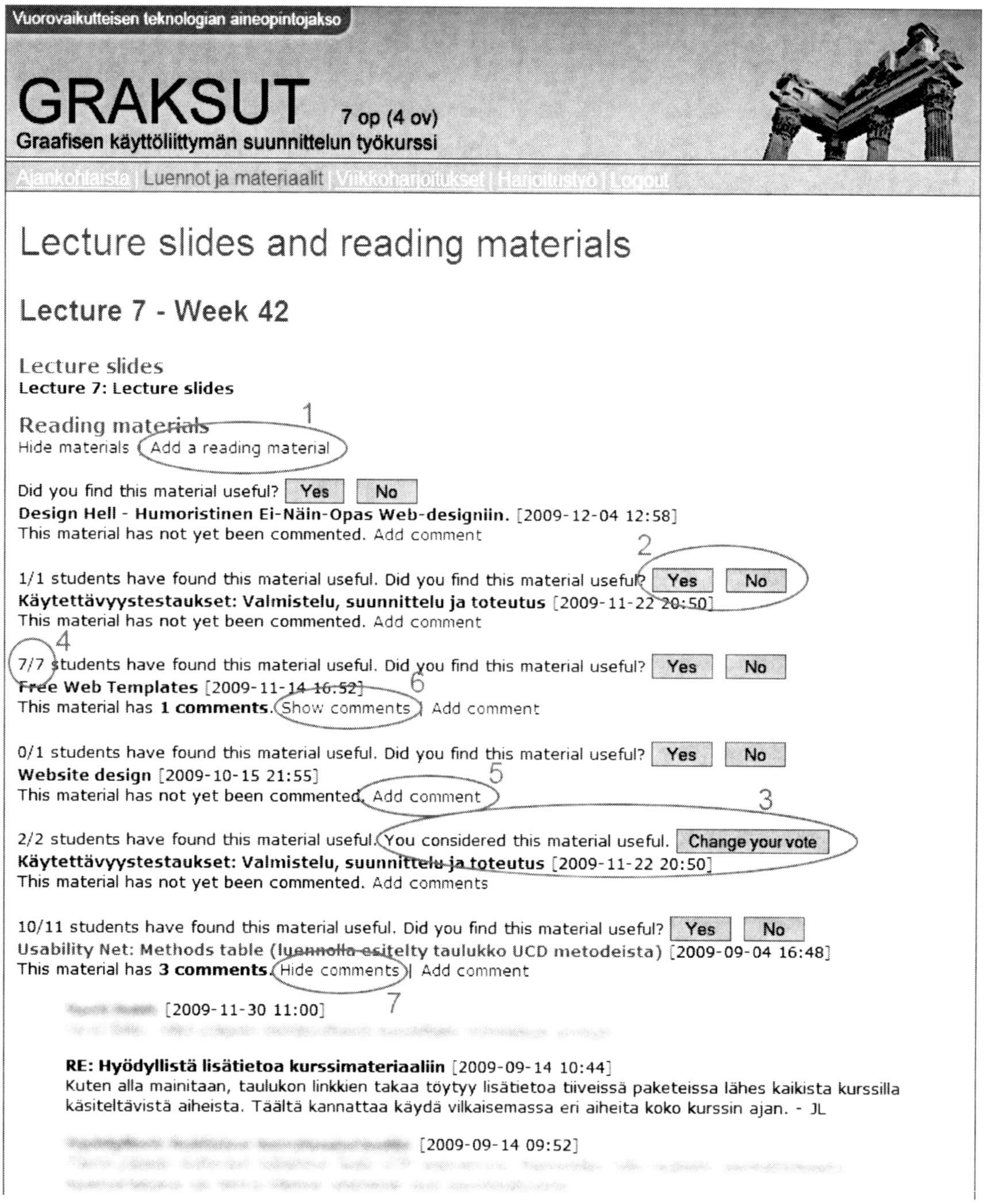


contributions were permitted. Adding a comment to a material (Figure 1:5) worked just like adding a material to a lecture. Comments could be modified but not deleted.

Comments were not visible by default to keep the page length manageable. Comments of a material could be opened from *Show comments* (Figure 1:6). The bottommost material in Figure 1 has its comments open and *Show comments* has changed into *Hide comments* (Figure 1:7).

The 23 students who filled out the questionnaire found the LSRM tools highly usable, with twenty rating them *very easy* (10) or *easy* (10) to use, two having no opinion and only one considering them somewhat difficult to use. Consequently, usability was unlikely to factor in other evaluations by the students.

# RESULTS AND DISCUSSION

## Adding Materials

As students had added few materials to LSRM when adding was voluntary (in both 2007 and 2008, only one student added one material), in 2009 students were required to add at least one material. Consequently, 23 students added 26 materials (three added two and others the required one) while the lecturer added 25 and teaching assistant one. The 52 materials were viewed 221 times; on average each student viewed 6.9 materials (STDEV 5.3; Max 19) and on average each material was viewed 4.3 times (STDEV 3.7; MAX 16). Eleven students viewed less than five materials. Students found the overall quality of materials good, with 21 considering them either *good* (20) or *very good* (1) and 2 having no opinion.

There was no undue rush towards the end to fulfill the requirement, as students added most materials in October (13) and November (7). Perhaps the majority needed to see others starting to use the system before joining in, as only 4 materials were added in September.

Students perceived the possibility of adding materials positively, with 17 students considering it *good* (14) or *very good* (3), four having no opinion, and only two considering it *bad*. The two students considering the possibility *bad* gave as reasons lack of time and the difficulty of finding high-quality materials. The students who perceived the possibility positively underlined that it made the course materials richer as "*nobody alone can know all the best links*." Some also spoke positively of the compulsoriness, saying that because of it they found "*surprisingly many new information sources*" and that it motivated them to read more articles.

Of the 26 materials added by students, three were PDFs, one was an online presentation (by Kevin Rose of Digg.com), one a flash interface example, and the rest normal web pages. Most were tutorials or how-tos but there were also blogs and articles (e.g. two articles from Nielsen's Alertbox). Some focused on specific aspects of designing (e.g. font issues, button designing) and some on wider issues (e.g. using personas, Internet designing). Two were resources (free templates and color-selecting tool). No research articles (journal articles or conference proceedings) were added by students.

The quality of the student-added materials was not inferior to the instructor-added materials: Most students had hard time telling which materials were added by other students and which by the lecturer. Moreover, the *useful* ratings also indicate that the material were perceived quite equally: The 26 materials added by the instructors received 93 *useful* votes (6 negative), were commented 8 times and viewed 110 times, while the 26 materials by students received 88 votes (4 negative), were commented 7 times and viewed 111 times.

Thus, the results encourage using students to complement instructor-added materials, as there were no quality problems and finding materials encouraged students to read at least some materials. Nevertheless, as students tended not to add research articles, instructors might be well advised to add research articles to complement the shorter and lighter materials students tend to add.

## Rating Materials

Students perceived the possibility of rating materials positively, with 16 seeing the feature as *very good* (2) or *good* (14) while 7 had no opinion.

Significantly, nobody saw the feature as *bad* or *very bad*. Those who rated the feature positively emphasized its guiding power in selecting materials.

Students gave altogether 180 *useful* votes (of which 10 negative). On average, each student gave 5.6 votes (STDEV 2.8; MAX 14). One student did not give any votes, seven gave less that the required five, nine gave the required five, and fifteen gave more than five. In addition, the teaching assistant also rated one material positively.

The requirement of five votes increased the number of votes significantly, as in 2007, only eleven votes were given by nine students, and in 2008, thirty votes were given by four students (one gave 26). Importantly, most students considered the number of votes high enough, as only three students thought that more votes would have made the system more useful, nine had no opinion, and eleven thought that more votes would have made only slight (8) or no difference at all (3).

Again, the beginning was hesitating, with only 7 votes given before Sept. 15, but after that, it continued solidly: 38 votes in September (thus, 31 votes after the mid-point), 62 in October, 77 in November, and 4 in December.

The rating coverage was extensive, as only five materials did not receive any ratings (average per material 3.5; STDEV 3.7; MAX 14). Seven items had negative votes (three had 2 and four had 1) but only four items had a negative rating (i.e. more negative than positive votes) and only two had only negative votes (each one).

The log data shows statistically significant correlation between the number of *useful* votes of a material and the number of students who viewed it ($r(n{=}52){=}0.818$, $p<0.000$) (all correlations in this Chapter are calculated as Pearson's correlation coefficient, as the tests were for linear dependency). While the correlation was statistically significant for both positive ($r(n{=}52){=}0.786$, $p<0.000$) and negative ($r(n{=}52){=}0.301$, $p<0.05$) votes, the correlation is understandably much stronger for positive votes. What is interesting is that the correlation for negative votes is also positive at all. This is partially explained by the fact that three items with negative votes had overwhelmingly positive overall rating (10/11, 8/10, and 4/5). For the four materials with negative overall rating, the average number of views is 4.3, thus the same as the average for all materials. Negative votes, perhaps due to their low number, do not appear to have discouraged viewing in LSRM.

However, the strong correlation does not necessarily mean that votes caused viewings. Other factors, such as material titles or information needs caused by assignments, could have directed students to view certain materials, and this could in turn have resulted in more ratings. In the questionnaire replies, 10 students thought that ratings had affected which material they read *very much* (3) or *much* (7) while another 10 considered the effect having been *not much* (8) or *not at all* (2), and three had no opinion. However, based on log data, the two groups are not that different: The correlation between the number of votes and materials viewed for *much/very much* group is $r(n{=}10){=}0.679$ ($p<0.000$) and for *not much/not at all* group $r(n{=}10){=}0.627$ ($p<0.000$).

Four students claimed to have selected materials based on titles, not ratings. As the same behavior has also been observed among Amazon users, some of whom selected books from the list page based on cover, title, and author independent of the star-rating (Leino & Räihä, 2007), this might at least partially explain the slightly lower correlation for the latter group.

Overall, we cannot conclude that votes caused viewings with absolute certainty although we note that the correlation makes it possible. The correlation and self-reports indicate that at least close to half of the students were affected by the ratings and that perhaps the other half was also influenced by them more than they realized. Moreover, in the Amazon study, the participants who did not pay much attention to the ratings on the list page did use them to evaluate the item on the item page (Leino & Räihä, 2007). Consequently, even if the ratings played a smaller role in scanning the LSRM page for interesting items for some students, the decision to open an interesting material may still have been influenced by the rating. For some students, ratings may have facilitated decision making more than item finding.

## Dishonest Ratings

Log analysis revealed that many students rated materials without viewing them. Altogether, 73 votes (40%) were given without viewing the material. The actual number of dishonest votes (i.e. votes given without having viewed the material) might, however, be somewhat lower, as some of the same links were also in the lecture slides; of the 32 materials that received dishonest votes, eight (representing 14 dishonest votes) were also in the lecture slides as links. Also, in four cases the dishonest voter had viewed the material's comment(s), and in all these cases, the vote seemed to follow the tone of the comment(s). Still, dishonesty was epidemic, as even in the best-case scenario (counting as honest the 14 votes with links in the lecture slides and the four votes based on comments), 30% of the votes were dishonest.

Altogether, 18 students (3 females) rated at least one item dishonestly and only 13 (6 females) rated every material honestly (not counting the one female who did not rate any materials). Fifteen voted dishonestly on more than half the time and 4 (all males) of them voted dishonestly every time. Interestingly, female students were significantly more likely to rate honestly: Out of nine females who rated items, six (67%) rated all materials honestly while only six males (27%) rated all honestly.

Although one might expect the students who made dishonest ratings to trust the ratings less, the opposite was actually true. It was the honest raters who claimed not to be greatly influenced by the ratings and dishonest ones who claimed to follow them (Table 1).

Dishonest votes did not necessarily distort the ratings quite as much as may first appear. Fifty-three (all positive) of the 73 dishonest votes were given according to the existing votes; on average, the materials already had 4.38 positive votes (STDEV 3.00) when the dishonest vote was given. Although two of these materials had a negative vote each, the ratio was nevertheless overwhelmingly positive in both cases (7/8 in both). The motivation seems to have been fulfilling the requirement rather than maliciousness.

Only in two cases were the votes given against the existing votes (once a positive vote to a material with a negative vote and once vice versa). The last 18 dishonest votes were given to materials that had no prior votes. These 20 votes can be seen as hurting the system's reliability to a larger degree. Thus, 11% of all votes were malicious from the system viewpoint even if not necessarily given with malicious intent.

There seems to be only two ways to tell dishonest votes from honest ones. One is obviously checking if the voter has viewed the material. While a relatively reliable way (minus the links

*Table 1. The effect of ratings by honesty level (the 23 students who filled out the questionnaire)*

| | | **How much rating influenced which ones read** | | | | | |
|---|---|---|---|---|---|---|---|
| **Honesty level** | | *Not at all* | *Not much* | *No opinion* | *Much* | *Very much* | **Total** |
| | *100% dishonest* | | | 1 | 2 | 1 | **4** |
| | *More than 50% dishonest* | | 2 | | 2 | 2 | **6** |
| | *Less than 50% dishonest* | | 1 | 2 | | | **3** |
| | *Honest* | 2 | 5 | | 3 | | **10** |
| | **Total** | **2** | **8** | **3** | **7** | **3** | **23** |

in the lecture slides), this nevertheless leads to a question of how to deal with such votes. If the vote is not displayed as given, the student may conclude that the system does not work. On the other hand, if the student is for instance directed to read the material before rating it (i.e. told the reason why the vote was not recorded), the student may simply learn how to game the system.

The other is to check the time difference between the current and the previous rating during the session. Students did most of their ratings during (on average) two sessions (STDEV 1.26; MAX: 6). When a dishonest vote was given, the time period from the previous vote was typically short. The shortest time between two honest votes was 14 seconds (average 3 min 40 sec with one outlier—over 27 minutes—removed) while the time between over half of the dishonest votes was less than 14 seconds (average 26 seconds with one outlier removed). Thus, over half of the dishonest votes in this sample could have been recognized with this simple measure.

Still, we face the question of what to do if dishonest voting is discovered. It is likely that compulsoriness of voting at least partially caused the large number of dishonest votes and so, if compulsoriness is used to make sure that enough votes are given, the issue needs to be confronted.

One way could be to present the rating indirectly in the interface, for instance gathering votes on one scale and showing them on another (e.g. have ratings done on binary scale and show them on five-star scale). This would allow weighting votes. Votes given without viewing the material could be nullified and votes given very fast after the previous rating, previous action, or opening the material could be weighted down in the final rating shown to students. If the student at the time of rating were told that the rating succeeded and the rating on the interface were updated to reflect the student's vote at face value, the student would be none the wise. In subsequent visits, the student would not notice the weighting as they could not know how many other students had rated the item afterwards. While this would not solve the original problem of dishonest voting, it would reduce its impact.

Naturally, there are many more complex approaches to reduce the effect of shilling in CF recommenders (e.g. Weng, Miao & Goh, 2005)—even if none of them works in all situations (Lam & Riedl, 2004; Weng et al., 2005)—but here we are interested in using ratings themselves as a recommender in e-learning setting. Also, the intent behind shilling in e-commerce is typically to gain advantage one way or another (e.g. promote own product or demote competing product) (Lam & Riedl, 2004) while here we are quintessentially dealing with self-professed laziness and lack of time as likely motivations for dishonest ratings.

## Commenting Materials

Ten materials were commented with altogether fifteen comments. Two materials had three comments, one had two and seven had one. Five comments were entered by the lecturer who signed his comments with his initial and ten were by seven students (one entered four, others one) who did not sign their comments in any way. Although few in number, the comments were viewed 134 times by 24 students (average per student who viewed comments 5.6; STDEV 4.5; MAX 15). Considering that the 52 materials had 221 views, the number of views for comments shows that what others said interested students.

Commenting was also viewed very positively, with fifteen students seeing it as *good* (14) or *very good* (1) and eight having no opinion. Again, nobody considered it *bad* or *very bad*. Many students in their questionnaire replies lamented the low number of comments while simultaneously admitting that they themselves did not contribute much, either. The importance of comments is underlined by the fact that when comparing the views for commented materials and the views for their comments, in all but one case the comments had received more views than the material itself after the addition of the first comment. The one exception is due to the fact that neither the comment nor the material was viewed after the commenting which took place at the end of the course.

The comments were on average 28 words (218 characters with white spaces excluded) long. Students' comments were typically shorter (on average 17 words/118 characters) than the lecturer's (on average 50 words/419 characters). The comments by students tended to express one idea about the material (e.g. the material helps with font problems or that the material gives information on interviewing). Only one student commented his own material while the lecturer commented three of his, twice in response to a student comment and once to give additional links on the topic. Only two comments were negative in content, one by student (link not working with Linux) and one by the lecturer (material title not corresponding to its content), and neither harshly so. Student comments did not bring forth conflicting viewpoints or problems in the material but tended to express approval.

In the questionnaire replies many students wished that the person adding a material or rating a material would have introduced the material (no student did) or discussed the reasons for the rating (one student did once). Four students even suggested making such commenting compulsory. At the same time, the selfsame people admitted not having done so themselves.

Only the lecturer responded to comments by others, as students even when commenting an already commented material simply said what they had in mind without referring to the previous comment(s). Thus, no actual discussions developed.

Students felt that comments effected what they viewed only slightly: Only three considered their influence *much*, four had no opinion, and sixteen claimed that their effect was *not much* (8) or *not at all* (8). Nevertheless, the correlation between the number of comments materials had and the number of students who viewed the material was statistically significant ($r(n=52)=0.688, p<0.000$). The correlation is even higher than that of *useful* votes if calculated only for the materials that had at least one comment ($r(n=10)=0.871, p=0.001$). Moreover, in over half the cases when a commented material was viewed, students viewed the comment(s) before viewing the material.

Not surprisingly, the correlation between the number *useful* votes and comments was also statistically significant ($r(n=52)=0.528$, $p<0.000$). Thus, commented materials typically had more *useful* votes on average (7) than non-commented materials (2.6) and more students viewed them on average (8) than non-commented materials (2.9), meaning that these materials were of special interest to students, be it due to the comments and *useful* votes or some other factor, such as title.

In fact, the best correlation between number of students who viewed a material and *useful* votes and comments was when the number of comments was weighted by multiplying it by 3 and added to the number of *useful* votes (both negative and positive). The correlation then reaches $r(n=52)=0.871$ ($p<0.000$). Thus, the number of *useful* votes and comments did tend to go hand in hand with the number of students who viewed the material, and if we try to use the number of votes and comments to explain the number of viewers, the comments appear to have a stronger explanatory power. However, as mentioned, causality has not been established in this study. Still, the correlations are so strong that the potential causality should be studied in the future.

There was no dishonesty in commenting; all students who commented a material had viewed it. This may be due to the fact that it is harder to cheat in commenting than in rating. Also, since commenting was not compulsory, there was little motivation for dishonesty.

## Eliciting Contributions with Compulsoriness

As seen, compulsory contributing increased the number of contributions significantly in comparison to 2007 and 2008 when contributing was voluntary, underlining the fact that providing tools alone is not enough (Neumann, 2007). However, the increase appears to have come at the cost of quality, given the number of dishonest votes. In contrast, commenting was voluntary and no material was commented without viewing it.

Compulsory ratings were meant to serve two purposes, 1) to encourage students to read additional materials, and 2) to allow the student community to determine what were the most pertinent materials to direct reading efforts to the best materials. As the system did not record right-clicking before 2009, we cannot compare the viewing rates with those of the previous two years. On the other hand, we do know that in 2008, the 44 students visited the LSRM page 1009 times while in 2009, 32 students visited it 779 times. Thus, on average in 2008 each student visited the LSRM page 22.9 times and in 2009, 28.3 times. Thus, per student average had increased by 19%. Compared to 2007 (when contributions were non-anonymous), the increase was 33.2%. While these are indirect measures and not too much emphasis should be placed on them, it appears that the first purpose may have been served to some extent. Some student comments also supported the idea that the first purpose was served at least to some degree: "*At least [compulsory ratings] forced me to read some articles and learn something.*"

Evaluating the successfulness of the second purpose is more problematic. On one hand, students saw the rating feature positively, felt that there were enough ratings, and almost half felt that it had affected which materials they read (and may have affected others, too, considering the correlations). On the other hand, since a large number of evaluations were dishonest, their value has to be questioned. While materials having numerous positive votes may have encouraged more students to read them (thus, serving the first purpose), as the results by Cosley et al. (2003) also imply, the materials read may not in fact have been the most pertinent ones.

Free-riding, i.e. using without contributing, is a common problem in RS (Neumann, 2007) and in fact affects many types of online communities. For instance, in peer-to-peer networks, large majority of users are free-riders with the top few percentage making disproportionate contributions (Feldman & Chuang, 2005). If most users in fact gravitate towards not contributing, forcing them to contribute may simply be a recipe for disaster. On the other hand, the more contributing users, the more useful RS tend to be (Neumann, 2007). Moreover, in many e-learning settings, large participation is a goal onto itself due to pedagogical considerations. Whether the approach of obligating all users to contribute in e-learning settings is viable remains an open question.

In the questionnaire replies, several students mentioned lack of time as a reason for making few contributions (especially beyond the compulsory), and some even stated that increasing the numbers of required contributions would be the only way to motivate them to contribute more.

As discussed, since over 70% of the dishonest votes were path-dependent, i.e. followed the previous votes, maliciousness does not seem to have been a motivating factor in much of the dishonest voting. In contrast, one student (ratings 70% dishonest, voted dishonestly against previous rating once, and made three dishonest first ratings) did admit having if not malicious then at least somewhat asocial motivations: "*I think I just wanted to fuck with some lousy comment and that's why I was an asshole about it.*" Thus, while apparently a small minority, some students' behavior may have been affected by more unpleasant motivations than just trying to get points without having to work for them.

Still, no student complained about having to add one material or rate five of them and some even suggested that compulsoriness should be extended so that ratings and material additions would need to be explained in comments. Furthermore, the compulsory adding of one material did not lead to low-quality contributions, as discussed. In fact, some even saw it as motivating, e.g. "*The possibility of adding materials was a good feature, because it motivated me to search for articles and, what's more, good articles, so that they'd be useful for others*" and "*I read materials added by others more actively since I had to add something myself, too.*" As compulsory adding of one material was also meant to get students to read more and make high-quality papers available to the community, compulsoriness there seems to have worked with fewer complications than in compulsory ratings. The reason may be that adding a material requires some investment of effort even if done carelessly (e.g. quick Google search and adding the first somewhat suitable material) and others can judge the contribution easily. Perhaps the problem with ratings was simply that cheating was too easy and the possibility of getting caught seemed minimal.

Interestingly, more students commented materials in 2009 (6 out of 32) than in 2008 (1 out of 44) or in 2007 (zero out of 45) even though it continued to be voluntary. While no hard conclusions can be drawn, it may be that increased compulsory activity also tends to leads to increased voluntary activity. Activating contributions more widely in a system with limited and selected compulsoriness is an interesting possibility that should be studied in the future, as that would work especially well in e-learning contexts where some compulsoriness can be a natural part of the course work.

In summary, using compulsoriness is not resented at least when used judiciously and it can help increase numbers of contribution to help make RS produce value in e-learning context. However, compulsoriness leads easily to large numbers of dishonest contributions, thus countermanding some of the benefits it brings. This has to be taken into consideration in e-learning when designing RS and deciding the level of compulsoriness to be used. While we feel that in case of LSRM, the benefits of compulsoriness did exceed problems in 2009, in part because most dishonest votes were path-dependant and many positive votes encouraging reading, the balance can be delicate.

## Social Presence

Recommender features can induce perceived social presence in e-commerce although different interface cues and textures induce different levels of perceived social presence in different users (Leino & Räihä, 2008). Perceived social presence both influences behavior and increases the number of contributions (Leino & Räihä, 2008; Nov & Ye, 2010).

While students were not directly asked about social presence in the questionnaire, some of the replies show a clear perception of others in the system and that this influenced behavior, e.g.

- "*On the other hand, I also wanted to read some materials that nobody had rated ... because I wanted that the person who had added the material would get at least some feedback for their work.*"
- "*I tried to read the materials carefully so that I could rate them (useful/useless) properly.*"
- "*Perhaps I was also a bit nervous about how others would see my comments.*"

Between the lines of many replies it shows that many students wanted to be responsible members of the community and considered other users in the system. Consequently, while it is hard to say if the perceived social presence increased the number of contributions in LSRM, it seems evident that at least for some students, it influenced their behavior positively, notwithstanding the dishonest votes and one student's self-professed misbehavior discussed above.

On the other hand, as the quote from the student worried about how others may perceive her comment shows, social presence may also have negative impact on more reserved students' willingness to participate, and consequently allowing anonymity or similar measures may be advisable.

Furthermore, the questionnaire comments show that recommenders function as social presence cues in two ways, first by showing cues of other users in the system and second by allowing participation and interaction, as some students mentioned: "*Possibility of commenting increases interaction*" and "*I felt that I could influence things.*" This supports the earlier suggestion that some compulsory activity to create an active environment (i.e. interface cues showing that others have contributed) may encourage further participation and contributing. Thus, social presence and active-looking environment together with some compulsory participation may lead to increased contributions.

## Overall Evaluation of LSRM

Overall, LSRM was a success from the student viewpoint, a central aspect in evaluating learning (López-Pérez et al., 2011). Students saw LSRM in positive light, considered the added materials good, liked the rating feature and almost half felt that ratings had clearly influenced their behavior, and they felt that the commenting feature was good but regrettably underused.

In addition, some students mentioned that the recommenders made the otherwise "*lifeless link-list*" more "*living*" and "*interesting.*" This is very significant, as the more fun and pleasant using a system is, the more it gets used (Harper et al., 2005, McNee et al., 2006). From the user experience viewpoint, then, the system was a success.

From the pedagogical viewpoint, too, the system faired reasonably well, as it appears to have encouraged reading materials. In a case study of a collaborative learning environment EDUCO, Ruohotie & Nokelainen (2003) found the number of documents viewed to the only viable indicator of the examination grade. In LSRM study, the correlation between students' total number of views (lecture slides, materials and comments) and the grade was statistically significant ($r(n=32)=0.442$, $p<0.05$). As there was no examination and all weekly assignments and the design assignment were done and graded as small groups with extra points for attendance constituting the only individual part of the grade, only in one small group all members did not get the same grade. Consequently, the correlation may be stronger than evident from the $r$ value, as some students are likely to have gotten higher than strictly speaking reserved grade, thus lowering the correlation. (As correlation can go both ways, it would be simplistic to take the correlation here to mean that more viewing resulted in better grade, as more conscientious students may have both worked harder on the assignments and read more additional readings etc.)

However, focusing solely on the grade fails to evaluate other skills and competences that may have been acquired (López-Pérez et al., 2011), such as improved information literacy due to having had to locate, select and evaluate materials (Kiliç-Çakmak, 2010) and getting feedback on the materials added from other students. As information literacy is the basis for lifelong learning and in higher education teaching should be arranged so as to allow students to acquire such skills (Kiliç-Çakmak, 2010), this aspect of LSRM should not be overlooked.

Also, final grade does not necessarily tell how much of the skill or knowledge is due to learning in a course and how much is based on prior skills and knowledge, as the starting point is typically not measured, only the end point. In fact, prior knowledge, in addition to class attendance and age, strongly determines the end-grade (López-Pérez et al., 2011).

López-Pérez et al. (2011) found that students' subjective perceptions and objective results (typically grade) are associated and that subjective can be used as a proxy for the objective. As students evaluated both LSRM and the course positively (in course feedback, 81% of the students were *satisfied* or *highly satisfied* with the course), we can extrapolate that learning took place both overall and in LSRM. In general, blended learning approach used here has been found to have positive effects on learning and learning experience, to reduce drop-out rates, and increase motivation (López-Pérez et al., 2011).

Judging LSRM for recommendation quality is more problematic. Bringing high-quality materials in from the Internet appears quite successful, as student considered the added materials good and many times could not tell apart the materials added by fellow students from those added by the lecturer. Commenting feature, even if underused, also appears to have served its function reasonably well. The most obvious problem lies in the large number of dishonest ratings. While the dishonest ratings may not have made the ratings useless—after all, positive ratings were repeatedly mentioned as attracting attention and resulting in reading in questionnaire comments—their high number does mean that the ratings did not necessarily attract students to the most pertinent material. In other words, students did read materials due to them but not necessarily the best materials.

Consequently, the rating recommender needs to be made robust against dishonest voting in e-learning. This study underlines that especially when students stand to gain something from making contributions (be it gaining extra points or avoiding losing points), a possibility of dishonest contributions exists and perhaps also a possibility of lower-quality contributions for instance in case of reviews. Thus, we need to be able to recognize dishonest contributions as such with high-enough accuracy and have appropriate ways to deal with them.

Furthermore, while in e-commerce, the motivation—and often the basis for recognizing the attack—is often either promoting (own) products or demoting (competing) products, in e-learning the motivation may often have nothing to do with promoting or demoting items but to get activity points. Thus, dishonest behavior may simply take the form of following the opinion of others, as it did in this case study with over 70% of dishonest votes following the current rating. This is very different behavior from what e-commerce RS typically guard against, and thus hardening e-learning recommenders against dishonest contributions may prove to be another ballgame altogether.

## FUTURE RESEARCH DIRECTIONS

Different e-learning contexts set different requirements for utilizing RS. For example, using RS to support formal learning in top-down learning management systems and to support informal learning in bottom-up learning networks represent vastly different contextual challenges. No one recommender approach will suffice and the research will also have to reflect this multiplicity.

In particular, the findings here encourage not limiting our thinking of RS only to such algorithmic approaches as CF, especially as user modeling in at least some e-learning contexts can be challenging (Granić & Adams, 2010). This case study underlines the viability of harnessing the collective intelligence of a learner community for providing and peer-reviewing learning resources. As students are already widely using online resources to support their learning and are ready to share these (Hage & Aïmeur, 2008), further studies to uncover the full potential of such recommendation approaches are necessary. However, the study also shows that dishonest contributions are not a rare exception. Consequently, we also need to study how to minimize the number and effect of dishonest contributions in e-learning RS.

Motivating contributions, here elicited with compulsoriness, also need to be studied further. In particular, social presence appears to both motivate contributing and induce social behavior (Leino & Räihä, 2008; Nov & Ye, 2010). As the results of this study also point to that direction, studying how to induce and use perceived social presence in e-learning appears to be a fruitful area of further study.

Also, using selective compulsoriness to elicit contributions should be studied further, as there were hints of compulsory contributing increasing contributing also in non-compulsory areas. As certain amount of compulsoriness is a natural part of e-learning at least in formal settings, understanding how to best use selective compulsoriness deserves a further look.

## CONCLUSION

LSRM enabled students to add materials to lectures to augment those added by the course instructors and then rate and comment the materials added. Students were required to add one material and rate five while commenting was voluntary. Based on student feedback, the system worked well. The individual features were seen in positive light as was the whole system, and students largely found ratings useful in selecting materials for reading. Importantly, compulsoriness was not resented and it increased the number of ratings to be high enough for students to perceive the system as useful. Indeed, some students suggested applying compulsoriness also to commenting.

Furthermore, many student replies in the questionnaire showed that others were perceived to be socially present in the system and that this affected behavior positively. Some students described how they wanted to read unrated materials to give feedback for the person who had added it and how they wanted to find and add materials that were useful for others.

As more students wrote comments in 2009 than before, it may be that compulsory activity leads to increasing activity also in non-compulsory areas. If further studies prove this to be the case, then judicious compulsoriness on contributions that are hard to do dishonestly without appearing as such to other users may solve some of the problems that compulsoriness created in this study.

The biggest problem in the current system was dishonest ratings, i.e. ratings made without viewing the material rated. While we discussed some means of recognizing dishonest votes, we did not manage to uncover any kind of a profile for dishonest users. In addition, recognizing the dishonest votes is not enough, because if the voter is told that they need to read the material first, they simply learn to game the system. One possible solution is abstracting the interface presentation of the rating, for instance by collecting ratings on one scale and presenting them on another. This way the dishonest voter cannot easily learn that the system was wise to him, especially if the immediate impact on the existing rating is given at face value to the voter and then subsequently the dishonest votes are eliminated or weighted down according to their likelihood of being dishonest.

However, while the above may solve the problem at least partially in LSRM, more generally the problem of dishonest votes points to the fact that in e-learners have different motives for dishonest contributions than users in e-commerce. Instead of trying to promote or demote items, e-learners may simply be trying to get activity points or avoid being penalized for lack of contributions. This type of dishonesty at least in this case study meant that many dishonest votes followed the existing rating and were probably not maliciously motivated. E-learning RS may need to be robust in different ways from those in e-commerce.

The lessons learned here may be applied in any e-learning setting where using CF approach to recommending is impossible and not all items, be they readings, postings, or suggestions, need to be viewed by all learners but the best ones should be. Using a community to find items and peer-review them seems a viable approach to e-learning but it is not without its challenges that future research needs to address.

Next to more theoretical work, including laboratory experiments and survey studies, we also need actual experiences of using RS in e-learning to better augment the e-learning process on the learners' terms to create an engaging e-learning experience. This case study is a step to that direction.

## REFERENCES

Amatriain, X., Pujol, J. M., Tintarev, N., & Oliver, N. (2009). Rate it again: Increasing recommendation accuracy by user re-rating. In *Proceedings of the Third ACM Conference on Recommender Systems* (pp. 173-180). New York, NY: ACM.

Cena, F., Vernero, F., & Gena, C. (2010). Towards a customization of rating scales in adaptive systems. In De Bra, P., Kobsa, A., & Chin, D. N. (Eds.), *Lecture Notes in Computer Science 6075* (pp. 369–374). Berlin, Germany: Springer.

Chevalier, J. A., & Mayzlin, D. (2006). The effect of word of mouth on sales: Online book reviews. *JMR, Journal of Marketing Research, 42*, 345–354. doi:10.1509/jmkr.43.3.345

Cosley, D., Lam, S. K., Albert, I., Konstan, J. A., & Riedl, J. (2003). Is seeing believing? How recommender system interfaces affect users' opinions. In *Proceedings of the SIGCHI Conference on Human Factors in Computing Systems* (pp. 585-592). New York, NY: ACM.

Drachsler, H., Hummel, H. G. K., & Koper, R. (2009). Identifying the goal, user model and conditions of recommender systems for formal and informal learning. *Journal of Digital Information, 10*(2), 4–24.

Feldman, M., & Chuang, J. (2005). Overcoming free-riding behavior in peer-to-peer systems. *SIGecom Exchanges, 5*(4), 41–50. doi:10.1145/1120717.1120723

Gadanho, S. C., & Lhuillier, N. (2007). Addressing uncertainty in implicit preferences. In *Proceedings of the 2007 ACM Conference on Recommender Systems* (pp. 97-104). New York, NY: ACM.

Garrison, D. R., & Kanuka, H. (2004). Blended learning: Uncovering its transformative potential in higher education. *The Internet and Higher Education, 7*, 95–105. doi:10.1016/j.iheduc.2004.02.001

Ghauth, K. I., & Abdullah, N. A. (2010). Learning materials recommendation using good learners ratings and content-based filtering. *Journal of Educational Technology Research and Development, 58*(6), 711–727. doi:10.1007/s11423-010-9155-4

Granić, A., & Adams, R. (2010). User sensitive research in e-learning: Exploring the role of individual user characteristics. *Universal Access in the Information Society, 10*(3). Retrieved September 30, 2010, from DOI: 10.1007/s10209-010-0207-7

Hage, H., & Aïmeur, E. (2008). Harnessing learner's collective intelligence: A Web2.0 approach to e-learning. In B. P. Woolf, E. Aïmeur, R. Nkambou & Lajoie (Eds.), *Lecture Notes in Computer Science 5091* (pp. 438-447). Berlin, Germany: Springer-Verlag.

Harper, F., Li, X., Chen, Y., & Konstan, J. (2005). An economic model of user rating in an online recommender system. In *Proceedings of the 10th International Conference on User Modeling* (pp. 307-216).

Hennig-Thurau, T., Gwinner, K. P., Walsh, G., & Gremler, D. D. (2004). Electronic word-of-mouth via consumer-opinion platforms: What motivates consumers to articulate themselves on the Internet? *Journal of Interactive Marketing, 18*(1), 38–52. doi:10.1002/dir.10073

Herlocker, J. L., Konstan, J. A., Terveen, L. G., & Riedl, J. T. (2004). Evaluating collaborative filtering recommender systems. *ACM Transactions on Information Systems, 22*(1), 5–53. doi:10.1145/963770.963772

Hu, N., Pavlou, P. A., & Zhang, J. (2006). Can online reviews reveal a product's true quality?: Empirical findings and analytical modeling of online word-of-mouth communication. In *Proceedings of the 7th ACM Conference on Electronic Commerce*. (pp. 324-330).

Kiliç-Çakmak, E. (2010). Learning strategies and motivational factors predicting information literacy self-efficacy of e-learners. *Australasian Journal of Educational Technology, 26*(2), 192–208.

Lam, S. K., & Riedl, J. 2004. Shilling recommender systems for fun and profit. In *Proceedings of the 13th International Conference on World Wide Web* (pp. 393-402). New York, NY: ACM.

Lang, J., Spear, M., & Wu, S. F. (2010). Social manipulation of online recommender systems. In In L. Bolc, M. Makowski, & A. Wierzbicki (Eds.), *Lecture Notes in Computer Science 6430* (pp. 125-139). Berlin, Germany: Springer.

Leino, J. (in press). Case study: Recommending course reading materials in a small virtual learning community. *International Journal of Web Based Communities, 6*(4).

Leino, J., & Räihä, K.-J. (2007). Case Amazon: Ratings and reviews as part of recommendations. In *Proceedings of the 2007 ACM Conference on Recommender Systems* (pp. 137-140). New York, NY: ACM.

Leino, J., & Räihä, K.-J. (2008). User experiences and impressions of recommenders in complex information environments. *A Quarterly Bulletin of the Computer Society of the IEEE Technical Committee on Data Engineering, 31*(2), 32–39.

López-Pérez, M. V., Pérez-López, M. C., & Rodríguez-Ariza, L. (2011). Blended learning in higher education: Students' perceptions and their relation to outcomes. *Computers & Education, 56*, 818–826. doi:10.1016/j.compedu.2010.10.023

Manouselis, N., Drachsler, H., Vuorikari, R., Hummel, H. G. K., & Koper, R. (2011). Recommender systems in technology enhanced learning. In Kantor, P. B., Ricci, F., Rokach, L., & Shapira, B. (Eds.), *Recommender systems handbook* (pp. 387–415). Berlin, Germany: Springer. doi:10.1007/978-0-387-85820-3_12

McNee, S. M., Riedl, J., & Konstan, J. A. (2006). Being accurate is not enough: How accuracy metrics have hurt recommender systems. In *CHI '06 Extended Abstracts on Human Factors in Computing Systems* (pp. 1097-1101). New York, NY: ACM.

Neumann, A. W. (2007). Motivating and supporting user interaction with recommender systems. In L. Kovács, N. Fuhr, & C. Meghini (Eds.), *Proceedings of the 11th European Conference on Research and Advanced Technology for Digital Libraries* (pp. 428-439). Berlin, Germany: Springer.

Nov, O., & Ye, C. (2010). Why do people tag? Motivations for photo tagging. *Communications of the ACM, 53*(7), 128–131. doi:10.1145/1785414.1785450

Rienties, B., Tempelaar, D., Van den Bossche, P., Gijselaers, W., & Segers, M. (2009). The role of academic motivation in computer-supported collaborative learning. *Computers in Human Behavior, 25*, 1195–1206. doi:10.1016/j.chb.2009.05.012

Ruohotie, P., & Nokelainen, P. (2003). Practical considerations of motivation and computer-supported collaborative learning. In Varis, T., Utsumi, T., & Klemm, W. R. (Eds.), *Global peace through the global university system* (pp. 226–236). Hämeenlinna, Finland: University of Tampere.

Santos, O. C., & Boticario, J. G. (2008). Users' experience with a recommender system in an open source standard-based learning management system. In Holzinger, A. (Ed.), *Lecture Notes in Computer Science 5298* (pp. 185–204). Berlin, Germany: Springer-Verlag.

Santos, O. C., & Boticario, J. G. (2010). Modeling recommendations for the educational domain. *Procedia Computer Science, 1*(2), 2793–2800. doi:10.1016/j.procs.2010.08.004

Schafer, J. B., Konstan, J., & Riedl, J. (1999). Recommender systems in e-commerce. In *Proceedings of the 1st ACM Conference on Electronic Commerce* (pp. 158-166). New York, NY: ACM.

Stefani, A., Vassiliadis, B., & Xenos, M. (2006). Behavioral patterns in hypermedia systems: A short study of e-commerce vs. e-learning practices. In Sirmakesis, S. (Ed.), *Adaptive and personalized Semantic Web* (pp. 57–64). Berlin, Germany: Springer. doi:10.1007/3-540-33279-0_4

Talwar, A., Jurca, R., & Faltings, B. (2007). Understanding user behavior in online feedback reporting. In *Proceedings of the 8th ACM Conference on Electronic Commerce* (pp. 134-142). New York, NY: ACM.

Tang, T., & McCalla, G. (2004a). Beyond learners' interest: Personalized paper recommendation based on their pedagogical features for an e-learning system. [Berlin, Germany: Springer.]. *Lecture Notes in Computer Science, 3157*, 301–310. doi:10.1007/978-3-540-28633-2_33

Tang, T., & McCalla, G. (2004b). Utilizing artificial learners to help overcome the cold-start problem in a pedagogically oriented paper recommendation system. [Berlin, Germany: Springer.]. *Lecture Notes in Computer Science, 3137*, 245–254. doi:10.1007/978-3-540-27780-4_28

Weng, J., Miao, C., & Goh, A. (2005). Protecting online rating systems from unfair ratings. In Katsikas, S. K., Lopez, J., & Pernul, G. (Eds.), *Lecture Notes in Computer Science 3592* (pp. 50–59). Berlin, Germany: Springer.

## ADDITIONAL READING

Chevalier, J. A., & Mayzlin, D. (2006). The Effect of Word of Mouth on Sales: Online Book Reviews. *JMR, Journal of Marketing Research, 42*, 345–354. doi:10.1509/jmkr.43.3.345

Cosley, D., Frankowski, D., Kiesler, S., Terveen, L., & Riedl, J. 2005. How oversight improves member-maintained communities. In *Proceedings of the SIGCHI conference on Human Factors in Computing Systems* (pp. 11-20). New York, NY: ACM.

Cosley, D., Lam, S. K., Albert, I., Konstan, J. A., & Riedl, J. 2003. Is seeing believing?: how recommender system interfaces affect users' opinions. In *Proceedings of the SIGCHI Conference on Human Factors in Computing Systems* (pp. 585-592). New York, NY: ACM.

Hage, H., & Aïmeur, E. (2008). Harnessing learner's collective intelligence: A Web2.0 approach to e-learning. In B. P. Woolf, E. Aïmeur, R. Nkambou & Lajoie (Eds.), *Lecture Notes in Computer Science 5091* (pp. 438-447). Berlin, Germany: Springer-Verlag.

Hennig-Thurau, T., Gwinner, K. P., Walsh, G., & Gremler, D. D. (2004). Electronic word-of-mouth via consumer-opinion platforms: What motivates consumers to articulate themselves on the Internet? *Journal of Interactive Marketing, 18*(1), 38–52. doi:10.1002/dir.10073

Herlocker, J. L., Konstan, J. A., Terveen, L. G., & Riedl, J. T. (2004). Evaluating collaborative filtering recommender systems. *ACM Transactions on Information Systems, 22*(1), 5–53. doi:10.1145/963770.963772

Hu, N., Pavlou, P. A., & Zhang, J. (2006). Can online reviews reveal a product's true quality?: empirical findings and analytical modeling of online word-of-mouth communication. In *Proceedings of the 7th ACM conference on Electronic Commerce*. (pp. 324-330).

Leino, J. (*in press*). Case study: Recommending course reading materials in a small virtual learning community. *International Journal of Web Based Communities, 6*(4).

Leino, J., & Räihä, K.-J. (2007). Case Amazon: Ratings and reviews as part of recommendations. In *Proceedings of the 2007 ACM Conference on Recommender Systems* (pp. 137-140). New York, NY: ACM.

Leino, J., & Räihä, K.-J. (2008). User experiences and impressions of recommenders in complex information environments. *A Quarterly Bulletin of the Computer Society of the IEEE Technical Committee on Data Engineering, 31*(2), 32–39.

López-Pérez, M. V., Pérez-López, M. C., & Rodríguez-Ariza, L. (2011). Blended learning in higher education: Students' perceptions and their relation to outcomes. *Computers & Education, 56*, 818–826. doi:10.1016/j.compedu.2010.10.023

McNee, S. M., Riedl, J., & Konstan, J. A. (2006). Being accurate is not enough: how accuracy metrics have hurt recommender systems. In *CHI '06 Extended Abstracts on Human Factors in Computing Systems* (pp. 1097-1101). New York, NY: ACM.

Neumann, A. W. (2007). Motivating and Supporting User Interaction with Recommender Systems. In L. Kovács, N. Fuhr, and C. Meghini (Eds.), *Proceedings of the 11th European Conference on Research and Advanced Technology for Digital Libraries* (pp. 428-439). Berlin, Germany: Springer.

Santos, O. C., & Boticario, J. G. (2010). Modeling recommendations for the educational domain. *Procedia Computer Science, 1*(2), 2793–2800. doi:10.1016/j.procs.2010.08.004

Schafer, J. B., Konstan, J., & Riedl, J. (1999). Recommender systems in e-commerce. In *Proceedings of the 1st ACM Conference on Electronic commerce* (pp. 158-166). New York, NY: ACM.

Talwar, A., Jurca, R., & Faltings, B. (2007). Understanding user behavior in online feedback reporting. In *Proceedings of the 8th ACM conference on Electronic commerce* (pp. 134-142). New York, NY: ACM.

Tang, T., & McCalla, G. (2004a). Beyond learners' interest: Personalized paper recommendation based on their pedagogical features for an e-learning system. [Berlin, Germany: Springer.]. *Lecture Notes in Computer Science, 3157*, 301–310. doi:10.1007/978-3-540-28633-2_33

## KEY TERMS AND DEFINITIONS

**Comment:** Here a textual remark or observation concerning a reading material.

**Community:** A group of people somehow tied together by a common interest or some other factor temporarily or permanently (here a group of students taking a course for the duration of the course).

**Rating:** A grade or rank that may be given for items on various scales (here binary *Useful/Not useful*).

**Reading Material:** Here any potential learning resource available on the Internet, be it video, text document, or audio recording.

**Recommender:** A system that facilitates recommending.

**Recommending:** An explicit or implicit act of presenting something as worthy or unworthy of some action or consideration.

**Social Presence:** A sense of somebody being present in a system (synchronously or asynchronously).

Section 4
# Challenges for Educational Recommender Systems

# Chapter 12
# Challenges to Use Recommender Systems to Enhance Meta-Cognitive Functioning in Online Learners

**Mingming Zhou**
*Nanyang Technological University, Singapore*

**Yabo Xu**
*Sun Yet-sen University, P. R. China*

## ABSTRACT

*A wealth of research has shown that meta-cognition plays a crucial role in the promotion of effective school learning. In most of the e-learning environment designs, however, meta-cognitive strategies have generally been neglected, and therefore, satisfactory uses of these strategies have rarely been realized. Most learners are not even aware of what they have been studying. If the learning system could automatically guide and intelligently recommend learning activities or strategies to facilitate student monitoring and control of their learning, it would favor and improve their learning process and performance. Unfortunately, nearly no e-learning systems to date have attempted to do so. In this chapter, we first described the need for enhancing meta-cognitive skills in e-learning environment, followed by an outline of major challenges for meta-cognitive activity recommendations. We then proposed to adopt data mining algorithms (i.e., content-based and sequence-based recommendation techniques) to meet the identified issues with a toy example.*

DOI: 10.4018/978-1-61350-489-5.ch012

## INTRODUCTION

A wealth of research has shown that meta-cognition plays a crucial role in the promotion of effective school learning and the improvement of ill-structured learning (Loizidou & Koutselini, 2007). We are pursuing a vision of learning in which students constantly engage in effective, efficient and fruitful learning. To achieve this vision, developing meta-cognitive expertise is crucial (White & Frederiksen, 2005) in fostering an individual's awareness of different cognitive, social, emotional, and meta-cognitive capabilities that are needed, knowledge of when and why they are useful, as well as development of regulatory skills, such as planning, monitoring, and reflecting.

In most of the e-learning environment designs, however, meta-cognitive strategies have generally been neglected and therefore satisfactory uses of these strategies have rarely been realized. Most learners are not even aware of what they have been studying (Kurt, 2007). Even when students monitor their learning, there is a broad theoretical notion that students experience illusions of competence (Bjork, 1999; Koriat & Bjork, 2005), which leads to inaccurate judgment of their learning progresses and outcomes. For these reasons, learners need to be guided towards reflecting on their learning and improving their cognitive models of expertise. The objectives of this chapter were, thus, to specify major challenges for meta-cognitive activity recommendations in e-learning systems and exemplify how the proposed data mining algorithms meet the identified challenges.

## BACKGROUND

Strategic selections among recommended learning resources and strategic processing of the selected materials are captured by the concept of *meta-cognition*. Meta-cognition has been defined as the process of "thinking about thinking" (Flavell, 1976, p 232). It refers to higher-order mental processes involved in learning such as creating learning plans, using appropriate skills and strategies to solve a problem, making estimates of performance, and calibrating the extent of learning (Dunslosky & Thiede, 1998). Examples of meta-cognitive activities are: I am engaging in meta-cognition if I notice that I am having more trouble learning A than B; I realize that this might not be the best way to do this task as I did not see much progress after spending many hours; or it strikes me that I should double check C before deciding to use it to support my argument.

Metacognition involves students' knowledge about their own cognitive processes and efficient use of the knowledge to regulate these cognitive processes. Accordingly, researchers distinguish between meta-cognitive knowledge and meta-cognitive regulation (Schraw & Dennison, 1994). The former is comprised of declarative knowledge (knowing which learning strategies work and which ones do not work), procedural knowledge (knowing how to use learning strategies), and conditional knowledge (knowing when and why to use strategies). The latter is more concerned with meta-cognitive monitoring and control, such as planning, information management strategies, comprehension monitoring, debugging strategies, and evaluation of progress and goals. Learners make judgments of their learning to monitor their progress and make conscious decisions about learning tasks and learning strategies to control (regulate) their own learning – how to proceed the task with the material, how well the material meets the goals, when and how to adjust the way the material is being used, and so forth. These two components of meta-cognition are highly correlated with each other, so it is possible that they work in unison to enhance academic performance (Schraw & Dennison, 1994). As Schunk and Zimmerman (2006) noted, "[Meta-cognition] requires that one understands what skills, strategies, and resources are required to complete a task as well as how and when to use those skills and strategies" (p. 360). It relates a learner's knowledge of personal characteristics, knowledge of the task to be completed and knowledge of the strategies available, to those strategies used to select, execute, monitor and control tasks (Flavell, 1979).

Research studies in the past three decades have documented the significance of metacognition, noting its positive effects on students' academic and personal development. Researchers have conveyed that metacognition is vital to knowledge construction as students who are able to effectively distinguish information they know and do not know are more likely to review and retain new information (Dunning, Johnson, Ehrlinger, & Kruger, 2003; Dunslosky & Thiede, 1998; Kruger & Dunning, 1999), and students who are able to think about their own thinking can track their progress and reflect on their learning become experts. Indeed, meta-cognitively active students plan, sequence, and monitor their learning in a way that directly enhances their performance (Schraw & Dennison, 1994; Schraw & Moshman, 1995). Such strategies have been found effective in a variety of areas such as reading comprehension, writing, attention, memory, problem-solving, social cognition, and various types of self-control and self-instruction (Flavell, 1992). Nonetheless, students are not typically meta-cognitive learners. A series of symptoms have been observed in these struggling students including difficulties in judging task difficulty and planning their learning activities, goal setting, monitoring their learning, selecting effective learning strategies, help-seeking (Azevedo, 2002), to name a few, which lead to unproductive approaches to their schoolwork (Joseph, 2010). In this chapter, we particularly focus on the skills of planning learning activities such as selecting and adapting learning strategies.

## Meta-Cognition in E-Learning Systems

Since all students do not spontaneously engage in meta-cognition, explicit training and coaching are required to learn such skills (Chi, Bassok, Lewis, Reimann, & Glaser, 1989; Lin & Lehman, 1999). Indeed, meta-cognitive training, even if administered for a short time, can improve performance considerably (e.g., Nietfeld & Schraw, 2002; Thiede, Anderson, & Therriault, 2003). E-learning environments have the potential to foster students' will and skill for learning about complex topics. The use of computer-based meta-cognitive support includes training general learning ability (Derry & Murphy, 1986); tutoring help-seeking strategies (Roll, Aleven, McLaren, & Koedinger, 2007); developing self-awareness through learning by teaching (Wagster, Tan, Biswas, & Schwartz, 2008); a reflection assistant for problem-solving (Gama, 2004); and encouraging learners to develop greater awareness of cognitive and meta-cognitive learning strategies (Bull, 1997). However, research indicated that students learn little in this type of environments as they do not deploy key self-regulatory processes and mechanisms such as effective cognitive and meta-cognitive strategies during learning (e.g. Azevedo & Cromley 2004; Hadwin & Winne 2001). As a consequence, different approaches in an e-learning environment have been developed to enhance students' metacognition during learning.

A group of researchers have investigated the effectiveness of computer-based instructional environments designed to support different subsets of meta-cognitive skills. SE-COACH (Conati & VanLehn, 2000) and Geometry Cognitive Tutor (Aleven & Koedinger, 2002) scaffolded self-explanation with the assumption that students can make good judgments about the difficulty of steps, and hence allow greater understanding of the subject. In the SE-COACH, students explain the steps in worked-out examples and construct explanations of problem-solving principles using a structured interface with menus and templates. In the Geometry Cognitive Tutor, students explain their own solution steps by naming the problem-solving principles that justify the step.

Another line of research investigated the ways to encouraging students to reflect such as using prompts (e.g., Bell & Davis, 2000; Davis & Linn, 2000). There are generally two basic types of reflection prompts. *Generic prompts* ask students to "stop and think", whereas *directed prompts* direct students toward planning for future activities and monitoring their understanding. The former assumes that students need to be reminded to reflect; the latter assumes that they need guidance in identifying productive avenues for reflection. Empirical findings showed that generic prompts appeared to encourage productive activities and to foster both reflection and knowledge integration.

Kramarski and Mevarech (2003) offered a metacognitive suite in the form of scaffolding self-questioning, eliciting explanations and providing feedback. The meta-cognitive questions included: (a) comprehending the problem; (b) constructing connections between previous and new knowledge; (c) using appropriate strategies for solving the problem; and (d) reflecting on the processes and the solution. Students can then refer to these questions when they solve mathematical problems, and provide explanations during discussions led by the teacher. Last, students are prompted to explain their reasoning on the computer and receive computer-generated feedback regarding the correctness of the task solution. This approach has been found to help students access and interact with the content functionality at a deeper level, think about the steps they need to take in their work, and make their thinking become explicit.

## Meta-Cognition in Recommender Systems

The above examples exemplified the efforts that have been made in this area. In spite of this success, there is room for improvement. Beyond explicit instructions and prompts, if the e-learning system could automatically guide and intelligently recommend learning activities or strategies to facilitate student monitoring and control of their learning, it would favor and improve their learning process and performance at a greater level. This goal can be achieved in a recommender system. A recommender system is a tool that helps users to identify interesting items from a large pool of objects. It has been widely used in many commercial sites for recommending books, movies, CDs, and news articles (e.g., Linden, Smith, & York, 2003; Marlin, 2003; Melville, Mooney, & Nagarajan, 2002; Rosset, Neumann, Eick, Vatnik, and Idan, 2002).

The success of these implementations has been inspiring for e-learning researchers. Multiple efforts have been made to design educational recommendation systems to recommend quality learning resources to learners to help reduce cognitive load and improve learning efficiency (e.g., Bobadilla, Serradilla, Hernando, & MovieLens, 2009; Chen, Lee, & Chen, 2005; Ghauth & Abdullah, 2011; Kerkiri, Manitsaris, & Mavridou, 2007; Khribi, Jemni, & Nasraoui, 2009; Ge, Kong, & Luo, 2006; Liu & Shih, 2007; Romero, Ventura, Zafra, & de Bra, 2009; Soonthornphisaj, Rojsattarat, & Yim-ngam, 2006; Tai, Wu, & Li, 2008; Tang & McCalla, 2005). Nonetheless, recommended items in learning can go beyond resources. In Zaïane's (2002) work, learning actions are recommended based on the actions of previous learners. The recommendation can be an on-line activity such as an action recommendation triggered by the learner's attempt to take a test or a shortcut recommendation in a course web site based on the current sequence of activities or pages visited by the learner and the frequent sequences of visited pages or learning activities other users did in the past. In addition, Santos, Pardo and Kloos (2006), and van den Berg, et al. (2005) use swarm-based sequencing techniques to identify, process and adapt the sequencing of learning paths presented to the student towards the attainment of learning goals.

In collaborative learning environments, meta-cognitive tools are also developed to monitor the state of interaction and provide collaborators with visualizations that can be used to self-diagnose the interaction. Effective collaborative learning involves both learning to effectively collaborate, and collaborating effectively to learn (Soller, Martínez-Monés, Jermann, & Muehlenbrock, 2005). Coaching or advising systems guide the collaborators by recommending actions they could take to improve their interaction and the effectiveness of the learning process (Jermann, Soller, & Muehlenbrock, 2001). For example, Barros and Verdejo (2000) developed an asynchronous discussion forum, wherein users are required to specify the type of contribution (e.g. proposal, question, or comment) each time they add to the discussion. The system constructs interaction models using various attributes such as cooperation, creativity, the mean number of students' contributions etc. to rate the collaboration among students, and make recommendations to improve their interaction, following an "if attribute-value then message" rule. In contrast to relying on users' ability to choose the correct contribution type, other systems adopt a finite state machine approach to model and advise collaborative learners (e.g., Inaba & Okamoto, 1996; McManus & Aiken, 1995). These systems compare users' conversation act sequences to those recommended in a number of finite state machines and generate advice through consideration of the dialog state and the roles of each group member.

## CHALLENGES TO MAKE RECOMMENDATIONS FOR META-COGNITIVE ONLINE ACTIVITIES

However, learning involves more than just shifts in cognitive states embedded in a computer-based learning environment; rather, it includes an intricate and complex interaction between neural, cognitive, motivational, affective, and social processes (Azevedo, 2002). What distinguishes the recommender systems in e-commerce sites from e-learning environment is, in the latter, the strong emphasis on the context or domain they operate in, the sheer complexity of the information about the learners (users) and learning activities (items), as well as the combination of different levels of complexity for the different learning situations the learners may be involved in (Drachsler, Hummel, & Koper, 2008). Learners need to attune themselves to different requirements in various phases of a learning journey by setting goals for their learning, monitoring, regulating, and controlling their cognition, motivation, and behavior. Given such a complicated process, if we aim to enhance learners' meta-cognitive functioning via recommender systems, many challenges are to be tackled. In this paper, we chose reading comprehension as our research field as it constitutes the most common context where learning occurs and focused on learning activity recommendation to improve students' strategy regulation skills in solo learning contexts.

Learners are the core drivers of providing personalized tutoring in an e-learning system (Bull & Kay, 2008). Student learning differs because learner traits and the way they learn differ. Good learners do not employ the same strategies (Stevick, 1989). Strategy choice may depend to some extent on learning style (Ehrman & Oxford, 1990), for example. Hence, there is no single set of strategies appropriate for recommendation to all learners (Gillette, 1987). Indeed, as Oxford (1994) comments, strategy training should be somewhat individualized. Thus, the recommender systems needs to structure the recommendations tailored to individualized application of learning strategies. Similar to the user profile in common commercial recommendation systems, a learner profile is to be established in educational recommender systems. It includes two parts. One is concerned with *learner attributes*, which includes such information as demographic information, learning goals, prior knowledge level in a specific domain/topic, learning preference (e.g., visual, auditory or textual learners), interest level, past performance and etc. The other is concerned with *learning sequence*, namely, a series of learning actions learners perform in a particular order for a given task. The first challenge is thus the need to consider both learner attributes and the learning sequences during recommendations, as both jointly determine how well the learner will learn. Hence, recommendations need to be based on the characteristics of learners as well as how learners have been studying up to the point a recommendation is to be made. For instance, some activities will be necessary for novice learners which can be redundant for more advanced learners. Similarly, some activities are effective for learners who focus on mastery of the content, but might not be useful for those who simply want to achieve higher scores.

Much of the social cognitive theory and research has emphasized students' efforts to understand and manage cognitive and meta-cognitive activities central to learning (Wolters, 2003). Nonetheless, the regulation of motivation is now recognized as a key aspect of effective learning across many different models (Sansone & Thoman, 2005; Winne & Hadwin, 2008). Motivational beliefs, attitudes, and values are critical in a planning stage of learning because they influence students' goal-setting and choices regarding task engagement, strategy selection and application. More significantly, motivational processes can be monitored and can be the subject of reflection and reaction or control (Wolters, 2003). Related to the learner profiles is that one's motivation and emotion constitute a different set of attributes as compared to cognitive elements such as prior knowledge and past performance level. One's motivation and social-emotion is not constant but changes as the task unfolds. From the social cognitive point of view of learning, one's motivation, emotion and cognition are intertwined with each other and jointly affect the learning process and performance. Researchers have found that the development of one's social emotional competence is believed to enable students to acquire an ability to self-monitor their behaviors and self-regulate their learning (Zins, Weissberg, Wang, & Walberg, 2004). Given that the recommendations should correspond to learner attributes in these dimensions, the system needs to devise a mechanism to detect a learner's motivation/emotion state to better inform what learning strategies to recommend.

There is much confusion about the definition of learning strategy. This multi-level construct is defined differently in different contexts for different purposes. It has been used to refer to (1) specific learning tactics such as rehearsal, imaging, and outlining; (2) more general types of self-management activities such as planning and comprehension monitoring; and (3) complex plans that combine several specific techniques (Derry, 1988). The variety of definitions of this construct poses challenges to compile, compare, and contrast different study results. The same applies to e-learning research. The third issue to be solved is the way learning strategies are operationalized in e-learning systems. In our view, each single mouse behavior can be taken as a learning action, e.g., type a URL to view a website, click on a button to access online dictionary. However, these actions alone do not constitute a learning strategy which is supposed to be defined at a higher level by involving a series of actions in a particular order with a particular purpose. Meta-cognitive learners not only choose to engage in selected learning actions but also engage in them in a strategic way. The recommender systems thus need to be sufficiently "intelligent" to detect meaningful learning *actions* and translate them into a *strategy* in order to evaluate current learning strategy use and subsequently formulate recommendations.

This leads to the fourth challenge about the nature of items to be recommended to foster meta-cognitive functioning in online learners. Meta-cognitive regulation skills involve a variety of executive functions such as resource allocation, monitoring, checking and error detection and correction (Brown, Bransford, Ferrara, & Campione, 1983). A common pattern of poor meta-cognition in novice students is that they seize on a solution strategy and fail to ask themselves if the strategy is leading to their goal (Schoenfeld, 1987). Hattie, Biggs, and Purdie (1996) reviewed 51 studies in which interventions aimed to enhance student learning by improving student use of either one or a combination of learning or study skills. The finding points to the conclusion that study skills training ought to take place with understanding of the conditions under which the strategy works, especially when the intention is to help students understand content with a view to applying it in a new context. Beyond recommending static learning resources (e.g., materials, websites), the system needs to suggest learning activities or strategies suitable for the current task which are more complex with multiple features–key actions involved in a learning strategy, the sequence of those actions, the context of a learning strategy application, the frequency of applying a particular strategy and so forth. In this way, learners can be prompted to be more meta-cognitive during learning and able to adjust meta-cognitive strategy use as the task varies. To meet this purpose, an inventory of "good strategies" should be established and constantly adapted while the amount of user data is growing such that the system has a sufficiently comprehensive reservoir of strategies to select and recommend to different learners.

The last challenge is the basis on which a recommendation can be made. The retrieval of ratings or preferences to learning strategies/activities is usually available in advance in commercial product recommender system such that the system will know what to recommend. In a learning situation, requiring learners to rate an initial set of learning activities based on intuition or experience does not seem feasible in that learning strategy is heavily context-sensitive and individual-specific, and the effectiveness of an activity or strategy will not be known until that strategy is applied and evaluated. Thus, the system is expected to generate such "ratings" in real-time to make decisions for learners by considering learner profiles, learning goals, tasks and contexts. Yet, recommendations alone do not ensure learning gain increase – how learners react to the recommended resources or activities defines the critical part of successful learning. Thus, the "ratings" need to be adapted according to the learner's progress and performance at different learning stages.

## USE OF DATA MINING TECHNIQUES IN RECOMMENDER SYSTEMS

To meet the above challenges, we propose to adopt data mining algorithms in the recommender systems. The objective of data mining is to discover new interesting and useful knowledge. It is a multidisciplinary area in which several computing paradigms converge: decision tree construction, rule induction, artificial neural networks, instance-based learning, Bayesian learning, logic programming, statistical algorithms, etc. (Klosgen & Zytkow, 2002). This technique has been applied in educational recommender systems. For instance, Zaïane (2002) used association rule mining to discover associations between user actions and URLs to recommend online learning activities or shortcuts in a course website. Lu (2004) used association fuzzy rules to discover associations between student's requirements and a list of learning materials in a personalized e-learning material recommender system.

Among these, sequential pattern mining (Agrawal & Srikant, 1995) attempts to find inter-session patterns such as the presence of a set of items followed by another item in a time-ordered set of sessions or episodes. Sequential patterns can especially reveal which content has motivated the access to other contents, or how tools and contents are entwined in the learning process (Romero & Ventura, 2007). For example, Romero and colleagues (2006) applied sequential pattern mining algorithms to discover the most used path by students and based on this information recommend links to new students while they browse in the course. We proposed data mining algorithms to address the aforementioned challenges for two reasons. First, recommender systems in e-commerce are mainly item-based, which can be translated into learning material, learning sources in learning contexts. However, the way students learn constitutes the most critical part when we aim to improve learning effectiveness and efficiency. Thus we argue for a sequence-based recommender system for learners. This relates to the second reason. When the system links learner profiles to recommendation strategies, we propose to take into account both learner attribute as well as their learning sequence attribute such that the recommendation will be truly personalized and adaptive as learning unfolds. In the following sections, we reported how (sequential) data mining techniques can help address the aforementioned concerns.

Most current recommender systems in e-learning are designed in the same way as in e-commerce without taking into account the specific attributes or conditions of the learners or the context of learning (Drachsler, et al., 2008). Learner profiles thus need to be established as a basis for recommendation. The *learner attribute profile* can either be collected through online surveys (self-reports), learners' actual data on past performance/failure on similar tasks, or traces. The first two can be easily collected before-hand, while the last applies only after learning begins. Note that this attribute profile is subject to change in terms of the task, the learning context, and other individual factors. Thus, new data will be collected when learning takes place in a different context. For the attributes that can be detected at the behavioral level, traces can be used, such as the goal-tracing methods developed by Zhou and Winne (2009) to use users' online goals to direct the recommendations. The *learning sequence profile* can be retrieved from the learner's history of learning as the learning task unfolds. The history of learning in this context comprises a learner's learning goals, specific learning actions as well as learning paths (learning patterns). This requires the recommender system to make online recommendations while monitoring learners' actions performed in the current task.

To use a learner's motivation/emotion state to inform learning strategy recommendation, the system can employ on-line measures to assess the learner's motivation/emotion level at different points during learning. Along with Ainley and Patrick's (2006) thought, single-item probes can be used to monitor learners' immediate experience of the task as they negotiate the learning activity. When the purpose of the measure is clear and unambiguous for the respondent and has a clear experiential focus, it can provide a valid indicator of the state being investigated. A Likert-type of probe can be "please indicate on the scale how you feel right now." This can be embedded in the system and prompt learners to report before a recommendation is made. Combined with other attributes of the learner, the recommendations for a learning activity are attuned to individual demands more effectively and accurately.

Behavioral definitions of learning strategies in e-learning systems can be obtained through a pre-defined *action library* (Zhou & Winne, 2009). The action library specifies how each multi-event action is defined in terms of fine-grained traces recorded in the log. For example, a strategy of self-questioning when reading an essay could contain the following sequence of actions: "Reading the first section → highlighting key terms and sentences → opening the "Question" tool → composing a question about the target section → labeling the difficulty level of the self-designed question →closing the "Question" tool → continuing the reading". This meta-cognitive strategy involves a series of cognitive learning actions (e.g., information selection, question design, and judgment of question difficulty levels). Once actions are identified by the action library, the system parses actions in each user's learning sequence to detect if there is such a strategy being employed. After all the actions are translated into learning strategies, it is possible to identify successful learners with certain characteristics and discover their learning strategy sequential patterns from their computer logs. The system can then determine whether or what to recommend to the current user based on his or her learner profile similarity. An important feature of the action library is its flexible control of grain size, i.e., the level of detail at which researchers decide *a priori* to model how individuals learn. In the action library, researchers can aggregate finer-grained learning events into bigger chunks. They can also divide coarser-grained events into smaller units to increase granularity. We believe this flexibility for exploring grain size is critical to new investigations of learning in multimedia environments (Zhou & Winne, 2009).

By linking the recommendations to each learner profile we could provide more personalized recommendations with regards to the type of strategy or activity. To address the fourth challenge, sequence matching can be employed to recommend learning strategies or activities such that learners' meta-cognitive thinking can be promoted. We can possibly automate the identification of the most salient patterns and present these to the students for their own learning. This aims to rectify ineffective patterns and consolidate effective ones. Essentially, it will enable us to provide regular feedback to students during their learning if their current work behaviour is more likely to be associated with positive or negative outcomes and where the problems are (Perera, Kay, Yacef, & Koprinska, 2007). If the recommendation is to be based on a group of other learners similar to the target learner, pattern matching can be used. Based on the similarity between learner profiles, the system can determine what to recommend. This is measured by a similarity metric which provides the means to determine the distance between two points. Learner attributes consist of a set of categorical learning attributes, e.g., learning goals, learning expectations, etc. Their distance can be measured by Jaccard distance. Two learners are considered similar if they share a certain number of common learning attributes. Learning sequence similarity is measured by edit distance wherein order is considered and the edit operations allow for insertion, deletion and substitutions of an item within a sequence (Ristad & Yianilos, 1997). The minimum number of point mutations required to change one sequence into the other with the edit operations is termed the edit distance of two sequences. It is worthy to note that the calculation of learner similarity does not happen only one time due to the dynamic variables (goal, motivation, emotion etc.) it involves. Thus, it will be executed as learners make progress on the task.

In addition to calculating the similarity of the target learner to other learners (according to their attributes and learning sequences), the effectiveness of a given learning activity also plays a role in determining whether or not to recommend it. No matter how many previous learners have adopted a strategy, it cannot be recommended if the strategy did not increase the mastery of learning (which could be measured by test performance). In respect of the last challenge, rather than retrieving other learners' or teachers' ratings on an activity, the evaluation of each learning activity is implicitly provided through the learner's own past performance after using the same activity or previous other learners' performance levels after engaging in these activities. If the performance is satisfying according to a pre-determined standard (e.g., scores above 85 out of 100), this activity will be assigned a higher rating, which means this activity is more effective for this learner in this context. This type of rating score is more objective and dynamic than receiving a static rating score by pooling a decent number of learners' performance for a certain activity. Also, the order of applying strategies needs to be taken into account. For the same type of learner, activity A might work well only after activity B is executed. Hence, if the system detects the engagement of activity C, activity A might not be recommended in the first place.

In summary, three factors need to be considered for the recommendation of a particular learning activity/strategy to a target user $u$:

- The *learner attribute similarity* between an existing user $u_i$ and the target user $u$, denoted as sim($u_i.p$, $u.p$), where $u_i.p$ indicates the learner attribute of $u_i$, and $u.p$ indicates the learner attribute of $u$;
- The *learning sequence similarity* between an existing user $u_i$ and the target user $u$, denoted as sim($u_i.s$, $u.s$), where $u_i.s$ indicates the learning sequence of $u_i$, and $u.s$ indicates the learning sequence of $u$;
- The performance level of an existing user $u_i$, denoted as $u_i.r$.

The first two factors can be combined as *learner profile similarity*, and represented by a single measurement, expressed as sim($u_i$, $u$) = $w_p$* sim($u_i.p$, $u.p$) + $w_s$*sim($u_i.s$, $u_i.s$), wherein $w_p$ and $w_s$ are the weight (or importance) of the learner attribute similarity and learning sequence similarity, respectively. Taken together, we use the formula below to compute the degree to which we would like to recommend a strategy $a$ to the target user $u$:

$$score(u,a) = \frac{\sum_{u_i \in U} sim(u_i, u) \times u_i.r}{\sum_{u_i \in U} sim(u_i, u)}$$

According to this formula, the recommendation of strategy $a$ to $u$ is based on other similar learners' task performance after applying strategy $a$. Both higher learner similarity scores and better performance after using a learning strategy contribute to a higher final score for recommendation. One interesting question remains unresolved how a system develops its initial study patterns in its first trial with first-time users. In this case, we suggest either pre-inserting effective study patterns for the task based on learning theories, or piloting the system with students whose academic performance in a designated subject area is notably high before it is applied to real cases. By analyzing their study patterns, the system pre-stores them as "ideal" learning strategies and recommends to other learners when necessary. This pool of "ideal" patterns is also updated as more and more high-performing learners contribute by enriching the variety of profiles and learning strategies. Below we present a toy example to show how the recommendation is performed when recommending learning strategies/activities. For ease of demonstration, the learner attribute similarity is provided and learning sequence similarity is computed in advance.

## A TOY EXAMPLE FOR LEARNING STRATEGY RECOMMENDATIONS

Assume the target user $u$ has learner attributes $p$, and his current learning sequence when reading an essay is $s$=<$a,b,c,d,e,f,g,h,x,y$>, wherein $a$ denotes a strategy of "highlight key terms"; $b$ denotes "click a hyperlink"; $c$ denotes "tag the hyperlink"; $d$ denotes "create a glossary term"; $e$ denotes "paraphrase term definitions"; f denotes "make a note"; $g$ denotes "link terms to notes"; $h$ denotes "revisit highlights"; $x$ denotes "update a note"; $y$ denotes "make a summary"; $v$ denotes "generate a question"; and $z$ denotes "create a concept map".

What activity to recommend next to the target user $u$? (For ease of calculation, suppose the weight of learner attributes and learning sequences in determining the similarity of two learner profiles is equal: $w_p$ =0.5 and $w_s$=0.5). Table 1 presents the learning history of previous learners $u_1$, $u_2$, $u_3$ and $u_4$.

In this example, suppose we consider $z$ and $v$ the two candidates for the next round of recommendation. To compute the recommendation score for a particular strategy, the system first locates all the users who have this learning strategy in their learning history (i.e. $u_1$, $u_2$ are located when the system considers recommending strategy $z$ in this example). To calculate learning sequence

*Table 1. Summarization of learner profiles and similarity scores*

| Learner | Learner Attribute | Learning Sequence | Performance Score | Learner Attribute Similarity | Learning Sequence Similarity |
|---|---|---|---|---|---|
| $u_1$ | $p_1$ | $s_1$ = a,b,c,d,e,f,g,h,x,y,z | $r_1 = 0.2$ | sim($p_1$, $p$) = 0.8 | sim($s_1$, $s$) = 1 |
| $u_2$ | $p_2$ | $s_2$ = b,d,f,g,g,x,y,z,c | $r_2 = 0.6$ | sim($p_2$, $p$) = 0.2 | sim($s_2$, $s$) = 0.6 |
| $u_3$ | $p_3$ | $s_3$ = a,b,c,d,f,g,h,x,q,v | $r_3 = 0.9$ | sim($p_3$, $p$) = 0.8 | sim($s_3$, $s$) = 0.8 |
| $u_4$ | $p_4$ | $s_4$= a,d,f,h,y,v,a,g | $r_4 = 0.4$ | sim($p_4$, $p$) = 0.2 | sim($s_4$, $s$) = 0.5 |

similarity, only the sequence of activities up to that strategy are considered.

Using the formula above, the recommendation score of learning strategy/activity $z$ can be computed as follows:

$$\text{sim}(u,u_1) = 0.5*\text{sim}(p_1, p) + 0.5*\text{sim}(s_1,s) = 0.5*0.8 + 0.5*1 = 0.9$$

$$\text{sim}(u,u_2) = 0.5*\text{sim}(p_2, p) + 0.5*\text{sim}(s_2,s) = 0.5*0.2 + 0.5*0.6=0.4$$

$$\text{score}(u,z) = [\text{sim}(u,u_1)* r_1 + \text{sim}(u,u_2)* r_2]/[\text{sim}(u,u_1)+ \text{sim}(u,u_2)]$$

$$= (0.9*0.2 + 0.4*0.6)/(0.9+0.4) = 0.32$$

Similarly, the recommendation score of learning strategy/activity $v$ can be computed based on the learning history of $u_3$ and $u_4$:

$$\text{sim}(u,u_3) = 0.5*\text{sim}(p_3,p) + 0.5*\text{sim}(s_3,s) = 0.5*0.8 + 0.5*0.8 = 0.8$$

$$\text{sim}(u,u_4) = 0.5*\text{sim}(p_4,p) + 0.5*\text{sim}(s_4,s) = 0.5*0.2 + 0.5*0.5 = 0.35$$

$$\text{score}(u,v) = [\text{sim}(u,u_3)*r_3 + sim(u,u_4)*r_4] / [\text{sim}(u,u_3)+\text{sim}(u,u_4)]$$

$$= (0.8*0.9 + 0.35*0.2)/(0.8+0.35) = 0.69$$

Because score($u$,$z$) < score($u$, $v$), between strategy $z$ and $v$, the system will recommend strategy $v$ ("generate a question") to the target user $u$.

In this example, it is clear that the similarity between the target learner and other learners alone does not determine the recommendation; the effectiveness of a strategy also accounts for the decision to a great extent. If the similarity of a new learner's profile to any existing learner profile is zero, the system will use pedagogical rules as guiding principles or pre-stored "ideal" strategies for meta-cognitive recommendations, mostly questions that get learners started on the right track, such as "Would you like to try the concept tool to make an outline first? "Would you like to read the task instruction first?" or "It is now a good time to get familiar with the tools available for you to use". After the learner starts his study, the system monitors his learning process by tracking his learning path and considers the learner attribute and learning sequence similarity, as well as the performance level of past learners after using the activity to be recommended. If the learner follows the recommendation and achieves well or the learner studies with a different strategy yet achieves good performance results, the system will update his or her learning profile in this particular context for future reference. When this learner studies next time, his or her past learning behavior as well as other learners' similar behavior constitute the bases for a new round of recommendation. It is noteworthy that learners' learning paths do not often match pre-stored strategies exactly in practice, thus the support of approximate matching will be desired in this case.

There is a caution that the system could mistakenly recommend ineffective strategies, if the recommendations are made solely based on a limited number of learners, as the calculation results could be highly skewed and biased by the small amount of data input. For instance, when the system recommends a strategy based on 10 high-performing users' data, among which 3 of them actually achieved well due to their strong short-term memory capabilities rather than the strategy use. When the system detects a need to recommend the same strategy for later users, their task performances are worse than expected. When the number of later users who perform poorly using the recommended strategy exceeds the number of initial users, the system will adjust its "rating" on that strategy and stop recommending the strategy in this situation. Hence, a sufficiently large user input will reduce the probability of making inaccurate recommendations.

## CONCLUSION

Research into meta-cognition suggests that learners need to become aware of the processes of their learning as distinct from the content of learning to improve their learning outcomes. Learners need to know how to monitor and regulate their own learning processes when working on tasks within an e-learning context. Meta-cognition helps learners exhibit cognitive processes that analyze and manage their own thinking in pursuit of knowledge acquisition in order to solve problems, gain insight and become critical thinkers (Gordon, 1996). Developing a system to enhance this skill, however, poses its own challenges. In this chapter, we reviewed five challenges to promote meta-cognitive activities with recommendations: i) the need to consider both learner attributes and the learning sequences during recommendations, ii) the need to detect the learners' motivation and social-emotion and their changes as the task unfolds and to inform what learning strategies to recommend, iii) the need to detect meaningful learning actions and translate them into a strategy in order to evaluate current learning strategy use and subsequently formulate recommendations, iv) the need to suggest learning activities or strategies which are more complex with multiple features instead of recommending static learning resources and v) retrieval of ratings or preferences to learning strategies/activities in advance by the system by considering learner profiles, learning goals, tasks and contexts and adapting them according to the learner's progress and performance at different learning stages.

These challenges highlight the difference between recommender systems in e-commerce and those for learning purposes. Most consumer recommender systems base their recommendations on a limited understanding of the users and items. Educational recommender systems, however, should look for the available data to decide on which strategy to select for which situation in order to improve the educational provision, taking into account the specific characteristics of learners (Drachsler et al., 2008) as well as the dynamic, multi-faceted nature of learning processes (e.g., the order of learning actions, the context of applying a certain learning strategy etc.). We thus proposed the use of data mining techniques to help address these issues as this technique attends to the sequence of the occurrence of learning actions and makes recommendation decisions based on learner behavior in the current context. To ensure the effectiveness and efficiency of the application of this algorithm, the recommendation engine has to be able to do online data mining automatically of online collection and analysis of user data (e.g., learning behavior, learner profile etc.) such that the system is able to work completely autonomously (Romero, et al., 2009) by recommending personalized activities to meet individual needs. These can assist learners to choose pertinent learning activities that should improve their learning process and performance.

## FUTURE RESEARCH DIRECTIONS

Knowledge about how students monitor and control their learning is useful to a recommender system only when it applies this knowledge to recognize specific situations that call for recommendation and make suggestions accordingly. Related to this is another issue that is not explored in this paper – the frequency of making recommendations. Recommender systems within e-learning should be able to cater for learners in different subject areas at different levels. Thus, future research needs to further analyze, for instance, 1) in what situation a recommendation needs to be made to maximize pedagogical gains; 2) how individual factors affect the frequency/ timing of providing recommendations (such as learner attribute and learning behavior); 3) what are contextual factors that affect the frequency/ timing of providing recommendations; and 4) how the frequency of making recommendations affect learning processes and outcomes. To address these questions, more studies are necessary to be conducted both theoretically and empirically.

This can in turn inform classroom teachers of the implementation of the recommendation principle and strategy outside e-learning systems.

## REFERENCES

Agrawal, R., & Srikant, R. (1995). Mining sequential patterns. In *Proceedings of Eleventh International Conference on Data Engineering* (pp. 3–14). Taipei, Taiwan: IEEE Computer Society Press.

Ainley, M., & Patrick, L. (2006). Measuring self-regulated learning processes through tracking patterns of student interaction with achievement activities. *Educational Psychology Review*, *18*, 267–286. doi:10.1007/s10648-006-9018-z

Aleven, V., & Koedinger, K. R. (2002). An effective metacognitive strategy: Learning by doing and explaining with a computer-based cognitive tutor. *Cognitive Science*, *26*(2), 147–179. doi:10.1207/s15516709cog2602_1

Azevedo, R. (2002). Beyond intelligent tutoring systems: Using computers as metacognitive tools to enhance learning? *Instructional Science*, *30*, 31–45. doi:10.1023/A:1013592216234

Azevedo, R., & Cromley, J. G. (2004). Does training of self-regulated learning facilitate student's learning with hypermedia? *Journal of Educational Psychology*, *96*, 523–535. doi:10.1037/0022-0663.96.3.523

Barros, B., & Verdejo, M. F. (2000). Analysing student interaction processes in order to improve collaboration. The DEGREE approach. *International Journal of Artificial Intelligence in Education*, *11*, 221–241.

Bell, P., & Davis, E. A. (2000). Designing Mildred: Scaffolding students' reflection and argumentation using a cognitive software guide. In B. Fishman & S. O'Connor-Divelbiss (Eds.), *Fourth International Conference of the Learning Sciences* (pp. 142-149). Mahwah, NJ: Erlbaum.

Bjork, R. A. (1999). Assessing our own competence: Heuristics and illusions. In Gopher, D., & Koriat, A. (Eds.), *Attention and performance XVII. Cognitive regulation of performance: Interaction of theory and application* (pp. 435–459). Cambridge, MA: MIT Press.

Bobadilla, J., Serradilla, F., & Hernando, A., & MovieLens. (2009). Collaborative filtering adapted to recommender systems of e-learning. *Knowledge-Based Systems*, *22*, 261–265. doi:10.1016/j.knosys.2009.01.008

Brown, A. L., Bransford, J. D., Ferrara, R. A., & Campione, J. C. (1983). Learning, remembering, and understanding. In J. H. Flavell & E. M. Markman (Eds.), *Handbook of child psychology (4th ed.): Cognitive development* (vol. 3, pp. 77-166). New York, NY: Wiley.

Bull, S. (1997). Promoting effective learning strategy use in CALL. *Computer Assisted Language Learning, 10*(1), 3–39. doi:10.1080/0958822970100102

Bull, S., & Kay, J. (2008). Metacognition and open learner models. In I. Roll & V. Aleven (Eds.), *Proceedings of Workshop on Metacognition and Self-Regulated Learning in Educational Technologies, International Conference on Intelligent Tutoring Systems* (pp. 7-20). Montreal, Canada.

Chen, C. M., Lee, H. M., & Chen, Y. H. (2005). Personalized e-learning system using item repository theory. *Computers & Education, 44*, 237–255. doi:10.1016/j.compedu.2004.01.006

Chi, M. T., Bassok, M., Lewis, M. W., Reimann, P., & Glaser, R. (1989). Self-explanations: How students study and use examples in learning to solve problems. *Cognitive Science, 13*, 145–182. doi:10.1207/s15516709cog1302_1

Conati, C., & VanLehn, K. (2000). Toward computer-based support of meta-cognitive skills: A computational framework to coach self-explanation. *International Journal of Artificial Intelligence in Education, 11*, 398–415.

Davis, E. A., & Linn, M. C. (2000). Scaffolding students' knowledge integration: Prompts for reflection in KIE. *International Journal of Science Education, 22*, 819–837. doi:10.1080/095006900412293

Derry, S., & Murphy, D. A. (1986). Designing systems that train learning ability: From theory to practice. *Review of Educational Research, 56*(1), 1–39.

Derry, S. J. (1988). Putting learning strategies to work. *Educational Leadership, 46*, 4–10.

Drachsler, H., Hummel, H. G. K., & Koper, R. (2008). Personal RS for learners in lifelong learning: Requirements, techniques and model. *International Journal of Learning Technology, 3*, 404–423. doi:10.1504/IJLT.2008.019376

Dunning, D., Johnson, K., Ehrlinger, J., & Kruger, J. (2003). Why people fail to recognize their own incompetence. *Current Directions in Psychological Science, 12*(3), 83–87. doi:10.1111/1467-8721.01235

Dunslosky, J., & Thiede, K. W. (1998). What makes people study more? An evaluation of factors that affect self-paced study. *Acta Psychologica, 98*, 37–56. doi:10.1016/S0001-6918(97)00051-6

Ehrman, M., & Oxford, R. (1990). Adult language learning styles and strategies in an intensive training setting. *Modern Language Journal, 74*(3), 311–327. doi:10.2307/327627

Flavell, J. (1976). Metacognitive aspects of problem-solving. In Resnick, L. (Ed.), *The nature of intelligence* (pp. 231–236). Hillsdale, NJ: Erlbaum Associates.

Flavell, J. H. (1979). Meta-cognition and cognitive monitoring: A new area of cognitive developmental inquiry. *The American Psychologist, 34*, 906–911. doi:10.1037/0003-066X.34.10.906

Flavell, J. H. (1992). Metacognition and cognitive monitoring: A new area of cognitive developmental inquiry. In Nelson, T. O. (Ed.), *Metacognition core readings* (pp. 3–8). Boston, MA: Allyn and Bacon.

Gama, C. (2004). Metacognition in interactive learning environments: The reflection assistant model. In J. C. Lester, R. M. Vicari & F. Paraguacu (Eds), *Intelligent Tutoring Systems: 7th International Conference* (pp. 668-677). Berlin, Germany: Springer-Verlag.

Ge, L., Kong, W., & Luo, J. (2006). Courseware recommendation in e-learning system. In *Advances in Web Based Learning ICWL2006* (pp. 10–24). Berlin, Germany: Springer.

Ghauth, K. I., & Abdullah, N. A. (2011). Learning materials recommendation using good learners' ratings and content-based filtering. *Educational Technology Research and Development*, *58*, 711–727. doi:10.1007/s11423-010-9155-4

Gillette, B. (1987). Two successful language learners. In Faerch, C., & Kasper, G. (Eds.), *Introspection in second language research* (pp. 268–279). Philadelphia, PA: Clevedon Multilingual Matters.

Gordon, J. (1996). Tracks for learning: Metacognition and learning technologies. *Australian Journal of Educational Technology*, *12*, 46–55.

Hadwin, A., & Winne, P. (2001). CoNoteS2: A software tool for promoting self-regulation. *Educational Research and Evaluation*, *7*, 313–334. doi:10.1076/edre.7.2.313.3868

Hattie, J., Biggs, J., & Purdie, N. (1996). Effects of learning skills interventions on student learning: A meta-analysis. *Review of Educational Research*, *66*, 99–136.

Inaba, A., & Okamoto, T. (1996). Development of the intelligent discussion support system for collaborative learning. In *Proceedings of ED-TELECOM'96 - World Conference on Educational Telecommunications* (pp. 137-142). Boston, MA: AACE.

Jermann, P., Soller, A., & Muehlenbrock, M. (2001). From mirroring to guiding: A review of the state of the art technology for supporting collaborative learning. In Dillenbourg, P., Eurelings, A., & Hakkarainen, K. (Eds.), *European perspectives on computer-supported learning* (pp. 324–331). Maastricht, The Netherlands: University of Maastricht.

Joseph, N. (2010). Metacognition needed: Teaching middle and high school students to develop strategic learning skills. *Preventing School Failure*, *54*, 99–103. doi:10.1080/10459880903217770

Kerkiri, T., Manitsaris, A., & Mavridou, A. (2007). Reputation metadata for recommending personalized e-learning resources. In *Proceedings of the Second International Workshop on Semantic Media Adaptation and Personalization* (pp. 110–115). Uxbridge, MA: IEEE Computer Society.

Khribi, M. K., Jemni, M., & Nasraoui, O. (2009). Automatic recommendations for e-learning personalization based on web usage mining techniques and information retrieval. *Journal of Educational Technology & Society*, *12*, 30–42.

Klosgen, W., & Zytkow, J. (2002). *Handbook of data mining and knowledge discovery*. New York, NY: Oxford University Press.

Koriat, A., & Bjork, R. A. (2005). Illusions of competence in monitoring one's knowledge during study. *Journal of Experimental Psychology. Learning, Memory, and Cognition*, *31*, 187–194. doi:10.1037/0278-7393.31.2.187

Kramarski, B., & Mevarech, Z. R. (2003). Enhancing mathematical reasoning in the classroom: Effects of cooperative learning and metacognitive training. *American Educational Research Journal*, *40*, 281–310. doi:10.3102/00028312040001281

Kruger, J., & Dunning, D. (1999). Unskilled and unaware of it: How differences in recognizing one's own incompetence lead to inflated self-assessments. *Journal of Personality and Social Psychology*, *77*(6), 1121–1134. doi:10.1037/0022-3514.77.6.1121

Kurt, M. (2007). *Activating meta-cognition through online learning log (OLL)*. Paper presented at the International Educational Technology (IETC) Conference, Nicosia, Turkish Republic of Northern Cyprus.

Lin, X. D., & Lehman, J. (1999). Supporting learning of a computer-based biology environment: Effects of prompting college students to reflect on their own thinking. *Journal of Research in Science Teaching*, *36*(7), 1–22. doi:10.1002/(SICI)1098-2736(199909)36:7<837::AID-TEA6>3.0.CO;2-U

Linden, G., Smith, B., & York, J. (2003). Amazon.com recommendations: Item-to-item collaborative filtering. *Internet Computing IEEE*, *7*(1), 76–80. doi:10.1109/MIC.2003.1167344

Liu, F., & Shih, B. (2007). Learning activity-based e-learning material recommendation system. In *Proceedings of the 9th IEEE International Symposium on Multimedia Workshops* (pp. 343–348). Washington, DC: IEEE Computer Society.

Loizidou, A., & Koutselini, M. (2007). Meta-cognitive monitoring: An obstacle and a key to effective teaching and learning. *Teachers and Teaching*, *13*, 499–519. doi:10.1080/13540600701561711

Lu, J. (2004). Personalized e-learning material recommender system. In *Proceedings of International Conference on Information Technology for Application* (pp. 374–379). Washington, DC: IEEE Computer Society.

Marlin, B. (2003). Modeling user rating profiles for collaborative filtering. In Thrun, S., Saul, L. K., & Schölkopf, B. (Eds.), *Advances in neural information processing systems* (pp. 627–634). Cambridge, MA: MIT Press.

McManus, M., & Aiken, R. (1995). Monitoring computer-based problem solving. *Journal of Artificial Intelligence in Education*, *6*(4), 307–336.

Melville, P., Mooney, R., & Nagarajan, R. (2002). Content-boosted collaborative filtering for improved recommendations. In *Proceedings of the 18th National Conference on Artificial Intelligence* (pp. 187-192). Menlo Park, CA: AAAI Press.

Nietfeld, J. L., & Schraw, G. (2002). The effect of knowledge and strategy explanation on monitoring accuracy. *The Journal of Educational Research*, *95*, 131–142. doi:10.1080/00220670209596583

Perera, D., Kay, J., Yacef, K., & Koprinska, I. (2007). Mining learners' traces from an online collaboration tool. *Workshop Educational Data Mining, Proceedings of the 13th International Conference of Artificial Intelligence in Education* (pp. 60-69). Marina del Rey, CA: IOS Press.

Ristad, E., & Yianilos, P. (1997). Learning string edit distance. In *Proceedings of the Fourteenth International Conference on Machine Learning* (pp. 287–295). San Francisco, CA: Morgan Kaufmann Publishers.

Roll, I., Aleven, V., McLaren, B. M., & Koedinger, K. (2007). Designing for metacognition - Applying cognitive tutor principles to the tutoring of help seeking. *Metacognition and Learning*, *2*, 125–140. doi:10.1007/s11409-007-9010-0

Romero, C. M., Porras, P. A. R., Ventura, S. S., Hervás, M. C., & Zafra, G. A. (2006). Using sequential pattern mining for links recommendation in adaptive hypermedia educational systems. *Current Developments in Technology-Assisted Education*, *2*, 1016–1020.

Romero, C. M., & Ventura, S. S. (2007). Educational data mining: A survey from 1995 to 2005. *Expert Systems with Applications*, *33*, 135–146. doi:10.1016/j.eswa.2006.04.005

Romero, C. M., Ventura, S. S., Zafra, G. A., & de Bra, P. (2009). Applying web usage mining for personalizing hyperlinks in web-based adaptive educational systems. *Computers & Education*, *53*, 828–840. doi:10.1016/j.compedu.2009.05.003

Rosset, S., Neumann, E., Eick, U., Vatnik, N., & Idan, Y. (2002). Customer lifetime value modeling and its use for customer retention planning. In *Proceedings of the 8th CM SIGKDD International Conference of Knowledge Discovery and Data Mining* (pp. 332-340). New York, NY: Association for Computing Machinery.

Sansone, C., & Thoman, D. (2005). Interest as the missing motivator in self-regulation. *European Psychologist, 10*, 175–186. doi:10.1027/1016-9040.10.3.175

Santos, S. G., Pardo, A., & Kloos, C. D. (2006). Some ideas for a collaborative search of the optimal learning path. *Lecture Notes in Computer Science, 4018*, 430–434. doi:10.1007/11768012_64

Schoenfeld, A. H. (1987). What's all the fuss about metacognition? In Schoenfeld, A. H. (Ed.), *Cognitive science and mathematics education*. Hillsdale, NJ: Lawrence Erlbaum Associates.

Schraw, G., & Dennison, R. S. (1994). Assessing metacognitive awareness. *Contemporary Educational Psychology, 19*, 460–475. doi:10.1006/ceps.1994.1033

Schraw, G., & Moshman, D. (1995). Metacognitive theories. *Educational Psychology Review, 7*, 351–371. doi:10.1007/BF02212307

Schunk, D. H., & Zimmerman, B. J. (2006). Competence and control beliefs: Distinguishing the means and ends. In Alexander, P. A., & Winne, P. H. (Eds.), *Handbook of educational psychology* (2nd ed., pp. 349–367). Mahwah, NJ: Erlbaum.

Soller, A., Martínez-Monés, A., Jermann, P., & Muehlenbrock, M. (2005). From mirroring to guiding: A review of state of the art technology for supporting collaborative learning. *International Journal of Artificial Intelligence in Education, 15*(4), 261–290.

Soonthornphisaj, N., Rojsattarat, E., & Yim-ngam, S. (2006). Smart e-learning using recommender system. *Computational Intelligence, 4114*, 518–523. doi:10.1007/978-3-540-37275-2_63

Stevick, E. W. (1989). *Success with foreign languages: Seven who achieved it and what worked for them*. London, UK: Prentice Hall.

Tai, D. W., Wu, H., & Li, P. (2008). Effective e-learning recommendation system based on self-organizing maps and association mining. *The Electronic Library, 26*, 329–344. doi:10.1108/02640470810879482

Tang, T., & McCalla, G. (2005). Smart recommendation for an evolving e-learning system. *International Journal on E-Learning, 4*, 105–129.

Thiede, K. W., Anderson, M. C., & Therriault, D. (2003). Accuracy of metacognitive monitoring affects learning of texts. *Journal of Educational Psychology, 95*, 66–73. doi:10.1037/0022-0663.95.1.66

van den Berg, B., van Es, R., Tattersall, C., Janssen, J., Manderveld, J., & Brouns, F. … Koper, R. (2005). Swarm-based sequencing recommendations in e-learning. In *Proceedings of the Fifth International Conference on Intelligent Systems Design and Applications,* (pp. 488–493). Washington, DC: IEEE Computer Society.

Wagster, J., Tan, J., Biswas, G., & Schwartz, D. (2007). *How metacognitive feedback affects behavior in learning and transfer.* Paper presented at 13th International Conference on Artificial Intelligence in Education. Los Angeles, CA.

White, B., & Frederiksen, J. (2005). A theoretical framework and approach for fostering metacognitive development. *Educational Psychologist, 40*(4), 211–223. doi:10.1207/s15326985ep4004_3

Winne, P., & Hadwin, A. (2008). The weave of motivation and self-regulated learning. In Schunk, D., & Zimmerman, B. (Eds.), *Motivation and self-regulated learning: Theory, research, and applications* (pp. 297–314). New York, NY: Taylor and Francis.

Wolters, C. (2003). Regulation of motivation: Evaluating an underemphasized aspect of self–regulated learning. *Educational Psychologist, 38*, 189–205. doi:10.1207/S15326985EP3804_1

Zaïane, O. R. (2002). Building a recommender agent for e-learning systems. In *Proceedings of the International Conference on Computers in Education* (pp. 55-59). Washington, DC: IEEE Computer Society.

Zhou, M., & Winne, P. H. (2009). Designing multimedia to trace goal-setting in studying. In Zheng, R. (Ed.), *Cognitive effects of multimedia learning* (pp. 288–311). Hershey, PA: IGI Global.

Zins, J. E., Weissberg, R. P., Wang, M. C., & Walberg, H. J. (Eds.). (2004). *Building academic success on social and emotional learning: What does the research say?*New York, NY: Teachers College Press.

## ADDITIONAL READING

Adomavicius, G., & Tuzhilin, A. (2005). Toward the next generation of recommender systems: A survey of the state-of-the-art and possible extensions. In []. Washington, DC: IEEE Computer Society.]. *Proceedings of IEEE Transactions on Knowledge and Data Mining Engineering, 17*(6), 734–749. doi:10.1109/TKDE.2005.99

Aroyo, L. (2006). *Learner models for web-based personalised adaptive learning: current solutions and open issues.* Electronic Version, http://knowgate.nada.kth.se:8080/portfolio/files/Prolearn-TUE/TUE/Participation/WorkPackages/WP_01_-_TUE/Deliverable_1.03/D1.3.pdf

Azevedo, R. (2005). Using hypermedia as a metacognitive tool for enhancing student Learning? The role of self-regulated learning. *Educational Psychologist, 40*(4), 199–209. doi:10.1207/s15326985ep4004_2

Choi, H. S., Jeong, Y.-S., & Jeong, M. K. (2010). A hybrid recommendation method with reduced data for large-scale application. *IEEE Transactions on Systems, Man and Cybernetics. Part C, Applications and Reviews, 40*(5), 557–566. doi:10.1109/TSMCC.2010.2046036

Corno, L. (1986). The metacognitive control components of self-regulated learning. *Contemporary Educational Psychology, 11*, 333–346. doi:10.1016/0361-476X(86)90029-9

Drachsler, H., Hummel, H. G. K., & Koper, R. (2008). Personal RS for learners in lifelong learning: Requirements, techniques and model. *International Journal of Learning Technology, 3*, 404–423. doi:10.1504/IJLT.2008.019376

Huffaker, D. A., & Calvert, S. L. (2003). The new science of learning: Active learning, metacognition, and transfer of knowledge in e-learning applications. *Journal of Educational Computing Research, 29*(3), 325–334. doi:10.2190/4T89-30W2-DHTM-RTQ2

Janssen, J., Berlanga, A., & Koper, R. (2009). How to find and follow suitable learning paths. In Koper, R. (Ed.), *Learning network services for professional development* (pp. 151–166). Berlin: Springer-Verlag. doi:10.1007/978-3-642-00978-5_9

Khribi, M. K., Jemni, M., & Nasraoui, O. (2007). Toward a Hybrid Recommender System for E-Learning Personalization Based on Web Usage Mining Techniques and Information Retrieval. In T. Bastiaens & S. Carliner (Eds.), In *Proceedings of World Conference on E-Learning in Corporate, Government, Healthcare, and Higher Education 2007* (pp. 6136-6145). Chesapeake, VA: AACE.

Khribi, M. K., Jemni, M., Nasraoui, O. (2009). Automatic recommendations for e-Learning personalization based on web usage mining techniques and information retrieval. *Journal of Educational Technology & Society, 12*(4,) 30-42,

Kim, J. (2006, Sep). *What is a recommender system?* Paper presented at The Present and Future of Recommender Systems '06 meeting, Bilbao, Spain.

Korhonen, V. (2004). Contextual orientation patterns as describing adults' personal approach to learning in a web-based learning environment. *Studies in Continuing Education*, *26*(1), 99–116. doi:10.1080/158037042000199470

Kurt, M. (2007, May). *Activating meta-cognition through online learning log (OLL)*. Paper presented at the International Educational Technology (IETC) Conference, Nicosia, Turkish Republic of Northern Cyprus.

Linton, F., & Schaefer, H. (2000). Recommender systems for learning: Building user and expert models through long-term observation of application use. *User Modeling and User-Adapted Interaction*, *10*, 181–208. doi:10.1023/A:1026521931194

Liu, F., & Shih, B. (2007). Learning activity-based e-learning material recommendation system. In *Proceedings of the 9th IEEE international symposium on multimedia workshops* (pp. 343–348). Washington, DC: IEEE Computer Society.

Melville, P., Mooney, R., & Nagarajan, R. (2002). Content-boosted collaborative filtering for improved recommendations," In *Proceedings of the 18th National Conference on Artificial Intelligence* (pp. 187-192). Menlo Park, CA: AAAI Press.

Narciss, S., Proske, A., & Koerndle, H. (2007). Promoting self-regulated learning in web-based learning environments. *Computers in Human Behavior*, *23*(3), 1126–1144. doi:10.1016/j.chb.2006.10.006

Rafaeli, S., Dan-Gur, Y., & Barak, M. (2005). Social recommender systems: Recommendations in support of e-learning. *International Journal of Distance Education Technologies*, *3*(2), 30–47. doi:10.4018/jdet.2005040103

Rashid, A. M., Albert, I., Cosley, D., La, S. K., McNee, S. M., Konstan, J. A., & Riedl, J. (2002). Getting to know you: learning new user preferences in recommender systems. In *Proceedings of the 7th International Conference on Intelligent User Interfaces* (pp. 127–134). NY: Association for Computing Machinery.

Tang, T., & McCalla, G. (2005). Smart recommendation for an evolving e-learning system. *International Journal on E-Learning*, *4*, 105–129.

Tsai, M.-J. (2009). The model of strategic e-Learning: Understanding and evaluating student e- learning from metacognitive perspectives. *Journal of Educational Technology & Society*, *12*(1), 34–48.

Veenman, M. V. J., Van Hout-Wolters, B. H. A. M., & Afflerbach, P. (2006). Metacognition and learning: Conceptual and methodological considerations. *Metacognition and Learning*, *1*(1), 3–14. doi:10.1007/s11409-006-6893-0

White, B., & Frederiksen, J. (2005). A theoretical framework and approach for fostering metacognitive development. *Educational Psychologist*, *40*(4), 211–223. doi:10.1207/s15326985ep4004_3

Zaïane, O. R. (2002). Building a recommender agent for e-learning systems. In *Proceedings of the International Conference on Computers in Education* (pp. 55-59). Washington, DC: IEEE Computer Society.

Zaïane, O. R., & Luo, J. (2001). Towards evaluating learners' behaviour in a web-based distance learning environment. In *Proceeding of IEEE International Conference on Advanced Learning Technologies* (pp. 357–360). Washington, DC: IEEE Computer Society.

## KEY TERMS AND DEFINITIONS

**Data Mining:** The process of searching for patterns and relationships with large volumes of data.

**Learning Pattern:** One particular sequence of learning actions that describe students in a group or one single student over multiple sessions.

**Meta-Cognition:** A notion of "cognition about cognition"; knowledge about when and how to use particular strategies to monitor and control learning.

**Meta-Cognitive Knowledge:** The knowledge about when, why and how to use a learning strategy and whether it is effective.

**Meta-Cognitive Regulation:** A meta-cognitive process to regulate one's learning, including assessing the task at hand, evaluating one's own strengths and weaknesses, planning the approach, applying strategies, and reflecting on the degree to which the current approach is working.

**Recommender System:** A tool that recommends to learners (users) learning objects (e.g., learning material, resources or activities) based on their profile (e.g., interest, goal, past performance etc.).

**Traces:** Logs generated by computer which record the context in which study actions occur as well as each action taken at its time point over the course of study.

**Similarity Metric:** An index of a similarity or dissimilarity (distance) score between two learning objects (e.g., learning patterns) for approximate matching or comparison.

# Chapter 13
# Providing Recommendations for Mobile Learning:
## Opportunities and Challenges from Context

**Chengzhi Liu**
*Norwegian University of Science and Technology, Norway*

**Monica Divitini**
*Norwegian University of Science and Technology, Norway*

## ABSTRACT

*At the interdisciplinary intersection of mobile computing and e-learning, mobile learning is a new paradigm that promises to revolutionize learning by supporting new pedagogical approaches and learning experiences. The unique advantage of mobile learning is to encourage learners to learn in an authentic environment with the help of their mobile devices. In mobile learning systems, recommendation technology can play an important role by providing suitable learning resources to learners according to their interests and preferences. However, the learning needs of learners are dynamically changing as they change their physical location and participate in different activities in the mobile learning environment. Recommendation results cannot reflect actual demands of learners if the learner's context is ignored. Integrating context into the recommendation process brings along opportunities to better understand the dynamic requirements of learners, but also challenges to constantly improve the existing recommendation mechanism. This chapter aims at providing an overview of these opportunities and challenges.*

DOI: 10.4018/978-1-61350-489-5.ch013

## INTRODUCTION

Mobile learning refers to "any sort of learning that happens when the learner is not at a fixed, predetermined location, or learning that happens when the learner takes advantage of the learning opportunities offered by mobile technologies" (O'malley et al., 2003, p.6). Mobile learning is a new paradigm that is expected to revolutionize learning forms by changing the ways of behavior and interaction of learners (Leung & Chan, 2003; Liu et al., 2003; Wang, Shen, Novak & Pan, 2009). At the early stage of mobile learning, learning materials were simply transferred from the previous E-learning systems to new mobile platforms (Cobcroft, Towers, Smith & Bruns, 2006). The main objective was to support learning anytime, anywhere by promoting a more flexible fruition of learning material on the move. Further development of mobile learning allowed to better understand the differences between E-learning and mobile learning. E-learning is suitable for distant education by supporting geographically distributed people to access large amounts of learning materials. Mobile learning is not just a mobile version of E-learning. Mobile learning is not suitable for the distribution of large learning contents due to the limitation of input and output of mobile devices and communication speed of wireless network. Rather, mobile learning can support new pedagogical approaches and learning experiences by encouraging students to leave the classroom and learn in authentic learning environments (Laurillard, 2007; Motiwalla, 2007). In this way, learning can be better integrated into learners' daily life and practices. Learners can find out what they desire to learn by walking around in the real environment and learn when and where they want. Learners can interact with the environment and collect environmental data with mobile devices and wireless network. Learners can discuss and share ideas with others when they need help.

In mobile learning systems, recommendation technology can play an important role by suggesting suitable learning resources to learners according to their interests and preferences, but also based on their specific situation and the possibilities that it offers. Recommendation technology refers to a type of information filtering system that attempts to recommend information items according to users' interests and preferences (Prem & Vikas, 2010). On the one hand, recommendation technology can be used in a specific domain to solve the problem of information overload. Mobile learning offers learners new learning experiences by supporting situated learning in local environment and communities. Suitable learning resources, such as learning content, tasks, activities and collaborators, should be suggested to learners in order to improve the satisfaction of learners and the efficiency of mobile learning systems. On the other hand, recommendation approaches should be improved or adapted according to the new requirements of mobile learning. The requirements of learners and the possibilities at their hands are dynamically changing when they move to different locations, take part in different tasks and activities, and collaborate with different partners. The dynamic of requirements challenges recommendation approaches on providing appropriate recommendation to learners. Recommendation results cannot meet actual demands of learners if their current situations are ignored, as in traditional recommendation approaches.

Context can be used to characterize the situations of a learner in a mobile learning environment. Integrating context into the recommendation process means both opportunities to better understand the dynamic requirements of learners and challenges to constantly improve the existing recommendation mechanism. Contextual information can be integrated into the recommendation process in order to understand the actual needs of learners. With the help of context, recommendation approaches can strengthen the advantages of mobile learning through providing suitable learning resources according to learners' current situations. However, the variability and complexity of context requires traditional recommendation mechanisms to be improved when context-based recommendation is realized in mobile learning settings.

The objective of this chapter is to systematically analyze the opportunities and challenges from context to provide suitable recommendations for mobile learning. From the analysis of opportunities, researchers can learn the importance and roles of context for the purpose of providing recommendation in mobile learning systems. From the analysis of challenges, researchers can understand the possible issues and promising research directions when context-based recommendation is applied to mobile learning systems. The rest of this chapter is organized as following. A brief introduction to mobile learning and recommendation systems is introduced in background section. Mobile learning encourages learners to learn in the authentic environment. The learning interests and preferences of learners are dynamic as they change their physical location and take part in different activities. The literature about applying recommendation technology in E-learning and mobile leaning shows that the adopted recommendation approaches can improve learning efficiency by meeting with the special requirements of learning systems. The next section discusses how learning resources can be effectively recommended by considering information about the context of learners. Opportunities and challenges from context are analyzed systematically in order to provide recommendations for mobile learning. Future research directions and conclusions are provided at the end of this chapter.

## BACKGROUND

### Mobile Learning

With the employment of mobile devices and wireless network, mobile learning takes learners from classrooms and homes to any places where hands-on learning can take place (Berri, Benlamri, & Atif, 2006; Ogata & Yano, 2004). Traditional education focuses on formal learning in classrooms where students can learn with predefined goals and activities. Internet-based E-learning systems allow geographically distributed learners to learn individually or collaboratively by sitting in front of computers. Now mobile devices and wireless technology bring learners new ways of learning in a variety of environments. Mobile learning does not simply transfer learning contents from a computer to a mobile device. Mobile learning facilitates new forms of learning with the change of infrastructure. E-learning can support geographically distributed people to learn distantly in online learning communities with large amounts of available learning resources. However, to deliver huge amounts of learning content is not the strength of mobile learning due to poor input and output capability of mobile devices and unstable communication of wireless network. The advantage of mobile learning is mobility, which allows learners to leave classroom or other fixed places and expand their learning to authentic environments in real life. Furthermore, mobile devices can easily be used to collect location and other environmental information with GPS and sensors. The learning status and process can be monitored through collecting learners' surrounding information in mobile learning systems.

Mobile learning will not replace traditional classroom learning and E-learning. Rather, it can support new ways of learning on the base of its unique characteristics and capabilities. The characteristics of mobile learning include (1) urgency of learning need; (2) initiative of knowledge acquisition; (3) mobility of learning setting; (4) interactivity of the learning process; (5) "situated" nature of instructional activities; and (6) integration of instructional content (Lavoie, 2006). Specific learning theory should be consistent with these characteristics. The mobility of learners changes the learning processes and practices by freeing learners from the constraints of classrooms and computers. Learners can find out what they desire to learn by walking around in the real environment and learn when and where they want. Learning is integrated into learners' daily life in order to support situated, collaborative and learner-centered personalized learning (Chen, Chang, & Wang, 2008).

Mobile learning provides new possibilities by integrating mobile computing into the learning environment. Mobile learning has the advantage of allowing learners to learn at anytime and anywhere. The advantage offers learners new learning experiences. The portability of mobile devices opens the door to new forms of learning, which are achieved through exploration of the environment, interaction with peers, and serendipitous encounters with people and learning resources. Learning activities in the real environment is closely connected to problems, tasks, environment and culture. The learning requirements arise from real problems and tasks. This provides learning motivation and collaborators with similar learning interests for mobile learners. Mobile learning has great potential to support learning in real settings, for example, museums tour or ecological survey in the river (Chu & Hwang, 2010). Learners can interact with the environment and collect environmental data by using the power of computation and communication of mobile devices. Meanwhile, learners can communicate with peers when they collect, analyze and record environmental data (Yang, 2006). In mobile learning, knowledge is presented in natural and authentic forms. It is important to account for local and remote social networks, both predefined and emerging, in order to support collaboration, but also to take advantage of serendipitous learning that might be triggered, for example, by co-located people (Canova Calori & Divitini 2009). Learners' surrounding information can be collected by mobile learning systems, such as where the learners are, what learning resources are available and who is qualified to solve learners' current problems. In the context of real world, rich information could be collected to represent the learners' surrounding environment (Economides, 2009). Efficient learning activities require an information filter mechanism to choose suitable information or services according to specific situations (Malek, Laroussi, & Derycke, 2006). Mobile learning systems can improve learners' learning experiences with recommendation approaches.

## Recommendation System

Recommendation technology originates in the domain of E-commerce (Resnick & Varian, 1997). Recommendation systems suggest appropriate products to customers according to their preferences and features of products. Customers can quickly find their favorite products in a large product space. Recommendation systems increase customers' satisfaction and loyalty. The accuracy and effectiveness of recommendation approaches is constantly improved with the drive of demand and the efforts of many researchers. Recommendation approaches are applied in many other domains that suffer from information overload. E-learning is one of the application domains where filtering out large amounts of unnecessary information with the help of recommendation technology has proved useful. The adopted recommendation approaches can improve the efficiency of e-learning systems by providing suitable learning resources and useful guidance to learners.

Recommendation approaches can help learners find appropriate learning contents, activities and tasks among countless learning objects (Manouselis, Vuorikari & Van Assche, 2010). With the analysis of one pilot study and two empirical studies, Recker et al. (2003) argue that collaborative filtering recommendation can be used as a promising means in helping learners find useful resources, bringing together people with similar interests and beliefs, and possibly as an aid to the learning process. Anderson et al. (2003) identify the challenge to find the most appropriate learning object for a given learner/purpose among countless e-learning objects and they argue that collaborative filtering recommendation can meet the demands of learners. An evolving web-based learning system is proposed by Tang and McCalla (2005) as an open learning environment. In this system, courses and learning materials come from the web and learning content is adapted according to the characteristics of learners. Adaptation is implemented with recommendation technology. In order to optimize the online learning process in a course web site, a recommender is used by Zaiane (2002) to recommend online learning activities or course navigation shortcuts in light of learners' access history.

However, E-learning has different recommendation requirements than E-commerce. These distinctive requirements bring big challenges to existing recommendation approaches. Drachsler et al. (2008) suggest that the challenge is the distinct differences of search behavior and needs for personalized recommendation between lifelong learners in e-learning and consumers in e-commerce. In order to meet with this challenge, memory-based recommendation techniques are adopted to recommend suitable learning activities for lifelong learners in the context of e-learning. Rafaeli et al. (2005) design an active recommender system to enhance knowledge sharing among learners. A number of challenges for recommendation systems stems from the differences between a learning context and a business environment. Learning resources should be valued in terms of learning needs. Recommendation results are determined on the base of pedagogical value, learning experiences, suitably for working task, and so forth.

In order to meet with the challenges, traditional recommendation approaches need to be adapted and new specialized recommendation approaches should be developed. For example, Sun et al. (2009) propose an approach to recommend appropriate learning activities through analyzing behavior pattern of learners through large amounts of web data. Klašnja-Milićević et al. (2010) question the approach common to most of contemporary e-Learning systems to display content and educational material in the same way to all learners. They suggest that recommendation systems can be used to suggest online learning activities or optimal browsing pathways to learners, based on their preferences, knowledge and the browsing history of other learners with similar characteristics. Nadolski et al. (2009) argue that recommender systems for e-learning demand specific pedagogy-oriented and hybrid recommendation strategies. They think that current systems do not seem appropriate for learning networks where distributed information is often not identifiable beforehand. So they suggest that new light-weight recommendation systems should be created to bridge this gap. A new learning content recommendation mechanism based on sequencing rules is proposed by Shen et al. (2004) to guild learners through the concepts of ontology of topics when gaps in the competencies of the learners are identified. Konstantinos et al. (2010) suggest that using recommendation systems in e-learning environments can help tutors to improve the performance of the teaching process and learners to find suitable online materials. In their approach, the e-learning system can recommend alternative educational resources on the base of student studying patterns by integrating semantic and ontological knowledge into recommendation systems.

## PROVIDING RECOMMENDATIONS FOR MOBILE LEARNING

As a new branch of E-learning, mobile learning also needs recommendation technology to provide appropriate information to learners. The goal of recommendation in mobile learning is to improve the efficiency of learning by recommending appropriate information of learning content, tasks and collaborators to learners against the huge alternative space. Recommendation is especially important for learners when mobile learning happens in an open and dynamically changing environment. It is necessary and possible for mobile learning systems to support learning with recommendation services. On the one hand, mobile learning has serious problems of information overload. A large amount of information is produced during the process of mobile learning in real settings. Learners are both producers and consumers of information. Information is produced and consumed when learners interact with others. Poor input and output capacity of mobile devices and unstable connection of wireless network limit the amounts of information that mobile learning system can support. On the other hand, the one-to-one relationship between a learner and his/her mobile device brings convenience to recommendation systems. It is easier for recommendation systems to collect individual information and provides personalized recommendation for learners. The information of the learning process could be recorded continuously in mobile learning systems. The location and environmental data of learners could also be read from sensors which are deployed in mobile learning environments. The collected information can be used as input data of recommendation systems.

The choice of recommendation approaches and the evaluation of recommendation performance depend on the requirements of specific domain. Recommendation service should strengthen the advantages of mobile learning and facilitates the enhancement of learning. How to provide suitable recommendation for mobile learning is decided by the unique characteristics and capabilities of mobile learning. Nowadays, many researchers are focusing on developing recommendation solutions to improve the efficiency of mobile learning systems. The recommendation objects can be classified into three categories: learning materials, tasks and collaborators. (1) Learning material. Large amounts of educational materials are put on a remote server in a digital learning environment. Learners can access these materials with their mobile devices and wireless network at anytime and anywhere (Luo, Dong, Cao, & Song, 2010). This does not refer only to traditional learning contents. A learning experience can itself be seen as useful learning material and should be shared with other learners (Ogata et al., 2010). It is difficult for learners to find suitable learning contents from the huge space of learning materials and various recommendation approaches can be used to suggest the suitable learning material according to learners' learning styles, knowledge level, interests and preferences (Yau & Joy, 2009; Andronico et al., 2003). (2) Learning tasks. Mobile learning encourages learners to learn in authentic learning environments, performing various tasks and activities. Different tasks have different preconditions that describe the specific situation and requirements. Learners should perform the right tasks or activities at the right time and in the right situation. To achieve the efficient learning, tasks should be conducted in the right sequence. Recommendation technology can help learners to choose the right tasks and optimize the sequence of learning tasks (Martín et al., 2006). (3) Learning collaborators and opportunities of collaboration. Mobile devices are used as learning tools in mobile learning environments. This can facilitate communication and collaboration among learners because learners usually take their mobile devices with them. With the help of their mobile devices, mobile learners can easily be involved in multiple learning communities, with co-located or geographically distributed members. But learners still need to spend a lot of time on finding a suitable learning partner. Even when they have the right learning partners, it is not easy to find the right time to collaborate without interfering with others' activities. Recommender systems might recommend matching collaborators and opportunities for learners in mobile learning systems (Bull, Cui, Robig & Sharples, 2005).

All the above recommendation objects are related to learners' current situation. The learners' surrounding information should be considered in order to provide effective recommendation. Traditional recommendation approaches, for example content-based recommendation and collaborative filter recommendation, just consider the interests and preferences of users. Traditional recommendation mechanisms do not recommend learning resources by taking into account the changing interests and preferences, which are arising from dynamic changing of the external environment. The impact of the external environment on learners and their learning resources is overlooked by traditional recommendation approaches. Traditional recommendation approaches cannot effectively reflect the actual requirements of mobile learners and provide accurate adaptation to mobile learning environments. The accuracy of recommendation results is very low when learner's interests change in a mobile environment. In order to deal with these problems, recommendation mechanisms that can exploit the learners' surrounding information during the recommendation process should be employed in mobile learning environments.

## Learning Context

Mobile learning offers learners a dynamic, continually changing setting. The circumstances of learners are dynamic as they change their physical location and take part in different collaboration activities. The accomplishments of learning activities and tasks will be affected by the current situations of learners. The learner's surrounding information can help understand the behavior of a learner and the current status of his/her learning process. Understanding the actual needs of learners is the key to provide right information to learners. Different learners have different preferences and requirements in different situations. The most appropriate learning activities, tasks, contents and services can be recommended to learners according to their current situations (Chan, Sharples, Vavoula, & Lonsdale, 2004; Malek, Laroussi & Derycke, 2006; Manasaweeet al., 2004). The situations of learner in mobile learning can be described by context, which is referred to any information that can be used to characterize the situation of an entity where an entity can be a person, place and a physical or computational object (Dey, 2001). Context provides a clue for mobile learning system to guide and support learners. Contextual information, for example the location or the current activities and tasks of learner, is very important for the purpose of improve the quality of learning experiences and collaboration (Nagella & Govindarajulu, 2007). Situated cognition theory argues that learning is simplified by embedding concept to the context where the concept will be used (Kirshner & Whitson, 1997).

Learning is greatly enhanced when it happens in a particular location or context. Learning is a continuous, life-long process resulting from acting in situations (Brown & Duguid, 1991). With the help of context, mobile learning systems can have a better understanding of learners and present personalized information and guidance to learners. Learning is embedded in the surrounding environment of a learner. The learner can flexibly access the required information as he/she moves in a physical learning environment. The learner can acquire knowledge from authentic learning activities and social contacts. Context is changing rapidly and continually when a learner moves between different locations and meets with localized resources, services and co-learners (Chan et al., 2004). The situations of a learner can be described from different perspectives with different levels of details (Derntl & Hummel, 2005).The concept of context should be redefined according to the requirements in mobile learning. A definition of learning context (Wang, 2004) is described as any information that can be used to characterize the situation of learning entities that are considered to be relevant to the interactions between a learner and an application. In another definition(Yang, 2006), learning context includes learner context and content context. Learner context includes the surrounding environment affecting learners' web content discovery and access and the content context includes the surrounding environment affecting Web content delivery and presentation.

In this chapter, context refers to any information that can be used to characterize the situation of a learner in mobile learning environments.

Context, which can be used to characterize the situations of a learner in a mobile learning environment, proposes opportunities to provide the suitable recommendation for mobile learning. Context can help to understand the behavior of learner and his/her surrounding environment. It is important to stress that the contextualization of learning. We refer to the notion of situated learning (Situated learning refers to "learning that is situated in a specific context and embedded within a particular social and physical environment".) introduced by Lave and Wenger (1991) to stress that learning does not happen in a vacuum but is situated in a given context. The acquisition of knowledge should not be fragmented and detached, but tied to a specific context (Lave & Wenger. 1991). Context is not only given by physical variables, like the location or temperature. More importantly, it has to take into account social aspects. In this perspective, the most interesting scenarios for mobile learning are the ones that provide a high degree of situatedness with respect to the social and physical context where the learning experience takes place (Canova Calori & Divitini, 2009). Contextual information should be integrated into the recommendation process to help compute the relevance degree between learners and various learning resources. Context-based recommendation is in coincidence with the dynamics nature of mobile learning environments. It can use real-time contextual information to accurately reflect the learning demands of learners.

There are also big challenges when contextual information is integrated into the process of recommendation in mobile learning systems. Recommendation approaches emerge in the domain of e-commerce. Recommendation approaches in e-commerce paid little attention to the situation of customers for a long time. Only recently, e-commerce began to consider the context of customers in order to provide more accurate recommendation (Cantador, Bellogin, & Castells, 2008; Liu, Cao, Zhao, & Yang, 2010). But the context still limited to the simple contextual information of users, for example the behavior of user webpage navigation, time and location. However, context is very complex in the mobile learning environment. Location and time are not the only important external elements that can affect recommendation performance. It is also necessary to take into account other elements, such as the physical and social environment, equipment, network settings and external events. In this perspective, the challenge becomes to design learning systems to be used *here* and *now*, rather than anywhere and anytime. This brings into the picture an understanding of contextual and situated aspects such as how to take advantage of the environments people inhabit temporarily; how the physical resources available in there may support a particular experience; how the people present there could provide unforeseen opportunities for collaboration; how relevant digital resources supplied by technologies can be accessed and used (Rossittom et al., 2010). This creates a large space of possibilities that learners have to choose from to assure an adequate and satisfying learning experience.

In mobile learning, learning requirements are dynamically changing as learners' context changes. The recommendation results can not reflect the actual demands of learners when the situations of learning activities are ignored in the process of recommendation. The characteristics of mobile learning bring both the unique advantages to support new forms of learning and new requirements to the current recommendation technology. New forms of learning supported by mobile learning systems propose new requirements to traditional recommendation approaches. Previous recommendation approaches need to be adapted or new recommendation approaches should be developed to meet with these requirements. Although some context-based recommendation approaches are proposed by researchers to solve some particular problems in mobile learning systems, there are still little attempts on systematically studying the opportunities and challenges that are posed by the unique nature of mobile learning. From the analysis of opportunities, researchers can learn the importance and roles of context for the purpose of providing the suitable recommendation in mobile learning systems. From the analysis of challenges, researchers can understand the possible issues and promising research directions when context-based recommendation is applied to mobile learning systems. The opportunities and challenges are outlined on four aspects. The opportunities and challenges from context, which are outlined in Figure 1, will be discussed in details in the following sections.

## Opportunities from Context

In mobile learning systems, contextual information should be integrated into the process of recommendation for the purpose of providing suitable recommendation according to the real requirements of learners. Context-based recommendation uses the context of learners to improve the effectiveness of recommendation. In an open and dynamic learning environment, context-based recommendation can help to provide more accurate recommendation by considering learners' surrounding information, learning status, preferences and the features of her/his mobile devices. What benefits can context-based recommendation bring to mobile learning? This question can be answered in the following four aspects.

### Supporting New Pedagogical Theories

Learning is embedded into learners' daily lives in mobile learning. The learning resources that learners use during the learning process are closely relevant with the context of learners. The impacts on learners and learning contents from the external environment are overlooked by previous pedagogical theories. Learners' interests and demands are constantly changing in the mobile learning environment. Both the requirements of collaboration among learners and learning tasks are related to context. New pedagogical theories for mobile learning put more attention to the external environment. Context-based recommendation can be used to support new pedagogical theories that emphasize the impact of environment. The environmental information can be used to improve the quality of learning. If the learning system can continually perceive the changes of the external environment, learners can establish a better relationship with the environment. Mobile learning systems can provide appropriate learning

*Figure 1. Providing recommendations for mobile learning: Opportunities and challenges from context*

resources by considering more environmental information. The information of relevant learning partners can also be seemed as a part of the context when mobile learning systems support collaboration among learners. For example, the current state of learners and available collaborative channels can be described in the context. Learners can efficiently work together through planning and reminding by mobile learning systems. New pedagogical theories need new learning systems to support. Contextual information is very important in the new learning theories because it represents the situation of learners. Contextual information can facilitate the integration of a learner with her/his surrounding environment (Wu et al., 2008; El-Bishouty, Ogata, & Yano, 2006). The right learning happens in the right environment. Contextual information can be used to determine whether students are available to collaborate with others, for example, the information of location, time and collaboration channels. So the context can promote the collaboration among learners.

Recommendation service can be used to replace a part of the teachers' duty in mobile learning systems. A learner-centered teaching can be achieved with the help of recommendation. Different learners have different learning styles, characteristics, needs and purposes. Personalized teaching can be implemented with recommendation according to learners' characteristics. Some teachers' tasks include recommending appropriate learning materials to their students. Recommendation can reduce the burden of teachers. When necessary, teachers can help learners and encourage them to learn effectively. The recommendation system can support students when teachers cannot stay with learners and help them in the specific circumstances.

Context-based recommendation can support new learning models, teaching methods and learning process in a mobile setting. Recommendations can help make full use of the advantages of mobility.

## Satisfying the Changing Requirements of Learners

Learning resources can be better adapted to the mobile learning environment by reflecting the dynamic learning interests of learners. Based on learners' surrounding information, available learning resources can be discovered without learner's explicit intervention. Dynamic implicit contextual information can be easily captured when learners take mobile devices with them all the time. So the dynamic changes of learners' demands can be captured and the suitable learning contents can be presented to learners. Without the automatic recommendation mechanism, learners have to explicitly request for these resources. Learning can be improved when learning resources are delivered according to learners' preferences and relevant contextual information. Learners can efficiently manage their own time with the help of recommendation. The required learning contents, tasks and collaborators are different in different learning environments. This will result in the large gap between the recommendation by traditional approaches and the actual requirements of learners. Contextual information can help the recommendation mechanism to timely respond to these changes and irrelevant information can be eliminated during the recommendation process.

The actual demands of learners can be accurately met based on real-time contextual information (Ogata et al., 2004; Yin, Ogata, Tabata & Yano, 2010). Mobile learning systems can understand the learner behavior and environmental parameters timely in the real world. Context-based recommendation can help improve the efficiency of learning. The learning context is used to describe the situation of learners. It can be used to search and adapt the learning resources in mobile learning systems. The context includes the characteristics of learners, ongoing activities, location, time, and the type of mobile devices. The benefits from context-based recommendation include the improvement of learning efficiency, providing the accurate learning contents, planning an appropriate learning schedule when learners have free time or appropriate learning opportunities. The current learning environment of learners can be discovered automatically by the recommendation mechanism. Then the suitable learning materials will be recommended to learners. Recommendation can create and maximize learning opportunities for learners in different situations. Learners should input their appropriate schedule rules in advance. When the specified conditions appear, the suitable learning contents and tasks will be proposed automatically. This will maximize the learning opportunities for learners. The suitable learning location, available learning tasks and collaborators are proposed by the recommendation mechanism. The maximization of learning productivity can be realized by making full use of learners' free time in their daily life.

Personalized information filtering mechanism can identify what resources are the most suitable for each leaner. The mechanism can offer an individual learning plan and tailor the learning contents according to the individual needs and interests of learners.

## Tackling Information Overload

In mobile learning systems, large amounts of data come from three sources. (1) Learning materials. Mobile learning systems are connected to Internet via mobile devices and wireless network. Extensive educational resources on the remote servers are available to mobile learners (Bull, et al., 2005). These resources could be in many forms, for example text, image, audio and video. They can be used as learning reference materials during the learning process. (2) The data generated by learners themselves. Mobile learning systems can help learners to record their learning experiences at anytime, anywhere (Bull, Cui, Robig, & Sharples, 2005). Learners use their mobile devices as learning tools. They can always record their ideas, insights, textual chats and the results of their own learning. Mobile learning system can support collaborative learning. Communication between learners is convenient when the communication tools, mobile devices, are used as learning tools. Collaborative learning encourages learner to interact and share ideas with others. Large amounts of information are produced during the process of communication. (3) The data provided by the environment. One advantage of mobile learning is that learners can learn in a real environment. The real learning objects and the virtual world of information could be connected by RFID (Radio Frequency Identification) tags and sensors. Learners in the real environment continually receive information from real learning objects (Lonsdale et al., 2004).

The portability of mobile devices is implemented at the expense of their input and output capabilities. Most of mobile devices have a small size screen, which can display limited contents. Moreover, network communication is conducted via wireless network. The network bandwidth and connection status also limit the amounts of data that is sent or received by mobile devices. If all the available information is sent to learners at the same time, not only it cannot provide benefits to learners, but also it will increase the burden of learners and reducing their enthusiasm to use mobile learning systems. How to filter and provide useful information to learners impacts on the employment of mobile learning systems. It is very important for effective mobile learning systems to provide an efficient approach to deal with information overload. The information is useful for learners when the data are sent, retrieved and reused in the right circumstances.

The context of learners can be used to determine what information is useful for learners (Bhaskar & Govindarajulu, 2008). The information, which are provided or produced in a situation, will usually be useful for other learners in the same or similar situation. Contextual information can be used as the information filtering criteria. Even if the learning contents is recommended by other recommendation approaches, contextual information can also be used to determine the right timing and ways to deliver learning resources without disturbing others (Ogata et al., 2010).

### Supporting the Variety of Mobile Devices

Mobile devices have different hardware, operation systems and software. The characteristics of mobile devices can be described as a part of the context (Zhao & Okamoto, 2008). The recommendation can be given according to both learners' dynamic interests and the characteristics of mobile devices. In this way, learners can receive learning contents with compatibility to their mobile devices. The recommendation results will be adapted according to the screen size of mobile devices before they are presented on mobile devices.

Learners can use traditional keyword search methods to find and acquire the most suitable resources. Because mobile devices have a limited input and output capacity, it is not suitable to input a large number of keywords, and navigate and search from lots for search results. In fact, these learning resources are relevant with the current context of learners. The number of input tasks will be reduced when some input contents are replaced by contextual information. Recommendation does not require learners to request or input data. It is a proactive method to present suitable resources to learners.

Contextual information can be used to replace the keywords. Compared with keyword search, context-based recommendation is a more convenient way to help learners access to their favorable learning materials. The input information can be automatically collected and only limited output are recommended to learners. The shortcoming of poor input and output capacity of mobile devices can be made up with context-based recommendation.

## Challenges from Context

A context-based recommendation system can recommend relevant learning resources to a learner against a huge alternative space based on her/his context. Context can play an important role in deciding what learning resources are useful to a learner. The importance of each context element is different in different situations. The complexity of context also proposes challenges for implementing context-based recommendation. The challenges for recommendation in mobile learning should be addressed from a systematic perspective. The existing recommendation approaches should be improved in many aspects that can affect the final recommendation results. The issues of creating learning context, designing recommendation algorithms, presenting recommendation results and evaluating recommendation performance are outlined as following:

### Creating Accurate Learning Context

In order to create accurate learning context for the purpose of recommendation, two questions should be answered: What contextual information should be included into the process of recommendation in mobile learning systems? How to collect, organize and use contextual data to provide accurate recommendation results?

A context model should be redefined from the learning and teaching perspective by determining what context information is associated with mobile learning. An effective context model should be created on the base of the combination of pedagogical theory and learning practices. It is a rather broad definition of context: any information that is relevant to describe the situation of a learner can be seemed as context. Many context elements should be taken into account in mobile learning systems (Kurti, Spikol, & Milrad, 2008). The recommendation should be given according to the model of learner, including personal information, knowledge and learning goal, tasks, ability and techniques. What context elements should be included in the context model? How to modeling context from the learning and pedagogical perspective to facilitate context-based recommendation? How to model the psychological and social state of learners? How to classify context elements with right abstraction levels and hierarchy? How to organize and store context in a good structure in order to facilitate the following recommendation? A standard of modeling context needs to be established in context-based recommendation for mobile learning.

The contextual data can be collected from different sources with different methods in mobile learning systems. The data sources include learner input (the navigation behavior of learners, input data, the records of chatting and discussion with other learners, learning tasks and activities), and sensors (location from GPS and other positioning systems, and the environmental data from sensors). Except for the data in mobile leaning systems, sensors and RFID are deployed in the mobile learning environment in order to provide a panoramic description of context (Beach et al., 2010). The raw data, which collected from different data sources, have different data types and formats. Different data need to be collected in different ways. The data from sensors or RFID can be seemed as the low-level context. The up-level context can be inferred from the low-level one. The records of chat and discussion and interpersonal relationships among learners can be used as a part of context to understand the social dimension of a learner. Hence, context may include different levels of information. The heterogeneity of data makes it difficult to collect and process context information. It is necessary to merge these data together when they are used as the input of recommendation. This is a big challenge for data collection, processing, storage and inference. What data can be used to represent the preferences of learning? What data can be used to represent the learning progress? In order to extract meaningful contextual information, the raw data need to be classified according to learning demands. The diverse data are merged together to describe the whole context of learners. It is a challenging problem of how to extract useful information from huge amounts of heterogeneous input data and organize them in a flexible format for context-based recommendation.

To create the accurate learning context for the purpose of providing suitable recommendations for mobile learning, the question of what elements are included in context model should be considered according to the real requirements (Yang, Huang, Chen, Tseng, & Shen, 2006). Learning context describes the situations of a learner in a mobile learning environment. Its model should be defined for the purpose of recommendation. The sufficient information is provided in order to present suitable recommendation to learners. The context elements that have important impacts on recommendation results are identified to better understand the relationship of learners, learning environment and recommendation objects. Context could include learning goal and tasks, knowledge and skills, environmental information and personal information. The useful and sufficient contextual data should be collected during the learning process (Luo, et al., 2010). Sufficient and orderly input data is the precondition of providing good recommendation. In context-based recommendation, data collection can be viewed as a process of obtaining the value of attributes, which are defined in a learning context model. The explicit collection can be conducted by monitoring learner behavior in mobile learning systems, which includes login or logoff, the participation of activities, the use of services. The inexplicit collection can be conducted by extracting the meaningful information from the raw data. Except for simple context elements, the context of the learning status, pedagogical model and learning progress should be included in the process of data collection. These contexts cannot be collected directly from the raw data and should be extracted from observing learning behaviors and the records of chat and discussion. More information will be produced in mobile learning than in other domains because learning happens in a real setting and learners can interact with both the environment and other learners. Currently, many approaches are adopted to deal with heterogeneous data and unstructured data in research and practice, for example linked data (Bizer, Heath, & Berners-Lee, 2009), ontology (Guarino, 1998), cloud computing (Armbrust et al., 2009) and folksonomy (Vander Wal, 2007). When accurate learning context is created for recommendation, these approaches can be referred, considered or adapted to simplify the data collection process.

## Designing Effective Recommendation Algorithms

In order to design effective recommendation algorithms, pedagogical issues should be included in the recommendation algorithms to guide how to enhance the learning experience and meet with the requirements of learners (Chen, Hsu, Li, & Peng, 2006). Context-based recommendation algorithm consists of input, filter mechanism and output. Contextual information is heterogeneous and usually described with a multi-dimension model. It is difficult to calculate the similarity of context because there different types of attributes in a context model. The different types and levels of granularity of heterogeneous input data make context-based recommendation more complex. How to apply contextual elements with different priorities and constraints in the recommendation process is a challenging problem. Context-based recommendation provides recommendation results by computing the relevance of a learner and learning resources on the base of context. Efficient context-based recommendation algorithms for mobile learning can be achieved by adapting existing recommendation approaches or creating novel algorithms.

1. The traditional recommendation algorithms are extended to involve contextual information into the recommendation process.

The challenge of this method is how to adapt existing approaches to provide recommendation by considering the factor of context. Context elements can be used as a part of input data in traditional recommendation approaches at pre-recommendation or post-recommendation stage. Traditional collaborative recommendation approaches can deal with the emergent and unknown learning contents because learners are involved in the recommendation process through user ratings. For example, a context-based recommendation algorithm is designed by integrating contextual information into collaborative recommendation. The collaborative recommendation provides suitable tasks on the base of the similarity of situations that are characterized with contextual information (Vo, Torabi, & Loke, 2009).

2. New context-based recommendation algorithms are created for mobile learning.

Most of current context-based recommendation approaches are rule-based inference algorithms, which combine inference rules with contextual information with the help of an inference engine (Zhao, Anma, Ninomiya, & Okamoto, 2008). The rules are set to predefine the content output under different contextual conditions. The rules are fired when the specific contextual condition occurs. In order to give the accurate recommendation, the rules should consider all situations in the learning progress according to the learning requirements. The challenge of this method is how to design inference rules to ensure the high efficiency of recommendation (Rubinsztejn, Endler, Sacramento, Goncalves, & Nascimento, 2004). For example, a context-based recommendation algorithm is designed with inference rules and engines. The current context is decided by searching the predefined context sets with a pattern matching method. Then the corresponding events are delivered to users based on context-aware rules (event type, time interval and context conditions). Each event represents a set of useful information about a topic, which can be statically defined by the system when generating the event instance, or dynamically defined through queries in the knowledge base (Kirsch-Pinheiro, Villanova-Oliver, Gensel, & Martin, 2005). The advantage of inference rules-based recommendation is that it can describe in details what should be recommended in what circumstances. Rule-based recommendation approaches use flexible rules, which can describe dynamic and complex context and propose different recommendation for different context. The inference rules can be used to customize the choice of learning materials. The weakness of rule-based approach is that rules must be designed in advance. It is not suitable to cope with unknown and emergent situations. On the one hand, it is complex and difficult to develop comprehensive rules for all the situations. On the other hand, conflicts of rule inference will increase with more and more rules being added to rule set.

Hybrid recommendation approaches, which combine several complementary recommendation approaches together to achieve better performance, could be a possible solution for context-based recommendation. For example, the initial recommendation objects can be selected with traditional recommendation approaches by considering the similarity of contents or learners. Then the final recommendation results are chosen with rule-based recommendation approaches according to the current context of learners.

## Properly Presenting Recommendation Results

The presentation of recommendation results in mobile learning systems is different from the presentation in E-commerce. In E-commerce, the presentation of recommendation results on the big-size computer screen is easy. The recommendation results are displayed in a list. Most of recommendation results are the same type of goods. And customers' preferences do not change in a short period of time. So the list is appropriate to present recommendation results in E-commerce. However, how to present recommendation results in mobile learning systems is a big problem. The presentation of recommendation results on small-size screens of mobile devices should be elaborately planned and organized. Accurate recommendation results need good presentation. Bad presentation will degrade the performance of recommendation and even disturb the learners' normal learning. Even the suitable recommendation results will disturb the normal learning when timing, frequency and amounts of recommendation are not right. The recommendation results may include many different kinds of learning resources in the changing learning context. Furthermore, the continually emerging recommendation results will interfere with the attention of learners.

The recommendation results can be presented in the following two ways:

1. Naturally integrating recommendation results into the learning process.

The presentation of the recommendation results to learners in mobile learning systems should be carefully designed since the recommendation results may distract learners when the recommendation results are pushed to learners' mobile devices (Martín & Carro, 2008). Criteria should be provided to guide when and how learners can be interrupted to inform them about new recommendations. The alert method should be considered to arouse the learners' attention. Alert rules can be designed in rule sets to support these criteria. Different rules apply to different learners and contextual conditions. The direct push method can be used to recommend the answers or references that learners currently need. The suitable collaborator can be suggested when learners are free or have mood to work with others. The feedback of learners for recommendation results should be collected by the feedback collection mechanism, which should be given when the recommendation results are presented. The behavior patterns of learners should be analyzed for the purpose of evaluating recommendation performance and improving recommendation efficiency. Contextual information can be used to determine the availability of some learning tasks. The decision can be made according to learners' previous reaction to the similar situations. The extent of interference should be considered to evaluate the recommendation performance. Quantitative experimental analysis should be used to find out the timing, ways and side effects of presentation. These experiments should be designed for different learning tasks. In order to naturally integrate the recommendation into the learning process, the pedagogical and learning methodology should be adopted to guide the presentation of recommendation results. The ways of presenting the recommendation results vary according to the learning contents, environment and learners' preference.

2. Appropriately reflecting the characteristics of mobile devices.

There are many kinds of mobile devices in mobile learning systems. Mobile devices have their characteristics on hardware, operation systems and application software. The characteristics of mobile devices should be considered during the recommendation process. The adaptation is very important for presenting the recommendation results because the screen size of mobile devices is very small. The number of recommendation results should be decided according to the size of small screen of mobile devices. The accuracy of recommendation results should be high. The learning materials should be present to learners in right forms according to the requirements of their mobile devices. Good navigation guidance should be given when too many recommendation results are presented to learners. The recommendation results can be displayed in a specific area. The layout of learning contents can be adjusted according to the recommendation degree. The items with highest recommendation degree can be put on the top. Color can be used to represent the recommendation level and degree. The recommended learning contents should be supported by the target mobile devices. For example, some media types cannot be supported by some type of mobile devices. Learning contents should be chosen according to the characteristics of mobile devices. The presentation of recommendation must adapt to the characteristics of mobile devices.

## Comprehensively Evaluating the Performance of Recommendation

The effectiveness and efficiency of context-based recommendation in mobile learning should be assessed with an evaluation framework. The purpose of evaluation of context-based recommendation is to understand the context's contribution to recommendation results. The evaluation results can be used to help identify and understand the problems that affect the effectiveness and efficiency of recommendation. The evaluation of the performance of context-based recommendation depends on the subjective relevance judgment. Multidimensional relevance cannot be decided by one single criterion. Learners need to evaluate the relevance of recommendation results with variable judgment criterion. Context-based recommendation happens in a context, which consists of the characteristic of learners, the tasks and activities, and the surrounding environment of learners. The relevance is multidimensional because context consists of multi elements and recommendation results are given on the base of multidimensional context. The evaluation of recommendation performance should be given from three perspectives. (1) The accuracy of recommendation. This evaluates the extent that recommendation results are accepted by learners. (2) The presentation of recommendation results. The following questions should be evaluated from this perspective: Are recommendation results presented in the right time and right way? Are the normal learning activities disturbed by the recommendation results? Are these recommendation services naturally embed into the learning process? (3) The contribution of context to recommendation. The recommendation results should be given on the base of specific contextual information.

The performance of recommendation approaches should be assessed with an evaluation framework (Luo et al., 2010). What are the advantages and disadvantages of existing evaluation methods when they are used to evaluate context-based recommendation? Evaluation methods should be critically reviewed in order to assure the effectiveness of evaluating context-based recommendation. In mobile learning, the interaction of learners with learning system, environment and other learners can change the content of context and the corresponding recommendation results. Recommendation results are dynamically changing with the interaction of learners. To include contextual information into the evaluation process requires the learner interaction to be involved into means the assessment process. Learners and their interaction, behaviors should be included into the evaluation framework. It is a big challenge for current evaluation methods when learners' context information is considered during the process of recommendation. The performance may be different for different context because of the dynamically changing requirements of learners in different learning situations. It is very hard that the evaluation results in a situation can be generic to other situations. The context of learner will affect the judgment of relevance of learner. The recommendation needs to be given in real time in order to react to the emerging context signal. And the signal should be triggered by learners in the real settings. The emergence and sequence cannot be guaranteed in real life in context-based recommendation. It is very hard to compare the performance of two context-based recommendations when dynamic interactions exist in mobile learning. The existing evaluation methods do not include learners and their surrounding environment in the scope of evaluation. Recall and Precision are widely used as evaluation indicators to measuring the effectiveness of recommendation. These evaluation methods cannot deal with the variability and complexity of context-based recommendation.

Novel evaluation strategies and measures should be designed to fill the gap of evaluation of context-based recommendation.

1. It should be a controllable evaluation framework that allows repeated experiments and comparison evaluation. Repeated experiments and comparison evaluation can help identify and understand the problems that affect the effectiveness and efficiency of recommendation.
2. It should consider both the recommendation performance and the satisfaction of learners. Context-based recommendation is a social activity and subjective in the background of learner interaction. The effectiveness of recommendation can be evaluated in the real settings by considering the requirements of learners in different context. The evaluation of recommendation approaches should meet with the requirements of learners. Therefore, learner-oriented and task-oriented assessment method could be used to evaluate the performance of context-based recommendation. Task-oriented evaluation can measure the satisfaction of learners for interaction, recommendation process and results.
3. The evaluation indicator should be chosen according to the requirement of mobile learning. Evaluation indicators are critical for the evaluation of recommendation performance. Accuracy is one of indicators but not the only indicator. For example, reaction time could be important when the recommendation should be given on the real time according

to context information. Recommendation performance may be evaluated in different situations with different indicators.

4. It should integrate the interaction of learners into the process of evaluation. The interaction of learners with system, environment and other learners can be defined in context simulation. Context simulation and user studies could be a part of evaluation framework. And comparable evaluation can be conducted in context simulation. The purpose of user study is to quantitatively evaluate the performance of context-based recommendation. The interaction of learners can be included in user study evaluation. The assessment can be conducted by user study through learner uses mobile learning systems and natural interaction.
5. Standard test data sets should be provided to compare the performance of different context-based recommendation algorithm. Contextual information is closely related to the specific environment and tasks. Classical dataset in different situations in mobile learning environments should be established for the purpose of evaluation.

## FUTURE RESEARCH DIRECTIONS

As a new branch of E-learning, mobile learning is continually developing on both theoretical and practical aspects. Suitable recommendation can improve learning by solving information overload problem during the learning process and helping a learner to shape a learning experience that takes advantage of the possibilities offered by the situation the learner is in. With the further development of mobile learning, there will be additional research questions in this area. Based on the above opportunities and challenges from context, the following research directions could be promising:

1. Recommendation requirements

With the development of mobile devices and wireless technology, mobile learning will be further integrated into learners' daily lives and support more learning forms. Different learning theories need different recommendation mechanisms to support. Context-based recommendation approaches should be designed to support mobile learning methodologies. New recommendation targets and requirements should be identified from the theory and practice perspectives. New recommendation requirements propose new opportunities and challenges for existing recommendation approaches.

2. Recommendation mechanism

In order to meet with the challenges of new recommendation requirements, the traditional recommendation mechanisms should be adapted or novel recommendation mechanisms should be created. Recommendation mechanisms should take into account the dynamic preference of learners in mobile learning environments. How to integrate context into recommendation process is still a hot research question. The advantage of mobile learning is the ability to support the high mobility of learning. The nature of mobility decides that the recommendation approaches in mobile learning systems should be context-based. Context is much more than location and time. More dimensions of context should be considered in the learning process. The development of other research areas, for example, image processing and analysis, learner observation techniques of physical activity and psychological impact on learners, will bring interesting research topics for context-based recommendation in mobile learning systems.

3. Recommendation evaluation

The appropriate evaluation matrix should be designed to assess both the performance of the recommendation system and its contribution to learning. The interaction of learners with the system, the physical environment and other learners must be considered in the process of evaluation. The designed evaluation mechanism should support comparable tests in mobile learning environments. This might be particularly challenging because mobile learning is often taking advantage of serendipitous encounters and exploration of opportunities that are highly context-based and therefore difficult to reproduce.

## CONCLUSION

In this chapter, opportunities and challenges from context are analyzed systematically in order to provide suitable recommendation for mobile learning. Mobile learning encourages learners to learn in authentic environments. The learning interests and preferences of learners are dynamic as learners change their physical location, join in different communities, and take part in different activities. Traditional recommendation approaches cannot provide accurate recommendation in a mobile learning environment because the recommendation process does not take into account the current situations of learners.

Context, which can be used to characterize the situations of a learner in a mobile learning environment, might improve the efficiency of mobile learning systems and promote richer and unplanned situated learning experiences. Recommendation approaches can provide appropriate recommendation by understanding the actual demands of learners with the help of context. Context-based approaches might offer the following opportunities: (1) Supporting new pedagogical theories. Context-based recommendation can support new learning models, teaching methods and learning process in a mobile setting. The recommendation can help make full use of the advantages of mobility. (2) Satisfying dynamic requirements of learners. The real learning demands of learners can be accurately met according to real-time contextual information. (3) Tackling Information Overload. Contextual information can be used as the information filtering criteria. Even if the learning resources are recommended by other recommendation approaches, contextual information can also be used to determine the right timing and ways to deliver learning resources. (4) The shortcoming of poor input and output capacity of mobile devices is made up with context-based recommendation. The input information can be automatically collected and only limited output are recommended to learners. Contextual information of learners needs to be modeled, collected and processed for the purpose of recommendation. Contextual information can be integrated into the recommendation process by adapting traditional recommendation algorithms or developing novel ones. Context-based recommendation can facilitate the interaction of learners with the system, the environment, and other learners by providing the suitable recommendation to learners in specific situations.

Context poses challenges to recommendation approaches concerning input data, context modeling, algorithm and evaluation. These challenges include: (1) Creating Accurate Learning Context. In order to create accurate learning context for the purpose of recommendation, two questions should be answered: What contextual information should be included into the process of recommendation in mobile learning systems? How to collect, organize and use contextual data to provide accurate recommendation results? (2) Designing Effective Recommendation Algorithms. In order to design effective recommendation algorithms, pedagogical methodologies, which guide how to enhance the learning experience and meet with the requirements of learners, should be included into the design process of recommendation algorithms. Context-based recommendation algorithm consists of input, filter mechanism and output. How to apply contextual elements with different priorities and constraints in the recommendation process is a challenging problem. (3) Properly Presenting Recommendation Results. The presentation of recommendation results on small-size mobile devices should be elaborately planned and organized. Accurate recommendation results need good presentation. Bad presentation will degrade the performance of recommendation and even disturb the learners' normal learning. Even the suitable recommendation results will disturb the normal learning when timing, frequency and amounts of recommendation are not right. (4) Comprehensively Evaluating the Performance of Recommendation. New evaluation mechanisms that allow repeated experiments and comparison evaluation in the dynamic learning environment should be developed to assess the performance of context-based recommendation.

Based on the analysis of opportunities and challenges from context, possible directions and questions are identified to guide future research. The application of context-based recommendation can facilitate the further development of mobile learning.

## ACKNOWLEDGMENT

This research is part of the NFR-project nr. 176841/SIO FABULA. More information about the project is available at http://fabula.idi.ntnu.no.

## REFERENCES

Anderson, M., Ball, M., Boley, H., Greene, S., Howse, N., Lemire, D., et al. (2003). RACOFI: A rule-applying collaborative filtering system. In *Proceedings of IEEE/WIC COLA'03*, Halifax, Canada, October 2003.

Andronico, A., Carbonaro, A., Casadei, G., Colazzo, L., Molinari, A., & Ronchetti, M. (2003). Integrating a multi-agent recommendation system into a mobile learning management system. In *Proceedings of Artificial Intelligence in Mobile System.* Retrieved from http://w5.cs.uni-sb.de/~krueger/aims2003/camera-ready/carbonaro-4.pdf

Armbrust, M., Fox, A., Griffith, R., Joseph, A. D., Katz, R. H., & Konwinski, A. … Zaharia, M. (2009). *Above the clouds: A Berkeley view of Cloud computing*. Technical report UCB/EECS-2009-28, Electrical Engineering and Computer Sciences, University of California at Berkeley, Berkeley, USA, February 2009.

Beach, A., Gartrell, M., Xing, X., Han, R., Lv, Q., Mishra, S., et al. (2010). Fusing mobile, sensor, and social data to fully enable context-aware computing, *Proceedings of the Eleventh Workshop on Mobile Computing Systems & Applications* (pp. 60-65).

Berri, J., Benlamri, R., & Atif, Y. (2006). Ontology-based framework for context-aware mobile learning. *Proceedings of the 2006 International Conference on Wireless Communications and Mobile Computing* (pp. 1307-1310).

Bhaskar, N. U., & Govindarajulu, P. (2008). A design methodology for acceptability analyzer in context aware adaptive mobile learning systems development. *International Journal of Computer Science and Network Security*, *8*(8), 130–138.

Bizer, C., Heath, T., & Berners-Lee, T. (2009). Linked data - The story so far. [IJSWIS]. *International Journal on Semantic Web and Information Systems*, *5*(3), 2009. doi:10.4018/jswis.2009081901

Brown, J. S., & Duguid, P. (1991). Organizational learning and communities-of-practice: Toward a unified view of working, learning, and innovation. *Organization Science*, *2*(1), 40–57. doi:10.1287/orsc.2.1.40

Bull, S., Cui, Y., Robig, H., & Sharples, M. (2005). Adapting to different needs in different locations: Handheld computers in university education. *Proceedings of the IEEE International Workshop on Wireless and Mobile Technologies in Education* (pp. 48-52).

Canova Calori, I., & Divitini, M. (2009). Reflections on the role of technology in city-wide collaborative learning. [iJIM]. *International Journal of Interactive Mobile Technologies*, *3*(2), 33–39.

Cantador, I., Bellogin, A., & Castells, P. (2008). Ontology-based personalised and context-aware recommendations of news items. *Proceedings of the 2008 IEEE/WIC/ACM International Conference on Web Intelligence and Intelligent Agent Technology* - volume 1 (pp. 562-565).

Chan, T., Sharples, M., Vavoula, G., & Lonsdale, P. (2004). Educational metadata for mobile learning. *Proceedings of the 2nd IEEE International Workshop on Wireless and Mobile Technologies in Education,* (pp. 197-198).

Chen, C. M., Hsu, S. H., Li, Y. L., & Peng, C. J. (2006). Personalized intelligent m-learning system for supporting effective English learning. *Systems, Man and Cybernetics, 2006. SMC, 06*, 4898–4903.

Chen, G. D., Chang, C. K., & Wang, C. Y. (2008). Ubiquitous learning website: Scaffold learners by mobile devices with information-aware techniques. *Computers & Education*, *50*(1), 77–90. doi:10.1016/j.compedu.2006.03.004

Chen, L., & Pu, P. (2010). User evaluation framework of recommender systems. *Proceedings of 2010 Workshop on Social Recommender Systems (SRS'10) at the ACM International Conference on Intelligent User Interfaces (IUI'10)*.

Chu, H. C., & Hwang, G. J. (2010). A location-aware mobile learning system to provide field learning guidance for natural science courses. *Informatics in Control, Automation and Robotics (CAR), 2010 2nd International Asia Conference* (vol. 3, pp. 291-294).

Cobcroft, R. S., Towers, S. J., Smith, J. E., & Bruns, A. (2006). Mobile learning in review: Opportunities and challenges for learners, teachers, and institutions. *Online Learning and Teaching (OLT) Conference 2006* (pp. 21-30).

Derntl, M., & Hummel, K. A. (2005). Modeling context-aware e-learning scenarios. *Proceedings of the Third IEEE International Conference on Pervasive Computing and Communications Workshops* (pp. 337-342).

Dey, A. K. (2001). Understanding and using context. *Personal and Ubiquitous Computing*, *5*(1), 4–7. doi:10.1007/s007790170019

Drachsler, H., Hummel, H. G. K., & Koper, R. (2008). Personal recommender systems for learners in lifelong learning networks: The requirements, techniques and model. *Int. J. Learn. Technol.*, *3*(4), 404–423. doi:10.1504/IJLT.2008.019376

Economides, A. A. (2009). Adaptive context-aware pervasive and ubiquitous learning. *International Journal of Technology Enhanced Learning*, *1*(3), 169–192. doi:10.1504/IJTEL.2009.024865

El-Bishouty, M. M., Ogata, H., & Yano, Y. (2006). Personalized knowledge awareness map in computer supported ubiquitous learning. *Proceedings of the Sixth IEEE International Conference on Advanced Learning Technologies* (pp. 817-821).

Guarino, N. (1998). *Formal ontology in Information Systems*. IOS Press.

Herlocker, J. L., Konstan, J. A., Terveen, L. G., & Riedl, J. T. (2004). Evaluating collaborative filtering recommender systems. *ACM Transactions on Information Systems, 22*(1), 5–53. doi:10.1145/963770.963772

Kirsch-Pinheiro, M., Villanova-Oliver, M., Gensel, J., & Martin, H. (2005). Context-aware filtering for collaborative web systems: Adapting the awareness information to the user's context. *Proceedings of the 2005 ACM Symposium on Applied Computing* (pp. 1668-1673).

Kirshner, D., & Whitson, J. A. (1997). *Situated cognition: Social, semiotic, and psychological perspectives*. Mahwah, NJ: Lawrence Erlbaum Associates.

Klašnja-Milićević, A., Vesin, B., Ivanović, M., & Budimac, Z. (2010). Integration of recommendations and adaptive hypermedia into Java tutoring system. *Computer Science and Information Systems 2010 OnLine-First Issue* (pp. 21-21).

Konstantinos, M., Penelope, M., Giannis, K., & Aglaia, L.-T. (2010). Semantic e-learning: Next generation of e-learning? *Next Generation Society: Technological and Legal Issues, 26*, 295–308. doi:10.1007/978-3-642-11631-5_27

Kurti, A., Spikol, D., & Milrad, M. (2008). Bridging outdoors and indoors educational activities in schools with the support of mobile and positioning technologies. *Int. J. Mob. Learn. Organ., 2*(2), 166–186. doi:10.1504/IJMLO.2008.019767

Laurillard, D. (2007). Pedagogical forms of mobile learning: framing research questions. In *Mobile Learning: Towards a Research Agenda, Occasional Papers in Work-based Learning* (pp. 153-175). London, UK: WLE Centre, Institute of Education.

Lave, J., & Wenger, E. (1991). Situated learning: Legitimate peripheral participation. In *Learning in doing: Social, cognitive and computational perspectives*. Cambridge, UK: Cambridge University Press.

Lavoie, M. (2006). *M-learning: Identifying design recommendations for a context-aware mobile learning system*. IADIS International Conference Mobile Learning.

Leung, C., & Chan, Y. (2003). Mobile learning: A new paradigm in electronic learning. *Third IEEE International Conference on Advanced Learning Technologies (ICALT'03)* (pp. 76-81).

Liu, N. N., Cao, B., Zhao, M., & Yang, Q. (2010). *Adapting neighborhood and matrix factorization models for context aware recommendation*. Paper presented at the Workshop on Context-Aware Movie Recommendation.

Liu, T. C., Wang, H. Y., Liang, J. K., Chan, T. W., Ko, H. W., & Yang, J. C. (2003). Wireless and mobile technologies to enhance teaching and learning. *Journal of Computer Assisted Learning, 19*(3), 371–382. doi:10.1046/j.0266-4909.2003.00038.x

Lonsdale, P., Baber, C., Sharples, M., Byrne, W., Brundell, P., & Beale, R. (2004). *Context awareness for MOBIlearn: Creating an engaging learning experience in an art museum*. MLEARN 2004.

Luo, J. Z., Dong, F., Cao, J. X., & Song, A. B. (2010). A context-aware personalized resource recommendation for pervasive learning. *Cluster Computing-the Journal of Networks Software Tools and Applications, 13*(2), 213–239.

Malek, J., Laroussi, M., & Derycke, A. (2006). *A multi-layer ubiquitous middleware for bijective adaptation between context and activity in a mobile and collaborative learning*. International Conference on Systems and Networks Communication (ICSNC'06), Tahiti, French Polynesia, 1-3 Novembre 2006.

Malek, J., Laroussi, M., & Derycke, A. (2006). A middleware for adapting context to mobile and collaborative learning. *Fourth Annual IEEE International Conference, Pervasive Computing and Communications Workshops,* (pp. 221-225).

Manasawee, K., Eamonn, O., Apos, N., & Bath Ba, A. (2004). *An integrated context model: Bringing activity to context.* In Workshop on Advanced Context Modelling, Reasoning and Management, UbiComp 2004, Nottingham, UK.

Manouselis, N., Vuorikari, R., & Van Assche, F. (2010). Collaborative recommendation of e-learning resources: An experimental investigation. *Journal of Computer Assisted Learning*, *26*(4), 227–242. doi:10.1111/j.1365-2729.2010.00362.x

Martín, E., Andueza, N., Carro, R. M., & Rodríguez, P. (2006). *Recommending activities in collaborative m-learning. Adaptive Hypermedia and Adaptive Web-based Systems* (pp. 197–204). Berlin, Germany: Springer.

Martín, E., & Carro, R. M. (2008). Supporting the development of mobile adaptive learning environments: A case study. *IEEE Transactions on Learning Technologies, 2*(1), 23-36. Jan-March 2009, doi: 10.1109/TLT2008.24

Motiwalla, L. F. (2007). Mobile learning: A framework and evaluation. *Computers & Education*, *49*(3), 581–596. doi:10.1016/j.compedu.2005.10.011

Nadolski, R., Van den Berg, B., Berlanga, A., Drachsler, H., Hummel, H., Koper, R., & Sloep, P. (2009). Simulating light-weight personalised recommender systems in learning networks: A case for pedagogy-oriented and rating-based hybrid recommendation strategies. *Journal of Artificial Societies and Social Simulation*, *12*(1), 4.

Nagella, U. B., & Govindarajulu, D. P. (2007). Adaptive approaches to context aware mobile learning applications. *International Journal of Computer Science and Security*, *2*(2), 15–27.

O'malley, C., Vavoula, G., Glew, J., Taylor, J., Sharples, M., & Lefrere, P. (2003). Guidelines for learning/teaching/tutoring in a mobile environment. *MOBIlearn WP4, 2003* (pp. 1-57).

Ogata, H., Akamatsu, R., Mitsuhara, H., Yano, Y., Matsuura, K., Kanenishi, K., et al. (2004). TANGO: Supporting vocabulary learning with RFID tags. *Proceedings of International Workshop Series on RFID.*

Ogata, H., Misumi, T., Bin, H., Mengmeng, L., El-Bishouty, M., & Yano, Y. (2010). Task recommendation for ubiquitous learning. *Informatics in Control, Automation and Robotics (CAR), 2010 2nd International Asia Conference on* (vol. 3, pp. 307-310).

Ogata, H., & Yano, Y. (2004). Context-aware support for computer-supported ubiquitous learning. *Proceedings of the 2nd IEEE International Workshop on Wireless and Mobile Technologies in Education (WMTE'04)* (pp. 27-34).

Prem, M., & Vikas, S. (2010). Recommender systems. In Sammut, C., & Webb, G. (Eds.), *Encyclopedia of machine learning, Springer, 2010.*

Rafaeli, S., Dan-Gur, Y., & Barak, M. (2005). Social recommender systems: Recommendations in support of e-learning. [IJDET]. *International Journal of Distance Education Technologies*, *3*(2), 30–47. doi:10.4018/jdet.2005040103

Recker, M. M., Walker, A., & Lawless, K. (2003). What do you recommend? Implementation and analyses of collaborative information filtering of web resources for education. *Instructional Science*, *31*(4), 299–316. doi:10.1023/A:1024686010318

Resnick, P., & Varian, H. R. (1997). Recommender systems. *Communications of the ACM*, *40*(3), 56–58. doi:10.1145/245108.245121

Rossitto, C., Canova Calori, I., Mamdouh, E., & Divitini, M. (2010). Considering the design of mobile applications for city-wide learning. [IRSI]. *International Reports on Socio-Informatics*, *7*(1), 134–140.

Rubinsztejn, H. K., Endler, M., Sacramento, V., Goncalves, K., & Nascimento, F. (2004). Support for context-aware collaboration. *Proceedings of Mobility Aware Technologies and Applications, LNCS, 3284*, 37–47. doi:10.1007/978-3-540-30178-3_4

Shen, L., & Shen, R. (2004). *Learning content recommendation service based-on simple sequencing specification. Advances in Web-Based Learning – ICWL 2004* (*Vol. 3143*, pp. 293–323). Berlin, Germany: Springer.

Sun, J., & Xie, Y. (2009). A recommender system based on web data mining for personalized e-learning. *International Conference on Information Engineering and Computer Science, 2009. ICIECS 2009.* (pp. 1-4).

Tang, T., & McCalla, G. (2005). Smart recommendation for an evolving e-learning system: Architecture and experiment. *International Journal on E-Learning*, *4*(1), 105–129.

Vander Wal, T. (2007). *Folksonomy coinage and definition*. Retrieved on October 1, 2007, from http://vanderwal.net/folksonomy.html

Vo, C. C., Torabi, T., & Loke, S. W. (2009). Towards context-aware task recommendation. *Pervasive Computing (JCPC), 2009 Joint Conferences* (pp. 289-292).

Wang, M., Shen, R., Novak, D., & Pan, X. (2009). The impact of mobile learning on students' learning behaviours and performance: Report from a large blended classroom. *British Journal of Educational Technology*, *40*(4), 673–695. doi:10.1111/j.1467-8535.2008.00846.x

Wang, Y. K. (2004). Context awareness and adaptation in mobile learning. *Proceedings of the 2nd IEEE International Workshop Wireless and Mobile Technologies in Education, 2004* (pp. 154-158).

Wu, T. T., Yang, T. C., Hwang, G. J., & Chu, H. C. (2008). Conducting situated learning in a context-aware ubiquitous learning environment. *Wireless, Mobile, and Ubiquitous Technology in Education, WMUTE* (pp. 82-86).

Yang, S. J. H. (2006). Context aware ubiquitous learning environments for peer-to-peer collaborative learning. *Journal of Educational Technology & Society*, *9*(1), 188–201.

Yang, S. J. H., Huang, A. F. M., Chen, R., Tseng, S.-S., & Shen, Y.-S. (2006). Context model and context acquisition for ubiquitous content access in u-learning environments. *Proceedings of the IEEE International Conference on Sensor Networks, Ubiquitous, and Trustworthy Computing*, vol. 2.

Yau, J. Y.-K., & Joy, M. S. (2009). A mobile context-aware framework for managing learning schedules — Data analysis from an interview study. *International Journal of Mobile and Blended Learning*, *1*(4), 29–55. doi:10.4018/jmbl.2009090803

Yin, C., Ogata, H., Tabata, Y., & Yano, Y. (2010). Supporting the acquisition of Japanese polite expressions in context-aware ubiquitous learning. *Int. J. Mob. Learn. Organ.*, *4*(2), 214–234. doi:10.1504/IJMLO.2010.032637

Zaiane, O. R. (2002). Building a recommender agent for e-learning systems. *Computers & Education, 51*, 55–59.

Zhao, X., Anma, F., Ninomiya, T., & Okamoto, T. (2008). Personalized adaptive content system for context-aware mobile learning. *IJCSNS International Journal of Computer Science and Network Security*, *8*, 153–161.

Zhao, X., & Okamoto, T. (2008). A device-independent system architecture for adaptive mobile learning. *Proceedings of the 2008 Eighth IEEE International Conference on Advanced Learning Technologies* (pp. 23-25). IEEE Computer Society.

Zhou, T., Kuscsik, Z., Liu, J.-G., Medo, M., Wakeling, J., & Zhang, Y.-C. (2010). Solving the apparent diversity-accuracy dilemma of recommender systems. *Proceedings of the National Academy of Sciences of the United States of America, 107*(10), 4511–4515. doi:10.1073/pnas.1000488107

## ADDITIONAL READING

Abowd, G., Dey, A., Brown, P., Davies, N., Smith, M., & Steggles, P. (1999). Towards a Better Understanding of Context and Context-Awareness. In H.-W. Gellersen (Ed.), *Handheld and Ubiquitous Computing* (Vol. 1707, pp. 304-307): Springer Berlin / Heidelberg.

Burke, R. (2002). Hybrid Recommender Systems: Survey and Experiments. *User Modeling and User-Adapted Interaction, 12*(4), 331–370. doi:10.1023/A:1021240730564

Cobb, P., & Bowers, J. (1999). Cognitive and Situated Learning Perspectives in Theory and Practice. *Educational Researcher, 28*(2), 4–15.

Cobcroft, R. S., Towers, S. J., Smith, J. E., & Bruns, A. (2006). Mobile learning in review: Opportunities and challenges for learners, teachers, and institutions. *Online Learning and Teaching (OLT) Conference 2006.*

Cui, Y., & Bull, S. (2005). Context and learner modelling for the mobile foreign language learner. *System: An International Journal of Educational Technology and Applied Linguistics., 33*(2), 353–367.

Economides, A. A. (2008). Context-Aware Mobile Learning. In Lytras, M. D., Carroll, J. M., Damiani, E., Tennyson, R. D., Avison, D., Vossen, G., & Ordonez De Pablos, P. (Eds.), *The Open Knowlege Society. A Computer Science and Information Systems Manifesto* (*Vol. 19*, pp. 213–220). Springer Berlin Heidelberg. doi:10.1007/978-3-540-87783-7_27

Henricksen, K., Indulska, J., & Rakotonirainy, A. (2002). Modeling Context Information in Pervasive Computing Systems. In F. Mattern & M. Naghshineh (Eds.), *Pervasive Computing* (Vol. 2414, pp. 79-117): Springer Berlin / Heidelberg.

Kuo, R., Wu, M. C., Chang, A., & Heh, J. S. (2007). Delivering Context-aware Learning Guidance in the Mobile Learning Environment based on Information Theory. *Seventh IEEE International Conference on Advanced Learning Technologies (ICALT 2007)*. (pp. 362-366).

Linton, F., & Schaefer, H.-P. (2000). Recommender Systems for Learning: Building User and Expert Models through Long-Term Observation of Application Use. *User Modeling and User-Adapted Interaction, 10*(2), 181–208. doi:10.1023/A:1026521931194

Liu, T. C., Wang, H. Y., Liang, J. K., Chan, T. W., Ko, H. W., & Yang, J. C. (2003). Wireless and mobile technologies to enhance teaching and learning. *Journal of Computer Assisted Learning, 19*(3), 371–382. doi:10.1046/j.0266-4909.2003.00038.x

Motiwalla, L. F. (2007). Mobile learning: A framework and evaluation. *Computers & Education, 49*(3), 581–596. doi:10.1016/j.compedu.2005.10.011

Pazzani, M. J., & Billsus, D. (2007). Content-based recommendation systems. In Peter, B., Alfred, K., & Wolfgang, N. (Eds.), *The adaptive web* (pp. 325–341). Springer-Verlag. doi:10.1007/978-3-540-72079-9_10

Resnick, P., & Varian, H. R. (1997). Recommender systems. *Communications of the ACM, 40*(3), 56–58. doi:10.1145/245108.245121

Rieger, R., & Gay, G. (1997). Using mobile computing to enhance field study, *Proceedings of the 2nd international conference on Computer support for collaborative learning.* Toronto, Ontario, Canada: International Society of the Learning Sciences. (pp. 218-226).

Schafer, J. B., Frankowski, D., Herlocker, J., & Sen, S. (2007). Collaborative filtering recommender systems. In Peter, B., Alfred, K., & Wolfgang, N. (Eds.), *The adaptive web* (pp. 291–324). Springer-Verlag. doi:10.1007/978-3-540-72079-9_9

Schmidt, A., Aidoo, K. A., Takaluoma, A., Tuomela, U., Van Laerhoven, K., & Van de Velde, W. (1999). Advanced Interaction in Context. *Lecture Notes in Computer Science, 1707*, 89–102. doi:10.1007/3-540-48157-5_10

Schmidt, A., Beigl, M., & Hans, W. (1998). There is more to Context than Location. *Computers & Graphics, 23*, 893–901. doi:10.1016/S0097-8493(99)00120-X

Sharples, M., Taylor, J., & Vavoula, G. (2005). Towards a theory of mobile learning. *Proceedings of MLearn 2005 conference*.

Sharples, M., Taylor, J., & Vavoula, G. (2010). A Theory of Learning for the Mobile Age. In Bachmair, B. (Ed.), *Medienbildung in neuen Kulturräumen* (pp. 87–99). doi:10.1007/978-3-531-92133-4_6

Tan, H. Y., Guo, J. F., & Li, Y. (2008). E-learning Recommendation System, *Computer Science and Software Engineering, 2008 International Conference on* (Vol. 5, pp. 430-433).

Ting, R. Y. L. (2005). Mobile Learning: Current Trend and Future Challenges. *Fifth IEEE International Conference on Advanced Learning Technologies, 2005. ICALT 2005* (pp. 603-607).

Trifonova, A., & Ronchetti, M. (2003). Where is Mobile Learning Going? In A. Rossett (Ed.), *World Conference on E-Learning in Corporate, Government, Healthcare, and Higher Education 2003* (pp. 1794-1801). Phoenix, Arizona, USA: AACE.

Uden, L. (2007). Activity theory for designing mobile learning. *Int. J. Mob. Learn. Organ., 1*(1), 81–102. doi:10.1504/IJMLO.2007.011190

van Kranenburg, H., Bargh, M. S., Iacob, S., & Peddemors, A. (2006). A context management framework for supporting context-aware distributed applications. *Communications Magazine, IEEE, 44*(8), 67–74. doi:10.1109/MCOM.2006.1678112

van Sinderen, M. J., van Halteren, A. T., Wegdam, M., Meeuwissen, H. B., & Eertink, E. H. (2006). Supporting context-aware mobile applications: an infrastructure approach. *Communications Magazine, IEEE, 44*(9), 96–104. doi:10.1109/MCOM.2006.1705985

Yang, S. J. H., Huang, A. F. M., Chen, R., Tseng, S.-S., & Shen, Y.-S. (2006). Context Model and Context Acquisition for Ubiquitous Content Access in ULearning Environments, *Proceedings of the IEEE International Conference on Sensor Networks, Ubiquitous, and Trustworthy Computing - Vol 2 - Workshops - Volume 02* (pp. 78-83).

Yau, J., & Joy, M. (2007). A Context-aware and Adaptive Learning Schedule framework for supporting learners' daily routines. *Second International Conference on Systems 2007. ICONS '07.* (pp. 31-37).

## KEY TERMS AND DEFINITIONS

**Context:** Context is referred to any information that can be used to characterize the situation of an entity where an entity can be a person, place and a physical or computational object.

**Mobile Learning:** Mobile learning is the interdisciplinary intersection of mobile computing and e-learning. Mobile learning refers to any sort of learning that happens when the learner is not at a fixed, predetermined location, or learning that happens when the learner takes advantage of the learning opportunities offered by mobile technologies.

**Recommendation System:** Recommendation System is an information filtering system that attempts to recommend possible interesting information to the user.

**Situated Learning:** Situated learning refers to learning that is situated in a specific context and embedded within a particular social and physical environment.

# About the Contributors

**Olga C. Santos** holds a PhD in Artificial Intelligence from the Computer Science School of the Spanish National University for Distance Education (UNED) and a MSc degree in Telecommunications Engineering specialized in Software Engineering from the Polytechnic University of Madrid (UPM). Since September 2001, she has been a researcher at the aDeNu Research Group at UNED, and since 2005, she is the R&D Technical Manager of the group. Her current research interests focus on taking into account recommendation strategies to provide open source educational accessible user-centered e-learning services for learners. She has participated in 11 international and national research projects, published over 100 papers in various international conferences and journals, and co-chaired workshops and conferences related to topics from her research.

**Jesus G. Boticario** is Professor of several courses at UNED concerning Artificial Intelligence subjects at the Computer Science School. He has been invited speaker at national and international conferences, forums and institutions. He has published over 200 research articles. He has participated in 19 R&D funded projects (Spain, USA, EU). He is head of aDeNu research group, and Scientific Coordinator in European and National funded projects in the areas of e-learning and e-inclusion. Jesus is Program Committee member at National and International Conferences. He has co-chaired International Workshops in the areas of user modeling and accessibility. He is reviewer of research projects and international journals. He has held several positions at UNED in the ICT area.

* * *

**Cristina Bender** received her Master in Computer Science at the Universidad de la República, Uruguay. She obtained her degree on Electronic Engineering at the Universidad Nacional de Rosario, Argentina. She is Professor and Researcher at the Department of Systems and Informatics of the Facultad de Ciencias Exactas, Ingeniería y Agrimensura of the Universidad Nacional de Rosario, and at the Facultad de Química e Ingeniería Rosario of the Universidad Católica Argentina. She participates in international and national research projects related to her research interests. Also, she is coauthor of many articles in international and national journals and conference proceedings, and is reviewer of some papers and journals. She participates as a researcher at the Research Group of Databases at the Facultad de Ciencias Exactas, Ingeniería y Agrimensura, Universidad Nacional de Rosario. Her research interests include databases technologies and information retrieval.

**Ig-Ibert Bittencourt** received his PhD in Computer Science at the Federal University of Campina Grande, Brazil. He is a Professor at the Federal University of Alagoas (UFAL), Brazil and head of Group of Optimization of the Web (GrOW). Additionally, Ig Ibert Bittencourt is the Vice-Director of Computing Institute at UFAL, IT Manager of the Distance Learning Department at UFAL, and Member of the Brazilian Computer Society, ACM, and IEEE. His research interests include artificial intelligence in education, software engineering in education, and social Semantic Web. He has served on the program committees for many international and national conferences, and as a reviewer for some journals.

**Constanta-Nicoleta Bodea** is Professor at the Academy of Economic Study Bucharest (ASE), Faculty of Cybernetics, Statistics and Economic Informatics, Economic Informatics Department. Currently, she teaches Artificial Intelligence, Data Mining, and Project Management. She coordinates numerous research projects at national level and achieved a high expertise in managing projects with multiple consortia. She was involved in research projects addressing topics related to competence management systems, technology enhanced learning, collaborative systems. She is author of 11 books and more than 50 papers on project management, Information Systems, and Artificial Intelligence, being honored by IPMA with the Outstanding Research Contributions in 2007. Her research interests include knowledge management, e-learning systems, ontology, recommender systems, and educational data mining.

**Patrick Brito** is Associate Professor at the Institute of Computing (IC), Federal University of Alagoas (UFAL) - Brazil, head of the Laboratory of Robust Software (LSR), and a member of the Cognitive Systems Engineering Research Group and the Group of Optimization of the Web (GrOW). He received the M.Sc. and PhD degrees from University of Campinas (UNICAMP) - Brazil, in 2005 and 2009, respectively. Patrick is also a Member of the Brazilian Computer Society, and his research interests include dependable software development methodologies, exception handling at the software architecture, component-based software development, and semantic and autonomous applications. Recently, Patrick is also working on the digital and social inclusion of Brazilian deaf people, especially children. The digital inclusion concerns the development of tools for facilitating the access to Web content by deaf people.

**Daniel Burgos** works as Head of User Experience Lab in the Research & Innovation Department of Atos Origin, Spain, since 2007. In addition, he is an Associate Professor in Technology-Enhanced Learning and ICT at the International University of La Rioja. His interests are mainly focused on adaptive elearning, elearning specifications, learning & social networks, and educational egames, and he is, or has been involved in the research projects Stellar, Gala, Go-MyLife, Grapple, Telma, GameTEL, Pauta, Unfold, Learning Network for Learning Design, ProLearn, TenCompetence, EU4ALL, NiHao, Kaleidoscope, Suma, Sister, Comeln, et cetera. He holds degrees in Communication (PhD), Computer Science (Dr. Ing), Education, and Business Administration.

**Ana Casali** received her PhD and her Master's degrees in Information Technologies at the University of Girona, Spain and she obtained her degree in Mathematics at the Universidad Nacional de Rosario (UNR), Argentina. She is Head of the Computer Science Department since 2007 and Professor at the Facultad de Ciencias Exactas, Ingeniería y Agrimensura, UNR since 1991. Also, she is Researcher in the Centro Internacional Franco Argentino de Ciencias de la Información y de Sistemas (CIFASIS). She has worked in several international cooperation research projects and her research interest includes agent architectures, knowledge representation, approximate reasoning, and recommender systems and their applications to education. She has participated as a member of the conference program committee in many scientific events, and she has been reviewer of different publications and journals. She also is author of many research articles, mainly in the field of Artificial Intelligence and its applications.

**Evandro Costa** received his Doctorate in Electrical Engineering at the Federal University of Paraiba, Brazil. He is currently an Associate Professor of the Computing Institute at the Federal University of Alagoas, Brazil and Director of the same Institute. He is also a collaborator Professor in the graduate program at Federal University of Campina Grande (UFCG), Paraiba, Brazil. His research interests include multiagent systems, knowledge representation and reasoning, ontology and semantic Web, e-learning systems, information retrieval, and recommender systems. He has published over 100 peer-reviewed papers. He has served on the program committees for many international and national conferences, and as a reviewer for some journals. He teaches several issues, such as, Artificial Intelligence, multiagent systems, data mining, and so on.

**Maria-Iuliana Dascălu** has a Master Degree in Project Management from the Academy of Economic Studies, Bucharest, Romania (2008) and a Bachelor Degree in Computer Science from the Alexandru-Ioan Cuza University, Iasi, Romania (2006). She is a PhD student in Economic Informatics at the Academy of Economic Studies, combining her work experience as a programmer with numerous research activities. Her research relates to computer-assisted testing with applications in e-learning environments for project management, competences development systems, and their benefits to adult education. Maria Dascălu is a Certified Project Management Associate (2008). She also conducted a research stage at the University of Gothenburg, Sweden, from October 2009 to May 2010.

**Claudia Deco** is Doctor in Engineering, Universidad Nacional de Rosario and she has a Master's Degree in Computer Science, Universidad de la República, Montevideo, Uruguay. She obtained her degree on Mathematics at the Universidad Nacional de Rosario. She is also a researcher in the Centro Internacional Franco Argentino de Ciencias de la Información y de Sistemas (CIFASIS), Rosario, Argentina, and professor and researcher at the Research Department, Facultad de Química e Ingeniería, Rosario, Universidad Católica Argentina. Furthermore, she coordinates the Research Group of Databases at the Facultad de Ingeniería, Universidad Nacional de Rosario. Her research interest includes database technologies and information retrieval. She participates in scientific events as a member of the conference program committee and as a reviewer of some papers and journals. She also is author of many research articles mainly in this area.

**Alicia Diaz** is a Professor at La Plata Nacional University (UNLP) since 1992 and she has also been working for LIFIA since 1988. Nowadays, she is a member of its Board of Directors. She graduated as Licentiate in Computer Science in 1992 and obtained a PhD in Computer Science at Université Henry Poincaré-Nancy I (France) in 2005. She is the author of more than 50 research articles mainly in the area of hypermedia, object oriented programming, databases, and knowledge management. At the moment, she is leading a research group which is working in the field of CSCW and Semantic Web. Furthermore, she actively participates in scientific events as a member of the conference program committee, workshops, and as a reviewer of some journals.

**Monica Divitini** is a Professor of Cooperation Technologies at the Department of Computer and Information Science, Norwegian University of Science and Technology. She holds a MSc. in Information Science from University of Milano, Italy, and a PhD in Computer Science from the University of Aalborg, Denmark. Her research interests lie primarily in the area of CSCW, mobile technology in learning communities, support for communities and loosely coupled groups, coordination support. She is currently involved in national and international projects for ICT enhanced learning in schools and workplaces. Focus of these projects is on creativity and reflection. Her special attention is on ICT solutions empowering learners to actively participate in cooperative process of knowledge creation.

**Lucas Drumond** is a PhD student at the Information Systems and Machine Learning Lab (ISMLL) at the University of Hildesheim, Germany, under the supervision of Prof. Dr. Lars Schmidt-Thieme and Dr. Tomas Horvath and is a scholarship holder of CNPq, an institution of the Brazilian government for the scientific development. He received a Bachelor degree in Computer Science and a Master's degree in Electrical Engineering from the Federal University of Maranhao, Brazil. He has been part of the Program Committee of Semantic Web and Applications track of the ACM Symposium on Applied Computing in 2010 and 2011. Currently his main research interests are in the field of machine learning, specifically factorization models, multi-relational learning, recommender systems, and statistical relational learning.

**James M. Foster** is pursuing a Ph.D. in Computer Science and Cognitive Science at the University of Colorado at Boulder. He completed a B.S. in Computer Science Engineering at the University of Florida in 2009 before joining CU-Boulder. Since then he has worked as a Research Assistant in the Computational Language and Education Research Lab (CLEAR). His research interests include cognitive modeling, lexical semantics, and educational technology. His current research projects include topics related to concept map creation in automatic tutoring systems, teacher knowledge and practice change with use of educational technology, cognitive modeling of analogical reasoning, and metaphorical extension of word senses.

**Valeria Gerling** has received a Computer Science Degree at the Universidad Nacional de Rosario, Argentina. She is Research Assistant in research projects at the Facultad de Ciencias Exactas, Ingeniería y Agrimensura, Universidad Nacional de Rosario, Argentina. She has worked in the international research Project "Jardin: Just an Assistant for Instructional Design" (LACCIR Projects, The Latin American and Caribbean Collaborative ICT Research, Microsoft). She is coauthor of several papers in international and national journals and conference proceedings about intelligent systems to assist the personalized search of learning objects. She is currently in charge of the Informatics Center of the Hospital Intendente Gabriel Carrasco that belongs to the Municipalidad Nacional de Rosario.

**Thieme Hennis** is a PhD researcher in the Systems Engineering Group of the Faculty of Technology, Policy, and Management of Delft University of Technology. Before joining the university, he was involved in the design of social software applications and environments to support professionals in their day-to-day tasks at Peers.me. In his research, he focuses on reputation as a social currency in online professional communities. More specifically, he researches the influence of reputation on interaction and contributions in communities, and focuses on building reputation standards that support the exchange and creation of knowledge in learning communities, improve relevancy of recommendations, and sustain self-organization.

**Olavo Holanda** is undergraduate student at Federal University of Alagoas in Computer Science. He is project researcher of the Group of Optimization of the Web - GrOW, Computing Institute, Federal University of Alagoas, Brazil. His research interests include recommender systems, social crawlers, Semantic Web, and multi-agent systems. Olavo is conducting a research project involving the development of a virtual learning environment based on Semantic Web services and intelligent agents. The environment adopts a component-based software architecture which modularizes the system functionalities and infrastructure control. His project uses Java programming language and Agent frameworks, such as JADE. Olavo Holanda should receive his B.Sc. degree in 2011.

**Tomáš Horváth** is a Post-Doc Researcher at the Information Systems and Machine Learning Lab (ISMLL) of the University of Hildesheim, Germany. He received a Master's degree in Computer Science at the Pavol Jozef Šafárik University in Košice, Slovakia in 2002. He is a member of the Institute of Computer Science (ICS) of the Pavol Jozef Šafárik University since 2003, where he obtained a PhD degree in Computer Science in 2008. He joined the ISMLL in 2009. His research interests include data mining, especially fuzzy rule-based learning and fuzzy inductive logic programming, monotone classification, user modeling and personalization techniques, recommender systems, and relational classification. He has co-authored 6 journal articles, 29 conference/workshop papers, and has co-edited one workshop proceedings. He is a member of the Slovak Society for Computer Science.

**Kinshuk** is Associate Dean of Faculty of Science and Technology and Professor of Computing and Information Systems at Athabasca University, Canada. He also holds NSERC/iCORE/Xerox/Markin Industrial Research Chair in Adaptivity and Personalization in Informatics. Before moving to Canada in August 2006, Kinshuk worked at German National Research Centre for Information Technology as Postdoctoral Fellow, and at Massey University, New Zealand as Associate Professor of Information Systems and Director of Advanced Learning Technology Research Centre. He has been involved in large-scale research projects for adaptive and mobile learning systems and by early 2011, he has published over 300 research papers in international refereed journals, conferences, and book chapters. He is the Founding Chair of IEEE Technical Committee on Learning Technology and Co-Editor-in-Chief of the SSCI indexed *Journal of Educational Technology & Society* (ISSN 1436-4522).

**Artus Krohn-Grimberghe** is a PhD student at the Information Systems and Machine Learning Lab (ISMLL), University of Hildesheim, Germany, under the supervision of Prof. Dr. Lars Schmidt-Thieme and Prof. Dr. Alexandros Nanopoulos. He graduated from the Karlsruhe Institute of Technology in 2006 and worked on business intelligence and data mining solutions in the industry before joining the ISMLL. His main research interests are multi-relational learning and the integration of Data Mining and OLAP technologies. Artus' publications appeared in several international conferences and a journal. Among them are ACM DOLAP, ACM RecSys, ACM SIGGRAPH, and IFCS. He recently acquired an EU-funded project which he currently works for.

**Juha Leino** is a part-time Teacher and Researcher at the School of Information Sciences (SIS) at the University of Tampere, Finland. He has an MSc in Interactive Technology from the University of Tampere, and he has lectured a course on user-centered design at the University of Tampere since 2006. His research interests center on human factors, in particular supporting human cognition, in complex information environments. In addition to the MSc, he has a BA in Film and Video Arts from the University of Regina, Canada, and he is currently completing an MA in Visual Journalism at the University of Tampere.

**Rafael-Ferreira Leite de Mello** is Master's candidate at Federal University of Pernambuco. He is external member of GrOW - Group of Optimization of the Web and member of OBIE - Ontology-Based Information Extraction. He has participated in projects involving interactive tools like video conferencing and virtual communities, but the main theme was explored Web 2.0 tools focused on blogs. Rafael also worked on the digital and social inclusion by given computer classes to children from public schools in Brazil. These classes had the objective to increase interest in computing and help children participate in the Brazilian Informatics Olympiad. His research interests include artificial intelligence, software engineering, and Semantic Web, all applied to Web 2.0 tools.

**Adina Lipai** has a Bachelor Degree in Informatics from the Academy of Economic Studies, Bucharest, Romania. She started as a junior researcher in a research institute in sports medicine, involved in several research projects. She also worked as Teaching Assistant at the artificial intelligence course. Adina Lipai earned a PhD in Economic Cybernetics and Statistics at the Academy of Economic Studies. Her doctoral research related to Web search clustering. She is working as a software developer in Holland, developing knowledge management systems. She is experienced in working in multinational projects. Her research interests include knowledge management, recommender systems, and innovative approaches for increasing the search performance.

**Chengzhi Liu** has been a postdoctoral fellow at the department of Computer and Information Science, Norwegian University of Science and Technology since December 2009. He received his Bachelor and Master's degrees in Computer Science from Shandong University, China in 2001 and 2005, respectively. He was awarded a PhD degree in Computer Science by Renmin University of China in 2009. During his PhD studies, he participated in two international projects of developing Ubiquitous Doctors Assistance System and Doctor Workstation System. He is currently involved in a NFR VERDIKT project for mobile collaborative learning in Trondheim, Norway. He focuses on facilitating collaboration among learners with context awareness and recommendation technology. His research interests include computer supported collaborative work, mobile learning, mobile commerce, context-aware computing, recommender system, and intelligent agent technology.

**Stephan Lukosch** is Associate Professor at the Delft University of Technology. His current research interests include collaborative design and engineering, collaborative storytelling for knowledge elicitation and decision-making, intelligent and context-adaptive collaboration support, and design patterns for computer-mediated interaction. In 2007, he published a foundational book on patterns for computer mediated-interaction. In 2003, he received a Dr. Rer. Nat. in Computer Science with distinction for his doctoral thesis on transparent and flexible data management for collaborative applications. His articles appeared in various journals including the *International Journal of Cooperative Information Systems, International Journal of Human Computer Studies,* and *Journal of Universal Computer Science*. Currently, he is a steering committee member of the special interest group on Computer-Supported Cooperative Work (CSCW) of the German computer science society and CRIWG conference on Collaboration and Technology. He further serves on the editorial board of the *International Journal of Cooperative Information Systems* (IJCIS).

**Aydano P. Machado** is Associate Professor of the Computing Institute at Federal University of Alagoas. He received his Ph.D. in Computer Science from Université Pierre et Marie Curie with the work performed at the Laboratoire d'Informatique de Paris 6-LIP6 (2009); his research foci are artificial intelligence, machine learning, knowledge transfer, multi-agent systems, and games. He also has experience in information technology and project management. This experience includes all phases of Systems Development Life Cycle (SDLC) with many kinds of software development methodologies. He has been worked on different types of information systems including interesting characteristics as: service-oriented architecture (SOA); networks and mobile systems; Internet and Web applications; Web services; mobile service and solutions; desktop applications; et cetera.

**Keith Maull** is pursuing a PhD in Computer Science at the University of Colorado at Boulder. He also holds an MS in Computer Science from the University of Colorado at Boulder and a BA in Computer Science from Indiana University at Bloomington. He has over 10 years of broad industry software development experience. He has worked for Fortune 100 companies such as Hewlett-Packard and IBM as well as start-up and non-profit companies. His research interests are in data mining, educational informatics, technology-enhanced pedagogy, and computational approaches to educational decision making, with particular focus on examining behavioral patterns in e-learning environments. His current research is in examining computational tools for examining and understanding teachers' behavioral patterns in curriculum planning environments and their impact on pedagogy.

**Christos G. Mettouris** is a graduate of the Computer Engineering & Informatics Department in the University of Patras. He holds a Master's degree of the same department. He has published his diploma thesis work in the 1st Hellenic Scientific Student Computing Conference, obtaining an award for presenting one of the 3 top papers. He has been a member of the e-Learning sector of the Research Academic Computer Technology Institute (RACTI). He is currently a member of the Software Engineering and Internet Technologies (SEIT) Lab of the Computer Science Dept. at the University of Cyprus. He was involved with the idSpace project and now is a member of the research team involved in CVN and Asterics projects while also pursuing a PhD degree at the University of Cyprus. His research interests include wireless technologies, mobile networks, ubiquitous computing, and context aware recommender systems.

**Regina Motz** holds a PhD in Computer Science from the Technische Universität Darmstadt, Germany (2004) and a Master of Science from the Federal University of Pernambuco, Brazil, (1990). She obtained a degree on Computing Engineering from the University of the Republic, Uruguay (1988). She currently serves as Full Professor at the Computer Science Institute, School of Engineering of the University of the Republic, Uruguay, where she coordinates the Information Systems Group. She holds a qualification of senior researcher in the National Reseracher System (SNI, National Agency of Research and Innovation, Uruguay) and in PEDECIBA (Program for the Development of Basic Science, Uruguay). Her research interests include ontology design, metadata, Semantic Web, and technology enhanced learning.

**Alexandros Nanopoulos** is currently Assistant Professor at University of Hildesheim, Germany. His research interests include ML/DM and Web Information Retrieval. He received the BSc and PhD degrees from the University of Thessaloniki, Greece, where he worked as a lecturer from 2004 to 2008. From 2005 to 2008, he was also an academic council of the Hellenic Open University, Greece. Dr. Nanopoulos is the coauthor of more than 100 articles in international journals and conference proceedings. He has also coauthored the monographs Advanced Signature Indexing for Multimedia and Web Applications, and R-Trees: Theory and Applications, both published by Springer Verlag. He has co-edited the volume Wireless Information Highways, published by Idea Group, Inc. He is also co-chair and program committee member of several international conferences on data mining and databases.

**Ifeyinwa Okoye** is pursuing a PhD in Computer Science and Cognitive Science at the University of Colorado at Boulder. She holds a Master's degree in Computer Science from the University of Colorado at Boulder and a Bachelor's degree in Computer Science specializing in software engineering from California State University East Bay (CSU East Bay). She has worked as a Research Assistant on a digital library project and a computer vision project at CSU East Bay. She has also worked as an intern for Sun Microsystems and IBM-Research. Her research interests span adaptive and personalization technology, user modeling, educational technology, and medical informatics.

**George A. Papadopoulos** (Ph.D.) holds the (tenured) rank of Professor in the Department of Computer Science. His research interests include software engineering, mobile and ubiquitous computing, multimedia systems, open and distance learning, distributed and high performance computing, e-business, e-health, internet technologies, and service oriented computing. He has published over 100 papers as book chapters or in internationally refereed journals and conferences, he serves in the Editorial Board of 5 international journals and has served as a Chair or Program Committee member in more than 100 international conferences. Professor Papadopoulos is a recipient of an 1995 ERCIM-HCM scholarship award. He has been involved or is currently participating, as coordinator or partner, in over 100 internationally and nationally funded projects (total budget for his participation around 7 MEURO). He is the Director of the Software Engineering and Internet Technologies Laboratory.

**Abelardo Pardo** received the M.Sc. degree in Computer Science from the Polytechnic University of Catalonia, Spain, in 1992, and the Ph.D. degree in Computer Science from the University of Colorado at Boulder in 1997. He is an Associate Professor of Telematics Engineering at the Carlos III University of Madrid. He has participated in numerous research projects both at international (Genius, E-LANE, iCOPER) and national (SIEMPRE, MOSAIC, Learn3) levels. He also has more than three years experience working for the computer industry in companies such as Mentor Graphics Inc. and AT&T Bell Labs. His research projects included topics related to technology enhanced learning, intelligent tutors, computer supported collaborative learning, and virtual learning environments. His current interests are in the area of computer-supported collaborative learning, adaptive hypermedia, and technology enhanced learning.

**Thiago Ribeiro** is an undergraduate student at the Institute of Computing (IC), Federal University of Alagoas (UFAL) - Brazil, and a member of the Cognitive Systems Engineering Research Group. He is a Junior Researcher in a project that aims to architect dependable software systems. His research interests include software engineering and graphical web development. Thiago is conducting a research project involving a specialist system for supporting the architectural design of robust software systems, based on trade-off analysis of quality attributes. His project uses Java programming language and the Adobe Flex technology. Thiago should receive his B.Sc. degree in 2011.

**Edelweis Rohrer** holds a MSc. in Computer Engineering from University of the Republic, Uruguay (2010). She obtained her degree on Computing Engineer Systems at the University of the Republic, Uruguay (2002). Furthermore, she has been part of the research project “Web Site Quality in the Health Area” (SALUS) of the Latin American Program of Science and Technology for Development (CYTED). She currently is a PhD student at the University of the Republic, Uruguay. Her research area is design of ontology networks and Semantic Web reasoning. Recently she has been awarded by Google with a fellowship to attend to the 20th International World Wide Web Conference, which took place in Hyderabad, India, from 28th March to 1st April, 2011. She also is part of the research project “Quality Health Information Retrieval” of the Latin American and Caribbean Collaborative ICT Research (LACCIR). Furthermore, she works as a Systems Analyst in the Ministry of Economy and Finance, Uruguay.

**Vicente Arturo Romero Zaldivar** received the M. Sc. Degree in Computer Science from the University of Las Villas, Cuba in 2001, the M. Sc Degree in Applied Mathematics from the University of Cienfuegos, Cuba in 2003 and the DEA (Advanced Studies Diploma) from the University of the Basque Country, Spain, in 2004. He works as Research Consultant at the User Experience Laboratory at the Research & Innovation Department of Atos Origin, Spain. Previously he has worked as Professor and Researcher at several Universities in Cuba and Spain. He has participated in several research projects: Telma, Gametel, Flexo, and Veritas. His interests are mainly focused on Recommender Systems and Learning & Social Networks.

**Lars Schmidt-Thieme** is a full Professor and leading the ISMLL, University of Hildesheim, Germany. He obtained his Diploma in Mathematics at the University of Heidelberg in 1999 and received his PhD at the University of Karlsruhe, Germany, in 2003. From 2003 to 2006 he was Professor at the Institute for Computer Science at the University of Freiburg, Germany. His main research interest is machine learning, especially classification and regression problems as well as recommender systems. He has published articles in top international conferences (e.g. IEEE ICDM, ACM KDD, UAI) and journals. He is member of program committees of international top conferences (e.g. ACM KDD, SIAM SDM, ECML/PKDD) as well as executive board member of the German Classification Society.

**Georgios A. Sielis** holds a Master of Science in Computer Science and Information Technologies from the University of Patras where he also received his BSc in Computer Engineering and Informatics. During his postgraduate studies, he was a member of the Pattern Recognition Laboratory of C.E.I.D. and his research was focused on the adaptive e-learning systems with computational intelligence algorithms. He worked as a Software Developer for two years and then joined the SEIT Lab as a Special Scientist. He is involved with the idSpace FP7 EU funded program and he is currently involved in COIN-EEU FP7 EU funded program. He is also pursuing a PhD degree at the University of Cyprus. His research interests are related to creativity and creativity support tools and in particular to the use of recommendation methods in creativity support tools for the enhancement of the creativity process.

**Tamara Sumner** is Executive Director of Digital Learning Sciences, a collaborative R&D center between the University of Colorado and the University Corporation for Atmospheric Research. Research there examines how cognitive tools, computational algorithms, and interactive media can improve learning outcomes and learner engagement. The aim is to invent successful technologies, processes, and know-how that can be replicated on a wider scale. Sumner is also an Associate Professor at the University of Colorado, with a joint appointment in Cognitive Science and Computer Science. She has extensive research publications in human-computer interaction, educational technology, digital libraries, and intelligent systems. Her teaching focuses on user-centered design and cognitive science research methods.

**Libertad Tansini** graduated as a Computer Engineer from University of the Republic, Uruguay in 1999 and obtained her Masters Degree in 2001. She pursued her PhD studies in Chalmers University of Technology in Gothenburg, Sweden, and graduated in 2008. She teaches at the Institute of Computer Science, Faculty of Engineering of the University of the Republic, Uruguay. Se has been working in the field of data mining to improve users search experience for more than 5 years, including algorithms for collaborative filtering in recommendation systems as well as classification and detection of user intent to improve search engines.

**Nguyen Thai-Nghe** is a PhD student at the Information Systems and Machine Learning Lab (ISMLL), University of Hildesheim, Germany, under the supervision of Prof. Dr. Lars Schmidt-Thieme and Dr. Tomas Horvath. He is sponsored by a scholarship of Cantho University, Vietnam and a fellowship of ISMLL. He received his BSc. in Informatics in 1999 at Cantho University and obtained the degree of Master of Engineering in Information Management at Asian Institute of Technology, Thailand, in 2006. His main interest research is machine learning, especially in classification for imbalanced data, educational data mining and educational recommender systems. He has published his papers at international conferences (e.g. IEEE-FIE, IEEE-ISDA, IEEE-ICALT).

**Aimilia Tzanavari** is Associate Professor at the Department of Design and Multimedia, University of Nicosia, Cyprus (2008-today). She holds a Ph.D. in Human Computer Interaction from the University of Bristol, United Kingdom. She has worked as a Special Scientist (2006-2008) and a Visiting Lecturer (2002-2004 and 2005) at the Department of Computer Science, University of Cyprus, Cyprus and as a Visiting Assistant Professor (2001-2002) at Miami University, OH, USA. She conducts research and publishes in the areas of human-computer interaction and e-learning and has served as program committee member and reviewer in various European and International workshops and conferences. She has participated in numerous research projects supported by the European Commission holding research and management positions.

**Jody S. Underwood** has spent over 20 years doing research and development of intelligent tutoring systems, digital learning environments, assessment design, and effective feedback. She received a Ph.D. in Science and Technology Education from the Technion-Israel Institute of Technology in 1998 and a M.S. in computer science from Rutgers University with a focus on artificial intelligence in 1987. Between her two advanced degrees, she did research and development of intelligent tutoring systems at Carnegie Mellon University and of AI applications at NASA Ames Research Center. Since earning her doctorate, Dr. Underwood has done R&D at Vanderbilt University's Learning Technology Center, the Math Forum (a renowned online mathematics education portal, now based at Drexel University), Educational Testing Service, and Pragmatic Solutions. At Intelligent Automation, she works on simulations and games for learning.

**Wim Veen** is full Professor of Education & Technology in the Systems Engineering Department of the Faculty of Technology, Policy and Management of Delft University of Technology. He has been involved in institutional strategies for educational innovations at his university. He researches the development of new concepts and models for ICT enabled learning in both the private and public sector. He introduced the concept of Homo Zappiens, a generation of learners with new learning strategies demanding flexible and participative education. Together with a multidisciplinary team of researchers he contributes to e-learning developments in organizations where new learning cultures are emerging for a knowledge intensive and creative economy. Key ideas in his view are: Game developers are excellent educationalists; learning and working are intimate lovers; knowledge is communication about meaning.

**Yabo Xu** is an Assistant Professor at School of Software, Sun Yat-sen University (P. R. China). His research focuses on large-scale data mining applications, web search, cloud computing, and information privacy. He is an expert on advanced analysis techniques and their applications in various domains, e.g. education, biology, and e-commerce. He has published widely on top data mining conferences and journals. Despite his proliferation in academia, he also has a keen interest in turning research ideas into successful products. He holds a patent for a summary-based search engine and co-founded a search engine startup. He is currently supervising the development of a general-purpose data analysis platform with a focus on large-scale data logging, collection, analysis, and real-time feedback.

**Mingming Zhou** is an Assistant Professor at Psychological Studies, National Institute of Education, Nanyang Technological University (Singapore). Her research interests include motivation, meta-cognition, pedagogy and educational technology. She has been working intensively and productively in researching how to use computer technology to improve teaching and learning effectiveness and efficiency. One of her major contributions to this field is the development of computer tracing methods to capture learning processes on the fly. She has been involved in many international projects, published in a series of books on intelligent learning systems and computer-based learning and presented in top conferences in e-learning. She is currently supervising the development of a computer tracking tool on web search in academic contexts.

# Index

## K



## L



## M



## N



## O

## P



## R



## S

## T



## U



## V



## W

CPSIA information can be obtained at www.ICGtesting.com
Printed in the USA
BVOW082325081111

275340BV00003B/3/P